Transnational Securities Law

Transnational Securities Law

Second Edition

Edited by
THOMAS KEIJSER

OXFORD
UNIVERSITY PRESS

Great Clarendon Street, Oxford, OX2 6DP,
United Kingdom

Oxford University Press is a department of the University of Oxford.
It furthers the University's objective of excellence in research, scholarship,
and education by publishing worldwide. Oxford is a registered trade mark of
Oxford University Press in the UK and in certain other countries

© The several contributors 2022

The moral rights of the authors have been asserted

First Edition published in 2014
Second Edition published in 2022

Impression: 1

All rights reserved. No part of this publication may be reproduced, stored in
a retrieval system, or transmitted, in any form or by any means, without the
prior permission in writing of Oxford University Press, or as expressly permitted
by law, by licence or under terms agreed with the appropriate reprographics
rights organization. Enquiries concerning reproduction outside the scope of the
above should be sent to the Rights Department, Oxford University Press, at the
address above

You must not circulate this work in any other form
and you must impose this same condition on any acquirer

Public sector information reproduced under Open Government Licence v3.0
(http://www.nationalarchives.gov.uk/doc/open-government-licence/open-government-licence.htm)

Published in the United States of America by Oxford University Press
198 Madison Avenue, New York, NY 10016, United States of America

British Library Cataloguing in Publication Data

Data available

Library of Congress Control Number: 2021946955

ISBN 978-0-19-285551-0

DOI: 10.1093/law/9780192855510.001.0001

Printed and bound in the UK by
TJ Books Limited

Links to third party websites are provided by Oxford in good faith and
for information only. Oxford disclaims any responsibility for the materials
contained in any third party website referenced in this work.

Foreword to the second edition

Seven years have passed since the publication of the first edition of this volume. This second edition is not a simple technical update. All the chapters have been carefully re-examined and substantially revised, and new chapters have been added. In particular, the regulatory response to the global financial crisis is examined and ground-breaking technological developments are analysed from a legal point of view in many of the chapters.

The developments that have marked both technology and the markets in recent years have been remarkable. In particular, digitalization in financial transactions has had a twofold impact. One effect has been that digital assets have an economic value, and as such are used as a means of payment, traded in the market as an object of investment, and used as collateral. The other is that digitalization is viewed as a process change, denoting the shift from analogue to digital. Financial transactions are moving from paper-based to digital-based dealings, and from transactions operated by hand to automation (from traditional contracts to 'smart contracts'). Thus, today, securities tokens are popular in many jurisdictions, where such tokens (ie, digital data) representing interests in investment securities are held, traded, and collateralized. Blockchain and other distributed ledger technology sometimes step in. Under a scheme generally called decentralized finance, the processes of contracting as well as collateralization and other financial transactions are automated and rendered autonomous by computer programmes and codes. These phenomena inevitably produce new legal and regulatory issues. Yet, the importance of investment securities remains unchanged. The volume of investment securities transactions remains huge, and they continue to play an important role in capital formation and resource allocation in the global economy. Today, new legal and regulatory issues are examined carefully in various fora in the global community, and new approaches and ideas surface almost every day.

In this second edition, Thomas Keijser again showed superb leadership in coordinating the revisions and additions made by the world eminent authors. The result is an updated, comprehensive, and reliable reference for all those who practise, study, or are otherwise interested in the legal and regulatory issues that arise with respect to investment securities in the global capital markets today.

Hideki Kanda
Emeritus Professor
University of Tokyo
August 2021

Foreword to the first edition

One notable innovation that has occurred in the world's capital markets in recent decades is the immobilization or dematerialization of investment securities. This development was made possible by technology. Nowadays, shares and bonds are no longer traded by moving certificates. Rather, they are held through intermediaries, typically banks and similar financial institutions, and those intermediaries manage book-entries by which 'intermediated securities' are held, traded, and collateralized.

Today, immobilization or dematerialization may be observed in almost all jurisdictions around the world. It helps to ensure the safety of transactions and to enable large volumes to be traded at less cost than where certificates move around. The phenomenon, in other words, is a simple one. Yet that simplicity does not mean that the legal and regulatory issues involved are simple as well. In fact, the legal and regulatory landscape is quite complex and varies from jurisdiction to jurisdiction. The doctrines of property law in this area vary even among common law jurisdictions and among civil law jurisdictions, as well.

Capital markets today are global. That is not to say there is only one, globe-spanning, single market. On the contrary, many markets coexist in a multi-layered fashion, ranging from local domestic markets to international wholesale markets. These multiple markets interact with one another. Moreover, financial transactions take place, and financial institutions act, across national borders in these multi-layered markets. In such a scenario, a risk that arises in one market is easily transmitted to another market, but from a legal and regulatory standpoint, controlling these multi-layered capital markets is anything but easy.

The international community has, over the past decades, come to recognize the legal risk associated with the intermediated holding of investment securities, and the global financial crisis that developed in 2007–2009 served as a potent reminder of the magnitude of that risk. The Hague Securities Convention and UNIDROIT's Geneva Securities Convention are tangible evidence of the attempts made by the international community to find ways of tackling the issue together. When I served as a member of the drafting committee at the diplomatic Conference and co-reporter on the Hague Securities Convention and as chairman of the drafting committee at the diplomatic Conference and co-author of the Official Commentary on the Geneva Securities Convention, I realized that these Conventions were the product of teamwork, of hard work by renowned experts from the participating jurisdictions who brought together their considerable expertise.

This book, also, is the product of teamwork. Thomas Keijser did a superb job coordinating the work of the first-class authors of the chapters that make up the volume, many of whom participated, in an official or other capacity, in the preparation of either or both the Hague and Geneva Securities Conventions. Together, they have produced a comprehensive and reliable reference for all those who practise, study, or are otherwise interested in the complex legal and regulatory issues connected with intermediated securities in the world's capital markets today.

Hideki Kanda
Professor of Law
University of Tokyo
October 2013

Preface

The importance of an international legal framework for investment securities is paramount. The intertwined cash and securities markets are at the core both of the global financial system and, as the global financial crisis of 2007 and onwards has made clear, of the socio-economic structure of many States. Securities have many applications. To name but a few, they are a principal means of funding for governments and corporate entities, they form one of the foundations on which central banks base their monetary policy operations, and they are frequently used as collateral in the context of commercial banking and investment activities. The markets for securities have increasingly become cross-border over the past decades.

The legal framework that has been developed for investment securities during that time reflects three basic paradigms: non-intermediated securities, intermediated securities, and crypto securities. Originally, securities were primarily held and traded in the form of certificates or by entries in the register kept by the issuer of shares. Such securities are sometimes referred to as directly held or non-intermediated securities, so as to distinguish them from securities held and traded in the intermediated systems that became popular when trading volumes became too large to be processed physically. In such intermediated systems, securities are commonly held in immobilized or dematerialized form at a central securities depository, while one or (often) more intermediaries provide an interface between the issuer and investors. Increasingly, the use of crypto securities based on distributed ledger or comparable technology is now being considered. Such technology allows direct contact between issuer and investors to be re-established, although some form of intermediation (for example, in relation to the custody of private keys or other services) may still continue to exist. All three forms of investment securities—non-intermediated, intermediated, and crypto—are relevant today for the different market segments in which they are held and traded.

At a time when securities were still primarily held and traded in the form of certificates, markets were largely national in scope and traditional legal concepts could be applied to these tangible assets. This has changed drastically due to the development, over the past several decades, of the now prevalent intermediated system, a development that has gone hand in hand with a steep increase in the volume of government and corporate securities held and traded in globalized markets. From a legal point of view, the new, multifaceted phenomenon of intermediated securities called for novel approaches in the fields of contractual, property, corporate, insolvency, regulatory, and international private law. Different jurisdictions have come up with their own solutions, leading to a variety of holding systems based on different legal approaches. In parallel, a fairly comprehensive international legal and regulatory framework for intermediated securities has been taking shape at the international level over the past two decades.

Back in 2000, the Hague Conference on Private International Law embarked on a project to identify the most appropriate conflict-of-laws approach in relation to intermediated securities, a project that resulted in the adoption, in 2002, of the Convention on the Law Applicable to Certain Rights in Respect of Securities Held with Intermediaries (also known as the Hague Securities Convention; HSC).[1] By then, the UNIDROIT Governing Council had already given the green light to start work on the harmonization of substantive law issues, which culminated in the 2009 UNIDROIT Convention on Substantive Rules for Intermediated Securities (Geneva Securities Convention; GSC). The GSC covers a wide array of issues, spanning various aspects of holding, transfer, and collateralization of intermediated securities, as well as the integrity of the intermediated system.[2] Although the hard-law rules of the GSC have not yet come into force as such,[3] while the HSC has come into force on the basis of just three ratifications,[4] the two Conventions serve as authoritative benchmarks, indicating best practice solutions and providing guidance to States that are developing infrastructure for intermediated securities.[5]

The two Conventions were complemented by a number of additional transnational instruments, including the 2013 UNIDROIT Principles on the Operation of Close-Out Netting Provisions and the 2017 UNIDROIT Legislative Guide on Intermediated Securities. The latter in particular provides concrete guidance to lawmakers and market participants on a broad range of policy choices regarding intermediated securities, also in respect of certain issues not covered in the Conventions, for example in the area of corporate, insolvency, and regulatory law. The various instruments developed by the Hague Conference and UNIDROIT are designed to dovetail with the work done by UNCITRAL on secured transactions and insolvency, as far as appropriate given the specifics of different types of asset.

Another important strain of work that has led to a considerable degree of harmonization in the international arena is the guidance provided by regulatory authorities such as the Basel Committee on Banking Supervision (BCBS), the Committee on Payments and Market Infrastructures (CPMI),[6] the Financial Stability Board (FSB), and the International Organization of Securities Commissions (IOSCO). The international regulatory guidance provided in the wake of the global financial crisis has proven to be a particularly successful driver of harmonization.

It should be borne in mind that the legal and regulatory framework for intermediated securities is complex for a variety of reasons. Besides a range of legal approaches relating to the set-up and operation of intermediated holding systems in different jurisdictions, intermediated chains may be long, a factor which may of itself increase legal

---

[1] For an in-depth, article-by-article analysis of the HSC, see Goode et al., *Explanatory Report*.
[2] For an in-depth, article-by-article analysis of the GSC, see Kanda et al., *Official Commentary*.
[3] See <https://www.unidroit.org/status> (accessed 15 August 2021).
[4] See <https://www.hcch.net/en/instruments/conventions/status-table/?cid=72> (accessed 15 August 2021).
[5] See Mooney, 'Geneva Securities Convention'; Bernasconi and Keijser, 'The Hague and Geneva Securities Conventions'.
[6] Until 1 September 2014, the CPMI was known as the Committee on Payment and Settlement Systems (CPSS).

PREFACE   xi

complexity. Moreover, national legal and regulatory approaches to the holding and transfer of intermediated securities are ideally, or should be, in tune with regional and international rules. The outlook is furthermore clouded by gaps in the international framework and the limited results of regional harmonization efforts on the substantive law front within, for example, the European Union[7] and the Organization of American States.[8] In addition, intermediated securities are a phenomenon that exists at the juncture of an assortment of legal, regulatory, and other issues, including taxation, accounting, and the technological and operational set-up of each separate intermediated system. Developing a comprehensive legal and regulatory framework capable of operating both domestically and in the context of the transnational holding and transfer of intermediated securities, while extremely important, therefore remains a challenge.

Crypto securities that are based on distributed ledgers, smart contracts, and comparable technologies have the potential to alleviate at least some of these complexities, although they also give rise to new risks and challenges. The market share of such securities is still relatively small but growing rapidly. Whereas some States have proactively promulgated a partial or more comprehensive legal and/or regulatory framework for crypto securities and other crypto assets, the international legal and regulatory framework for these assets is still at a nascent stage.[9] Various aspects of such a framework are discussed in different chapters of this volume, including in relation to corporate actions processing, the integrity of securities holdings, insolvency, other substantive law issues, regulation, and the conflict of laws.

In considering the issues at stake, the focus of this entirely revised edition is first and foremost on international instruments. The legal and regulatory set-up in individual States and regional organizations, such as the US or the European Union, is referred to particularly where it promotes the identification of best practice standards or policy developments at the transnational level.

In Chapter 1, Michel Deschamps examines what the rules for non-intermediated securities should be. Such securities continue to play a role in several sectors of the economy. Deschamps identifies the *lex ferenda* in relation to issues such as the creation of non-intermediated securities, the validity and effectiveness of their transfer, priority rules, and the conflict of laws. He considers the rules for non-intermediated securities in the

---

[7] The reports by the Giovannini Group of November 2001 and April 2003; the advice of the EU Legal Certainty Group of August 2006 and August 2008; and the subsequent consultations on 'Securities Law Legislation' did not result in a comprehensive legal framework for intermediated securities in the EU. See <https://ec.europa.eu/info/business-economy-euro/banking-and-finance/financial-markets/post-trade-services/securities-and-claims-ownership_en> (accessed 15 August 2021).

[8] The proposal to place investment securities on the agenda of the seventh Inter-American Specialized Conference on Private International Law (CIDIP VII) did not bear fruit. See Permanent Council of the Organization of American States, Committee on Juridical and Political Affairs, CP/CAJP-2094/03 add 7 rev 1 (27 February 2004) and add 7-a (17 December 2004).

[9] For a plea to develop transnational rules for crypto assets so as to prevent the legal fragmentation per State as is typical for non-intermediated securities, see Lehmann, 'National Blockchain Laws as a Threat to Capital Markets Integration'.

2016 UNCITRAL Model Law on Secured Transactions and, where relevant, compares how rules for non-intermediated securities sit with those for intermediated securities.

Chapter 2, by Guy Morton, Matthias Haentjens, and the undersigned, deals with financial collateral, a phenomenon that has become *the* lubricant for financial markets over the past decades. Until the global financial crisis, the focus was on private law reform geared to creating a special regime for the provision (whether by transfer or by vesting a security interest) and enforcement of financial collateral. The crisis has led to a notable shift to regulatory law reform aimed at addressing risks related to collateralization, including the provision of too little or too much collateral and the treatment of such collateral in insolvency and resolution proceedings.

Marcel Peeters elaborates on the issue of enforcement of financial collateral arrangements in Chapter 3 on close-out netting, with a critical assessment of the UNIDROIT Principles on the Operation of Close-out Netting Provisions against the background of the global financial crisis. He provides invaluable insight in the debate on the pros and cons of the special treatment of close-out netting, including its systemic impact.

In Chapter 4, Spyridon V. Bazinas enriches the analysis in the preceding chapters by considering the issue of enforcement more generally. He does so by comparing the United Nations Convention on the Assignment of Receivables in International Trade, the UNCITRAL instruments on secured transactions and insolvency, the GSC, and the HSC. He also critically assesses the ongoing UNIDROIT project on 'Best Practices for Effective Enforcement'.

In Chapter 5, Eva Micheler examines drawbacks of the intermediated system against the backdrop of English law. She argues that the system has become unnecessarily complex, with too many intermediaries and other participants in the holding chain, leading to erosion of the rights of ultimate investors. One of the solutions that Micheler discusses in depth is the international debate on applying distributed ledger (or comparable) technology to reduce anomalies in the intermediated system and give investors a more pivotal role.

This plea for structural reform is echoed in Chapter 6, in which Maria Vermaas and the undersigned examine the processing of corporate actions. Income payments, voting rights, and the distribution of information are essential to investors. The introduction of the intermediated system has given rise to a chain that may involve a considerable number of intermediaries and other players, which often complicates the processing of corporate actions between the issuer, at one end of the chain, and the investor, at the other end. The chapter discusses initiatives that have been taken to address such problems that are inherent in the intermediated system and pays particular attention to making optimum use of new technological opportunities with a view to ensuring the efficient processing of corporate actions.

Another set of issues that determines the integrity of the intermediated system is the intermediary's obligation to hold or have available sufficient securities for its account holders, the proper allocation of these securities (notably by way of segregation), the mechanisms to correct any imbalances, and the way in which losses are dealt with in the event of insolvency. In Chapter 7, Guillermo Caballero, Erica Johansson, Maria Vermaas, and myself show that a variety of legal approaches and market practices in respect of these issues exists in different jurisdictions. The chapter also considers how these issues may play out in a setting of crypto securities.

Insolvency is the acid test of the various aspects of holding, transfer, and integrity discussed in the preceding chapters, as became all too obvious during and in the aftermath of the global financial crisis. On the basis of this experience, in Chapter 8, Charles Mooney Jr, Guy Morton, and Karen Saperstein set out the core components of an effective insolvency law framework for intermediated securities. They also look ahead by considering issues such as the treatment of crypto securities in insolvency, as well as possible modifications of the current infrastructure for the holding of intermediated securities based on advances in technology with a view to achieving greater transparency and (a level of) disintermediation.

The global financial crisis has had a major impact on the market infrastructure, which is now characterized by much more stringent regulation, supervision, and oversight in order to guarantee the stability of the financial system. In Chapter 9, Klaus Löber elaborates on this key development, which affects many of the topics discussed in earlier chapters, including financial collateral, close-out netting, the treatment of client assets, and insolvency.

Chapter 10 on crypto securities and other digital assets is an entirely new chapter by Hans Kuhn and Klaus Löber, in which they provide a wealth of information regarding the nascent substantive and regulatory legal framework for such assets. They discuss the pioneering work carried out in this field in a number of jurisdictions and by different international standard setters.

Chapter 11 concludes with an analysis of the conflict-of-laws rules for intermediated securities, the subject matter which sparked the global harmonization process. One of the reasons why the HSC has not found widespread acceptance is the ongoing debate on this topic in the European Union. Francisco Garcimartín, Florence Guillaume, and the undersigned examine the issues at stake and look 'beyond' by proposing ways of breaking the current deadlock, as well as by paying attention to the need for a conflict-of-laws framework for crypto assets.

Teamwork is the keyword that characterizes the process that led to this revised edition. Inspired by the working methods of the 'Intermediation and Beyond' research group led by Louise Gullifer, Guy Morton, and Jennifer Payne,[10] the contributors to the present volume exchanged information, views, and expertise during a series of online colloquia in which the different chapters were discussed. The team also includes Hideki Kanda,

---

[10] This work resulted in the book Gullifer and Payne, *Intermediation and Beyond*.

to whom I owe thanks for what were invariably inspiring talks; Peter Werner, who gave expert advice in relation to Chapter 2 on financial collateral and Chapter 3 on close-out netting; Corjo Jansen who, as Chairman of the Business Law Institute of the Radboud University Nijmegen, gave this project his full support; Patricia de Seume-Nissing, who carried out an outstanding English-language edit of a considerable number of chapters; and the staff at Oxford University Press, notably Rachel Mullaly and John Smallman, for their most pleasant and constructive cooperation. Without the ties of friendship and joint ventures with Herbert Kronke, who stood at the cradle of the UNIDROIT capital markets projects and who has made groundbreaking contributions to transnational commercial law generally, this work would not have seen the light of day.

A clear roadmap is indispensable in order to navigate national, regional, and international securities markets. It is hoped that the signposts offered in this volume will prove useful to the reader.

Thomas Keijser
August 2021

Contents

Table of Cases	xix
Table of Legislation	xxi
List of Contributors	xxxiii
List of Abbreviations	xxxix

1 THE BEST RULES FOR NON-INTERMEDIATED SECURITIES
Michel Deschamps

A. Introduction	1.01
B. Terminology and Concepts	1.07
C. Creation of Non-intermediated Securities	1.20
D. Validity of a Transfer between the Parties	1.23
E. Effectiveness of a Transfer against the Issuer	1.30
F. Effectiveness of a Transfer against Third Parties	1.40
G. Horizontal Priority Rules	1.56
H. Vertical Priority Rules	1.90
I. Conflict of Laws	1.96
J. Conclusion	1.108

2 FINANCIAL COLLATERAL: FROM PRIVATE TO REGULATORY LAW REFORM
Matthias Haentjens, Thomas Keijser, Guy Morton

A. Introduction: Development of the Markets and the Legislative Framework	2.01
B. Over- and Undercollateralization	2.26
C. Collateral in Insolvency and in Resolution	2.63
D. Concluding Remarks	2.91

3 ON CLOSE-OUT NETTING
Marcel Peeters

A. Introduction	3.01
B. A Brief Analysis of Close-out Netting	3.08
C. Principles, Policies, and the Practice of Close-out Netting	3.26
D. Harmonization of Close-out Netting Regimes	3.53
E. Concluding Remarks	3.80

4 ENFORCEMENT OF SECURITY INTERESTS IN SECURITIES UNDER UNIFORM LAW
Spyridon V. Bazinas

A. Introduction	4.01
B. Scope and Definitions	4.04
C. Enforcement	4.44
D. Conclusions	4.128

5 THE NO-LOOK-THROUGH PRINCIPLE: INVESTOR RIGHTS, DISTRIBUTED LEDGER TECHNOLOGY, AND THE MARKET
Eva Micheler

A. Introduction	5.01
B. The Problem	5.11
C. Distributed Ledger Technology	5.15
D. Barriers to Change	5.29
E. Possible Solutions	5.37
F. Conclusion	5.51

6 CORPORATE ACTIONS PROCESSING: BRIDGING THE GAP BETWEEN ISSUER AND INVESTOR
Thomas Keijser, Maria Vermaas

A. Introduction	6.01
B. General Meetings	6.10
C. Income Distributions	6.24
D. Provision of Information	6.33
E. Outlook: New Technologies	6.45
F. Conclusion: Current Status and the Way Forward	6.64

7 SUFFICIENT SECURITIES, SEGREGATION, AND LOSS SHARING
Guillermo Caballero, Erica Johansson, Thomas Keijser, Maria Vermaas

A. Introduction and Terminology	7.01
B. Causes of Imbalances	7.07
C. Requirement of Sufficient Securities	7.13
D. Segregation of Securities	7.19
E. Correction Methods	7.54
F. Loss Sharing in Insolvency	7.71
G. Outlook: New Technologies	7.94
H. Conclusion	7.108

8 PRINCIPLES OF INSOLVENCY LAW FOR INTERMEDIATED SECURITIES
Charles W. Mooney Jr., Guy Morton, Karen Saperstein

A. Introduction	8.01
B. Scope and Objectives of an Effective Insolvency Law Regime for Intermediated Securities	8.17
C. Related Regimes: Special Resolution of Systemically Important Financial Institutions	8.71
D. Selected Additional Issues	8.88
E. Conclusion	8.132

9 REGULATION, SUPERVISION, AND OVERSIGHT
Klaus Löber

A. Introduction	9.01
B. Function and Scope of Regulation, Supervision, and Oversight	9.04
C. Requirements for Central Securities Depositories and Securities Settlement Systems	9.37
D. Market-wide Recommendations and Requirements for Intermediaries	9.94
E. Concluding Remarks	9.146

10 CRYPTO SECURITIES AND OTHER DIGITAL ASSETS: ASPECTS
   OF SUBSTANTIVE AND REGULATORY LAW
   Hans Kuhn, Klaus Löber
A.	Introduction	10.01
B.	Definitions and Key Concepts	10.06
C.	Legislative Developments in Selected Jurisdictions	10.20
D.	Core Elements of a Legal Framework for Digital Securities	10.68
E.	Regulation of Crypto Securities	10.103
F.	Conclusions	10.204

11 CONFLICT-OF-LAWS RULES
   Francisco Garcimartín, Florence Guillaume, Thomas Keijser
A.	Introduction	11.01
B.	Internationality of a Situation Involving Intermediated Securities	11.02
C.	History of the Hague Securities Convention	11.06
D.	Scope of the Hague Securities Convention	11.11
E.	Choice of Law as the Primary Rule	11.22
F.	Fall-back Rules	11.36
G.	Factors to be Disregarded When Determining the Applicable Law	11.41
H.	Third-party Rights	11.43
I.	Relationship between the Hague Securities Convention and the UNIDROIT Instruments for Intermediated Securities	11.51
J.	Problems of the Hague Securities Convention: the European Debate	11.65
K.	Outlook: New Technologies	11.103

Bibliography	391
Index	415

Table of Cases

Bernard L Madoff Inv Securities LLC, In re 654 F 3d 229 (2d Cir 2011) 8.35 n.72
Boston Trust Co Ltd v Szerelmey Ltd [2020] EWHC 1136 (Ch)........................ 5.50 n.101
Boston Trust Co Ltd v Szerelmey Ltd [2020] EWHC 1352, [2020] BusLR 1647........... 5.50 n.103
Brittania Bulk plc v Pioneer Navigation Ltd and others [2011] EWHC 692 (Comm) 3.22 n.31
Byers v Chen [2021] UKPC 4 .... 5.48 n.99

Ciban Management Corporation v Citco (BVI) Ltd [2020] UKPC 21..................... 5.48 n.99
Commissioners for Her Majesty's Revenue & Customs v Enron Europe Ltd
    [2006] EWHC 824 (Ch) 3.22 n.30

Duomatic Ltd, Re [1969] 2 Ch 365 .... 5.48, 5.48 n.98, 5.49

Eckerle v Wickeder Westfalenstahl GmbH [2013] EWHC 68 (Ch);
    [2014] Ch 196................................. 5.11 n.9, 5.11 n.11, 5.30 n.57, 5.31, 5.43 n.86

Hunter v Moss [1993] 1 WLR 934.. 8.28 n.57

Jafari-Fini v Skillglass Ltd [2004] EWCA 3353 (Ch) 5.50 n.103

Lehman Brothers International (Europe) (in administration), Re [2009] EWHC 2545 (Ch);
    [2009] EWHC 2141 (Ch); [2009] EWCA 1161; [2012] UKSC 6..... 2.31 n.59, 2.33 n.63, 8.28 n.58

MF Global Inc., In re No. 11–2790 (Bankr. S.D.N.Y. June 4, 2012)...................... 8.45 n.95

Ruscoe v Cryptopia Ltd (in Liquidation) [2020] NZHC 728......................... 8.130 n.258
Ryan v Picard, 567 US 934 (25 June 2012) 8.35 n.73

Satyam Enterprises Ltd v Burton [2021] EWCA Civ 287............................. 5.48 n.99
SEC v Howey Co, 328 US 293 (1946) 10.161 n.153
Secure Capital SA v Credit Suisse AG [2015] EWHC 388 (Comm) 25 February 2015 ...... 5.12 n.12
Secure Capital SA v Credit Suisse AG [2017] EWCA Civ 1486 (6 October 2017) 5.12 n.14,
                                                      5.30 n.58, 5.31, 5.42 n.84, 5.48 n.100
Sirius Minerals plc, Re [2020] EWHC 1447 (Ch).................................... 5.13 n.15
SL Claimants v Tesco plc [2019] EWHC 2858 (Ch), [2020] Bus LR 250 .... 5.47 n.95, 8.28 n.58
Sterling Equities Associates v. Picard, certiorari dismissed, 566 US 1032 (4 June 2012) 8.35 n.73

Velvel v Picard, 567 US 934 (25 June 2012) 8.35 n.73

Table of Legislation

Unless explicitly mentioned otherwise, the legislation in this table is stated as it applied on 1 July 2021, including earlier amendments, corrections, etc.

FRENCH LEGISLATION

Code de commerce
   Art L.229-1 .... 10.21
Code monétaire et financier
   Art L.211-1 .... 10.24
   Art L.211-3 .... 10.23, 10.26
   Art L.211-4 .... 10.21, 10.25
   Art L.211-7 .... 10.25
   Art L.211-20 .... 10.23
   Art R.211-1-5 .... 10.26
   Art R.211-9-4 .... 10.26, 10.70
   Art R.211-9-7 .... 10.26, 10.70
   Art R.211-1-5 .... 10.70
Décret n° 2018-1226 du 24 décembre 2018 relatif à l'utilisation d'un dispositif d'enregistrement électronique partagé pour la représentation et la transmission de titres financiers et pour l'émission et la cession de minibons 10.22, 10.171
Loi de finance n° 81-1160
   Art 94-II. 10.21
Ordonnance n° 2016-520 du 28 avril 2016 relative aux bons de caisse ('Minibons Ordinance'). 10.22
   Art L.223-6 .... 10.22, 10.171
Ordonnance n° 2017-1674 du 8 décembre 2017 relative à l'utilisation d'un dispositif d'enregistrement électronique partagé pour la représentation et la transmission de titres financiers ('DLT Regulation') 10.22, 10.171
Securities Act 2001
   Art 1(1)-(2) L.1.8.2001 .... 10.28
   Art 1(3) L.1.8.2001 .... 10.30
   Art 3(7) L.1.8.2001 .... 10.28
   Art 18bis L.1.8.2001 ...... 10.29, 10.30

GERMAN LEGISLATION

Act on Electronic Securities (eWpG) 10.54
   § 1 .... 10.56
   § 2 .... 10.57
   § 2(1) 10.59
   § 2(2) 10.57
   § 2(3) 10.58
   § 4(1)–(2). 10.59
   § 4(2) 10.55
   § 4(3) 10.55
   § 7 .... 10.60, 10.70
   § 7(1) 10.60
   § 7(2)–(3). 10.60
   § 12(2) 10.55
   § 16 .... 10.55, 10.59, 10.62, 10.70
   § 16(2) 10.60
   § 17 .... 10.70
   § 18 .... 10.70
   § 19(1) 10.60
   § 20(1) 10.61
   § 20(2)–(3) 10.61
   § 21(1) 10.78
   § 21(2) 10.78
   § 23 .... 10.59
   § 24 .... 10.66
   § 25 .... 10.66
   § 26 .... 10.67, 10.90, 10.92
   § 27 .... 10.58, 10.67
   § 28 .... 10.67
   § 32 .... 10.101
Capital Investment Code
   § 95 .... 10.56
Civil Code
   § 90 .... 10.58
Covered Bond Act
   § 4(5) 10.56
   § 8(3) 10.56
Handelsgesetzbuch (Commercial Code; HGB)
   § 443(3) 10.54
   § 475c(4) 10.54
   § 516(2)–(3) 10.54
Insolvenzordnung (Insolvency Statute; InsO)
   § 47 .... 10.58
Kreditwesengesetz (Banking Act) 2.73
   § 1(1a) 10.63

TABLE OF LEGISLATION

§ 2(7b) 10.63
§ 25h............................ 10.63
§ 25k............................ 10.63
Restrukturierungsgesetz
   (Restructuring Act) 2.73

GIBRALTAR LEGISLATION

Financial Services (Distributed
   Ledger Technology Providers)
   Regulations 2017 .... 10.168

ITALIAN LEGISLATION

Testo Unico della Finanza
   Art 57.3-bis 7.83

LIECHTENSTEIN LEGISLATION

Persons and Company Act (Personen- und
   Gesellschaftsrecht; PGR)
   § 81a............................ 10.37
   § 81a(1) 10.37
   § 81a(3) 10.37
   § 81a(4) 10.37
   § 81a(5) 10.37
Token and Trusted Technology Service
   Provider Act (Token- und VT-
   Dienstleiter-Gesetz; TVTG)
   Art 1 .... 10.33
   Art 2(a) 10.33, 10.70, 10.166
   Art 2(1)(c) 10.34
   Art 2(c) 10.10
   Arts 3–10 .... 10.32, 10.34
   Art 3 .... 10.100
   Art 3(2) 10.100
   Art 3(2)(b) 10.100
   Art 3(3) 10.34
   Art 4 .... 10.100
   Arts 4–6 .... 10.34
   Art 5(1) 10.15, 10.34
   Art 5(2) 10.15, 10.34
   Arts 6(1)(c) 10.35
   Art 6(2)(a)–(c) 10.35
   Art 6(2)(a) 10.94
   Art 7 .... 10.36
   Art 7(1) 10.36
   Art 7(2) 10.36
   Art 8 .... 10.36
   Art 9 .... 10.34–5, 10.90, 10.92
   Art 10 .... 10.36
   Arts 11–29 .... 10.32
   Art 30 .... 10.32, 10.166

MALTA LEGISLATION

Innovative Technology Arrangements
   and Services Act (ITASA) (2018) 10.170
Virtual Financial Assets Act
   (VFAA) (2018) 10.169

NETHERLANDS LEGISLATION

Civil Code
   Art 7:53(3) 2.55
Faillissementswet (Bankruptcy Act) 2.76
Interventiewet (Intervention Act) 2.73, 2.76
Wet op het financieel toezicht (Financial
   Supervision Act; Wft)
   Art 3:267f(4)(b) 2.88

SINGAPORE LEGISLATION

Securities and Futures Act of 2006 (SFA) ... 10.175

SOUTH AFRICAN LEGISLATION

Companies Act 71 of 2008
   s 57(1) 6.10
   s 59 .... 6.19

SPAIN LEGISLATION

Texto refundido de la Ley del Mercado de
   Valores
   Art 154 .... 7.83

SWISS LEGISLATION

Banking Act of 8 November 1934
   Art 16 n°1bis 7.107
   Art 37d 7.107
Code of Obligations (CO) 10.38, 10.39
   Art 165(1) 10.40
   Art 899 .... 10.44
   Art 935 .... 10.91
   Art 967(1) 10.15
   Art 973c(1) 10.40
   Art 973c(4) 10.40
   Art 973d 10.38, 10.42
   Art 973d(1) 10.15, 10.42, 10.84
   Art 973d(2) 10.42, 10.70, 10.78, 10.81
   Art 973d(3) 10.70
   Art 973e(1) 10.84
   Art 973e(1)–(2) 10.43
   Art 973e(3) 10.43, 10.90, 10.92
   Art 973e(4) 10.43
   Art 973f(1) 10.43
   Art 973g 10.44

TABLE OF LEGISLATION   xxiii

Art 973g(1) 10.44, 10.94
Art 973g(2) 10.44
Federal Act of 11 April 1889 on Debt
  Enforcement and Bankruptcy
  Art 242a 7.107
  Art 242b 7.107
Federal Act on Adapting Federal Law to
  Developments in Distributed Ledger
  Technology (DLT Act) 10.38–10.39,
                                  10.44, 10.70, 10.84
Federal Intermediated Securities
  Act (FISA)
  Art 3(1) 10.41
  Art 6(1) 10.41
  Art 6(2) 10.41
  Art 11(2) 7.17
  Art 19(1) 7.85
  Art 19(1) 7.85
  Art 29(1)–(2) 7.63
Private International Law Act (PILA)
  Art 108c 11.09
  Art 145a 10.99
Swiss Civil Code
  Art 899 . . . . 10.40
  Art 900(1) 10.40

UNITED KINGDOM LEGISLATION

Banking Act 2009 . . . . 2.73, 8.38, 8.73, 8.85
  ss 232–236 . . . . 8.38
  s 232 . . . . 8.38
Banking Act 2009 (Restriction of Partial
  Property Transfers) Order 2009 . . . . 2.88
  Art 4 . . . . 2.88
Companies Act 1989
  Pt VII 8.70
Companies Act 2006 . . . . 5.04
  s 98 . . . . 5.11
  s 98(4)–(5) 5.11
  s 112(2) 5.04
  s 145 . . . . 5.14
  s 127 . . . . 5.04
  s 145(1) 5.43
  s 146(2) 5.44
  s 153 . . . . 5.45
  s 153(1)(a) 5.45
  s 153(1)(b) 5.45
  s 153(1)(ba) 5.45
  s 153(1)(c) 5.45
  s 153(1)(d) 5.45
  s 153(2)(e) 5.45
  s 327(2) 6.19
  s 899 . . . . 5.13

Financial Services and Markets Act 2000 . . . . 8.03
  s 90A 5.47
  s 137B 8.26, 8.38
  ss 212–24A 8.30
  Sch 10A 5.47
Insolvency Rules 2016
  r 14.24 . . . . 8.98
  r 14.25 . . . . 8.98
Investment Bank (Amendment of
  Definition) and Special Administration
  (Amendment) Regulations 2017
  (IBSARS) 8.41
  reg 10 . . . . 8.42
  reg 10(5) 8.43, 8.52
  reg 10A 8.42
  reg 10B–G 8.42, 8.61
  reg 11 . . . . 8.42, 8.51
  reg 12 . . . . 8.42–8.43
  regs 12B–12F 8.42
  reg 12B 8.51
  reg 12B(3) 8.51
  reg 14 . . . . 8.42
  reg 19A 8.57
Investment Bank Special Administration
  (England & Wales) Rules 2011
  r 139 . . . . 8.51
  r 134(1)(a) 8.57
  r 135(1) 8.57
Investment Bank Special Administration
  Regulations 2011 . . . . 8.39, 8.42–3, 8.51,
                                        8.57, 8.61
  reg 10 . . . . 8.42
  reg 10(5) 8.43, 8.52
  reg 10A 8.42
  reg 10B–G 8.42, 8.61
  reg 11(3) 8.51
  reg 12 . . . . 8.43
  reg 12B 8.42, 8.51
  reg 12B(3) 8.51
  reg 12F 8.42
  reg 14 . . . . 8.42
  reg 19A 8.57
Uncertificated Securities Regulations 2001
  reg 41(1) 6.19

UNITED STATES LEGISLATION

Bankruptcy Code 2.70, 2.72, 3.34, 3.42,
                         3.49, 8.56, 8.88–91, 8.97, 9.139
  § 1106 . . . . 3.42
Code of Federal Regulations
  12 CFR § 380.61 . . . . 8.81
  17 CFR § 240.8c-1(a)(3) 2.35, 8.25
  17 CFR § 240.15c2-1(a)(3) 2.35, 8.25

xxiv TABLE OF LEGISLATION

17 CFR § 240.15c3-3 ....8.25
17 CFR § 240.15c3-3(a) 8.25
17 CFR § 240.15c3-3(e)(1) 8.25
17 CFR § 240.15c3-3(f) 8.25
17 CFR § 302.101 ....8.81
17 CFR § 302.102 ....8.81
12 CFR § 380.62 ....8.81
Dodd-Frank Act, Title II 2.72–3, 8.78–9, 8.84
Foreign Account Tax Compliance
  Act (FATCA) 6.32
Securities Act of 1933................ 10.161
Securities and Exchange
  Commission (SEC) rules
  r 14a-13 ....6.14
  r 14b-1 ....6.14
  r 14b-2 ....6.14
Securities Exchange Act of 1934
  s 17A(b)(1) 8.105
  r 15c3-3 .... 10.161
Securities Investor Protection Act 1970
  (SIPA) 2.35, 8.03, 8.08, 8.22, 8.29,
    8.34–7, 8.42, 8.44–5, 8.53–4, 8.56, 8.60,
    8.68–9, 8.79, 8.81–4, 8.88, 8.101, 8.105
Supplemental Commercial Law for
  the Uniform Regulation of
  Virtual-Currency Businesses
  Act (SCL-URVCBA) 10.48–9
Uniform Commercial Code
  (UCC) 1.15, 1.22–3, 1.44, 1.50, 1.62,
    1.101, 4.012, 6.14, 8.32, 8.44, 8.63, 10.45
  § 7-204............................1.79
  Art 8...........1.23, 4.08, 7.22, 8.32, 8.127,
    10.46, 10.50, 10.53
  § 8-102(a)(2).......................1.15
  § 8-102(a)(15)..................... 10.51
  § 8-102(4) 10.46
  § 8-102(18) 10.46
  § 8-106(a) 8.63
  § 8-106(d) 8.63
  § 8-110(d) 1.101
  § 8-113...........................1.27
  § 8-207(a) 1.30
  § 8-303...........................1.94
  § 8-304...........................1.53
  § 8-501.................. 7.90, 10.46, 10.47
  § 8-501(d) 1.22
  § 8-503........................... 10.47
  § 8-503(b) 8.32, 8.44
  § 8-504........................... 10.47
  § 8-506...........................6.14
  § 8-511...........................8.63
  § 8-511(a) 8.63
  § 8-511(b) 8.63
  Art 9......... 1.27, 4.08. 4.102, 4.127, 10.53

§ 9-309...........................1.87
§ 9-313...........................1.49
§ 9-328......................1.44, 1.62
Uniform Regulation of Virtual-Currency
  Businesses Act (URVCBA)......... 10.47
  § 102(25) 10.47
  § 502......................10.47, 10.48
  § 502(a) 10.47
  § 502(b) 10.47
United States Code (USC)
  11 USC §§ 101....................8.56
  11 USC § 362(b)(6) 2.70, 8.90
  11 USC § 362(b)(7) 2.70, 8.90
  11 USC § 362(b)(17) 2.70, 8.90
  11 USC § 362(b)(27) 2.70, 8.90
  11 USC § 362(o) 2.70
  11 USC § 365(e) 2.83
  11 USC § 506(a)(1)................8.97
  11 USC § 546(e) 8.90
  11 USC § 553.....................8.97
  11 USC § 555–556 ....2.70, 8.90
  11 USC § 555.....................8.90
  11 USC §§ 559–561 ....2.70, 8.90
  11 USC § 556.....................8.90
  11 USC § 559.....................8.90
  11 USC § 561.....................8.90
  12 USC §§ 5381–5394 .... 2.73, 8.73, 8.78
  12 USC § 5381(a)(7)...............8.79
  12 USC § 5382(a) 8.80
  12 USC § 5382(a)(1)(v) 8.80
  12 USC §§ 5383(a)(1)(B)...........8.80
  12 USC §§ 5383(a)(2)..............8.80
  12 USC §§ 5383(c) 8.80
  12 USC § 5384....................8.78
  12 USC § 5384(b) 8.78
  12 USC § 5385....................8.79
  12 USC § 5385(a)(1)...............8.81
  12 USC § 5385(a)(2)(A)............8.81
  12 USC § 5385(b)(1) 8.84
  12 USC § 5385(f)(1)............. 8.83–4
  12 USC § 5385(f)(2)............. 8.83–4
  12 USC § 5390(a)(1)(O) 8.82
  12 USC § 5390(h)(2)(H)(iv) 8.82
  15 USC §§ 78aaa..................8.03
  15 USC § 78fff....................8.08
  15 USC § 78fff-1–4................8.08
  15 USC § 78fff-2(a)(3).............8.53
  15 USC § 78fff-2(b) 8.34
  15 USC § 78fff-2(c)(1).............8.34
  15 USC § 78fff-2(c)(2).........8.34, 8.36
  15 USC § 78fff-2(f)............8.60, 8.83
  15 USC § 78fff-3(a)................8.60
  15 USC § 78fff-3(a)(1).............8.29
  15 USC § 78fff-3(b) 8.56, 8.60

15 USC § 78fff-3(a)(5)	.8.29
15 USC § 78*lll*(2)	8.22, 8.34
15 USC § 78*lll*(2)(B)(i), (iii)	.8.22
15 USC § 78*lll*(3)	.8.34
15 USC § 78*lll*(4)	.8.34
15 USC § 78*lll*(4)(A)	.8.44
15 USC § 78*lll*(4)(E)	.8.44
15 USC § 78*lll*(11)	.8.34
15 USC § 78*lll*(14)	8.105

INTERNATIONAL INSTRUMENTS

Convention on International Factoring... 4.130
Geneva Securities Convention (GSC); UNIDROIT Convention on Substantive Rules for Intermediated Securities 1.02, 1.04, 1.06–07, 1.11–12, 1.16, 1.18–19, 1.22, 1.26–7, 1.29, 1.37–9, 1.44–6, 1.52–4, 1.57, 1.65, 1.75, 1.79, 1.88, 1.91, 1.93–4, 1.108, 2.14–5, 2.24, 2.27, 2.30, 2.32, 2.89–90, 3.06, 3.09, 3.29, 3.31, 3.59, 3.60–1, 4.01–03, 4.05–12, 4.16–17, 4.19, 4.29, 4.32, 4.34–41, 4.44, 4.46–7, 4.49, 4.111, 4.119, 4.128, 4.131–2, 6.07, 6.17, 6.23, 6.65, 7.02, 7.11, 7.14–20, 7.25–32, 7.57, 7.63, 7.64–5, 7.72–3, 7.79–81, 7.83, 7.85, 7.90, 7.92, 7.110, 8.01–03, 8.12–13, 8.17–21, 8.31–3, 8.36, 8.43, 8.63, 8.70, 8.77, 8.96, 8.99–101, 8.126, 9.96–8, 9.119, 11.01, 11.51–2, 11.54–7, 11.59, 11.60–2

Chs II–IV	.2.14
Ch III	4.01, 4.1, 4.35
Ch V	.2.14–15, 2.24, 2.89–90, 3.06, 3.59, 4.01, 4.11, 4.35, 4.44, 4.111
Art 1	1.07, 1.26
Art 1(1)	.1.53
Art 1(a)	1.18, 4.14, 4.34, 8.03
Art 1(b)	4.14, 4.34, 8.03
Art 1(c)–(e)	.8.03
Art 1(h)	3.29, 7.73, 8.18
Art 1(i)	.3.29
Art 1(k)	.4.39–40, 8.20
Art 1(m)	4.05, 11.60
Art 1(n)–(p)	.4.12
Art 1(n)	.8.70
Art 2	4.06, 11.55
Art 2(a)	4.06, 11.53
Art 2(b)	.4.06
Art 3	11.55
Art 4	.7.73
Art 4(2)(f)–(g)	.4.39
Arts 6–10	.4.08
Art 7	.8.19
Art 9	1.22, 6.07, 6.65, 11.59
Art 9(1)	6.07, 9.96, 10.17
Art 9(1)(a)	.6.07
Art 9(2)(b)	.6.07
Art 9(3)	.8.01
Art 10	1.22, 6.65, 9.96–7, 11.59, 11.61
Art 10(1)	6.07, 9.96
Art 10(2)	6.07, 9.96
Art 10(2)(e)	.6.07
Art 10(2)(f)	.6.07
Arts 11–13	.4.10
Art 11	.1.27, 1.46, 1.75, 4.08, 8.18, 11.59
Art 12	1.46, 1.54, 1.75, 4.08, 8.18, 8.20, 8.63, 11.59
Art 12(1)	.8.20
Art 12(3)	1.53, 8.20
Art 12(5)	.4.09
Art 12(7)	.4.09
Art 13	1.65, 8.01
Art 14	4.10, 8.18, 8.20, 11.59
Art 14(1)	.8.20
Art 14(2)	.1.88
Art 14(2)(b)–(c)	.8.20
Art 14(3)	.8.20
Art 14(4)	.1.88
Art 15	.9.96
Art 15(1)(c)	.8.01
Art 16	4.08, 7.63
Art 18	.1.29, 1.37–8, 1.65, 1.75, 1.79, 1.91–1.93, 4.09–10, 7.63, 10.90
Art 18(3)	1.75, 1.79, 1.93–4
Art 18(4)	.1.75
Art 19	1.44, 1.65, 1.75, 1.91, 4.09–10
Art 19(2)	.1.65
Art 20	.4.10
Art 20(1)	.8.63
Art 20(2)	1.02, 8.63
Art 21	.8.19–20, 11.59
Art 21(1)	.8.19, 8.21
Art 21(2)	.8.18, 8.21
Art 21(3)	.8.19
Art 24	.7.02, 7.14, 7.85, 8.43, 9.96, 9.119
Art 24(1)	.7.14, 8.31
Art 24(1)(a)	.7.27, 8.31
Art 24(2)	.7.27, 7.14
Art 24(2)(d)	.7.16, 7.20
Art 24(3)	.7.17
Art 24(4)	.7.17
Art 25	7.19, 7.26, 7.85, 9.96, 9.119
Art 25(1)	.7.26, 7.28, 7.30–1, 7.79, 8.31, 8.43
Art 25(2)	.7.28
Art 25(3)	.7.29
Art 25(4)	.7.20

Art 25(5)	7.30–1, 7.85, 8.43	Art 2(1)(a)–(g)	11.15, 11.57–8
Art 25(6)	7.28	Art 2(1)(b)–(g)	11.15
Art 26	7.73, 7.79–80, 8.31, 8.100	Art 2(3)(a)	11.19, 11.57
Art 26(1)	7.81, 8.11, 8.33	Art 2(3)(b)	11.19
Art 26(2)	7.79, 8.31	Art 2(3)(c)	11.20, 11.88
Art 26(2)(b)	7.83	Art 3	4.13, 11.02, 11.11
Art 26(3)	7.81	Art 4	10.97, 11.11, 11.38–9, 11.41, 11.43, 11.45, 11.58
Art 27	7.63, 8.70	Art 4(1)	4.50, 4.51, 11.24, 11.26, 11.29, 11.33
Art 27(a)–(b)	8.70		
Art 28	6.07, 9.97	Art 4(1)(a)–(b)	11.31
Art 28(1)–(2)	7.32	Art 4(1)(a)	4.50
Art 28(4)	6.73	Art 4(2)(a)–(d)	11.31
Art 29	11.59	Art 4(3)	11.25
Art 29(2)	6.17	Art 5	4.51, 11.11, 11.33, 11.36, 11.41, 11.58
Art 30	8.96, 8.99		
Art 31	1.16, 4.11	Art 5(1)	11.38
Art 31(3)	8.31	Art 5(2)	11.39
Art 31(3)(a)–(c)	4.35, 6.23	Art 5(3)	11.40
Art 31(3)(d)	2.15	Art 6	11.11, 11.41
Art 31(3)(j)	3.08, 4.34	Art 6(a)–(d)	11.42
Art 31(f)–(g)	4.36	Art 7	11.11, 11.85
Art 31(h)	4.38	Art 7(3)	11.45, 11.47
Art 32	4.11, 4.46	Art 7(4)	11.46–7
Art 33	2.89, 4.11	Art 7(4)(a)–(c)	11.46
Art 33(1)	4.44	Art 7(5)	11.46
Art 33(2)	3.60, 4.44	Art 8	11.11
Art 33(3)	4.45	Art 8(1)	11.49
Art 34	2.27, 2.30, 2.32, 4.11, 4.49	Art 8(2)	11.50
Art 34(1)	2.32	Art 9	11.11, 11.17, 11.60
Art 34(2)	2.32	Art 10	11.11
Art 35	3.61, 4.11, 4.47. 4.111	Art 11	11.11, 11.95
Art 36(1)	4.49	Art 11(1)	11.17
Art 36(2)	2.89	Art 11(2)	11.21, 11.35
Art 38	2.15, 2.89, 4.11. 4.111	Art 11(3)	11.43
Art 42(1)	2.15	Art 108c	11.09

Hague Securities Convention (HSC);
    Hague Convention of 5 July 2006 on the Law Applicable to Certain Rights in Respect of Securities Held with an Intermediary

International Insolvency Institute (III)
    Model Provisions on Secured Transactions for Intermediated Securities

Art 1(1)(a)	4.14, 4.34, 11.13	Art 1	4.113
Art 1(1)(b)	4.14	Art 2	4.113
Art 1(1)(c)	4.14, 11.13	Art 27bis	4.114
Art 1(1)(f)	4.14, 11.13	Art 51bis	4.115
Art 1(1)(g)	11.16	Art 51ter	4.115
Art 1(1)(h)	4.14, 11.13	Art 51quater	4.115
Art 1(1)(j)	11.30	Art 71	4.116
Art 1(2)(a)–(c)	11.16	Art 97bis	4.118
Art 1(3)	11.13	Art 98	4.118
Art 1(3)(b)	11.93		
Art 1(4)	11.13		

UN Convention on Electronic Communications

Art 9(3)	4.08

UNCITRAL Legislative Guide on Insolvency Law (LGIL) 3.06, 3.62, 3.64, 4.01, 4.77

Art 2	11.11, 11.95
Art 2(f)	4.13
Art 2(1)	11.14, 11.16, 11.18, 11.27–8, 11.42–4, 11.58, 11.60
Rec 88	4.77

Rec 101	3.62
Rec 101	3.62
Rec 101-3	3.62
Rec 101-4	3.31
Rec 101-5	3.62
Rec 101-7	3.6
Rec 102	3.62, 3.64, 4.77
Rec 102	3.62, 3.64, 4.77
Rec 103	4.77
Rec 104	4.77
Rec 105	4.77
Rec 106	3.63
UNCITRAL Legislative Guide on Secured Transactions (LGST)	3.67, 4.01, 4.03, 4.05, 4.08, 4.11, 4.15, 4.18, 4.20–2, 4.31–2, 4.33, 4.36, 4.37, 4.52, 9.119
Rec 1(h)	4.52
Rec 1(k)	4.102
Rec 2	4.15, 4.36
Rec 3	4.18
Rec 4	4.36
Rec 11	3.67
Rec 12	4.08, 9.119
Rec 31	4.74
Rec 32	4.74
Rec 33	4.74
Rec 34	4.74
Rec 35(a)	4.75
Rec 39(a)	4.75
Rec 46(b)	4.75
Rec 49	4.75
Rec 50	4.75
Rec 52(a)–(b)	4.75
Rec 55	4.75
Rec 58	4.75
Rec 65-7	4.77
Rec 88	4.76
Rec 94	4.86
Rec 102	4.77
Rec 103	4.77
Rec 104	4.77
Rec 105	4.77
Rec 126	4.78
Rec 131	4.47
Rec 152	4.78
Rec 153	4.78
Rec 172	4.79
Rec 179	4.79
Rec 188	4.79
Rec 235	4.82
Rec 236	4.82
Rec 237	4.83
Rec 238	4.84
Rec 239	4.85
Rec 240	4.86
Rec 241	4.87
Rec 242	4.88
UNCITRAL Model Law on Secured Transactions ('MLST')	1.05
Art 1	4.113
Art 1(1)	4.06, 4.15–17
Art 1(2)	4.06, 4.18
Art 1(3)	1.87
Art 1(3)(a)	4.22
Art 1(3)(c)	4.07, 4.16–17, 4.22, 4.113
Art 1(3)(d)	4.15–7
Art 1(5)	4.15
Art 2	1.87, 4.113
Art 2(3)(d)	4.34
Art 2(b)	4.33
Art 2(d)	1.14–15
Art 2(e)	1.17, 4.42
Art 2(g)	4.40
Art 2(j)	4.54
Art 2(k)	4.33, 4.36
Art 2(m)	4.34
Art 2(t)	4.17
Art 2(u)	4.17
Art 2(o)	4.36
Art 2(v)	4.34
Art 2(w)	1.08, 4.34
Art 2(z)	4.08
Art 2(aa)	4.42
Art 2(dd)	4.17–18, 4.32, 4.36
Art 2(ff)	4.36
Art 2(gg)	4.37
Art 2(hh)	4.34
Art 2(kk)(i)	4.15
Art 2(kk)(ii)	4.18
Art 2(ll)	4.17
Art 2(mm)	1.15
Art 2(nn)	4.08
Art 2(uu)	4.15
Art 3(3)	4.89
Art 4	4.47, 4.60, 4.69
Art 6	4.33
Art 6(1)	4.08, 4.17
Art 10(1)	4.17
Art 13(1)	4.70
Art 14	4.70
Art 18	1.49, 4.33
Art 18(1)	4.17
Art 19(1)	4.17
Art 25	4.17, 4.65
Art 27	1.40
Art 32	4.17
Art 35	4.15, 4.71
Art 36	4.15
Art 37(1)	4.107
Art 43	4.86

TABLE OF LEGISLATION

Art 47	4.17
Art 48	4.17
Art 51	1.67
Art 51(1)	4.107
Art 55	4.70
Art 65(1)–(2)	4.08
Art 71	1.38, 4.58
Arts 72–81	4.53
Art 72(1)	4.54
Art 73(1)	4.55, 4.90
Art 73(2)	4.55
Art 73(3)	4.57
Art 74	4.54, 4.67, 4.92
Art 75	4.54, 4.68, 4.94
Art 76(1)	4.69
Art 76(2)	4.69
Art 77–79	4.54
Art 77	4.96
Art 77(1)	4.55
Art 77(2)	4.57
Art 77(3)	4.57
Art 77(4)	4.57
Art 78	4.65, 4.97
Art 78(2)	4.55
Art 78(4)	4.59
Art 78(5)	4.59
Art 79	4.98
Art 79(1)	4.55–6
Art 79(2)–(3)	4.61
Art 80	4.54, 4.65, 4.99
Art 80(1)	4.62
Art 80(2)–(3)	4.62
Art 80(4)	4.62
Art 80(5)	4.62
Art 80(6)	4.54, 4.62
Art 81	4.100
Art 81(1)	4.56
Art 81(3)	4.63, 4.68
Art 81(5)	4.63
Art 82	4.17, 4.117
Art 82(1)	4.54, 4.58
Art 82(5)	4.66
Art 89	4.17
Art 96	1.101
Art 92	4.06
Art 94	4.72
Art 96	4.06, 1.100
Art 97	4.17, 4.12
Art 98	1.103, 4.106, 4.118
Art 100	1.100–1, 1.103, 1.105, 4.102
Art 100(1)	4.103
Art 100(2)	4.104
UNIDROIT Legislative Guide on Intermediated Securities	8.01
para 269	8.59
para 271	8.64
para 272	8.65
paras 275–6	8.67
para 276	8.67
Annex 1	8.01
Annex 2	8.01
Annex 3	8.01
UNIDROIT Principles of International Commercial Contracts (PICC)	
Art 8.1	3.11
Art 8.5	3.11
Art 7.3.1	3.19
Art 7.3.5	3.19
UNIDROIT Principles on the Operation of Close-Out Netting Provisions (PCON)	3.06, 3.09, 3.12, 3.27, 3.31, 3.36, 8.65, 9.61, 9.89
Principles 2–8	3.06
Principle 2	3.73
Principles 5–8	3.71
Principle 5	3.71
Principle 6	3.72
Principle 7	3.72
Para 2 3	3.09
Para 4(1)	3.12
Para 4(1)(a)(ii)	3.07
Para 4(2)(b)	3.12
Paras 6	3.06, 3.31
Para 6(1)(a)	3.27
Para 7	3.06, 3.31
Para 7(1)(a)–(b)	3.36
Para 8	2.89
United Nations Convention on the Assignment of Receivables in International Trade (CARIT)	4.01
Art 1(1)(a)–(b)	4.26
Art 1(3)	4.27
Art 2(a)	4.28, 4.36
Art 2(b)	4.16
Art 4	4.36
Art 4(2)(a)	4.34
Art 4(2)(a)–(e)	4.29
Art 4(2)(b)	4.16
Art 4(2)(f)–(g)	4.39
Art 4(2)(f)	4.17
Art 5(g)	4.43
Art 5(k)–(l)	4.34
Art 5(l)	4.24, 4.29
Art 5(m)(i)	4.26
Arts 8–10	4.108
Art 9	4.70
Art 10	4.70
Art 13	4.108
Art 14	4.17, 4.38
Art 14(1)	4.109

Art 17(1)–(2)	4.27
Art 17(2)–(7)	4.27
Art 17(8)	4.27
Art 22	4.31, 4.109
Art 24	4.17, 4.4.110
Art 24(1)	4.110
Art 24(2)	4.110
Arts 26–32	4.30

United Nations Convention on the Use of Electronic Communications in International Contracts

Art 9(3)	4.08

EU LEGISLATION

Directives

Alternative Investment Fund Managers Directive (AIFMD); Directive 2011/61/EU of the European Parliament and of the Council of 8 June 2011 on alternative investment fund managers and amending Directives 2003/41/EC and 2009/65/EC and Regulations (EC) No 1060/2009 and (EU) No 1095/2010 .... 2.30, 2.34, 2.59, 7.44, 7.46, 7.52

Recital 32	7.44
Recital 40	7.44
Recital 49	2.59
Art 21(8)(a)(ii)	7.44
Art 14(3)	2.30, 2.34, 2.59
Art 15(4)	2.30, 2.59
Art 21(8)(a)(ii)	7.44
Art 21(10)	2.30, 2.59
Art 21(11)(d)(iii)	7.44, 7.46
Art 21(11)(d)(iv)	2.30, 2.34, 2.59
Art 23(1)(a)	2.30, 2.34, 2.59
Art 23(1)(o)	2.30, 2.34, 2.59
Art 23(5)(a)	2.30, 2.59
Art 24(4)	2.30, 2.34, 2.59

Bank Recovery and Resolution Directive (BRRD); Directive 2014/59/EU of the European Parliament and of the Council of 15 May 2014 establishing a framework for the recovery and resolution of credit institutions and investment firms 2.71, 2.73, 3.75, 7.74, 8.85

Art 2(67)	2.77
Art 2(71)–(71b)	2.75
Art 2(98)	3.08, 3.78
Art 33a	2.86
Art 33a(4)	2.87
Art 33a(10)	2.87
Art 34(1)(g)	2.74
Arts 38–39	2.82
Arts 40–1	2.82
Arts 42	2.82
Art 44	2.77
Art 44(1)	2.76
Art 44(1)–(2)	3.77
Art 44(2)(b)	2.77, 3.77
Art 44(3)	2.76
Art 44(3)(c)–(d)	3.77
Art 45	2.80
Art 45f	2.81
Art 45f(3)	2.81
Art 49	2.77
Art 49(2)	3.78
Art 49(3)	2.77, 3.78
Art 49(4)	3.28, 3.78
Art 49(5)	3.78
Art 64(1)(f)	2.84
Art 68	3.57–76
Art 68(1)	2.88
Art 70(1)	2.87
Art 70(2)	2.75
Art 71	3.57
Art 71(1)–(2)	2.86–7, 3.76
Art 73	2.74
Art 76(2)(a)	2.83
Art 77	3.78, 9.139
Art 77(1)	2.83–4, 3.76
Art 78(1)	2.83
Art 78(1)(d)	2.84
Art 108	2.74
Art 117	3.56–7
Art 118(1)	2.88

Bank Recovery and Resolution (BRRD II); Directive 2019/879 .... 2.79

Banks Insolvency Directive (BID); Directive 2001/24/EC of the European Parliament and of the Council of 4 April 2001 on the reorganisation and winding up of credit institutions 3.07, 3.55–6, 11.74

Art 3	3.56
Art 9(1)	3.56
Art 10	3.56
Art 23	3.56
Art 24	11.68
Art 25	3.07, 3.57
Art 26	3.57

Capital Requirements Directive (CRD V); Directive 2019/878 .... 2.79

Commission Delegated Directive 2017/593 (MiFID II RTS) 7.42, 8.27

Arts 2–3	7.42
Arts 5–8	7.42
Art 2(1)(a)–(d)	7.43

XXX   TABLE OF LEGISLATION

Art 2(1)(d)..........................8.27
Art 3...............................8.27
Deposit Guarantee Scheme Directive (recast);Directive 2014/49/EU of the European Parliament and of the Council of 16 April 2014 on deposit guarantee schemes................7.93
Directive 2002/21/EC on a common regulatory framework for electronic communications networks and services
Recital 18........................10.112
Directive 2009/44/EC amending the Settlement Finality Directive and the Financial Collateral Directive
Recital 5............................2.11
Directive 2018/843 5th AML-Directive
Art 3(18).........................10.11
Directive 2019/1023 of the European Parliament and of the Council of 20 June 2019 on preventive restructuring frameworks, on discharge of debt and disqualifications, and on measures to increase the efficiency of procedures concerning restructuring, insolvency and discharge of debt, and amending Directive (EU) 2017/1132
Recital 43...........................8.91
Financial Collateral Directive (FCD); Directive 2002/47/EC of the European Parliament and of the Council of 6 June 2002 on financial collateral arrangements.......3.06, 4.11, 4.16, 6.23, 8.91, 9.60, 11.74
Recital 15...........................2.69
Art 2(1)(a)–(c).....................6.23
Art 2(1)(d)–(e).....................2.11
Art 2(1)(f).........................2.15
Art 2(1)(l).........................3.09
Art 2(1)(n).........................3.08
Art 3.........................2.10, 3.71
Art 4(4)............................2.10
Art 4(5)............................2.67
Art 4(6).......................3.61, 3.73
Art 5................2.10, 2.27, 2.30–1
Art 5(1)............................2.32
Art 5(2)......................2.32, 3.60
Art 5(5)............................3.60
Art 6...............................2.10
Art 6(2)...........2.68, 2.88, 3.31, 3.60
Art 7(2)............................2.68
Art 8...............................2.67
Art 8(1)............................2.67
Art 8(1)(a).........................2.67
Art 8(1)(a).........................2.67

Art 8(2)............................2.67
Art 8(3)............................2.67
Art 8(4)............................2.67
Art 9...............................2.12
Art 9(1)...........................11.69
Art 21(l)...........................3.09
Art 21(n)...........................3.08
Arts 31–33..........................3.31
Investor Compensation Scheme Directive; Directive 97/9/EC of the European Parliament and of the Council of 3 March 1997 on investor-compensation schemes..............7.93
Markets in Financial Instruments Directive (MiFID); Directive 2004/39/EC of the European Parliament and of the Council of 21 April 2004 on markets in financial instruments amending Council Directives 85/611/EEC and 93/6/EEC and Directive 2000/12/EC of the European Parliament and of the Council and repealing Council Directive 93/22/EEC
Art 5...............................9.29
Art 13(7)...........................2.59
Markets in Financial Instruments Directive (MiFID II); Directive 2014/65/EU on markets in financial instruments (recast).....7.52, 8.28, 8.106–7
Recital 51..........................2.59
Recital 52..........................2.59
Art 16.......................8.26, 9.29
Art 16(8)–(10)......................2.59
Art 16(8).....................7.41, 8.26
Art 24(1)...........................9.29
Art 39.............................8.107
Annex I, s B(1).....................9.28
MiFID Implementing Directive; Commission Directive 2006/73/EC of 10 August 2006 implementing Directive 2004/39/EC of the European Parliament and of the Council as regards organisational requirements and operating conditions for investment firms and defined terms for the purposes of that Directive
Art 5...............................9.29
Second Banking Directive; Directive 89/646/EEC on the coordination of laws, regulations and administrative provisions relating to the taking up and pursuit of the business of credit institutions and amending Directive 77/780/EEC (no longer in force)......3.56

Settlement Finality Directive (SFD);
    Directive 98/26/EC of the European
    Parliament and of the Council of 19
    May 1998 on settlement finality in
    payment and securities settlement
    systems 2.08, 2.12–13, 3.57,
                              7.63, 8.91, 11.74
  Arts 3–5. . . . . .8.70
  Art 9(1) 2.08
  Art 9(2) 2.12, 11.67
Shareholder Rights Directive (SRD);
    Directive 2007/36/EC of the
    European Parliament and of the
    Council of 11 July 2007 on the exercise
    of certain rights of shareholders in
    listed companies. 6.12, 6.56, 6.58, 11.88
  Recital 10. . . . . .6.14
  Recital 11. . . . . .6.02
  Art 2(b) 6.08
  Art 3(a)–(c). 6.08, 6.65
  Art 3(a)(4)–(6) 6.12, 6.58
  Art 3(c) 6.12
  Art 3(c)(2). 6.56
  Art 5. 6.12, 6.20, 6.22
  Art 7. . . . . .6.17
  Art 7(1)(b). 6.17
  Art 7(2) 6.17
  Art 8. . . . . .6.22
  Art 9. . . . . .6.22
  Art 10. . . . . .6.12
  Art 10(1)–(3). 6.17
  Art 10(3)–(4). 6.14
  Art 10(4) 6.21
  Art 11. . . . . 6.12, 6.22
  Art 12. . . . . .6.20
  Art 13. . . . . .6.20
  Art 13(4)–(5). 6.17
  Art 14. . . . . .6.20
Undertakings for Collective Investment
    (UCITS); Directive 2009/65/EU
  Art 22(7) 2.59
Undertakings for Collective Investment
    (UCITS V); Directive 2014/91/EU
  Art 22. . . . . .7.44

Regulations

Capital Requirements Regulation (CRR II);
    Regulation (EU) 2019/876 . . . . .2.79
CCP Recovery and Resolution Regulation;
    Regulation (EU) 2021/23 of the
    European Parliament and of the
    Council of 16 December 2020 on
    a framework for the recovery and
    resolution of central counterparties 7.74

Commission Delegated Regulation (EU)
    231/2013 of 19 December 2012
    supplementing Directive 2011/61/EU
    of the European Parliament and of the
    Council with regard to exemptions,
    general operating conditions,
    depositaries, leverage, transparency,
    and supervision (AIFMD RTS)
  Art 89. . . . . .7.45
Commission Delegated Regulation (EU)
    2016/1401 supplementing the Bank
    Recovery and Resolution Directive
    2014/59/EU
  Art 6. . . . . .3.78
Commission Delegated Regulation (EU)
    2016/1450 supplementing the Bank
    Recovery and Resolution Directive
    2014/59/EU 2.79
Commission Delegated Regulation (EU)
    2016/2251 supplementing the European
    Market Infrastructure Regulation
    No 648/2012. . . . . .7.36
Commission Delegated Regulation (EU) 2017/
    392 of 11 November 2016 supplementing
    Regulation (EU) No 909/2014 of the
    European Parliament and of the Council
    with regard to Regulatory Technical
    Standards on Authorisation, Supervisory
    and Operational Requirements
  Art 25. . . . . .7.61
  Arts 59– 65 . . . . .7.61
Commission Implementing Regulation
    (EU) 2018/1212 implementing the
    Shareholder Rights Directive
    2007/36/EC. 6.08
  Recital 12 6.58
  Art 10. . . . . .6.58
Commission Delegated Regulation (EU) 2017/
    867 on classes of arrangements to be
    protected in a partial property transfer 2.83
Commission Delegated Regulation (EU)
    2018/1619 of 12 July 2018 amending
    Delegated Regulation (EU) 2016/438
    as regards safe-keeping duties of
    depositaries. 7.46
CSD Regulation (CSDR); Regulation
    (EU) No 909/2014 of the European
    Parliament and of the Council of 23 July
    2014 on improving securities settlement
    in the European Union and on central
    securities depositories and amending
    Directives 98/26/EC and 2014/65/EU
    and Regulation (EU) No 236/2012)
  Recital 2. . . . . .7.61

Recital 57 . . . . 11.76
Art 2(1)(1) 9.49
Art 5 . . . . 7.69, 9.116
Art 7 . . . . 7.67, 9.117
Art 8 . . . . .7.51
Art 37 . . . . .7.61
Art 38 . . . . .7.51
Art 52 . . . . .9.49
European Market Infrastructure
  Regulation (EMIR); Regulation
  (EU) No 648/2012 of the European
  Parliament and of the Council
  of 4 July 2012 on OTC derivatives,
  central counterparties and trade
  repositories 2.30, 2.59, 7.36, 7.47,
               7.49, 7.51–2, 8.91, 9.35
Recital 64 . . . . .7.47
Art 11 . . . . .2.42
Art 18 . . . . .9.35
Art 39 . . . . .7.47
Art 39(6) 7.49
Art 39(7) 7.49
Art 39(7) 7.47
Art 39(8) 2.30, 2.59
Art 52(1) 2.30, 2.59
Art 53(2) 2.30, 2.59
Insolvency Regulation (EU) 2015/848 of
  the European Parliament and of the
  Council of 20 May 2015 on insolvency
  proceedings
Art 7 . . . . 8.101
Proposed CSD Regulation (pCSDR);
  Proposal for a Regulation of the
  European Parliament and of the
  Council on improving securities
  settlement in the European Union and
  on central securities depositories (CSDs)
  and amending Directive 98/26/EC
  (Brussels, 7.3.2012; COM(2012) 73
  final; 2012/0029 (COD))
Art 46 . . . . 11.76
Proposed Regulation on Markets in
  Crypto-assets (MiCA); Proposal for a
  Regulation of the European Parliament
  and of the Council on Markets in
  Crypto-assets, (Brussels, 24.9.2020;

COM(2020) 593 final, 2020/0265
  (COD)) 7.105, 8.106, 8.107, 10.64
Title V 8.106
Recital 38 . . . . 7.106
Recital 51 . . . . 8.107
Arts 2(5)–(2) 8.107
Art 3(1) 7.106
Art 3(2) 8.106
Art 3(3) 7.106
Art 3(21) 7.106
Art 53(1) 8.107
Art 63 . . . . 11.105
Art 63(1) 8.106
Art 67 . . . . 8.106
Regulation (EU) 260/2012 establishing
  technical and business
  requirements for credit transfers
  and direct debits in euro 10.112
Rome I Regulation; Regulation (EC) No
  593/2008 of 17 June 2008 on the law
  applicable to contractual obligations
  (Rome I) 11.61
Securities Financing Transactions
  Regulation (EU) 2015/2365 . . . . .2.59
Recital 8 . . . . .2.59
Recital 10 . . . . .2.59
Recitals 21–25 . . . . .2.59
Art 2(1)(d) 2.59
Art 3(12) 2.59
Art 4(9)(b) 2.59
Art 15 . . . . .2.59
Single Resolution Mechanism
  Regulation (SRMR); Regulation
  (EU) 806/2014 . . . . 2.71, 2.73, 2.79, 8.86
Recital 1 . . . . .2.78
Art 5 . . . . .8.86
Art 12 . . . . .2.80
Art 12(g) 2.81
Art 12(g)(3) 2.81
Art 12k 2.79
Art 24 . . . . .2.81
Art 25 . . . . .2.82
Art 26 . . . . .2.82
Single Resolution Mechanism
  Regulation (SRMR II);
  Regulation (EU) 2019/877 . . . . .2.79

List of Contributors

Thomas Keijser is Senior Researcher at the law faculty of the Radboud University in the Netherlands. From 2007–2012, he worked as Senior Officer, later Consultant, at UNIDROIT. He contributed to the Official Commentary on the Geneva Securities Convention and the UNIDROIT Legislative Guide on Intermediated Securities, and published widely in the field of financial law. He was visiting faculty at universities in Germany, Greece, Japan, the Russian Federation, and the United States, and organized several international conferences. He is admitted to the Dutch Bar and worked as a legal officer at a project of the European Union in the Russian Federation. He holds a doctoral degree in law from Radboud University and a master's degree in Russian literature from the University of Amsterdam (cum laude).

Spyridon V. Bazinas is a lecturer, author, and independent consultant advising States and national and international organizations on trade law reform matters. He has been the Secretary of the UNCITRAL Working Group VI (Security Interests) when it prepared the Guide to Enactment of the UNCITRAL Model Law on Secured Transactions (2017), the UNCITRAL Model Law on Secured Transactions (2016), the UNCITRAL Guide on the Implementation of a Security Rights Registry (2013), the Supplement on Security Interests in Intellectual Property Rights (2010), and the UNCITRAL Legislative Guide on Secured Transactions (2007). He also served as Secretary of the Working Group on International Contract Practices, when it prepared the draft Convention on the Assignment of Receivables in International Trade (2001). He has also been involved in the Commission's work on insolvency, bank guarantees, procurement, and electronic commerce. He has also provided technical assistance to States and lectured all over the world on a variety of UNCITRAL work topics. For a number of years, he has been teaching a course on secured financing (including insolvency and private international law) at the Law Schools of the University of Vienna and Sigmund Freud University in Vienna, Austria. Mr Bazinas has co-authored or co-edited more than ten books and has published more than fifty articles on various international trade law topics and, in particular, on secured financing.

Guillermo Caballero is Professor of Law at the University of Chile, Santiago, Chile, and was formerly Professor of Law at the Carlos III University, Madrid, Spain and Adolfo Ibáñez University, Santiago, Chile. Caballero graduated in Law from the Catholic University of Valparaíso, Chile (1996), post-graduated in Economy and Finance from the University of Chile (2002) and obtained his *Juris* Doctor degree *cum laude* from the Autónoma University of Madrid, Spain (2010). His main areas of specialization are commercial law, corporate law, insolvency law, and securities regulation. He published *La adquisición a non domino de valores anotados en cuenta* (*The Acquisition A Non Domino of Intermediated Securities*) (Madrid: Civitas, 2010) and *La custodia en el mercado de valores* (*The Custody of Intermediated Securities*) (Santiago: Thomson Reuters, 2016).

Michel Deschamps is counsel at the Canadian law firm McCarthy Tétrault LLP and associate professor at the Law Faculty of the University of Montreal, where he teaches banking law. He participates as Canadian delegate or expert in law reform projects in the area of secured transactions sponsored by UNCITRAL and UNIDROIT. Deschamps chairs the editorial board of the Québec Bar law review and the secured transactions committee of the Québec Bar. He is a fellow of the American College of Commercial Finance Lawyers. He also appears in most leading lawyers' guides as one of the leading lawyers in Canada in areas of banking and financial services. In October 2013, he received a doctorate *honoris causa* from the University of Montreal.

Francisco Garcimartín is a Chair Professor of Private International Law at Universidad Autónoma of Madrid. He has published in most of the leading law journals on different aspects of private international law and cross-border transactions. He has represented the Spanish Government in different international organizations, such as UNIDROIT, UNCITRAL, The Hague Conference, and the Council of the European Union. He collaborates as consultant for Linklaters SLP.

Florence Guillaume is a Full Professor of civil and private international law at the Faculty of Law of the University of Neuchâtel (Switzerland) since 2006. Her research and publications cover a wide array of topics, including international intermediated securities law, international corporate law, national and international succession law, international trust disputes, and legal issues of digitalization. In 2020, she founded the LexTech Institute, which is an academic centre dedicated to research and training in digital technologies. Before entering academics, Professor Guillaume practiced as a lawyer at the Geneva Bar and the Zurich Bar. She also worked as a Deputy to the Head of the Private International Law Department at the Swiss Federal Ministry of Justice.

Matthias Haentjens is a full professor of law at Leiden Law School and director of the Hazelhoff Centre for Financial Law since 2012. Prior to joining Leiden Law School, he was an attorney with De Brauw Blackstone Westbroek. Matthias Haentjens obtained a Master degree in Greek and Latin at the University of Amsterdam. He obtained his PhD in law also at the University of Amsterdam and was a visiting scholar at Université de Paris II (Panthéon-Assas), Harvard Law School, New York University School of Law, and Ghent University. He has been a member of the Expert Group on Securities and Claims at the European Commission, of the Consultative Working Group on Investment Management at ESMA, and a short term consultant with the World Bank. Since 2016, he has been appointed a deputy judge in the Court of Amsterdam.

Erica Johansson is working as a Legal Counsel at Swedbank AB (publ) in Stockholm. She has extensive experience in derivatives transactions, clearing, capital markets transactions, and regulatory matters. Prior to joining Swedbank AB (publ), she worked as a Senior Legal Counsel at the Swedish Securities Markets Association and prior to that at Nasdaq in Stockholm. She has worked as a Partner at one of the larger Swedish law firms and at two international law firms in London. She holds a Master of Laws from Stockholm University and a PhD from London University on *Property Rights in Investment Securities and the Doctrine of Specificity*. She is a leading expert in the area of intermediated securities and has acted as a legal consultant to the World Bank.

Hideki Kanda is Emeritus Professor at the University of Tokyo. His main areas of specialization include commercial law, corporate law, banking regulation, and securities regulation. Mr Kanda served as Visiting Professor of Law at the University of Chicago Law School in 1989, 1991, and 1993, and Visiting Professor at Harvard Law School in 1996. He is chairman of the Financial Council at the Financial Services Agency of Japan. Mr Kanda's recent publications include Reinier Kraakman et al., *The Anatomy of Corporate Law* (Oxford: 3rd edn, Oxford University

Press, 2014) and Hideki Kanda et al., *Official Commentary on the UNIDROIT Convention on Substantive Rules for Intermediated Securities* (Oxford: Oxford University Press, 2012). He has also written many articles in English in the areas of commercial law, corporate law, banking regulation, and securities regulation.

Hans Kuhn is a practicing attorney in Zurich (Switzerland). He specializes in banking and financial market law with a focus on banking and fintech regulation and blockchain law. He is also advising a number of blockchain-based digital asset projects and worked with the governments in Liechtenstein and Switzerland on blockchain legislation. Before joining private practice in 2014, he served as chief legal counsel for Swiss National Bank, Switzerland's central bank, for more than thirteen years. He has extensive experience as a member of national and international expert groups on matters such as securities law, bank resolution, derivatives, and netting legislation. He is the author of a number of books and numerous articles on securities and secured transactions law. He has been teaching secured transactions law and financial and monetary law at Lucerne University. A graduate of the University of Zurich in 1993, Hans Kuhn was admitted to the bar in Switzerland in 1995. In 1998 he received his doctorate summa cum laude from University of Zurich. He holds an LLM-Degree from Tulane University School of Law (New Orleans, 2001).

Klaus Löber is the Chair of the CCP Supervisory Committee (CCPSC) at the European Securities Markets Authority in Paris. The CCPSC is responsible for enhancing supervisory convergence in respect of EU central counterparties (CCPs) and ensuring a resilient CCP landscape. It is also responsible for the new supervisory responsibilities of ESMA regarding third-country CCPs, with the objective to ensure an adequate monitoring and management of the risk they may pose to the EU. Previously, Löber was Head of Oversight at the European Central Bank in charge of safeguarding the safety and efficiency of payment, clearing, and settlement arrangements as well as Head of Secretariat of the Committee on Payment and Market Infrastructures (CPMI), a global standard-setting body for financial market infrastructures hosted at the Bank for International Settlements in Basel, Switzerland. Earlier work practice also includes the European Commission DG Internal Market, the Deutsche Bundesbank, and private practice. Löber was a founding Secretary of the European Financial Markets Lawyers Group. He is co-editor of various legal journals and has written numerous publications on financial market legal and regulatory issues.

Eva Micheler is a Reader in Law at the London School of Economics (LSE) and Universitätsprofessor at the University of Economics in Vienna where she took Habilitation in 2003. She is also a member of the board of the Institute of Central and East European Business Law in Vienna, and teaches regularly at the University of Vienna, the Wirtschaftsuniversität Wien, and the Bucerius Law School in Hamburg. Before joining LSE, Micheler was also a fellow at the Faculty of Law at the University of Oxford in the context of the EU Training and Mobility of Researchers (TMR) Programme. She has written widely on company and comparative law in both English and German. Her work was cited by the UK Supreme Court in 2010 and by the Austrian Oberster Gerichtshof on numerous occasions. She contributed to Gower and Davies, *Principles of Modern Company Law* (Sweet and Maxwell, 2012) and to *Gore-Browne on Companies* (Jordan Publishing).

Charles Mooney is a leading legal US scholar in the fields of commercial law and bankruptcy law. He is the Charles A Heimbold, Jr Professor of Law at Pennsylvania University School of Law. He served as US Delegate at the diplomatic Conference for the Cape Town Convention on International Interests in Mobile Equipment and the Aircraft Protocol thereto and at the diplomatic Conference for the Geneva Securities Convention, where he was a member of the Drafting Committee. He is co-author and co-editor of the Official Commentary on the Geneva Securities Convention. Mooney was honoured for his contributions to the uniform law process by the Oklahoma City School of Law and was awarded the Distinguished Service Award by the American College of Commercial Finance Lawyers.

Guy Morton is an English solicitor and was, until his retirement, a partner in Freshfields Bruckhaus Deringer LLP. He was Senior Partner of the firm from 2006 to 2010 and for many years before that led the firm's financial services group. He served on the European Commission's Forum Group on Collateral and assisted with the preparation of the Financial Collateral Directive; he was also a member of the Commission's Legal Certainty Group on EU clearing and settlement and is a former member of the UK Financial Markets Law Panel. He represented the United Kingdom in the development of the Hague Securities Convention and the Geneva Securities Convention, in each case serving also as a member of the Drafting Committee.

Marcel Peeters is not only a lawyer but also an economist, having received his PhD in economics from Cambridge University in 1984. He held university lectureships in economics before taking his law degree at Leiden University in 1994, when he switched to the legal profession. Initially, he focused on Supreme Court litigation *(cassatie)* at the Dutch law firm Houthoff. Subsequently, and in particular after his move to NautaDutilh (where he worked until 2012), he specialized in financial law (both private law and regulatory), with an emphasis on derivatives law and capital and liquidity requirements. He was Professor of Derivatives Law at the University of Amsterdam from 2010 until 2020.

Karen Saperstein is a securities clearing expert and is currently the Vice President-Operations for the Securities Investor Protection Corporation.[11] Ms Saperstein served as General Counsel for National Securities Clearing Corporation. During her tenure she developed and brought to market many products including ACATS and Fund/Serv. While at NSCC, Ms Saperstein created and obtained regulatory approval from the FSA for European Central CounterParty, a UK based clearing corporation, and negotiated international clearing agreements with The London Stock Exchange, Caja de Valores, Japan Securities Clearing Corporation, The Stock Exchange of Singapore, and Monte Titoli. Ms Saperstein has been a featured speaker at the Federal Reserve Bank of New York Annual Payment Systems Conference. Ms Saperstein has a JD degree from Fordham University School of Law, served as an arbitrator for the NYC Small Claims Court, and is a certified mediator.

Maria Vermaas obtained academic qualifications in South Africa at the University of Pretoria (BLC, 1981; LLB, 1983) and the University of South Africa (LLM, 1987; LLD, 1995). She earned her doctorate with a thesis entitled *Aspects of the Dematerialisation of Listed Shares in South African Law*. Vermaas held the position of Head of Legal and Regulatory at Strate Ltd, South Africa's Central Securities Depository and serves as an Executive Member of this organization. Maria represented South Africa in the UNIDROIT meetings relating to the Geneva Securities Convention, where she served on various sub-committees and as a Vice-President

---

[11] The Securities Investor Protection Corporation, as a matter of policy, disclaims responsibility for any private publication by any of its employees. The views expressed herein are those of the author and do not necessarily reflect the views of SIPC or of the Author's colleagues upon the staff of SIPC.

of the diplomatic Conference that adopted the Convention. Vermaas retired at Strate in 2019 and is currently acting as legal consultant to the World Bank and National Treasury on financial market legal matters in South Africa.

Advisor

Peter Werner, Senior Counsel, International Swaps and Derivatives Association.

List of Abbreviations

AFME	Association for Financial Markets in Europe
AH	account holder
AIF	alternative investment fund
AIFMD	Alternative Investment Fund Managers Directive (EU)
ALI	American Law Institute (US)
AMF	*Autorité des marchés financiers* (Financial Markets Regulator; France)
AML	anti-money laundering
APP	Asset Purchase Programme
ASIC	Australian Securities and Investments Commission
ASX	Australian Stock Exchange
BaFin	*Bundesanstalt für Finanzdienstleistungsaufsicht* (German Federal Financial Supervisory Authority)
BCBS	Basel Committee on Banking Supervision
BID	Banks Insolvency Directive (EU)
BIS	Bank for International Settlements
BLMIS	Bernard L. Madoff Investment Securities LLC
BNY	The Bank of New York
BRRD	Bank Recovery and Resolution Directive (EU)
CA 2006	Companies Act 2006 (UK)
CARIT	[United Nations] Convention on the Assignment of Receivables in International Trade
CASS	client assets
CC	Civil Code (Switzerland)
CCAF	Cambridge Centre for Alternative Finance
CCP	central counterparty
CER	controllable electronic record
CESR	Committee of European Securities Regulators
CFR	Code of Federal Regulations (US)
CFT	combating the financing of terrorism
CFTC	Commodity Futures Trading Commission (US)
CIDIP	*Conferencia Interamericana de Derecho Internacional Privado* (Inter-American Specialized Conference on Private International Law)
CIPF	Canadian Investor Protection Fund
CMF	Code monétaire et financier (France)
CO	Code of Obligations (Switzerland)
CPMI	Committee on Payments and Market Infrastructures
CPSIPS	Core Principles for Systemically Important Payment Systems
CPSS	Committee on Payment and Settlement Systems
CRMPG	Counterparty Risk Management Policy Group
CRD	Capital Requirements Directive (EU)
CRR	Capital Requirements Regulation (EU)

LIST OF ABBREVIATIONS

CSA	Canadian Securities Administrators
CSA	Credit Support Annex
CSD	central securities depository
CSDR	CSD Regulation (EU)
CTP	crypto asset trading platform
CUSIP	Committee on Uniform Securities Identification Procedures
DG	Directorate-General (EU)
DLT	distributed ledger technology
DORA	Digital Operational Resilience Act (EU)
DTC	Depository Trust Company
DTCC	Depository Trust and Clearing Corporation
DvP	delivery versus payment
E&C	Explanation and commentary
EBA	European Banking Authority
EBRD	European Bank for Reconstruction and Development
EC	European Commission [previously: Commission of the European Communities]
ECB	European Central Bank
ECSDA	European Central Securities Depositories Association
EEA	European Economic Area
EIOPA	European Insurance and Occupational Pensions Authority
EMEA	Europe, the Middle East, and Africa
EMIR	European Market Infrastructure Regulation (EU)
ESCB	European System of Central Banks
ESMA	European Securities and Markets Authority
EU	European Union
eWpG	*Gezetz über elektronische Wertpapiere* (Act on Electronic Securities; Germany)
FATCA	Foreign Account Tax Compliance Act (US)
FATF	Financial Action Task Force
FCA	Financial Conduct Authority (UK)
FCD	Financial Collateral Directive (EU)
FCIC	Financial Crisis Inquiry Commission (US)
FDIC	Federal Deposit Insurance Corporation (US)
FICC	Fixed Income Clearing Corporation
FINMA	Financial Market Supervisory Authority (Switzerland)
FINRA	Financial Industry Regulatory Authority (US)
FISA	Federal Intermediated Securities Act (Switzerland)
FMI	financial market infrastructure
FMLC	Financial Markets Law Committee (UK)
FOCP	fund of customer property (US)
FSA	Financial Services Authority (UK)
FSAP	Financial Sector Assessment Program
FSB	Financial Stability Board
FSCS	Financial Services Compensation Scheme (UK)
FSMA	Financial Services and Markets Act 2000 (UK)
FSTB	Financial Services and the Treasury Bureau (Hong Kong)
GFMA	Global Financial Markets Association
GFSC	Gibraltar Financial Services Commission
GMRA	Global Master Repurchase Agreement

LIST OF ABBREVIATIONS xli

GMSLA	Global Master Securities Lending Agreement
GOSA	gross omnibus segregated account
G-SII	global systemically important institution
G-SIB	global systemically important bank
GSC	Geneva Securities Convention
HCCH	Hague Conference on Private International Law
HGB	*Handelsgesetzbuch* (Commercial Code; Germany)
HM Treasury	Her Majesty's Treasury (UK)
HSC	Hague Securities Convention
IA collateral	independent amount collateral
IBSARs	Investment Bank and Special Administration Regulations 2017 (UK)
ICMA	International Capital Market Association
ICO	Initial Coin Offering
ICR	insolvency and creditor/debtor rights
ICT	information and communication technology
IFI	International Financial Institution
IFSE	International Federation of Stock Exchanges
IIF	Institute of International Finance
IMF	International Monetary Fund
IOSCO	International Organization of Securities Commissions
IP	intellectual property
IPBA	International Prime Brokerage Agreement
ISDA	International Swaps and Derivatives Association [previously: International Swap Dealers Association]
ISIN	International Securities Identification Number
ISMA	International Securities Market Association
ISO	International Organization for Standardization
ISSA	International Securities Services Association
ITA	innovative technology arrangement
ITASA	Innovative Technology Arrangements and Services Act (Malta)
JPMC	JPMorgan Chase Bank NA
KWG	*Kreditwesengesetz* (Banking Act; Germany)
LBHI	Lehman Brothers Holdings Inc
LBI	Lehman Brothers Inc
LBIE	Lehman Brothers International (Europe)
LEI	Legal Entity Identifier
LGIL	[UNCITRAL] Legislative Guide on Insolvency Law
LGIS	[UNIDROIT] Legislative Guide on Intermediated Securities
LGST	[UNCITRAL] Legislative Guide on Secured Transactions
LSOC	legal segregation with operational commingling
MAS	Monetary Authority of Singapore
MDIA	Malta Digital Innovation Authority
MEFISLA	Master Equity and Fixed Interest Stock Lending Agreement
MFA	Managed Funds Association
MFSA	Malta Financial Services Authority
MGESLA	Master Gilt Edged Stock Lending Agreement
MiCA	Markets in Crypto Assets
MiFID	Markets in Financial Instruments Directive (EU)

MLST	[UNCITRAL] Model Law on Secured Transactions
MNA	Model Netting Act
MREL	minimum requirement for own funds and eligible liabilities
MTA	minimum transfer amount
MTM	mark-to-market or mark-to-model
NIS	non-intermediated securities
NOSA	net omnibus segregated account
NSCC	National Securities Clearing Corporation
NY	New York
OCC	Options Clearing Corporation
OECD	Organisation for Economic Co-operation and Development
OJ	Official Journal of the European Union
OLA	orderly liquidation authority
OSLA	Overseas Securities Lender's Agreement
OTC	over-the-counter
PACTE	*Plan d'Action pour la Croissance et la Transformation des Entreprises* (Action Plan for Business Growth and Tranformation; France)
PAM	private asset management
PB	prime brokerage
PBA	prime brokerage account
PBC	People's Bank of China
PCON	[UNIDROIT] Principles on the Operation of Close-Out Netting Provisions
PEPP	Pandemic Emergency Purchase Programme
PFMI	Principles for Financial Market Infrastructures
PICC	[UNIDROIT] Principles of International Commercial Contracts
PILA	Private International Law Act (Switzerland)
PIM	private investment management
PIRR	[LBI Trustee's] Preliminary Investigation Report and Recommendations
PRA	Prudential Regulation Authority (UK)
PRIMA	place of the relevant intermediary approach
PSA	Public Securities Association
RBA	risk-based approach
RBI	Reserve Bank of India
RCCP	Recommendations for Central Counterparties
RSSS	Recommendations for Securities Settlement Systems
RTS	regulatory technical standards
SA	*société anonyme*
SAR	special administration regime
SCL-URVCBA	Supplemental Commercial Law for the Uniform Regulation of Virtual-Currency Businesses Act (US)
SCS	securities clearing system
SEC	Securities and Exchange Commission (US)
SFA	Securities and Futures Act (Singapore)
SFC	Securities and Futures Commission (Hong Kong)
SFD	Settlement Finality Directive (EU)
SFT	securities financing transaction
SFTR	Securities Financing Transactions Regulation (EU)
SIFI	systemically important financial institution

SIFMA	Securities Industry and Financial Markets Association
SIMM	Standard Initial Margin Model
SIPA	Securities Investor Protection Act (US)
SIPC	Securities Investor Protection Corporation (US)
SRD	Shareholder Rights Directive (EU)
SRMR	Single Resolution Mechanism Regulation (EU)
SSS	securities settlement system
STP	straight through processing
SWIFT	Society for Worldwide Financial Interbank Telecommunication
T2S	TARGET2-Securities
TLAC	total loss-absorbing capacity
TT	trustworthy technologies (see also TVTG and VT)
TVTG	*Token- und VT-Dienstleiter-Gesetz* (Token and Trustworthy Technology Service Provider Act; Liechtenstein)
UCC	Uniform Commercial Code (US)
UCITS	undertakings for the collective investment in transferable securities
UK	United Kingdom
ULC	Uniform Law Commission (US)
UN	United Nations
UNCITRAL	United Nations Commission on International Trade Law
UNIDROIT	International Institute for the Unification of Private Law
UNSGSA	United Nations Secretary-General's Special Advocate for Inclusive Finance for Development
URVCBA	Uniform Regulation of Virtual-Currency Businesses Act (US)
US	United States of America
USC	United States Code
VA	virtual asset
VASP	virtual asset service provider
VFA	virtual financial asset
VFAA	Virtual Financial Assets Act (Malta)
VT	*vertrauenswürdige Technologien* (trustworthy technologies; see also TVTG)
Wft	*Wet op het financieel toezicht* (Financial Supervision Act; Netherlands)
WTO	World Trade Organization
XBRL	eXtensible Business Reporting Language

1

THE BEST RULES FOR NON-INTERMEDIATED SECURITIES

A.	Introduction	1.01	G. Horizontal Priority Rules	1.56
B.	Terminology and Concepts	1.07	(1) Horizontal general priority rules	1.60
C.	Creation of Non-intermediated		(a) Certificated securities	1.60
	Securities	1.20	(b) Uncertificated securities	1.64
D.	Validity of a Transfer between the		(2) Qualifications or exceptions	1.73
	Parties	1.23	(a) Transfer not for value	1.74
E.	Effectiveness of a Transfer against		(b) Judgment creditor or insolvency	
	the Issuer	1.30	administrator	1.84
F.	Effectiveness of a Transfer against		H. Vertical Priority Rules	1.90
	Third Parties	1.40	I. Conflict of Laws	1.96
	(1) Certificated securities	1.48	(1) Certificated securities	1.98
	(2) Uncertificated securities	1.52	(2) Uncertificated securities	1.104
			J. Conclusion	1.108

A. Introduction

Securities used to be held directly by the investor, with the latter being entitled to exercise its rights against the issuer directly and, depending on applicable laws and practices, with a certificate being issued by the issuer to the investor. In addition, the investor holding directly-held securities was registered in the issuer's books as security holder, except for bearer securities. Over time, the holding of securities through intermediaries has become more common practice, at least for securities intended to be sold and traded on capital markets. In a simple case, the intermediary is registered in the issuer's books as security holder and maintains an account for the investor into which the securities are credited; a certificate may or may not have been issued by the issuer to the intermediary, but the investor itself does not hold a certificate and is not registered in the issuer's books as the security holder. **1.01**

Yet a large number of securities continue to be held by investors other than with intermediaries, in particular where the issuer is a 'private' entity. Moreover, there are still investors in publicly traded securities which continue for various reasons[1] to prefer to **1.02**

---

[1] For example, an investor may wish to avoid the application of the rule whereby a security interest granted by an intermediary may impair the rights of an account holder of that intermediary. See Art 20(2) GSC and the

be registered in the issuer's books. The investor then has a direct relationship with the issuer and its interest is recorded in the issuer's books. Even for such securities, the paper form has often been abandoned and in some cases, the issuance of certificates is prohibited by corporate law.

1.03 This chapter deals with non-intermediated securities, that is to say, securities not held with intermediaries. As just stated, non-intermediated securities may, or may not, be represented by certificates.

1.04 In its early development, at least in some States, the legal framework for intermediated securities consisted of a transposition or adaptation of the rules governing certificated securities directly held by the investor. Many States have now implemented laws on intermediated securities which are no longer a mere transposition of their old rules on certificated securities. At the international level, this is illustrated by the Geneva Securities Convention (GSC) with respect to substantive law matters and the Hague Securities Convention (HSC) with respect to conflict-of-laws matters.

1.05 Ironically, the existence of a new legal regime for intermediated securities has raised the question of whether new rules also need to be in place for non-intermediated securities. In other words, should the law on non-intermediated securities borrow from the law on intermediated securities, in particular where non-intermediated securities are dematerialized (in other words, are not represented by a certificate)? In principle, there should be a level playing field for all holders of securities, intermediated or not. Some States have already adopted this approach. The 2016 UNCITRAL Model Law on Secured Transactions ('MLST')[2] also proposes a level playing field for secured transactions involving certificated and uncertificated non-intermediated securities; intermediated securities are outside the scope of the MLST.

1.06 This chapter attempts to set out, in a harmonization context, the legal framework applicable (or which should be applicable) to non-intermediated securities, with a comparison to the rules established by the GSC and, at times, the MLST. Section B deals with terminology and concepts. Section C examines how non-intermediated securities are created or established. Sections D, E, and F address various issues relating to the transfer of non-intermediated securities: the requirements for a transfer to be effective between the parties (section D), against the issuer (section E), and against third parties (section F). Sections G and H consider priority issues. Finally, section I discusses the conflict-of-laws rules to apply to non-intermediated securities.

---

discussion in Kanda et al, *Official Commentary*, 20–2. The same rule exists in some States which have laws conceptually similar to the GSC.

[2] Adopted by the United Nations Commission on International Trade Law in 2016.

B. Terminology and Concepts

The GSC defines intermediated securities as 'securities credited to a securities account'; the term 'securities account' is defined as 'an account maintained by the intermediary to which securities are credited'. A person who holds intermediated securities is described as an account holder.[3]

It follows from these definitions that non-intermediated securities are securities not held through a securities account. Article 2(w) MLST contains a similar statement. This statement is not, however, sufficient to describe the principal feature of non-intermediated securities, namely that the holder of such securities has a direct relationship with the issuer. Moreover, the holder of non-intermediated securities needs to be registered in the issuer's books in order to be entitled to exercise the rights attached to the securities, except for bearer securities. This chapter will sometimes use the term 'security holder' to refer to the holder of non-intermediated securities and the term 'registered holder' to refer to a security holder registered in the issuer's books. Indeed, the word 'holder' does not necessarily indicate that the person so designated has physical possession of the securities (or, more accurately, of a certificate representing them); clearly, dematerialized non-intermediated securities are not capable of physical appropriation.

It is worth noting that a fact pattern involving intermediated securities generally involves non-intermediated securities. If issuer A issues and registers securities in its books in favour of intermediary B, which in turn credits these securities (or a portion of them) to a securities account of C, then B will hold non-intermediated securities whereas C will hold intermediated securities. This example shows that securities may be viewed as being both non-intermediated (at the A-B level) and intermediated (at the B-C level), to the extent that under the applicable law account holder C is considered as enjoying a property right in the underlying securities issued by A. On the other hand, in legal systems where intermediated securities are characterized essentially as a contractual right against the intermediary (as opposed to a *sui generis* property or real right in the underlying securities), the intermediated securities credited to the account of C in the example are not the same securities as the non-intermediated securities held by intermediary B.

The term 'securities entitlement' is used in some legal systems as the term corresponding to intermediated securities. To some extent, the term 'securities entitlement' implies that the account holder is not an indirect holder of the underlying securities.

The GSC seeks to take a neutral approach as to the legal nature of intermediated securities and avoids characterizing them as a property right or a contractual right, or a combination of both. For this reason, the GSC does not describe intermediated securities as indirectly held securities. Likewise, the HSC does not take a stand on the

---

[3] See the definitions in Art 1 GSC.

characterization of intermediated securities (referred to in the HSC as 'securities held with an intermediary').[4]

1.12 It is also implicit from the neutral approach taken by the GSC and the HSC that the term 'directly-held securities' is not a substitute for non-intermediated securities. Nonetheless, the legal relationship between the issuer and the registered holder of non-intermediated securities is still a direct relationship; therefore, this chapter will on occasion refer to non-intermediated securities as 'directly held'. It is worth noting that securities do not cease to be directly held if a third party acts as the issuer's agent to record the investors' interests or any transfers of securities from one security holder to another.

1.13 Other concepts or terms relevant to this chapter are 'certificated securities', 'uncertificated securities', 'transfer', and 'competing claimant'.

1.14 Certificated securities are securities represented by a certificate issued by the issuer. In such cases, possession of the certificate is normally required to permit the security holder fully to exercise the rights conferred by the securities concerned. Certificated securities may be in registered or bearer form. They are in registered form where the certificate specifies the name of the person entitled thereto. They are in bearer form where the certificate states that the bearer thereof is the security holder.[5] Certificated securities are designated by Article 2(d) MLST as 'certificated non-intermediated securities'.

1.15 Uncertificated securities are securities which are issued in favour of a person registered in the issuer's books as the holder of the securities but are not represented by a certificate. This term is preferred to the term 'dematerialized securities', as in common parlance the latter is sometimes used also to encompass intermediated securities. Article 2(mm) MLST defines uncertificated securities as 'non-intermediated securities not represented by a certificate'. Uncertificated securities cannot constitute bearer securities and Article 2(d) MLST recognizes that conceptually, a certificate is required to hold non-intermediated bearer securities; § 8-102(a)(2) of the Uniform Commercial Code (UCC) of the United States is to the same effect.

1.16 The term 'transfer' will be used to include not only an outright (or absolute) disposition but also a transaction whereby a security interest or other limited interest is granted in non-intermediated securities.[6] Whenever appropriate, the discussion will distinguish between outright transfers and security interests.

---

[4] An elaboration of this neutral approach is found in Bernasconi and Keijser, 'The Hague and Geneva Securities Conventions', 549. See also discussions on the nature of intermediated securities in Kanda et al, *Official Commentary*, 9–3; Thévenoz, 'Geneva Securities Convention'; Paech, 'Market Needs'; Dupont, 'Rights of the Account Holder'; Segna, 'Impact on German Law'; and Garcimartín, 'A Spanish Perspective'.

[5] For instance, a bond payable to bearer. Many corporate laws prohibit the issuance of shares in bearer form.

[6] The term 'security interest' is used in a broad sense to denote 'the grant of an interest other than full ownership in ... securities for the purpose of securing the performance of ... obligations'. The quoted language comes from the definition of 'security collateral agreement' in Art 31 GSC.

The term 'competing claimant' will be used in the context of priority disputes between a   1.17
transferee of securities and another person claiming rights in the securities superior to
those of the transferee. The other person may be another transferee, a judgment creditor of the transferor, or an insolvency administrator in insolvency proceedings relating
to the transferor. Article 2(e) MLST contains a definition of competing claimant which
is to the same effect. Priority disputes often arise in the area of secured transactions; as
noted, the term 'transfer' will be used in this chapter as a generic term which includes
the grant of a security interest. Therefore, the discussion on priority issues will also
cover disputes involving a creditor to which a security interest in securities has been
granted.

This chapter does not attempt to define the various categories of rights or interests to be   1.18
considered as 'securities' for the purposes of harmonized rules on non-intermediated
securities. Paraphrasing Article 1(a) GSC, the term should generally include shares,
bonds, or other, similar equity interests or debt instruments the transfer of which may
be registered in the issuer's books or that are capable of being represented by a certificate in bearer form.

As the goal of this chapter is to propose harmonized rules for non-intermediated se-   1.19
curities in comparison to the GSC rules, specific references are not made to national
laws, with the exception of the UCC. The UCC in effect has been a source of inspiration
for some other States which have modernized their laws on intermediated and non-
intermediated securities. At the international level, in addition to the GSC, reference
is made to the HSC and the MLST. As mentioned in paragraph 1.05, the MLST does
not deal with intermediated securities but has rules on non-intermediated securities.
Harmonized rules on non-intermediated securities, in particular for security interests
in such securities, must therefore take into account the provisions of the MLST.

C. Creation of Non-intermediated Securities

Non-intermediated securities are created or established where the issuer agrees to issue   1.20
securities in favour of another person in conformity with applicable law (for example,
corporate law) and with the terms and conditions governing their issuance. Nothing
more than an agreement between the issuer and that person should, in principle, be required to create non-intermediated securities. The issuer usually maintains a securities
register in which the issue is recorded. The person to whom the securities have been
issued will then become a security holder (and a registered holder unless the securities
are in a certificated bearer form). A frequent corporate law requirement is that securities cannot be issued unless they are fully paid.

The delivery of a certificate should not be a condition for the validity of the creation   1.21
of non-intermediated securities. Thus, for those jurisdictions that permit the issuance
of certificates, such issuance should be an option, not a requirement. Indeed, where a

certificate is issued, the possession of the certificate may become necessary to attain full enjoyment of the rights attached to the securities.

1.22 It is beyond the scope of this chapter to discuss whether an issuer may challenge the validity of securities that have not been issued in compliance with the applicable law or the terms and conditions governing their issue, where the security holder is unaware of the non-compliance. Approaches on this difficult question differ, and distinctions can be made between shares and debt obligations or between non-compliance with applicable law and non-compliance with the terms and conditions of the securities. Suffice it to say that in similar circumstances, the holder of intermediated securities might enjoy greater protection than the holder of non-intermediated securities (provided the intermediary remains solvent). In its relationship with the account holder, an intermediary will as a rule be precluded from contending that the underlying securities have not been validly issued. This is so regardless of the legal characterization of intermediated securities, because by crediting the securities account the intermediary incurs the obligation to procure to an account holder the rights purporting to result from the credit.[7]

D. Validity of a Transfer between the Parties

1.23 A transfer of securities, whether or not intermediated, may occur in a variety of circumstances, as for any other type of property. The term 'validity' is used here to refer to the effectiveness of a transfer between the parties thereto (and not third parties). The validity of a transfer as between the transferor and the transferee should be outside the scope of laws intended to establish rules on the right of transferees against third parties or the issuer; Article 8 UCC is an example of such laws and does not in general address validity issues.

1.24 Therefore, the law of obligations (including contract law) and property law will determine whether a transfer is valid. If a transfer is made by way of a sale and if, under the applicable law, no more than an agreement is required for a sale to take place, the transfer will be effective upon the parties reaching that agreement. If the transfer results from a contract the validity of which is subject to the fulfilment of formalities, the transfer will occur only once these formalities have been fulfilled. This may be the case in those States which subject the validity of a gift or a security interest to form requirements.

1.25 A transfer may also occur by operation of law; for example, the bankruptcy of a security holder will result in the assets of the bankrupt being vested in an insolvency administrator (for example, a trustee in bankruptcy). In addition, a transfer may be made through a judicial process further to a seizure by a creditor of the security holder.

---

[7] Articles 9 and 10 GSC; § 8–501(d) UCC is clearer on this.

Special rules exist in some States on the enforcement of creditors' rights with respect to securities.

The above remarks may also apply to the validity of a transfer of intermediated securi- **1.26** ties. The GSC does not deal explicitly with the issue of the validity of a transfer between the parties thereto; the matter is left to the non-Convention law, that is, the law in force in a Contracting State other than the provisions of the GSC.[8]

It is, however, possible to construe Article 11 GSC as implying that nothing more than **1.27** an agreement (even oral) is needed for the validity of a consensual transfer giving rise to a credit to a securities account; under that interpretation, the validity of the transfer could not be challenged on the grounds of non-compliance with form requirements that would otherwise apply to an agreement of the same type (for example, a requirement that the agreement be notarized).[9]

At first glance, a defective or invalid transfer of non-intermediated securities should **1.28** have no effect against third parties. For example, if the transferor has been induced by fraud to consent to the transfer, the transfer is subject to annulment and the transferee would then have no property right to enforce against a subsequent transferee of the transferor. The same analysis applies to an invalid security interest: the security interest, being invalid, would not rank ahead of the claims of the transferor's other creditors.

However, as will be discussed in section H, this analysis does not necessarily hold true **1.29** in a scenario where the transferee under an invalid transfer has retransferred the non-intermediated securities to a third party. A third party in good faith which acquires non-intermediated securities from the transferee under the invalid transfer should be protected in the same manner as an innocent acquirer under Article 18 GSC.

E. Effectiveness of a Transfer against the Issuer

The law under which non-intermediated securities are issued generally states that an is- **1.30** suer may treat the registered holder as the person entitled to exercise the rights attached to the securities.[10] It follows from that rule that a transfer will not be effective against the issuer until the transfer is registered in its books.

Indeed, the rule cannot apply to bearer securities, that is to say, securities represented **1.31** by a certificate in bearer form (for example, bonds payable to the bearer thereof). In that case, the only condition for the effectiveness of the transfer will be the delivery of

---

[8] See the definition of 'non-Convention law' in Art 1 GSC.
[9] The above interpretation of Art 11 GSC is probably too far-reaching given its scope. § 8–113 UCC and the laws of some other States specifically provide that no writing is required for 'a contract for the sale or purchase of a security' to be enforceable. This provision of the UCC is, however, subject to the form requirement that may apply to a security agreement under Art 9 UCC.
[10] See, eg, § 8–207(a) UCC. Note that the UCC term is 'registered owner' and not 'registered holder'; however, the person so registered is not always an owner and the term 'holder' as used in this chapter is more neutral.

the certificate to the transferee, and possession of the certificate will be sufficient for the transferee to be recognized by the issuer as the security holder.

1.32 Securities that must be registered in the issuer's books for its holder to be empowered to exercise its rights against the issuer are often designated as registered securities. For these securities, any discussion of the effectiveness of a transfer against the issuer must first examine the question as to whether the issuer is bound to give effect to any request for a transfer or whether it may impose conditions on the registration of the transfer. Common sense dictates that the issuer should be entitled to impose conditions to be fulfilled by the transferee, and most existing laws regulate this matter to that effect. What are (or what should be) these conditions? Distinctions must first be made between certificated securities and uncertificated securities.

1.33 For certificated securities, it goes without saying that the transferee must surrender the certificate to the issuer in order to be registered as the new security holder and to obtain a new certificate in its name. In addition, the issuer should not be compelled to register the transfer unless the transferee provides reasonable proof that it has become the security holder. An endorsement of the certificate by the transferor constitutes such proof, but the laws of many legal systems often provide that the endorsement may be replaced by a separate document signed by the transferor evidencing the transfer. In each case, the issuer should also be allowed to satisfy itself that the transferor's signature or that of its representative is genuine; in the case of a signature affixed by a representative of the transferor, evidence of that representative's power may also be required by the issuer.

1.34 For uncertificated securities, the basic requirements prescribed by the issuer to register the transfer should in substance be the same as those for certificated securities, except for the surrender of a certificate. Thus, the issuer should be permitted to require proof that the existing registered holder has authorized the transfer and that the authorization is genuine.

1.35 In addition to evidence that a transfer has been effected, the transferee may have to meet other conditions in order for the issuer to be required to register the transfer. These other conditions do not depend on whether the securities are certificated or uncertificated. Rather, they relate to any restrictions on transfers that may be found in the applicable law or the terms under which the securities have been issued. For example, the applicable law or the constitutive documents of the issuer may require that a transfer be authorized by the governing body of the issuer (eg, its board of directors) or that the transferee belong to a specified class of persons (eg, due to the regulatory framework applicable to the issuer). In such case, the issuer will subject registration of the transfer to the fulfilment of the relevant requirements.

1.36 The registration by an issuer of an unauthorized transfer should not deprive the previous registered holder from its rights in the related securities. For instance, if a purported transferee of non-intermediated securities causes the issuer to register the transfer and if the purported transferor's endorsement or authorization has been forged, the issuer will remain liable to provide the true owner of the securities with equivalent securities. This general rule may, however, be subject to exceptions in certain circumstances: for example, if the issuer has taken steps to satisfy itself of the genuineness of an endorsement on a certificate surrendered for transfer purposes and if the true owner of the securities failed to notify the issuer of the loss within a reasonable time, the issuer should be relieved from liability to the true owner.

1.37 A related question is whether a transferee in good faith should still be able, further to an unauthorized transfer registered in the issuer's books, to enforce rights against the issuer after the latter has discovered that the transfer was not authorized. This may happen where the transferee has dealt with a person believed in good faith to be a representative of the true owner. Applying the provisions of Article 18 GSC on innocent acquisition by analogy would result in the good faith transferee being empowered to exercise the rights attached to the securities against the issuer, except if the transfer was 'made by way of gift or gratuitously'.

1.38 Another analogy may, however, be made with the law of negotiable instruments. Under the laws of some States, a forged endorsement on a promissory note in non-bearer form will preclude the purported endorsee, even if in good faith and for value, from being entitled to claim payment from the maker of the note. In order to achieve results in the area of non-intermediated securities similar to those contemplated by the GSC, the rule of Article 18 GSC should prevail over a solution based on an analogy with the law of negotiable instruments. It should be noted that the MLST does not deal with the issue and its Article 71 refers to the law of the enacting State relating to the obligations of the issuer of non-intermediated securities.

1.39 Indeed, the consequence of the GSC approach, as applied to non-intermediated securities, is that the number of outstanding securities of the issuer may exceed those initially issued. To the extent that this over-issue would not be permitted under applicable law or the terms of the securities, the law should provide means to compensate the previous registered owner.[11]

F. Effectiveness of a Transfer against Third Parties

1.40 A transfer that is effective against an issuer will as a rule also be effective against third parties. However, consistent with the MLST,[12] the law should permit a transferee to achieve third-party effectiveness by means other than registration in the issuer's books. For the sake of concision, the term 'perfection' (or any correlative term) will on occasion be used hereafter as an equivalent to effectiveness against third parties.

---

[11] See Ch 7.
[12] The MLST provides that perfection of a security interest in certificated non-intermediated securities may be achieved by possession or by registration in the registry for security rights, while for uncertificated non-intermediated securities, registration in that registry or control (in a broad sense—see Art 27 MLST) is a mode of perfection.

1.41 This section examines the requirements, if any, to be met for a valid transfer to be effective against third parties which are competing claimants. Competing claimants include another transferee of the transferor, a judgment creditor of the transferor, or an insolvency administrator in insolvency proceedings relating to the transferor.[13] Should steps be taken in order for the transferee to be able to set up its transfer against these persons?

1.42 Under the traditional *nemo dat* rule, third parties cannot acquire or claim better rights than those of the transferor. Under that rule, a transfer that is effective between the parties to the transfer should be effective against third parties. For example, if a person sells goods to a buyer, that person is no longer the owner of the goods and a judgment creditor of the seller cannot seize the goods after the sale. In principle, the *nemo dat* rule has the same outcome if the seller subsequently resells the goods to a second buyer, as the second buyer has nothing to acquire.[14] Likewise, goods sold by a person who subsequently becomes bankrupt are not vested in the trustee in that person's bankruptcy. In most legal systems, the *nemo dat* rule is, however, subject to many exceptions. Real property law is an example: the purchaser of a land the title to which is registered in the land registry will generally prevail over a previous purchaser with an unregistered title; a registered mortgage will rank ahead of a prior mortgage that has not yet been registered.

1.43 The MLST and the laws of many States on security interests in movable property also contain many examples of exceptions to the *nemo dat* rule: certain steps usually need to be taken in order for a security interest to be effective against third parties, with the result that security interests do not necessarily derive their ranking from the time when they were granted. In the same vein, many legal systems subject the third-party effectiveness of an outright assignment of receivables to the fulfilment of certain formalities.

1.44 The GSC provisions on the effectiveness against third parties of an acquisition of intermediated securities also disregard the *nemo dat* rule in many respects.[15] The underlying policy reason for these provisions applies to non-intermediated securities, as it is intended to ensure certainty where third-party effectiveness is achieved by the acquirer.[16] This is also dictated by the need for a level playing field for intermediated and non-intermediated securities. For securities represented by certificates, it is worth noting that the *nemo dat* rule has been displaced for a long time: a sale or other transfer of the securities will be ineffective against a subsequent purchaser in good faith to which the certificate has been endorsed and delivered.

---

[13] This section does not consider whether a defect in a transfer may be raised against a subsequent transferee which has obtained the securities in good faith from the transferee under the defective transfer. This issue will be examined in s H.

[14] Although sale law will often provide exceptions to that result, in particular where the first buyer has not taken delivery of the goods and the seller delivers them to the second buyer.

[15] For example, under Art 19 GSC, if A sells intermediated securities to B and thereafter sells the same intermediated securities to C and enters into a control agreement with the intermediary, the sale to C will be effective against B despite the *nemo dat* rule.

[16] The UCC Official Commentary contains a discussion on that policy in the comments on § 9–328.

So what would be the best rules for the perfection of a transfer of non-intermediated securities? Should they parallel the GSC rules and if so, how? To what extent should they be comparable to those of the MLST or, in the case of certificated securities, to the rules governing negotiable instruments? **1.45**

A preliminary question is whether the same methods should be available to perfect both an outright transfer and a security interest. In principle, this question should be answered in the affirmative. First, it is not always easy to characterize a transfer as absolute or only made for security purposes; allowing for the use of different methods for outright transfers and security interests would not determine the applicable perfection method with certainty. Secondly, complications would ensue in resolving priority disputes between an outright transferee and a second creditor, if the outright transferee were able to achieve third-party effectiveness under a perfection mechanism not available to a secured creditor. It must be noted that the methods of perfection provided by Articles 11 and 12 GSC are available for any kind of transfer. **1.46**

As uncertificated securities are purely intangible property and certificated securities may, in some fashion, be assimilated to negotiable instruments, the perfection mechanisms cannot be the same for both types of securities. **1.47**

(1) Certificated securities

It is generally recognized that the transfer of a certificated security may be made effective against third parties by the delivery of the certificate to the transferee (or another person acting on behalf of the transferee). This long-standing rule has its roots in negotiable instruments law. After delivery of the certificate to the transferee, the transferor cannot usually transfer real benefits to another person. **1.48**

In the case of a certificate in registered form, should the certificate also be required to be endorsed by the transferor? A certificate in registered form is a certificate issued in favour of a person named on the certificate as the holder thereof (as opposed to a bearer certificate). Without the transferor's endorsement, the transferee will be unable to compel the issuer to record the transfer in its books. On the other hand, after an unendorsed certificate in registered form has been delivered to the transferee, it is impossible for the transferor to deliver and endorse the certificate in favour of another person. Therefore, it appears that delivery of the certificate should be sufficient to make the transfer effective against third parties.[17] Requiring endorsement could imply that third parties may disregard the transfer even if the certificate is no longer in the hands of the transferor. **1.49**

---

[17] This is implied by Art 18 MLST on the effectiveness against third parties of a security interest in a tangible asset, which term includes certificated non-intermediated securities. § 9–313 UCC has the same effect.

1.50 Consistent with the law of negotiable instruments, a transfer with delivery of a certificate in registered form should require the transferor to provide any missing endorsement.[18] If the transferor fails to do so, the courts should be empowered to issue an order allowing for the transfer to be registered in the issuer's books.

1.51 In the area of secured transactions, the MLST and many legal systems provide that registration in a security interest registry is a method of achieving third-party effectiveness, including for assets capable of being the subject of a possessory security interest. There is no reason why such a method could not be allowed for a security interest in certificated securities as well. As will be discussed in section G, a possessory security interest in certificated securities should nonetheless prevail over a non-possessory security interest previously registered in a security interest registry.

(2) Uncertificated securities

1.52 Uncertificated securities cannot be the subject of physical appropriation; accordingly, possession cannot be a means of perfecting a transfer of uncertificated securities. In many ways, uncertificated securities resemble intermediated securities, except that the former are held directly with the issuer. But for that distinction, they are conceptually similar. Therefore, the legal framework of the GSC for the effectiveness against third parties of an acquisition of intermediated securities appears to be an appropriate template to model the rules on the effectiveness against third parties of a transfer of uncertificated securities.

1.53 Under that approach, a transferee of uncertificated securities may render its transfer effective against third parties, either by causing the issuer to register the transfer in the issuer's books or by obtaining control of the securities through a control agreement.[19] These two methods should be available not only to an outright transferee but also to a transferee which is a secured creditor. Both methods play the same role as the delivery of the related certificate to a transferee of certificated securities. In the case of a security interest in uncertificated securities, a control agreement is a functional equivalent to possession of a certificate representing the securities.

1.54 In the context of uncertificated securities, a control agreement is an agreement between the transferee, the registered holder, and the issuer whereby the transferee becomes empowered either to prevent a disposition of the securities by the registered holder or to dispose of them without any further consent by the registered holder. Article 12 GSC also provides that a control agreement perfects an acquisition of intermediated securities.

---

[18] § 8–304 UCC provides for such obligation on the part of a transferor of a certificate in registered form.
[19] Article 12(3) GSC also contemplates that an outright transferee or a secured creditor may perfect its interest through a designating entry. Under Art 1(l) GSC, a designating entry has the same effect as a control agreement.

As has been proposed with respect to certificated securities, it should also be possible for a secured creditor to achieve third-party effectiveness through registration of its security interest in a security interest registry. The MLST recognizes this possibility. **1.55**

G. Horizontal Priority Rules

This section deals with the rules intended to resolve a priority dispute between a transferee of non-intermediated securities and another person claiming a right or interest in the securities as a result of dealings with the transferor or other action taken against the transferor. A dispute of this kind may be described as a horizontal priority dispute: both the transferee and the competing claimant invoke a right or interest deriving from that of the transferor.[20] **1.56**

At first glance, a priority dispute between a transferee and a competing claimant may be resolved using one single rule: a transfer, once made effective against third parties, would necessarily have priority over another right or interest not yet so effective. However, for policy and efficiency reasons, neither the GSC, the MLST, nor many legal systems have adopted this straightforward approach, in particular where more than one method to achieve third-party effectiveness exists under the applicable regime. **1.57**

Another issue is whether any third party may assume that the securities still belong to the transferor where no perfection requirement has been fulfilled. In other words, should a non-perfected transfer still have some effects? The question notably arises in the event of a dispute between an outright transferee and a judgment creditor or the administrator of the transferor's insolvency. **1.58**

The horizontal priority rules relating to non-intermediated securities must take the above considerations into account. **1.59**

(1) Horizontal general priority rules

(a) Certificated securities
Consistent with the expectations of the parties that possession of a certificate normally entitles the holder thereof to exercise the rights attached to the related securities, two basic priorities rules should apply for certificated securities. **1.60**

First, a transferee whose transfer is effective against third parties by delivery of the certificate should have priority against any competing claimant. Secondly, a transferee whose transfer is effective against third parties by registration in a public registry **1.61**

---

[20] By contrast, a 'vertical priority dispute' is a dispute where a competing claimant asserts against the transferee an interest not deriving from the transferor. If securities owned by A are stolen by B, who subsequently sells them to C, a claim by A against C gives rise to a vertical priority dispute.

should have priority against any competing claimant other than a transferee in possession of the certificate. The combined effect of these two rules is that perfection achieved by possession of the certificate will trump perfection by registration in a public registry, even if the registration occurred prior to the delivery of the certificate. In the area of secured transactions, the MLST and the UCC provide for the same result.

1.62 For the sake of simplicity, the super-priority resulting from the delivery of a certificate to a transferee should not be made conditional on the certificate being endorsed in favour of the transferee. This is a matter relevant to a transferee's ability to compel the issuer to give effect to the transfer, but not to the priority against competing claimants of a transferee in possession of the certificate. Providing for two levels of priority by possession depending on whether the certificate has or has not been endorsed by the transferor would lead to unwarranted complexity and would call for sub-rules dealing with a scenario where two competing transferees would be treated as having possession (actual or constructive) of the same certificate.[21]

1.63 Registration in a public registry as a method of achieving third-party effectiveness is usually reserved for a transfer made for security purposes, namely a security interest. However, nothing should prevent a legal system from providing that the third-party effectiveness of an outright transfer may also be achieved by registration in a public registry (for example, in a bulk transfer of the securities portfolio of a business).

(b) Uncertificated securities

1.64 The similarities between intermediated securities and uncertificated securities dictate the adoption of a priority regime for the latter similar to that applicable to intermediated securities.

1.65 The GSC essentially determines the priority of an acquisition (including through a security interest) in accordance with the following hierarchy:

(i) an acquirer whose securities account is credited with the securities prevails over any competing claimant;[22]

---

[21] It should be noted that in such cases, § 9–328 UCC provides for two levels of priority in the area of secured transactions: a transferee in possession of an endorsed registered certificate has priority over a transferee in possession of an unendorsed registered certificate. This is so because of the UCC priority rule providing that control of a certificated security (that is, possession of an endorsed certificate) prevails over mere possession. Indeed, such a hypothesis may materialize only in a situation where the law deems both transferees to be in possession of the same certificate. Still, in normal circumstances it would be rare for a certificate to be considered as endorsed with respect to one party and unendorsed with respect to the other party. However, this may occur where a certificate is held by a third party on behalf of the two transferees and has been endorsed in favour of one of these; the latter would have control while the other transferee would have mere possession.

[22] Article 18 GSC.

(ii) a transferee which has obtained control of securities credited to and remaining in the securities account of the transferor prevails over another person claiming an interest in the securities credited to that account;[23]

(iii) a transferee which has achieved third-party effectiveness under a method of perfection not established by the GSC will have such priority as is afforded by the law outside the GSC, but cannot prevail over a transferee which has priority under the GSC.[24]

1.66 The same approach may be adopted in relation to uncertificated securities; the priority of a transferee of uncertificated securities should therefore be the following:

(i) First, a transferee of uncertificated securities which perfects its transfer by becoming the registered holder in the books of the issuer will prevail over any competing claimant (the 'first level priority rule').

(ii) Secondly, a transferee which has obtained control of the securities by a control agreement will prevail over any competing claimant other than a transferee which becomes the registered holder of the securities (the 'second level priority rule'). As between two transferees with which the issuer may have concluded a control agreement, priority would be accorded to the transferee whose control agreement is concluded first in time.

(iii) Thirdly, a transferee which achieves third-party effectiveness only by registration in a public registry will prevail over a competing claimant other than a transferee which has already perfected or subsequently perfects its interest by control or by becoming the registered holder of the securities (the 'third level priority rule'). As between two transferees relying only on registration in a public registry, the first in time to register will have priority over the other.

1.67 Several observations must be made on these rules, the substance of which has been implemented by Article 51 MLST.

1.68 Under the first level priority rule, a transferee which becomes the registered holder of the securities will have priority even against another transferee with which the issuer may previously have concluded a control agreement.

1.69 The following example illustrates the application of the first level priority rule. Suppose that A is the registered holder of uncertificated securities issued by issuer X and transfers the securities to B; instead of causing the transfer to be registered in X's books, A and B enter into a control agreement with X, whereby X is only permitted to follow transfer instructions from B. Subsequently, A transfers the securities to C and, despite the control agreement, issuer X registers the transfer in its books in favour of C. The result of the first level priority rule will be that the transfer by A to C will have priority over the transfer by A to B.

---

[23] Article 19 GSC.
[24] See Arts 13 and 19(2) GSC, read together. Registration in a public registry is the best example of a method of perfection not established by the GSC.

1.70 However, this result would not relieve the issuer from liability if, as in the example, the control agreement did not permit the issuer to accept transfer instructions from the person who was the registered holder at the time the control agreement was made. As a practical matter, in most cases, the previous transferee (B, in the example) is unlikely to suffer a loss as a result of its transfer being subject to the first level priority rule. Either the issuer is solvent, in which case the previous transferee will have recourse against the issuer for the loss arising from the breach by the issuer of its obligations under the control agreement, or the issuer is insolvent, in which case the previous transferee would not have been better off in absence of the breach (at least if the securities are shares in the equity of the issuer). It is worth mentioning that the use of control agreements to achieve third-party effectiveness of a transfer will be more frequent in the area of secured transactions. An outright transferee will generally prefer to rely on the greater protection afforded by registration of its transfer in the issuer's books.

1.71 An example of the operation of the second level priority rule is where A, the holder of securities registered in its name in the issuer's books, grants a security interest in the securities in favour of B and subsequently grants another security interest in favour of C. In each case, a control agreement is entered into between A, the secured creditor concerned, and the issuer. The respective priorities of B and C will depend on the order in time of their respective control agreements, and not on the order in time of their respective security interests. Indeed, a prudent issuer which has concluded a control agreement with a transferee will not become party to another control agreement with another transferee without appropriate safeguards; in particular, the issuer will insist on the provisions of the second control agreement being subject to the first control agreement. Allowing for the possibility of more than one control agreement is a useful tool in lending transactions where all parties contemplate that the same uncertificated securities will serve as collateral for loans made by two lenders. By achieving perfection through a control agreement, each of the first and second lenders will ensure that they rank ahead of another secured creditor perfecting its security interest by registration only.

1.72 The following example illustrates the purpose and application of the third level priority rule. The assets of company A include a manufacturing business and investments in uncertificated securities. Company A has granted a security interest to a lender in all its present and future assets. For practical reasons, company A is unwilling to spend the time and incur the costs associated with convincing each issuer of the uncertificated securities to conclude a control agreement with the lender. The lender is prepared to abstain from obtaining a control agreement and to rely on the honesty of company A and on the 'negative pledge'[25] provisions of the loan agreement. Nonetheless, the lender still wants protection in the event of the insolvency of company A. Achieving third-party effectiveness by registration in a public registry will in that case ensure that

---

[25] The term 'negative pledge' is shorthand for a covenant by a borrower not to encumber its assets with security interests in favour of persons other than the lender.

the lender's security interest in the uncertificated securities will be enforceable against the administrator of the insolvency of company A if the latter becomes subject to insolvency proceedings.

(2) Qualifications or exceptions

The above priority rules apply to any transferee and to both an outright transfer and a transfer by way of a security interest. The question arises whether qualifications or distinctions would be appropriate for a transfer which is not made for value or where an outright transferee competes with a judgment creditor or an insolvency administrator. **1.73**

(a) Transfer not for value

Should a transfer be for value in order for the transferee to benefit from the priority rules stated above? An outright transfer may be made gratuitously (for example, as a result of a gift). A security interest is typically granted for value, but even in that case the issue is not entirely moot.[26] **1.74**

A review of the GSC indicates that the provisions of Articles 11 and 12 on the methods of achieving third-party effectiveness apply to any acquisition of intermediated securities, regardless of the nature of the agreement under which the securities have been acquired; there is no requirement that the acquisition be for value. In the same vein, the provisions of Article 19 GSC on priority between interests in the same intermediated securities do not distinguish between an acquisition for value or one not for value. It is only in Article 18 GSC, which deals with the protection of an innocent acquirer, that such a distinction appears, albeit in a limited way. Article 18(3) and (4) provides that the rule protecting an innocent acquirer 'does not apply to an acquisition of intermediated securities, other than the grant of a security interest, made by gift or otherwise gratuitously'; in such a case, 'the applicable law determines the rights ... of the acquirer'. **1.75**

The issue may arise in the following scenario. A, the holder of uncertificated securities, donates the securities to B, and B makes its transfer effective against third parties by becoming the registered holder. Suppose that A subsequently transfers the same securities to C under a transfer for value. Would C be entitled to defeat the transfer in favour of B and obtain a court order compelling the issuer to cancel B's title? **1.76**

There is no policy reason specific to the law on intermediated or non-intermediated securities which mandates that C be given priority merely because B has acquired the securities under a gift (namely, not for value). The better view is to leave the matter to the law on donations: to the extent that the donation is valid and effective under that **1.77**

---

[26] In the rare case where a security interest secures a promise to make a donation, the question of whether the promise constitutes value or consideration depends on the law of obligations of the relevant legal system.

law, transferee B should be entitled to benefit from the priority rules governing non-intermediated securities.

1.78 The same analysis may be made to determine the priority of a donee against a judgment creditor or insolvency administrator. A transfer not for value may be subject to avoidance under creditors' rights or insolvency laws, but, again, this is not a matter falling under the rules on intermediated or non-intermediated securities. If the transferee is insolvent, the gift could be set aside by a judgment creditor or an insolvency administrator of the donor as a result of the prejudice caused to the creditors of the donor. However, this is not a ground for imposing a requirement that the third-party effectiveness of a transfer be conditional upon the transfer being for value.

1.79 Such a requirement would also create uncertainty and add an unnecessary layer of complexity to the area of priority rules. The concept of value or consideration is not the same in all legal systems and significant differences exist between the common law and the civil law.[27] In the case of a security interest, different approaches are possible on whether the security interest has been granted for value. One position is that the grantor itself must have received value; under another position, it is sufficient that value be given either to the grantor or a third party.[28] This difficulty has not gone unnoticed by the drafters of the GSC: Article 18 on the protection of an innocent acquirer does not apply to an acquisition effected gratuitously except for an acquisition by way of a security interest.[29] Other difficulties include the treatment of nominal value and of a transfer made in satisfaction of an antecedent debt.[30]

1.80 In addition, requiring that value be given in order for a transfer to be effective as against third parties would clash with the rules on the effectiveness of a transfer against the issuer. An issuer is under an obligation to register a transfer (whether or not for value) in its books, if the transferee provides reasonable evidence that the transfer has been authorized. If the title of a registered transferee which obtained the securities through a gift could be defeated by a subsequent transfer for value, the rule that an issuer may treat a registered holder as 'true owner' would need to be relaxed to take into account that possibility: an exception to the rule would have to be provided to deal with the rights and duties of an issuer receiving a request for registration by a subsequent transferee for value claiming that the previous transfer was not for value. This would increase the risk of the issuer becoming involved in litigation resulting from circumstances beyond its control.

---

[27] Under the civil law, the concept of 'consideration' (as understood in the common law) as a requirement for the enforceability of a 'simple contract' (another common law concept) is unknown. See McKendrick, *Goode on Commercial Law*, 73.

[28] Under the common law, consideration must move from the promisee (the grantee, in our context), but need not move to the promisor (the grantor).

[29] Article 18(3) GSC.

[30] Under the traditional common law concept of consideration, a transfer in satisfaction of an antecedent debt is not made for a valuable consideration. This approach has been overridden by many statutes in common law States. See § 7–204 UCC.

1.81 Should the above analysis also apply to a competition between B and C, in a variant of the example in paragraph 1.76 where C, instead of being a subsequent transferee, is a previous transferee? In other words, if the gift in favour of B is subsequent to the transfer for value in favour of C, should B prevail over C in a situation where B (the donee) is the first in time to perfect its transfer (for example, by becoming the registered holder of the securities)?

1.82 To the extent that giving value is not a factor relevant to the determination of the priority of a transferee, B should prevail in the second scenario as well. It is true that, in this second scenario, the application of the priority rule would trump the *nemo dat* rule: transferor A has donated to B securities previously transferred for value to C. However, priority rules are intended to provide certainty and it is generally recognized that they may have the effect of displacing the *nemo dat* rule. Again, the consequence of a transfer not being made for value should be a matter left to the legal principles governing gratuitous transfers of property or fraudulent conveyances.

1.83 As a practical matter, the scenario where a gift subsequent to a transfer for value would have priority does not necessarily yield an unfair result. First, a prudent buyer of securities would normally subject the payment of the purchase price to its transfer having been made effective against third parties; if this cannot be done, the purchaser will not pay the seller. Secondly, the transferor would still be liable against the transferee for value, on the basis of a legal or contractual warranty; if the transferor is unable to honour the warranty because of its insolvency, the transferee would likely be able to attack the gift as being a fraudulent conveyance.

(b) Judgment creditor or insolvency administrator

1.84 Secured transactions laws generally provide that an unperfected security interest does not have priority over a judgment creditor or an insolvency administrator of the grantor of the security interest. The policy underlying the rule is that creditors may assume that their debtor's assets are free from security interests unless the latter have been perfected.

1.85 Should the same rule apply to an outright transferee? For example, if the buyer of securities has not perfected its transfer and if the transferor subsequently becomes bankrupt, would the buyer be entitled to invoke the transfer against the trustee in the bankruptcy of the transferor?

1.86 In general, the buyer of goods does not need to take steps to ensure that the transaction will be effective against the creditors of the seller; if the goods have not been delivered at the time of the bankruptcy of the seller, the buyer will be entitled to claim the goods from the trustee. In the area of immovable property, some legal systems take the same approach: an immovable which has been sold prior to the bankruptcy of the seller is not vested in the trustee even if the sale has not been registered in the appropriate land registry. In such case, the trustee is treated as a successor (not as a third party) and cannot have greater rights in the immovable than those held by the bankrupt.

1.87 On the other hand, the MLST and many legal systems apply to an outright assignment of receivables[31] the same regime as for a security interest: an outright assignment is not effective against an insolvency administrator of the assignor if perfection steps are not taken. This facilitates the resolution of priority disputes between an outright assignee and the holder of a security interest in the receivable. It is noteworthy, however, that other forms of intangible property (eg, intellectual property) are not subject to such a uniform regime. Moreover, even for receivables, the MLST and the legal systems which contain perfection requirements for an assignment of receivables contemplate exceptions to such requirements for certain types of receivables (eg, certain financial receivables).[32]

1.88 In relation to intermediated securities, the GSC does not take position on whether steps must be taken to render an acquisition (including a security interest) effective against an insolvency administrator. The GSC provides that an interest made effective against third parties by credit or by control is also effective against an insolvency administrator.[33] It does not state, however, that failure to do so results in the interest being unenforceable in insolvency proceedings. The matter is left to law outside the GSC.[34]

1.89 Therefore, the principle that assets not belonging to an insolvent debtor are not vested in its insolvency administrator should apply to an unperfected transfer of non-intermediated securities. There is no compelling reason to treat non-intermediated securities differently. To some extent, the MLST and some legal systems assimilate an outright assignment of receivables to a security assignment. This is not the case, however, for an outright transfer of other types of asset.

H. Vertical Priority Rules

1.90 A vertical priority dispute occurs where the interest of a transferee is challenged by a person whose claim is not derived from dealings with the transferor of that transferee. A typical scenario is as follows: A delivers and endorses to B certificated securities in a pledge transaction; B is not authorized under the transaction to transfer the securities to another person. Notwithstanding the foregoing, B grants to C a security interest in the securities and delivers the certificate to C. After discharging its obligations to B, would A be entitled to demand that C return the certificates (assuming B's obligations to C have not been satisfied)?

---

[31] The term 'receivables' is used in a broad sense, namely a right to obtain payment of a monetary obligation.
[32] See the definition of receivables in Art 2 MLST and the exclusions in its Art 1(3). See also § 9–309 UCC, which provides that filing is not required for the perfection of certain categories of receivables (eg, the sale of a loan is not subject to perfection formalities).
[33] Article 14(2) GSC.
[34] Article 14(4) GSC. In light of the limited scope of the GSC on insolvency matters, this article cannot be read as requiring that the law outside the GSC must also prescribe the fulfilment of perfection requirements in an insolvency context.

1.91 The GSC addresses a similar question in Article 18 ('Acquisition by an innocent acquirer'). Essentially, the GSC provides that a good faith acquirer of intermediated securities is immune from a claim by another person asserting an interest in the securities. The protection afforded by Article 18 is confined to vertical priority disputes; horizontal priority disputes[35] are dealt with by Article 19 (priority to the transferee which is the first in time to obtain control).

1.92 Applied to the above scenario, Article 18 would protect C: its security interest in the securities would be effective against A even if B did not have the right to transfer these securities to C. It is worth noting that the provisions of Article 18 are not new in this regard; they transpose to intermediated securities an existing rule in the area of certificated securities. The origin of the rule is found in the law of negotiable instruments: a 'holder in due course' obtains good title to the instrument even if the previous holder had a defective title or acted fraudulently in negotiating the instrument. It must also be pointed out that the standards that apply to the question of whether an acquirer should investigate the transferor's title in order to be protected by Article 18 are similar to those that have been developed under negotiable instrument laws for a holder in due course (at least in common law jurisdictions).

1.93 Therefore, in a law reform context, a transferee of non-intermediated securities should benefit (or continue to benefit) from the same protection as that contemplated by Article 18 GSC for intermediated securities. For the transferee to be protected, its interest must have become effective against third parties. However, in addition to being in good faith, must the transferee have given value? Article 18 excludes 'an acquisition of intermediated securities, other than the grant of a security interest, made by way of gift or otherwise gratuitously'.[36] The security interest exception renders irrelevant the question of whether a security interest granted by a person other than the debtor of the obligation secured is accorded gratuitously. But for that exception, a secured creditor would not qualify as a protected acquirer in circumstances where the security interest is treated under the applicable law as a gratuitous transaction.

1.94 Thus, should a transferee of non-intermediated securities have given value in order to be protected in the event of a vertical priority dispute (assuming that a secured creditor is treated as giving value to the extent of the obligation secured)? In line with the UCC[37] and other existing laws on the issue, as well as the GSC[38] and the law of negotiable instruments,[39] this requirement appears appropriate.[40] Faced with a choice between a donee and an owner of securities which is the victim of an unlawful action, the law

---

[35] A dispute between two persons who acquire the same securities from the same transferor.
[36] Article 18(3) GSC.
[37] § 8–303 UCC (definition of protected purchaser).
[38] Article 18(3) GSC, *a contrario*.
[39] To be a 'holder in due course' under negotiable instruments statutes in effect in States of a common law tradition, the holder must have given value.
[40] The concept of value should, however, be defined or understood in a way that avoids the difficulties alluded to in para 1.79.

should accord precedence to the victim. The donee would not suffer a real loss as a result of the gift being declared ineffective; the value of its assets (prior to the gift) would remain the same. Giving priority to the donee would be an unjustified windfall for the donee in a situation where B, a thief, steals bearer certificates belonging to A and donates the certificates to C.

1.95 It is true that in horizontal priority disputes, giving value is not a prerequisite for the priority of a transferee which meets the relevant priority requirements. However, the policy reasons for not stipulating this condition in the case of a horizontal priority dispute are different. Among other things, a transferee for value whose transfer might be defeated by a subsequent transfer made gratuitously is in a position to protect itself against the occurrence of such an event; for instance, a lender which lends in reliance of a security interest in securities may postpone the disbursement of the loan until its security interest has been perfected by a method ensuring that the security interest will be first-ranking.

I. Conflict of Laws

1.96 This section examines the conflict-of-laws rules that should apply to the effectiveness against the issuer and third parties and to the priority of a transfer of non-intermediated securities.[41] The factors that determine the law applicable (the connecting factors) to an outright transfer and a security interest must be the same. Otherwise, in the event of a priority dispute between an outright transferee and a secured creditor, it might be impossible for a court to resolve the dispute: this would be the case, for example, if the priority of the outright transfer is subject to the law of State X (under which the outright transfer would prevail over the security interest) and the priority of the security interest is subject to the law of State Y (under which the security interest would prevail over the outright transfer).

1.97 Certificated securities are in many respects assimilated to tangible property: the rights attached to these securities are embodied in certificates. Uncertificated securities are entirely dematerialized. Therefore, even if the relevant conflict rule is the same for an outright transfer and a security interest, in many legal systems the factor most closely connected to the perfection and priority of a transfer of certificated securities is different from that connected to the perfection and priority of a transfer of uncertificated securities. The MLST takes a different view on this issue: as indicated below, Article 100 MLST determines the applicable law on all secured transactions issues by making

---

[41] The issue of the law applicable to the validity of the transfer as between the parties will not be discussed, although many legal systems apply the same connecting factor to validity issues as for perfection and priority issues (at least for security interests); this is also generally the approach of the MLST. Another approach is to apply to validity issues the law governing the agreement under which the transfer is made; this is to some extent the UCC approach.

a distinction between equity securities and debt securities, rather than between certificated and uncertificated securities.

(1) Certificated securities

The traditional *lex rei sitae* or *lex situs* rule is applied in many States to certificated securities, as is the case for negotiable instruments or negotiable documents of title. Because of the similarities between certificated securities and negotiable instruments, at first glance there seems to be no compelling reason to take a different approach in uniform conflict-of-laws rules that attempt to deal comprehensively with non-intermediated securities. These similarities could dictate that the law applicable to the perfection and priority of a transfer of certificated securities be the law of the State in which the certificate is located. Thus, if a transferee obtains delivery of a certificate in State X, the law of State X will determine the priority of the transferee for as long as the certificate remains in State X.

1.98

The effectiveness of the transfer against the issuer cannot, however, be governed by the law of the place where the certificate is physically held. An issuer has no means of knowing where a certificate is held and needs to be able to rely on one single law to ascertain its duties and obligations to security holders. In addition, many of these duties and obligations may come under the corporate law governing the issuer. The situs of a certificate cannot be an appropriate connecting factor to determine the law applicable to the effectiveness of a transfer against the issuer.

1.99

The factor best connected to the situation appears to be law under which the issuer has been formed or constituted (the 'issuer's constitutive law').[42] Therefore, the relationship between the transferee and the issuer should be governed by the issuer's constitutive law, including the conditions to be met for the registration of the transfer and the obligations of the issuer to a previous security holder in the event of wrongful registration.

1.100

A different approach may, however, be envisioned for debt securities. In the area of receivables, many legal systems provide that the law applicable to the effectiveness of an assignment of a receivable against the debtor of the receivable is the law governing the receivable; in the case of a receivable arising out of a contract, the applicable law is the law governing the contract.[43] Debt securities are receivables in a broad sense and it is arguable that the applicable law for debt securities (as proposed by Article 100 MLST) should be the law governing the terms and conditions of these securities. In line with that approach, some legal systems provide that the law applicable to the relationship of

1.101

---

[42] It should be noted that in most cases, third parties which have no direct dealings with the security holder cannot ascertain the physical location of a certificate. Therefore, it can be argued that the issuer's constitutive law should also apply to the perfection and priority of a transfer of certificated securities, which is the approach of Art 100 MLST for non-intermediated equity securities (whether or not certificated).

[43] The MLST proposes such a conflict-of-laws rule in Art 96.

the issuer with a security holder (including a holder of equity securities) is the issuer's constitutive law unless the issuer selects another applicable law in the terms and conditions of the securities.[44]

1.102 The difficulty with giving the issuer an option to select the applicable law is that some matters relating to the effectiveness of a transfer against the issuer may fall under corporate law, especially where the securities are equity securities. At first glance, a solution reconciling the receivables approach and the issuer's constitutive law approach might be to allow the issuer to determine the applicable law only for debt securities. However, this would not provide certainty since the distinction between equity securities and debt securities may be blurred (for example, debentures convertible in equity). Moreover, debt securities may still be subject to the issuer's constitutive law for certain matters relevant to the relationship between the issuer and the holders of these securities.

1.103 For the sake of certainty, it is preferable not to make exceptions to the issuer's constitutive law as the law applicable to the effectiveness of a transfer of certificated securities against the issuer. A more drastic view on referring to the issuer's constitutive law is found in Article 100 MLST; this article applies that law not only to the effectiveness against the issuer of a security interest in non-intermediated equity securities but also to the creation, perfection, priority, and enforcement of a security interest in all non-intermediated equity securities, whether certificated or not (subject to the limited exception of Article 98 MLST which refers to the grantor's location law for perfection by registration if that law recognizes registration as a mode of perfection).

(2) Uncertificated securities

1.104 With respect to uncertificated securities, the traditional conflict rule in some legal systems points to the issuer's constitutive law for the effectiveness of the transfer against the issuer and for perfection and priority. As to the effectiveness against the issuer, the reasons discussed above for selecting the issuer's constitutive law in relation to certificated securities lead to the same conclusion with respect to uncertificated securities. Matters concerning the relationship between a security holder and the issuer are essentially the same whether the securities are certificated or not certificated. It follows that the law applicable to that relationship could be the same for each type of non-intermediated securities.

1.105 The effectiveness against third parties and the priority of a transfer of uncertificated securities are likewise issues that could be governed by the issuer's constitutive law. It should, however, be noted that for such issues, Article 100 MLST refers to the law governing the securities for debt securities.

---

[44] See § 8–110(d) UCC.

1.106 The perfection and priority of a transfer of uncertificated securities will be achieved principally by registration of the transfer in the books of the issuer or by a control agreement with the issuer. Both registration of a transfer and entering into a control agreement require the participation of the issuer. Both methods of perfection are dependent on the transferee's ability to effect or block a disposition under the law governing the effectiveness of a transfer against the issuer. The logical consequence of the foregoing is that the issuer's constitutive law could be the law applicable to the perfection and priority of a transfer of uncertificated securities. The novel approach of the MLST referring to the governing law of non-intermediated debt securities (certificated or not) for all relevant issues is different, but it is unlikely that an issuer would agree to debt securities being governed by a law inconsistent with its constitutive law. As a practical matter, the proposal of the MLST to apply the law governing the securities for non-intermediated debt securities should not raise any concerns.

1.107 The MLST approaches are simple and, though deviating from tradition in some respects, they avoid interpretation difficulties in the application of other conflict rules referring to different connecting factors on the relevant issues.

J. Conclusion

1.108 The preparation and negotiation of the GSC has been a challenging exercise. From a superficial point of view, national laws on non-intermediated securities do not need to be substantially modified or revised, as they are based on a system that has been in effect for a long time and still applies to such securities. However, this chapter shows that modernization and harmonization are also desirable in the area of non-intermediated securities, in particular to ensure uniformity at the international level and consistency with the law on intermediated securities. As has been seen, there are several issues pertaining to non-intermediated securities where the law is not clear, so that different approaches may be taken. Providing for certainty on these issues would be a significant achievement. In the conflict of laws, consideration should be given to the MLST proposals outlined above.

2
FINANCIAL COLLATERAL: FROM PRIVATE TO REGULATORY LAW REFORM*

A. Introduction: Development of the Markets and the Legislative Framework	2.01	(c) The position of the provider of independent amount collateral	2.47
(1) *Lex mercatoria*: two forms of collateralization	2.02	(5) Overcollateralization: possible responses	2.50
(2) Private law reform	2.06	(a) Private law responses	2.51
(a) The European Union	2.08	(b) Regulatory restrictions	2.57
(b) Geneva Securities Convention	2.14	(c) Concluding remarks	2.62
(3) Regulatory law reform	2.16	C. Collateral in Insolvency and in Resolution	2.63
(4) Further contents of this chapter	2.21	(1) General	2.63
B. Over- and Undercollateralization	2.26	(2) Safe harbours	2.67
(1) Introduction	2.26	(3) Bank resolution	2.71
(2) Title transfer and right of use devices compared	2.30	(4) Resolution tools	2.76
(3) The case of Lehman: overcollateralization from a legal policy perspective	2.33	(a) Bail-in	2.76
		(b) Ensuring loss-absorbing capacity: TLAC and MREL	2.78
(4) Overcollateralization in the form of independent amounts	2.37	(c) Sale of business, bridge institution, and asset separation tools	2.82
(a) Introduction	2.37	(d) Modification of contracts	2.84
(b) Independent amounts: factual and contractual aspects	2.41	(5) Limitations to termination rights	2.85
		D. Concluding Remarks	2.91

A. Introduction: Development of the Markets and the Legislative Framework

2.01 The decades preceding the onset of the global financial crisis that started in 2007 were a period of liberalization and rapid expansion of the financial markets. A steep increase in the collateralization of financial transactions, the development of market standard documentation, and private law reform in relation to such transactions were an integral part of this trend. Financial collateral became a key component of the financial markets. The provision of such collateral, consisting of money and transferable securities, plays a crucial role in the wholesale financial markets, for example where it is used to secure exposures

---

* The version of this chapter included in the first edition of this book (and the updates thereof for the Oxford Legal Research Library) have benefited greatly from the contribution by Marcel Peeters and helpful comments by Ed Murray and Peter Werner. The authors of the current version are also grateful to Peter for his input regarding this text. They are of course wholly responsible for its final content.

under derivative transactions. It is also a cornerstone of monetary policy operations through repurchase ('repo') agreements. As a result, the amount of money and securities involved in financial collateral arrangements has skyrocketed.[1] However, the global financial crisis brought to light issues in respect of financial collateral arrangements, mainly concerning systemic risk and investor protection, which resulted in a variety of regulatory initiatives. This chapter considers the development of the legal framework for financial collateral from the application of 'traditional' law to the private law reform that marked the 1990s and the early years of the new millennium, as well as the layer of financial regulation that was added notably in the wake of the global financial crisis.

(1) *Lex mercatoria*: two forms of collateralization

The expansion of the collateral markets went hand in hand with the increased use of market standard documentation for different types of collateral arrangements. The first standardized agreements, which may be considered as a *lex mercatoria* for the financial sector,[2] were developed in the US, where these markets were first active. Somewhat later, in the course of the 1990s, agreements were developed that reflect the legal and operational features of international transactions.

2.02

Space does not permit an exhaustive listing of all relevant market standard documentation, but the following are particularly noteworthy. Repo agreements are commonly documented under a PSA/ISMA (now SIFMA/ICMA) Global Master Repurchase Agreement (GMRA).[3] A standard agreement for securities lending agreements is the Global Master Securities Lending Agreement (GMSLA),[4] which followed on earlier— now largely obsolete—agreements such as the 1996 Master Equity & Fixed Interest Stock Lending Agreement (MEFISLA), the 1996 Master Gilt Edged Stock Lending Agreement (MGESLA), and the 1994/1995 Overseas Securities Lender's Agreement (OSLA). Standard documentation for derivatives and related agreements was developed by ISDA in the form of a Master Agreement,[5] with various associated definitions, and English and New York law credit support documentation.[6,7] There are also other

2.03

---

[1] See, eg, the annual Margin Surveys by the International Swaps and Derivatives Association (ISDA; formerly the International Swap Dealers Association), and the European Repo Market Surveys, carried out at the request of the European Repo Council of the International Capital Market Association (ICMA).

[2] Cf Collins, 'Flipping Wreck'; Eidenmüller, '*Lex Mercatoria*'.

[3] See the 1992, 1995, 2000, and 2011 versions; <http://www.icmagroup.org> (accessed 7 July 2021).

[4] See the 2000, 2009, and 2010 (title transfer) and 2018 (security interest) versions; <http://www.isla.co.uk> (accessed 7 July 2021).

[5] See the 1987, 1992, and 2002 versions.

[6] The credit support documentation includes the 1994 Credit Support Annex (New York law; 'NY Annex'), the 1995 Credit Support Annex (English law; 'English Annex'), and the 1995 Credit Support Deed (English law; 'Deed'). In 2001, 2013, and 2014, ISDA published revised credit support documents, which, although differing on a number of points, are broadly based on the same principles; however, in practice, the 1994/1995 documentation has remained predominant. After the global financial crisis, documentation was developed to accommodate new regulatory requirements concerning margin provided in the context of OTC derivatives. For further details, see Murray, in Yeowart and Parsons, *Law of Financial Collateral*, 17.56–75 and para 2.45 below.

[7] Repos and securities lending transactions can, in principle, also be made subject to an ISDA Master Agreement.

multi-product standard documents, such as the European Master Agreement,[8] which can be used for repos, securities lending, and derivatives alike.[9] More recently, various industry associations which first developed these master agreements have started discussing the alignment and integration of the documentation and operational processes for derivatives and securities financing transactions.[10]

2.04 There are two basic forms of collateralization: collateral is provided either by way of a title transfer or by granting a security interest. If agreed, a security interest may be granted together with a 'right of use', conferring a right of disposal on the collateral taker like that of an owner. As discussed in section B(2), this is a hybrid containing elements of both basic forms. Under many market standard agreements, including the GMRA, the GMSLA, and under ISDA's English Annex, collateral is provided by way of the title transfer method. ISDA's English Deed is an example of an instrument creating a security interest without a right of use. The ISDA NY Annex is an example of a standardized agreement combining a security interest with the possibility of a collateral taker's right of use.[11]

2.05 Prime brokerage agreements, under which an investment bank or securities dealer provides a client, such as a hedge fund, with a range of services, including financing, trade execution, and custody, will usually provide that the client's assets held with the prime broker are available as collateral for the client's obligations, either by way of title transfer or by way of security interest with a right of use. In the light of experience during the global financial crisis of the potential risks of making client assets available to prime brokers without imposing a limit, it now appears to have become more common to opt for a security interest with right of use, and to restrict the extent of the right of use to a specified proportion (for example 140%) of the client's indebtedness to the prime broker.

(2) Private law reform

2.06 Developments in the collateral markets over the past decades have also, in a number of countries, brought to light aspects of substantive private law, or of traditional conflict-of-laws principles, which many market participants considered were not, or were insufficiently, attuned to novel financial techniques and transactions, in particular where they involved two or more jurisdictions. These market pressures resulted in various proposals for private law reform at national, EU, and international level.

---

[8] See the versions of 2001, 2004, 2013, and 2020, available at <https://www.ebf.eu/home/european-master-agreement-ema/> (accessed 7 July 2021).
[9] See also UNIDROIT 2011–S78C–Doc. 2, para 6.
[10] See, eg, ISDA, *Collaboration and Standardization Opportunities in Derivatives and SFT Markets.*
[11] Paragraphs 2 and 6(c) of the NY Annex.

Some special features of financial collateral have driven such reforms. Financial collateral is typically easy to transfer, value, and realize, all of which operations are aspects of its liquidity.[12] For these reasons, financial collateral is especially well adapted to financial transactions that may be (very) short term, such as repos, and/or give rise to exposures that may vary substantially over a (very) short period of time (such as derivatives), and have to be collateralized regularly. Private law reforms since the end of the 1990s have been directed at enhancing this liquidity.

2.07

(a) The European Union

The first relevant law reform measure in the EU was the 1998 Settlement Finality Directive (SFD). This Directive includes several features that were later applied more widely in the EU Financial Collateral Directive (FCD), notably the protection of collateral against invalidation under rules of insolvency law.[13] The SFD was, however, narrowly targeted at payment and settlement systems rather than constituting a general law reform measure.

2.08

More important in the context of this chapter is the FCD, which was part of the European Commission's Financial Markets Action Plan.[14] The FCD entered into force in 2002 and had to be implemented by Member States by 27 December 2003.

2.09

The FCD required Member States to protect financial collateral arrangements from a number of possibly conflicting provisions of domestic law (including insolvency law).[15] The key protections are summarized below:

2.10

(i) the effective creation or enforcement of a financial collateral arrangement must not depend on the performance of formal acts such as registration or official notification;[16]

(ii) if a security financial collateral arrangement provides for a right of use, the right must be effective;[17]

(iii) a title transfer financial collateral arrangement must take effect in accordance with its terms (and must therefore be protected from being 'recharacterized' as a traditional pledge or other security arrangement);[18]

(iv) the effectiveness of close-out netting must be recognized;[19]

(v) to a specified extent, traditional rules of insolvency law, such as automatic claw-back provisions, may not be invoked to invalidate a financial collateral

---

[12] Gullifer, 'Financial Collateral', 380; Keijser, *Financial Collateral* (2006), 2.4.
[13] See in particular Art 9(1) SFD. See also Keijser, 'Financial Collateral' (2017), I.2.
[14] See EC, *Financial Markets: Action Plan*. The Action Plan was issued in May 1999 in response to a request from the Cardiff European Council meeting in June 1998. See also ISDA, *Need for National Law Reform*; Keijser, 'Financial Collateral' (2017), I.3.
[15] For an explanation of the rationale underlying these protections, see the European Commission's Proposal for a Directive on financial collateral arrangements, 27 March 2001 (COM(2001) 168 final; 2001/0086(COD)).
[16] See Arts 3 and 4(4) FCD.
[17] Article 5 FCD.
[18] Article 6 FCD.
[19] Article 7 FCD.

30 FINANCIAL COLLATERAL

arrangement entered into, or collateral provided, before or around the commencement of insolvency proceedings.[20]

2.11 The original FCD covered the provision of collateral in the form of both cash and securities.[21] In 2009, the scope of the FCD was extended to cover collateral in the form of credit claims,[22] following the decision of the European Central Bank to make credit claims eligible as collateral for Eurosystem credit operations from 2007.[23]

2.12 Both the SFD and the FCD also contained conflict-of-laws provisions determining the law applicable to 'book entry' securities collateral, and dispositions thereof.[24] Conflict-of-laws issues will be further discussed in Chapter 11.

2.13 At the time when the SFD and FCD reforms were being introduced, legal attention was becoming directed more generally to the implications of modern market practice in holding and dealing in securities—in particular the fact that most securities had come to be held through accounts with intermediaries, rather than being held directly by the beneficial owner in the form of certificates or entries on the register maintained by the issuer. There was concern that substantive and private international law might not fully have kept pace with market practice, and that traditional rules of law which had evolved by reference to the direct holding pattern might be unclear or impractical when applied to modern practice. As part of this process, the European Commission formed a group of legal experts to advise it and, if appropriate, suggest measures to amend or clarify the law. This group, called the Legal Certainty Group, issued its final report in 2008.[25] The European Commission's subsequent work on 'Securities Law Legislation' repeatedly considered issues relating to financial collateral, but this project has, unfortunately, not crystallized.[26]

(b) Geneva Securities Convention

2.14 At the international level, UNIDROIT instituted a project on Substantive Rules regarding Intermediated Securities (Study LXXVIII) in 2002, which led to an agreed text of the Geneva Securities Convention (GSC) in October 2009. Chapter V GSC relates to

---

[20] Article 8 FCD.
[21] For the definitions of 'cash' and 'financial instruments', see Art 2(1)(d) and (e) FCD. We use the term 'securities' rather than the FCD term 'financial instruments' in order to (i) avoid confusion with market practice and MiFID terminology, where 'financial instruments' has a much broader coverage (including derivatives), and (ii) facilitate comparison with the Geneva Securities Convention (GSC).
[22] Directive 2009/44/EC (OJ 2009 L146/37), effective 30 June 2009, with a transposition date of 30 December 2010.
[23] See recital (5) of Directive 2009/44/EC.
[24] Article 9(2) SFD and Art 9 FCD.
[25] Legal Certainty Group, *Second Advice*.
[26] See <https://ec.europa.eu/info/business-economy-euro/banking-and-finance/financial-markets/post-trade-services/securities-and-claims-ownership_en> (accessed 7 July 2021). Specific issues regarding conflict of laws were again taken up by the Expert Group set up by the Commission in 2017: see the same website. Unfortunately, the work of this group did not crystallize into a binding legal instrument for securities either, although an official proposal for a Regulation on the law applicable to the third-party effects of assignments of claims did result from this initiative: <https://eur-lex.europa.eu/legal-content/EN/TXT/?qid=1520854606250&uri=COM:2018:96:FIN> (accessed 7 July 2021).

financial collateral transactions. This chapter is a self-contained, optional part of the Convention, which differs significantly from the main body of the GSC (which sets out a basic framework of minimum harmonized provisions governing the rights conferred by the credit of securities to an account with an intermediary, the means by which such rights can be disposed of, the integrity of the intermediated system, and related matters).[27] Chapter V GSC applies specifically to collateral transactions and contains a set of liberalizing provisions modelled closely on those of the FCD.[28]

Since the GSC as a whole deals with intermediated securities, it is not surprising that the scope of Chapter V is limited to collateral in the form of intermediated securities and therefore not as broad as the scope of the FCD. In other respects, the scope of Chapter V GSC is more extensive than that of the FCD. For example, the personal scope of Chapter V is unlimited, and the relevant obligations secured or otherwise covered by collateral are not restricted to obligations that give a right to cash settlement and/or delivery of financial instruments.[29] A Contracting State may, however, impose limits in respect of these issues by way of declaration.[30] Another aspect of practical importance is that of implementation: the FCD had to be implemented by all EU Member States by the end of 2003, but the GSC has so far only been signed by Bangladesh[31] and has accordingly not yet entered into force.[32]

2.15

(3) Regulatory law reform

The global financial crisis has added new dimensions to the legal analysis of financial collateral arrangements. Regulatory concerns have arisen as a result of a number of prominent insolvencies and near insolvencies of financial market participants and the resulting systemic effects. Policy-makers and financial market participants have reviewed a wide range of issues concerning the law and regulation of financial markets, some of them relating to collateral and collateral transactions.[33]

2.16

Particular questions raised include whether the rapid expansion of the securities financing markets, in particular through the techniques of title transfer and the re-use of collateral, which have been facilitated by the private law reforms described in section A(2), has given rise to undesirable risks.

2.17

Such risks can in principle be divided into two categories. First, there are possible risks to the stability of the financial system, in particular risks arising from the extensive use

2.18

---

[27] See Chs II–IV GSC.
[28] See Kanda et al, *Official Commentary*, V-1; Keijser, 'Financial Collateral' (2017), I.5.
[29] Article 31(3)(d) GSC; cf Art 2(1)(f) FCD.
[30] See Art 38 GSC.
[31] See <https://www.unidroit.org/status> (accessed 7 July 2021).
[32] See Art 42(1) GSC. For a further comparison of the FCD and Chapter V FCD, see Keijser, Kyrkousi, and Bakanos, 'The Legal Framework of the European Union and UNIDROIT Compared'.
[33] Haentjens, *Financial Collateral*, ch 9; Keijser, 'Financial Collateral' (2017), ss 7, 8, 10–12.

of securities financing transactions and collateralized derivatives in both the regular banking and the 'shadow banking' sector.[34] Secondly, there are investor protection risks arising from the fact that title transfer arrangements and arrangements involving the grant of security coupled with a right of use (to the extent that the right of use is exercised) give rise to a credit exposure of the collateral provider to the collateral taker, if and to the extent that the value of the collateral exceeds that of the liabilities covered at any point in time. These two categories of risk are distinct and require different measures to address them.

2.19 As regards possible risks to financial stability, it seems clear that the rapid contraction of repo credit when market confidence was shaken was a factor in accelerating the onset and increasing the severity of the global financial crisis, in particular in light of the frequent rollover and (ultra) short-term nature of these securities financing transactions and the systemic effect of even modest increases in the 'haircuts' applied to securities collateral. For example, a 'repo run' occurred in the case of Bear Stearns: Bear's repo counterparties were not willing to rollover short-term, mainly overnight, repos, which thus reduced the funding available to the investment bank.[35] Following the Lehman insolvency, some clients restricted the rights (in particular the right of use) granted to their brokers, and this, coupled with a more general loss of confidence and heightened caution, caused market participants to reduce their repo and other securities financing activities, with a major, systemic impact on market liquidity as a result.[36]

2.20 Generally, the global financial crisis was followed by a period of relative scarcity of collateral, for reasons that included a trend towards more extensive collateralization and other aspects of greater 'systemic risk aversion'. This may be illustrated by a considerable decrease in unsecured intra-bank lending, an increase in collateral required due to mandatory central clearing of OTC derivatives, dependence of banks on repo lending by central banks, central bank asset purchase programmes, and new prudential regulations both for banks (notably the Basel III framework) and (in future) also for certain categories of investment firms.[37] The resulting greater demand for high-quality collateral goes hand in hand with collateral transformation processes, in which lower-quality collateral is channelled to other parts of the system.[38]

---

[34] See Ch 3, s C(5).
[35] See Cohan, *House of Cards*, 32–53 and 76–8; FCIC, *Financial Crisis Inquiry Report*, 153 and Ch 15.
[36] See EC, *10th Discussion Paper*, paras 20–36; Lucas and Stokey, *Liquidity Crises*; Scott, *Interconnectedness and Contagion*; Senior Supervisors Group, *Risk Management Lessons*. For an economically oriented analysis of developments regarding rehypothecation and the collateral markets generally since Lehman, see the following IMF working papers: Singh and Aitken, *Deleveraging after Lehman*; Singh and Aitken, *Shadow Banking*; Singh, *OTC Derivatives*; Singh, *Velocity*; Singh, *The (Other) Deleveraging*; Singh, *Changing Collateral Space*.
[37] See eg Corradin, Heider, and Hoerova, *On Collateral*, ss 1 (and Figure 1), 2.4; FSB, *Re-hypothecation and Collateral Re-use*, 2.2; Haentjens, *Financial Collateral*, 3.01; Levels and Capel, *Is Collateral Becoming Scarce?*.
[38] On the related risks, see, eg, Bank of England, *Collateral Upgrade Transactions*.

(4) Further contents of this chapter

A key thread running through this chapter is the interaction of phenomena that were, until recently, largely considered to be part of the realm of private law, including insolvency law, with regulatory concerns that have emerged in the wake of the global financial crisis. **2.21**

An obvious question is whether (and if so, to what extent) the framework of the *lex mercatoria* and private law-oriented legislation, which was largely developed before the global financial crisis, has withstood the impact of the resulting financial turbulence, including the failure of major market participants. The standard perspective, albeit often implicit, is that of the collateral *taker* wishing to make optimal use of the portfolio of securities to which it has access or to enforce its rights under collateral arrangements, following the insolvency of, or any other event of default with respect to, the collateral provider. In contrast, section B approaches the question from the perspective of both collateral taker *and* collateral provider confronted with insolvency of their counterpart. Both parties may be under- or overcollateralized in the context of either security or title transfer collateral arrangements.[39] This section pays specific attention to overcollateralization[40] such as occurred in the context of the Lehman insolvency and as is typical in initial margin arrangements. **2.22**

Another lesson learned from the global financial crisis is that traditional insolvency regimes did not function well when applied to a failing bank. Section C considers the development of regulatory measures to ensure effective pre-insolvency restructuring and resolution of banks, and the treatment of collateral in that context. **2.23**

The following exposition focuses mainly on transnational and European legal developments. The European origin of the authors of this chapter partly explains this focus on European law, while the inspiration drawn from the FCD in the drafting of Chapter V GSC is another explanation. In only a few contexts will attention be given to other legal systems, US law in particular. **2.24**

This chapter does not take into account the impact of the recent Covid pandemic. Although the pandemic has had some consequences for the ways in which financial collateral is channelled through the financial system (for example, in light of price **2.25**

---

[39] In principle, the collateral provider under a bare security financial collateral arrangement should not incur any credit exposure to the collateral taker, but, as discussed in para 2.49, credit risk may in practice arise under the guise of operational risk if collateral is not properly identified and segregated.

[40] In the discussion that follows we use the term 'overcollateralization' in a purely factual sense, to refer to any situation in which, at a given point in time, the value of the collateral provided exceeds that of the value of the secured liabilities or transactions and therefore exposes the collateral provider to risk in the event of the insolvency of the collateral taker at that time (at least where the collateral is provided by way of title transfer, or by a security interest with a right of use, after the exercise of the right of use). The existence and level of overcollateralization may arise from a number of economic and legal considerations, including the credit standing of the parties, the nature (and market volatility) of the collateral and the secured liabilities, the economic advantages to the collateral taker of having free use of the collateral, and the extent to which these advantages are reflected in the financing terms negotiated between the parties. We consider in s B(5) whether there should be legal or regulatory intervention to limit the risks to which, as the global financial crisis has shown, overcollateralization can give rise.

swings in the market,[41] additional central bank swap and repo lines,[42] and the role of financial collateral in central bank asset purchase programmes[43]), no relevant structural legal/regulatory reform is currently in the offing. Likewise, this chapter does not discuss the potential impact on collateral management of (distributed ledger) technology and smart contracts.[44]

B. Over- and Undercollateralization

(1) Introduction

2.26 The global financial crisis, in particular the failure of Lehman in September 2008, brought to light some notable instances of overcollateralization of the collateral taker (Lehman), with major consequences for the parties involved and for the markets in general. This has led to considerable debate in legal and financial literature, and among legislators and regulators. These debates are not concerned only with the pros and cons of a collateral taker's right of use, but range more widely, covering, among other things, overcollateralization and protection of the rights of collateral providers in general.[45]

2.27 Collateral, including excess collateral, may be provided by way of a 'bare' security interest,[46] a security interest combined with a collateral taker's right of use, or an 'outright' or 'title' transfer. When referring specifically to the collateral taker's right to dispose of collateral provided in connection with a security interest, we apply the 'use' or 'right of use' terminology set out in Article 5 FCD and Article 34 GSC. 'Rehypothecation' is a term that is sometimes used to refer to disposals by the collateral taker based on either a right of use or a title transfer.[47] Although this is not strictly accurate,[48] we follow this

---

[41] See, eg, ISDA, *Coronavirus and SIMM* [Standard Initial Margin Model], <https://www.isda.org/2020/04/08/coronavirus-and-the-simm/> (accessed 7 July 2021).
[42] On the extension of the ECB's swap and repo lines in light of the pandemic, see Panetta and Schnabel, *ECB Swap and Repo Operations*.
[43] See, eg, Corradin, Heider, and Hoerova, *On Collateral*, ss 1, 2.4; ECB, *Securities Lending of Holdings under the Asset Purchase Programme (APP) and Pandemic Emergency Purchase Programme (PEPP)*, <https://www.ecb.europa.eu/mopo/implement/omt/lending/html/index.en.html> (accessed 7 July 2021); ECB, *Pandemic Emergency Purchase Programme (PEPP)*, <https://www.ecb.europa.eu/mopo/implement/pepp/html/index.en.html> (accessed 7 July 2021).
[44] See eg ECB Advisory Group, *The Potential Impact of DLTs*, s 8 (Collateral Management and DLTs); as well as several reports by ISDA on smart derivatives contracts and DLT, available at <https://www.isda.org/2019/10/16/isda-smart-contracts/> (accessed 7 July 2021), including *Legal Guidelines for Smart Derivatives Contracts: Collateral* (September 2019).
[45] See, for example, BCBS, *Cross-border Bank Resolution*; BCBS and IOSCO, *Margin Requirements* (2020); EC, *10th Discussion Paper*, paras 38–47, mentioning different other forums FSB, *Key Attributes*; FSB, *Shadow Banking: Securities Lending and Repos*; Senior Supervisors Group, *Risk Management Lessons*.
[46] Cf FCA Handbook, CASS 3.1.4.
[47] For different interpretations of the terms 'use', 're-use', 'right of use', and 'rehypothecation' (and the resulting confusion), see EC, *10th Discussion Paper*, para 18 and Annex 2; FSB, *Shadow Banking: Securities Lending and Repos*, 3.2; FSB, *Re-hypothecation and Collateral Re-use*, 2.1; Haentjens, *Financial Collateral*, ch 6 (also on US law); Keijser, 'Financial Collateral' (2017), II.18; Kettering, 'Repledge and Pre-Default Sale', 1111–12; Singh, *Velocity*, 9 (Box 1).
[48] Strictly speaking, 'hypothecation' refers to the creation of a pledge or another security interest.

usage in the discussion below. The similarities between the title transfer and right of use devices are discussed further in section B(2).

2.28 Of course, under- or overcollateralization of either party to a collateral transaction may occur simply because of market developments: the collateralized exposure may fluctuate in value and the same is true of the collateral provided. Sections B(3) and (4), however, address overcollateralization that is the structural, intended effect of collateral arrangements under past and current market practice. Section B(3) focuses on unrestricted rights of use, exemplified by the Lehman case, while section B(4) relates to overcollateralization in the particular setting of the provision of initial margin. Section B(5) assesses possible responses to the issues identified.

2.29 A general point needs to be made in connection with these issues. A party that has provided collateral by title transfer (and one that has granted a security interest with a right of use, once the right of use has been exercised) is protected against failure of its collateral-taking counterparty to the extent of the collateral taker's exposure to it. This is because, upon the insolvency (or comparable failure) of the collateral taker, leading to termination of outstanding transactions, that exposure can be netted against the market value of collateral provided (assuming the effectiveness of close-out netting provisions).[49] As a result, the collateral provider has de facto security for its claim to the extent of the collateral taker's exposure. However, to the extent that there is insufficient collateral, the collateral taker is exposed to the collateral provider, and to the extent that there is excess collateral, the collateral provider is exposed to the collateral taker. In both instances this typically results in an unsecured claim for the exposure after netting.[50]

(2) Title transfer and right of use devices compared

2.30 Historically, the device of a security interest combined with a right of use has its origin in the margin lending practice of US stockbrokers in the early decades of the twentieth century, when client agreements commonly stipulated that the stockbroker had repledge rights over margin posted by the client.[51] Modern prime brokerage agreements have broadened the broker's repledge rights in respect of assets pledged by clients to a general right to use, in particular to sell, or otherwise dispose of, margin securities to third parties. This practice has a parallel in the collateralization of OTC derivatives, where the standard 1994 ISDA Credit Support Annex under New York law envisaged such a right of use.[52] The main drivers for the introduction of this new device are the pressure on market participants to make optimal use of their portfolios, advantages

---

[49] See Ch 3, paras 3.13–17.
[50] In the absence of special statutory provisions to the contrary; see, eg, para 2.55.
[51] See Kettering, 'Repledge Deconstructed'; Kettering, 'Repledge and Pre-Default Sale'.
[52] See paras 2 and 6(c) of the NY Annex. For analysis, see Johnson, 'Rehypothecation Failure'; Kettering, 'Repledge Deconstructed'; Kettering, 'Repledge and Pre-Default Sale'.

for an institution's funding costs, and for market liquidity generally. In 2002, the right of use was also given a legal basis in the FCD,[53] and in 2009, in the GSC, in a similar manner.[54]

2.31 Economically speaking, a title transfer and a security interest combined with a right of use serve broadly equivalent functions. This economic similarity is underlined by legal interpretations of the right of use under various legal systems. With respect to US law, Johnson and Kettering have analysed the conceptual challenges surrounding the 'missing *res*', and the incompatibility of the right of use with the equity of redemption and the collateral taker's duty of reasonable care.[55] Benjamin and Gullifer have pointed out a number of principles of traditional English law that are not easy to square with a right of use, such as 'once a mortgage, always a mortgage', the rule against collateral benefits, and, to a lesser extent, the prohibition of clogs on the equity of redemption. These commentators express differing views about whether, absent Article 5 FCD, this tension would call into question the effectiveness of the right of use.[56] Johnson points out incompatibilities relating to the equity of redemption and the duty to ensure safe custody in the UK and Australia.[57] In other, civil law jurisdictions, such as Denmark, Germany, and Italy, the device should arguably, under general principles of law (absent Article 5 FCD), be characterized as an 'irregular pledge', which implies an immediate transfer of title.[58] Common to most of these analyses of the right of use is its effect on the traditional allocation of proprietary rights with respect to collateral between the collateral provider and collateral taker in security interests, and the approximation to the title transfer technique.[59]

2.32 However, the circumstance that the right of use is usually based on contract and that a collateral taker therefore only has a right of use 'if and to the extent that the terms of the collateral agreement so provide', as both the FCD and the GSC put it,[60] leaves a level of control to the collateral provider to determine the level of its credit exposure to its counterparty by agreement. Another difference between a title transfer and a security

---

[53] Article 5 FCD; on the legislative history, see Keijser, *Financial Collateral* (2006), IV.1.3.3. Cf references to a right of use in other EU legislation, eg, Arts 39(8), 52(1), last para, 53(2) European Market Infrastructure Regulation (EMIR); recital (49), Arts 14(3), 15(4), 21(10), last para, 21(11)(d)(iv), 23(1)(a), 23(1)(o), 23(5)(a), 24(4) of the Alternative Investment Fund Managers Directive (AIFMD).

[54] See Art 34 GSC, commented upon in Kanda et al, *Official Commentary*, 34–1 to 34–18.

[55] See Johnson, 'Rehypothecation Failure'; Kettering, 'Repledge Deconstructed'; Kettering, 'Repledge and Pre-Default Sale'. See also Keijser, *Financial Collateral* (2006), IV.2.

[56] See Benjamin, *Interests in Securities*, 5.46–70; Gullifer, 'Financial Collateral', 394–6. See also Johansson, 'Reuse Revisited', 155; Keijser, *Financial Collateral* (2006), IV.3. Cf Gullifer, *Goode on Legal Problems*, 6–30, expressing the view that a right of use in accordance with normal market practice is effective in the absence of opression, and that 'the very existence of art.5 should make it abundantly clear that conferment of a right of re-use is standard international practice and is not open to attack on public policy grounds'.

[57] Johnson, 'Collateral', 14.

[58] See Carrara and Fulvio (Italy), Keijser (Germany and the Netherlands), and Nivaro (Denmark), in Keijser, *Report on a Right of Use*; Haentjens, *Financial Collateral*, ch 6 (Germany, Belgium, and the Netherlands); Keijser, *Financial Collateral* (2006), IV.4.

[59] Gullifer, 'Ownership of Securities', 21, fn 120, notes, however, that Briggs J rejected the qualification of a security interest combined with a right of use as an outright transfer in *Re Lehman Brothers International (Europe) (in administration)* [2009] EWHC 2545 (Ch), paras 60–3.

[60] See Art 5(1) FCD and Art 34(1) GSC.

interest combined with a right of use, as provided for under the FCD and the GSC, is the moment in time when full title passes. In the event of an outright transfer, title to securities passes immediately to the counterparty. In line with Article 5(2) FCD and Article 34(2) GSC, the collateral provider loses title at the later moment of exercise of the right of use, while the collateral taker at that moment incurs an obligation to provide replacement collateral.[61]

(3) The case of Lehman: overcollateralization from a legal policy perspective

Rehypothecation featured prominently in the Lehman insolvency. Briefly, Lehman Brothers International (Europe) (LBIE), the principal trading company of the Lehman group in Europe, with headquarters in London, had obtained unrestricted rights of rehypothecation (ie, not restricted by reference to the level of the secured liabilities) in relation to a considerable number of client portfolios, leading to overcollateralization in many cases.[62] Rehypothecation had its origin in two types of documentation, based on title transfer and a charge with a right of use, respectively.[63] Upon insolvency, clients found that their assets, or assets they considered theirs, could not be retrieved because they had been rehypothecated. To the extent of overcollateralization, close-out netting and similar arrangements provided no protection, leaving the clients with a contractual claim for the excess only. Clearly, this was merely one of several, interrelated factors. For instance, whereas only some of the keener clients had negotiated a cap on the right of use, many clients which had contractually agreed to an unrestricted right of use had not been sufficiently alert to realize its consequences; legal documentation was poor (containing uncertainties as to rehypothecation rights, and written with client insolvency in mind, not that of Lehman itself); many of the securities involved were part of poorly administered, non-segregated asset pools, making it difficult to determine which assets were actually rehypothecated and to identify the rights of clients in the remaining assets; in addition, given that the assets had been provided as security for the clients' obligations to Lehman, it was necessary to establish the extent of clients'

2.33

---

[61] On traditional security interests, the irregular pledge, a security interest combined with a right of use, and title transfers, see Keijser, *Financial Collateral* (2006), IV.

[62] Singh and Aitken, *Deleveraging after Lehman*, I, noted, in 2009, that '[e]very Customer Account Agreement or Prime Brokerage Agreement with a prime brokerage client will include a blanket consent to this practice [ie, use of client collateral by a prime broker for its own purposes] unless stated otherwise'. See also EC, *10th Discussion Paper*, para 68.

[63] Cf *Re Lehman Brothers International (Europe) (in administration)* [2009] EWHC 2545 (Ch), para 8: 'LBIE offered its prime brokerage services pursuant to a range of alternative standard form agreements … Of those alternatives, the two most important (as least for present purposes) were the Title Transfer IPBA [International Prime Brokerage Agreement] and the Charge IPBA. The essential difference between the two was that, pursuant to the former, LBIE was to have all right, title and interest in and to securities delivered by or on behalf of the client, whereas under the latter LBIE was to hold securities as custodian, upon the basis that, subject to important exceptions, they were described as continuing to belong to the client, subject to a charge in favour of LBIE to secure all and any actual or contingent indebtedness of the client to it.' On the charge structure combined with a right of use, see Haentjens, *Financial Collateral*, 6.52–6.

38   FINANCIAL COLLATERAL

liabilities in order to quantify their possible claims against the pool of client assets, and in many cases this proved a complex and time-consuming process. The combination of these factors gave rise to extensive litigation.[64]

2.34 There are therefore good arguments, from the standpoint both of financial stability and investor protection, for imposing or enhancing standards (and ensuring their implementation) relating to proper administration (including the technology in place for that purpose), client asset segregation, market transparency generally (eg, regarding portfolio movement and risk profile reporting to clients and/or supervisors), and, more specifically, a duty to inform collateral providers as to the consequences of a security interest combined with a right of use.[65] Section B(5) considers whether there should be more extensive changes that would restrict the scope for, or the extent of, overcollateralization.

2.35 One of the main issues identified in the LBIE cases is that the legal and regulatory system in the UK (and in other European jurisdictions) did not include measures for protecting clients corresponding to mechanisms applicable in the US.[66] In the US, the recognition of a security interest combined with a right of use is accompanied by a set of checks and balances, which, in effect, protect customer assets and place a cap on their use. Briefly, Securities and Exchange Commission (SEC) regulations (i) impose limitations on an individual account holder's securities available for use (essentially, securities that have been fully paid for are not available for use, whereas pledged securities bought 'on margin' may be used up to 140 per cent of the value of the secured debt; the rest must be kept in possession or under control by the broker-dealer), (ii) contain an aggregate 'hypothecation restriction' (no use of pledged account holder securities if this 'exceeds the aggregate indebtedness of all customers in respect of securities carried for their accounts'[67]), and (iii) determine the treatment of the monetary proceeds of use in the context of calculating a Reserve Bank Account that must be available for the direct benefit of account holders. These SEC rules are complemented by distributional rules in insolvency, set out in the Securities Investor Protection Act (SIPA), which in effect mutualize any shortfalls among all account holders of the insolvent intermediary.[68] It

---

[64] On the Lehman cases and rehypothecation, see: Benjamin, Morton, and Raffan, 'The Future of Securities Financing'; FSB, *Re-hypothecation and Collateral Re-use*, especially 4.1; Van den Hoek, 'Voorkomt Ulpianus de crisis?', 7; Gullifer, 'Ownership of Securities', 1.IV.B (in particular pp 20–2), 1.VII; Johansson, 'Reuse Revisited'; Zacaroli, 'Taking Security'.

[65] See, eg, EC, *10th Discussion Paper*, paras 74–85; FSB, *Shadow Banking: Securities Lending and Repos*, s 2 (for policy recommendations related to improvement in transparency), and s 3.2 and Recommendations 7–8 (focusing on rehypothecation); FSB, *Consultative Document: Application of Key Attributes*, Appendix III, s 4 (segregation, securities lending, rights of use) and s 8 (information requirements and record keeping); Johansson, 'Reuse Revisited', 6.VI–VII; Senior Supervisors Group, *Risk Management Lessons*, 17 ('Segregation of Margin') on provision by prime brokers of frequent (sometimes daily), detailed information to their hedge fund clients concerning rehypothecated assets; the reporting requirements in relation to the right of use under Arts 14(3), 23(1)(a), 23(1)(o), 23(5)(a), and 24(4) AIFMD; in the UK, Financial Conduct Authority (FCA), *CP 13/5*, Ch 6 (client reporting and information). See also Ch 9, s D(4) and, specifically on segregation, Ch 7, s D.

[66] See Johansson, 'Reuse Revisited'; Singh and Aitken, *Deleveraging after Lehman*. See also Ch 8, s B(2).

[67] 17 CFR § 240.8c-1(a)(3) and 17 CFR § 240.15c2-1(a)(3). See Mooney, 'Shortfall', 174.

[68] For an illuminating explanation of the intricate SEC and SIPA regime, see Mooney, 'Shortfall', 7.3.3, with further references. See also Singh and Aitken, *Deleveraging after Lehman*, II.

should be noted that these checks and balances apply to the broker-dealer market segment, but not to bank intermediaries, and were originally developed for the repledge practice, with account holder protection as a key underlying rationale.

The FCD also embraced the concept of a right of use, but, as an instrument aimed at harmonizing private law, it is confined to private law aspects of that right, while not setting out any regulatory checks and balances as developed in the US. **2.36**

(4) Overcollateralization in the form of independent amounts

(a) Introduction
Financial collateral arrangements typically take the mark-to-market or mark-to-model exposure ('MTM exposure') of the parties as the reference point for their collateral obligations. MTM exposure, if applicable thresholds are met, generally gives rise to a transfer of (variation) margin in order to reduce or eliminate that exposure. This section, however, examines overcollateralization that may occur where the collateral arrangement contains provisions to the effect that at least one of the parties may be obliged to post collateral with a value *in excess of* the other party's actual MTM exposure. In the context of derivatives, such excess collateral is typically called 'initial margin' or 'independent amount collateral', while in the context of securities financing transactions 'haircuts'[69] fulfil largely the same function.[70] For ease of discourse (including the ability to refer to well-known ISDA standard forms), this section is mainly concerned with collateral to secure derivatives exposures. The exposition transposes to other contexts without material changes. **2.37**

The principal purpose of excess collateral such as 'initial margin' or 'independent amount collateral' is to provide cover for potential future exposure that may arise from the time of the last posting of collateral until such time as the collateralized position may have to be closed out by the collateral taker (the close-out interval).[71] The required amount of excess collateral clearly depends on assumptions about the length of the interval, volatility of positions, etc.[72] Where exposure is stable in the short run (for example, the exposure of a bank to a borrower under an ordinary loan), the risk that exposure will increase during the relatively short time until close-out is small or non-existent. However, exposures relating to derivatives positions are typically **2.38**

---

[69] 'Haircut' is the colloquial term used by market participants to refer to an agreed ratio by which the value of collateral must exceed that of the obligation of the collateral provider (the value of the collateral being 'trimmed' by this ratio for the purposes of calculation). Market agreements use more technical defined expressions, for example 'Margin Ratio' (GMRA) or 'Required Collateral Value' (GMSLA).

[70] For regulatory guidance on margin in the context of OTC derivatives, see BCBS and IOSCO, *Margin Requirements* (2020); for regulatory guidance on haircuts in the context of securities financing transactions, see FSB, *Haircuts*. See also extensively Haentjens, *Financial Collateral*, ch 3.

[71] BCBS and IOSCO, *Margin Requirements* (2020), 3(d); ISDA, MFA, and SIFMA, *Independent Amounts*, s 3.

[72] The BCBS and IOSCO, *Margin Requirements* (2020), 3.1, recommend taking 'an extreme but plausible estimate of an increase in the value of the instrument that is consistent with a one-tailed 99 per cent confidence interval over a 10-day horizon'. Cf FSB, *Haircuts*, 2.1(i).

subject to substantial short-term variations,[73] and overcollateralization is therefore more common in relation to such transactions.[74]

2.39 The terminology differs according to the relevant area: 'initial margin' is the term of art to describe overcollateralization in respect of exchange-traded, centrally cleared transactions and positions,[75] but this term was rarely used in practice in connection with OTC derivatives. Instead, the term 'independent amount' (which has its origin in the ISDA credit support documents referred to below) was often employed to refer to the value of collateral that is or should be posted in addition to collateral covering actual MTM exposure under all OTC transactions subject to a single master agreement.[76] In recent years, however, 'initial margin' is increasingly being used in connection with OTC transactions, probably because of the regulatory focus on central clearing and collateralization in the OTC space.[77] While undue weight should not be given to the particular terms used, it should be noted that both terms may, in their respective contexts, be confusing: 'initial margin' may also refer to margin (or collateral) that is or must be posted during the course of a transaction or after certain positions have been taken (for example, because the initial margin is calculated in relation to a portfolio of trades, and not trade by trade); an 'independent amount' will often depend on several factors, which may vary over time.

2.40 In the remainder of this section, which concentrates on OTC derivatives and associated collateral arrangements, our preferred (though not exclusive) term is 'independent amount collateral' or 'IA collateral'.[78]

(b) Independent amounts: factual and contractual aspects

2.41 Traditionally, (positive) independent amounts were a rare occurrence within the OTC derivatives markets and were mainly confined to dealer/end-user transactions.[79] In fact, in the period preceding the global financial crisis, *under*collateralization (including no collateralization at all) was a much more common phenomenon in these markets. Many OTC collateral arrangements stipulated that exposures needed to be secured by collateral only if, and to the extent that, they exceeded agreed threshold values. Overcollateralization (through initial margining) has assumed much greater importance in relation to exchange-traded and centrally cleared derivatives.

---

[73] See Ch 3, s C(4).
[74] An example of non-derivative transactions for which initial margin will typically be required is a short sale; see, eg, Hull, *Risk Management*, 5.3.1.
[75] As well as 'variation margin' to describe security provided to cover actual MTM exposure.
[76] ISDA, MFA, and SIFMA, *Independent Amounts*, 2.2; ISDA, *Smart Derivatives Contracts: Collateral*, 13 and 15.
[77] Cf Murphy, *OTC Derivatives*, 44. Eg, BCBS and IOSCO, *Margin Requirements* (2020), uses initial margin terminology in connection with OTC derivatives transactions.
[78] We use these terms to refer to 'excess collateral' (cf para 2.38) in general and their scope is therefore broader than that of 'Independent Amount' as defined in the ISDA credit support documents.
[79] ISDA, MFA, and SIFMA, *Independent Amounts*, 5–6; Murphy, *OTC Derivatives*, 44.

2.42 The global financial crisis has led to substantial changes, both qualitative and quantitative.[80] First, the crisis has triggered an increased risk awareness on the part of market participants in general. This in turn has led to a much wider coverage by way of collateralization agreements,[81] including coverage by independent amounts (and equivalent mechanisms). In addition, overcollateralization is an (intended) side-effect of the global regulatory initiative geared to moving many OTC derivatives to central clearing, where initial margining is a standard feature of clearing arrangements.[82] Finally, derivatives that are not centrally cleared are increasingly becoming subject to regulatory requirements, including independent amounts.[83]

2.43 This section takes the ISDA credit support documentation, which is used by the great majority of OTC market participants, as a starting point.[84] As mentioned in paragraphs 2.03–4, there are several ISDA 'credit support documents', which are relevant in this context since they cover the whole of the relevant range of collateral arrangements: (i) the 1995 English Annex, which is a *title transfer* arrangement; (ii) the 1995 English Deed, which, as a *bare security* arrangement, does not allow for a right to use posted collateral;[85] and (iii) the 1994 NY Annex, which is a *security* arrangement that does allow for a *right of use*.[86,87]

2.44 These documents do not differ as regards the determination (calculation) of exposure and collateral amounts (both amounts actually posted and required).[88] Under all three of the 1994/1995 credit support documents, a positive independent amount applicable to a party has the effect of an 'add-on' to collateral linked to exposure.[89] It should, however, be noted that the credit support documents may be modified so as to eliminate the offset of independent amounts.[90] Such a modification has the effect of ensuring that a

---

[80] This development has strengthened the secular trend toward the increased use of collateral agreements and collateralization; see the ISDA Margin Surveys and their predecessors (n 1).
[81] See para 2.20.
[82] For a critical analysis of (unintended) systemic effects of central clearing, see Pirrong, *CCPs and Systemic Risk*.
[83] See, eg, BCBS and IOSCO, *Margin Requirements* (2020), p 4 and Elements 1–3; cf Art 11 EMIR.
[84] The ISDA documents and standard collateral documentation published by other trade organizations operate on broadly similar principles, though with numerous differences of detail; for an example of a 'non-ISDA' standard collateral arrangement, see the Margin Maintenance Annex (Edition 2020) to the European Master Agreement, available at <https://www.ebf.eu/home/european-master-agreement-ema/> (accessed 7 July 2021).
[85] As explicitly provided ('[f]or the avoidance of doubt') in para 6(d) of the Deed; cf ISDA, MFA, and SIFMA, *Independent Amounts*, 12. Of course, the Deed predates the FCD and its implementation in the UK.
[86] See para 6(c) of the NY Annex; in the sequel we assume that the parties to an NY Annex have not excluded or restricted this right of use in any way (cf para 13(g)(ii)).
[87] For a clear general discussion of these documents, see Murray, in Yeowart and Parsons, *Law of Financial Collateral*, 17.56–75. The user's guides published by ISDA also provide helpful introductions: see ISDA, *User's Guide to the 1994 ISDA Credit Support Annex*; and ISDA, *User's Guide to the ISDA Credit Support Documents under English Law*.
[88] In this context the principal defined terms are: 'Exposure', 'Credit Support Amount', 'Credit Support Balance', 'Threshold', and, of course, 'Independent Amount'. Each credit support document takes as its point of departure that the collateral to be posted by a party must have a value at least equal to: the exposure of its counterparty; *minus* the applicable threshold; *plus* the sum of all independent amounts applicable to that party; *minus* the sum of the independent amounts applicable to the counterparty.
[89] ISDA, *User's Guide to the 1994 ISDA Credit Support Annex*, 6; ISDA, *User's Guide to the ISDA Credit Support Documents under English Law*, 21, 36. As stated in ISDA, MFA, and SIFMA, *Independent Amounts*, 1.5: 'Exposure and Independent Amounts are simply two of several terms netted together in the expression that yields the overall Credit Support Amount. . . . under the ISDA CSA there is technically just a single pool of collateral.'
[90] ISDA, *User's Guide to the 1994 ISDA Credit Support Annex*, Appendix C; ISDA, *User's Guide to the ISDA Credit Support Documents under English Law*, Appendix B.

party is always required to post at least the sum of its independent amounts as collateral, irrespective of the level of exposure, and that both parties should post such independent amount collateral.

2.45 Lately, in order to accommodate new regulatory guidelines, notably by the BCBS and the Board of IOSCO,[91] ISDA has developed several documents for the provision of regulatory variation and initial margin, such as the ISDA 2016 Credit Support Annex for Variation Margin (English law), which is a title transfer arrangement; the ISDA 2016 Credit Support Annex for Variation Margin (New York law), which is a security arrangement; as well as a wide range of standard documents to cover the provision of regulatory initial margin, often on a two-way gross basis.[92] It is fair to say that this new documentation conceptually builds on the original documentation of the mid-1990s.

2.46 The legal position in respect of all posted collateral is determined by the nature of the relevant credit support document: title transfer arrangement or security arrangement, and in the latter case with or without a right of use.

(c) The position of the provider of independent amount collateral

2.47 The relevance of overcollateralization, including the provision of IA collateral, is that it leads to credit risks run by the *provider* of excess collateral. Of course, even within the context of the ISDA credit support documents, positive independent amounts are not the only possible cause of overcollateralization. Collateral *haircuts* may also lead to an excess of the realized value (actual or hypothetical) of collateral over the exposure that the collateral is supposed to cover. Haircuts play a role similar to independent amounts: whereas the latter primarily reflect possible changes of MTM exposure during the close-out interval, haircuts reflect (at least in theory) the variability of the value of posted collateral during that interval.[93]

2.48 The nature of the risks run by the collateral provider differs according to the type of collateral arrangement between the parties. Under a *title transfer arrangement*, such as the English Annex, the excess claim (ie, the value of collateral minus exposure at close-out) is unsecured and therefore corresponds to the full extent of (unmitigated) credit risk of the collateral provider. Similar considerations apply to a *security arrangement that includes a right of use*, such as the NY Annex, if that right of use has been exercised by the collateral taker (leading to a loss of title of the collateral provider).

---

[91] BCBS and IOSCO, *Margin Requirements* (2020).

[92] See further: ISDA, *Navigating Initial Margin Documentation*; ISDA, *Smart Derivatives Contracts: Collateral*, 15–16 and 25–26; ISDA, *User's Guide to the 2018 & 2019 ISDA Regulatory Initial Margin Documentation*.

[93] Overcollateralization may also result from non-zero 'minimum transfer amounts' (MTAs), the principal purpose of which is to avoid transfers (postings and returns) of small amounts of collateral. In practice, however, one may encounter substantial MTAs (in combination with zero thresholds), which clearly have another purpose, more akin to thresholds. This may lead to comparably substantial overcollateralization. For example, suppose that in the initial situation party A's exposure of 100 is fully collateralized by party B under their collateral arrangement. Let the applicable MTA be 20. If A's exposure drops to, say, 85, A is not required to return any collateral: the exposure drop of 15 is less than the MTA. (Of course, in different circumstances *under*collateralization may result from a non-zero MTA: if A's exposure to B increases by 15 (to 115), B is not required to post extra collateral, and A's exposure will be undercollateralized by the same amount.)

Under a *bare security arrangement*, such as the English Deed, the legal position should, in principle, be different. Collateral posted should be identifiable as belonging to the collateral provider (and subject to the security interest of the collateral taker), and should therefore be recoverable as the provider's property in the insolvency of the collateral taker. In practice, however, credit risk may return under the guise of operational risk, notably where the collateral taker has failed to arrange for the proper holding of security collateral as property of the provider subject to a security interest.

2.49

(5) Overcollateralization: possible responses

In the debate on overcollateralization among market participants, legislators, and regulators, a central theme concerns possible ways of mitigating the associated risks. As discussed in paragraphs 2.33–4 and 2.49, this includes a number of operational and related issues, in particular concerning the accuracy of records, client asset segregation, transparency, and the client's understanding of risk. The focus of this section, however, is on overcollateralization as such. We therefore examine whether, and if so how, overcollateralization should be restricted by changes to the legal or regulatory framework.

2.50

(a) Private law responses

This raises the fundamental question of the appropriate role of the general framework of private law. Preceding the global financial crisis, the approach adopted in many jurisdictions has been that the law should provide a clear and predictable framework for transactions that business people in fact choose to enter into, as reflected in the *lex mercatoria*.[94] However, if some such transactions entail undue (systemic) risks or require additional safeguards against unfairness, private law and regulatory approaches are available. For the latter see section B(5)(b). In this section we focus on private law responses developed in the market, by the legislator, and by scholars.

2.51

One possible response is to reconsider the legal techniques applied in the market. In case of a title transfer, and that of a grant of security with a right of use to the extent that the right of use is exercised, the collateral provider loses title to the collateral provided and receives instead an unsecured claim of a contractual nature, which will usually rank *pari passu* with other unsecured liabilities in insolvency.[95]

2.52

Given the crucial place of title transfer collateral arrangements in the wholesale financial markets (including central bank operations), it is neither possible nor desirable to

2.53

---

[94] One desirable element of such framework is clarity regarding any risk of invalidity under regulatory or private law due to non-compliance with any restriction on overcollateralization in general, or on the right of use in particular. Such invalidation should be approached with caution, since it may give rise to uncertainty, legal risk, and unintended consequences for innocent parties.

[95] It should be noted that 'segregation' of collateral title transferred to, and not (yet) transferred further by, the collateral taker as somehow 'belonging' to the collateral provider would be misdirected and may actually introduce recharacterization risks. Cf ISDA, MFA, and SIFMA, *Independent Amounts*, 13.

completely replace title transfer arrangements and security arrangements including a right of use by bare security arrangements. A less drastic response, which may be practicable in some cases, would be to move to *dual* collateral arrangements, that is, to split such arrangements and the resulting pool of collateral into two parts: a title transfer arrangement or a security collateral arrangement with a right of use, which applies to collateral covering actual MTM exposure, and a bare security collateral arrangement governing the provision of excess collateral.[96]

2.54 As part of this debate, some propose abolishing the right of use and structuring the market exclusively on the basis of 'traditional' outright transfers and security interests.[97] Opinions on the merits of the right of use diverge.[98] Here we merely wish to note two points in its favour. First, the comparable device of the irregular pledge, implying a transfer of title, is no legal novelty and has been applied in a number of jurisdictions over time.[99] Secondly, if there is an actual need in the market for a 'hybrid' device that offers collateral takers more rights than traditional security interests (and therefore less protection to collateral providers), this need should arguably be catered for. Indeed, it seems likely that the practical effect of the abolition of the right of use would be increased use of title transfer collateral arrangements.[100]

2.55 Another possible way of mitigating the negative consequences of overcollateralization for the collateral provider is to give its contractual claim for the delivery of equivalent collateral some kind of priority over the claims of other creditors.[101] This solution, however, has its own complications and drawbacks, and in particular represents a significant shift in the balance between the claims of clients which have provided collateral (in circumstances where, in principle, they have the ability to control their exposure by limiting the degree of overcollateralization) and those of other unsecured creditors.

2.56 Gullifer approaches the issue from a private law perspective, by attempting to determine the limits that should apply to the carve-outs from generally applicable private law rules under the FCD regime for financial collateral arrangements by way of 'blue sky thinking'.[102] She concludes that the right of use (and other features of this regime) should only be available to large businesses trading on the wholesale financial markets.[103]

---

[96] ISDA, MFA, and SIFMA, *Independent Amounts*, 33–5 (esp. Recommendations 4 and 5).
[97] One of the solutions identified in Keijser, *Financial Collateral* (2006), IV.4.3. See also EC, *10th Discussion Paper*, esp. para 63, which is critically assessed in Yates and Montagu, *Global Custody*, 7.190.
[98] See, in favour of a security interest with a right of use, Benjamin, Morton, and Raffan, 'The Future of Securities Financing'; and, critical, Keijser, *Financial Collateral* (2006), IV; Kettering, 'Repledge and Pre-Default Sale'; Kettering, 'Repledge Deconstructed'.
[99] See para 2.31. On the comparable irregular deposit or *mutuum* under Roman law, see Benjamin, Morton, and Raffan, 'The Future of Securities Financing', D; see also Carrara and Fulvio (n 58) p 46, s 6 (Italian law); Nivaro (n 58) p 25, s 2.1 (Danish law).
[100] Singh and Aitken, *Deleveraging after Lehman*, I, fn 3 note that hardly any empirical work has been done on the cost aspect of the alternative approaches of security interest combined with a right of use under prime brokerage agreements, on the one hand, and title transfer under repos, on the other.
[101] See, eg, art 7:53(3) Dutch Civil Code. On US and English law, see Johansson, 'Reuse Revisited', 6.V.
[102] See Gullifer, 'Financial Collateral', 378.
[103] See Gullifer, 'Financial Collateral', 394–6. In the same vein, Keijser, *Financial Collateral* (2006), IV.5.5 and VI.4.2.

(b) Regulatory restrictions

2.57 Another option is to develop a system of regulatory checks and balances in order to mitigate the potentially disruptive consequences, and investor protection risks, of substantial overcollateralization, including reasonable restrictions on rehypothecation. Inspiration for such an approach can be found in the US regime applicable to broker-dealers, outlined in paragraph 2.35. In practice, too, some market participants have negotiated various measures, including caps and limits on rehypothecation.[104]

2.58 At the international level, the BCBS Cross-border Bank Resolution Group recommended in 2010 that '[c]onsideration should be given to adopting limits on rehypothecation of customer or other collateral'.[105] In 2013, the Financial Stability Board (FSB) established a number of recommendations relating to the rehypothecation of client assets.[106] Pursuant to Recommendation 7, authorities should ensure that (i) clients whose assets are rehypothecated should be informed of the resulting exposure in the event of failure of the intermediary; (ii) intermediaries should not rehypothecate client assets for own-account activities; and (iii) only entities that are subject to adequate regulation of liquidity risk should be allowed to rehypothecate client assets. The FSB also investigated the possible further harmonization of rules, including limits on rehypothecation, which resulted in a report on rehypothecation and collateral reuse in 2017.[107] In this report, the FSB concluded that it currently saw no immediate case for further harmonizing regulatory approaches to rehypothecation of client assets, but encouraged the observance of its earlier Recommendation 7 as well as the monitoring of collateral reuse in the global financial system so as to enhance the understanding of this phenomenon.[108] Moreover, the BCBS and IOSCO Board prescribed a set of conditions that should be met for rehypothecation to be allowed to take place, albeit only in the context of initial (but not variation) margin provided in respect of non-centrally cleared derivatives.[109]

2.59 In the EU, in the wake of the global financial crisis, a patchwork of provisions was enacted with different approaches to rehypothecation. See, for example, Article 13(7) of the 2004 Markets in Financial Instruments Directive (MiFID); recitals (51) and (52), and Articles 16(8)–(10) of the 2014 recast of the Markets in Financial Instruments Directive (MiFID II); Article 22(7) of the 2009 UCITS Directive;[110] recital (49) and

---

[104] Johansson, 'Reuse Revisited', 6.V; Harris, 'Use of Customer Securities'; Senior Supervisors Group, *Risk Management Lessons*, 16 ('Limits on Rehypothecation of Client Securities'); Singh and Aitken, *Deleveraging after Lehman*, IV.
[105] See BCBS, *Cross-border Bank Resolution*, Recommendation 8 (cf para 108).
[106] See FSB, *Shadow Banking: Securities Lending and Repos*, 3.2 and Recommendations 7–8, discussed in Keijser, 'Financial Collateral' (2017), I.7(c). See also Ch 9, s D(4).
[107] See FSB, *Re-hypothecation and Collateral Re-use* (January 2017). On the work towards this report, see FSB, *Shadow Banking: Securities Lending and Repos* (August 2013), 3.2, Recommendation 8; FSB, *An Overview of Progress* (November 2015), 10–11; FSB, *Possible Measures of Non-cash Collateral Re-use* (February 2016), 1; Keijser, 'Financial Collateral' (2017), I.7(c).
[108] On this latter topic, see FSB, *Non-cash Collateral Re-use: Measure and Metrics* (January 2017). These guidelines are part of a broader global securities financing data collection initiative.
[109] BCBS and IOSCO, *Margin Requirements* (2020), Element 5, notably 5(v).
[110] The reuse provision in the UCITS Directive was introduced by way of Directive 2014/91/EU.

46   FINANCIAL COLLATERAL

Articles 14(3), 15(4), 21(10), last paragraph, 21(11)(d)(iv), 23(1)(a), 23(1)(o), 23(5)(a), and 24(4) of the 2011 Alternative Investment Fund Managers Directive (AIFMD); Articles 39(8), 52(1), last paragraph, and 53(2) of the 2012 European Market Infrastructure Regulation (EMIR); and recitals (8), (10), (21)–(25), and Articles 2(1)(d), 3(12), 4(9)(b), and 15 of the 2015 Securities Financing Transactions Regulation (SFTR).[111] These provisions cover a variety of topics, ranging from the use of assets only with consent to limitations on or prohibitions of use in specific contexts, risk management, and disclosure, notification, and reporting requirements towards clients and regulators. They are not always consistent with each other.[112] Different types of caps and limits on rehypothecation were also considered in the EU debate on securities law legislation.[113]

2.60 In legal literature, Johansson has raised the question of whether national authorities should consider limitations on rehypothecation after Lehman, such as were imposed in the US after comparable events in the first half of the twentieth century.[114] Van den Hoek is in favour of a cap on the right of use on the basis of an analysis of traditional repledge rights, similar to Johnson's earlier analysis under US law.[115] One could also ask whether the mechanisms relating to the US broker-dealer market segment should be extended to bank intermediaries.[116]

2.61 A major drawback of the regulatory approach is that it leads to a legal framework that consists of three interacting layers based upon diverging principles: the 'traditional' private law that tries to strike a fair balance between the parties involved in a transaction; the reform of aspects of the private law regime for financial collateral transactions with an emphasis on the interests of collateral takers and liquid markets; and the regulatory regime that imposes rules to address both inter-party and structural aspects of collateralized transactions. Putting it mildly, this layering leads to a challenging legal environment from the practitioner's point of view.[117]

(c) Concluding remarks

2.62 Rehypothecation enhances the liquidity of the financial markets but, where no limits on the rehypothecation of excess collateral are imposed, may give rise to substantial exposure of collateral providers, which might contribute to threats to systemic stability and raise concerns as to appropriate investor protection. While the US has developed a set of checks and balances in relation to overcollateralization of broker-dealer exposures,

---

[111] Keijser, 'Financial Collateral' (2017), I.11.
[112] Ibid, II.18.
[113] See EC, *10th Discussion Paper*, paras 71–3.
[114] See Johansson, 'Reuse Revisited', 6.VI–VII. In relation to the UK, Johansson carefully notes the argument that flexible legislation enhances the competitiveness of London's financial markets, and states that the consensus view in the UK, reflected in proposals from the Treasury and the FSA, seems to be that the issue of a cap on rehypothecation should be left to contract rather than imposing limitations by law. See also Gullifer, 'Ownership of Securities', 21–2.
[115] See Van den Hoek, 'Voorkomt Ulpianus de crisis?'. Cf Johnson, 'Rehypothecation Failure'.
[116] Cf Mooney, 'Shortfall', 7.3.3.3.
[117] On the complications arising as a result of these three 'mindsets', see Keijser 'Financial Collateral' (2017).

there is no comparable overall regime in Europe, though, as mentioned in paragraph 2.59, a number of specific new measures now apply to rights of rehypothecation. There are several possible ways to limit overcollateralization or its effects, including various private law and regulatory-inspired solutions. In all cases, the general law and regulatory framework should balance the objectives of maximum flexibility for market participants, minimal complexity of the applicable legal framework, appropriate protection of clients, and protection of the stability of the financial system more generally.

C. Collateral in Insolvency and in Resolution

(1) General

2.63 The preceding sections have focused on the provision of collateral outside of the insolvency context, ie assuming both parties to the transaction have not entered formal reorganization or liquidation proceedings. However, and as our discussion of the Lehman bankruptcy in paragraph 2.33 illustrated, in insolvency the credit risk materializes from which collateral is intended to protect, whilst other risks may materialize that jeopardize the enforcement of collateral. Insolvency is thus an important perspective to take when considering the legal positions of the parties to a collateral transaction.[118] More strongly put, it is primarily in the insolvency context that collateral transactions must prove their worth, that is, they must show whether they are indeed effective in reducing or limiting the credit risk which the collateral taker runs on the collateral provider.[119] In this section, we will further discuss the way in which legislators, initially, sought to facilitate the enforcement of financial collateral by the collateral taker in the collateral provider's insolvency, and then curbed that enforcement where the insolvent is a financial institution.[120]

2.64 The enforcement of collateral before maturity of the collateral transaction in question, ie the early termination of financial collateral transactions and the enforcement, by the collateral taker, of its rights in the assets provided as collateral, involve specific legal issues. First, the majority of financial collateral transactions provide for 'close-out netting' as a way of enforcement. Close-out netting thus replaces traditional enforcement mechanisms of security interests such as public auction. More specifically, close-out netting refers to the technique by means of which, upon default by one of the parties: (i) the agreement is 'closed out', that is terminated or cancelled, and all outstanding obligations incurred under the agreement are accelerated so that they become immediately payable; (ii) all these payable obligations are valued and, where necessary, converted into monetary claims in terms of a single currency; so that (iii) these monetary claims

---

[118] See, eg, Haentjens, 'Dispossession and Segregation', 263 et seq.
[119] Haentjens, *Financial Collateral*, 8.01, and our discussion of the Lehman insolvency above.
[120] Sections C(1) and C(2) are based on Haentjens, *Financial Collateral*, 8.01 et seq. See also Keijser, 'Financial Collateral' (2017), especially ss I.1, 3, 7(e), 8, 9, 10, and II.19, 20.

can be set off or 'netted' against one another. As a consequence, only a 'net' balance or aggregate amount needs to be paid by the party owing a higher amount to the other.[121]

2.65 An important point to make is that the netting technique just discussed may involve not only the set-off of one (monetary) claim against one (monetary) obligation—which is a legal technique long known to most jurisdictions—but also the aggregation of multiple claims and obligations that may have been incurred under the multiple transactions concluded under the umbrella of one or more master agreements such as the General Master Repurchase Agreement (GMRA) or General Master Securities Lending Agreement (GMSLA).[122] In essence, the technique of netting thus represents a contractual enhancement of what is possible under some national set-off laws, whilst some jurisdictions even consider netting a separate legal concept.[123]

2.66 In a number of jurisdictions, the termination of financial collateral transactions and close-out netting in particular is protected by 'safe harbours', which means that they are shielded from insolvency law rules that would otherwise be applicable. These safe harbours thus serve to protect the parties' enforcement of the contractual arrangements against insolvency law rules. Specifically, close-out netting has been made possible on insolvency, where in various jurisdictions insolvency set-off would not be possible under general property and insolvency laws. The concepts of close-out netting and safe harbours are therefore connected. The regulatory responses to the global financial crisis, however, narrowed those safe harbours where these are applied in bank failures.

(2) Safe harbours

2.67 As stated above, several jurisdictions protect the termination of financial collateral transactions and close-out netting by 'safe harbours', which means that they are shielded from insolvency law rules that would otherwise be applicable. Under EU law, for instance, as mentioned in paragraph 2.10, the FCD requires the disapplication of certain insolvency provisions under national Member States' laws. In essence, it requires that:[124]

(i) any zero-hour rule be disapplied with respect to financial collateral transactions as defined in the FCD (financial collateral arrangements, or FCAs) and to financial collateral provided under an FCA (Article 8(1) FCD). Under a zero-hour rule, insolvency proceedings commonly apply retroactively from 00:00 hours of the day that insolvency has been declared or insolvency proceedings have formally commenced. This means that FCAs and financial collateral provided thereunder

---

[121] On close-out netting, see Ch 3, especially para 3.10.
[122] See more specifically, Haentjens, *Financial Collateral*, ch 3, ss 3.3.3.5 (for repos), 3.4.2.7 (for securities lending).
[123] See on this topic, extensively, Muscat, *Insolvency Close-out Netting*.
[124] For a more detailed account of Art 8 Collateral Directive and its implementation into various Member States' national laws, see Haentjens, *Financial Collateral*, 8.13 et seq; see also Keijser, *Financial Collateral* (2006), ch V.

cannot be invalidated because they have been concluded or provided, respectively, on the day of the commencement of insolvency proceedings (Article 8(1)(a) FCD), or within a prescribed period earlier than that (Article 8(1)(b) FCD);
(ii) freezes be disapplied with respect to FCAs and financial collateral provided under an FCA (Article 4(5) FCD). Under a freeze, commonly, a creditor is temporarily not allowed to exercise its right to take recourse against assets that are part of the insolvency estate; and
(iii) the provision of financial collateral under an FCA after the commencement of insolvency proceedings be valid, provided that the collateral is provided on the day of such commencement, and that the collateral taker can prove that he was not aware, nor should have been aware, of the commencement (Article 8(2) FCD).

These rules apply not only to the provision of financial collateral, but also to the provision of additional financial collateral (also called 'margin') and to the substitution or replacement of financial collateral under a financial collateral arrangement (Article 8(3) FCD). Finally, Article 8(4) FCD provides that, without prejudice to Article 8(1), (2), and (3), the general rules of national insolvency laws relating to the voidance of transactions entered into during a prescribed period as defined in Article 8(1) and in Article 8(3) FCD be unaffected. This means that the FCD regime allows national laws to continue to sanction fraudulent conveyance or fraudulent preference rules, so that FCAs and the provision of financial collateral thereunder, –whether initially provided, provided as top-up collateral, or as substitute collateral—may still be considered invalid where this has been intentionally done to the detriment of creditors during a prescribed period.

2.68 In addition to the safe harbour rules described above, Article 7(1) FCD introduced a safe harbour for close-out netting arrangements by providing that a close-out netting provision should take effect in accordance with its terms, notwithstanding: (i) the commencement or continuation of winding-up proceedings or reorganization measures in respect of the collateral provider and/or the collateral taker; and (ii) any purported assignment, judicial or other attachment, or other disposition of or in respect of 'such rights' (from the face of the provision, it is not immediately clear what 'such rights' refers to, but this must concern any of the claims that are to be set off under the netting arrangement). In addition, the operation of a close-out netting provision may not be subject to formalities such as court approval (Article 7(2) FCD).[125]

2.69 Article 7 FCD takes a functional approach. It requires that EU Member States allow close-out netting arrangements and provides that certain formalities may not be applied in respect to such arrangements. It does not harmonize the requirements for netting as such. Recital (15) FCD makes clear that it has been left to the applicable national law to determine the requirements for (close-out) netting. For example, the recital says that it is for the applicable national law to determine whether claims must be

---

[125] Haentjens, *Financial Collateral*, 8.29 et seq.

considered reciprocal and therefore eligible for netting. Also, under this same recital (15), it remains a prerogative of national law to determine whether a party is allowed to invoke (close-out) netting in light of its knowledge of the future commencement of insolvency proceedings of its counterparty. This means that the rules of national law relating to fraudulent conveyance (*actio pauliana*) remain untouched by the Directive. Finally, all (other) issues that Article 7 FCD does not specifically regulate, such as the moment when parties' claims must be valued, must be considered to have remained subject to national law.[126]

2.70   Under US laws, similar safe harbour rules as just discussed for the EU apply. More specifically, certain securities and commodities contracts, swaps, forwards, and repos are exempt from the US Bankruptcy Code's automatic stay.[127] A party's insolvency typically constitutes an 'event of default' under the relevant contract and the insolvency of the party's parent or affiliate typically constitutes a 'cross-default'. Both will trigger enforcement rights on the part of the counterparty, allowing it to immediately terminate the contract, net obligations, and/or liquidate collateral. The Bankruptcy Code's 'safe harbor' provisions will allow such rights to be exercised immediately, notwithstanding the automatic stay, which would otherwise preclude such exercise.[128]

(3) Bank resolution

2.71   As stated in paragraph 2.66, the safe harbours discussed in the preceding subsection have been narrowed as a (regulatory) response to the global financial crisis. This crisis was a banking crisis mainly, so that these limitations to the safe harbours were initially geared to failing banks specifically. Since the introduction of new specialist regimes for the recovery and resolution of failing banks, however, initiatives have been undertaken to have these regimes also apply, *mutatis mutandis*, to other categories of financial institutions such as investment firms, insurance companies, and central counterparties.[129] Likewise, the safe harbours that otherwise apply to collateral transactions have been modified in these instruments (or draft instruments) of legislation. We will now proceed to discuss these modifications in more detail, but before we do so, some brief comments on the introduction of the relatively recent, specialist regime for the resolution of banks and the rationale for that introduction may be in order. The focus will be on

---

[126] Keijser, *Financial Collateral* (2006), 293 and 304 et seq.
[127] 11 USC §§ 362(b)(6), (7), (17), (27), 362(o), 555–56, 559–61.
[128] Sykes, *Regulatory Reform 10 Years After the Financial Crisis*, 24.
[129] Certain categories of investment firms are included in the BRRD and SRMR. Insurance companies are covered by national instruments such as the Dutch Act on Recovery and Resolution of Insurance Companies (*Wet herstel en afwikkeling van verzekeraars*, Stb. 2018, 489)), 489), which has largely been based on the BRRD. This may change if and when an EU recovery and resolution regime is adopted for insurance companies. See, eg, the EIOPA consultation including a recovery and resolution regime for insurance companies in the Solvency II Directive: <https://www.eiopa.europa.eu/content/consultation-paper-opinion-2020-review-of-solvency-ii_en> (accessed 7 July 2021). For Financial Market Infrastructures, the EU Proposal for a Regulation on a framework for the recovery and resolution of central counterparties (COM/2016/0856 final – 2016/0365 (COD)) is still pending in parliament.

the EU Bank Recovery and Resolution Directive (BRRD),[130] primarily because this accords with the discussions centred on the EU collateral legislation in section B, but also because the BRRD (and the Single Resolution Mechanism Regulation or 'SRMR')[131] set out a fully developed resolution regime, which reflects and incorporates earlier legislative and regulatory initiatives.

Already early in the global financial crisis, widespread agreement[132] was found to exist that restructuring banks in financial difficulty is very difficult to achieve through normal insolvency proceedings. Banking revolves around trust and solvency—trust *in* solvency—and the commencement of insolvency proceedings destroys, at the very least, the appearance of both. As a result, the chances of preserving viable parts of a failing bank as a going concern are slim once it has entered insolvency.[133] This aspect of insolvency is relevant to banks of any size and may be termed the 'firm-specific risks' of an insolvency filing.[134] In the case of banks that are deemed systemically important, it is also necessary to consider the 'systemic risks' of a filing,[135] which may be so great that the failure of such a bank is not an acceptable option. In the absence of statutory regimes specifically aimed at rescuing failing banks, ad hoc rescues 'by deal'[136] and bail-outs using public funds ('taxpayers' money') are then the only remaining options. For various reasons bail-outs are generally considered undesirable,[137] while improvised interventions by deal are fraught with practical difficulties, as dramatically illustrated by the failure of the US authorities to procure the rescue of Lehman.[138]

2.72

Since the global financial crisis, international agenda setters and regulators have therefore investigated the design of special resolution regimes for failing banks (or banks

2.73

---

[130] Directive 2014/59/EU.
[131] Regulation (EU) No 806/2014.
[132] Widespread, but not universal agreement. See, eg, Ayotte and Skeel, 'Bankruptcy or Bailouts', for a nuanced view, although it should be borne in mind that this article concerns US Chapter 11 proceedings, which do not apply to deposit-taking banks (cf Hynes and Watt, 'Banks and Bankruptcy').
[133] Bates and Gleeson, 'Bank Bail-ins', 264.
[134] Ayotte and Skeel, 'Bankruptcy or Bailouts', 470.
[135] Ibid, 471.
[136] Cf Davidoff and Zaring, 'Regulation by Deal'.
[137] Reference should be made to the very extensive literature and official pronouncements on this subject, but in summary the main objections, in addition to the cost to the taxpayer, are the 'moral hazard'—that is, the incentive for irresponsible risk-taking—created by the expectation of public rescue of a systemically important ('too big to fail') institution, and the competitive distortion arising from the fact that the expectation of public rescue enables systemically important institutions to benefit from substantially better terms than those available to institutions that are not expected to be rescued.
[138] With respect to the failed attempts to save Lehman, see, eg, FCIC, *Financial Crisis Inquiry Report*, 324–43; Sorkin, *Too Big to Fail*, 296–375. However, it should also be noted that a large (and presumably viable) part of Lehman, comprising its US investment banking operations, was sold to Barclays within a week of its Chapter 11 filing, followed a few days later by a sale of its Europe, Middle East, and Africa (EMEA) operations to Nomura. Ayotte and Skeel adduce these transactions as evidence that 'the bankruptcy process has been remarkably effective in many respects' ('Bankruptcy or Bailouts', 481–2). For a counterfactual analysis of a resolution of Lehman under Title II of the Dodd-Frank Act, see FDIC, *Orderly Liquidation of Lehman*; cf EC, *BRRD Impact Assessment*, 176 ('Lehman's case under bail-in'). The rescue of Bear Stearns, though ultimately effective, is another illustration of such practical difficulties. The sale of Bear Stearns to JP Morgan at a price of USD2 per share, agreed during the weekend of 15 and 16 March 2008, had to be amended during the following weekend in order to repair substantial defects in the original deal. See Cohan, *House of Cards*, 92–107 and 131–42; FCIC, *Financial Crisis Inquiry Report*, 290.

that are likely to fail),[139] and many jurisdictions have adopted legislation introducing such regimes. Some examples of the latter are, in chronological order of enactment:

- the UK Banking Act 2009;[140]
- Title II of the Dodd-Frank Act;[141]
- the German *Restrukturierungsgesetz*;[142]
- the Dutch *Interventiewet*;[143] and
- the EU Bank Recovery and Resolution Directive (BRRD) and (for the eurozone) the Single Resolution Mechanism Regulation (SRMR).

The adoption and implementation of the BRRD and SRMR have led, to a large extent, to replacement and amendment of the preexisting national regimes of the EU Members States, including the UK Banking Act 2009, the German *Restrukturierungsgesetz*, and the Dutch *Interventiewet*.

2.74 By way of an advance synopsis of and conclusion from what follows, it may be stated that the impact of resolution on collateral transactions is likely to be fairly limited in general. The basic explanation for this is that, as noted above, the reason for the introduction of a formal resolution regime is a *practical* one: normal insolvency regimes appear to be unable to deal with failing banks. Principles and policies underlying insolvency law, however, remain an important benchmark for resolution. This is reflected in the resolution principle that no creditor of a resolved bank should be worse off in comparison with the hypothetical situation in which the bank would have been allowed to fail and to be liquidated under a normal insolvency regime ('no creditor worse off principle').[144] A related principle is that where resolution has an impact on the rights of creditors and shareholders (for instance, if a bail-in instrument is applied to effect resolution),[145] their ordinary insolvency hierarchy should in principle be respected. Since, at least in theory, secured or collateralized creditors should not feel the negative effects of insolvency—to the extent that their claims are covered by security interests and collateralization—the same should be true of resolution based on these principles.[146]

2.75 A separate (though related) reason for supposing that the impact of resolution on collateral transactions is likely to be small is the recent regulatory emphasis on more extensive—and 'intensive'—collateralization, which has the objective of reducing

---

[139] See BCBS, *Cross-border Bank Resolution*; FSB, *Key Attributes*.
[140] 2009 c. 1.
[141] 12 USC §§ 5381–94.
[142] *Bundesgesetzblatt*, 2010, Teil 1, Nr 63, 1900–32. The 'Restructuring Act' sets out a new recovery and reorganization regime and includes amendments of, *inter alia*, the *Kreditwesengesetz* (Banking Act).
[143] The official short title of this 'Intervention Act' is the *Wet bijzondere maatregelen financiële ondernemingen* (Financial Institutions Special Measures Act), *Staatsblad* 2012, 241. The Intervention Act amended the *Wet op het financieel toezicht* (Wft; Financial Supervision Act) and the *Faillissementswet* (Bankruptcy Act).
[144] See FSB, *Key Attributes*, 11 ('no creditor worse off than in liquidation'); Arts 34(1)(g) and 73 BRRD.
[145] For bail-in, see paras 2.76–7.
[146] This is not to say that resolution regimes did not harmonize and amend the ranking of creditors' priority under national laws. See, eg, Art 108 BRRD.

systemic effects of bank failures in common with the new resolution regimes.[147] This might suggest that resolution regimes are framed so as not to have substantial negative impacts on collateralized transactions and positions. On the other hand, collateral transactions were found to have played a central and procyclical role in the Lehman insolvency, which led policy makers to reconsider the liberalized regime for, specifically, close-out netting arrangements under collateral transactions.[148] Consequently, bank resolution regimes now do limit, albeit not in a fundamental manner, the fairly liberal rules applying to collateral transactions. As described in more detail below, the limitations are narrowly defined, and are essentially directed to ensuring that the automatic or discretionary triggering of termination or default provisions cannot prevent resolution authorities from effectively exercising powers under the resolution regime, for example the power to transfer viable parts of the failing institution's business to another, solvent institution. These limitations are all the more significant in practice, because in a majority of collateral transactions, at least one, if not both of the contracting parties qualifies as a bank.

(4) Resolution tools

(a) Bail-in

The BRRD is the first major piece of legislation to include an explicit, fully developed bail-in tool, aimed primarily at recapitalizing a failing bank with no or minimal use of public funds. This tool was included in the BRRD after lengthy consultations and discussions, the substance of which falls largely outside the scope of this chapter.[149] In the preparatory phase, powers to write down or convert only specific types of debt were considered,[150] but the BRRD (and SRMR) now provides for *generic* bail-in powers to be exercised by resolution authorities, extending in principle to *all* liabilities of the failing bank except those specifically excluded (ie, to all 'eligible liabilities').[151] In addition, in

2.76

---

[147] See, eg, BCBS, *Cross-border Bank Resolution*, 36–40, which includes the recommendation (at 39) that '[j]urisdictions should promote the use of risk mitigation techniques that reduce systemic risk and enhance the resiliency of critical financial or market functions during a crisis or resolution of financial institutions. These risk mitigation techniques include enforceable netting agreements, collateralisation, and segregation of client positions.' An illustration of this shared objective is Art 70(2) BRRD, which exempts from a possible regulatory stay of enforcement of security interests 'any security interest of systems or operators of systems designated for the purposes of [the SFD], central counterparties . . . , and central banks over assets pledged or provided by way of margin or collateral by the institution under resolution'. Another example of the greater importance being attributed lately to collateralization is the role collateral transactions may play in the context of (compliance with) MREL requirements, discussed in paras 2.78 et seq

[148] See eg *Derivatives in Cross-border Insolvency Proceedings*; Haentjens, *Financial Collateral*, 3.63 et seq and 8.05 et seq; Keijser, 'Financial Collateral' (2017), s 20; Mokal, 'Liquidity, Systemic Risk, and the Bankruptcy Treatment of Financial Contracts'.

[149] The discussions about bail-in can be traced through the following EC papers: *Crisis Management* (2009); *Crisis Management* (2010); *Bank Resolution Funds; Resolution: Technical Details; Bail-in*. See also EC, *BRRD Impact Assessment*, Annex XIII ('Debt write-down (bail-in) and ex-ante funding') and Annex XVIII ('Results of targeted discussions on bail in').

[150] See EC, *Resolution: Technical Details*, Annex 1, where 'comprehensive' (generic) and 'targeted' (specific) approaches are described in some detail.

[151] Article 44(1) BRRD; cf Art 2(71)-(71b) BRRD.

'exceptional circumstances' the resolution authority may exclude certain eligible liabilities from bail-in.[152]

2.77 The crucial provision with regard to collateral transactions is Article 44(2)(b) BRRD, which excludes 'secured liabilities' from the scope of the bail-in tool. This is a broad concept including not only liabilities covered by genuine security interests but also liabilities under title transfer collateral arrangements.[153] Collateralized claims of a counterparty of a failing bank are therefore in principle protected against bail-in. However, to the extent that liabilities of the failing bank are *under*collateralized they remain subject to bail-in (if not excluded from bail-in under Article 44 BRRD).[154] This is not surprising in view of the resolution principles set out in paragraph 2.74 and, moreover, unlikely to have a substantial impact on collateral practice, since the unsecured or uncollateralized part of a creditor's claim would also be affected in ordinary insolvency[155] and the 'no creditor worse off' safeguard applies anyway.

(b) Ensuring loss-absorbing capacity: TLAC and MREL

2.78 For the bail-in instrument as just described to be effective and credible, banks would need to have sufficient 'bail-inable' liabilities, that is, have sufficient liabilities to write down or convert into equity so as to absorb balance sheet losses.[156] Specifically for this purpose, the 2013 G20 St. Petersburg Summit called on the Financial Stability Board (FSB) to develop proposals on the adequacy of global systemically important institutions' (G-SIIs) loss-absorbing capacity when they fail.[157] The FSB's efforts focused on increasing the markets' confidence that systemically important banks are truly no longer 'too big to fail' and resulted in the Total Loss-Absorbing Capacity (TLAC) term sheet, published in November 2015.[158] The 21 principles set out in the TLAC term sheet specify their objective to ensure that in and immediately following a G-SIB resolution critical functions can be continued without taxpayers' funds or financial stability being put at risk.[159] Thus, the TLAC principles must be understood in the context of preventing bailouts and reducing systemic risk. Substantially, this should ensure the effective use of the bail-in mechanism, if needed.[160]

---

[152] Article 44(3) BRRD.
[153] Article 2(67) BRRD.
[154] Similarly, where liabilities of the failing bank under derivative transactions are concerned, only the 'liability arising from those transactions on a net basis in accordance with the terms of the [relevant netting] agreement' may be subject to bail-in. See Art 49(3) BRRD. Bail-in of derivative liabilities pursuant to Art 49 BRRD is further discussed in Ch 3, paras 3.77–8.
[155] Bates and Gleeson, 'Bank Bail-ins', 268, make a similar point with respect to senior unsecured debt that may be affected by partial property transfers.
[156] The following paragraphs have been based on M. Haentjens, 'Commentary on Arts. 12-12k' in J.-H. Binder et al, *Brussels Commentary on the European Banking Union* (Nomos and others, forthcoming 2021).
[157] FSB, *G20 Leaders' Declaration* (September 2013), para 68 at p 17, <https://www.fsb.org/wp-content/uploads/g20_leaders_declaration_saint_petersburg_2013.pdf> (accessed 7 July 2021).
[158] FSB, *Principles on Loss-absorbing and Recapitalisation Capacity of G-SIBs in Resolution*, p 3.
[159] Ibid., at p 9. See also recital (1) SRMR II.
[160] On the functioning of the MREL within the bail-in mechanism, see Janssen, 'Bail-in from an Insolvency Law Perspective', 464–6.

In the EU legislative context, the TLAC standard for G-SIBs has been implemented **2.79** within the existing framework of the minimum requirement for own funds and eligible liabilities (MREL), which is applicable to all banks, regardless of their G-SIB status. This required several amendments to the existing MREL framework. In addition, many highly technical MREL related subjects previously dealt with by Commission Delegated Regulation (EU) 2016/1450 have now been transposed into level 1 EU legislation. This led to the amendment of the SRMR by Regulation (EU) 2019/877 (SRMR II), which has been applicable from 28 December 2020 onwards.[161] Together with amendments to the BRRD,[162] the Capital Requirements Regulation,[163] and the Capital Requirements Directive[164] these changes in European banking law are collectively part of what is known as the banking reform package.

Articles 45 et seq. BRRD and 12 et seq. SRMR in essence prescribe that the resolution **2.80** authority must determine, per entity or group, a 'minimum requirement for own funds and eligible liabilities' (MREL). As already alluded to above, MREL has to be understood in the context of the write-down and conversion powers and of the bail-in tool. To put it very simply, the write-down and conversion of capital instruments, which must precede bail-in or may be applied together with bail-in, intend to restore a failing entity's or failing group's capital structure by writing down—possibly to zero—shares and/or liabilities, and/or converting liabilities into shares of the entity or group in question. As stated in paragraph 2.76, the bail-in tool is broad and applies to all liabilities that are not explicitly excluded. This could open a loophole to entities enabling them to structure their liabilities in such a manner that the bail-in tool cannot be applied to them by relying on forms of funding consisting entirely of excluded, ie non-bail-inable, liabilities. Similarly, investors may prefer excluded liabilities, which are not susceptible to be written down or converted into shares, since those liabilities reduce their exposure on the entity. However, such a strategy would adversely affect the effectiveness of the bail-in tool, so that the avoidance of reliance on public financial support (one of the resolution objectives) would become illusory. Thus, in order to preclude entities and investors from structuring the relevant entity's or group's capital so as to consist primarily of excluded liabilities, Articles 45 et seq. BRRD and 12 et seq. SRMR prescribe that entities and groups must at all times meet a minimum requirement for own funds and eligible liabilities which may be written down or converted into shares.[165]

In the context of collateral transactions, Articles 45f BRRD and 12g SRMR are of spe- **2.81** cific relevance. Pursuant to Article 45f(3) BRRD and 12g(3) SRMR, so-called 'internal' MREL can also be satisfied by a guarantee provided by the resolution entity in the

---

[161] Pursuant to Art 2(2) SRMR II. Notwithstanding specific transitional arrangements provided pursuant to Art 12k SRMR.
[162] By way of Directive 2019/879 (BRRD II).
[163] By way of Regulation (EU) 2019/876 (CRR II).
[164] By way of Directive 2019/878 (CRD V).
[165] See further Moss, Wessels, and Haentjens, *EU Banking and Insurance Insolvency*, 244–5; Schelo, *Bank Recovery and Resolution*, 6.02., *Too Complex to Work; Why MREL Won't Help Much*.

same resolution group as the entity subject to the internal MREL requirement. From Articles 45f(3) BRRD and 12g(3) SRMR, it must be inferred that under this guarantee, the resolution entity would pay to the subsidiary (the entity subject to internal MREL) the amount that would otherwise be bailed in at the resolution entity. This guarantee must be secured through a collateral arrangement as defined in the FCD for at least 50 per cent.

(c) Sale of business, bridge institution, and asset separation tools

2.82 An important instrument in the resolution toolkit is the power of a resolution authority to transfer assets and/or liabilities of a failing bank. A partial property transfer may be aimed at preserving viable or systemically important parts of a bank's operations by transferring them either to another (but solvent) bank ('sale of business tool')[166] or to a bridge bank ('bridge institution tool').[167] The remainder will be a 'bad bank', which may subsequently be liquidated under normal insolvency law. Conversely, the BRRD and SRMR also envisage that bad ('toxic') assets may be lifted out of an otherwise viable bank and transferred to an asset management vehicle, which is then run off in isolation from the bank ('asset separation tool').[168]

2.83 The BRRD and SRMR provide a high level of protection for collateral transactions and positions in the event of a partial property transfer. The fundamental safeguard is that liabilities secured under a security arrangement and the assets upon which they are secured (and the benefit of those security interests) must either *all* be transferred (as a whole) or all left at the bank under resolution.[169] Where the realization of collateral is by close-out netting,[170] transactions under a single netting agreement must either be transferred as a whole (together with the netting agreement) or not at all. This safeguard is of special relevance to title transfer collateral arrangements,[171] but also applies to 'security arrangements, under which a person has by way of security an actual or contingent interest in the assets or rights that are subject to transfer, irrespective of whether that interest is secured by specific assets or rights or by way of a floating charge or similar arrangement'.[172]

(d) Modification of contracts

2.84 The BRRD and SRMR provide for a resolution power, 'ancillary' to the transfer powers, to 'cancel or modify the terms of a contract' to which the failing bank is a party.[173] This may clearly have substantial effects on the contracts concerned. However, special

---

[166] Articles 38–9 BRRD and 24 SRMR.
[167] Articles 40–1 BRRD and 25 SRMR.
[168] Articles 42 BRRD and 26 SRMR.
[169] Article 78(1) BRRD.
[170] See also paras 2.63 et seq.
[171] Article 77(1) BRRD.
[172] Article 76(2)(a) BRRD. The scope of this safeguard, ie which categories of transactions are covered by this safeguard, is further set out in Commission Delegated Regulation (EU) 2017/867 on classes of arrangements to be protected in a partial property transfer.
[173] Article 64(1)(f) BRRD.

safeguards protect title transfer financial collateral arrangements and netting arrangements, as well as security arrangements.[174]

(5) Limitations to termination rights

Since one of the objectives of resolution regimes is to protect viable parts of an institution under resolution, such regimes must deal with the rights of the institution's counterparties to terminate financial contracts. The continued operation of any of these contracts may be essential, separately or in combination, to the viability of parts of the institution's business that resolution measures are seeking to preserve, and/or to critical functions of the institution involved. It will, therefore, come as no surprise that the BRRD and other resolution regimes impose limitations on the exercise of termination rights of counterparties of an institution in resolution, not least since the demise of Lehman was precipitated by margin calls under, and the close-out of its collateral transactions.[175] As a matter of principle, limitations on the exercise of termination rights of counterparties of an institution in resolution therefore now also apply to collateral transactions, so that no carve-outs or safe harbours allow collateral transactions to be terminated in the context of resolution. These restrictions on party autonomy, however, are limited in scope. 2.85

The restrictions imposed by the BRRD and SRMR are twofold. The first is the invalidation of *ipso facto* clauses, which make 'the fact itself' of the commencement of resolution measures an event of default and thus a ground for termination of the relevant contract (but this does not affect termination on other grounds, such as actual default, for example failure to make a payment or meet a margin call).[176] The second is a temporary prohibition (or 'stay') on the ability of counterparties to invoke default or termination provisions (on whatever ground, including actual breach) during a brief 'window'. This stay may be imposed by the relevant resolution authority or authorities, either as a temporary moratorium before an institution or an entity is put into resolution, or following the commencement of resolution.[177] 2.86

The restriction of a stay is basically a practical measure providing resolution authorities with a window of opportunity in which to decide on specific resolution actions, in particular which financial transactions to transfer, and to put the necessary measures into effect.[178] It is therefore limited to a brief period that either starts upon the publication of a notice of suspension (in case of a moratorium) or upon the commencement of resolution. In both instances, the BRRD provides that the stay ends at midnight on the business day following the publication of a notice of suspension, or the announcement 2.87

---

[174] Articles 77(1) and 78(1)(d) BRRD, respectively.
[175] See, eg, Haentjens, *Financial Collateral*, ss 3.68 et seq.
[176] Article 68 BRRD. Cf 11 USC § 365(e); Skeel and Jackson, *Transaction Consistency*, fn 24.
[177] Articles 33a and 71(1)–(2) BRRD, respectively.
[178] See BCBS, *Cross-border Bank Resolution*, 40–2.

of resolution, respectively.[179] The BRRD also imposes a regulatory stay (of the same duration) on enforcement of security interests against the bank.[180]

2.88 In so far as they limit or stay the operation of contractual termination and default provisions, the resolution measures envisaged by the BRRD and SRMR run counter to the pre-crisis trend towards liberalization of statutory rules governing close-out netting, in particular in relation to collateral transactions.[181] For instance, the FCD stipulates that close-out netting provisions will be recognized according to their terms, whereas a regulatory stay and the invalidation of *ipso facto* clauses entail that such provisions shall *not* be recognized in certain circumstances. For this reason, both the Netherlands and the UK exempted financial collateral arrangements covered by the FCD from the scope of certain resolution provisions of their respective resolution regimes, as originally enacted.[182] The BRRD follows a route that was not (yet) available to these national legislators, in that it provides that special resolution measures will not be recognized as FCD enforcement events, and also includes a carve-out from Article 7(1) FCD (which provides for the enforceability of close-out netting provisions in accordance with their terms).[183]

2.89 Chapter V of the GSC, although agreed *post*-crisis, is in substance a *pre*-crisis regime. In particular, the GSC does not reflect the recent regulatory and legislative developments regarding resolution.[184] Furthermore, the GSC does not provide for a generic exception for regulatory intervention. In fact, the tenth recital of the GSC appears explicitly to deny this, as it states that the Convention 'does not limit or otherwise affect the powers of Contracting States to regulate, supervise or oversee the holding and disposition of intermediated securities or any other matters expressly covered by the Convention, *except in so far as such regulation, supervision or oversight would contravene the provisions of this Convention*'.[185] Resolution measures such as invalidation of *ipso facto* clauses and regulatory stays therefore contravene the core enforcement provisions of Article 33 GSC. An amendment to the GSC along the lines of Principle 8 of the UNIDROIT Principles on the Operation of Close-Out Netting Provisions would therefore seem necessary to adapt the GSC to the new reality of resolution.[186]

---

[179] Articles 33a(4) and 71(1)–(2) BRRD, respectively. See Mokal, 'Liquidity, Systemic Risk, and the Bankruptcy Treatment of Financial Contracts', 93–4, for the view that a longer period of ten to twenty days may be more appropriate.
[180] Articles 33a(10) and 70(1) BRRD.
[181] Cf Ch 3, paras 3.80–1.
[182] See Art 3:267f(4)(b) Wft and Art 4 Banking Act 2009 (Restriction of Partial Property Transfers) Order 2009, as originally enacted.
[183] See Arts 68(1) and 118(1) BRRD, respectively.
[184] See Ch 3, paras 3.69–74 for a discussion of similar issues arising in connection with the UNIDROIT Principles on the Operation of Close-Out Netting Provisions, which take regulatory developments into account in Principle 8. This provides that '[t]hese Principles are without prejudice to a stay or any other measure which the law of the implementing State, subject to appropriate safeguards, may provide for in the context of resolution regimes for financial institutions'.
[185] Kanda et al, *Official Commentary*, P-11 (emphasis added).
[186] The technical solution of a partial opt-out in respect of Art 33 GSC alone is not available. See Arts 36(2) and 38 GSC and Kanda et al, *Official Commentary*, 38-1 et seq.

2.90 The above analysis shows that in the context of enforcement, as in the context of under- and overcollateralization (see paragraph 2.61), essentially three layers of legislation apply: general insolvency law based on the equal treatment of creditors; liberal rules specifically facilitating collateral arrangements and the position of collateral takers (including the Financial Collateral Directive and Chapter V of the GSC); and regulatory rules enacted in the wake of the global financial crisis that narrow such liberal regime.

D. Concluding Remarks

2.91 Over the past decades, financial collateral has become a central component of the financial system. Detailed standardized agreements have been developed in order to document the provision of collateral in the context of securities financing transactions and derivatives, while there has also been a considerable effort to reform private law (including insolvency law) applicable to such systemically important transactions.

2.92 The global financial crisis of 2007 and onwards has led to the identification of an array of areas where adjustments of market practice, in some cases by regulatory intervention, were considered appropriate. This chapter has focused on the issues of over- and undercollateralization and the treatment of collateral in the context of the resolution of a failing bank.

2.93 Unlimited overcollateralization may give rise to substantial exposures of collateral providers, which raises concerns both as to its heightening the threat to systemic stability and to appropriate investor protection. Various private law and regulatory responses are available to address these concerns. Any such response should ensure the certainty and predictability of the general law governing collateral transactions, including its ability to cover transactions that market participants in fact wish to enter into.

2.94 Collateral arrangements are largely protected in the event of measures aimed at the resolution of a failing bank. Important exceptions are the invalidation of *ipso facto* provisions referring to resolution, and the temporary stay on the exercise of all powers of termination and enforcement during a short period—both restrictions being regarded as essential to enable the authorities to protect viable parts of an institution under resolution.

2.95 Financial collateral is a complex area of the law due to the co-existence of different conceptual frameworks that apply to collateral transactions and that may not square with one another. These frameworks include 'ordinary' private and insolvency law, more liberal rules tailored to specific private and insolvency law issues concerning such transactions, and subsequent regulatory qualifications of these liberalized rules. One wonders whether this has resulted in an optimal legal framework for practitioners operating in this crucial market segment.

3
ON CLOSE-OUT NETTING

A. Introduction	3.01	(4) The interaction of market risk and credit risk		3.39
B. A Brief Analysis of Close-out Netting	3.08	(5) Systemic risk		3.43
(1) Introduction	3.08	D. Harmonization of Close-out Netting Regimes		3.53
(2) Three common elements	3.10	(1) Introduction		3.53
(3) Three types of close-out netting	3.11	(2) EU Banks Insolvency Directive		3.56
(a) Type A: 'close-out set-off'	3.11	(3) EU Financial Collateral Directive and Geneva Securities Convention		3.59
(b) Type B: set-off of accelerated and converted obligations	3.13	(4) UNCITRAL Legislative Guide on Insolvency Law		3.62
(c) Type C: netting of replacement values	3.18	(5) FSB Key Attributes of Effective Resolution Regimes for Financial Institutions		3.65
(4) Qualifications	3.23	(6) UNIDROIT Principles on the Operation of Close-Out Netting Provisions		3.69
C. Principles, Policies, and the Practice of Close-out Netting	3.26	(7) Close-out netting and resolution: the EU regime		3.75
(1) Obstacles to enforceability of close-out netting	3.26	E. Concluding Remarks		3.80
(2) Master agreements and the single agreement concept	3.32			
(3) Credit risk	3.36			

A. Introduction

3.01 Close-out netting is a legal technique of great importance to the operation of the financial markets. There are various forms that this technique may take, but by way of a brief introduction (and ignoring the differences between the forms) it may be said that 'close-out netting' generally refers to the early termination of financial transactions between two parties upon the occurrence of an event of default (or similar event), followed by the determination of a final net amount due from one of the parties to the other in respect of that termination.

3.02 Viewed from an historical perspective on private law, close-out netting is a relatively novel technique that came to prominence concomitantly with the explosive development of the OTC derivatives markets in the 1980s and 1990s. During that period close-out netting provisions quickly became an integral, indeed a central part of standardized industry documentation for OTC derivatives and of the *lex mercatoria* of the financial markets in general.[1]

---

[1] See Ch 2, para 2.03 for more details on standard documentation (including close-out netting provisions) for financial transactions.

INTRODUCTION   61

The relative novelty of close-out netting should not, however, obscure the fact that the   **3.03**
technique, in its different forms, combines pre-existing, often much older, legal concepts and techniques.[2] Indeed, the innovative aspect of close-out netting is to be found predominantly in the specific combination of these classical concepts and techniques and their adaptation to financial market practice. One of the purposes of this chapter is to describe in some detail the various forms that close-out netting may take. This is the subject of section B, where common characteristics as well as distinctive features of three types of close-out netting are analysed.

Initially, the widespread use of relatively novel close-out netting provisions led to uncertainty about their effectiveness under various national systems of law. This legal uncertainty was especially undesirable since the economic interests involved were very substantial. The financial industry itself responded with several initiatives, including commissioning legal opinions on the validity and enforceability of standardized close-out netting provisions[3] and by extensively and intensively lobbying legislators to enact legislation that would ensure the enforceability of close-out netting provisions, in particular against an insolvent counterparty. Prominent among the initiatives directed at netting legislation were the influential 'Model Netting Acts' (MNAs) promulgated by the International Swaps and Derivatives Association (ISDA).[4]   **3.04**

These attempts to integrate the financial *lex mercatoria* into national systems of law   **3.05**
raise a number of questions on the principles and policies underlying the latter, some of which may conflict with unrestricted enforceability of close-out netting. Some of these matters of principle are considered in section C, which also looks at the legal and non-legal contexts of close-out netting provisions, thus fleshing out the conceptual analysis in section B.

A detailed analysis of netting legislation at national level falls outside the scope of this book,[5]   **3.06**
but several relevant international instruments now exist. Close-out netting was the subject of various provisions of the 2002 EU Financial Collateral Directive (FCD) and Chapter V of the 2009 Geneva Securities Convention (GSC).[6] The 2004 UNCITRAL Legislative Guide

---

[2] See, eg, UNIDROIT 2011–S78C–Doc. 2, para 46, referring to the 'ready association [of close-out netting] with existing legal concepts'.
[3] See, eg, the netting opinions commissioned by the International Swaps and Derivatives Association (ISDA) and the opinions on repo master agreements commissioned by the International Capital Market Association (ICMA). These opinions are, however, only made available to members of these trade organizations.
[4] See the 1996, 2002, 2006, and 2018 MNAs. The 2018 MNA was published by ISDA in Appendix A to ISDA, *2018 MNA and Guide*. Cf Biggins and Scott, 'ISDA, the State and OTC Derivatives Market Reform', 328–32; Herring, 'Resolving Cross-Border Financial Institutions', 866–7 (where Herring judges that 'the widespread adoption of the ISDA model laws is probably the most successful international harmonization achievement over the last two decades'); Werlen and Flanagan, 'The 2002 Model Netting Act'.
[5] Various national close-out netting regimes are considered in: Böger, 'Close-out Netting Provisions (I)'; Böger, 'Close-out Netting Provisions (II)'; Muscat-Gatt, *Insolvency Close-out Netting*; UNIDROIT 2011–S78C–Doc. 2, paras 55–80; Wood, *Set-off and Netting*, 144–70. Appendix D of ISDA, *2018 MNA and Guide*, contains an overview of the 'Status of Netting Legislation' in more than 85 countries. Of course, jurisdiction opinions on standardized close-out netting provisions commissioned by trade organizations contain extensive and detailed analyses of national regimes, but these opinions are only available to members of these organizations (cf n 3).
[6] Cf Ch 2, paras 2.09–15.

on Insolvency Law (LGIL) contained recommendations with regard to close-out netting. The UNIDROIT 'Principles on the Operation of Close-Out Netting Provisions' (PCON) were adopted in 2013.[7] These (and other) international harmonization projects are considered in section D, but they—in particular the UNIDROIT Principles—also inform the discussion in sections B and C. Some concluding remarks are made in section E.

3.07 For reasons of space the following exposition had to be limited mainly to a few central, substantive, private-law themes and issues; with one exception[8] conflict of laws rules are not discussed. The focus of the exposition is on financial transactions, in particular OTC derivatives and securities financing transactions (SFTs),[9] between professional parties; specific questions of material and personal scope are only discussed where they are directly relevant to the central substantive issues. Only bilateral, contractual forms of close-out netting are considered; both statutory and multilateral close-out netting fall outside the scope of this chapter,[10] but central clearing is covered to the extent that it makes use of bilateral close-out netting agreements between the central counterparty (CCP) and its clearing members and between the latter and their clients (or between the CCP and those clients themselves). Payment and settlement netting are also not considered: these techniques are applied more or less continuously as part of everyday, normal processes of clearing and settling financial transactions, whereas close-out netting provisions are actually applied only (and exceptionally) if an event of default or other contractually agreed trigger event occurs with respect to one of the parties to the agreement of which these provisions form part.

B. A Brief Analysis of Close-out Netting

(1) Introduction

3.08 This section elaborates on the brief description of close-out netting in paragraph 3.01 by providing a short, analytical account of the various legal techniques that are often subsumed in legislation and the legal literature under the catch-all term 'close-out netting'. For example, UNIDROIT Principle 2 defines a close-out netting provision as:

> a contractual provision on the basis of which, upon the occurrence of an event predefined in the provision in relation to a party to the contract, the obligations owed by the

---

[7] Available at <http://www.unidroit.org/english/principles/netting/netting-principles2013-e.pdf> (accessed 7 July 2021). The official publication of the (eight) Principles also contains an 'Explanation and commentary' (E&C) in numbered paragraphs, as well as 'Key considerations' in respect of each of the Principles 2–8 (combined in the case of Principles 6 and 7).

[8] See s D(2) on the EU Banks Insolvency Directive (BID), but here too the focus is on the substantive implications of the relevant conflict-of-laws rule (Art 25 BID).

[9] SFTs include repos and securities lending transactions; see BCBS, *Basel II*, 19 (fn 15) (and para 3.39); and para 4(1)(a)(ii) PCON, in conjunction with E&C, paras 65–70.

[10] As does multi-branch close-out netting within a bilateral relationship, where at least one of the parties operates in several jurisdictions through branches with no legal personality; cf Pt II 2018 MNA.

parties to each other that are covered by the provision, whether or not they are at that time due and payable, are automatically or at the election of one of the parties reduced to or replaced by a single net obligation, whether by way of novation, termination or otherwise, representing the aggregate value of the combined obligations, which is thereupon due and payable by one party to the other.

Other international instruments considered in section D set out similar functional definitions,[11] which are intended to capture the various forms that close-out netting may take in practice.[12] The principal purpose of this section is to describe what these various forms have in common and to analyse their differences by distinguishing different types of close-out netting (and the legal techniques involved) that are or may be covered by such broad definitions. The various types and techniques are illustrated by close-out netting provisions set out in the standard master agreements for derivatives and SFTs, respectively, but it should be made clear at the outset that the point is not that these widely used provisions should always be interpreted in exactly the manner set out below, nor that there is a one-to-one correspondence between type of master agreement and type of close-out netting.[13] The purpose of the remainder of this section is to present useful theoretical constructs for the analysis of legislation and market practice.

In the interest of conciseness, in what follows a contractually agreed event triggering close-out[14] (either automatically or upon the exercise of a party's right to close-out transactions) will mostly be referred to as an 'event of default', the party with respect to which an event of default occurs as the 'defaulting party' and its counterparty as the 'non-defaulting party', while 'termination amount' refers to the amount payable as the final result of the close-out netting process. It should be noted that the occurrence of such an event of default does not imply that the defaulting party has defaulted on any of its payment or delivery obligations in a strictly legal sense; for example, a credit downgrade of a party may constitute a mutually agreed 'event of default' irrespective of whether the downgraded party continues to perform all its obligations vis-à-vis its counterparty.

3.09

(2) Three common elements

Whatever the specific form close-out netting takes, it can generally be considered to consist of three constituent elements (or stages), each of which may take a different form depending on the standard documentation or specific contract in which it appears:[15]

3.10

---

[11] See: the corresponding definitions of 'close-out netting provision' in Art 2(1)(n) FCD and Art 31(3)(j) GSC; and the definition of 'netting arrangement' in Art 2(98) BRRD. Cf LGIL, 156 (para 210) and the definitions of 'netting' and 'netting agreement' in s (I)(1) 2018 MNA.
[12] Cf the first two 'Key considerations' in respect of UNIDROIT Principle 2.
[13] Cf para 3.25.
[14] Cf: 'an event predefined in the [close-out netting] provision in relation to a party to the contract' (para 2 PCON, quoted in para 3.08); 'enforcement event' as defined in Art 2(1)(l) FCD.
[15] See, eg, UNIDROIT 2011–S78C–Doc. 4, paras 17 and 39; ISDA, *2018 MNA and Guide*, 1.2; Mengle, *Importance of Close-out Netting*, 3. The second element, valuation, may be split into two: valuation of each outstanding

(i) The first element is, of course, close-out: *early termination* of transactions or obligations subject to the relevant close-out netting provisions upon the occurrence of an event of default that either gives the non-defaulting party the right to effect such termination or leads to termination automatically.

(ii) The next element is the *valuation* of the closed-out transactions or obligations in terms of a single currency, which has the effect of making all valued 'items' commensurable.

(iii) The final element is the *netting* of these items to determine the final net obligation of one of the parties to pay the termination amount to the other party.

These three elements are employed in the next section to structure the description of the different types.

(3) Three types of close-out netting

(a) Type A: 'close-out set-off'

3.11 As the commentary on the UNIDROIT Principles notes, 'close-out netting is often understood as resembling the classical concept of set-off applied upon default or insolvency of one of the parties'.[16] Although the interesting, 'novel' versions of close-out netting differ from a straightforward application of classical set-off, this resemblance means that it is useful to look first at a type of close-out netting that is basically (classical) set-off upon close-out. Concepts of set-off differ between systems of law, but in keeping with the purpose of this volume, set-off may be functionally defined as a technique of discharging an obligation by bringing a cross-obligation of the counterparty of the same kind into account; see, for example, Articles 8.1 and 8.5 of the UNIDROIT Principles of International Commercial Contracts (PICC).

3.12 This type of close-out netting is particularly relevant to traditional financial transactions, such as loans and deposits. Consider, for example, a bank with a claim for repayment of an ordinary loan (at maturity in normal circumstances) against a borrower, where the borrower has placed a term deposit (in the same currency as the loan) at the bank. The bank and the borrower have agreed that their respective payment obligations under the loan and the deposit become due and payable upon an event of default with respect to either of them. In this case *early termination* is therefore simple acceleration; *valuation* is trivial (or may be skipped) as the amounts of the loan and the deposit are

---

transaction in terms of a currency specific to the transactions being valued and, if there are multiple 'transaction currencies', conversion of all values thus determined into a single 'termination currency'; see, eg, point (ii) of the netting-definition of the 2018 MNA. Since both these operations involve valuation of some sort, they are here merged into one.

[16] E&C, para 3.

either given or easy to establish; and *netting* is in this case achieved through set-off of the respective payment obligations.[17]

(b) Type B: set-off of accelerated and converted obligations

This type of close-out netting is often encountered in connection with SFTs. Its first and third element—early termination and netting—stay very close to the corresponding elements of the type of close-out netting described in the previous section: acceleration and set-off, respectively. This is not surprising in view of the nature of many SFTs. A repo transaction may serve as illustration. From an economic viewpoint a repo is a secured loan. The purchase price paid by the buyer to the seller constitutes the principal of the loan, the difference between the repurchase price and the purchase price is the amount of interest payable by the seller, and the securities sold and delivered (and repurchased) by the seller constitute collateral provided by the seller to secure his obligation to repay the loan plus interest (ie, the repurchase price) at maturity of the transaction. **3.13**

The economic similarities between a repo and a loan render it possible to apply the standard technique of acceleration to achieve *early termination* in this context, as is illustrated clearly by paragraph 10(b) of the Global Master Repurchase Agreement (GMRA) 2000: **3.14**

> The Repurchase Date for each Transaction hereunder shall be deemed immediately to occur and, subject to the following provisions, all Cash Margin (including interest accrued) shall be immediately repayable and Equivalent Margin Securities shall be immediately deliverable.[18]

The *valuation* element looks forward to the way netting proceeds in this case, namely by set-off. Under the repurchase leg of a repo, the basic obligations of the (original) buyer and the (original) seller are clearly not commensurable: the seller has an obligation to pay money to the buyer, the buyer an obligation to deliver securities to the seller. This is why close-out netting at this point involves a contractually agreed conversion of the delivery obligation of the buyer into an obligation to pay the (market) value of securities to be delivered to the seller if close-out occurs after an event of default. More generally, upon close-out of an SFT or several SFTs, all obligations to deliver securities are converted into obligations sounding in money (and in the same currency). Paragraphs 10(b) and 10(c)(ii) of the GMRA 2000 illustrate this where they say that 'performance of the respective obligations of the parties with respect to the delivery of Securities' must be effected 'on the basis that each party's claim against the other in respect of **3.15**

---

[17] It should be noted here that loans and deposits are *not* included in the 'default' material scope of the UNIDROIT Principles, although implementing States are free to extend the coverage of their national close-out netting rules to include them; see paras 4(1) and (2)(b) PCON and E&C, paras 88–91. Likewise, the definition of 'qualified financial contract' of the 2018 MNA does not include 'conventional loans'; see ISDA, *2018 MNA and Guide*, 4.7.

[18] Cf GMRA 2011, paras 10(b) and 10(c). Similar provisions appear in securities lending documentation: see, eg, Global Master Securities Lending Agreement (GMSLA) 2000, para 10.2 and GMSLA 2010, para 11.2. See Ch 2, para 2.03 for more information on these master agreements for repos and securities lending transactions.

the transfer to it of Equivalent Securities or Equivalent Margin Securities under this Agreement equals the Default Market Value therefor'.

3.16 Finally, since all accelerated and converted obligations are now commensurable, *netting* may be effected as set-off of these obligations to determine the termination amount due as well as the party that must pay this amount. Again, paragraph 10(c)(ii) of the GMRA 2000 may be quoted as illustration:

> an account shall be taken (as at the Repurchase Date) of what is due from each party to the other under this Agreement ... and the sums due from one party shall be set off against the sums due from the other and only the balance of the account shall be payable (by the party having the claim valued at the lower amount pursuant to the foregoing).

3.17 An important observation is that this type of close-out netting may be economically and functionally equivalent to traditional manners of taking recourse on the collateral by the collateral taker in the event of a default by the collateral provider. However, it is also important to note that this is not the whole point of these contractual provisions, as the collateral provider may be the non-defaulting party and invoke close-out netting to have the value of the collateral posted returned to it in whole or in part.[19]

(c) Type C: netting of replacement values

3.18 The nature of derivative transactions is such that early termination by simple acceleration would not in general be appropriate (if at all possible). For example, how should one 'accelerate' the contingent obligation of the seller of a European call option which the buyer was only allowed to exercise some time after the early termination date? Similarly, how can one accelerate the obligations of the parties to a weather derivative under which a payment due depends on the average temperature at a certain location during a period that has not yet commenced on the early termination date?

3.19 *Early termination* of derivatives therefore often takes another form, that of extinguishing (rather than accelerating) obligations under outstanding transactions (and thus the transactions themselves) upon the occurrence of an event of default.[20] Section 6(c)(ii) of the ISDA Master Agreements[21] describes these extinguishing effects of close-out:

> Upon the occurrence or effective designation of an Early Termination Date, no further payments or deliveries... in respect of the Terminated Transactions will be required to be made.[22]

---

[19] Cf Ch 2, paras 2.29 and 2.48.
[20] Cf UNIDROIT 2011–S78C–Doc. 9, para 82, esp. fn 80.
[21] Cf Ch 2, para 2.03.
[22] The remainder of s 6(c)(ii) refers to s 6(e) pursuant to which '[t]he amount, if any, payable in respect of an Early Termination Date shall be determined'. Subject to what was said at the end of para 3.08 about the 'theoretical' purpose of the present exposition, s 6(e) may be seen as comprising the valuation and netting elements of this type of close-out netting; see paras 3.20–1.

Once again, we encounter a traditional contractual technique, that of termination of a contract upon default (as laid down, for example, in Articles 7.3.1 and 7.3.5 PICC).[23]

The *valuation* element of this type of close-out netting may be described[24] as the determination (estimation) of the costs that the non-defaulting party would incur or the gains it would experience if it were to replace the terminated transactions by economically equivalent transactions with third parties. Usually, the non-defaulting party will determine these replacement values, for example by asking dealers for quotes for replacement transactions[25] ('marking-to-market') or by using valuation models to estimate these costs and gains[26] ('marking-to-model'). The result is a series of replacement values which may be positive and negative: at the time of close-out (or, more precisely, at the time as of which the transactions are valued) some transactions may have been in-the-money for the non-defaulting party (these have a positive replacement value for this party[27]), while others may have been out-of-the-money (with negative replacement values as a result).   **3.20**

Finally, in the *netting* stage a simple calculation of the balance of these positive and/or negative replacement values from the perspective of the non-defaulting party will be made to determine the termination amount. This value may be positive or negative: on balance, the non-defaulting party may also be said to be in-the-money or out-of-the-money, respectively. Close-out netting provisions of this type usually stipulate that, if the non-defaulting party is in-the-money 'overall', the defaulting party must pay it the termination amount, but if the balance of the replacement values is negative, the non-defaulting party must pay the absolute value of the termination amount to the defaulting party.[28]   **3.21**

Clearly, netting of this type differs from classical set-off: after early termination nothing remains to be set off, as the original obligations under the derivative transactions were extinguished.[29] The obligation to pay emerges only as the final result of the netting of replacement values of the terminated transactions. This type of close-out netting   **3.22**

---

[23] In view of the various forms and consequences of termination for breach under different systems of law, it is relevant to note that the close-out discussed here is forward-looking and has no retroactive effect. Obligations that have become due before (or on) the early termination date are not extinguished. Performances already rendered of obligations that became due before that date do not become undue retroactively and, to the extent that such obligations had not yet been performed by then, they must still be performed. The full close-out netting mechanism set out in the ISDA Master Agreements takes account of this aspect by including amounts that had become due before or as of the early termination date in the netting stage as 'Unpaid Amounts' (as defined in s 14 of the ISDA Master Agreements).

[24] Other approaches to valuation are, of course, possible; cf the 'payment measure' 'Loss', as defined in s 14 of the 1992 ISDA Master Agreement, which may be considered as a more straightforward calculation of 'damages' (however, see also para 3.22).

[25] Cf the 'payment measure' 'Market Quotation', as defined in s 14 of the 1992 ISDA Master Agreement.

[26] Cf the references to such models in s 14, 'Close-out Amount', of the ISDA 2002 Master Agreement.

[27] Since the non-defaulting party would have to pay a third party 'compensation' for entering into a replacement transaction that would be out-of-the-money from the latter's perspective.

[28] The defaulting party is therefore given credit for transactions that were in-the-money for it, but this does not mean that payment of the termination amount will leave the defaulting party no worse off as a result of the close-out. In practice, the defaulting party *will* be worse off if only because the replacement values are determined from the perspective of its (non-defaulting) counterparty and from the latter's side(s) of the market(s).

[29] Cf ISDA, *2018 MNA and Guide*, 3.20; Murray, *Use of Close-out Netting*, 17.47.

resembles the way termination for breach is settled under many systems of law: by the payment of damages by the defaulting party.[30] However, in practice there is an important difference, and a novel aspect, of this type of close-out netting, since the netting process may lead to the result that the non-defaulting party must pay the termination amount to the defaulting party. Many systems of law impose a duty on a non-defaulting party claiming damages to account for gains it derives from a breach of contract. Such gains may reduce the damages to which the non-defaulting party is entitled. However, these systems do not go as far as requiring in general that any net gains should be paid to the defaulting party.[31]

(4) Qualifications

3.23 So far, the different types of close-out netting have been described as resulting more or less naturally from certain characteristics of the underlying transactions and obligations: loans and repos are accelerated, derivatives are extinguished, and so on. But, especially where the second and third types are concerned, an element of arbitrariness is involved. For example, repos and securities lending transactions may be governed by an ISDA Master Agreement instead of an SFT master agreement and would then be subject to close-out netting of Type C.[32] Conversely, it is theoretically possible to design a Type B mechanism applicable to derivative transactions, including netting by set-off as its third constituent element. For example, instead of estimating replacement values of terminated transactions, the parties could agree that, upon close-out, every one of their outstanding future and possibly contingent obligations will be converted by the application of an agreed valuation model into corresponding due and payable obligations to pay the respective expected present values of those obligations. The obligation to pay the termination amount would be arrived at by setting off these converted obligations. The results may be economically similar, if not identical, to the result of a determination of net replacement values under Type C close-out netting.

3.24 This suggests a certain arbitrariness in the contractual choice of type. Considerations the parties may have in this regard include that it may be advisable to opt for, or on the contrary avoid any reference to, a specific technique such as set-off, for example (in the latter case) because they both operate under a system of law that imposes strict

---

[30] In the words of Lightman J: the result of close-out netting is 'essentially compensation for the termination calculated on damages principles' (*Commissioners for Her Majesty's Revenue & Customs v Enron Europe Ltd* [2006] EWHC 824 (Ch), para 20); cf Paech, 'Enforceability of Close-out Netting', 13; UNIDROIT 2011–S78C–Doc. 2, 3.

[31] Bilateral termination payments are envisaged under the ISDA 2002 Master Agreement and, if the 'Second Method' has been elected, under the 1992 Master Agreement. By contrast, the 'First Method' 'reflects the position that applies at common law, where damages are never payable to the party in breach. In other words, if First Method has been chosen and the calculation has a negative value, no payment is due to either party. Such a provision is often referred to as a walkaway clause because it means that the Defaulting Party forfeits the embedded value of the transactions that have been closed out': Firth, *Derivatives*, 11.157; quoted approvingly by Flaux J in *Brittania Bulk plc v Pioneer Navigation Ltd and others* [2011] EWHC 692 (Comm), para 15.

[32] Cf n 33.

limitations on set-off in insolvency. This is not so much a point regarding risks of recharacterization (for example, of close-out netting as, in truth, being a form of set-off). It is a point about the relationship between, and resemblances of, various forms of close-out netting. A particular point, relevant to the discussion in the next sections, is that a jurisdiction's law of set-off, and the principles and policy considerations supporting that law, may have implications for the treatment of close-out netting in that jurisdiction.

3.25 Matters are further complicated because any contract may incorporate two or even all three types of close-out netting. For example, where derivatives exposures are collateralized, a Type C mechanism will usually determine the amount due in respect of the closed-out derivatives transactions themselves. The obligation to pay this amount may then be 'set off' against the obligation to pay the market value of securities posted as collateral—which (under a Type B mechanism) is the accelerated and converted obligation to return those securities—to arrive at the overall termination amount.[33] Another example is provided by Section 6(f)—'Set-Off'—of the ISDA 2002 Master Agreement which allows the non-defaulting party to set off the termination amount determined pursuant to the master agreement against amounts due under other agreements (eg, a deposit or loan). Depending on the actual circumstances of a close-out, Section 6(f) may thus lead to application of a Type A mechanism in combination with the core Type C netting provisions of the master agreement.

C. Principles, Policies, and the Practice of Close-out Netting

(1) Obstacles to enforceability of close-out netting

3.26 This section reviews the main legal obstacles to the enforceability of close-out netting provisions and some of the principles and policies that underlie such obstacles, or that would permit their removal. With respect to close-out netting applied against a *solvent* (defaulting) party, the principle of freedom of contract is usually considered a sufficiently strong basis for the enforceability of mutually agreed close-out netting provisions. The transactions that are typically subject to such provisions, as well as the nature of the typical parties to those transactions—broadly speaking, financial transactions and professional parties active on the financial markets—should not necessitate significant restrictions on the freedom of contract,[34] as the commentary on the UNIDROIT Principles notes:

---

[33] Conversely, in addition to the Type B mechanism described in s B(3)(b), both the GMRA 2000 and the GMRA 2011 also provide for, *inter alia*, compensation of losses (or gains) the non-defaulting party incurs (or makes) if it enters into transactions to replace the accelerated repos; see GMRA 2000, para 10(k), and GMRA 2011, para 10(l).

[34] Clearly, invoking freedom of contract is not sufficient on its own. Systems of law based on that principle standardly constrain the rights to 'close out' certain (non-financial) contracts outside insolvency (eg, employment contracts, rent agreements, energy contracts with consumers).

A close-out netting provision is a provision within a bilateral contractual relationship. Outside insolvency proceedings or resolution regimes, such a close-out netting provision rarely clashes with policy considerations so that there is scant reason to prohibit or limit its use.[35]

3.27 However, one important qualification is in order here. Traditionally, taking recourse on assets provided as security for a debt ('realizing' those assets) has been an area where mandatory rules may override contractually agreed realization mechanisms both outside and within insolvency of the defaulting debtor against which recourse is taken (such rules may provide, for example, for judicial control of the process of realization or for the observance of certain formalities). As noted in paragraph 3.17, close-out netting may function as a mechanism for realizing collateral (in particular under a title transfer collateral arrangement) and at least in theory it would therefore be reasonable to consider the application of such mandatory rules—either directly or by analogy—in such cases, which could lead to constraints on the operation of close-out provisions. This is an issue that is best considered as part of the more general question as to the validity and enforceability of title transfer collateral arrangements as a whole (including, but not limited to, their respective close-out netting provisions), in particular against the background and in the context of the law of security interests. For reasons of space and in order to avoid duplication with the treatment of collateral and enforcement issues in Chapters 2 and 4 respectively, this particular issue is not considered further here.[36]

3.28 The situation is, in any case, fundamentally different if the defaulting party is insolvent. Insolvency law is largely mandatory law reflecting public policies and principles, such as the equal treatment of equally ranked creditors, coordinated management of the insolvency estate as a 'common pool', and the preservation of assets of the debtor in the interest of the creditors and, if applicable, of an efficient reorganization. It is useful to list some of the main potential legal obstacles to the exercise of close-out netting rights against an insolvent counterparty using the three constituent elements distinguished in section B(2):[37]

(i) With respect to *early termination*, creditors may be prohibited from exercising close-out rights by a 'stay' that may automatically result from the commencement of insolvency proceedings or be imposed by the insolvency administrator or the insolvency court. A less far-reaching prohibition is a ban on *ipso facto* clauses—which make 'the fact itself' of the commencement of insolvency proceedings an event of default and thus a ground for termination of the relevant contracts—but to allow close-out during insolvency on other grounds.

(ii) In relation to *valuation*, insolvency laws may prescribe specific valuation procedures and methods, which may differ from contractual valuation rules. For

---

[35] E&C, para 114. Cf UNIDROIT 2011–S78C–Doc. 2, paras 19 and 44.
[36] For a discussion of these and related issues, see also Gullifer, 'Financial Collateral'; cf para 6(1)(a) PCON in conjunction with E&C, paras 118–9.
[37] Cf, eg, E&C, paras 123–30; ISDA, *2018 MNA and Guide*, 1.2.

PRINCIPLES, POLICIES, AND THE PRACTICE OF CLOSE-OUT NETTING   71

example, with regard to the determination of the values of creditor claims in general, the LGIL notes that '[a]s to timing of the valuation, many insolvency laws require it to refer to the effective date of commencement of proceedings'—whereas the ISDA and GMRA close-out netting provisions provide the non-defaulting party with appreciably more leeway.[38] Another example is that, under the relevant insolvency law, the insolvency administrator may be responsible for making the final valuation despite contractual provisions stipulating that the non-defaulting party will determine the value of its claim.[39]

(iii) From a *netting* perspective, a fundamental obstacle arises where the insolvency regime allows the insolvency administrator to decide whether to assume or to repudiate individual outstanding—'executory'—contracts one by one, irrespective of a close-out netting provision that applies to them all. Other constraints have less far-reaching effects, but these may still be substantial, such as restrictions on insolvency set-off that are either directly relevant (in those cases where netting is set-off or includes a set-off component; see Types A and B described in section B(3)), or by analogy.[40]

3.29 A terminological remark is in order here. In this chapter, unless indicated otherwise, the expressions 'insolvency proceeding' and 'insolvency administrator' have a general, functional meaning, similar (but not necessarily identical to) the meaning of the corresponding GSC terms: see Article 1(h) and (i) GSC. The same applies to other terms referring to 'insolvency'. Insolvency proceedings thus comprise both reorganization and liquidation proceedings, and include in particular resolution proceedings discussed in sections D(5)–(7).

3.30 National legal systems display—or have in the past displayed—different approaches to the issues identified in paragraph 3.28. Since the main interest here is with legal *obstacles* to close-out netting, it should be clarified at the outset that many traditional national insolvency laws did not constrain close-out netting, or constrained it only to an insignificant degree.[41] Here it is useful to refer to the frequently made distinction between pro-creditor and pro-debtor jurisdictions based on 'two fundamentally irreconcilable concepts of fairness'.[42] Pro-creditor, 'netting-friendly' jurisdictions view it as *un*fair that a debtor or the debtor's insolvency administrator could require payment from a creditor while simultaneously refusing to pay a cross-claim. Set-off and netting

---

[38] LGIL, 259 (para 38). For another 'timing' example, see UNIDROIT 2011–S78C–Doc. 4, para 71 (referring to provisions of German insolvency law prescribing valuation of assets as of the fifth day after commencement of insolvency proceedings).
[39] Cf Art 49(4) BRRD, discussed in para 3.78.
[40] For general observations on the nature and prevalence of set-off restrictions in insolvency (such as 'connexity' of the obligations to be set off), see LGIL, 155 (paras 205–6). For more details, see, eg, Wood, *Set-off and Netting*.
[41] The Netherlands provides an example of a system of insolvency laws that did not constrain close-out netting (with the possible exception of the contractually agreed timing of valuation of closed-out transactions in bankruptcy, about which some doubts—as yet unresolved—were expressed). See, eg, Nijenhuis and Verhagen, 'Netting' and Nijenhuis, 'Close-out netting en insolventie', both published in the 1990s. Unsurprisingly, the Netherlands has not adopted any specific netting legislation; cf ISDA, *2018 MNA and Guide*, 52 (fn 78) and 60.
[42] Bergman et al, 'Netting, Financial Contracts, and Banks', 2.1.

may then be considered to be generally conducive to (greater) fairness and significant obstacles to the netting element are unlikely to arise. In contrast, pro-debtor jurisdictions look at the insolvency estate and the interests of general creditors therein and consider it unfair that a creditor could deploy set-off and netting techniques in order to deny to the estate assets (eg, cross-claims of the estate; derivative transactions that are in-the-money for the estate) that should 'in fairness' (to the other creditors) belong to it. Similar principled considerations may determine whether or not a jurisdiction restricts close-out rights—depending on its weighing of debtor, counterparty, and general creditor interests in the preservation of the debtor's assets.

3.31 The drift of the main international instruments considered in section D (and many national 'netting acts') is and has been to *remove* (or at least to reduce) legal obstacles to the operation of close-out netting provisions.[43] One may ask what is so special about close-out netting that justifies the loosening of these, often principled constraints, even their abolition. Why should the *lex mercatoria* prevail in this fashion?[44] Why do we treat close-out netting differently?[45] In order to provide some background to possible answers to these questions, sections C(2)–(5) consider the legal and economic contexts in which close-out netting operates, and associated matters of policy and principle.

(2) Master agreements and the single agreement concept

3.32 So far, the analysis has focused on close-out netting provisions as such. In practice, the contractual relationship between the parties that have agreed such provisions and have entered into financial transactions governed by them is usually broader: typically, both the transactions and the close-out netting provisions form part of a *master agreement*, which invariably includes a single agreement clause.[46] If this way of looking at the legal relationship is adopted unreservedly, the effect on cherry-picking powers is obvious and radical: there is only a single cherry to pick, and the insolvency administrator should only be able to assume or repudiate all transactions as a whole (as a 'netting set'), but not individual transactions. It is also worth noting that the single agreement concept may also be relevant where other constraints on set-off and netting apply, for example under a system of insolvency law that only allows insolvency set-off of obligations arising under the same contract.

---

[43] Paragraphs 6 and 7 PCON; Recommendations 101–4 LGIL; Art 7(1) FCD; Arts 31–3 GSC. See s D for more details.
[44] Of course, ISDA's Model Netting Acts all promote the enforceability of close-out netting.
[45] To paraphrase Gullifer's question regarding financial collateral under the FCD regime; see Gullifer, 'Financial Collateral', 378. Cf Edwards and Morrison, 'Derivatives and the Bankruptcy Code', the full title of which includes the question: 'Why the Special Treatment?'.
[46] A typical single agreement clause is set forth in s 1(c) of the ISDA Master Agreements: 'All Transactions are entered into in reliance on the fact that this Master Agreement and all Confirmations form a single agreement between the parties (collectively referred to as this "Agreement"), and the parties would not otherwise enter into any Transactions'. For other examples of such clauses, see GMRA 2000/2011, para 13 and GMSLA 2010, para 17.

PRINCIPLES, POLICIES, AND THE PRACTICE OF CLOSE-OUT NETTING 73

The strength of this argument against cherry-picking will depend on how much legal and economic substance corresponds to the form of the single agreement.[47] The principal argument against attaching much weight to the single agreement concept in this context is that, in practice, individual transactions retain their identity, not only economically but also legally. For example, it is market practice to allow novation of (individual) derivative transactions or termination of a transaction before maturity by mutual agreement.[48] Valuation of transactions forming part of a single agreement will typically proceed by determining the respective values of individual transactions. The close-out methodology of the ISDA Master Agreements, for example, is based on the same principle;[49] see also the description of Type C close-out netting in paragraph 3.20. If the parties are able to pick and choose among transactions, why should an insolvency administrator not be able to do the same? **3.33**

Another argument in favour of cherry-picking by an insolvency administrator (and against safe harbours for close-out netting under the US Bankruptcy Code) has been put forward by Lubben, who states 'that parties can always "cherry pick" which contracts to perform outside of bankruptcy' (and that cherry-picking within bankruptcy is therefore not special).[50] However, this argument seems incorrect: the relevant master agreements apply the single agreement approach consistently across all situations. Typically, the non-defaulting party is contractually prohibited from cherry-picking the transactions to be closed out if an event of default occurs with respect to the counterparty, both within and outside insolvency.[51] This implies that, if the counterparty opts to breach a single outstanding transaction outside insolvency, the other party may only respond to this event of default by terminating *all* transactions,[52] effectively negating the cherry-picking attempt of its counterparty to (breach and) terminate only the selected transaction. **3.34**

Under a single agreement a default under any individual transaction constitutes a default in respect of all transactions.[53] The single agreement concept does therefore have some legal substance and it is not possible to dismiss it as wholly 'form without **3.35**

---

[47] Cf Firth, *Derivatives*, 5.043–5, who concludes that there is not enough substance to the single agreement approach for it to override (by itself) mandatory insolvency provisions allowing cherry-picking. See also Wood, *Set-off and Netting*, 12–010.

[48] Cf BIS, *Lamfalussy Report*, 8: 'In contrast to what occurs in the case of [netting-by-]novation, the individual transactions are not "blended" into running accounts but retain their specific terms, rates and maturities so that they can be individually assigned or terminated'.

[49] See in particular the definitions of 'Market Quotation' and 'Close-out Amount' set out in the 1992 and 2002 Master Agreements, respectively (cf nn 25 and 26, respectively).

[50] Lubben, 'Derivatives and Bankruptcy', 62 and 68–73, where this ability to cherry-pick (or 'option to breach') is considered as resulting from the general view of a contract 'as a choice between fulfilling a promise or breaching and paying damages' (69).

[51] Where master agreements exceptionally allow for termination of some, but not all, outstanding transactions, they typically do so to address disruptive events outside the parties' control—as opposed to a deliberate breach of a transaction. See, eg, 'Illegality' and 'Force Majeure Event', set out in ss 6(b)(i)–(ii) of the ISDA 2002 Master Agreement; cf, eg, the 'mini close-out' provisions of paras 10(h)-(i) of the GMRA 2011, which are mainly concerned with the consequences of ('technical') settlement fails.

[52] See, eg, s 6(a) of the ISDA Master Agreements and para 10(b) of the GMRA 2011 which grant the non-defaulting party close-out rights with respect to '*all* outstanding Transactions' (emphasis added).

[53] Cf GMRA 2000/2011, para 13.

74   ON CLOSE-OUT NETTING

substance'. However, on balance—taking into account the continued economic and legal separateness of individual transactions noted above—it seems unlikely that the concept can, on its own, provide a strong argument in favour of the special treatment of close-out netting.

(3) Credit risk

3.36   In an important sense, close-out netting is all about credit risk and credit risk management. From this perspective, the worst-case scenario (in particular where derivative transactions are concerned) is probably an insolvency regime combining an automatic stay with insolvency administrators empowered to cherry-pick individual transactions.[54] Credit risk with respect to a counterparty subject to such a regime would have to be calculated on a gross, rather than net basis. Exposure to that party would be the sum of the values of all transactions that are in-the-money for its counterparty, as the latter runs no credit risk in respect of transactions that are currently out-of-the-money (since it loses nothing if those transactions are not performed). Conversely, if close-out netting is effective, credit risk is reduced, as the absolute aggregate value of all out-of-the-money transactions may be subtracted from gross exposure. In practice, the difference between gross and net exposures is very substantial: estimates of the aggregate impact of netting on OTC derivatives exposures, for example, are usually in the order of 80 per cent.[55]

3.37   When conducting risk management, rational institutions will therefore take into account whether and to what extent close-out netting is effective in relation to their various counterparties. It is not surprising that close-out netting, as a technique of credit risk mitigation, has also for some time been part of prudential regulation of banks and other financial institutions, in particular the successive 'Basel' capital requirements, which have been implemented worldwide. Initially, in 1988, when the original Basel Accord was adopted, close-out netting was still a recent innovation and the Basel Committee on Banking Supervision (BCBS) was not yet prepared to acknowledge its risk-reducing effects.[56] The Committee changed its position after the publication of two influential reports under the auspices of the Bank for International Settlements (BIS),[57] which were favourable to close-out netting. The 1994 and 1995 amendments

---

[54] Cf paras 7(1)(a)–(b) PCON.
[55] For example, in 2010, Mengle, referring to the global OTC derivatives statistics of the Bank for International Settlements (BIS), put the difference at 'over 85 percent as of mid-2009' (*Importance of Close-out Netting*, 1). By 2018 that percentage had fallen to a (still substantial) low of 75%, but BIS reported an increase to 80% at end-December 2019 (BIS, *OTC Derivatives (YE 2019)*, 2 and Graph A1, reporting the corresponding exposures after netting at 25% and 20%, respectively)—with a slight drop to 78.5% by the end of 2020 (BIS, *OTC Derivatives (YE 2020)*, 2 and Graph A1).
[56] This was because '[t]he effectiveness of such agreements in an insolvency has not yet been tested in the courts, nor has it been possible to obtain satisfactory legal opinion that liquidators would not be able to overturn them'. The Committee added, however, that it did not wish to discourage market participants from employing close-out netting clauses and that it would 'continue its work to assess the acceptability of various forms of netting'. See BCBS, *Basel I*, p 27.
[57] BIS, *Angell Report*; BIS, *Lamfalussy Report*.

to the original Accord recognized close-out netting under a number of conditions, including the condition that the relevant bank provide its supervisor with legal opinions that demonstrated the validity and enforceability of close-out netting under the laws of all relevant jurisdictions.[58] In the Basel II Accord and its revision by Basel III this approach was retained and extended with some modifications to cross-product netting agreements.[59]

In view of the very substantial reduction of credit risk and capital requirements, enforceable close-out netting is clearly 'good for business' in the relevant financial markets: 'enforceable netting (and collateral) provisions are a major contributor to the large size and substantial liquidity of derivative markets'.[60] With a given amount of capital a bank or other financial institution subject to those (or comparable) capital requirements[61] will be able to support a much larger derivatives book or volume of SFTs. A concomitant effect is the substantial reduction of collateral required to cover derivatives exposures on a net rather than a gross basis. The policy implications are important: effective close-out netting is likely to improve the liquidity, and thereby, arguably, also the efficiency, of the financial markets, in particular the markets for derivatives and SFTs.[62] As Chapter 2 has shown in relation to collateral laws, this is—or at least used to be—an extremely important consideration of legal policy. Clearly, the global financial crisis of 2007–2009 has had an impact on the persuasiveness of arguments based on the effects on liquidity and the size of the financial markets, as will be further detailed in section C(5).   **3.38**

(4) The interaction of market risk and credit risk

An essential characteristic of derivatives and SFTs is the interaction of credit risk (with respect to counterparties) and market risk (of these transactions). The value—the mark-to-market or mark-to-model (MTM) value—of a derivative transaction fluctuates in the short (often very short) run with the value of the underlying asset, index, or statistic. SFTs have similar characteristics, as illustrated by the definition set out in the Basel II Accord: **3.39**

> Securities Financing Transactions (SFT) are transactions such as repurchase agreements, reverse repurchase agreements, security lending and borrowing, and margin

---

[58] BCBS, *1994 Amendment*; BCBS, *1995 Amendment*.
[59] BCBS, *Basel II*, Annex 4; BCBS, *Basel III: Capital*.
[60] Bergman et al, 'Netting, Financial Contracts, and Banks', 4.1.1; see also, eg, LIGL, 156 (para 209): 'Debtors often enter into multiple financial contracts with a given counterparty in a single course of dealing and the availability of credit is enhanced if rights under those contracts are fully enforceable in accordance with their terms, thereby permitting counterparties to extend credit based on their net exposure from time to time after taking into account the value of all "open" contracts.'
[61] Or, if an institution is not subject to such requirements, rational risk management will presumably have similar effects on its *economic* capital calculations.
[62] See Paech, 'The Value of Financial Market Insolvency Safe Harbours', 859–60 and 867–72.

lending transactions, where *the value of the transactions depends on the market valuations* and the transactions are often subject to margin agreements.[63]

3.40 Close-out netting will only actually be applied in exceptional situations—if events of default occur. However, day-to-day management of credit risk is based on hypothetical defaults of counterparties and the resulting exposures at default. Since credit risk under derivatives and SFTs is determined by, among other things, the MTM values of the transactions and collateral posted, one of the prerequisites of prudent risk management is the ability to value transactions and collateral more or less continuously (as MTM values may change substantially within hours or even seconds) in order to determine exposures at default. It is worth remarking that this ability to value is not a fortuitous by-product of derivatives and SFTs. On the contrary, the ability is an essential part of the development of these markets for such transactions. For example, many derivatives would not be offered if they could not be priced relatively objectively and accurately—that is, in a manner acceptable not just to the institution doing the pricing but also to its counterparties, regulators and supervisors, and other interested third parties.[64] Efficient collateralization also requires a large measure of consensus on the valuation of the transactions and collateral (in particular, securities collateral).

3.41 These considerations go some way towards supporting the enforceability of the valuation component of close-out netting. It may be argued that this is an instance where private, professional market participants should be allowed to conduct their own business—in this case, the micro-management of risk—without interference from insolvency laws,[65] especially if the latter would introduce uncertainty by giving an insolvency administrator discretion as to valuation (including its timing). However, there seems to be no reason why constraints on the valuation of a precise and predictable nature should not be permitted, for example a rule that all valuations should be made as of a date a fixed number of business days (which number may be zero) after the commencement of insolvency proceedings.[66] Such valuation parameters could easily be incorporated in valuation methods and models. More importantly, they could thus be conducive to greater predictability and/or fairness of the treatment of the general creditors of the debtor—in the case of a rule prescribing a fixed valuation date, by removing the possibility of 'speculating' against the insolvency estate.

3.42 Furthermore, almost any valuation method will necessarily leave some room for the valuer's discretion. Under normal circumstances, this creates no special problems: valuations done by one party may not directly affect its counterparty (for example, where their derivative transactions are not collateralized) or, if they do, the effects of valuations

---

[63] BCBS, *Basel II*, fn 15 (emphasis added).
[64] A large part of the economic literature on derivatives is concerned with pricing models, such as the classical Black-Scholes model for stock options. See, eg, Hull, *Options, Futures, and Other Derivatives*, passim.
[65] Cf Collins, 'Flipping Wreck'.
[66] Cf para 3.28 and n 38.

may be reversible (for example, collateral must eventually be returned in such normal circumstances). However, after close-out, the valuations will determine the termination amount in respect of final settlement.[67] It could be argued that insolvency laws should provide some control of valuation processes, by imposing general requirements of commercial reasonableness and good faith on the valuer, and perhaps also requirements more specific to valuation.[68] For example, Grove argues that the principles of transparency, consistency, and independence 'should govern the valuation of "hard-to-value" assets and liabilities'.[69,70]

(5) Systemic risk

A further observation with respect to market risk, in particular market risk of derivatives, is that risks of this type will typically be hedged by dealers running a matched book; non-dealer financial institutions may also employ derivatives to hedge other transactions or positions. In such a context, effective close-out netting is itself an important risk management tool because it allows the non-defaulting party to insulate itself as much as possible from the default (in particular: the insolvency) of its counterparty, by closing out its hedges with this counterparty and re-establishing those hedges with third parties and/or liquidating positions that were hedged by the terminated hedges. This aspect has been central to discussions of close-out netting as an effective mitigant of systemic risk in the financial sector.

3.43

---

[67] It is no surprise that in such 'irreversible' situations, the often large degree of discretion the valuer has (or claims to have) leads to valuation disputes. Grove, 'Valuation', 149, observes that '[t]he financial crisis of the past few years has spawned an unprecedented number of disputes relating to swaps and other privately negotiated derivatives transactions.... In many, if not all, of these disputes, valuation of the relevant derivatives is a central issue'.

[68] Cf the following exception to enforceability of contractually agreed valuation considered in the *travaux préparatoires* of the UNIDROIT Principles: 'if the valuation method was one-sidedly favouring one party, namely if the input parameters were not taken from objective sources but from the sphere of the determining party' (UNIDROIT 2011–S78C–Doc. 9, para 74). The basic point to be made here is that such subjective inputs are unavoidable in practice (and are normally permitted under standard master agreements). For example, the non-defaulting party will usually have some discretion as to the timing of close-out and/or valuation, and may reject 'objective inputs' that would normally be used in a valuation process if using them in the actual situation after close-out would not produce a commercially reasonable result. In practice, general statutory valuation requirements would often not or not significantly constrain contractually agreed valuation methods as several such requirements are in fact incorporated in standard master agreements. See, eg, the references to commercial reasonableness and good faith in s 14, 'Close-out Amount', of the ISDA 2002 Master Agreement.

[69] Grove, 'Valuation', 154.

[70] In her detailed review of the valuation and final settlement of Lehman's derivatives that were closed out by its counterparties, Summe points out that 'the legal obligations imposed on the administrator are such that a high standard of care is required before claims can be finalized for settlement. The statutory duties of the trustee in a Chapter 11 case are set forth in § 1106 of the U.S. Bankruptcy Code. In addition, case law imposes fiduciary obligations on a trustee, including treating all beneficiaries fairly and equally' (Summe, 'Lehman Brothers' Derivatives Portfolio', 92; footnotes omitted). The end result was that virtually all counterparties settled their claims in accordance with the *Derivatives Claims Settlement Framework* (27 May 2011), available at <http://dm.epiq11.com/LBH/document> (accessed 7 July 2021), proposed by Lehman. This framework departed at various important points from the valuation methodology under the ISDA Master Agreements governing the derivatives transactions; eg, Lehman, despite being the defaulting party, determined the termination amounts on the basis of *mid-market* values as of certain *fixed* valuation dates and times (Summe, 'Lehman Brothers' Derivatives Portfolio', 94–8).

3.44 The reduction of systemic risk is perhaps the single most important rationale given for much of the netting legislation reviewed in section D, as well as for the special treatment of derivatives and SFTs under national laws.[71] The principal argument in support of close-out netting as a mitigant of systemic risk runs along the following lines. If close-out is not allowed against an insolvent debtor because an automatic stay applies, or for any other reason, this creates uncertainty about the effectiveness of the counterparties' hedging strategies and transactions. 'Stays would effectively lock counterparties into long-term positions of rapidly changing value, thus making it difficult for solvent counterparties to manage their own exposures.'[72] These difficulties may lead to liquidity and solvency problems, not only for the direct counterparties of the insolvent debtor but also for their counterparties, and so on. If these effects are substantial, the stability of the financial system may be endangered. In the case of OTC derivatives these systemic risks are considered so great because of the large degree of interconnectedness of, in particular, the major (and very large) derivatives dealers; in the case of SFTs, especially repos, because these have become a major funding instrument for many financial institutions.[73]

3.45 A related argument in favour of close-out netting is that, in view of these negative effects of constraints on the operation of close-out netting in insolvency, counterparties of a debtor in financial problems (but not yet formally insolvent) may be tempted to close out transactions (or not to roll them over) if they do not have the right to terminate them once insolvency proceedings have commenced; conversely, if the right to close-out (and to net) were not constrained in insolvency, this may prevent 'runs' on a debtor and its subsequent collapse into insolvency with potentially systemic effects if the debtor is systemically important by itself or together with other failing institutions affected by common risk-factors.[74]

3.46 These arguments have not remained uncontested, and the challenges have only increased and intensified after the global financial crisis. This is especially true of legal and economic academic literature originating in the United States, where the special position of derivatives and SFTs under insolvency law is most prominent due to specific safe harbour provisions of the Bankruptcy Code.[75] Various arguments have been

---

[71] See, eg, Adams, *Derivative Exemptions*, 3 and 15–16; BCBS, *Cross-border Bank Resolution*, 36–8; Bergman et al, 'Netting, Financial Contracts, and Banks', 4.2.1; Bliss and Kaufman, 'Derivatives and Systemic Risk', 1; E&C, para 5; Edwards and Morrison, 'Derivatives and the Bankruptcy Code', 103–4 and 107–8; LGIL, 157–8; Lubben, 'Repeal the Safe Harbors', 326–8; Lubben, 'Transaction Simplicity', 195; Roe, 'Financial Crisis Accelerator', 545; Morrison and Riegel, 'Financial Contracts and the New Bankruptcy Code', 642–3; Paech, 'Enforceability of Close-out Netting', 16.

[72] Bergman et al, 'Netting, Financial Contracts, and Banks', 4.2.1.

[73] See also Ch 2, paras 2.18–19.

[74] For this distinction between systemic risk arising from individual and collective failure, respectively, see Acharya and Öncü, 'Resolution of Systemically Important Assets and Liabilities', 292; cf Crockett, 'Discussion of "Resolution of Systemically Important Assets and Liabilities"', 351–3. Note that these two perspectives on systemic risk are not mutually exclusive (as Acharya and Öncü point out themselves) and that, arguably, the failure of even a relatively small financial institution may, in certain circumstances, have systemic effects, if only through 'irrational' contagion.

[75] Footnote 8075 to Ch 3 in the first edition of this book contained a selection of contributions to the debate about the pros and cons of close-out netting. To these may be added a number of articles published since

PRINCIPLES, POLICIES, AND THE PRACTICE OF CLOSE-OUT NETTING

advanced to show that the safe harbours (and other netting-friendly provisions or regimes) are too broad in scope or that they should even be abolished because they may actually increase systemic risk or have other substantial negative effects. The following is a brief synopsis of the main arguments against the unconstrained enforceability of close-out netting in insolvency.

Liquidity. Several authors have turned the argument that close-out netting is good for business and liquidity[76] on its head and have argued in various ways that larger transaction volumes (and concomitantly larger, including too-big-to-fail, financial institutions) are not necessarily more beneficial from an economic and social point of view. It is not surprising that this type of reasoning frequently adduces experiences of the global financial crisis.[77]   **3.47**

Runs and fire sales. Enforceable close-out netting may diminish the propensity of counterparties to 'run' before insolvency, but it does so by allowing them to run once insolvency has been declared. Not only may this harm the prospects of reorganizing the debtor and/or saving viable parts of its enterprise, with possible systemic effect if the debtor is relatively large, but fire sales of derivatives and collateral may also by themselves have serious systemic effects on financial markets.[78] Both the Financial Stability Board (FSB) and the Basel Committee have acknowledged these risks in their recent publications on resolution regimes.[79]   **3.48**

Arbitrage. Combining these two types of arguments, Acharya et al. have argued that the safe harbours encourage regulatory arbitrage by providing parties with incentives to design products and strategies to shift assets from the banking book to the trading book, increasing systemic risks.[80] Similarly, Lubben has argued that the safe harbours   **3.49**

---

then: Johnson, 'The case against close-out netting'; Mokal, 'Bankruptcy Treatment of Financial Contracts'; Mooney, 'The Bankruptcy Code's Safe Harbors'; Morrison et al, 'Rolling Back the Repo Safe Harbors'; Paech, 'The Value of Financial Market Insolvency Safe Harbours'; Schwarcz and Sharon, 'The Bankruptcy-law Safe Harbor for Derivatives': Sołtysiński, 'The Importance of the Principles of Equality'.

[76] See para 3.38.
[77] See, eg, Edwards and Morrison, 'Derivatives and the Bankruptcy Code', IV.A, who argued—pre-crisis—that enhanced liquidity 'is less obviously a social good when it is the product of a government subsidy, paid for by other creditors' (which are not able to profit from the protection of a safe harbour). See also Mokal, 'Bankruptcy Treatment of Financial Contracts', in particular s V; Mokal 'draws attention to the importance of distinguishing [liquidity] from froth, with which liquidity is often damagingly confused' (ibid, 20); here 'froth' refers to the 'state in which assets are persistently and/or progressively overvalued and in which negative net value projects obtain funding' (ibid, 16).
[78] See, eg, Ayotte and Skeel, 'Bankruptcy or Bailouts?', V; Perotti, *Systemic Liquidity Risk*.
[79] FSB, *Key Attributes*, Annex 4, 1.1; and BCBS, *Cross-border Bank Resolution*, 40–2 (including Recommendation 9). Edwards and Morrison, 'Derivatives and the Bankruptcy Code', 102–3, note the 'irony' of the intervention by the Federal Reserve 'to avoid a systemic meltdown that might arise from [Long Term Capital Management's] liquidation—a liquidation made possible by the Bankruptcy's Code special treatment of derivative contracts...designed to avoid systemic risk'; see also 109–16, where they express doubts regarding the effectiveness of the Code to mitigate systemic risk.
[80] Acharya et al, 'Resolution Authority', as quoted in Sołtysiński, *Report*, 51. Cf Edwards and Morrison, 'Derivatives and the Bankruptcy Code', IV.B, who point to rent-seeking behaviour by banks and other institutions using derivatives instead of ordinary loans to finance debtors in order to profit from the safe harbours.

for derivatives and repos under the US Bankruptcy Code lead to socially inefficient subsidization of such transactions to the detriment of 'normal' financial contracts.[81]

3.50 *Firm-specific and illiquid assets.* Edwards and Morrison reject the systemic-risk rationale for the safe harbours, but suggest an alternative: the special treatment of derivatives and SFTs may be justified because these transactions and related collateral securities are not 'firm-specific assets', but money-like, liquid assets.[82] Since such transactions and securities are usually easy to replace, it is, arguably, not necessary to preserve them through a stay on close-out. Edwards and Morrison themselves point out that this argument is of doubtful general validity. Other authors have argued that at least some derivatives and collateral securities *are* firm-specific or illiquid and that these should therefore not fall within the scope of a safe harbour or that counterparties should not be able to realize such assets unrestrictedly.[83]

3.51 *Market discipline.* Another argument is that protection of close-out netting may lead to a reduction in market discipline by reducing the incentive for parties to derivatives and SFTs to monitor their counterparties without a commensurate increase in monitoring by other general creditors of these counterparties.[84]

3.52 It is clearly impossible to do justice to these arguments and counterarguments within the confines of this chapter, let alone to evaluate them. It should be said that there is little formal economic analysis of the various arguments[85] or quantitative empirical research that is directly relevant. It is difficult to see that or how this debate will evolve (much) further and whether it will have more than the very limited impact on close-out netting regimes it may have had so far.[86]

D. Harmonization of Close-out Netting Regimes

(1) Introduction

3.53 Little of the debates and conflicting ideas regarding close-out netting touched upon in the preceding section is reflected in the international and transnational legal instruments reviewed below. The instruments dealing with substantive law are squarely based on the principle that close-out netting should be generally enforceable, a feature that they share with many national legal systems. This lack of legislative acknowledgement

---

[81] Lubben, 'Transaction Simplicity', 195–6 and 199; cf Mokal, 'Bankruptcy Treatment of Financial Contracts', V; Perotti, *Systemic Liquidity Risk*.
[82] Edwards and Morrison, 'Derivatives and the Bankruptcy Code', I–II (rejection of the systemic risk rationale; cf n 77) and III ('A Better Reason for Treating Derivatives Differently').
[83] See, eg, Acharya and Öncü, 'Resolution of Systemically Important Assets and Liabilities', 298–9 and 331–6; Duffie and Skeel, 'Dialogue on Automatic Stays', 164–5.
[84] Bergman et al, 'Netting, Financial Contracts, and Banks', 4.1.2; Roe, 'Financial Crisis Accelerator', passim.
[85] One exception is Bolton and Oehmke, 'Should Derivatives Be Privileged in Bankruptcy?', although their formal analysis is limited to a highly stylized 'toy model'.
[86] The short resolution stay (see ss D(5)–(7)) can be viewed as building on some of the arguments against full enforceability of close-out netting provisions.

of countervailing ideas is perhaps not surprising since legislation is a practical, not a theoretical activity. This may be particularly important in relation to close-out netting, where there is, and has been for some appreciable time, a well-established market practice, including a detailed *lex mercatoria*, and where industry organizations were actively—and successfully—promoting the removal of legal obstacles to that practice.

Furthermore, a substantial number of national law systems had never put up any significant obstacles to close-out netting anyway (even absent special close-out netting legislation), including the legal systems of jurisdictions, such as England,[87] that were home to important financial centres and major financial market participants. In addition, from the 1990s onward, 'Wall Street' and American financial institutions in general were able to benefit from expanding netting safe harbours enacted in the United States. Clearly, such jurisdictions enjoyed competitive advantages in comparison with less netting-friendly States, which may well have led the latter to amend their laws to reduce or eliminate those advantages.[88] The recognition of close-out netting by the Basel Committee in the mid-1990s is an indication that around that time there existed a critical mass of legal systems that permitted effective close-out netting and that under the pressure of competition in the financial sector other jurisdictions simply had to follow suit and accommodate close-out netting. In any case, in 2003, Bergman et al. were already able to observe that '[w]hile harmonization of bankruptcy laws has languished, harmonization of the treatment (and protection) of close-out netting now encompasses virtually all major derivative markets'.[89] One also surmises that the perceived complexity of these areas of *haute finance* has played a substantial role in convincing legislators to defer to the *lex mercatoria* that had been developed by specialist practitioners.[90]

3.54

Of course, the global financial crisis has had some impact on the more recent instruments discussed in this section, despite their continuing adherence to principles and rules conducive to close-out netting. That impact has turned out to be limited so far, which was probably to be expected in view of the very substantial financial interests involved and against the background of other (restrictive) post-crisis legislation and regulation aimed at the financial sector, including Basel III and mandatory central clearing regimes. For example, writing in 2010 (before the introduction of much more stringent collateralization regimes), Mengle estimated that 'without the benefits of netting, banks worldwide might face a capital shortfall of over $500 billion' and that '[w]ith regard to collateral, it simply would not be feasible to raise $22 trillion of additional collateral'

3.55

---

[87] See ISDA, *Netting Legislation: Status*: 'In England, the enforceability of netting is widely accepted without the need for specific statutory recognition'; cf Gullifer, 'Financial Collateral', 396; ISDA, *2018 MNA and Guide*, Appendix D, 52 (fn 78) and 64; Yeowart and Parsons, *The Law of Financial Collateral*, 10.05.

[88] For example, ISDA, *2018 MNA and Guide*, ii, refers to ISDA's 'experience over the past 30 years of dialogue with lawmakers, regulators and other government officials in countries around the world, from a variety of legal traditions, seeking to implement netting legislation locally in order to strengthen and modernize their national financial markets and to ensure the competitiveness of their leading financial institutions and other professional financial market participants in the global marketplace'.

[89] Bergman et al, 'Netting, Financial Contracts, and Banks', 4.2.1.

[90] Cf Collins, 'Flipping Wreck'.

required to cover gross instead of net exposures.[91] To these quantitative effects must be added other possible (negative) systemic consequences of substantive changes to close-out netting regimes—especially after the introduction of mandatory central clearing of large classes of OTC derivatives, since close-out netting is an integral part of central clearing structures—as well as the inconclusiveness of the recent academic debate on close-out netting. It is therefore not surprising that the only significant, though limited, inroad on the enforceability of close-out netting provisions has been in the context of resolution measures, as discussed in sections D(5)–(7).

(2) EU Banks Insolvency Directive

3.56 In 2001, the Banks Insolvency Directive (BID) introduced a harmonized insolvency regime for EU banks ('credit institutions')[92] that took its inspiration from the principle of home-State supervision laid down in the Second Banking Directive 89/646/EEC and its successors. The insolvency analogue of this principle[93] consists of two parts: (i) only the home Member State may institute insolvency proceedings against a bank (including its branches in other Member States); and (ii) the laws of the home State govern those insolvency proceedings unless otherwise provided in the BID.[94]

3.57 The BID legislators refrained from a harmonization of substantive insolvency law, but the Directive did set out several conflict-of-laws rules, of which at least two[95] are directly relevant to close-out netting. Article 25 BID provides that '[n]etting agreements shall be governed solely by the law of the contract which governs such agreements'. Article 26 contains a similar provision with regard to 'repurchase agreements'. The terminology is not entirely clear: 'netting agreement' is not defined in the BID and has, in the past, been interpreted as referring only to netting agreements that form part of a system within the meaning of the Settlement Finality Directive (SFD). This interpretation appears to be too narrow, however, and 'netting' in Article 25 must be assumed to encompass close-out netting, in particular after its amendment by Article 117 BRRD, which inserted a reference to Articles 68 and 71 BRRD in Article 25 BID.[96] Furthermore, the use of 'solely' in both provisions may be taken to mean that these

---

[91] See Mengle, *Importance of Close-out Netting*, 1, 4.
[92] The BRRD has extended the scope of the BID to include, *inter alia*, investment firms that may be subject to resolution pursuant to the BRRD; see Art 117 BRRD.
[93] Cf recital (4) BID.
[94] Articles 3, 9(1), and 10 BID.
[95] Cf Art 23 BID on set-off.
[96] The narrow interpretation has been put forward by Marks, 'Regulating Financial Services and Markets in the EU', 7.84, and also formed the basis for the implementation of the BID in the Netherlands (criticized as faulty by Bertrams, 'EU-richtlijn sanering en liquidatie kredietinstellingen'). An argument for a broader interpretation may be found in the *travaux préparatoires* of the BID. For example, the Council stated in its Common Position (see OJ C300/29) that the provisions of Arts 25 and 26: concern contractual netting agreements (agreements to set off positive and negative balances) between a credit institution and its counter party and repurchase agreements (an agreement between a seller and a buyer of securities where the seller agrees to repurchase the securities at an agreed price)

articles refer to the system of law governing the agreement *including* the insolvency law provisions of that system of law.[97]

3.58 In practice, these conflict-of-laws provisions may have important substantive effects: a bank (or any other party subject to the BID) and its counterparty to a projected netting agreement or repurchase agreement could choose a netting-friendly system of law (for example, English or Dutch law[98]), which would have to be accepted by the insolvency court (in the bank's home State). The parties could thereby ensure that close-out netting would be effective in the event of insolvency of the bank, at least within the confines of the EU.[99]

(3) EU Financial Collateral Directive and Geneva Securities Convention

3.59 The FCD and Chapter V of the GSC have already been discussed in Chapter 2 (where it was explained why these collateral regimes may both be characterized as essentially reflecting *pre*-crisis ideas and concerns)[100] and are only considered here to the extent that they apply to close-out netting. Chapter V GSC is modelled closely on the FCD and adds very little of substance in this context; the following paragraphs discuss only the FCD, but what is said there applies analogously to the close-out netting rules of the GSC.[101]

3.60 In paragraph 3.17 it was observed that close-out netting may be used, in effect, to enforce rights of the collateral taker in respect of collateral provided. Article 6(2) FCD acknowledges this aspect with regard to title-transfer arrangements.[102] In relation to a security arrangement including a right of use, Article 5(5) FCD similarly provides that if that right has been exercised, the obligation to transfer equivalent collateral to the collateral provider may be the subject of a close-out netting provision upon the occurrence of an enforcement event.[103] Article 7(1) FCD ensures that these mechanisms of

---

respectively.... Such agreements are commonly used on the financial markets and the Council considers that the special function of such contracts requires a derogation from the principle of universal application of home Member State law in order to protect the functioning of the financial markets and to ensure legal certainty for the contracting parties.See also BCBS, *Cross-border Bank Resolution*, para 107; Böger, 'Close-out Netting Provisions (I)', 255–6.

[97] See Böger, 'Close-out Netting Provisions (I)', 256–7 (with further references).
[98] Cf nn 87 and 41, respectively.
[99] For a similar argument see ISDA, *2018 MNA and Guide*, Chapter 6.
[100] See Ch 2, paras 2.09–11 and 2.89, and s B.
[101] Chapter V GSC is of course only concerned with collateral in the form of intermediated securities. The FCD also covers cash collateral and collateral in the form of credit claims resulting from banking business; see Ch 2, para 2.11. For a detailed analysis of the (minor) other differences between the close-out netting regimes of both instruments, see Keijser et al, 'Financial Collateral: EU and UNIDROIT Compared', VI.
[102] Cf Art 33(2) GSC.
[103] Cf Art 33(2) GSC. See also Art 5(2), second para FCD.

'realizing' collateral are enforceable in accordance with the terms of the relevant close-out netting provisions, both outside and within insolvency.[104]

3.61 With respect to valuation issues, Article 4(6) FCD enables national legislatures to make some inroads on enforceability, since it provides that Articles 4–7 FCD 'shall be without prejudice to any requirements under national law to the effect that the realisation or valuation of financial collateral and the calculation of the relevant financial obligations must be conducted in a commercially reasonable manner'.[105] In practice, Article 4(6) is probably not very significant as most standard documentation already includes obligations to value in a commercially reasonable manner. In fact, this FCD provision seems to raise the question of whether other statutory duties may be imposed on the valuing party—for example, a duty to value in good faith[106]—or whether that would be inconsistent with the FCD regime.

(4) UNCITRAL Legislative Guide on Insolvency Law

3.62 The LGIL was adopted in 2004 and published in 2005.[107] Recommendations 101–7 deal with close-out netting and are preceded by explanatory paragraphs 208–15 and a description of the purpose of legislative provisions on close-out netting.[108] The core Recommendations 101–3 of the LGIL provide for enforceability of close-out netting arrangements and explicitly recommend exempting them from stays on close-out (Recommendation 101) or set-off restrictions (Recommendation 102).[109]

3.63 A significant aspect of the LGIL is its unlimited personal scope: Recommendation 106 states that 'Recommendations 101–105 should apply to all transactions that are considered to be "financial contracts," whether or not one of the counterparties is a financial institution'. According to the accompanying footnote, the reason is that '[e]ven if a given financial contract does not involve a financial institution, the impact of the insolvency of a counterparty could entail systemic risk'.

3.64 The LGIL description of close-out netting may seem too narrow if taken literally, especially where it makes set-off a constituent element of the technique:

> 'Close-out netting' embraces two steps: firstly, termination of all open contracts as a result of the commencement of insolvency proceedings (close-out); secondly, the

---

[104] Thus, removing any possibility of applying traditional mandatory rules with respect to realization to collateral arrangements covered by the Directive; cf para 3.27.
[105] Cf Art 35 GSC. On this standard of commercial reasonableness, see Franciosi, 'Commercial Reasonableness' and Graziadei, 'Many Faces of Reasonableness'.
[106] See, eg, CRMPG III, *Containing Systemic Risk*, 121: 'a clear consensus has emerged around three principles that must be associated with any close-out methodology. These are: (1) commercial reasonableness; (2) duty of good faith; and (3) fair dealing'. See also para 3.42.
[107] See LGIL, i–iii. Cf Ch 4, paras 4.23–5.
[108] See LGIL, 156–8.
[109] See also Ch 4, para 4.77.

set-off of all obligations arising out of the closed out transactions on an aggregate basis (netting).[110]

See also Recommendation 102 for the apparent equation of netting with set-off. However, other sections of the Guide make it clear that set-off and netting should be distinguished.[111]

(5) FSB Key Attributes of Effective Resolution Regimes for Financial Institutions

After the global financial crisis, international regulatory forums and both national and international legislators have designed methods that will allow (f)ailing financial institutions to be 'resolved' while preserving systemic stability and without the need for State-sponsored bail-outs.[112] At a global level the BCBS and the FSB (of which the BCBS is of course a member) have formulated resolution principles and recommendations, some of which are directly relevant to close-out netting.[113]   **3.65**

Those principles and recommendations are based on unequivocally positive assumptions about the effects of close-out netting on systemic risk reduction. For example, in 2010 the BCBS included 'enforceable netting agreements' among 'risk mitigation techniques that reduce systemic risk and enhance the resiliency of critical financial or market functions during a crisis or resolution of financial institutions' with a recommendation that '[n]ational authorities should promote the convergence of national rules governing the enforceability of close-out netting and collateral arrangements with respect to their scope of application and legal effects across borders'.[114] Only in the event of resolution of a financial institution should the relevant authority be able 'to temporarily delay immediate operation of contractual early termination clauses in order to complete a transfer' of the underlying contracts to another institution.[115] Termination rights should otherwise be preserved.   **3.66**

The FSB followed the same approach in its 2011 *Key Attributes*,[116] which have since become the global standard for resolution regimes: 'the legal framework governing set-off rights, contractual netting and collateralisation agreements... should be clear, transparent and enforceable during a crisis or resolution of firms, and should not hamper   **3.67**

---

[110] LGIL, 156 (para 210). Cf s B.
[111] See para I(20)(g) of Part One; Recommendation 7(g); and the definition of 'netting agreement' in para 12(aa) of the Introduction.
[112] See Ch 2, s C(3).
[113] BCBS, *Cross-border Bank Resolution*; FSB, *Key Attributes*.
[114] BCBS, *Cross-border Bank Resolution*, 39 (Recommendation 8) and para 106, quoted and discussed in ISDA, *2018 MNA and Guide*, 1.8.
[115] BCBS, *Cross-border Bank Resolution*, 42 (Recommendation 9).
[116] The *Key Attributes* were updated in 2014 by additional implementation guidance. However, Key Attribute 4 dealing with close-out netting was unchanged and 2014 Annex I-5 ('Temporary Stays on Early Termination Rights') is identical to 2011 Annex 4.

the effective implementation of resolution measures'.[117] The influence of crisis experiences can be discerned in the possibility that certain constraints are imposed on the operation of close-out netting (invalidation of *ipso facto* clauses and a short stay, subject to 'adequate safeguards'),[118] where this may be conducive to successful resolution, but not in any more stringent constraints that would reflect some of the criticisms directed at close-out netting that were reviewed in section C(5). In this context it is interesting to note that the FSB has elsewhere[119] cautiously acknowledged some academic ('theoretical') criticism of safe harbours for repos, but that this was accompanied with the following recommendation:

> Changes to bankruptcy law treatment... may be viable theoretical options but should not be prioritised for further work at this stage due to significant difficulties in implementation.[120]

The FSB has produced no 'further work' on this and related issues since.

3.68 The regulatory resolution standard set by FSB Key Attribute 4 has quickly become part of a broader consensus, including market participants and their trade organizations. The most substantial change in ISDA's 2018 MNA relative to its 2006 precursor, for example, is the addition of sub-clause (j) to the core enforceability provision, section (I)(4); this sub-clause covers financial institutions subject to resolution in line with the FSB recommendations.[121,122] Under some regulatory pressure, ISDA has also created various Resolution Stay Protocols to enable market participants to opt in contractually to resolution regimes that stay and, in certain cases, override close-out rights. These Protocols address the 'concern that stays of termination under national resolution regimes would not be recognized by courts in other jurisdictions, particularly if the governing law of the derivatives contract or credit enhancement is not the law of the resolution jurisdiction'.[123]

(6) UNIDROIT Principles on the Operation of Close-Out Netting Provisions

3.69 The UNIDROIT Principles[124] are the outcome of a project that originated in an ISDA proposal dated 2008; the project was put on ice as the global financial crisis deepened,

---

[117] FSB, *Key Attributes*, 4.1.
[118] FSB, *Key Attributes*, 4.2–4.
[119] FSB, *Shadow Banking: Securities Lending and Repos*, 18.
[120] FSB, *Shadow Banking: Securities Lending and Repos*, 18–19, in particular Recommendation 11; cf Ch 9, s D(4)(d).
[121] Cf ISDA, *2018 MNA and Guide*, 1.9–10.
[122] Another example is provided by the World Bank's *Principles for Effective Insolvency and Creditor/Debtor Regimes*. At least as far as close-out netting is concerned, the relevant recommendations simply follow those of the FSB (and their implementation in the BRRD and the PCON); see World Bank, *ICR Principles*, C10.4 and endnote 9 in particular.
[123] Mayer Brown, *The ISDA Resolution Stay Protocol*.
[124] See n 7 for a description of the structure of the official publication of the Principles.

but it was reactivated in May 2010.[125] The Principles are therefore truly a post-crisis instrument, although the impact of 'lessons learned' from the crisis appears to be limited. In connection with this aspect, it is also surprising to observe that there is very little attention, either in the commentary[126] or the *travaux préparatoires*, to critical approaches in the legal and economic literature to close-out netting, which, though not all originating in the experience of the crisis, have certainly been informed by it.[127] As a result, the Principles themselves do not reflect these critical ideas either. It appears that this 'non-critical' approach is mainly due to the fact that the Principles are intentionally based on the international regulatory consensus with respect to close-out netting (which was, to a large extent, to be expected) and that, as already noted in section D(5), this shared opinion is that—despite recent crisis experiences and criticisms—close-out netting generally contributes to system stability and a reduction of systemic risks.[128]

3.70 Consistent with the recommendations issued by the FSB and the BCBS—discussed in section D(5)—the commentary on the UNIDROIT Principles states that their objective is 'to improve the *enforceability* of close-out netting…in order to provide a sound basis, in commercial and insolvency law terms, for risk management and mitigation by financial institutions and for the application of regulatory policies in the international context'.[129]

3.71 Thus, enforceability is the main substantive concern of the Principles themselves, the substance of which is otherwise relatively limited.[130] The first four Principles, including the definition of 'close-out netting provision', are more properly viewed as provisions limiting the scope of the (genuine) Principles 5–8. Principle 5 prohibits formal requirements for the operation of close-out netting provisions. An analysis of this provision

---

[125] See UNIDROIT 2012–CD (91) 15, para 50; UNIDROIT 2013–CD (92) 6(a), para 2; Sołtysiński, *Report*, para 2. The first tangible preparatory work was UNIDROIT 2011–S78C–Doc. 2, a 'Preliminary draft Report on [t]he need for an international instrument on the enforceability of close-out netting in general and in the context of bank resolution', prepared by Paech; cf Paech, 'Framework for Netting'. Loizou, 'Close-out Netting' and Paech, 'Enforceability of Close-out Netting' discuss draft versions of the Principles.

[126] Ie the E&C and the Key considerations; see n 7.

[127] Indeed, there is a remarkable comment by the Chairman of the Study Group, Professor Sołtysiński, that 'he did not think the Principles reflected the deep divisions among legal scholars and economists about netting as an institution, to which the Group's report made no reference' and that 'he felt [the Principles] to be one-sided, representing as they did 90% of the view of the interested segment of the industry' (UNIDROIT 2012–CD (91) 15, para 56, further explained in the equally remarkable critical sections of his report appended to this document (Sołtysiński, *Report*, 48–53)).

[128] See, eg, the reference to the '*agreement*, notably amongst the regulatory community, that netting is one of the primary risk mitigation tools and therefore should be available in all financial markets' (UNIDROIT 2011–S78C–Doc. 2, para 117; emphasis added). This is followed by the statement that '[t]his regulatory suggestion is the basis on which the analysis in this study is built'—as well as the basis for much of the subsequent legislative discussion and the Principles themselves, one may add. The Study Group that prepared and debated the first drafts of the Principles was of the opinion that it was not necessary to explain in detail why netting was 'an efficient risk-mitigation mechanism', since this was the consensus among regulators (UNIDROIT 2011–S78C–Doc. 4, para 21). See also E&C, para 5, and Paech, 'Enforceability of Close-out Netting', 18.

[129] E&C, para 11 (emphasis added).

[130] The 'small scope' of the Principles was noted in the preparatory phase: UNIDROIT 2012–CD (91) 15, para 55; note that the scope of the final Principles is even smaller because in that phase the draft Principles still contained conflict-of-laws provisions (cf para 64 of the same document).

88   ON CLOSE-OUT NETTING

falls outside the scope of this chapter, but note its similarity to Article 3 FCD, which bans such requirements in relation to financial collateral arrangements.[131]

3.72 The core principles are Principles 6 and 7, which together[132] provide for the enforceability of close-out netting provisions, both outside and within insolvency. There is, however, one important exception because Principle 7, which deals with insolvency proceedings, is subject to Principle 8, which incorporates the international regulatory consensus with regard to resolution principles and provides that the Principles are without prejudice to measures 'which the law of the implementing State may provide for in the context of resolution regimes for financial institutions'. The 'Key considerations' in respect of Principle 8 refer to the *Key Attributes* of the FSB as the 'current international consensus for such resolution regimes', but permit any national resolution regime to constrain close-out netting, 'subject to appropriate safeguards'. The final 'Key consideration' acknowledges that:

> ... international standards on the appropriate treatment of close-out netting in the context of resolution regimes for financial institutions and their implementation under national law are still evolving. The policy underlying such resolution regimes is still subject to changes in the future and the references in Principle 8 and the commentary should therefore be understood as being dynamic and contingent.

3.73 The Principles lack any explicit provision with regard to statutory valuation requirements, analogous—in the context of close-out netting—to Article 4(6) FCD, discussed in paragraph 3.61. However, the commentary suggests that such a rule is in fact implicit in the Principles and that it can be based on Principle 2 in particular. This 'principle' contains the definition of 'close-out netting provision' quoted in paragraph 3.08 (and nothing else). According to the commentary, the element of the definition that the result of close-out netting is a single net obligation 'representing the aggregate value of the combined obligations' is in fact a substantive requirement. The commentary notes:

> No specific additional criteria are laid down in the definition of the term 'close-out netting provision' and the implementing States retain some discretion as to the precise conditions to be fulfilled by a valuation mechanism in order to satisfy this requirement. Some legal systems, for instance, require an element of commercial reasonableness for the enforceability of close-out netting provisions.[133]

The reasoning here appears to be that a valuation mechanism that does not satisfy a statutory requirement falling within the discretion allowed to implementing States—for example, a requirement that the valuation is commercially reasonable—must be regarded, for that reason, as *not* resulting in a single net obligation representing the

---

[131] The FCD ban (or rather its UK implementation) is critically assessed by Gullifer, 'Financial Collateral', 385–94.
[132] Earlier drafts contained just one provision covering enforceability; see, eg, UNIDROIT 2012–CGE/Netting/1/ WP.2, p 19 (draft Principle 7).
[133] E&C, para 39.

('true') aggregate value of the netted obligations or transactions. Therefore, the contractual close-out netting agreement that includes such a valuation mechanism does not constitute close-out netting provisions to which the Principles apply, and the relevant implementing State may refuse to recognize its enforceability.

Apart from this aspect, the Principles, the commentary, and the preparatory documents are virtually silent on the admissibility of statutory constraints regarding the valuation element of close-out netting. In view of the clear statement of enforceability-in-principle it must be assumed that the Principles prohibit most statutory constraints on contractually agreed valuation parameters that are not of a general nature (such as requirements of good faith and commercial reasonableness). However, because of the paucity of information about the relevant legislative intentions, it is not clear why this should be so and where the boundary between admissible and prohibited constraints should be drawn.[134]

3.74

(7) Close-out netting and resolution: the EU regime

This section looks at specific constraints on close-out netting, and the related safeguards, set out in the EU Bank Recovery and Resolution Directive (BRRD), which also reflect the FSB and BCBS recommendations on close-out netting, described in section D(5). A more detailed exposition of various aspects of the BRRD is provided in Chapter 2, sections C(3)–(5).

3.75

The BRRD affects close-out netting in several ways already discussed in Chapter 2:

3.76

(i) it invalidates *ipso facto* clauses that purport to provide a party with close-out rights on the ground of any resolution action with regard to its counterparty or that would lead to automatic close-out on that ground;[135]
(ii) it provides for a brief stay of close-out rights (at the election of the resolution authority);[136]
(iii) transactions subject to a close-out netting agreement may be the subject of a partial property transfer, but such a transfer must preserve netting sets and therefore either transfer a netting set as a whole or not at all.[137]

An important feature of the BRRD is its detailed bail-in tool. After lengthy discussions, European legislators agreed that liabilities arising under derivative transactions should, in principle, be subject to bail-in.[138] However, in 'exceptional circumstances'

3.77

---

[134] See para 3.42 (including the footnotes thereto), where various constraints, principles, and duties in relation to valuation were discussed; see also para 3.61 on valuation under the FCD.
[135] Article 68 BRRD; see Ch 2, para 2.86.
[136] Article 71(1)–(2) BRRD; see Ch 2, paras 2.86–7.
[137] Article 77(1) BRRD; see Ch 2, para 2.83.
[138] Article 44(1)–(2) BRRD; cf Ch 2, para 2.77, where it is also noted that 'secured liabilities' (which include liabilities under title transfer collateral arrangements) are excluded from the scope of the bail-in tool pursuant to Art 44(2)(b) BRRD.

the resolution authority may exclude or partially exclude certain liabilities from bail-in. Exclusion may be called for to avoid widespread and disruptive contagion (for example, negative systemic effects of the bail-in of derivatives liabilities), or if the bail-in of these liabilities would lead to a net value destruction for other creditors.[139]

3.78 If the derivatives liabilities of the institution under resolution are bailed in, several (additional) inroads on the relevant (close-out) netting agreements[140] are possible. Since, pursuant to Article 49(2) BRRD, bail-in may only take place upon or after close-out of the relevant derivatives, the resolution authority will be granted a statutory close-out right for this purpose, which the authority will presumably exercise on behalf of the institution under resolution. This feature (in effect, close-out by a defaulting party) is linked to the safeguard that close-out netting agreements will be respected in so far as only the net liability of the institution under resolution may be bailed in.[141] Another possible deviation from the relevant close-out netting agreements in the event of a bail-in of derivatives concerns valuation: Article 49(4)–(5) BRRD provides that the resolution authority shall determine the net derivatives liabilities in accordance with valuation 'methodologies' and 'principles' to be promulgated by the European Commission in a delegated regulation. Thus, the resolution authority is not bound by the valuation method agreed between the parties, although Article 49(5) BRRD stipulates that, in drafting the delegated regulation, the European Banking Authority (EBA) 'shall take into account the methodology for close-out set out in the netting agreement'. The relevant delegated regulation[142] does not refer explicitly to any contractually agreed valuation methodology, but Article 6 of the regulation ('Determination of the close-out amount') is substantially in accordance with the methodology set out in the definition of 'Close-out Amount' in Section 14 of the ISDA 2002 Master Agreement.[143]

3.79 The impact of resolution under the BRRD on close-out netting is likely to be limited (except, possibly, if the bail-in tool is used), which is the same conclusion drawn in Chapter 2 with respect to the impact of resolution on collateralization. The basis for these conclusions is to be found in the various safeguards that form part of the resolution regime of the BRRD (and the BCBS and FSB recommendations, on which the

---

[139] Article 44(3)(c)–(d) BRRD.

[140] As noted in n 11, the relevant BRRD defined term is 'netting arrangement' (see Art 2(98) BRRD). Despite this, the BRRD appears to use the terms 'netting arrangement' and 'netting agreement' interchangeably; 'netting arrangement' occurs seven times and 'netting agreement' eight times. See, for example, Art 77 BRRD, the heading of which reads 'Protection for financial collateral, set-off and netting *agreements*', whereas its first paragraph requires 'appropriate protection for title transfer financial collateral arrangements and set-off and netting *arrangements*' (emphasis added in both cases).

[141] Article 49(3) BRRD. In other words, there will be no cherry-picking of derivative contracts in order to subject them to bail-in. Counterparties of the institution under resolution that are out-of-the-money 'overall' (cf para 3.21) will not be subject to bail-in.

[142] Commission Delegated Regulation (EU) 2016/1401 supplementing Directive 2014/59/EU . . . with regard to regulatory technical standards for methodologies and principles on the valuation of liabilities arising from derivatives.

[143] The valuation methodology applied by the valuer in a resolution situation may therefore deviate materially from the methodology agreed between the institution under resolution and any of its counterparties if their relevant derivatives netting agreement is not an ISDA 2002 Master Agreement.

BRRD is based), the main one of which is the safeguard, itself a resolution principle, that no creditor of an institution under resolution should be worse off in comparison with the hypothetical liquidation of the institution under normal insolvency proceedings. Resolution under the BRRD (therefore) respects the integrity of netting sets under all circumstances. Furthermore, the constraints on close-out are limited in time (a short stay of at most two business days) and in scope (only *ipso facto* clauses referring to resolution measures are invalidated).

E. Concluding Remarks

Close-out netting has become a well-established part of the law of international finance. In the period since its introduction on the OTC derivatives markets, national and international legislators and regulators worldwide have gradually removed obstacles to its operation, culminating in the adoption of the UNIDROIT Principles. **3.80**

In the first edition of this book, this chapter ended with the tentative conclusion that it was unlikely that this area of law will show little further development from this point on. This conclusion was a reflection of the fact that the global financial crisis had led to more critical approaches to close-out netting. It now appears that those criticisms have remained largely confined to academic circles and that they have had little impact on legislation and regulation. In any case, the secular 'netting-friendly' trend of the period prior to the global financial crisis has not really been reversed in recent years, although it should be noted that internationally accepted resolution principles now acknowledge that unconstrained close-out netting may in certain situations increase rather than mitigate systemic risks. **3.81**

4

ENFORCEMENT OF SECURITY INTERESTS IN SECURITIES UNDER UNIFORM LAW

A. Introduction	4.01	(a) Enforcement outside insolvency	4.52
B. Scope and Definitions	4.04	(b) Enforcement in insolvency	4.71
(1) The Geneva Securities Convention	4.05	(c) Enforcement and alternative dispute resolution	4.89
(2) The Hague Securities Convention	4.13	(d) The law applicable to enforcement	4.102
(3) The Secured Transactions Model Law	4.15	(4) Enforcement under the Receivables Convention	4.108
(4) The Secured Transactions and the Insolvency Law Legislative Guides	4.21	(5) Enforcement: the Secured Transactions Model Law as non-Convention law under the Geneva Securities Convention and required amendments	4.111
(5) The Receivables Convention	4.26
(6) Differences in scope and terminology	4.32
C. Enforcement	4.44
(1) Enforcement under the Geneva Securities Convention	4.44
(2) The law applicable to enforcement under the Hague Securities Convention	4.50	(6) Enforcement: the UNIDROIT project	4.120
(3) Enforcement under the Secured Transactions Model Law and the Secured Transactions and Insolvency Guides	4.52	D. Conclusions	4.128

A. Introduction

4.01 This chapter deals with the enforcement of security and other (eg, title) interests in intermediated and non-intermediated securities under uniform law. The uniform law discussed includes the UNIDROIT[1] Convention on Substantive Rules for Intermediated Securities, Chapters III and V (hereinafter referred to as the 'Geneva Securities Convention' or the 'GSC'),[2] the Convention of 5 July 2006 on the Law Applicable to Certain Rights in Respect of Securities Held with an Intermediary (hereinafter referred

---

[1] UNIDROIT is short for International Institute for the Unification of Private Law, an independent intergovernmental organization outside the United Nations system with 63 Member States (<https://www.unidroit.org/about-unidroit/overview>, accessed 5 April 2021).

[2] The GSC is accompanied by: (i) the *Official Commentary on the UNIDROIT Convention on Substantive Rules for Intermediated Securities*, written by Hideki Kanda, Charles Mooney, Luc Thévenoz, Stephane Béraud, and Thomas Keijser, Oxford University Press, 2012 (hereinafter referred to as 'Kanda et al, *Official Commentary*'); and (ii) the UNIDROIT Legislative Guide on Intermediated Securities (hereinafter referred to as the 'LGIS'). The GSC and the LGIS are available on the UNIDROIT website under <https://www.unidroit.org/instruments/capital-markets/geneva-convention> and <https://www.unidroit.org/instr-capitalmarkets-legislative-guide> respectively (both accessed 5 April 2021).

to as the 'Hague Securities Convention' or the 'HSC'),[3] the UNCITRAL Model Law on Secured Transactions (hereinafter referred to as the 'Model Law' or the 'MLST'),[4] the UNCITRAL Legislative Guide on Secured Transactions (hereinafter referred to as the 'Secured Transactions Legislative Guide' or the 'LGST'),[5] the UNCITRAL Legislative Guide on Insolvency Law (hereinafter referred to as the 'Insolvency Law Legislative Guide' or the 'LGIL'),[6] and the United Nations Convention on the Assignment of Receivables in International Trade (hereinafter referred to as the 'Receivables Convention' or the 'CARIT').[7]

4.02 There are two reasons for this discussion and comparison of the above-mentioned uniform law texts. One reason is the fact that the GSC does not fully address all the matters that it covers but rather refers several to the law of a Contracting State other than the GSC, such as general secured transactions and insolvency law, which may be based on the above-mentioned texts (see paragraph 4.05). Thus, a State that decides to adopt the GSC may also wish to implement those other texts to ensure that the matters referred by the GSC to non-Convention law are adequately covered.[8] Another reason is that, for a State to have a comprehensive regime on security and other interests in securities, simply adopting all those uniform law texts is not enough. It would, in addition, need to introduce some amendments to its enactment of the MLST or to adopt a new comprehensive law on security and other interests in securities, building on all the uniform law texts under consideration (see paragraphs 4.111–19).

4.03 Section B of this chapter discusses the scope and key definitions of the relevant uniform law texts. Section C discusses: (i) the enforcement of security and other interests in intermediated securities under Chapters III (transfer of intermediated securities) and

---

[3] <https://www.hcch.net/en/instruments/conventions/full-text/?cid=72> (accessed 5 April 2021).
[4] United Nations publication, Sales No V.16-04667, 2016. The MLST is accompanied by: (i) the UNCITRAL Model Law on Secured Transactions: Guide to Enactment (hereafter referred to as the 'Guide to Enactment'; United Nations publication, Sales No V.17-07549); and (ii) the UNCITRAL Practice Guide to the Model Law on Secured Transactions (hereinafter referred to as the 'Practice Guide'; United Nations publication, Sales No: E.20.V.6). The MLST is also supplemented by the LGST (n 5) and the LGIL (n 6). All texts of UNCITRAL on security interests are available on the UNCITRAL website under <https://uncitral.un.org/en/texts/securityinterests> (accessed 5 April 2021). The LGIL is available on the UNCITRAL website under <https://uncitral.un.org/sites/uncitral.un.org/files/media-documents/uncitral/en/05-80722_ebook.pdf> (accessed 5 April 2021).
[5] The LGST (United Nations publication, Sales No E.09.V.12, 2010) and the LGST: Terminology and Recommendations (United Nations publication, Sales No E.09.V.13, 2009) are accompanied by (i) the UNCITRAL Legislative Guide on Secured Transactions: Supplement on Security Interests in Intellectual Property (hereinafter referred to as the 'IP Supplement'; United Nations publication, Sales No E.11.V.6, 2011); and (ii) the UNCITRAL Guide on the Implementation of a Security Rights Registry (hereinafter referred to as the 'Registry Guide'; United Nations publication, Sales No E.14.V.6, 2014). The LGST deals with the enforcement of security interests both within and outside insolvency, building on the LGIL (n 6).
[6] United Nations publication, Sales No E.05.V.10, 2005. The LGIL deals also with the enforcement of security interests in insolvency.
[7] United Nations publication, Sales No E.04.V.14, 2004, available at <http://www.uncitral.org/uncitral/en/uncitral_texts/security/2001Convention_receivables.html> (accessed 5 April 2021).
[8] This is the purpose of the joint publication of UNCITRAL, UNIDROIT, and the Hague Conference on Private International Law entitled UNCITRAL, Hague Conference, and UNIDROIT, *Texts on Security Interests* (United Nations publication, Sales No V.12-51563, 2012). This publication shows the enormous co-ordination efforts jointly undertaken by these three organizations and makes the point that, as a result, States seeking a comprehensive and coherent secured transactions regime may adopt them all. Hopefully, this publication will be updated soon to include a comparison of the more recent texts of UNCITRAL and UNIDROIT on security interests (eg, the MLST and the Cape Town Convention Protocol on Mining, Agriculture, and Construction Equipment).

V (special provisions in relation to collateral transactions) of the GSC (section C(1)); (ii) the law applicable to enforcement under the HSC (section C(2)); (iii) the enforcement of security interests in non-intermediated securities (hereinafter referred to as the 'NIS') under the MLST, the LGST, and the LGIL, outside and within insolvency, as well as enforcement and alternative dispute resolution (hereinafter referred to as 'ADR') (section C(3)); (iv) the enforcement of security in and outright transfers of receivables under the CARIT (section C(4)); (v) the application of the MLST as non-Convention law under the GSC and the necessary amendments for the MLST to apply to security and other interests in securities or a new uniform law text, in both cases building on all the above-mentioned uniform law texts (section C(5)). Section C(6) concerns the ongoing UNIDROIT project on enforcement. Section D contains the conclusions of this chapter.

B. Scope and Definitions

4.04 In order better to understand the common characteristics and the gaps of the relevant uniform law texts, it is important first to recognize the different aspects of their scope of application and definitions.

(1) The Geneva Securities Convention

4.05 The GSC is intended to regulate the holding and disposition of intermediated securities (preamble). As it is an international convention addressed to States with different legal traditions and at different levels of economic development, the GSC leaves a number of issues that do not lend themselves to unification at the international level to the law of a Contracting State other than the GSC ('non-Convention law', Article 1(m)).[9] Such non-Convention law may be secured transactions law (including law enacting the MLST and the CARIT), insolvency law (including law enacting the recommendations of the LGST and the LGIL), or conflict-of-laws law (including the HSC and the relevant conflict-of-laws provisions of the MLST).

4.06 The GSC leaves its territorial scope to non-Convention law. It applies where the law of a Contracting State is applicable by virtue of the conflict-of-laws rules of the forum State, which may or may not be a Contracting State (Article 2(a)).[10] If the forum State has

---

[9] 'In recognising the diversity of legal concepts underlying securities holding around the world, the Convention embraces a core and functional harmonization approach in order to accommodate different legal systems and traditions within a unitary framework'; see LGIS, para 65. For a discussion of some of those issues, see Deschamps, 'Selected Issues', 703.

[10] LGIS, para 75, 'applicable law'. Deschamps, 'Selected Issues', 704. Deschamps expresses the view that, while Art 2 GSC is silent on whether *renvoi* is permitted, the words contained in the definition of applicable law—'law in force in a Contracting State as the applicable law'—lead to the conclusion that *renvoi* is not permitted. This interpretation is in line with the purpose of the GSC. It would have been clearer, however, if *renvoi* had been explicitly excluded in Art 2 GSC, as is done in MLST Art 92.

enacted the MLST, the conflict-of-laws provisions of the MLST would apply but only with respect to the law applicable to security interests in cash and non-intermediated securities (MLST Articles 1(1), (2), and (3)(c)). The GSC may also apply, in purely domestic situations, if the circumstances do not lead to the application of any law other than the law of the Contracting State (Article 2(b)).[11] However, in order fully to understand the territorial scope of the GSC, it is necessary to examine the declarations that a Contracting State may make.[12]

The substantive scope of application of the GSC is not addressed in a single article but instead becomes evident through a combination of definitions and operative rules. In this regard, it should be noted that, in general, the GSC focuses on the rights and obligations of the account holder and the intermediary; thus, the GSC leaves the position of the issuer—the third key participant in an intermediated holding system—largely unaffected.[13] More concretely, the GSC applies to a wide range of securities transactions as the term 'securities' is defined very broadly to include any financial assets capable of being held in the intermediated holding system, except cash.[14] In particular, the GSC applies to third-party effectiveness, priority, and enforcement of interests in intermediated securities, resulting from title transfers and the establishment of security[15] or other interests, such as usufructus or a life interest.

4.07

What constitutes a valid credit or a valid grant of a security or other interest is left to non-Convention law (Article 16).[16] In other words, the GSC does not deal with creation issues, leaving them to non-Convention law.[17] However, Articles 11 and 12 may be read as implying that an agreement is necessary between the seller and the buyer, or between the collateral provider and the collateral taker.[18] As to the content and form of the agreement, if a Contracting State enacted the MLST without excluding intermediated securities (as long as the GSC prevails over non-Convention law), the MLST provisions on these matters could apply as non-Convention law (Articles 6–10).[19] Thus, a security or other interest in intermediated securities could be created by agreement between the grantor and the secured creditor; the agreement need be signed (electronic signature is intended to be covered)[20] only by the grantor and must be in writing (writing includes

4.08

---

[11] Kanda et al, *Official Commentary*, 2–6 to 2–11.
[12] LGIS, paras 76–7. Bernasconi and Keijser, 'The Hague and Geneva Securities Conventions', 556.
[13] LGIS, paras 71–3. Bernasconi and Keijser, 'The Hague and Geneva Securities Conventions', 557.
[14] Kanda et al, *Official Commentary*, 1–7.
[15] What qualifies as a security interest is left to other law outside the GSC. See Kanda et al, *Official Commentary*, 12–4.
[16] Under Art 8 of the US Uniform Commercial Code (UCC), which may apply as non-Convention law, acquisition occurs by a book entry indicating that a financial asset has been credited to a securities account or even, under certain circumstances, in the absence of a book entry. See Mooney and Kanda, 'Core Issues', 85.
[17] Kanda et al, *Official Commentary*, 11–10. See also Deschamps, 'Selected Issues', 707, where Deschamps expresses the view that no more than an agreement is required.
[18] Deschamps, 'Security Interest Provisions', 337 and 339, fn 10.
[19] In the US, the principal State law relating to intermediated securities consists of UCC Art 8 ('Intermediated Securities') and UCC Art 9 ('Secured Transactions'). See Mooney and Kanda, 'Core Issues', 80.
[20] For the purpose of those articles of the MLST that refer to signature (ie, Arts 6(1) and 65(1)–(2)), the enacting State is advised that it will have to consider whether to include in its enactment of the MLST an article along the lines of Recommendation 12 of the LGST, which is based on Art 9(3) of the UN Convention on Electronic Communications (Guide to Enactment, para 70).

an electronic communication; Article 2(nn)). A writing is not required if possession of certificated intermediated securities is given to the secured creditor. However, as possession is defined in the MLST as 'actual possession of a tangible asset' (Article 2(z)), it does not amount to control; thus, to create a security interest in uncertificated intermediated securities, a written security agreement is always required.

4.09 In addition, while dealing with key priority issues in several articles (for example, Articles 18 and 19), the GSC leaves other priority issues to non-Convention law (for example, the priority of non-consensual interests, which is a matter addressed in the MLST but only with respect to security interests in NIS). Moreover, the fact that Contracting States may make declarations under Article 12(5) and (7) opens the door to complex combinations of the GSC and non-Convention law. In view of the diverging approaches adopted in different legal systems, other issues left to non-Convention law are the legal characterization of intermediated securities as a personal or property right[21] and the question of whether they may even include directly-held securities in some cases.[22]

4.10 Chapter III of the GSC deals with transfers of, as well as security interests and other limited interests in, intermediated securities. The following matters dealt with in Chapter III are particularly relevant for the comparison of the GSC with the MLST and the CARIT: acquisition and disposition by book entry to the relevant securities account and other methods under the GSC, as well as under non-Convention law (Articles 11–13); effectiveness in insolvency (Article 14); acquisition by an innocent person (Article 18); priority among competing interests (Article 19); and priority of interests granted by an intermediary (Article 20).[23]

4.11 Chapter V of the GSC, which is based on the EC Financial Collateral Directive (FCD) and is subject to an opt-out by States (Article 38 GSC), contains special provisions relating to collateral transactions entered into, for example, pursuant to repurchase, securities lending, and derivatives agreements.[24] In particular, Chapter V deals with the following matters relevant to the comparison of the GSC with the MLST and the CARIT: scope and definitions (Article 31); recognition of title transfer collateral arrangements (Article 32); enforcement (Article 33); right to use collateral securities (Article 34); and requirements of non-Convention law relating to enforcement (Article 35).[25]

---

[21] Securities are assets of a particular kind, issued for circulation in a liquid market, which distinguishes them from other types of fungible asset and justifies exceptions to property law. See Micheler, 'The Legal Nature of Securities', 148.
[22] Deschamps, 'Selected Issues', 706.
[23] For a detailed discussion of Ch III of the GSC, see Kanda et al, *Official Commentary*, commentary on Ch III.
[24] For a detailed discussion of Ch V of the GSC, see Kanda et al, *Official Commentary*, commentary on Ch V.
[25] For a schematic comparison of the GSC, the CARIT, and the LGST, see UNCITRAL, Hague Conference, and UNIDROIT, *Texts on Security Interests* (n 8). Of course, if UNIDROIT prepares a model law on factoring, as it has decided, the basic premise of this joint publication can no longer apply. A State may not enact a functional and comprehensive law like the MLST and then undermine the comprehensive nature of that law with one or more stand-alone laws on factoring or any other financing practice.

SCOPE AND DEFINITIONS   97

In addition, the GSC refers several matters to the law applicable by virtue of the conflict-of-laws rules of the forum State ('applicable law'). Moreover, the GSC recognizes the uniform rules of securities clearing systems (SCSs) and securities settlement systems (SSSs), which may derogate from or supplement the rules of the GSC (Article 1(n)–(p)).[26]   **4.12**

(2) The Hague Securities Convention

The HSC[27] applies to a range of issues in respect of securities held with an intermediary, including the legal nature and effects of a disposition of an interest in intermediated securities against the intermediary and third parties, the requirements for the perfection of a disposition, as well as the priority and the enforcement of an interest in intermediated securities (Article 2(f)). For the HSC to apply, there must be a choice between the laws of different States, that is, an element of internationality (Article 3).   **4.13**

The term 'securities' means any shares, bonds, or other financial instruments or financial assets (other than cash), or any interest therein (Article 1(a)). The term 'securities held with an intermediary' means the rights of an account holder resulting from a credit of securities to a securities account (Article 1(f)). The term 'disposition' means any transfer of title, whether outright or by way of security, and any grant of a security interest, whether possessory or non-possessory (Article 1(h)). The term 'securities account' means an account maintained by an intermediary to which securities may be credited or debited (Article 1(b)). The term 'intermediary' means a person that in the course of a business or other regular activity maintains securities accounts for others or both for others and for its own account and is acting in that capacity (Article 1(c)).   **4.14**

(3) The Secured Transactions Model Law

To simplify secured transactions law and to avoid the fragmentation that would result from having each asset or practice governed by a separate law and that typically leads to gaps and inconsistencies, the MLST takes a unitary, functional, and comprehensive approach.[28] Thus, it applies to security interests in any type of movable asset (Article   **4.15**

---

[26] For a discussion of the different sources of law outside the GSC referred to in the GSC, see UNIDROIT 2010–S78B/CEM/1/Doc 3 ('Accession Kit'), 94–100 and LGIS, paras 75–9.
[27] The HSC is available on the Hague Conference website under <https://assets.hcch.net/docs/3afb8418-7eb7-4a0c-af85-c4f35995bb8a.pdf> (accessed 5 April 2021). The HSC is accompanied by an Explanatory Report on the 2006 HCCH Securities Convention, written by Roy Goode, Hideki Kanda, Karl Kreuzer with the assistance of Christophe Bernasconi (available under <https://assets.hcch.net/docs/d1513ec4-0c72-483b-8706-85d2719c11c5.pdf>, accessed 7 July 2021).
[28] Guide to Enactment, para 17. Legislation based on or influenced by the Model Law has been adopted in eight States (Australia, Colombia, Fiji, New Zealand, Nigeria, Papua New Guinea, Philippines, and Zimbabwe); see <https://uncitral.un.org/en/texts/securityinterests/modellaw/secured_transactions/status> (accessed 5 April 2021). The Model Law is also being considered for adoption by a number of other States (eg, Bahrain, Paraguay, St Lucia, and Trinidad and Tobago).

1(1)), with limited exceptions, such as intermediated securities and payment rights arising from or under financial contracts governed by netting agreements (Article 1(3)(c)–(d)). In addition, the MLST uses a generic concept of 'security interest' rather than various different terms (eg, pledge, mortgage, transfer for security purposes, assignment of receivables).[29] Moreover, the term 'security interest' is defined in functional terms by reference to a property right which is created by an agreement[30] to secure payment or other performance of an obligation, regardless of whether the parties have identified it as a security interest, of the type of asset, of the status of the grantor or secured creditor,[31] or of the nature of the secured obligation (Article 2(kk)(i)).[32] As a result, the MLST applies also to transfers of title for security purposes, retention-of-title sales and financial leases, whether the grantor is an incorporated or unincorporated business or a consumer (the latter subject to consumer protection legislation; Article 2(5)).

4.16 Unlike the GSC and the HSC, the MLST does not apply to intermediated securities, but does apply to security interests in, albeit not to outright transfers of, NIS (Articles 1(1) and 1(3)(c)). The reason for the coverage of NIS in the MLST is twofold. First, NIS are typically part of commercial finance transactions (not of capital market transactions). Secondly, unlike intermediated securities which are regulated in the GSC and the HSC, there is no uniform law that covers security interests in NIS.[33] Thus, the MLST may not apply as non-Convention law to security and other interests in intermediated securities or to outright transfers of NIS, unless it is properly amended (see section C(5)). However, both the MLST and the CARIT apply to a receivable arising from or under a financial contract governed by a netting agreement arising upon the termination of all outstanding transactions (MLST Article 1(3)(d) and CARIT Article 4(2)(b)). Still, there cannot be any overlap between the GSC, on the one hand, and the domestic law of a State that has enacted the provisions of the MLST or the CARIT, on the other hand.

4.17 In addition, unlike the GSC and the HSC, the MLST applies to cash in the form of money as a tangible asset (eg, Articles 1(1), 2(t), (u), and (ll), 6(1), and 48); the MLST applies also to rights to the payment of funds credited to a bank account (eg, Articles 1(1), 6(1), 18(1), 25, 47, 82, and 97), both as originally encumbered assets and as proceeds (eg, Articles 1(1), 10(1), 19(1), 32, and 89). The CARIT applies to cash in the form of money only as proceeds of receivables (Articles 14 and 24) and does not apply to

---

[29] The term 'security right' is used in the MLST as it is easier to translate to the other five official languages of the UN, that is, Arabic, Chinese, French, Spanish, and Russian (Art 2(uu)). For ease of reference, however, this chapter uses the term 'security interest'.
[30] But priority conflicts with statutory preferential rights are also addressed (Arts 35 and 36).
[31] As a legal or a natural person, including a consumer, subject to consumer protection legislation (Art 1(5)).
[32] See also LGST Recommendation 2. For a discussion of the salient features of the LGST, see Bazinas, 'UNCITRAL Legislative Guide on Secured Transactions'.
[33] Guide to Enactment, para 26. For a discussion of the interaction of the rules of the draft Model Law on security interests in NIS with those of the EU Financial Collateral Directive (FCD), see Keijser, 'A European View on the Draft UNCITRAL Model Law'.

bank accounts (Article 4(2)(f)). Thus, if a Contracting State of the GSC were to enact the MLST and the CARIT, their provisions with regard to security interests in cash would apply as non-Convention law and fill this gap in the GSC. Similarly, the provisions of the MLST could apply as non-Convention law, provided that receivables arising under or from intermediated securities and financial contracts were not excluded from the scope of the MLST (Article 1(3)(c)–(d)) and appropriate amendments were made to the MLST (see section C(5)).[34]

4.18 The MLST also applies to all types of receivables finance transaction, including those involving an outright transfer of receivables by agreement (eg, factoring and securitization), without re-characterizing them as secured transactions (Articles 1(2) and 2(kk)(ii)).[35] The rationale of this approach is the need to ensure that the same third-party effectiveness and priority rules apply to all types of receivables finance transactions, in particular as it may be extremely difficult for third parties to know whether a prior receivables finance transaction involves a secured transaction or an outright transfer of receivables by agreement. However, the enforcement chapter of the MLST does not apply to the collection or other enforcement of receivables that are the subject of an outright transfer by agreement. In this respect, it should be noted that, unlike the CARIT, which applies only to contractual receivables, the MLST covers any right to payment of a monetary obligation, including non-contractual receivables (Article 2(dd)).

4.19 The MLST is intended to be enacted into domestic law that would apply if the law of the enacting State is the law applicable to a security interest by virtue of the conflict-of-laws rules of the forum State. If the forum State has enacted the conflict-of-laws rules of the MLST,[36] they would apply. If the State whose law is applicable has enacted the provisions of the MLST (without excluding intermediated securities and having made the necessary amendments), the MLST will be part of the non-Convention law under the GSC.

4.20 The MLST is accompanied by the Guide to Enactment and the Practice Guide. The Guide to Enactment briefly explains the thrust of each provision of the MLST and its relationship with the other UNCITRAL texts on security interests, that is, the LGST, the IP Supplement, and the Registry Guide. The Practice Guide is intended to provide practical guidance to parties involved in secured transactions in States that enact the MLST.[37] Taken together, these texts, supplemented by the LGIL with respect to the treatment of security and other interests in insolvency, provide comprehensive guidance to States with respect to legal and practical issues that need to be addressed in a modern secured transactions and insolvency regime.[38]

---

[34] MLST Art 2(dd).
[35] See also LGST Recommendation 3 and Ch I, paras 25–31.
[36] Bazinas, 'Harmonization of Conflict-of-laws', 1–15.
[37] Practice Guide, para 1.
[38] Guide to Enactment, paras 1–4.

(4) The Secured Transactions and Insolvency Law Legislative Guides

4.21 The LGST deals with all issues to be addressed in a modern and efficient law on secured transactions, including their creation, third-party effectiveness, the registry system, priority, rights and obligations of the parties and third-party obligors and enforcement of a security interest within and outside insolvency, acquisition finance, the law applicable to a security interest and transition. The LGST does so by discussing all the relevant issues and the approaches followed in modern and efficient secured transactions legislation. The discussion of each issue concludes with a recommendation to the legislator with options on a number of issues. The MLST implements the recommendations of the LGST, offering some options but not as many as the LGST. As the MLST has already been discussed above, this part of this chapter is limited to an issue that is not addressed in the MLST at all: the enforcement of a security interest in the case of the grantor's insolvency. The LGST addresses this issue in line with the recommendations of the LGIL.

4.22 It should be noted that, on the one hand, the LGST does not address some of the issues contemplated by the MLST (eg, security interests in NIS; Article 1(3)(c)), and, on the other hand, does tackle various matters not addressed in the MLST (eg, security interests in rights to receive the proceeds under an independent undertaking; Article 1(3)(a)) or not addressed specifically (eg, security interests in attachments to encumbered movable assets, which are addressed by way of the general rules), or at all (eg, security interests in attachments to immovable property).[39] States in which rights to receive the proceeds under an independent undertaking may be used as security for credit could enact the relevant recommendations of the LGST.[40]

4.23 The LGIL is intended to provide guidance to legislators with respect to insolvency law, with an emphasis on reorganization. The first part of each chapter contains commentary identifying key issues and possible approaches; the second part of each chapter offers recommendations to the legislator. With respect to cross-border insolvency issues, the LGIL includes the text and the Guide to Enactment of the UNCITRAL Model Law on Cross-Border Insolvency.[41]

4.24 The LGIL uses its own neutral terminology. For example: (i) the term 'insolvency estate' means 'assets of the debtor that are subject to insolvency proceedings'; (ii) the term 'insolvency proceedings' means 'collective proceedings, subject to court supervision, either for reorganization or liquidation'; (iii) the term 'insolvency representative' means 'a person or body, including one appointed on an interim basis, authorized in insolvency proceedings to administer the reorganization or the liquidation of the insolvency

---

[39] Ibid, paras 32–4.
[40] Ibid, para 24.
[41] LGIL, paras 1–3. The Model Law has been adopted in 49 States in a total of 52 jurisdictions; see <https://uncitral.un.org/en/texts/insolvency/modellaw/cross-border_insolvency/status> (accessed 5 April 2021).

estate'; (iv) the term 'netting' means the setting-off of monetary and non-monetary obligations under financial contracts; (v) the term 'netting agreement' means a form of financial contract between two or more parties

> that provides for one or more of the following: (i) The net settlement of payments due in the same currency on the same date whether by novation or otherwise; (ii) Upon the insolvency or other default by a party, the termination of all outstanding transactions at their replacement or fair market values, conversion of such sums into a single currency and netting into a single payment by one party to the other; or (iii) The set-off of amounts calculated as set forth in [subparagraph (ii) of this definition] under two or more netting agreements[42]

and (vi) the term 'security interest' means 'a right in an asset to secure payment or other performance of one or more obligations'.

4.25 The LGIL deals also with the treatment of secured creditors in insolvency proceedings (eg, exceptions to the *lex fori concursus*, treatment of assets subject to a security interest upon commencement of an insolvency proceeding, use and disposal of encumbered assets, treatment of cash proceeds, post-commencement finance, and priorities) and, for the ease of the reader, contains an annex that includes references to the relevant commentary and recommendations.

(5) The Receivables Convention

4.26 The CARIT applies to assignments of international receivables (assignor and debtor located in different States) and to international assignments of receivables (assignor and assignee located in different States), if the assignor is located in a Contracting State at the time the contract of assignment is concluded (Article 1(1)(a)).[43] It also applies to domestic assignments of domestic receivables, if: (i) they are part of a chain of assignments, one of which is an assignment to which the CARIT applies, so that the same law applies to all assignments in a chain of assignments (Article 1(1)(b)); and (ii) they are in competition with an assignment to which the CARIT applies so that all priority competitions are covered by the CARIT (Article 5(m)(i)).

4.27 The CARIT does not, however, affect the rights and obligations of the debtor of the receivable unless, at the time of the original contract from which the assigned receivables arise, the debtor is located in a Contracting State (Article 1(3)). Debtor issues are clearly distinguished in the CARIT from third-party effectiveness and priority issues. The reason is that, once the receivable has been assigned to another party, the debtor of the receivable

---

[42] Cf CARIT, Art 5(l). The CARIT has been ratified by two States (Liberia and the United States of America). Although there is no study on the matter, empirical information suggests that it has influenced national assignment law adopted all over the world in the past 20 years. It has certainly influenced the MLST.

[43] For a brief discussion of the CARIT, see Bazinas, Kohn, and Del Duca, 'Uniform Receivables Financing Law', 277–316.

needs to have a clear way to discharge its debt; it cannot be expected to determine which assignment has been made effective and has priority as against third-party competing claimants. Under the CARIT, the debtor of the receivable is discharged if, before notification, it makes payment according to the contract giving rise to the receivables and, after notification, it makes payment as instructed in the notification (Article 17(1)–(2)). The CARIT contains a complete set of rules to address multiple notifications (Article 17(2)–(7)) and does not affect national law rules under which the debtor may discharge its obligation by paying to a judicial or other authority or to a public deposit fund (Article 17(8)).

4.28 The CARIT defines 'assignment' as a transfer (without drawing a distinction between outright transfers and fiduciary transfers), but adds that the creation of a security interest in a receivable is also deemed to be a transfer (Article 2(a)). As a result, the same rules apply to outright transfers, transfers by way of security, and security interests in receivables. The rationale underlying this approach is the same as that of the MLST for its own approach. Receivables finance transactions take the form of a transfer (outright or fiduciary) or a security interest in a receivable. If different rules were to apply to these types of transaction, third parties would need to check the underlying transaction to ascertain whether an outright transfer or a secured transaction was involved, a process that would be both time-consuming and costly if several receivables were involved and impossible at the time of transaction in the case of future receivables. More importantly, no rules would provide a sufficient degree of certainty unless they addressed all priority conflicts, including a priority conflict between an outright transferee of a receivable and a creditor with a security interest in that receivable.

4.29 The CARIT does not apply to transactions on a regulated exchange, financial contracts governed by netting agreements, foreign exchange transactions, and transactions for the transfer of security interests in, sale or loan of, or agreement to repurchase securities or other financial assets or instruments held with an intermediary (Article 4(2)(a)–(e)). As already mentioned, the reasons are that securities transactions are capital market transactions, not receivables finance transactions, and they are covered in the GSC and the HSC. The term 'financial contract' is defined to mean 'any spot, forward, future, option or swap transaction involving interest rates, commodities, currencies, equities, bonds, indices or any other financial instrument, any repurchase or securities lending transaction, and any other transaction similar to any transaction referred to above entered into in financial markets and any combination of the transactions mentioned above'. The term 'netting agreement' is defined in equally broad terms (Article 5(l); see paragraph 4.24(v)).

4.30 The CARIT also contains both substantive law and conflict-of-laws rules. The main reason for this approach is that, while States were able to reach agreement on a substantive law approach to a range of matters (for example, effectiveness of bulk assignments, assignments of future receivables, and assignments made despite an anti-assignment agreement, and rights and obligations of the debtor of the receivable), they failed to agree on a substantive law third-party effectiveness and priority rule. Thus, a conflict-of-laws third-party effectiveness and priority rule was generally considered to be the second-best solution. This rule is intended to eliminate the uncertainty as to the law applicable to the third-party effectiveness and priority of assignments of receivables currently prevailing in many States. As a result of this uncertainty, assignees in international receivables finance transactions are left to guess the State in which a conflict of priority may arise and make their assignments effective against third parties in those jurisdictions. This is a process that may take time and entail significant costs, a problem that could be addressed by a uniform conflict-of-laws rule along the lines of the rule in the CARIT. The conflict-of-laws third-party effectiveness and priority rule of the CARIT is supplemented by an optional annex with alternative substantive law rules from which States may choose (based on the time of the assignment, the time of debtor notification, or the time of notice registration). It is also supplemented by a set of optional conflict-of-laws rules (a mini conflict-of-laws convention within a substantive law convention) that deal with the law applicable to other aspects of an assignment (Articles 26–32).[44]

4.31 With respect to receivables, the provisions of the MLST are substantially based on the recommendations of the LGST, which in turn are based on the provisions of the CARIT. A State that ratifies or accedes to the CARIT but does not yet have an efficient and modern secured transactions law will need to enact the MLST as well, mainly because the CARIT does not provide substantive rules on third-party effectiveness and priority but instead refers these matters to the applicable domestic law, that is, the law of the assignor's location (Article 22). Conversely, a State enacting the MLST would be well advised to ratify or accede to the CARIT as well, in order to promote effective international receivables finance, the more so as a convention provides a higher level of uniformity and transparency than a model law. For example, if the States where the assignor, the assignee, and the debtors of the receivables are located all ratify or accede to the CARIT, lenders are likely to be more willing to extend receivables finance to exporters and at more affordable cost, because they will understand the legal rules that apply to the receivables owed to the exporters and thus will be more confident that they will be able to collect them.[45]

(6) Differences in scope and terminology

4.32 The GSC and the HSC apply to security and other interests (eg, title transfers) in intermediated securities. They do not apply to interests in cash or funds credited to a bank account. The MLST and the LGST apply to security interests in movable assets (including cash and funds credited to a bank account) and outright transfers of receivables by agreement. They do not apply to security or other interests in intermediated

---

[44] For a comparison of the conflict-of-laws rules of the CARIT with the relevant rules in the US and Canada, see Deschamps, 'Conflict-of-laws Rules on Assignments of Receivables'.
[45] Guide to Enactment, paras 11–15.

securities. The MLST applies to security interests in, but not to outright transfers of, NIS or any asset other than receivables, which are defined broadly to include a right to payment of a monetary obligation but exclude a right to payment evidenced by a negotiable instrument, a right to payment of funds credited to a bank account, and a right to payment under a non-intermediated security (Article 2(dd)). This is because, with respect to these types of receivables, the MLST contains asset-specific rules on several matters, such as third-party effectiveness, priority, and enforcement.

4.33 In all these uniform law texts, the terminology used is neutral, in the sense that it is not derived from any specific jurisdiction.[46] Even when a term appears to be the same as that used in a particular legal system, that term may be given a different meaning.[47] For example, the MLST refers to the creation and third-party effectiveness of a security interest, not to the attachment and perfection of a security interest (Articles 6 and 18), to encumbered assets, not to collateral (Article 2(k)), and to acquisition security interests, not to purchase money security interests (Article 2(b)).

4.34 Both the GSC and the HSC define 'securities held by an intermediary' by reference to any financial assets capable of being credited in a securities account (GSC Article 1(a)–(b) and HSC Article 1(a) and (f)). The MLST contains a broad neutral definition of the term 'securities' referring also to national securities law (Article 2(hh)). Following the definition of the term 'securities held with an intermediary' in the GSC and the HSC, the MLST defines NIS as 'securities other than securities credited to a securities account and rights in securities resulting from the credit of securities to a securities account' (Article 2(w)). Both the MLST and the CARIT define and exclude receivables arising under or from 'financial contract' in a very broad manner to include, *inter alia*, 'any spot, forward, future, option or swap transaction involving... or any other financial instrument, any repurchase or securities lending transaction, and any transaction referred to above entered into in financial markets...' (MLST Article 2(m) and CARIT Article 5(k)). They also define 'netting agreement' (MLST Article 2(v) and CARIT Article 5(l)), because financial contracts are excluded only if covered by a netting agreement (MLST Article 2(3)(d) and CARIT Article 4(2)(a)). The definition of 'netting agreement' is so broad as to include the net settlement of payments due, close-out netting (which is defined more generally than in Article 31(3)(j) GSC), and the set-off of amounts due upon default under two or more netting agreements.

4.35 Chapter III GSC refers to acquisition of a full interest (title) and to acquisition of a security or other limited interest. In Chapter V GSC, 'collateral agreement' is defined by reference to security collateral agreements and title transfer collateral agreements (Article 31(3)(a)–(c)). No distinction is drawn between outright transfers and transfers for security purposes, however. While title transactions are distinguished from secured transactions, the basic rules of the GSC are the same for both title transactions and

---

[46] Bernasconi and Keijser, 'The Hague and Geneva Securities Conventions', 556.
[47] Introduction to the LGST, para 15.

secured transactions (which may not be the case where non-Convention law applies) and, most importantly, the notion of 'security interest' is not defined and hence left to non-Convention law. Where a State enacted the provisions of the MLST without excluding securities (provided the GSC prevailed over non-Convention law), the notion of 'security interest' ('security right')[48] in the MLST could apply as a notion of non-Convention law and fill this gap in the GSC. In this regard, as already noted, the functional approach adopted by the MLST means that it covers pledges (whether possessory or non-possessory), as well as transfers of title for security purposes, retention-of-title sales and financial leases, and outright transfers of receivables by agreement (but not outright transfers of any other type of asset).

4.36 The 'collateral provider' in the GSC (Article 31(g)) is the 'grantor' in the MLST (Article 2(o)), which includes a transferor in an outright transfer of receivables by agreement,[49] and the 'assignor' in the CARIT (Article 2(a), which includes an assignor in an outright or security transfer of receivables and in a security agreement relating to receivables). The 'collateral taker' in the GSC (Article 31(f)) is the 'secured creditor' in the MLST, which includes a transferee in an outright transfer of receivables by agreement (Article 2(ff)),[50] and the 'assignee' in the CARIT (Article 2(a), which includes an assignee in an outright or security transfer of receivables and in a security agreement relating to receivables). The 'collateral' consists of 'intermediated securities' in the GSC, and tangible or intangible 'encumbered assets', including contractual and non-contractual receivables, and NIS in the MLST (Article 2(k) and (dd)) and contractual 'receivables' in the CARIT (Article 2(a), subject to the exclusions and limitations in Article 4). It should be noted, however, that the term 'receivable' in the MLST does not include a right to payment evidenced by a negotiable instrument, a right to payment of funds credited to a bank account, and a right to payment under an NIS. This means that the provisions of the MLST that apply to receivables do not apply to these types of asset (which are addressed by different asset-specific rules in the MLST).[51]

4.37 The 'relevant obligation' in the GSC is the 'secured obligation' in the MLST, in which the singular includes the plural, and vice versa (Article 2(gg)).[52] However, the provisions of the MLST that refer to a secured obligation do not apply to an outright transfer of receivables by agreement.[53] As it treats all assignments of receivables as transfers (but only for the application of its rules), the CARIT makes no reference to a secured obligation.

4.38 The GSC refers to an 'enforcement event' as a condition of enforcement, in the sense of an event of default or other similar event which, under the collateral agreement, allows the collateral taker to realize the collateral securities or proceed with close-out netting

---

[48] Supra n 29.
[49] Introduction to the LGST, s B, 'Terminology and interpretation'.
[50] Ibid.
[51] LGST, Terminology and Recommendation 2, subject to the exceptions in Recommendation 4.
[52] Introduction to the LGST, s B, 'Terminology and interpretation', para 17.
[53] Guide to Enactment, para 64.

(Article 31(h)). The MLST refers to the enforcement of a security interest in the case of default (and with respect to receivables and some other types of asset, even before default with the agreement of the grantor). In principle, 'enforcement' means the repossession of certificated NIS, their sale or other disposition, the use of the proceeds to satisfy the secured obligation, the acquisition of the NIS in total or partial satisfaction of the secured obligation (Articles 77–80), and the collection from the issuer of uncertificated NIS (Article 81). In addition, while the MLST does define 'default', it leaves the exact determination of its meaning to the parties to the security agreement and the law governing that agreement (Article 2(j)). The CARIT refers to the payment of the assigned receivable. As between the assignor and the assignee and unless otherwise agreed, the assignee may retain the proceeds of payment if the debtor pays the assignee and claim them if the debtor pays the assignor or a third party, albeit only if the assignee has priority over that party, which is a matter left to the law of the assignor's location (Article 14).

4.39 Both the GSC and the MLST (for the purposes of security interests in bank deposits and NIS which, however, are excluded from the scope of application of the CARIT: Article 4(2)(f)–(g)) define the term 'control agreement', although the definitions differ slightly. 'Control agreement' under the GSC means an agreement in respect of intermediated securities: (i) between an account holder, the relevant intermediary, and another person; (ii) between the account holder and the relevant intermediary; or (iii) between the account holder and another person from whom the intermediary receives notice. Such an agreement must include one or both of the following provisions: (i) the relevant intermediary may not follow the instructions of the account holder without the consent of that other person; (ii) the relevant intermediary must follow the instructions of that other person without the further consent of the account holder (Article 1(k)). The related term 'designating entry' in Article 1(l) GSC has no equivalent either in the CARIT or in the MLST.[54]

4.40 Under the MLST, 'control agreement' means an agreement between a depositary bank or the issuer of uncertificated NIS, a grantor, and a secured creditor, evidenced by a signed writing, according to which the depositary bank or the issuer agrees to follow the instructions of the secured creditor with respect to the right to receive payment of funds credited to a bank account or with respect to NIS without the further consent of the grantor.[55] So, while the essence of the 'control agreement' is the same in the GSC (Article 1(k)) and MLST (Article 2(g)), in the MLST: (i) it refers to rights to payment of funds credited to a bank account and to uncertificated NIS; (ii) while it is a tripartite agreement, it involves different parties (that is, the depositary bank or the issuer, the grantor, and the secured creditor); and (iii) there is no choice and the depositary

---

[54] While the terms 'designating entry' and 'control agreement' share a number of common characteristics, they differ in one important respect: a designating entry is a book entry. See Kanda et al, *Official Commentary*, 12–29.
[55] Introduction to the LGST, s B, 'Terminology and interpretation'.

bank or the issuer must follow the instructions of the secured creditor without the further consent of the account holder.

4.41 The GSC uses the term 'priority' generically, without defining it. The concept is not used in the case of a transfer, where instead the issue is whether the transferee acquires the securities free of or subject to a security or other interest (based on the *droit de suite* accompanying a security interest or the *nemo dat* principle). In addition, the GSC does not use the term 'competing claimant' but refers to 'competing interests'; and priority or quasi-priority issues arising in the context of a transfer are dealt with in a way that is not necessarily easy to understand (for example, under the heading of 'innocent acquisition').

4.42 The MLST defines these terms somewhat differently. 'Priority' is defined by reference to the right of a person in an encumbered asset in preference to the right of a competing claimant (Article 2(aa)); 'competing claimant' is defined by reference to another secured creditor with a security interest in the same encumbered asset (including a retention-of-title seller or financial lessor), another creditor of the grantor with an interest other than a security interest in the same encumbered asset, the administrator in the insolvency of the grantor, and a buyer, lessee, or licensee of the encumbered asset (Article 2(e)).[56] Thus, while reference is always made to priority conflict among *rights* of competing claimants, this broad definition of 'competing claimant' covers all possible priority conflicts.

4.43 The CARIT defines 'priority' as the right of a person in preference to the right of another person and, to the extent relevant, includes the determination of whether the right is a personal or property right, whether it is a security interest, and whether any steps must be taken to render that right effective against third parties (Article 5(g)). This is a complex method (in particular, as priority includes third-party effectiveness), but it is arguably justified by the convenience of reference. The CARIT also defines 'competing claimant' as another assignee of the same receivable from the same assignor, a person acquiring a right in the assigned receivable by operation of law, another creditor of the assignor, or the administrator in the assignor's insolvency (Article 5(m)).

C. Enforcement

(1) Enforcement under the Geneva Securities Convention

4.44 The GSC contains a set of provisions in an optional Chapter V on the enforcement of collateral (title or security) transactions. If a State opts into Chapter V, where an enforcement event occurs, the collateral taker may enforce its interest in the securities by one of the following three methods. First, where the securities are given under a

---

[56] Ibid.

security agreement, the collateral taker may, subject to the terms of the security collateral agreement, sell them and apply the net proceeds towards the discharge of the relevant obligations. Secondly, if the collateral agreement foresees and regulates this method of enforcement, it may retain the securities in satisfaction of the relevant obligations. Thirdly, where an enforcement event occurs and obligations remain outstanding, the collateral taker may exercise its rights under a close-out netting provision (Article 33(1)–(2)).[57]

4.45 Unless otherwise agreed by the parties in the collateral agreement, such enforcement action may be taken without prior notice, approval of the terms of enforcement by a court or other authority, or a public auction. In addition, such enforcement action cannot be stayed in the case of insolvency proceedings with respect to the collateral provider or the collateral taker (Article 33(3); with respect to a regulatory stay, see Chapter 2, section C(5)).[58]

4.46 As the GSC recognizes a title transfer agreement in accordance with its terms (Article 32), a transferee may exercise its rights as an owner and retain any surplus left after satisfaction of the relevant obligation.[59]

4.47 The GSC does not affect any requirement of non-Convention law that enforcement must be conducted in a commercially reasonable manner (Article 35). Such a requirement would exist where non-Convention law includes rules enacting the provisions of the MLST, as the MLST subjects the exercise of any right and the performance of any obligation under the MLST to the standards of good faith and commercial reasonableness (Article 4).[60]

4.48 As a rule, a collateral taker under a security agreement may sell or encumber the securities in which it has an interest only after default of the collateral provider (which remains the owner and thus retains a right to sell or encumber the assets). If an enforcement event occurs after disposition and before replacement of the collateral securities, the collateral taker's obligation to provide replacement securities and the relevant (secured) obligation may be the subject of close-out netting.[61]

4.49 However, if so agreed in the security collateral agreement, the collateral taker may, even prior to default and enforcement, sell or encumber the securities as if it were the owner (or beneficial owner) but has an obligation to replace any securities thus disposed of. The replacement securities will be subject to an interest in the same way as the original collateral securities and in all other respects will be subject to the terms of the relevant security collateral agreement (Article 34). The purpose of this provision is to 'enhance market liquidity and promote secured finance' in the sense that a collateral provider

---

[57] Kanda et al, *Official Commentary*, 33–1.
[58] Ibid, 33–3.
[59] Ibid, *Official Commentary*, 33–17 and 33–18. See also Deschamps, 'Security Interest Provisions', 344.
[60] LGST Recommendation 131. See also Franciosi, 'Commercial Reasonableness', 483–95; Graziadei, 'Many Faces of Reasonableness', 497–506.
[61] Kanda et al, *Official Commentary*, 34–15.

may need to dispose of the collateral securities. This approach raises no problems as long as the collateral provider has agreed to it and the collateral securities are replaced.[62]

(2) The law applicable to enforcement under the Hague Securities Convention

The HSC refers the matters to which it applies, including the enforcement ('realisation') of a security or other interest in intermediated securities, primarily to the law of the State expressly agreed in the account agreement as the State whose law governs the account agreement or, if the account agreement expressly provides that another law is applicable to all such issues, to that other law (Article 4(1)). This law applies only if the relevant intermediary has, at the time of the agreement, an office in that State which meets certain conditions, such as whether it effects or monitors entries to securities accounts, administers payments or corporate actions relating to securities held with the intermediary, or is otherwise engaged in a business or other regular activity of maintaining securities accounts (Article 4(1)(a)). 4.50

Article 5 of the HSC also contains a number of fall-back rules that apply if the applicable law is not determined in accordance with the primary rule. For example, when it is expressly and unambiguously stated in a written account agreement that the relevant intermediary entered into the account agreement through a particular office, under the first fall-back rule, the law applicable to all the issues to which the HSC applies is the law in force in the State in which that office was then located, provided that such office satisfies the conditions mentioned above (Article 4(1)).[63] 4.51

(3) Enforcement under the Secured Transactions Model Law and the Secured Transactions and Insolvency Guides

(a) Enforcement outside insolvency
With a view to facilitating efficient enforcement of security interests, which is one of the key objectives of an efficient secured transaction law (LGST Recommendation 1(h)),[64] the MLST deals with the enforcement of a security interest in some detail. The underlying policy of the MLST is to minimize the time, cost and difficulty involved in enforcing a security interest so as to avoid a negative effect on the availability and cost of credit. The enforcement regime of the MLST is summarized in the following paragraphs. 4.52

---

[62] Ibid, 34–1 and 34–12 to 32–14. See, however, Ch 2 for problems caused by under-and overcollateralization and by non-replacement of securities. For top-up collateral agreements, see Art 36(1) GSC.
[63] See further Ch 11.
[64] The key objectives of the LGST are also the key objectives of the MLST (Guide to Enactment, para 16).

110 ENFORCEMENT OF SECURITY INTERESTS

4.53 The general enforcement provisions of the MLST (Articles 72–81) also apply to the enforcement of a security interest in NIS, as supplemented by a provision dealing with the right of a secured creditor to collect 'liquid' encumbered assets such as receivables, negotiable instruments, funds credited to a bank account, and NIS from the debtor of the receivables, the obligor under the negotiable instrument, the deposit-taking institution, or the issuer of the NIS (Article 82).

4.54 Generally, the secured creditor may enforce its security interest in the encumbered asset only upon default of the debtor in performing the secured obligation. 'Default' is generally defined by reference to the failure of the debtor to pay or otherwise perform the secured obligation and to the terms of the security agreement (Article 2(j)). Thus, in the case of default, the secured creditor may: (i) obtain possession, sell or otherwise dispose of the encumbered assets and use the sales proceeds to satisfy the secured obligation (Articles 77–79); (ii) propose to acquire the encumbered assets in full or partial satisfaction of the secured obligation (Article 80); (iii) collect from the issuer of the encumbered NIS (Article 82(1)); or (iv) exercise any right under the security agreement or the law (Article 72(1)). The grantor may: (i) apply to a court for relief (Article 74); (ii) pay the secured obligation in full and obtain a release (Article 75); (iii) propose to the secured creditor to acquire the encumbered assets in full or partial satisfaction of the secured obligation (Article 80(6)); or (iv) exercise any right under the security agreement or the law (Article 72(1)).

4.55 Enforcement may take place in court, including through summary proceedings (Article 73(1)). Judicial enforcement is governed by the enforcement provisions of the MLST and the civil procedure rules of the enacting State (Article 73(2)). Thus, the secured creditor may obtain possession of encumbered certificated NIS, sell or otherwise dispose of them in a public auction and distribute the proceeds of the sale by order of a court or other authority in accordance with the MLST and the general judicial enforcement provisions of the relevant jurisdiction. However, distribution of the sales proceeds must also be in accordance with the provisions of the MLST on priority (Articles 77(1), 78(2), and 79(1)).

4.56 In addition, if a person acquires encumbered NIS in a court-supervised or ordered public auction, whether the buyer or other transferee acquires them free of any rights or not is left to the relevant law of the jurisdiction enacting the MLST (Article 81(1)). However, as already noted, the requirement that the distribution of the proceeds of a judicial sale or other disposition be made in accordance with the priority rules of the MLST means that all secured creditors are entitled to share in the proceeds according to their order of priority (Article 79(1)). As a result, an enacting State should specify that a buyer or other transferee acquires the encumbered asset free of any security interests, including security interests ranking higher in priority to that of the enforcing secured creditor.[65]

---

[65] Guide to Enactment, para 460.

Extra-judicial enforcement is also possible and is regulated in detail in the MLST (Article 73(3)). Thus, to obtain possession of encumbered certificated NIS out of court, a secured creditor must have ensured that adequate provision for this option is made in the security agreement, that the grantor and any person in possession of the NIS is duly notified, and that, at the time of repossession, the person in possession does not object (Article 77(2)). The rationale underlying these rules is the need to ensure the protection of the grantor and all parties in possession of the encumbered NIS and to avoid disturbance of public order, while no party is deprived of their constitutionally protected access to the courts.[66] To forestall loss of value, notice need not be given if the encumbered NIS is likely to decline in value rapidly (Article 77(3)). In addition, if a higher-ranking secured creditor is in possession, a lower-ranking secured creditor is not entitled to obtain possession of the encumbered NIS (Article 77(4)). The main reason for this provision is the need to ensure that the lower-ranking secured creditor cannot interfere with the exercise of the enforcement rights of the higher-ranking secured creditor,[67] while not unduly interfering with the enforcement rights of the lower-ranking secured creditor. In any case, the lower-ranking secured creditor may exercise its right to dispose of the encumbered asset without obtaining possession, for example, by selling it extrajudicially.[68]

4.57

Out-of-court collection from the issuer is not subject to these conditions (Article 82(1)). However, as against the issuer of encumbered NIS, this right of collection is subject to the rights and obligations of the issuer under the relevant securities law (Article 71).[69]

4.58

In the case of an out-of-court sale or other disposition of encumbered NIS, the enforcing secured creditor must notify the grantor, the debtor (if different from the grantor), any person with a right in the encumbered NIS who notifies the secured creditor in writing, any other secured creditor who registered a notice in the security interest registry, and any other secured creditor who was in possession at the time of repossession of the securities by the enforcing secured creditor (Article 78(4)). The notice must be given at least several days (eg, 10–15 days) before the out-of-court disposition of the encumbered NIS and must include a description of the encumbered securities, a statement of the outstanding amount of the secured obligation, including interest and reasonable cost of enforcement, a statement that the grantor, and any other person with a right in the encumbered NIS is entitled to terminate enforcement by paying the secured obligation in full, and a statement of the date of the sale and, in the case of a public sale, the time, place, and manner of sale (Article 78(5)).[70]

4.59

In any case, the enforcing secured creditor must act in good faith and in a commercially reasonable manner (Article 4).[71] A breach of this obligation may result in liability for damages and other consequences that are left to the relevant law of the enacting State.[72]

4.60

---

[66] Ibid, paras 430–1.
[67] Ibid, para 444.
[68] Ibid, para 445.
[69] Ibid, para 420.
[70] Ibid, para 449.
[71] Ibid, para 450.
[72] Ibid, para 76.

The concept of 'commercial reasonableness' is not defined in MLST but it is generally understood to refer to actions that a reasonable person would take in circumstances similar to those encountered in a particular case by a person exercising a right or performing an obligation under MLST.[73] For example, if there is a recognized market in which large volumes of similar assets are bought and sold between many different sellers and buyers, and accordingly prices are set by the market and not negotiated between individual market participants, such as a commodity exchange, the enforcing secured creditor must avoid selling the encumbered assets outside that market.

4.61 Once the encumbered NIS are disposed of out of court, the enforcing secured creditor must apply the net proceeds (after deducting the reasonable cost of enforcement) to the secured obligation; if there is a shortfall, the grantor remains liable but the secured creditor then has the position of an unsecured creditor,[74] whereas any surplus remaining must be turned over to the grantor or to other creditors announced during the enforcement proceedings, or, if there is doubt, be deposited with a competent judicial or other authority or with a public deposit fund (Article 79(2)–(3)). For these provisions to operate, the secured creditor must provide an account, specifying the amount of proceeds realized, how they were distributed and the amount of any surplus or deficiency.[75]

4.62 The secured creditor may, on its own initiative or at the request of the grantor, propose to the grantor in writing to acquire the encumbered NIS in total or partial satisfaction of the secured obligation (Article 80(1) and (6)). Notice of such a proposal must be given to the same parties and contain all the information referred to above (Article 80(2)–(3)). If the secured creditor made a proposal to acquire the encumbered NIS in full satisfaction of the secured obligation, the secured creditor acquires them unless it receives an objection in writing from any addressee of the proposal within a short period of time after the proposal is received by the relevant addressee (Article 80(4)). If, however, the secured creditor made a proposal to acquire the encumbered NIS in partial satisfaction of the secured obligation, the secured creditor acquires them only if it receives in writing the positive consent of all addressees of the proposal within a short period of time after the proposal is received by each of the addressees (Article 80(5)). The requirement of positive consent is intended to protect the debtor, since, in the case of partial satisfaction of the secured obligation, the debtor would remain liable for the balance of the obligation. It is also intended to protect any lower-ranking claimant, since its rights would be extinguished (Article 81(3)). In any case, if the secured creditor's proposal is unsuccessful, the secured creditor may enforce its security interest by disposition or collection.

4.63 To ensure finality of the rights acquired pursuant to an out-of-court disposition of encumbered NIS, the MLST provides that the buyer or other transferee acquires the encumbered NIS free of any security interests that are subordinate to the security interest of the enforcing secured creditor, but subject to any security interests with priority over the security interest

---

[73] Ibid, para 77.
[74] Whether the debtor has a claim or counter-claim reducing or extinguishing the secured obligation is a matter left to other law of the enacting State (Guide to Enactment, para 453).
[75] Guide to Enactment, para 454.

of the enforcing secured creditor (Article 81(3)). If the secured creditor sells or otherwise disposes of the encumbered NIS in violation of the provisions of the MLST, the buyer or other transferee acquires them as just mentioned, but only if it had no knowledge of a violation that materially prejudiced the rights of the grantor or another person (Article 81(5)).

4.64 The secured creditor may only collect from the issuer of encumbered NIS (the debtor of an encumbered receivable, the obligor of an encumbered negotiable instrument or the deposit-taking institution of an encumbered right to payment of funds credited to a bank account) after default, unless the grantor consented to collection before default (Article 82(1)–(2)). The secured creditor is also entitled to enforce any personal or property rights, such as a personal guarantee or standby letter of credit, that secures or supports payment (Article 82(3)).

4.65 If the encumbered asset is a right to payment of funds credited to a bank account made effective against third parties solely by registration, the secured creditor is only entitled to collect or otherwise enforce, for example, through a sale under Article 78 or through a proposal under Article 80 if it obtains a court order or the deposit-taking institution consents. This limitation does not apply if the security interest was made effective against third parties by a method other than registration, that is: (i) automatically by the security interest being created in favour of the deposit-taking institution itself; (ii) by the conclusion of a control agreement between the deposit-taking institution, the grantor (account holder) and the secured creditor; or (iii) by the secured creditor becoming the account holder, a method that requires the consent of the institution (Article 25). This provision is intended to protect deposit-taking institutions from having to violate their obligations under other law not to accept instructions with respect to a bank account from any person other than the account holder unless the institution has actively consented to the creation of that security interest.[76]

4.66 The right of collection is subject to the rights of debtors of receivables, obligors under negotiable instruments, deposit-taking institutions and issuers or NIS under the relevant law (eg contract, negotiable instrument, banking or securities law; Article 82(5)).

4.67 The MLST also foresees certain additional rights of the secured creditor or the grantor and other affected persons. First, the MLST provides a right of judicial relief in the event of non-compliance with the enforcement provisions of the MLST. Enacting States can choose between two options (Article 74, option A and option B). The first option addresses non-compliance only by the secured creditor and provides that relief may be sought by the grantor, the debtor (if the debtor is a different person from the grantor) or any other person with a right in the encumbered asset whose rights are affected by the non-compliance. The second option is broader, addressing non-compliance by any person, and giving any person affected by that non-compliance the right to seek relief (eg, a competing claimant, a guarantor of the secured obligation, or a co-owner of an asset in which another co-owner has created a security interest).

---

[76] Ibid, para 465.

4.68 Secondly, the grantor or the debtor (if the debtor is a different person from the grantor) or any other person with a right in the encumbered NIS is entitled to terminate the enforcement process by paying or otherwise performing the secured obligation in full, including the reasonable cost of enforcement (Article 75). The right of termination (or the right of redemption of the encumbered asset, as it is known in some jurisdictions) may be exercised until the earlier of the sale or other disposition, acquisition or collection of the encumbered NIS by the secured creditor and the conclusion of an agreement by the secured creditor for the sale or other disposition of the encumbered NIS. The reason for this time limitation is that, after that particular point of time, the enforcement process has advanced so far that it is no longer possible for the higher-ranking secured creditor to take over. However, if the lower-ranking creditor has sold the encumbered assets out of court, the buyer or other transferee of the encumbered NIS acquires its rights subject to the security interest of the higher-ranking secured creditor (Article 81(3)).

4.69 Thirdly, the secured creditor whose security interest has priority over the security interest of the enforcing secured creditor may take over the enforcement process at any time before the earlier of the sale or other disposition, acquisition or collection of the encumbered NIS by the enforcing secured creditor and the conclusion of an agreement by that secured creditor for the sale or other disposition of the encumbered NIS (Article 76(1)). The secured creditor with priority may either continue with the same enforcement method (eg, by applying to a court or other authority) or follow a different method (eg, without applying to a court or other authority) (Article 76(2)). However, the secured creditor must act in good faith and in a commercially reasonable manner, so that it should, for example, avoid incurring unreasonable additional enforcement costs (Article 4).

4.70 In addition, whether before or after default, the secured creditor may assign the secured obligation and with it the security interest, even if a non-assignment clause is included in the agreement from which the secured obligation arises, and any personal or property rights securing payment of the secured obligation follow automatically (Articles 13(1) and 14, reproducing Articles 9 and 10 of the CARIT). Moreover, the secured creditor in possession of the encumbered assets may make reasonable use of them and apply any revenues from that use to the secured obligation and a secured creditor not in possession may inspect the encumbered assets (Article 55).

(b) Enforcement in insolvency

4.71 The MLST does not deal with the enforcement of a security interest in the event of the grantor's insolvency. It does, however, include two rules that are applicable in the event of the grantor's insolvency, one substantive law and one conflict-of-laws rule. Under the former, a security interest retains its third-party effectiveness and priority even if the grantor is declared insolvent (Article 35). Thus, this rule is intended to create a degree of certainty sufficient to enable a potential financier to price the insolvency risk involved in a secured transaction.[77] However, this rule cannot override any mandatory

---

[77] Ibid, para 312.

insolvency law rules that may give priority to the interests of other parties even over a security interest (eg, the insolvency administrator for the costs of the insolvency proceedings), provided these mandatory rules are stated in the law in a clear and transparent manner.

Under the conflict-of-laws rule of the MLST, the law applicable to a security interest continues to apply even if the grantor is declared insolvent (Article 94). This rule is intended to preserve certainty as to the applicable law, but it also has its limits in that it cannot set aside mandatory law provisions of the law of the State in which the grantor is declared insolvent (eg, provisions on the avoidance of fraudulent or preferential transactions, the treatment of secured creditors, the ranking of claims and the distribution of proceeds).[78] **4.72**

With regard to the treatment of security interests in insolvency, the MLST is supplemented by a number of recommendations provided by the LGIL that are also reiterated in the LGST. These recommendations are discussed in the following paragraphs. **4.73**

The law of the State in which insolvency proceedings are commenced (*lex fori concursus*) applies, *inter alia*, to the treatment of secured creditors and the ranking of claims (Recommendation 31). However, this rule does not apply to the effects of insolvency proceedings on the rights and obligations of the participants in a payment or settlement system or in a regulated financial market, which should be governed solely by the law applicable to that system or market (Recommendation 32). Similarly, this rule does not apply to the effects of insolvency proceedings on rejection, continuation, and modification of labour contracts, which may be governed by the law applicable to the contract (Recommendation 33). Any other exceptions should be limited and clearly set out in insolvency law (Recommendation 34). **4.74**

Encumbered assets are part of the insolvency estate (Recommendation 35(a)). However, the insolvency court may provide relief to secured creditors where relief is needed to protect the value of encumbered assets or the interests of secured creditors (Recommendations 39(a) and 46(b)). Protection may be offered to the secured creditor from a fall in value of the encumbered assets and may take the form of cash payments from the estate, provision of additional security interests, and any other means as the court may determine (Recommendations 49 and 50). The insolvency court may permit the use and disposition of assets of the estate, including encumbered assets, in the ordinary course of business, except for cash proceeds, and outside the ordinary course of business subject to certain requirements, such as notice, due process, and protection of the priority of the security interest (Recommendations 52(a)–(b), 55, and 58). **4.75**

In principle, post-commencement finance does not have priority over pre-commencement finance. However, the court may grant such priority after hearing pre-commencement secured creditors, the insolvent debtor proves that it cannot obtain finance in any **4.76**

---

[78] Ibid, para 500.

other way, and the interests of pre-commencement secured creditors are protected (Recommendations 65–7).

4.77 Like any other transaction, a secured transaction may be avoided if it is fraudulent or preferential (Recommendation 88). Netting and set-off should be allowed where financial contracts of the insolvent debtor are terminated by a counterparty and should be exempted from any stays of individual actions (Recommendation 102). Counterparties should be allowed to enforce their security interests arising out of financial contracts (Recommendation 103). Certain routine pre-insolvency transfers consistent with market practice, such as putting up of margins for financial contracts and transfers to settle financial contract obligations, should be exempt from avoidance (Recommendation 104). The finality of netting, clearing, and settlement of financial contracts through payment and settlement systems should be recognized and protected (Recommendation 105).

4.78 Secured creditors are entitled to participate in insolvency, to submit their claims and vote on the plan in reorganization proceedings (Recommendation 126). Secured creditors may be bound to the plan against their will where certain conditions are satisfied, such as that requisite approvals have been obtained, the approval process has been properly conducted, under the plan, creditors will receive as much as they would have received in liquidation, and their ranking under insolvency law will be properly recognized (Recommendations 152 and 153).

4.79 Insolvency law should specify whether secured creditors are required to submit claims and the insolvency administrator should evaluate encumbered assets to determine the portion of a secured claim that is secured (Recommendations 172 and 179).

4.80 Secured claims should be satisfied subject to any claims superior in priority, which should be minimized and clearly set out in insolvency law (Recommendation 188).

4.81 Moreover, the LGST includes a number of insolvency-related recommendations applicable in the case of the grantor's insolvency, which are discussed in the following paragraphs.

4.82 Assets of the insolvency estate acquired after the commencement of insolvency proceedings are not subject to a security interest in after-acquired assets (Recommendation 235). If this were the case, the secured creditor would unfairly benefit from the increase of the encumbered assets to the detriment of other creditors, without providing further credit to the estate.[79] This rule does not apply to encumbered assets that constitute proceeds of assets encumbered before the commencement of insolvency proceedings (Recommendation 236). Otherwise, the extension of a security interest to the proceeds of an encumbered asset would be meaningless and, as a result, potential lenders would

---

[79] LGST, ch XII, para 22.

be disinclined to extend credit or would extend credit on less advantageous terms for potential borrowers.[80]

4.83 If insolvency law provides that, upon the commencement of insolvency proceedings with respect to the grantor of a security interest, an obligation is terminated or its maturity accelerated, this may not render unenforceable or invalidate a contract clause relieving a creditor from an obligation to make a loan or extend credit or other financial accommodations to the insolvent debtor (Recommendation 237). It would be unfair to require a secured creditor to extend credit knowing that the prospect of repayment was greatly diminished, which would be the case in particular if no additional encumbered assets were provided after commencement of insolvency proceedings with respect to the grantor.[81]

4.84 If a security interest is effective against third parties at the time of commencement of insolvency proceedings, the secured creditor may take any measure necessary to preserve third-party effectiveness, such as renewing a registration (Recommendation 238). This results from the principle that the third-party effectiveness of a security interest should not be affected by the commencement of insolvency proceedings with respect to the grantor.[82]

4.85 A security interest retains the priority it had prior to the commencement of insolvency proceedings, except if priority is given pursuant to insolvency law to another claim (Recommendation 239).

4.86 Subordination agreements entered into before the commencement of insolvency proceedings remain effective even after commencement (Recommendation 240). However, the main principle is that subordination agreements between two creditors should not affect the rights of third parties (Recommendation 94; see also MLST Article 43).

4.87 Reasonable costs and expenses incurred by the insolvency representative to preserve the value of the encumbered assets may be paid from their value on a first priority basis (Recommendation 241).

4.88 In determining the value of encumbered assets in reorganization proceedings, consideration is to be given to their use and the purpose of the valuation, and their value may be based on their value as a going concern (Recommendation 242).

(c) Enforcement and alternative dispute resolution

4.89 The MLST provides that nothing in it 'affects any agreement to use alternative dispute resolution, including arbitration, mediation, conciliation and online dispute resolution' (Article 3(3)).

---

[80] Ibid, para 23.
[81] Ibid, para 41.
[82] Ibid, para 13.

4.90 In addition, the MLST deals with the enforcement of a security interest by application to a court or other authority vested with adjudicative power or without such an application (Article 73(1)). Thus, it deals with enforcement by an alternative dispute resolution method (hereinafter referred to as 'ADR'), such as arbitration, mediation, or conciliation.

4.91 The MLST does not provide that disputes arising from secured transactions are arbitrable. It assumes that: (i) disputes arising from secured transactions are arbitrable to the same extent any other contractual dispute is arbitrable, unless otherwise provided in law; and (ii) the real issue in this respect is the protection of the rights of third parties where the secured creditor seeks to enforce against the encumbered asset an arbitral award ordering the debtor of the secured obligation to pay.[83]

4.92 The MLST addresses this issue with a set of provisions in respect of third-party rights. First, a person whose rights are affected by the non-compliance by another person with the enforcement provisions of the MLST is entitled to apply for relief to a court or other authority specified by the enacting State, including expeditious relief (Article 74, option B).

4.93 Secondly, any person with a right in the encumbered asset may terminate the enforcement process by paying or otherwise performing the secured obligation in full (Article 75).

4.94 Thirdly, a third-party higher-ranking secured creditor is entitled to take over enforcement before the sale or disposition of the encumbered asset or before the conclusion of an agreement for the sale or other disposition of the encumbered asset, whichever occurs first (Article 76).

4.95 Fourthly, to obtain possession of an encumbered asset by application to a court or other authority, a secured creditor must follow the order of the court or other authority and abide by the relevant procedural rules that should protect the rights of third parties (Article 73(2)).

4.96 Fifthly, to obtain possession of the encumbered asset out of court, a secured creditor must have ensured that the security agreement provided for that right and must give notice to the grantor and any person in possession of the encumbered asset; that latter person must not raise objections at the time of repossession; and if a third-party higher-ranking secured creditor is in possession, the enforcing lower-ranking secured creditor may not take possession (Article 77).

4.97 Sixthly, to dispose of an asset by application to a court or other authority, a secured creditor must follow the instructions of the court or other authority and the relevant procedural rules that should protect the rights of third parties. To do so out of court, the secured creditor must give advance written notice to the debtor, the grantor (if the

---

[83] Guide to Enactment, para 75.

latter is a different person) and all third parties with a right in the encumbered asset (Article 78).

Seventhly, to distribute the proceeds of a judicial sale, a secured creditor must follow the instructions of the court or other authority and the relevant procedural rules that should protect the rights of third parties. However, under the MLST, payment must be made first to a third-party higher-ranking secured creditor. To distribute the sale proceeds out of court, a secured creditor must pay the secured obligation and turn over any remaining balance to any subordinate third-party secured creditor that notified the enforcing secured creditor of its claim and then to the grantor (Article 79). **4.98**

Eighthly, to acquire the encumbered asset in full satisfaction of the secured creditor, a secured creditor must give advance written notice to the debtor, the grantor (if the latter is a different person), and any third party with a right in the encumbered asset. To acquire the encumbered asset in partial satisfaction of the secured obligation, a secured creditor must first obtain the consent of all those persons in writing (Article 80). **4.99**

Ninthly, if an encumbered asset is sold or otherwise disposed of in court, the person acquiring the encumbered asset typically acquires it free of any other rights. However, if the asset is sold or otherwise disposed of out of court, the person acquiring the encumbered asset typically acquires it subject to any higher-ranking rights (Article 81). **4.100**

In view of the above, a regime that includes the provisions of the MLST should have a sufficiently high level of third-party creditor protection and make possible the enforcement of an arbitral award against an encumbered asset. **4.101**

(d) The law applicable to enforcement
The MLST also contains conflict-of-laws rules, as one of its key objectives is to harmonize secured transactions laws, including conflict-of-laws rules, and thus to facilitate trade financing and with that, trade across national borders (LGST Recommendation 1(k)).[84] The MLST departs from the traditional conflict-of-laws rules of the location of the asset for certificated NIS (*les situs* or *lex rei sitae*) and the location of the grantor for uncertificated NIS and adopts one conflict-of laws rule that applies to all matters, drawing a distinction between equity NIS (eg, shares of a corporation)[85] and debt **4.102**

---

[84] There are several reasons for including conflict-of-laws rules in the MLST. First, in practice, the first question arising with respect to any secured transaction typically relates or should relate to asking what jurisdiction's law is applicable to the issue involved. Second, harmonization of substantive secured transactions law will take time. Until that time, conflict-of-laws rules would be useful in providing ex ante certainty as to the law applicable to a secured transaction, which may in itself have a beneficial impact on the availability and the cost of credit. Third, even after harmonization of substantive secured transactions law has been achieved, conflict-of-laws rules would be necessary to identify the law of which State that would apply, for example, to the third-party effectiveness (perfection) and priority of a security interest. See Bazinas and Smith, 'UNCITRAL Model Law and UCC Article 9 Conflict-of-laws Rules Compared'.
[85] The term 'equity' is not defined in the Model Law but is understood as referring to participation rights in the capital of the issuer (Guide to Enactment, para 516).

NIS (eg, bonds), rather than between certificated and uncertificated securities.[86] The reason for this departure is twofold. First, it provides a clear and simple rule that would apply to all issues, distinguishing only between debt and equity securities; and, secondly, it prevents the secured creditor from manipulating the applicable law by moving certificated securities from State to State.[87]

4.103 Thus, the law applicable to the creation, effectiveness against third parties, priority, and enforcement of a security interest in non-intermediated equity securities, as well as to its effectiveness against the issuer, is the law under which the issuer is constituted (Article 100(1)). For a corporation, it is the law under which it was incorporated; for a partnership, it is the law under which the partnership was created.[88]

4.104 In addition, the law applicable to the creation, effectiveness against third parties, priority, and enforcement of a security interest in non-intermediated debt securities, as well as to its effectiveness against the issuer, is the law governing the debt securities (Article 100(2)). This is typically the law selected by the parties as the law governing their contractual rights and obligations arising from these debt securities. In the absence of such a choice of law (which would be extremely rare for debt securities), the forum will determine the applicable law under its own conflict-of-laws rules.[89]

4.105 The distinction between equity and debt securities is left to the corporate or enterprise law (not accounting or other law) of the issuer's State. Thus, preferred shares (ie, shares that entitle the holder to a fixed dividend, whose payment takes priority over that of common share dividends) are to be treated as equity securities if they are so considered under the corporate or enterprise law of the issuer's State, even if under accounting or other rules of that State they are classified as liabilities. Similarly, subordinated debt securities (eg, debt payable only after satisfaction of obligations owing to certain creditors) are to be treated as debt securities if they are so considered under the corporate or enterprise law of the issuer's State, even if they are viewed as equity securities under accounting or other law.[90]

---

[86] The term 'debt securities' is not defined in the Model Law but is understood as denoting a payment obligation (Guide to Enactment, para 519).

[87] Report of the 49th session of UNCITRAL (2016), A/71/17, para 87. The version of Art 100 that was before the Commission provided for the application of different laws to different matters; see A/CN.9/884/Add.4, Art 97 under <https://uncitral.un.org/en/commission#49> (accessed 5 April 2021).

[88] Where the issuer may be constituted either under a federal law of a federal State or a law of one of its territorial units, applying by analogy Art 95, the internal conflict-of-laws rules of the federal State (or of the territorial unit which is the forum) should determine the territorial unit's law to be applicable to the issues falling under Art 100 where all or some of these issues are not dealt with by the federal law of the constitution of the issuer (Guide to Enactment, para 517).

[89] The question of whether the parties may select a governing law that has no connection with the issuance of the securities is left to the conflict-of-laws rules on contractual obligations of the forum State (Guide to Enactment, para 518).

[90] Guide to Enactment, para 520. Upon the issuance of convertible debt securities and until conversion, the law governing these securities is the law applicable to a security interest. If and when they are converted into equity securities, the law of the issuer's constitution becomes the law applicable to a security interest. This possible change in applicable law makes it necessary for enacting States to adopt grace periods preserving third-party effectiveness and priority and rules for the relevant time for determining the place of the issuer's constitution or a choice of law by the parties (Guide to Enactment, para 523).

4.106 There is one exception to these conflict-of-laws rules. If the law of the State in which the grantor is located recognizes registration of a notice as a method of achieving effectiveness against third parties of a security interest in certificated non-intermediated securities, the law of that State is the law applicable to the third-party effectiveness of the security interest in this type of asset by registration (Article 98).

4.107 Thus, with respect to certificated NIS, a secured creditor may rely on the law of the location of the grantor to make its security interest effective against third parties by registration (rather than the law of the location of the certificated NIS). It should be noted, however, that, if the priority rules of the applicable law are based on the priority rules of the MLST, achieving third-party effectiveness by registration would only yield a lower-ranking priority in the case of a priority conflict with a competing secured creditor who achieved third-party effectiveness, for example, by possession of a certificated non-intermediated (Article 51(1)). However, the security interest with respect to which a notice was registered in the Registry under the law of the grantor's location would have priority over the right of: (i) the grantor's insolvency representative or the general body of creditors (subject to the applicable insolvency law; Articles 35 and 36); and (ii) judgment creditors, if registration took place before a judgment creditor took the steps required to acquire a right in the encumbered assets (Article 37(1)).[91]

(4) Enforcement under the Receivables Convention

4.108 To the extent that the provisions of the CARIT have been incorporated in the provisions of the MLST, it is worth briefly referring to the enforcement regime under the CARIT. In the event of default, as between the assignor and the assignee, unless otherwise agreed, the assignee may notify the debtor and collect the assigned receivable; the assignee may also reassign the assigned receivables and with them any right securing their payment, even if an anti-assignment clause is included in the agreement from which the assigned receivables arise (Articles 8–10). As between the assignor and the assignee, the assignee may have these rights even prior to default (Article 13).

4.109 In addition, if payment of an encumbered receivable is made to the secured creditor, the secured creditor is entitled to retain the proceeds of payment; if payment is made to the debtor of the receivable, the secured creditor is entitled to claim the proceeds of payment; and, if payment is made to a third party, the secured creditor is entitled to claim the proceeds of payment, provided it has priority over that third party (Article 14(1)). Priority is subject to a conflict-of-laws rule that refers the matter to the law of the assignor's location (Article 22).

4.110 Moreover, the CARIT contains a limited substantive law rule dealing with the secured creditor's (assignee's) right to retain the proceeds of payment of an encumbered receivable in preference to competing claimants (Article 24). Under this rule, if the proceeds

---

[91] Guide to Enactment, paras 510, 511, and 524.

are received by the secured creditor, the secured creditor may retain them, if it had priority over a competing claimant in the encumbered receivable (Article 24(1)); if the proceeds are received by the grantor, the secured creditor has priority and may claim them from the grantor if: (i) the grantor received the proceeds under instructions from the secured creditor to hold them on behalf of the secured creditor and (ii) the proceeds are held by the grantor for the benefit of the secured creditor separately and are reasonably identifiable from the grantor's assets, such as where they are held in a separate deposit or securities account (Article 24(2)).

(5) Enforcement: the Secured Transactions Model Law as non-Convention law under the Geneva Securities Convention and required amendments

4.111 Chapter V GSC is optional, since a Contracting State may declare that this chapter shall not apply or shall not apply with respect to collateral agreements entered into by certain categories of persons or with respect to certain categories of obligations, or with respect to non-traded intermediated securities (Article 38). In that case, a Contracting State opting out of Chapter V GSC may apply its own enforcement regime, generally or only with respect to the excluded categories of persons, obligations, or securities, which regime may include rules based on the provisions of the MLST, if the enacting State does not exclude intermediated securities, or of the CARIT with respect to cash, if it is an international transaction to which the CARIT applies. Even if a Contracting State does not opt out of Chapter V GSC, law based on the provisions of the MLST may still apply as part of non-Convention law (for example, as provided in Article 35 GSC), if the enacting State does not exclude intermediated securities, at least to the extent that the GSC refers to non-Convention law.

4.112 However, for the MLST to apply to security and other interests in intermediated securities, several amendments would need to be made. These amendments are discussed in the following paragraphs.

4.113 Article 1(3)(c) excluding intermediated securities should be deleted.[92] A new paragraph should be added to Article 1 to ensure that the MLST applies not only to security interests in, but also to outright transfers of, intermediated securities. Several definitions should be added to Article 2 ('account agreement', 'account holder', 'control agreement', 'designating entry', 'intermediary', etc).[93]

4.114 A new article should be added to provide that a security interest in intermediated securities could be made effective against third parties by a credit of securities to the secured creditor's securities account, the creation of a security interest in favour of the relevant

---

[92] Article 1 of the Model Provisions on Secured Transactions for Intermediated Securities, published and made available by the International Insolvency Institute, prepared by Charles W Mooney, Jr (the 'STMP').
[93] Ibid, Art 2.

intermediary, the conclusion of a control agreement, a designating entry in favour of the secured creditor or a notice with respect to the security interest in the Registry.[94]

New articles should be added to deal with: (i) the acquisition of securities by an innocent person;[95] (ii) the priority of a security interest in intermediated securities according to the method of third-party effectiveness;[96] and (iii) the priority of interests granted by an intermediary.[97] **4.115**

Reference should be made in Article 71 to intermediated securities deferring to the relevant securities law with respect to the rights of a secured creditor against the issuer.[98] **4.116**

Article 82 should be revised to apply to the collection of intermediated securities from the issuer after default or before default if the grantor/collateral provider consents. **4.117**

In the conflict-of-laws chapter: (i) a new article should be added to deal with the law applicable to security and other interests in intermediated securities (the law of the relevant intermediary or the approach followed in the HSC);[99] and (ii) reference should be made in Article 98 to intermediated securities to ensure that the law of the grantor's location applies to third-party effectiveness of a security interest in intermediated securities, if it recognizes registration.[100] **4.118**

Alternatively, a new uniform law on securities could be prepared by the relevant international legislative standard formulating agencies (ie, UNCITRAL, UNIDROIT, and the Hague Conference). Such a uniform law should build on the GSC, the HSC, the MLST, the CARIT, and all relevant uniform law texts. This option presents certain advantages. First, it is based on the distinction between commercial finance transactions and capital market transactions, which justified their treatment in separate laws. Secondly, it does not require amendment of the MLST so soon after its finalization and adoption by UNCITRAL, which could unnecessarily slow down the adoption process. Thirdly, this option minimizes the co-ordination issues as, in light of its work on securities, UNIDROIT could take the lead in preparing a new uniform law on securities and simply co-ordinate its work with UNCITRAL and other relevant organizations. **4.119**

(6) Enforcement: the UNIDROIT project

UNIDROIT is working on a text on best practices for effective enforcement of a creditor's claim against the obligor.[101] It is envisaged that this document will: (i) take the form of **4.120**

---

[94] Ibid, Art 27bis.
[95] Ibid, Art 51bis.
[96] Ibid, Art 51ter.
[97] Ibid, Art 51quater.
[98] Ibid, Art 71.
[99] Ibid, Art 97bis.
[100] Ibid, Art 98.
[101] For the background of this project, see UNIDROIT 2020–Study LXXVIB-W.G.1–Doc 2, November 2020, <https://www.unidroit.org/english/documents/2020/study76b/wg-01/s-76b-wg-01-02-e.pdf> (accessed 5 April 2021), paras 5–9.

a guidance document, not a model law or detailed rules or principles (analysis without recommendations, analysis with recommendations, or general principles with comments);[102] (ii) be named 'Best Practices for Effective Enforcement';[103] (iii) clarify the meaning of enforcement or execution in a functional rather than a technical manner, and the various enforcement or execution procedures (eg, judicial and extra-judicial recourse against an obligor or against an encumbered asset, excluding the foreign law elements of the recognition and enforcement of foreign decisions and the process of obtaining a legal judgment against a defaulting obligor);[104] (iv) focus on commercial contractual claims, monetary and non-monetary, unsecured and secured;[105] (v) also address consumer claims;[106] (vi) include discussion of the enforcement of claims in insolvency, at least in an ancillary part, including enforcement against an insolvent debtor conducted outside an insolvency proceeding;[107] (vii) discuss provisional and protective measures;[108] (viii) consider additional factors that may influence enforcement (eg, mechanisms that may serve as an incentive not to default on obligations, thereby limiting the need to resort to enforcement proceedings, such as debtor registries);[109] and (ix) consider the impact of technology on enforcement (eg, electronic service, enforcement of smart contracts).[110]

4.121 At its first meeting, the UNIDROIT Working Group on Best Practices for Effective Enforcement considered the above-mentioned issues and made some preliminary decisions, but mostly raised issues for further study. The Working Group agreed, *inter alia*, that: (i) its general mandate was to 'identify current challenges for the enforcement of creditors' rights, particularly in relation to contractual rights, and develop solutions in the form of global best practices';[111] (ii) it would use a functional notion of enforcement and develop typical examples of enforcement procedures (judicial and non-judicial enforcement against an obligor and an encumbered asset);[112] (iii) in principle, enforcement of arbitral awards should not be excluded from the scope as there was no substantial difference in respect of enforcement of a judicial decision once the arbitral award was recognized in a jurisdiction;[113] (iv) 'pure' self-help enforcement should not be excluded;[114] (v) secured claims should be included but a decision on how the relevant questions would be presented in the final

---

[102] Ibid, paras 11–13.
[103] Ibid, para 14.
[104] Ibid, paras 24–31.
[105] Ibid, paras 33–7.
[106] Ibid, para 38.
[107] Ibid, paras 39–40.
[108] Ibid, paras 41–2.
[109] Ibid, paras 43–4.
[110] Ibid, paras 46–54. Discussion of issues related to the impact of technology on enforcement will be included in a separate preliminary report (Study LXXVIB–WG 1–Doc 3) which was not available on the UNIDROIT website by 18 February 2021.
[111] Ibid, para 7.
[112] Ibid, para 13.
[113] Ibid, para 18.
[114] Ibid, para 20.

document should be postponed;[115] (vi) the project would not cover the procedure through which a decision rendered in one country was recognized as enforceable in another country but would have to address the execution or enforcement phase of the enforceable decision, irrespective of whether it derived from a cross-border or a purely domestic situation;[116] (vii) digital assets could be addressed in the same and not in an alternative framework, while the issue would be 'how to best integrate technology in existing procedures, which may influence the nature of the proceedings';[117] (viii) the process of obtaining a legal judgment against a defaulting obligor should not be addressed but the possible relationship between the execution procedure and the process of determination of the merits should be considered; [118] (ix) the focus would be on commercial claims, monetary and non-monetary, secured and unsecured, but consumer claims would also be covered;[119] (x) the main focus would be on enforcement in general, and insolvency-related enforcement should be discussed at a later stage and with caution (while issues of material insolvency law could be avoided, *inter alia*, an efficient mechanism to transition between individual and collective enforcement could be discussed);[120] and (xi) consider the impact of technology on enforcement.[121]

4.122 With respect to the impact of technology on enforcement, several issues were raised at that first meeting of the working group. One such issue was whether technology-related issues should be part of the guidance document or be included in a separate instrument. Another issue was whether a proposal of a taxonomy identifying the different levels or layers of impact of technology should be made as an analytical framework to conduct the work (platforms for electronic auctions, processes and procedures, including 'smart performance', 'self-enforcement', and 'dynamic enforcement', digital assets, and technology-based remedies enhancing effectiveness).[122]

4.123 It is premature to comment on the substance of this work as it is 'work in progress'[123] and the discussion by the working group 'had mostly been conducted at an abstract level', and 'it might be helpful to have more concrete examples on how technology is put to use'.[124] However, this is the main problem of this project (and perhaps the typical problem of many projects). It was initiated prematurely on the basis of a brief proposal (by the World Bank)[125] without a detailed desirability and feasibility study to identify the problems and the way in which they might be resolved. This means that taxpayers'

---

[115] Ibid, para 21.
[116] Ibid, para 25.
[117] Ibid, para 29.
[118] Ibid, para 30.
[119] Ibid, paras 35–42.
[120] Ibid, para 45.
[121] Ibid, paras 46–7.
[122] Ibid, paras 48–9.
[123] Ibid, para 47.
[124] Ibid, para 54.
[125] Ibid, para 2.

money is being spent on meetings and travel expenditure of experts appointed by member States and representatives of intergovernmental organizations essentially to prepare this desirability and feasibility study; and the quality of the result will be as good as that of the process by which it was produced.[126]

4.124 All these issues should first be discussed in detail in a study that should identify the issues to be addressed and demonstrate the desirability of future work, that is, the problem that has not yet been addressed but needs to be addressed. The study should also generally describe the manner in which those issues could or should be addressed to ascertain whether agreement by States in the context of the relevant international legislative standard-setting organizations (ie, UNCITRAL, UNIDROIT, and the Hague Conference) is feasible within a reasonable period of time. Following that, Member States could decide whether scarce taxpayer resources should be devoted to the preparation of yet another text on enforcement and whether it should include the enforcement of security interests, within and outside insolvency.

4.125 To lay a solid foundation for the project, the process, and the future involvement of the relevant organization, the proposed guidance document should address real issues and avoid duplication of efforts, which would be a waste of resources and create overlap and conflicts with existing texts. This objective could be achieved, for example, if any work were limited to the enforcement of unsecured contractual claims or to the impact of technology on enforcement (eg, on the notifications and other procedural steps to be taken upon default, on the valuation of assets and the determination of what is commercially reasonable).[127]

---

[126] The problem with this process is the lack of equal participation of States with developing economies and the excessive influence of States with developed economies, either directly, or through governmental organizations (eg, the World Bank), non-governmental organizations (eg, industry groups), or private individuals (eg, renowned academics). The rest of the world finds it difficult to participate at all or on an equal footing, in particular when powerful industry groups or organizations, such as the World Bank, show their preference for a certain approach or solution. By not confining itself to providing trade law reform assistanceand by attempting to legislate either directly, preparing itself international legislative standards (eg on insolvency), or indirectly, through another organization, such as UNIDROIT the World Bank may exceed its mandate, antagonizes essentially UNCITRAL, and creates problems of coordination (for the turf fight between UNCITRAL and the World Bank on insolvency and secured transactions law, see Block-Lieb and Halliday, *Global Lawmakers*). In addition, by attempting to legislate or to exercise excessive influence over the international legislative process, the World Bank is said to have a clear conflict of interest, as it considers it part of its work to invest even in industry sectors regulated by laws the preparation of which it has itself influenced (see Provost and Kenard, 'The World Bank Is Supposed to Help the Poor'). This is the case with the UNIDROIT Model Law on International Leasing (on the IFC's role in promoting leasing in Sub-Saharan Africa and in the African Leasing Foundation 'Africalease', see <https://www.ifc.org/wps/wcm/connect/REGION__EXT_Content/Regions/Sub-Saharan+Africa/Advisory+Services/AccessFinance/AfricaLeasingFacility/FAQsLeasing/> and <https://africalease.org/en/presentation-of-africalease/> (both accessed 5 April 2021)). The model law on international factoring that UNIDROIT is preparing at the suggestion of the World Bank presents similar problems of coordination, excessive influence, and perhaps even a conflict of interest of the World Bank (see Bazinas, 'Does the World Need Another Uniform Law on Factoring?').

[127] For a discussion of these issues, see Keijser, 'The Potential Impact of Technology on the Enforcement of Security Interests'. For a discussion of how specific digital technologies could increase the efficiency of secured transactions systems (eg, through automatic, self-executed remedies implemented through an ecosystem of smart contracts and smart devices) and a fully automatic electronic (eg, blockchain-based) registry, see Rodríguez de las Heras Ballell, 'Digital Technology-Based Solutions for Enhanced Effectiveness of Secured Transactions Law'.

4.126 Another way to avoid duplication of efforts, overlap, and conflicts, not only with the UNCITRAL uniform law texts discussed above but also with the World Bank Insolvency and Creditor/Debtor Rights Standard (the 'ICR Standard'), which contains the main recommendations of the LGIL and the World Bank Principles,[128] would be to ensure that any part of the work that related to issues addressed in an UNCITRAL text was undertaken in co-operation with UNCITRAL and the resulting text submitted to UNCITRAL for consideration and approval.[129]

4.127 In any case, the proposed guidance document should not attempt to amend or supplement the MLST by addressing issues not specifically addressed in the MLST, such as security interests in digital assets (eg, virtual currency, electronic promissory notes, and securities maintained electronically on a distributed ledger, often called a 'blockchain'). Attempting to amend a uniform law text just a few years after it was first prepared is bound to undermine its broad adoption, a goal to which member States will have devoted significant time and cost. In addition, attempting to address an issue as complex as security in digital assets, which is not yet addressed even in jurisdictions with developed financial markets and sophisticated secured transactions laws, would, at the present time, be premature.[130] Moreover, once the time is ripe for international legislative work on security interests in digital assets, the matter should be addressed in the context of a comprehensive text such as the MLST[131] in order to avoid reproducing the problem of fragmentation of secured transactions law which the MLST is intended to address.[132]

---

[128] It should be noted that an amended version of the ICR Standard including the relevant recommendations of the LGST is still pending completion. As noted in the report of the 49th session of UNCITRAL in 2016, 'The Commission noted with appreciation the efforts of the Secretariat in coordinating and cooperating with a number of organizations active in the area of security interests. It was noted that the Secretariat had provided comments on the World Bank Principles contained in the World Bank Insolvency and Creditor Rights Standard (the "Standard") and was expecting to receive the comments of the World Bank on a revised draft of the Standard that contained the key recommendations of the Secured Transactions Guide (see A/71/17, para. 126)'.

[129] As was done for the work on warehouse receipts, with respect to which a Study Group to be convened by UNIDROIT in co-operation with UNCITRAL will prepare a draft model law and submit it to UNCITRAL for consideration; see Report of UNCITRAL on the work of its 53rd session, 2020, A/75/17, Part 2, para 61, available under <https://undocs.org/en/A/75/17> (accessed 5 April 2021).

[130] Even in the US, only in 2019 the American Law Institute and the Uniform Law Commission formed a study group to 'examine whether any amendments to the Uniform Commercial Code (the "UCC"), enacted in all states and the District of Columbia, are needed to accommodate emerging technological developments including digital assets'. In view of this work and 'initiatives already undertaken or being considered by a number of states to enact digital asset legislation impacting on the UCC and otherwise establishing commercial and property law rules for digital assets', the ULC 'recommends states refrain from enacting digital asset legislation pending the work of the Study Committee. To ensure the continued uniformity of state commercial laws, states are instead encouraged to send representatives to join in the work of the Study Committee and in the drafting of any legislation recommended by the Study Committee'. See <https://www.uniformlaws.org/blogs/edwin-smith/2019/03/13/ucc-and-digital-assets-legislative-initiatives> (accessed 5 April 2021).

[131] In fact, in the context of its future work discussion, UNCITRAL has already begun considering issues relating to security interests in digital assets (A/CN.9/1012/Add.3, paras 25 and 26, available under <https://undocs.org/en/A/CN.9/1012/Add.3>, accessed 5 April 2021) and has 'reaffirmed that UNCITRAL plays a central and coordinating role within the United Nations system in addressing legal issues related to the digital economy and digital trade' in the Report of UNCITRAL on the work of its 53rd session, 2020, A/75/17, Part 2, (n 131), para 76.

[132] In the US, the matter under consideration involves necessary amendments to UCC Art 9, not the preparation of a separate law.

D. Conclusions

4.128 The GSC is a significant first step in the harmonization of securities law at the international level. At the same time, the GSC has its limitations. Several issues are referred to non-Convention law, since they do not lend themselves to unification or harmonization at the international level, so that consensus on these issues among States was beyond reach.

4.129 The MLST has already influenced or resembles the law of several States,[133] and law in general.[134] It is also being considered for enactment by a number of States.[135]

4.130 While the CARIT has not been widely adopted, its ratification by the United States of America in 2018 and the possibility that its main conflict-of-laws provision may be enacted in an EU regulation has created new momentum for the CARIT to enter into force and produce a universal uniform regime on international receivables finance.[136] In any case, the CARIT has already significantly influenced the development of the law, as its principles have been implemented in the domestic law of many States[137] and have also been incorporated in the provisions of the MLST. Thus, as the influence of the MLST grows, so will the influence of the CARIT, as the MLST has incorporated the latter's provisions.

4.131 There is no conflict or overlap between the GSC, on the one hand, and the MLST or the CARIT, on the other hand. Most importantly, to the extent that the provisions of the MLST (which, with respect to insolvency, include the relevant Recommendations of the LGST and the LGIL) are implemented by a Contracting State of the GSC, those provisions may form part of non-Convention law and apply to matters left by the GSC to non-Convention law.

4.132 The MLST provides additional guidance to States with respect to matters referred by the GSC to non-Convention law. However, the MLST does not apply to security interests in, or outright transfers of, intermediated securities, unless a State enacts it without excluding intermediated securities. To do so, a State would need to modify the MLST to address security interests in intermediated securities. Another option may the preparation of a separate uniform law on security and other interests in intermediated

---

[133] For example, Australia, Canada, Colombia, Mexico, New Zealand, Nigeria, and the United States of America.
[134] For example, the Draft Common Frame of Reference, Book IX; Bazinas, 'Harmonization of Conflict-of-laws', fn 10.
[135] For example, Bahrain, Paraguay, St Lucia, Trinidad, and Tobago.
[136] Bazinas, 'The Law Applicable to Third-party Effects of Assignments of Claims'.
[137] While a good study on the matter is still missing, a good example is the Japanese Act Concerning the Exceptional Cases of the Civil Law for the Perfection of Assignment of Receivables that foresees the registration of assignment of receivables, which was prepared by the Japanese delegate to the relevant UNCITRAL Working Group, Prof Masao Ikeda. This act influenced similar laws in other countries, such as China and South Korea. Another good example is the German law of 1994 rendering ineffective anti-assignment agreements that opened the way for the ratification of the Convention on International Factoring by Germany (see Brink, 'New German Legislation Opens Door to Ratification of UNIDROIT Factoring Convention').

CONCLUSIONS 129

securities on the basis of the GSC, the HSC, the MLST (including the LGST and the LGIL), and the CARIT. This last option may be preferable for a variety of reasons, including that it places the focus on capital market transactions, which are distinct from commercial finance transactions, and it does not create significant co-ordination issues, as these matters are not the main focus of the MLST. Also, in view of its work on the GSC, this project would fall clearly within the mandate and expertise of UNIDROIT.

5

THE NO-LOOK-THROUGH PRINCIPLE: INVESTOR RIGHTS, DISTRIBUTED LEDGER TECHNOLOGY, AND THE MARKET

A. Introduction	5.01	D. Barriers to Change	5.29
B. The Problem	5.11	E. Possible Solutions	5.37
C. Distributed Ledger Technology	5.15	F. Conclusion	5.51

A. Introduction

5.01 This chapter explores English law as an example of a particular model for the analysis of intermediated securities. Like other jurisdictions, England uses a no-look-through approach. The rights of investors are analysed through the lens of trust law rather than through bailment. This chapter discusses the advantages and disadvantages of the no-look-through model.

5.02 From a structural perspective, intermediated holding structures in the UK are similar to those operating elsewhere. There is a Central Securities Depositary (CSD) to which everyone interested in investing in UK securities needs to connect. In the UK, the CSD is referred to as CREST and operated by Euroclear.[1] CREST does not store paper documents but rather operates a central register for recording ownership to securities issued in the UK. Investors can hold securities directly through an account with CREST, but most investors hold securities in intermediated form through custodians. There may be more than one custodian operating between an issuer and an investor. Like elsewhere, a custody chain in the UK looks like this:

Investor
Custodian 1
Custodian 2
Custodian 3

---

[1] <https://www.euroclear.com/services/en/settlement/settlement-euroclear-uk-ireland.html> (accessed 7 July 2021).

CREST (Euroclear)
Issuer

To understand the position of an investor who holds securities through such a chain, English law distinguishes between legal ownership and equitable or beneficial ownership. **5.03**

The legal owner is the person whose name is entered on the securities register maintained by the issuer. Under English law, the issuer is currently only able to recognize the legal owner as the holder of shares or other securities.[2] An investor whose name is not registered cannot exercise or enforce rights against an issuer. **5.04**

In a custody chain, custodians, who hold securities for investors, are considered to be trustees. The terms of the trust are set out in the contract agreed upon between the investor and its custodian (Custodian 1 in the example above). Custodian 1 (C1) has a contract with Custodian 2 (C2). C2 has another contract with Custodian 3 (C3). C3 has a contract with CREST. These four contracts are independent of one another and are negotiated separately from each other. On the basis of these contracts, the property rights of the participants in the chain are analysed as follows. **5.05**

C3, whose name is registered on the CREST register, is considered the legal owner of these securities. On the terms set out in the contract with C2, C3 is also a trustee, holding the legal ownership in the securities for the benefit of C2. C2 is the beneficiary of this trust and is referred to as beneficial or equitable owner. That beneficial ownership gives C2 the right to claim the securities as its own in the insolvency of C3, but it is not good enough to cause the issuer to recognize C2 as entitled to exercise rights. This analysis continues along the chain. C2 is also a trustee holding the beneficial interest for the benefit of C1. The terms of that trust arrangement are set out in the contract agreed between C2 and C1. C1 again has two roles. It is both the beneficiary of a trust managed by C2 and also a trustee holding a beneficial interest for the investor. The ultimate investor is the beneficial owner of the beneficial interest held by C1. **5.06**

The effect of this analysis is that an indirect investor has a beneficial ownership interest over a beneficial ownership interest, which attaches to another beneficial ownership interest, which in turn attaches to a legal interest. Ultimate investors thus have a right in another right, but they do not have a right in the underlying securities. This is sometimes referred to as the no-look-through approach. **5.07**

This no-look-through approach is convenient for issuers, who thus have one certain record for the identification of those who are entitled to exercise rights against them. The no-look-through approach also helps custodians, who are able to use contracts to regulate the relationships with their immediate clients without having to deal with investors or custodians elsewhere in the custody chain.[3] **5.08**

---

[2] Companies Act 2006, ss 112(2), 127.
[3] Micheler, 'Custody Chains and Asset Values'.

5.09 From the perspective of investors, the arrangement has the advantage of enabling them to use just one account to hold securities in different jurisdictions. Custodians also provide administrative services.[4] The downside of the no-look-through model, however, is that investor rights are modified when securities are held through a custodian or through a chain of custodians. If securities are held in a custody chain, the rights of an investor are reduced to the least favourable custody term operating in the chain. In effect, an investor's rights 'revert to the lowest denominator. Any term in a custody chain that qualifies or limits the rights of a sub-custodian also reduces the rights of the investor'.[5] Indirectly held assets can be significantly reduced in value in comparison to directly held assets. The longer the chain of custodians, the greater the erosion of investor rights.

5.10 This effect of custody chains was recently highlighted by the UK Law Commission.[6] In a Scoping Paper published in November 2020, the Law Commission observed that the intermediated holding system has certainly made trading quicker, more cost effective, and more convenient. It has, however, also caused problems in relation to corporate governance, transparency, and uncertainty as to the legal rights and remedies available to the ultimate investor.[7] The Law Commission concluded that the current system adversely affects ultimate investors who, after all, are the ones who invest their money and take the financial risk.[8]

B. The Problem

5.11 The problem associated with English law can be illustrated by reference to three recent cases. In *Eckerle v Wickeder Westfalenstahl GmbH*, investors owned shares issued by a UK-registered company, DNick Holding plc.[9] The issuer was taken over by a group of shareholders who decided to transform the company from a public into a private one. Mr Eckerle was an investor who opposed this. He held a sufficient number of shares to be able to rely on Companies Act (CA) 2006, s 98, which permits 5 per cent of the nominal value of the company's issued share capital to apply to court to request the cancellation of a shareholder resolution transforming the company from a public to a private one. On such an application, the court may make an order as it thinks fit and, in particular, can order the company to buy the shares of any of its members and to reduce its capital accordingly.[10] Notwithstanding the size of his holding, Mr Eckerle was unable to invoke CA 2006, s 98 because his shares were held indirectly through a custody chain running through Postbank, Clearstream Banking Luxembourg, Bank of New York Mellon, and ending at Crest (Euroclear). He was therefore not the legal owner of these shares but rather, as described above, the holder of 'the ultimate economic interest'.[11]

---

[4] Twemlow, 'Why are Securities Held in Intermediated Form?', 85.
[5] Micheler, 'Custody Chains and Asset Values', 507.
[6] Law Commission, *Who Owns Your Shares?*.
[7] Ibid, p 5.
[8] Ibid, 8.
[9] [2013] EWHC 68 (Ch); [2014] Ch 196.
[10] CA 2006, s 98(4)–(5).
[11] *Eckerle v Wickeder* [2013] EWHC 68 (Ch); [2014] Ch 196, para 14(g).

5.12 Likewise, in *Secure Capital SA v Credit Suisse AG*[12] an investor was unable to claim against the issuer for breach of disclosure obligations in relation to a longevity bond. This was because the investor was unable to present the bearer certificate representing the bond. The issuer held the bond through a chain consisting of RBS Global Banking (Luxembourg) SA, Clearstream Banking (Luxembourg), and Bank of New York Mellon. Under Luxembourg law, Secure Capital would have had standing against Credit Suisse, notwithstanding the fact that there was more than one custodian between the investor and the asset. The bond was, however, governed by English law.[13] The Court of Appeal held that the claim was of a contractual nature and so English law determined who was entitled to claim.[14] The claim failed because Secure Capital was unable to deliver the bond.

5.13 Another example demonstrating how custody chains can prevent investors from enforcing their rights against issuers is the decision in *Sirius Minerals plc*.[15] The case concerned a mining company which submitted a scheme of arrangement to the court. Such schemes need to be approved by the shareholders of the company. Under Companies Act 2006, s 899, two majority requirements need to be met. The scheme needs to be sanctioned by a majority of members present at the meeting either in person or by proxy (headcount test), which together represent 75 per cent of the members (value test). At the meeting, 812 out of 1,314 members present voted to approve the scheme, with 502 members voting against the scheme. The votes in favour represented over 80 per cent of the value of shares voted. Both the headcount test and the majority in value test were satisfied.[16] When the company applied to the High Court to sanction the scheme pursuant to Companies Act 2006, s 899, objections were raised including claims that individual ultimate investors had not had a voice at the meeting at which members voted to approve the scheme, since the former did not appear on the company's membership register. Mr Justice Fancourt held that the fact that many ultimate investors did not have the opportunity to vote was not 'directly relevant to an assessment of fair representation of members, because beneficial shareholders are not members'. He further said that, 'If sufficient numbers of beneficial shareholders had given instructions to their nominees to vote against the scheme, the outcome of the vote might have been different, but the company cannot be blamed for that. As the law stands, it had no obligation to communicate with the beneficial owners of its shares.'

5.14 The above cases illustrate how the no-look-through approach disconnects indirect investors from issuers. This is an unattractive and surprising outcome in particular for a market with the calibre of that of the United Kingdom. It is also clear that none of these cases involved connections with remote financial markets, where some disruption might be expected. Both Germany and Luxembourg are advanced economies with

---

[12] [2015] EWHC 388 (Comm) 25 February 2015.
[13] Ibid, paras 3, 4, 7–11, 23–8.
[14] *Secure Capital SA v Credit Suisse AG* [2017] EWCA Civ 1486 (6 October 2017).
[15] *Re Sirius Minerals plc* [2020] EWHC 1447 (Ch).
[16] Ibid, para 17.

correspondingly mature legal systems in close geographical proximity to the UK, and those serving the investment industry in these countries have good command of the English language.

C. Distributed Ledger Technology

5.15 I argued in 2015 that, in light of the unappealing consequences of the no-look-through approach, it is worth exploring the possibility of crypto-securities.[17] Since then, a number of academic contributors have further endorsed this idea. Their contributions will be examined in this section.

5.16 Academic scholars agree with the proposition that a technological solution can be found that address the problems associated with the current intermediated holding structure. Emilios Evouleas and Aggelos Kiayias criticize the current market infrastructure and observe that distributed ledger technology could benefit end-investors as well as other end-users of financial services.[18] Frederico Panisi, Ross P Buckley, and Douglas W Arner observe that distributed ledger technology has the capacity to streamline the entire shareownership architecture, enabling the tracking of share ownership through the complete settlement cycle, and enhancing shareholder democracy and corporate governance.[19] They point out that the technology is associated with certain risks, which will have to be mitigated, and conclude by setting out tasks to be addressed by regulation.[20] Along similar lines, Christoph Van der Elst and Anne Lafarre state that a permissioned distributed ledger can be used to enable shareholders to exercise their voting rights.[21] Georg Geis also focuses on the ability of shareholders to exercise governance rights. He predicts that distributed ledger technology will bring about traceable shares leading to a detailed and traceable record of title for every single share. This will have a profound impact on corporate law, changing the structure of shareholder lawsuits, altering the allocation of corporate governance rights, and requiring law makers to rethink the fundamental principles of shareholder responsibility for corporate misdeeds.[22]

5.17 Delphine Nougayrède adds a further dimension to the debate. She is primarily concerned with questions of taxation, money laundering, and sanction compliance, and observes that the intermediated holding system impedes the public policy aims of the respective rules. She also notes that end-investor transparency would produce benefits for the governance of companies and, referring to the possible use of distributed

---

[17] Micheler, 'Custody Chains and Asset Values', 519.
[18] Avgouleas and Kiayias, 'The Promise of Blockchain Technology for Global Securities and Derivatives Markets', 105–6.
[19] Panisi, Buckley, and Arner, 'Blockchain and Public Companies'.
[20] Ibid, 15–16.
[21] Van der Elst and Lafarre, 'Blockchain and Smart Contracting for the Shareholder Community', 125–33.
[22] Geis, 'Traceable Shares and Corporate Law', 273.

ledger technology, recommends that end-investors hold securities transparently at CSD level.[23]

5.18 There are also sceptics. Philipp Paech has warned that the Bitcoin model is unsuitable for financial markets. He observes that a permissionless distributed ledger undermines existing regulatory strategies, which rely on identifying individual participants and their bilateral relationships. He also believes that immutable records and self-executing smart contracts are capable of undermining the ability of the law to review transactions and enforce policy goals. He therefore concludes that the blockchain revolution will primarily introduce new ways of transaction processing, recording, and reporting that will render financial markets significantly more efficient. He urges governments to involve themselves in the governance of such networks to ensure that the technology is used for the benefit of all market participants.[24]

5.19 Edmund Schuster also points out that the disruptive nature of distributed ledger technology has been greatly overstated. He argues that any implementation of the technology is necessarily accompanied by design choices that undermine the logic of the Bitcoin model leading to applications that are 'blockchains in name only'.[25] He observes that the benefits generally associated with distributed ledger technology could be achieved by any technological upgrade intended to increase the interoperability of legacy systems. His conclusion is that it would be beneficial for the economy if the 'excitement surrounding' distributed ledger technology encouraged 'business to rebuild and update legacy systems sooner and in a more co-ordinated way'.[26]

5.20 Notwithstanding their scepticism in relation to the, now receding, hype around distributed ledger technology as adopted by Bitcoin, both Philipp Paech and Edmund Schuster concede that it is possible to design a more efficient technological infrastructure for financial markets.

5.21 David Donald and Mahdi Miraz add a further dimension to the debate by making a granular proposal for a distributed-ledger-based system that would facilitate both trading and settlement. In this proposed system, nodes would need permission to be able to join. Investors would hold securities directly. The authors' main concern is the fragmentation of trading, which has made it difficult for investors to ascertain price, while the intermediated holding model has also obscured ownership of securities, thereby damaging investor rights. They propose a permissioned distributed ledger system since this would avoid the cumbersome consensus mechanism associated with permissionless systems such as Bitcoin. Securities would be held directly on an issuer register.

---

[23] Nougayrède, 'Towards a Global Financial Register?', 305–6.
[24] Paech, 'Governance of Blockchain Financial Networks'.
[25] Schuster, 'Cloud Crypto Land', 20–1.
[26] Ibid, 31.

5.22 Charles W Mooney also makes granular suggestions. He has published a request for a proposal to the FinTech industry. He does not state a preference for any particular technology but nevertheless observes that distributed ledger technology has benefits that could overcome the problems associated with the current intermediated infrastructure.[27] He stresses the importance for any new system to take account of the resistance to change of the providers of the existing infrastructure. Their 'enormous influence' should not prevent regulators and law makers from coming on board.[28] His contribution contains parameters designed to provide FinTech developers with a granular starting point from which to develop a technological solution. In his proposal, the operator of the system does not maintain a register but facilitates the entry of securities-related transactions on a globally shared record where investors hold securities directly.[29] The system should serve the needs of all market participants that are currently addressed by the intermediated holding system.[30] For example, investment companies are currently required to hold securities through custodian banks. In a direct holding model, the banks could continue to oversee investments held directly by such companies.[31] End-investors nevertheless would be identified by name or through another identifier at master record level.[32] This would enable investors to exercise voting rights and claim against issuers. The system would also accommodate securities lending by facilitating the designation of securities released by investors for that purpose.[33] Investors would retain an option to use an intermediary particularly in a cross-border context.[34] The system would work globally and so require 'substantial co-operation, coordination, and harmonization of laws, regulation and operations'.[35] Existing organizations are, however, well suited to organize the necessary processes of harmonization for the implementation of such a system.[36]

5.23 Randy Priem provides an in-depth review on how distributed ledger technology could be made to work against the background of the current market infrastructure. In particular, he believes that the technology could be used to reduce the long custody chains that are involved in cross-border transactions of exchange-traded securities.[37] Because such a system would involve fewer intermediaries, many of the currently repetitive reconciliations would be eliminated.[38] He observes that, while several proof of concept projects have succeeded, no full-scale DLT system is as yet fully operative and so the wider implications of DLT in terms of business model impacts are not yet known.[39]

---

[27] Mooney, 'Beyond Intermediation', 443–6.
[28] Mooney, 'Beyond Intermediation', 426.
[29] Ibid, 427–31 and 442.
[30] Ibid, 428.
[31] Ibid, 451.
[32] Ibid, 430.
[33] Ibid, 433–4.
[34] Ibid, 435.
[35] Ibid, 435.
[36] Ibid, 435.
[37] Priem, 'Distributed Ledger Technology for Securities Clearing and Settlement', 3.
[38] Ibid, 12.
[39] Ibid, 2, 7.

Priem nevertheless predicts that in a DLT-based system, trading and post-trading (clearing and settlement) could become more intertwined. He analyses the current infrastructure and on that basis develops a DLT-based model into which the current infrastructure could be transformed.[40] He envisages a permissioned system, which would require gatekeeper licensing nodes. The ledger would be updated through a consensus mechanism administered by those licensed nodes.[41] He observes that CCPs and CSDs, whose current role would be redundant, could adapt to perform functions such as co-ordinating evolution of the software, the management and safekeeping of private keys, the management of the introduction and cancellation of tokens on the ledger, as well as the licensing and operation of nodes.[42] He also identifies regulatory challenges that currently hinder the adoption of a DLT-based system.[43]

5.24 Sarah Green and Ferdisha Snagg observe that securities could be tokenized on a distributed ledger.[44] For debt securities, there would no longer be a global paper certificate. Instead, they would be issued directly onto the distributed ledger with issuers committing to recognizing the holder of the token as the owner of the securities. For equity securities, the law would have to change to allow for members to be identified by reference to that distributed ledger.[45] This would make it possible for the owners of securities to be identified without the need for assets to be 'pooled with other investors' assets' or 'mirrored across cascading tiers of holders'.[46] It would also eliminate the possibility of one investor's securities inadvertently being used by an intermediary to settle another's transaction.[47] The authors also observe that a distributed ledger for securities could be linked with the payment system. This would further reduce settlement risk by linking the delivery of securities with the payment of the purchase price, which is currently possible only at the level of the CSD but can be difficult to achieve for investors who hold securities indirectly.[48] They also endorse the observation that a distributed ledger would reduce systemic risk by removing the current reliance of the system on the CSD as one central operator. A distributed system has 'as many redundant backups as there are contributers to the network'.[49]

5.25 Green and Snagg further acknowledge that investors may decide to hold securities through wallet providers but point out that it is not necessary, as a matter of law, to characterize the relationship between the provider of the wallet and the investor as a trust. They argue that it would be possible to analyse that relationship in terms of bailment, which would give the investor a right in the underlying asset rather than a right

---

[40] Ibid, 10–14.
[41] Ibid, 11–14.
[42] Ibid, 14–15.
[43] Ibid, 15–20; for an analysis of issues relating to insolvency law, see Mangano, 'Blockchain Securities, Insolvency Law and the Sandbox Approach'.
[44] Law Commission, *Who Owns Your Shares?*, 9.67.
[45] Green and Snagg, 'Intermediated Securities and Distributed Ledger Technology', 341.
[46] Ibid, 341; see also Paech, 'Securities, Intermediation and the Blockchain'.
[47] Green and Snagg, 'Intermediated Securities and Distributed Ledger Technology', 342.
[48] Ibid, 342–8.
[49] Ibid, 342.

in the right held by the custodian.[50] This argument relies on a number of contributions by Sarah Green, who reasons that the concept of possession is not intrinsically linked with the concept of tangibility. Like the possessor of a tangible, the holder of cryptosecurities can exclude others from using them and their interest can also be completely exhausted.[51] They should be characterized as negotiable securities by commercial usage.[52]

5.26 I have advanced a similar argument elsewhere in relation to German and Austrian law, where it is also possible to conclude that negotiability is independent of tangibility, justifying the conclusion that securities are negotiable irrespective of whether they are represented by paper documents or through electronic entries.[53]

5.27 Overall, we may conclude that there are reservations in relation to the ability of the original unpermissioned Bitcoin model to suit the infrastructure requirements of financial markets. Still, these reservations do not undermine the conclusion that it would be possible to develop a technology that enfranchises indirect investors while retaining the ability of investors to make their securities available for lending and other financing transactions.[54]

5.28 The conclusion that distributed ledger technology can inspire an upgrade of the current technological infrastructure is further supported by the recent proposal by the European Commission of a pilot regime for the development of a DLT multilateral trading facility and also by the decision of the Australian Stock Exchange (ASX) to adopt a new settlement system inspired by distributed ledger technology.[55]

D. Barriers to Change

5.29 So far we have seen that alternative technological solutions are possible. The hype associated with Bitcoin has supplied momentum for reform.[56] We have also come some way towards defining the characteristics of an alternative system that could enfranchise investors. Unfortunately, however, the business case for switching from the current

---

[50] Ibid, 344–5.
[51] Green, 'To Have and to Hold?'; Green and Snagg, 'Intermediated Securities and Distributed Ledger Technology', 346.
[52] Green, 'To Have and to Hold'; Green and Snagg, 'Intermediated Securities and Distributed Ledger Technology', 348.
[53] Micheler, 'The Legal Nature of Securities'; see also Micheler, *Wertpapierrecht zwischen Schuld—und Sachenrecht*.
[54] On such transactions, see Ch 2.
[55] Proposal for a Regulation of the European Parliament and of the Council on a pilot regime for market infrastructures based on distributed ledger technology, COM(2020) 594 final, <https://eur-lex.europa.eu/legal-content/EN/TXT/PDF/?uri=CELEX:52020PC0594&from=EN> (accessed 7 July 2021); for a critical assessment of the proposal see Ringe and Ruof, 'The DLT Pilot Regime'. On developments at the ASX, see ASX CHESS Background, <https://www.asx.com.au/services/chess-replacement.htm#consultation-papers> (accessed 7 July 2021); McDowell, 'ASX to Replace Equity Post-trade Systems with Blockchain'; Digital Asset, *The Digital Asset Platform*.
[56] For an analysis of English language news media articles in relation to distributed ledger technology, see Perdana et al, 'Distributed Ledger Technology'.

intermediated model to a direct holding model is less clear. A number of problems arise in this connection.

5.30 The first problem is that the structure of custody chains is difficult to rationalize from an economic perspective. Admittedly, some elements of a custody chain can be explained by reference to economies of scale. In the *Eckerle* case, the custody chain consisted of Postbank, Clearstream Banking Luxembourg, Bank of New York Mellon, and CREST (Euroclear).[57] Postbank may not have enough customers to justify membership in Crest and therefore uses Clearstream Banking Luxembourg as an intermediary to connect it to the UK. What is much less clear is why Mr Eckerle benefitted from Clearstream Banking Luxembourg using Bank of New York Mellon to connect to CREST. Clearstream Banking Luxembourg is a large international custodian and so is likely to have sufficient traffic with the UK to justify membership in CREST. The *Secure Capital* case poses a similar puzzle. The participants in the custody chain in that case were RBS Global Banking (Luxembourg), Clearstream Banking Luxembourg, and Bank of New York Mellon. Secure Capital bought a bespoke bond. There were no other investors. Bank of New York Mellon acted as the depositary for the bearer notes.[58] RBS, Secure Capital's immediate custodian, may not have had the facilities to store a bearer bond. It is less clear, however, why it was in the interest of Secure Capital for RBS to use Clearstream to connect to Bank of New Mellon rather than to contract with a provider of a storage facility directly.

5.31 We can only assume that the presence of Bank of New York Mellon in the *Eckerle* case and that of Clearstream Banking (Luxembourg) in the *Secure Capital* case served an economic rationale of the custodians delegating custody to them, but it is difficult from the outside to articulate this rationale.

5.32 The second point to make here is that developing new technology and adapting legacy systems to that technology is costly.[59] Intermediaries are only able to shoulder the cost associated with the development of a new technology if they are persuaded that the necessary investment will be justified by future return.[60] It has already been mentioned that Charles W Mooney predicts robust opposition from incumbent custodians to any change that undermines their position in the market.[61] Ghiath Shabsigh, Tanai Khaionarong, and Harry Leinonen have published a survey of experiments conducted by incumbent infrastructure providers testing distributed ledger technology for clearing and settlement purposes.[62] They observe that these experiments were all based on the assumption that the current market infrastructure would stay the same and that

---

[57] *Eckerle v Wickeder* [2013] EWHC 68 (Ch).
[58] *Secure Capital SA v Credit Suisse AG* [2017] EWCA Civ 1486, para 14.
[59] Law Commission, *Who Owns Your Shares?*, 9.65.
[60] Manning, Sutton, and Zhu, 'Distributed Ledger Technology in Securities Clearing and Settlement', 33.
[61] Mooney, 'Beyond Intermediation', 426.
[62] For a list of the projects surveyed see: Shabsigh, Khaionarong, and Leinonen, *Distributed Ledger Technology Experiments in Payments and Settlements*, 10. Note, however, that the authors have only examined projects conducted by participants in the existing market infrastructure.

exchanges, dealers, CCPs, CSDs, custodians, and the central bank would operate in similar or near-similar roles as they do today and in a multi-layered registration structure. None of these projects analysed a flatter market structure or DvP processing at the end-investor level or other radical structural changes in the market.[63] This evidences a preference on the part of incumbent service providers to retain the business model associated with the status quo.[64]

5.33 We can also learn from history. In the UK, the current settlement system was implemented following the disastrous collapse of the Taurus project. The Taurus project was launched in the late 1980s to replace paper-based settlement with electronic settlement. The initial design did not integrate a role for registrars, who had previously handled paper documents and maintained paper registers. The project had to be abandoned in the face of their robust opposition.[65]

5.34 I have mentioned elsewhere that the settlement infrastructure suffers from a lack of oversight from investors. Individual investors do not have the bargaining power enabling them to insist on better custody terms.[66] We can further observe that very few investors hold individual securities. Since the middle of the twentieth century, investment has become increasingly institutionalized.[67] Individual investors have been replaced by funds. These include pension funds but also funds held by individual savers who, in earlier times, would have invested in individual securities. Counterintuitively the institutionalization of investment does not appear to result in greater oversight for custodians. Custody is a back office function. We would need empirical research to improve our understanding of the perspective of pension trustees and asset managers acting for funds. We may speculate that these service providers tend to focus on identifying appropriate assets and that custody arrangements do not receive the same amount of careful attention.[68]

5.35 In 2001, the Lamfalussy Report and, a little later, two Giovannini Reports called on the market to create a more efficient solution for clearing and settlement in the EU.[69] At the time, the problem was complexity leading to high settlement cost. Since then, complexity has increased and intermediation has emerged as a new, additional challenge. In 2017, the European Post Trade Forum Report stated that the barriers highlighted in the Giovannini Reports continued to exist and that investor rights in custody chains constitute an impediment to the Capital Markets Union.[70]

---

[63] Shabsigh, Khaionarong, and Leinonen, *Distributed Ledger Technology Experiments in Payments and Settlements*, 3–4.

[64] The authors do not appear to have conducted a survey of projects conducted by potential disrupter FinTech firms; for a study surveying a broader range of distributed ledger projects, see Rauchs et al, *2nd Global Enterprise Blockchain Benchmarking Study*.

[65] <http://calleam.com/WTPF/?p=3474> (accessed 7 July 2021).

[66] Micheler, 'Intermediated Securities from the Perspective of Investors', 247–8.

[67] Davies Evans, 'A Requiem for the Retail Investor?'; Judge, 'Intermediary Influence'; Gilson and Gordon, 'Agency Costs of Agency Capitalism'; Moore and Petrin, *Corporate Governance*, 99–109.

[68] Micheler, 'Intermediated Securities from the Perspective of Investors', 248.

[69] Lamfalussy, *Final Report*; Giovannini, *Cross-Border Clearing and Settlement Arrangements*; Giovannini, *Second Report*.

[70] EPTF, *Report*, 12–13.

In the UK, the problems associated with intermediated shareholders were discussed by the Steering Group drafting the Companies Act 2006. At the time, the Steering Group accepted assurances from the custody industry that it would be 'very soon ... feasible, at low cost', for indirect investors to vote in shareholder meetings.[71] The Law Commission observes that this has yet to come to pass.[72] The fact that the market is finding it difficult to create an overall, efficient infrastructure is also evident from the aforementioned Taurus project. After the first attempt failed due to opposition by registrars, a second attempt to design a computer-based settlement system was likewise unsuccessful. That design aimed to please all incumbent actors but was so complex that it proved unworkable.[73] In light of the market's persistent failure to produce a solution, it is time for the government to step in.

E. Possible Solutions

In principle, the UK government should be motivated to improve the legal position of indirect investors in UK securities. The disenfranchisement of indirect investors under English law is a reputational problem. Having left the European Union, the UK is now orienting itself towards attracting a more global audience. It is still interested in appealing to European investors, who need to overcome the barriers created by Brexit to benefit from UK financial services. A situation where English law and market practices design indirect holdings so as to deprive investors of the ability to exercise their rights is not helpful in that respect. Investors with bargaining power may insist on opting out of English law.[74] Others could decide to invest their money in other jurisdictions.

The recent Scoping Paper by the UK Law Commission suggests that the UK government is aware of the problem.[75] The Law Commission puts forward two approaches. The first is either to remove intermediation altogether and operate a 'name on register' structure or to retain intermediation but create an affordable avenue for investors to hold securities directly if they wish.[76] The alternative would be to adopt a range of targeted solutions enhancing the rights of ultimate investors and improving corporate governance.[77] The Law Commission also discusses the idea that a Code of Best Practice could be created, which would initially apply on a voluntary basis but could, with time, evolve to establish itself along the same line as the UK Corporate Governance Code or the UK Stewardship Code.[78] The principles contained in such a Code of Best Practice would cover the relationships between intermediaries and both retail and institutional

---

[71] The Company Law Review Steering Group, *Final Report*, 7.1, 7.3, and 3.51.
[72] Law Commission, *Who Owns Your Shares?*, 9.3–8.
[73] <http://calleam.com/WTPF/?p=3474> (accessed 7 July 2021).
[74] Micheler, 'Intermediated Securities from the Perspective of Investors', 250.
[75] Law Commission, *Who Owns Your Shares?*.
[76] Ibid 8.4, 8.36–86.
[77] Ibid 10.6–7.
[78] Ibid 9.14.

investors. Examples of matters to be included in the Code are the provision of information to an ultimate investor as well as a commitment on the part of intermediaries to facilitate the exercise of investors' rights.

5.39 It is worth pointing out that the current situation could be remedied without resorting to technological, legislative, or regulatory change. The root of the problem is the terms used by intermediaries.[79] These terms can be changed, but this is unlikely to happen without governmental pressure. The Law Commission reports that, in light of the failure of previous industry-led initiatives, stakeholders, including intermediaries, have indicated that 'the industry requires an incentive, such as a legislative or regulatory obligation, in order to change its current practices'.[80]

5.40 I have previously suggested that such an incentive could be provided by requiring investor custodians to insist on certain terms in their outsourcing contracts. Those terms could be required to be filtered through the chain of any sub-custodians. It would also be possible to require synchronized reconciliations along the custody chain and to introduce more robust rules holding investor custodians liable for the conduct of custodians further down the chain.[81]

5.41 Another solution would be for regulators to insist that custodians require their sub-custodians to use identifiers in records that can be traced back to individual investors. This practice could be referred to as 'earmarking' or 'colouring' securities. International Bank Account Numbers can serve as a role model here. Similar, alphanumeric identifiers might be developed that would not only be uniquely associated with individual ultimate investors but also identify securities available for financing transactions. Custodians could then be required to insist in their contracts that such identifiers be associated with securities records held throughout the chain.[82]

5.42 In addition, the UK could solve the problem of the no-look-through approach by adopting legislation enabling indirect investors to claim against issuers. Other jurisdictions have gone down that path. Germany and Austria, for example, put in place legislation following their paper crunch in the 1930s.[83] The *Secure Capital* case centred around an issue of private international law. The investor's argument was that Luxembourg law determined ownership in the securities. Under Luxembourg law, the investor would have been able to claim against the issuer.[84]

5.43 UK company law has started to take into account the phenomenon of indirect investment. For example, it is now possible for an issuer to adopt provisions in its articles enabling a registered member to nominate another person to 'enjoy or exercise all or any specified rights of the member in relation to the company'.[85] In the *Eckerle*

---

[79] Micheler, 'Custody Chains and Asset Values', 509–12; Law Commission, *Who Owns Your Shares?*, 9.22–5.
[80] Law Commission, *Who Owns Your Shares?*, 9.4.
[81] Micheler, 'Intermediated Securities from the Perspective of Investors', 253–8.
[82] Ibid, 257.
[83] Micheler, *Property in Securities*, 193–222.
[84] *Secure Capital SA v Credit Suisse AG* [2017] EWCA Civ 1486 (6 October 2017).
[85] CA 2006, s 145(1).

case, the issuer's constitution did contain such provisions, which would have enabled Clearstream Interest Holders to exercise shareholder rights. Unfortunately, Mr Eckerle did not hold Clearstream Interests, which were held by another custodian acting for Mr Eckerle.[86] Those drafting provisions for the constitution of a company could learn from that case and use more careful language. Ultimately, however, the length of a custody chain falls outside the influence of issuers and investors alike, so that it is very difficult to word the constitution with a view to empowering end-investors, however far removed from the issuer though they be.

Under CA 2006, s 146(2) a registered member of a traded company can nominate another person to 'enjoy information rights'.[87] A registered holder of shares can also exercise rights in different ways upon the instructions of different indirect investors.[88] Both provisions go some way towards assisting indirect investors. **5.44**

Moreover, English law is beginning to show signs suggesting that it might be able to find a way of recognizing indirect investors. The Companies Act 2006 contains rules that could be expanded. CA 2006, s 153 enables a hundred or more indirect investors to exercise certain shareholder rights. These rights are: the power to require the circulation of a statement,[89] the power to require circulation of a resolution for an AGM of a public company,[90] the power to include matters in business dealt with at an AGM of a traded company,[91] the power to require an independent report on a poll,[92] and the power to require website publication of audit concerns.[93] In order to be able to benefit from CA 2006, s 153, the investors need to submit a statement: **5.45**

(i) of the full name and address of a person ('the member') who is a member of the company and holds shares on behalf of that person;
(ii) that the member is holding those shares on behalf of that person in the course of a business;
(iii) of the number of shares in the company that the member holds on behalf of that person;
(iv) of the total amount paid up on those shares;
(v) that those shares are not held on behalf of anyone else or, if they are, that the other person or persons are not among the other persons making the request;
(vi) that some or all of those shares confer voting rights that are relevant for the purposes of making a request under the section in question; and
(vi) that the person has the right to instruct the member how to exercise those rights.

---

[86] *Eckerle v Wickeder* [2013] EWHC 68 (Ch); [2014] Ch 196, paras 14 and 29–31.
[87] CA 2006, s 146(2).
[88] Ibid, s 152.
[89] Ibid, s 153(1)(a).
[90] Ibid, s 153(1)(b).
[91] Ibid, s 153(1)(ba).
[92] Ibid, s 153(1)(c).
[93] Ibid, s 153(1)(d).

In addition, the request must be accompanied by 'such evidence as the company may reasonably require'.[94]

5.46 Admittedly, the provision is very limited in scope. It requires a hundred or more shareholders to co-operate and is only available to a very small number of shareholder rights. Also, it is not clear what type of evidence the company is entitled to require from indirect investors. Finally, investors who hold securities through a custody chain can only benefit from the provision if they can find a way of identifying the registered holder to whom they are ultimately connected and can persuade that holder to supply them with the evidence required by the company. The provision is therefore unlikely to have much traction in practice. It is nevertheless a starting point from which a wider regime enabling indirect investors to exercise rights against issuers could be developed.

5.47 The courts have also recently shown a willingness to recognize indirect investors holding securities through a custody chain. In *SL Claimants v Tesco plc*,[95] ultimate investors brought a claim under section 90A of the FSMA, claiming loss in connection with false and misleading statements made by Tesco in relation to its commercial income in 2014. Under Schedule 10A paragraph 8, a person who holds 'any interest in securities' is entitled to claim. Tesco argued that, since the claimants held the securities through a chain of intermediaries, they only had rights that could be asserted against the person immediately preceding them in the chain, and that this was not enough to constitute an 'interest' in the underlying securities.[96] Hildyard J rejected that argument. He characterized the position of an investor as the owner of 'a right to a right' held through 'a waterfall or chain of equitable relationships which is unaffected by the insolvency of its intermediary, and enables it ultimately, even if indirectly, to enjoy the benefit of the bundle of rights which the securities represent to the exclusion of others'.[97] As a result, the ultimate investors had standing to claim against Tesco under FSMA, section 90A.

5.48 The courts have, moreover, been prepared to recognize beneficial owners of companies in the context of the *Duomatic* principle. Under that principle, unanimous decisions taken by all shareholders are recognized even though the formalities usually associated with shareholder meetings have not been complied with.[98] In three recent decisions, the courts have held that the consent of the ultimate beneficial owner of all the shares in a company is sufficient for the *Duomatic* principle to apply.[99] The principle was applied notwithstanding the fact that the names of the respective beneficial owners were not entered on the shareholder register. These cases shared some distinct features. In all three, one individual was the beneficial owner of all the shares in a company. The

---

[94] Ibid, s 153(2)(e).
[95] [2019] EWHC 2858 (Ch), [2020] Bus LR 250.
[96] Ibid, para 37.
[97] Ibid, paras 81, 85.
[98] *Re Duomatic Ltd* [1969] 2 Ch 365.
[99] *Ciban Management Corporation v Citco (BVI) Ltd* [2020] UKPC 21; *Byers v Chen* [2021] UKPC 4; *Satyam Enterprises Ltd v Burton* [2021] EWCA Civ 287.

trustees were not financial services providers, but individual off-shore companies set up for the purpose of facilitating the investor's indirect ownership. This is very different from the situation analysed in this contribution. This chapter is concerned with cases where individuals hold a relatively small number of securities through a financial service provider.[100]

More generally, the *Duomatic* principle gives license to the court to override the formal requirements for shareholder decisions contained in the Companies Act. While the courts neither discussed nor accepted this point, the requirement for registration may be characterized as such a formal requirement for the taking of shareholder decisions. Against this backdrop, the approach adopted in these recent cases is unlikely to be applied successfully in other areas of company law. It is nevertheless worth noting that the recognition of beneficial shareholders is not an unheard-of measure in the realm of English company law. 5.49

Another avenue for the recognition of indirect investors was recently opened up by the decision in *Boston Trust Co Ltd v Szerelmey Ltd*.[101] In that case, an investor filed a derivative claim at common law, arguing that it had been validly appointed as replacement trustee of the shares in the company. At first, the case was struck out on the basis that the claimant was not the legal owner of the securities and could not show a beneficial interest, either.[102] A second application, however, succeeded, with the court granting conditional permission to continue the derivative claim. That conditional permission was granted because the court was satisfied that there was 'a good prospect' of the claimant succeeding at having the register rectified 'within a tolerable time frame'.[103] As it stands, this decision is only of use to investors able to show they are entitled and have applied to have their names registered as the legal owners of shares. To this effect, the custodian forming part of the custody chain would have to agree that the chain can be collapsed, not an easy thing to achieve. From our perspective, the case at issue nevertheless contributes to the overall picture, showing that ways can be found to ensure that indirect holders of securities can fully enjoy the rights associated with their securities. 5.50

F. Conclusion

This chapter set out to demonstrate that the intermediated holding structure that has evolved across the world does not sit comfortably with English law, which is currently unable to recognize indirect investors and allow them to exercise the rights associated with their securities. In the short term, the problem can be resolved by bond 5.51

---

[100] *Secure Capital SA v Credit Suisse AG* ([2017] EWCA Civ 1486), of course, was a case where one investor held all the units of a particular issues of debt securities.
[101] [2020] EWHC 1136 (Ch).
[102] Ibid.
[103] *Boston Trust Co Ltd v Szerelmey Ltd* [2020] EWHC 1352, [2020] BusLR 1647, para 72 (which case is currently under appeal); see also *Jafari-Fini v Skillglass Ltd* [2004] EWCA 3353 (Ch), paras 38, 41–3.

investors contracting out of English law. Equity investors can opt to hold securities directly through personal accounts with the CSD. Remedies might also be found through changes in the technology. In light of previous failed attempts on the part of the market to craft more efficient solutions, this contribution concludes that it is time for the government to step in, and suggests ways in which this might be done. The recent Scoping Study conducted by the UK Law Commission combined with the UK Government's ambition to attract a global pool of investors suggests that the UK Government is motivated to address the problem.

6

CORPORATE ACTIONS PROCESSING: BRIDGING THE GAP BETWEEN ISSUER AND INVESTOR[*]

A. Introduction	6.01	
B. General Meetings	6.10	
(1) Who votes and how?	6.10	
(2) Challenges in the exercise of voting rights	6.11	
(a) Direct rights against the issuer	6.11	
(b) Instructions to intermediaries and proxy voting	6.12	
(c) Transparency and omnibus/individual accounts	6.16	
(d) Split voting	6.17	
(e) Timelines	6.18	
(f) Processing errors and 'lost votes'	6.20	
(g) The role of technology	6.22	
(h) Collateral	6.23	
C. Income Distributions	6.24	
(1) Income: what, to whom, and how?	6.24	
(2) Challenges in the distribution of income	6.28	
(a) Identifying the investor	6.29	
(b) Timelines	6.30	
(c) Income processing errors	6.31	
(d) Withholding tax	6.32	
D. Provision of Information	6.33	
(1) Provision of information: what, to whom, and how?	6.33	
(2) Challenges in the provision of information	6.35	
(a) Identifying the recipients	6.36	
(b) Content of information	6.37	
(c) Interpretation	6.39	
(d) Regulatory probes or proceedings	6.40	
(e) Timelines and technology	6.41	
E. Outlook: New Technologies	6.45	
(1) New technologies: DLT and smart contracts	6.45	
(2) Consistency and common standards	6.50	
(3) Information processing	6.53	
(4) Reconciliation	6.54	
(5) Immutability	6.55	
(6) Transparency	6.56	
(7) Other factors	6.59	
F. Conclusion: Current Status and the Way Forward	6.64	

A. Introduction

During the lifecycle of securities, issuers and investors must effectively liaise with regard to the rights attached to securities, including rights concerning (i) general meetings, notably voting rights; (ii) the distribution of income (such as payment of dividend on shares, interest on bonds, or other distributions); and/or (iii) the provision of information. We refer to these events as corporate actions.[1] The processing of corporate actions may be complicated when

6.01

---

[*] We wish to thank Nora Rachman for her contribution to the version of this chapter included in the first edition of this book (and the updates thereof for the Oxford Legal Research Library).

[1] The term 'corporate' actions is used in the context of securities issued by corporations or other private entities, such as shares or private bonds, as well as by governments or government agencies, such as public bonds. See Simmons and Dalgleish, *Corporate Actions*, 3, defining a corporate action as 'an event in the life of a security

an intermediated chain is involved. Such a chain is typically composed of several actors.[2] At the 'top' of the chain one may find issuers, the issuer's registrar,[3] and central securities depositories (CSDs). The 'bottom' of the chain is composed of ultimate account holders or investors.[4] One or more intermediaries provide the interface between issuers and investors, and process corporate actions 'up' and 'down' the chain. Depending on how the system is set up, there may thus be a 'disconnect' between the issuer and end investors.[5] The longer the chain of intermediaries, the more complex it may become, increasing the likelihood of errors, delays, or other complications. In a worst-case scenario, investors are cut off from their rights.[6] This chapter examines these complications and possible solutions.

6.02 A key issue is identification of the economic beneficiary of intermediated securities (the ultimate account holder or investor), so as to enable it to exercise the rights attached to the securities, including voting rights, income, and information.[7] However, under corporate law, the person entitled to the economic stake may not always be the registered holder (with legal or registered title) as indicated on the register.[8] Depending on the set-up of a particular legal system, there may thus be a discrepancy between who is legally entitled to the rights attached to the securities (for example, the first intermediary in the chain from the issuer's perspective) and who is economically entitled to these rights (the ultimate investor).[9] If issuers of intermediated securities do not know who is ultimately entitled to their securities, they may need to rely on the intermediaries in the holding chain to process corporate actions.[10]

(typically) instigated by the issuer, which affects a position in that security'. Another definition is that of the Legal Certainty Group, *Second Advice*, 79: 'all kinds of action triggered by the issuer or by the terms of a security and affecting the security (equity or debt)'.

[2] Cf UNIDROIT Legislative Guide on Intermediated Securities, para 22.

[3] A registrar maintains the register of shareholders/bondholders/investors to identify those entitled to the rights attached to the securities, so as to facilitate corporate actions processing. Registrar services may be rendered by the issuer, but in practice the issuer often appoints another entity for that specific purpose. Registrar services include identifying who holds securities in certificated form or in book-entry form. In some States, eg, South Africa, a securities issue may consist of both certificates and dematerialized securities, although the law requires compulsory dematerialization for new listings traded on the exchange and settled in the CSD. Where the registrar maintains the register for certificated securities and another entity such as a CSD maintains the register for dematerialized securities, these registers may need to be reconciled. See Legal Certainty Group, *Second Advice*, 15.2.2.2. On reconciliation, see Ch 7, s E(2).

[4] In this chapter, an 'investor' may be an account holder, shareholder, bondholder, other holder of securities, or beneficiary, at the end of or outside the holding chain. Cf the definitions in the UNIDROIT Legislative Guide on Intermediated Securities, para 22; Legal Certainty Group, *Second Advice*, 79.

[5] For different intermediated securities holding models, see UNIDROIT Legislative Guide on Intermediated Securities, paras 39–53. There are models, notably 'transparent' ones, in which issuers and investors are directly connected. For more information on transparent systems, see Kanda et al, *Official Commentary*, Int-28 to Int-30 and commentary on Art 7.

[6] Donald, *Rise and Effects*, 23–5; Panisi, Buckley, and Arner, 'Blockchain and Public Companies', III.

[7] A discussion of 'empty voting' and 'hidden ownership', where there is a discrepancy between the voting rights and economic interests of an account holder (eg, in the case of short selling or stock lending), is outside the scope of this chapter. On collateral, see para 6.23.

[8] Kahan and Rock, 'Hanging Chads of Corporate Voting', 1233, 1240–3; Paech, 'The UNIDROIT Project', 1144; Payne, 'Right to Vote in the UK', I, III.

[9] See Kanda et al, *Official Commentary*, 8–7, 9–3, 9–16, 29–3.

[10] Recital (11) SRD; Kahan and Rock, 'Hanging Chads of Corporate Voting', 1244; Legal Certainty Group, *Second Advice*, 13.5; Myners, *Report* (2007), 15; Paech, 'The UNIDROIT Project', 1144, 1150. On shareholder identification, see Enriques, Gargantini, and Novembre, 'Shareholding Disclosure', 714–5, 718–20, 724–7; Rachman, 'Trends and

INTRODUCTION 149

6.03 Intermediated chains may be more complex or less so because of the legal, regulatory, and market infrastructure in the jurisdictions involved. Intermediated chains often cross borders, which means that several legal and regulatory frameworks may be involved that need to be compatible.[11] Moreover, in a cross-border context, additional actors, such as global custodians, may be added to the intermediated chain to manage the complexity of an international portfolio. These factors may increase the time needed for and the likelihood of errors in processing corporate actions to and from the ultimate account holders and investors.[12]

6.04 National frameworks for the exercise of voting rights need to be compatible. Problems may, for example, arise where the law of State X: (i) does not allow omnibus accounts, while a foreign intermediary may be unable to provide voting services to an account holder in an individual segregated account; or (ii) attributes legal consequences to registered title, but only if both the account and the intermediary are governed by the domestic law of State X.[13] Where such rules discriminate as regards the exercise of voting rights because of a specific holding pattern or choice of a foreign account or intermediary, they hamper the development of global financial markets.[14]

6.05 Likewise, income processing across borders requires compatibility, for example where agreements and the legal framework in different States envisage different types of income. Here, too, time is of the essence: distributions of income to investors may be delayed if payments need to be carried out across borders.[15]

6.06 These examples underline the importance of enhancing corporate actions processing within and across borders.[16] Operational and other challenges in this context have prompted a number of studies that have led to national and international recommendations.[17] Possible solutions include legislation/regulation, self-regulation by the market, and/or the application of new technologies.

6.07 An example of legislation at the international level is the GSC, which deals with corporate rights of account holders, including income and voting rights (Article 9(1)), which

---

Patterns', 840–3. But see for example on the unwillingness of intermediaries to engage, Law Commission, *Who Owns Your Shares?*, 3.62–66, 3.87, 3.130–2, 3.142.

[11] Expert Group on Cross-Border Voting, *Report*; Legal Certainty Group, *Second Advice*, 12.3; Zetzsche, 'Shareholder Passivity', 289. On the position in the UK, see Law Commission, *Who Owns Your Shares?*, 1.49.
[12] Benjamin, *Interests in Securities*, 10.04 and 10.63.
[13] Legal Certainty Group, *Second Advice*, 13.2.2.
[14] Kanda et al, *Official Commentary*, 29–20, 29–26; Legal Certainty Group, *Second Advice*, Recommendation 13, 13.1–5.
[15] On the impact, in the early 2000s, of delayed, cross-border dividend payments, including from emerging markets, see Oxera, *Corporate Action Processing*, 30–1.
[16] See Paech and Löber, 'Securities Holding and Transfer', 15; Zetzsche, 'Corporate Governance in Cyberspace', 48–61.
[17] ECSDA, *Response: Corporate Actions*; EPTF, *Report*, 28–33 (EPTF Barrier 1: Fragmented corporate actions and general meeting processes); Giovannini Group, *Second Report*, 9–10 (on removing Barrier 3); Group of Thirty, *Global Clearing and Settlement*, Recommendation 8; ISSA, *Global Principles*; Legal Certainty Group, *Second Advice*, Part II; Oxera, *Corporate Action Processing*; and, specifically on shareholder voting in the UK, Myners, *Report* (2004); Myners, *Report* (2007); Law Commission, *Who Owns Your Shares?*.

may be exercised against an intermediary or the issuer (Article 9(2)(b)).[18] The pendant to Article 9 is Article 10(1) GSC, which obliges an intermediary to enable its account holders to receive and exercise their rights specified under Article 9(1) GSC.[19] Article 10(2)(e) GSC specifically addresses the question of how information is passed on to account holders, while Article (10(2)(f) deals with the payment of income.[20] The scope of the GSC is, however, limited. To begin with, corporate rights do not arise under the GSC, as it is only concerned with how rights attached to securities flow through the chain of intermediaries.[21] An ultimate account holder is entitled to exercise the rights attached to securities 'through the tiers'. Moreover, the GSC does not confer corporate rights on investors which, although economically entitled, fall outside the holding chain.[22] Whether such an investor can in fact exercise corporate rights is subject to domestic 'corporate law'. If the corporate law recognizes only certain account holders, but not investors with an economic entitlement, corporate law prevails, although this is not to say that benefits such as dividends should not be passed on to investors.[23]

6.08 In Europe, several interconnected initiatives aim at streamlining corporate actions processing. Initial key initiatives towards this end in Europe are the 2009/2015 Market Standards for Corporate Actions Processing[24] and the 2010 Market Standards for General Meetings,[25] as well as, based on and aligned to these market standards, the complementary TARGET2-Securities (T2S) standards on corporate actions.[26] These initiatives are complemented by the 2017 amendment of the Shareholder Rights Directive (SRD)[27] (notably new Articles 3a-c) and the Commission Implementing Regulation[28] in connection therewith, which address issues such as the identification of shareholders, transmission of information, and facilitation of the exercise of shareholder rights, primarily in the context of intermediated chains.[29] However, the SRD does not provide a uniform definition of 'shareholder', so that domestic corporate law remains crucial in this context as well.[30]

---

[18] Kanda et al, *Official Commentary*, 9–14 to 9–17; Combs, 'U.C.C. Versus UNIDROIT', 406–8.
[19] On the obligations of an intermediary under Art 28 GSC, see Kanda et al, *Official Commentary*, Art 28. Liabilities arising in the context of processing corporate actions are outside the scope of this chapter.
[20] There is thus a certain 'mismatch' between Article 9(1)(a) GSC (which explicitly mentions voting and income rights) and Article 10(2) (which mentions information and income).
[21] Kanda et al, *Official Commentary*, 9–14.
[22] Kanda et al, *Official Commentary*, 9–15.
[23] Corporate rights are also reflected in the UNIDROIT Legislative Guide on Intermediated Securities, especially ss 24, 30, 35, 85, 90–3, 100–01, 110–13, 230–50.
[24] Revised version 2012 (updated 2015), available at <https://www.ecb.europa.eu/paym/target/t2s/governance/html/casg.en.html> (accessed 7 July 2021).
[25] Available at <https://www.ebf.eu/wp-content/uploads/2017/07/Market-Standards-for-General-Meetings.pdf> (accessed 7 July 2021).
[26] See the T2S Corporate Actions Standards on 'market claims' (2013), 'buyer protection' (2013), and 'transformations' (2016), available at <https://www.ecb.europa.eu/paym/target/t2s/governance/html/casg.en.html> (accessed 7 July 2021). On the market and T2S standards, see also EPTF, *Report*, 28–33 (EPTF Barrier 1).
[27] Directive 2007/36/EC, as amended.
[28] Commission Implementing Regulation (EU) 2018/1212.
[29] ECB Advisory Group, *Potential Use Cases for Innovative Technologies*, s 1; EPTF, *Report*, 28–33 (EPTF Barrier 1) and 52–9 (EPTF Barrier 5). On issues arising in the context of the SRD's implementation, see Broadridge, *Shareholder Rights Directive II*.
[30] Article 2(b) SRD defines 'shareholder' as 'the natural or legal person that is recognised as a shareholder under the applicable law'. See also EPTF, *Report*, fn 66 (recommending that 'the term should have the meaning of an end

In the remainder of this chapter, we explore bottlenecks in the intermediated system **6.09** and ways to address them in relation to different types of corporate actions, ie, in relation to general meetings, including voting rights (section B), income distributions (section C), and the provision of information (section D). These corporate actions appeared to us to have sufficiently distinct characteristics to justify separate treatment, although they clearly also have elements (and problematic issues) in common. The possible impact of (new) technologies is the topic of section E.

B. General Meetings

(1) Who votes and how?

The register indicating registered holders may be used as a starting point to determine **6.10** who is entitled to participate and vote in general meetings.[31] However, as mentioned in paragraph 6.02, in the context of intermediated systems, many States separate registered (legal) and beneficial title. Where corporate law deals only with the representation rights of registered holders against issuers in general meetings, issuers and intermediaries may not be interested in the rights of investors.[32] This may not be of concern in some, notably transparent systems, where investors may exercise voting rights directly against issuers. However, matters may be more of a problem in 'tiered', non-transparent systems where issuers and investors are connected via intermediaries, which should ensure the proper exercise of voting rights. Even if it is understood in practice that ultimate investors should be able to vote,[33] tiered systems may give rise to significant legal and operational problems.[34] Each intermediary only knows the identity of its immediate account holder and voting instructions should accordingly be passed along each constituent of the chain. As a result of this 'disconnect' between issuers and ultimate investors, voting processes have become inefficient, expensive, and complex.[35] Voting

---

investor . . . '); Keijser and Mooney, 'Intermediated Securities Holding System Revisited', 314; Payne, 'Right to Vote in the UK', 214–5.

[31] Kanda et al, *Official Commentary*, 18-1 to 18-2 and 18-12 to 18-14 (esp. Examples 8-1 and 8-2); Nolan, 'Continuing Evolution', 93–4. However, Kanda, 'Case No. 19', 204, mentions that for book-entry shares in Japan the books of intermediaries may be more relevant than the issuer's shareholder register.

[32] On ways in which UK law enfranchised investors (and the limits thereto), see Payne, 'Right to Vote in the UK', IV. Nolan, 'Indirect Investors', C, discusses various aspects of forcing issuers to recognize and enfranchise investors other than their 'registered owners'. Although this may imply considerable costs for issuers, a counter-argument is that there may be circumstances where these costs are worth incurring to achieve a desired corporate goal. The matter is not clear-cut. See also Zetzsche, 'Corporate Governance in Cyberspace', 38–9.

[33] Legal Certainty Group, *Second Advice*, 4.2.1, 13.2.1.

[34] On voting by investors in the Netherlands, see Struycken and Schim, 'Aandelen vanachter het girale gordijn'; on the position of 'beneficial shareholders' in Japan, see Kanda, 'Legal Rules', 272; for the UK, see Payne, 'Right to Vote in the UK' and Law Commission, *Who Owns Your Shares?*, s 3; see also s 57(1) of the South African Companies Act 71 of 2008, which contains a definition of 'shareholder', which differs from the definition of 'shareholder' in s 1 of the Act and which purports, purely for the purposes of exercising voting rights, to establish a direct connection between the issuer and the end investor with the beneficial interest. See also Donald, *Rise and Effects*, 25–8.

[35] Kahan and Rock, 'Hanging Chads of Corporate Voting', 1279; Myners, *Report* (2004), 6–11, for diagrams on voting; Myners, *Report* (2007), 9–13. Donald, *Rise and Effects*, 21 and Donald, 'Heart of Darkness', 41–100, specifically 72–9, state that information can be distorted.

may not function properly and votes may go astray.[36] Questions may therefore arise as to the level of due care that intermediaries need to meet and this may lead to disputes.[37] In such a setting, the investor—intermediary–issuer relationship deserves special attention.[38]

(2) Challenges in the exercise of voting rights

(a) Direct rights against the issuer

6.11 There seems to be no single solution to the problem of the disconnect between issuers and investors in matters of voting. One possible way forward is to ensure that an ultimate account holder or investor can exercise (as a default right) its voting rights directly against the issuer, irrespective of the specific intermediated holding model or registered holder status.

(b) Instructions to intermediaries and proxy voting

6.12 Where the ultimate account holder or the investor is not able to vote directly, instructions to and proxy appointments by intermediaries may provide solace.[39] Proxies used to be brought into play to attend and vote at meetings in accordance with the wishes of registered holders; nowadays, they are widely used in intermediated systems to permit ultimate account holders or investors to exercise voting rights through the intermediated chain.[40] The effectiveness of indirect voting processes based on instructions or proxy voting relies on the cooperation of every intermediary in the chain.[41]

6.13 As mentioned in paragraph 6.10, corporate law may determine that only a registered holder (the 'higher' tier intermediary or account holder), but not the ultimate investor, can attend and vote at meetings or have the right to appoint a proxy to do so in its name.[42] A core problem in this connection is that issuers and intermediaries may not be required to ensure effective voting processes by seeking voting instructions from or giving proxy rights to ultimate investors.[43] Standard account (or custody) agreements do not necessarily include voting services. An intermediary may therefore have little incentive to exercise voting rights on behalf of its account holders. Unless specifically agreed,[44] or as required by regulation, intermediaries may thus choose not to perform voting services and/or vote at their discretion.[45]

---

[36] For the UK, see Myners, *Report* (2007), 13–15; Payne, 'Right to Vote in the UK', especially at 199.
[37] Payne, 'Right to Vote in the UK', 213, points out that the investor is potentially in a weak position.
[38] See Nolan, 'Indirect Investors', D; and, for a custodian's perspective, Yates and Montagu, *Global Custody*, 6.86–90.
[39] Articles 3c, 5, 10, 11 SRD. For earlier developments in the UK, see Nolan, 'Indirect Investors', E.3.
[40] See Donald, *Rise and Effects*, 21–8 World Economic Forum, *The Future of Financial Infrastructure*, 104–5.
[41] Likewise, such cooperation in the intermediated chain is needed for effective income and information processing. See ss C and D.
[42] See Donald, *Rise and Effects*, 30–4. On the development of proxies in the UK, see Nolan, 'Continuing Evolution', 98–109.
[43] For the US, see Donald, *Rise and Effects*, 25–8.
[44] See Payne, 'Right to Vote in the UK', 207.
[45] Yates and Montagu, *Global Custody*, 6.77–90.

GENERAL MEETINGS 153

6.14 The terms and conditions in the contracts between the parties in the intermediated chain play a crucial role.[46] Investors should ensure—if their bargaining position allows them to do so—that their account agreements contain specific voting service standards, such as a right to give instructions to or receive a proxy right from their intermediary.[47] The downside is that such rights reflect a mere contractual arrangement between the parties, so ideally they should be complemented by legal/regulatory requirements concerning (i) the enhancement of transparency regarding investors' identity, and (ii) the execution of voting instructions or the provision of proxy rights by intermediaries as a standard practice.[48] Specifically in relation to proxy rights, it should be noted that even if the goal is to enable ultimate investors to vote, the interest of the appointing shareholder may still play a role.[49]

6.15 Any of these approaches (direct voting, instructions, proxy voting) can be enhanced by giving effect to CSD or SSS rules that enable them, thus providing legal and procedural certainty.[50] Another (complementary) solution could be the development of best practice principles for the industry.[51]

(c) Transparency and omnibus/individual accounts

6.16 There are those who link the role of intermediaries and the 'pooling' of intermediated securities in omnibus accounts to negative externalities, such as the disconnect between issuers and investors, diminished transparency throughout the holding chain, and a reduction of the governance function of registered shares.[52] Transparency and accountability in the context of voting could be enhanced by recognizing holdings by individual investors on individual accounts (as opposed to omnibus accounts).[53] This could contribute to an effective 'flow-through' structure connecting issuers, intermediaries, and investors, in the context of voting and other corporate actions.

(d) Split voting

6.17 Split voting may occur when an intermediary is the person legally entitled to vote (as registered holder) for different account holders. For example, B-bank acts as an intermediary for two account holders, AH-1 and AH-2. Both account holders prefer B-bank to convey their vote to the general meeting through the chain of intermediaries, but

---

[46] Law Commission, *Who Owns Your Shares?*, 9.22–37.
[47] Myners, *Report* (2004), 12; Payne, 'Right to Vote in the UK', 217.
[48] Payne, 'Right to Vote in the UK', IV, VII. See also Donald, *Rise and Effects*, 35; Kahan and Rock, 'Hanging Chads of Corporate Voting', 1273–9 (on the 'Spanish' model); Law Commission, *Second Seminar*, 1.281–300; US Uniform Commercial Code (UCC), § 8–506 (duty of securities intermediary to exercise rights as directed by entitlement holder).
[49] In this vein, see Recital (10) and Art 10(3)-(4) SRD. See Donald, 'Heart of Darkness', 63–6, on the US 'shareholder communication' rules (Securities and Exchange Commission (SEC) rules 14a-13, 14b-1, 14b-2) which require intermediaries to pass along proxy packets to their clients for a fee.
[50] See Einsele, 'Modernising', 260–1.
[51] Law Commission, *Who Owns Your Shares?*, 9.9–21.
[52] Donald, 'Heart of Darkness', 61–5, 71–3, 81 explains voting as the legal channel to exercise control over the company and asserts that the direct governance relationship between issuers and investors, as envisaged in corporate law, is disturbed by the indirect holding structure. See also Ooi, *Conflicts of Laws*, 3.09, 3.18–19, 5.44, 6.20.
[53] Myners, *Report* (2004), 15–6; see also Myners, *Report* (2007), 5–6, on cost aspects.

AH-1 wishes to vote in favour of a specific resolution and AH-2 wishes to vote against it. If the issuer's law regards B-bank as the registered holder entitled to vote, some argue that B-bank is not entitled to split its vote to reflect the diverging instructions of AH-1 and AH-2, since a single person cannot have a split opinion. However, such an argument against split voting does not reflect the economic reality of intermediated systems. To address this concern, many State laws allow split voting.[54] Article 29(2) GSC also permits split voting as a matter of principle.[55]

(e) Timelines

6.18 There is generally a time lapse between the meeting notice, the record date, and the date of the general meeting. In a meeting notice, an issuer calls a general meeting.[56] The record date is a fixed date preceding the general meeting at which the identity and holdings of those entitled to participate and vote in general meetings are determined.[57] Securities may be sold or lent between the record date and the date of the actual meeting, but the seller or lender then retains the right to exercise the attached voting and other general meeting-related rights.[58]

6.19 Setting the record date is a fine art.[59] Communicating the meeting notice and the record date to investors through the intermediated chain in good time may present a challenge in light of the brief periods between the announcement of the record date, the record date itself, and the general meeting.[60] The number of rights in the register should be reconciled with the actual holders at the record date, so as to detect and solve instances of inflation of securities in a timely manner.[61] New technologies may facilitate the immediate processing of information and reconciliation.[62]

(f) Processing errors and 'lost votes'

6.20 Current voting processes are marked by inefficiencies. The timely passing of voting instructions through the chain in advance of a meeting is a major concern. Likewise, processing and checking proxies is complex but deadlines are short. Votes may be delayed, lost, or misattributed due to processing errors in especially long holding chains.[63]

---

[54] See Arts 10(1)–(3) and 13(4)–()–(5) SRD, also on the number of proxy holders. See also Legal Certainty Group, *Second Advice*, 13.3; Payne, 'Right to Vote in the UK', 213.
[55] See Kanda et al, *Official Commentary*, 29–3, 29–20, 29–25.
[56] Market Standards for General Meetings (n 25) Definitions.
[57] See Art 7 SRD; ISSA, *Global Principles*, p 10 and Glossary; Market Standards for General Meetings (n 25) Definitions. Cf. the description of 'record date' and other key dates in para 6.30.
[58] Article 7(1)(b) and (2) SRD. See Kahan and Rock, 'Hanging Chads of Corporate Voting', 1263–5; Turing, *Clearing and Settlement*, 20.11–13. See also para 6.23 on financial collateral.
[59] Myners, *Report* (2007), 8.
[60] Kahan and Rock, 'Hanging Chads of Corporate Voting', 1249–51.
[61] For the UK, see Companies Act 2006, s 327(2); Uncertificated Securities Regulations 2001 (SI 2001/3755), reg 41(1); Myners, *Report* (2004), 17–9. For South Africa, see Companies Act 71 of 2008, s 59; Companies Regulations 2011, reg 37. See also Ch 7, s E(2).
[62] See ss E(3) ('Information processing') and E(4) ('Reconciliation').
[63] Donald, 'Heart of Darkness', 74–5, 88–91, indicates how intermediaries and proxy service companies benefit from the inefficiencies related to tiered systems, and states, at 62–3, that the 'pass-it-along technique…is so inefficient that it spawned its own industry—the proxy service companies—which feed off the difficulties issuers and shareholders experience under the SEC regime'. See also Donald, *Rise and Effects*, 34; Kahan and Rock, 'Hanging

While the ultimate account holder may be unable to trace its votes through the chain of intermediaries to the issuer, issuers face similar problems in tracing votes on account of client confidentiality and cost.[64] A clear end-to-end audit trail is necessary, but sadly absent in many States.[65] The situation may be improved by permitting voting by correspondence in advance of the meeting,[66] disclosure to the issuer of the identity of investors and the number of shares they hold,[67] and disclosure by the issuer of voting results.[68] Transparency along the tiers of intermediation would reduce errors, the possibility of intermediaries misusing votes, and over-voting.[69]

Over-voting is the situation where more votes are cast than are recorded in the issuers' register. Over-voting may, for example, occur in the context of pooling in omnibus accounts when account holders innocently, but incorrectly, exercise votes belonging to the registered holder without that holder's agreement.[70] Such discrepancies should be corrected forthwith, on pains of such incorrect votes being wholly disregarded by the issuer. The votes then become 'lost' votes.[71] **6.21**

(g) The role of technology
Technology can improve the processing of meeting notices, proxy appointments, voting instructions, and other information along the intermediated chain.[72] Electronic voting and the participation of investors (including foreign investors) in general shareholder meetings via electronic media has become more commonplace over the past years, in particular in the wake of the Covid pandemic.[73] Electronic voting and modern technology can enhance efficiency and accuracy in the short term. In the longer term, **6.22**

Chads of Corporate Voting', 1251–5. Myners, *Report* (2007), 4–5, proposes automated straight-through processing of electronic voting. See also the industry initiative for harmonization: Broad Stakeholder Group, *Dismantling Giovannini Barrier 3*.

[64] See Myners, *Report* (2007), 5; Ooi, *Conflict of Laws*, 6.28–33.
[65] Kahan and Rock, 'Hanging Chads of Corporate Voting', 1253–5, describe the process as a 'nightmare of verification'.
[66] Articles 5, 12 SRD.
[67] Article 13 SRD.
[68] Article 14 SRD.
[69] Payne, 'Right to Vote in the UK', 217.
[70] Myners, *Report* (2007), 5.
[71] See Kahan and Rock, 'Hanging Chads of Corporate Voting', 1255–63.
[72] Kobler, 'Shareholder Voting', 689–700; Myners, *Report* (2007), 4–5; Nolan, 'Continuing Evolution', 106–9; Zetzsche, 'Corporate Governance in Cyberspace', 41–4.
[73] See Arts 5, 8, 9, 11 SRD; ISSA, *Global Principles*, p 8 (Principle 10). Donald, *Rise and Effects*, 48–59, describes how technology allows a return to a system of 'direct issuer–shareholder' relationships via a direct registration system. Zetzsche, 'Corporate Governance in Cyberspace', 21–9, identifies barriers to the widespread adoption of electronic voting processes and virtual shareholder meetings. HLS Forum, *Istanbul Stock Exchange*, describes Turkey as the first country to require companies listed on the Istanbul Stock Exchange to enable voting at general shareholder meetings via an electronic platform. It saves costs as compared to a dual process of paper and electronic means. Birnhak, 'Online Shareholder Meetings', describes the positive example of technology applications and online meetings held in Delaware, as well as negative shareholder sentiment elsewhere regarding online meetings. Boros, 'Virtual Shareholder Meetings', 265–88, points out the need for corporate legislative guidance regarding virtual meetings and electronic ballots. See also Fairfax, 'Virtual Shareholder Meetings', 1382–95; High Level Group of Company Law Experts, *Report*, 49–53; Nolan, 'Continuing Evolution', 119; Nolan, 'Indirect Investors', 91; Zetzsche, 'Shareholder Passivity', 323–5.

technology may add transparency to the intermediated chain by linking securities to the person ultimately entitled to vote in connection with them.[74]

(h) Collateral

6.23 Collateral may be provided by a collateral provider to a collateral taker by way of a title transfer or the vesting of a security interest.[75] This may imply that the person entitled to vote (or to receive income or information) is no longer the collateral provider but the collateral taker. Since only one party should be able to exercise corporate rights against the issuer, the correct identification of the entity which may exercise these rights is crucial. The parties may contractually agree that corporate rights are 'passed on' from one party to the other.[76]

C. Income Distributions

(1) Income: what, to whom, and how?

6.24 Income distributions, such as dividend or interest, are a remuneration to investors in securities that may affect the price of securities and their trading. Income is usually an amount of money paid that does not affect the number of securities originally issued, although income may also be distributed in the form of additional securities. The first form of income is common in both corporate securities (for example, shares, equity, or bonds) and government securities (for example, bonds), while the second form of income generally relates to corporate securities only. Other examples of distributions, although these may not qualify as 'income', are redemption sums paid where securities cease to exist and the transfer of (additional) securities as a result of corporate events such as a merger, spin-off, or takeover.

6.25 Several other distinctions may be made in addition to the kind of income earned (money or additional securities) and the type of securities to which the income relates (corporate or government securities). It is important to consider who distributes the income: the issuer or a third party, as in a takeover. Another distinction is that between so-called (i) 'mandatory' corporate actions, in which no decision is required by the investor (such as in case of dividend or interest payments, redemption, or a merger without options), (ii) mandatory actions with options (for example, where there is a choice between dividend in the form of cash or securities); and (iii) 'voluntary' corporate actions, which require an instruction or decision by an investor (for example, in case of appraisal rights, or in a restructuring offer or takeover bid).[77] Understanding

---

[74] Myners, *Report* (2007), 15; Payne, 'Right to Vote in the UK', 217. See also s E.
[75] On the legal constructions, see Art 31(3)(a)-(c) GSC; Art 2(1)(a)-(c) EU Financial Collateral Directive; Benjamin, *Interests in Securities*, 119–21. See also Ch 2.
[76] See, eg, paragraph 6 Global Master Securities Lending Agreement (2010) and paragraph 5 Global Master Repurchase Agreement (2011); cf EPTF, *Report*, 31–2; Payne, 'Right to Vote in the UK', 203.
[77] Generally, mandatory corporate actions apply to securities of both public and private issuers, whereas voluntary corporate actions may not apply to government securities. For further information on the classification of corporate actions, see Oxera, *Corporate Action Processing*, 2.1; Simmons and Dalgleish, *Corporate Actions*, 1.5, ch 2.

the nature of each type of income is essential to appreciate the complexity of processing throughout intermediated chains.

As a matter of principle, income should be distributed to investors that are economically entitled to receive it. As in the case of rights related to general meetings, a range of entities may be involved in the passage of income through the intermediated chain, the most important of these entities being the issuer, the registrar, the CSD, intermediaries, and the ultimate investors. Their exact roles depend on the jurisdiction involved. Yet other entities, such as SSSs, custodians, fund managers,[78] paying agents, and banks may also be responsible for aspects of income processing. Investors may delegate responsibility for the processing of corporate actions to one or more of these entities (unless they wish to manage them themselves, as happens with institutional investors).[79] Clearly, this is a simplified image of a complex reality, in part because the analysis of the legal and economic rights to the income may vary depending on the jurisdiction in play.

6.26

Key elements of processing income payments are: (i) determining the amount of distributable income by the issuer; (ii) identifying the recipients of the income; (iii) income distribution along the chain; and (iv) processing-related corporate action notifications, either 'downstream', for example in relation to payment dates, or 'upstream', when an instruction or decision of the investor in a voluntary corporate event is involved. Intermediaries play a key role in transmitting these flows up and down the chain.

6.27

(2) Challenges in the distribution of income

Distributing income through the intermediated chain may involve errors and other failures, often operational in nature. They may damage the reputation of the intermediaries involved and have financial consequences.

6.28

(a) Identifying the investor

Identifying the investor to which the income will be distributed is a critical issue. In legal systems that require such identification for income payments, identification failures may arise, among other things, from the nature of the holding system (for example, whether it is a transparent or a non-transparent holding system), through misstatement of the name of an ultimate account holder or investor, or from the absence of registration of a transfer or a security interest on securities. Errors may also result from investors' failure to provide information (for example, in legal successions, following a merger or a consolidation process), failures in the intermediaries' systems and 'know

6.29

---

[78] Fund managers are often appointed by investors to manage their investment portfolio with broad powers, including receipt of income and taking decisions on corporate actions.
[79] The services related to the processing of income and related corporate actions are commonly referred to as 'asset services'. See Chan et al, *Securities Custody System*; Austen-Peters, *Custody of Investments*, 9.17.

158   CORPORATE ACTIONS PROCESSING

your customer' obligations, or the issuers' failure to process information. If investors have not been correctly identified, they may not get something to which they were entitled (for example, in mandatory corporate actions), or not be given the opportunity to send relevant instructions (in voluntary corporate actions).

(b) Timelines

6.30 As with other corporate actions, processing income within strict timelines may be a challenge. The following key income-processing dates can be distinguished: (i) the announcement date, on which the issuer announces the corporate action; (ii) the ex date, from which the securities are traded without the rights attached to them;[80] followed by (iii) the record date, on which the investors with rights in respect of the corporate actions announced are identified, and their positions recorded at the issuer level;[81] and (iv) the payment date, on which payment is due.[82] New technologies may facilitate the immediate processing of the different steps involved.[83]

(c) Income processing errors

6.31 Passing income and related information up and down the intermediated chain is complex, as it may involve a range of actors and challenging timelines. Errors may occur in the proper identification of subsequent recipients throughout the chain, including correct information about their respective bank and securities accounts. Operational errors, such as erroneous amounts, may also occur. A failed, insufficient, or untimely transfer of income through the chain to intermediaries and investors may cause investors to sustain losses. Such losses may, for example, occur where the amounts corresponding to the income are assigned by the investor to investment strategies even though actual payment is still pending.[84]

(d) Withholding tax

6.32 Payment of dividend or interest is usually subject to income tax withheld at source, that is, funds are paid to investors net of taxes. Issuers often withhold tax directly or through CSDs. The investor's actual tax status should be determined in the light of applicable legal rules, including in light of treaties to avoid double taxation in cross-border situations. Fragmented formats for the communication of the investor's tax status and consequent tax reduction or refund procedures, which may differ from jurisdiction to jurisdiction, as well as other tax-related reporting requirements,[85] may

---

[80] Market Standards for Corporate Actions Processing (n 24) Glossary.
[81] Market Standards for Corporate Actions Processing (n 24) Glossary.
[82] On these and some other relevant dates, see also ISSA, *Global Standards*, p 10 and Glossary; Market Standards for Corporate Actions Processing (n 24) especially pp 12 (cash distributions) and 17 (securities distributions); Simmons and Dalgleish, *Corporate Actions*, 8.2.2, 9.5, 9.7.
[83] See s E(3).
[84] On the associated risks of settlement of income payments by FMIs in central or commercial bank money, see CPSS and IOSCO, *Principles for FMIs*, Principle 9, 67–9. These risks are also at play at the European level in the context of the T2S project; see <http://www.ecb.europa.eu/paym/t2s/html/index.en.html> (accessed 7 July 2021).
[85] Eg, the US Foreign Account Tax Compliance Act (FATCA) generally requires foreign financial institutions to report on information about financial assets held by their US account holders, while US persons are required to

involve considerable compliance costs. Moreover, operational errors may occur in processing the relevant filings and other information through the intermediated chain by the different actors involved.[86]

D. Provision of Information

(1) Provision of information: what, to whom, and how?

As a rule, issuers are required to provide a minimum set of information for the proper exercise of corporate rights. This includes information regarding meeting calls, the distribution of income, and other relevant decisions or material facts. Information provided by the issuer enables investors to make investment decisions, guarantees the realistic pricing of securities, allows the accurate and efficient exercise of rights attached to the securities (such as rights related to voting or receiving income), and thus contributes to investor protection.[87] Hence, it is important that issuers provide adequate information in a timely manner.

6.33

While the issuer is essential as an originator of information, intermediaries play an important role in disseminating information relating to the securities throughout the intermediated chain to the ultimate account holder and investors. In addition to these actors, data vendors play a role in information disclosure. These companies buy and receive corporate information from issuers or CSDs and broadcast it through their own channels to market participants. In some markets, other entities such as regulators, stock exchanges, or CSDs also disseminate issuers' public information through their platforms.

6.34

(2) Challenges in the provision of information

The main challenges associated with the processing of information disclosed by issuers include: (i) identifying the investors/recipients of that information; (ii) determining the content of the information; (iii) interpreting the information, and (iv) actually processing the information (timing and technology).[88]

6.35

(a) Identifying the recipients
Identifying investors with a view to providing corporate information to these investors may be difficult in practice. Particularly when information needs to be processed

6.36

---

report, depending on the value, their foreign financial accounts and foreign assets; see <https://www.irs.gov/businesses/corporations/foreign-account-tax-compliance-act-fatca> (accessed 7 July 2021).

[86] EPTF, *Report*, 101–09 (EPTF Barrier 12).
[87] Hertig, Kraakman, and Rock, 'Issuers', 289.
[88] ECB Advisory Group, *Potential Use Cases for Innovative Technologies*, s 4.2.

160   CORPORATE ACTIONS PROCESSING

through different entities in the intermediated chain, this may result in problems regarding access to information and unequal treatment of investors. This issue should be addressed by harmonizing the legal and operational framework relating to information processing, which should include mandatory disclosure obligations on issuers so as to ensure adequate access to relevant information.[89]

(b) Content of information

6.37 Decisions as to the content of the information to be provided on corporate events can be a complex matter as the events covered may be diverse and require a case-by-case analysis. A range of administrative, corporate, investment, operational, tax, and other aspects may be involved.

6.38 The language in which information on corporate actions is provided should also be considered. In cross-border settings, many issuers provide information in their mother tongue, accompanied by an English-language version. In addition to the risks involved in interpretation, translation may also entail longer disclosure times, thereby further curtailing the time available to investors to make their decisions.

(c) Interpretation

6.39 Information transmitted by issuers is subject to interpretation by its recipients throughout the chain. Besides investors, which may use the information to adjust securities prices and make their trading and investment decisions, these recipients may include a variety of asset service providers, such as CSDs, intermediaries, and data vendors. Such entities enter information into their systems, process and often interpret it, either performing these tasks themselves or outsourcing them. A complicating factor is that the terms used in corporate actions disclosure tend to be specific to a given market or financial investment. The information flow through a variety of channels at different times can generate inconsistencies, which may require considerable effort to set straight in a practice known as 'scrubbing' of information.[90] Accordingly, information processing and interpretation require time and qualified personnel. To streamline the process, the entities involved should focus on transmitting such information as is directly relevant to investors in each corporate action, and avoid providing useless or confusing data.[91] Misinterpretation or other failures may lead to incorrect or late payments, mispricing, and sub-optimal trading decisions, and may thus have financial and reputational consequences for the actors involved.[92]

(d) Regulatory probes or proceedings

6.40 Regulators and supervisors may require detailed information to initiate a probe or proceedings. This may be problematic both in domestic and cross-border holdings where

---

[89] See Hertig et al, 'Issuers', 289.
[90] Oxera, *Corporate Action Processing*, 11.
[91] ISSA, *Global Principles*, p 7 (Principle 4); Legal Certainty Group, *Second Advice*, 14.3.1.
[92] Oxera, *Corporate Action Processing*, s 3.

neither the issuer nor the intermediary has full information on the ultimate account holders or investors, or where they have been unable to communicate that information under their contractual arrangements. Late or incomplete information can involve regulatory risks, which may be mitigated by guaranteeing some form of information-sharing between regulators.[93]

(e) Timelines and technology

6.41 Information should be disclosed at such intervals as are set out in State laws. Different timeframes may apply to regular accountability duties and other situations, whether arising from the issuer's own activities (including business conduct or resolutions taken by corporate bodies) or taking place outside the company, such as acts of third parties that materially affect the issuer's activities.

6.42 Timelines may prove difficult to meet where information needs to be processed through the intermediated chain, for example in the context of instructions regarding voluntary corporate actions, in particular if these instructions must be handled manually. A large number of intermediaries in a chain and the presence of several fund managers working on behalf of a particular client may further complicate matters, resulting, for example, in inconsistent instructions from the same investor (for example, if transmitted to the same issuer by different fund managers) and difficulties in managing deadlines to process information upstream.

6.43 One solution would be to extend the deadlines for instructions. However, this would probably require amending corporate laws. In addition, longer deadlines could have undesirable side-effects in that they might allow new errors to creep into the processes. Moreover, fluctuations in market prices associated with longer timeframes would seem to suggest that this is an inefficient method.

6.44 The development of technological solutions therefore seems a more feasible way of ensuring the timely processing of information between the different actors in the intermediated chain. Helpful technological initiatives towards this end include, for example, the standards developed by the International Organization for Standardization (ISO) aimed at standardizing communication flows between different financial market participants, also in relation to corporate actions processing,[94] as well as electronic messaging tools such as those developed by SWIFT[95] and those in XBRL format.[96] These initiatives are constantly being improved upon and new electronic communication tools and rules are being developed. Although announcements, notices, and

---

[93] See, eg, IOSCO, *Multilateral Memorandum of Understanding*.
[94] ISO standard 20022 (and its predecessor ISO 15022) contains a set of rules to build messages. See <https://www.iso20022.org> (accessed 7 July 2021). The ISO standards play a key role in, eg, ISSA's *Global Principles*; the European Market Standards for Corporate Actions Processing (n 24) and for General Meetings (n 25). See also Broadridge, *Shareholder Rights Directive II*.
[95] See ISSA, *Global Principles*, p 14; Simmons and Dalgleish, *Corporate Actions*, 22, 45, 117.
[96] XBRL (eXtensible Business Reporting Language) is a global standard for sharing business and financial information, which may be used by issuers and other participants in the intermediated chain for corporate actions-related communications. See <http://www.xbrl.org> (accessed 7 July 2021); ISSA, *Global Principles*, p 18.

instructions are increasingly communicated electronically, information on corporate actions may be so specialized and complex as to require manual intervention throughout the chain. However, particularly in relation to more typical corporate actions, further steps should be taken to optimize 'straight-through processing' of such actions and to achieve market-wide adoption of common messaging standards.[97]

E. Outlook: New Technologies

(1) New technologies: DLT and smart contracts

6.45 A promising way forward in tackling the many operational shortcomings in corporate actions processing is to optimize the benefits of technological innovation. Any such future initiative should ideally reflect a multi-facetted approach that not only considers specific corporate action problems in isolation, but places them within the context of the financial infrastructure as a whole. Although the technological landscape is still changing rapidly and has not taken definite shape, this section discusses some of the challenges and benefits ahead with a focus on corporate actions processing.

6.46 DLT[98] and/or smart contracts[99] could play a meaningful role in the development of a reshaped corporate action system and related services. Blemus and Guégan mention potential benefits such as improved transparency and more accurate identity verification; instant communication between securities holders and management; online voting in real time; efficient involvement of securities holders; greater shareholder participation; speedier decision-making; lower voting costs; modification or disintermediation of the role of proxy firms; and deterrents to empty voting and other undesirable practices.[100] While DLT and smart contracts may reduce or mitigate certain risks in corporate actions processing, they may also create or exacerbate others.[101]

6.47 DLT and smart contracts are distinct technologies that can operate separately or in combination with one another. DLT can function as a platform to host and execute smart contracts.[102] Smart contracts can leverage on DLT. For example, shareholder

---

[97] Giovannini Group, *Second Report*, 7–8 (on removing Barrier 1); EPTF, *Report*, 7–8 (EPTF Barrier 2); ISSA, *Global Principles*.
[98] For a short explanation of the terminology, see Blemus and Guégan, 'ICOs, Tokenization and Corporate Governance', 193–5. DLT is the general term used to refer to methods of maintaining a distributed ledger on networks of computers and 'blockchain' represents one type of DLT. See also ISDA and Linklaters, *Whitepaper*, 7–8. The technology allows participants in the network to validate new transactions or information or blocks thereof and append them to the chain of previously validated ones; see Pinna and Ruttenberg, *Distributed Ledger Technologies in Securities Post-trading*, 15.
[99] Essential elements of smart contracts are automated self-execution of pre-programmed steps agreed between the parties; see ISDA and Linklaters, *Whitepaper*, 8–9.
[100] Blemus and Guégan, 'ICOs, Tokenization and Corporate Governance', 203–4.
[101] For an overview of the use and potential implications of DLT, see FINRA, *Report on Distributed Ledger Technology*.
[102] ISDA and Linklaters, *Whitepaper*, 8–9, 19.

information, information about proxies, and access rights could be encrypted in smart contracts as input for an automatically executed voting process, which may be reflected in real time on the DLT platform.[103] New information resulting from the execution of (corporate actions embedded in) smart contracts could automatically be made available on the ledger. A smart contract thus ensures that voting, including by way of proxies, takes place in a streamlined process without the need for further human intervention, while the DLT ensures that the necessary information is available to all the actors concerned. This reduces the time, manual processes, and other inefficiencies currently involved, as well as, possibly, the need for third party intermediaries/service providers and associated fees.

Smart contracts could be used to encode automated procedures for any part in a lifecycle event, although there may be reasons not to opt for automation.[104] Selection criteria such as standardization, complexity, externalities, common functions, and legal effect can help in determining whether the automation of processes is efficient.[105] A level of automation could, for example, be applied in the context of calculating and processing dividend or interest payments from the issuer to investors.[106] 6.48

As a quick fix, DLT and smart contracts could help to optimize the least efficient processes in the current market structure. In this scenario, the technologies leave (parts of) the conventional intermediated system intact and certain existing business standards or rules may continue to apply. For example, DLT and smart contracts could be used to improve the processing of information, currently complex and cumbersome due to a series of contractual arrangements put in place to mitigate the risk to the relevant parties of incorrect data being used along the intermediated chain.[107] A more radical solution would be to apply DLT and smart contracts for the processing of corporate actions between the parties at source (the issuer) and at the end point (the ultimate investor), without the need for intermediaries. This would obviate the need to pass data up and down the various tiers of the holding chain, 'since the concept of a hierarchical chain of intermediaries would be replaced by direct interaction between all permissioned actors in the DLT'.[108] End-to-end platforms with integrated process automation would make the corporate action infrastructure and process more efficient and cost-effective and ensure accurate and timely information for issuers, investors, and other parties involved. 6.49

---

[103] Blemus and Guégan, 'ICOs, Tokenization and Corporate Governance', 204. On the components of the 'e-proxy voting process', see CSD Working Group on DLT, *Proxy Voting on Distributed Ledger*, 2.2.
[104] See Clack and McGonagle, *Smart Derivatives Contracts*, s 5.3; ISDA and Linklaters, *Whitepaper*, 17–18.
[105] See Clack and McGonagle, *Smart Derivatives Contracts*, 30–1; ISDA and King & Wood Mallesons, *Smart Derivatives Contracts: From Concept to Construction*, 14–15; ECB Advisory Group, *Potential Use Cases for Innovative Technologies*, 4.3.1.
[106] For a discussion of automating dividend payments, see ISDA, *Equity Derivatives*, 10–13, 17–18.
[107] ECB Advisory Group, *Potential Impact of DLTs*, s 9, especially at 76.
[108] ECB Advisory Group, *Potential Impact of DLTs*, 9.2.1. 'Permissioned' or 'private' DLT (with membership restricted to known entities) is likely better suited to the needs of highly regulated securities markets; see Pinna and Ruttenberg, *Distributed Ledger Technologies in Securities Post-trading*, 2.2.

(2) Consistency and common standards

6.50 A critical factor in the adoption of new technology should be the development of and compliance with a high level of technical consistency and common standards, both currently lacking throughout the intermediated chain between different actors, platforms, and systems.[109] New technology provides an opportunity to interconnect various actors and sources of information relevant to corporate action processing.[110]

6.51 Currently, local market practices mean that information concerning corporate actions is available in a rather unstructured and non-standardized format, which makes it difficult to process.[111] For example, corporate action notifications to facilitate the exercise of shareholder rights may be transmitted by intermediaries downstream from the issuer to the account holder in the form of published, unstructured text, in XBRL format, or as an ISO standard message (see paragraph 6.44).[112] Those relying on such information must first interpret the data, at times manually, before they can pass on instructions. Likewise, different, non-standardized processing mechanisms for dividend payments from one market to another cause inefficiencies and considerable costs. Although progress has been made in developing consistent legal and operational market standards for corporate actions processing in Europe, especially in T2S markets (see paragraph 6.08), national differences in the rules governing corporate actions processing remain a key concern of successful European post-trade reform and cross-border market integration.[113]

6.52 When adopting new technologies, all relevant stakeholders should therefore collaborate to develop harmonized legal, technical, and business standards and processes, including common definitions, so as to ensure compatibility among market participants.[114] An additional challenge is that of guaranteeing the interoperability of various legacy solutions with harmonized DLT models where these functionalities (temporarily) co-exist.[115]

---

[109] ECB Advisory Group, *Potential Use Cases for Innovative Technologies*, 4.3.5; ECB Advisory Group, *Potential Impact of DLTs*, 9.2.3 and, specifically on the harmonization of settlement cycles, 15.1 at 114; ISDA and King & Wood Mallesons, *Smart Derivatives Contracts: From Concept to Construction*, 6–8.

[110] Eg, DLT has the potential of connecting a corporate action announcement by an issuer with information about the holdings of investors; see ISSA, *Crypto Assets*, 10, 34. On the use of business standards, see ISSA, *Distributed Ledger Technology: Principles*, 23–7.

[111] ECB Advisory Group, *Potential Use Cases for Innovative Technologies*, 4.2, 4.3.5, 4.4.

[112] On the compatibility of ISO 20022 with DLT, see CSD Working Group on DLT, *Proxy Voting on Distributed Ledger*, 4.3.

[113] EPTF, *Report*, 28–33 (EPTF Barrier 1).

[114] For various aspects of corporate actions processing that may benefit from standardization in a DLT environment, see ECB Advisory Group, *Potential Impact of DLTs*, 9.2.3 at 83; ISSA, *Distributed Ledger Technology: Principles*, Appendix 1, 62–6. On industry initiatives for standardization of token protocols, see OECD, *Tokenisation of Assets*, p 14, Box 2.1.

[115] ECB Advisory Group, *Potential Impact of DLTs*, 9.2.3 at 83, 15.1 at 114; Pinna and Ruttenberg, *Distributed Ledger Technologies in Securities Post-trading*, 27.

(3) Information processing

6.53 In contrast to information processed through a long intermediated chain, a DLT network could render information on corporate actions accurate, reliable, up-to-date, and rapidly available. Such a network could be used for information flows in both directions, that is to say, downstream from the issuer, for example, to notify investors of the possibility of providing instructions, and upstream when instructions are submitted by or on behalf of investors.[116] The technology could ensure that data on general meetings, (proxy) voting, income distributions, and other asset servicing-related processes stem from a validated single source ('golden' or 'trusted' copy) and are accessible to all interested actors.[117] As a DLT application may capture, store, and update corporate action information in a structured format, it can help to standardize and streamline communications and carry out sequential steps in relation to various corporate actions in accordance with strict reference dates. The technology could, for example, speed up the processing of income distributions or voting instructions and reduce the timespan between the record date and a general meeting (a desirable goal from a good governance perspective), as information can be made immediately available and does not have to be processed through long intermediated chains.[118]

(4) Reconciliation

6.54 Individual databases in an intermediated chain may give rise to inconsistencies that need to be reconciled in a timely manner. This may not always be feasible, in particular where long intermediated chains and/or manual processes are involved, a circumstance that may impair the accurate processing of corporate actions. By adopting DLT, the actors in play could resolve such timing and operational issues by sharing a common, transparent, digital representation of securities holdings on the distributed ledger, which can be continuously updated.[119] This would reduce, simplify, or remove the current need for intermediaries to reconcile information, often manually.[120] For example, DLT could be instrumental in reconciling the number of securities issued with the number of voting and proxy instructions given by investors on a continuous basis in the run-up to the general meeting, obviating the need for extra time to carry out checks up and down the intermediated chain. New technologies could also play a role in reducing and correcting errors by providing real-time, uniform information, for example, when an excessive number of votes has been cast (inflation).[121] The DLT system may thus reduce or eliminate errors, inefficiency, and risk.

---

[116] ECB Advisory Group, *The Potential Impact of DLTs*, 9.2.1.
[117] ECB Advisory Group, *Potential Impact of DLTs*, 9.2.1 at 78–9, 15.2 at 117; ECB Advisory Group, *Potential Use Cases for Innovative Technologies*, 4.1, 4.3.1, 4.3.3–4. Information provided by the issuer directly onto the DLT network would obviate current complications in putting together a 'golden copy' of a corporate event from multiple sources; see ISSA, *Distributed Ledger Technology: Principles*, Appendix 1, 3.4.
[118] ECB Advisory Group, *Potential Impact of DLTs*, 9.1 at 76, 9.2 at 79.
[119] CSD Working Group on DLT, *Proxy Voting on Distributed Ledger*, 2.3.3 (Requirement No.124).
[120] ISSA, *Distributed Ledger Technology: Principles*, Appendix 1, 2.2.
[121] ESMA, *Report: Distributed Ledger Technology*, 3.1.

(5) Immutability

6.55 In contrast to processes in the intermediated chain, immutability may be built in as a feature of blocks in the blockchain (ie, assets are represented digitally in an immutable ledger). Cryptography may ensure that it is impossible to tamper with, modify, or destroy any data, such as voting right allocations, proxy assignment instructions, and final vote counts.[122] The immutable ledger should reflect information regarding the issue and from the source (a node) with the most up-to-date information. For example, an intermediary may assign tokenized voting rights to voting parties on the ledger, as mirrored and backed by the securities issued and in accordance with ownership records (and in compliance with relevant issuer rules and national laws).[123] Likewise, smart contracts can count votes and ensure that they are valid by comparing the number of votes cast with the number of securities issued and ownership data at the time of voting. Thus, instead of having to rely on time-consuming correction or other validation processes, an immutable, automatically reconciled, correct copy of all data is reflected in the blockchain.[124]

(6) Transparency

6.56 New technology may impact transparency issues. Currently, a specific step or series of steps in a specific type of corporate action may not be sufficiently transparent. More transparency could render corporate actions processing more efficient and enhance the availability of the evidence to be adduced in the event of a legal challenge. For example, intermediaries may be obliged to confirm to their clients that their votes in regard to their securities holdings have been received and cast in accordance with instructions given.[125] DLT could provide the required transparency among the different actors involved, for example in the context of shareholder transparency by way of an 'Investor Data Directory', the availability of information regarding corporate actions (in the form of a 'golden' or 'trusted' copy), electronic voting, or by making voting results transparent during shareholder meetings.[126]

6.57 Transparency is also relevant in terms of infrastructure. The current financial infrastructure lacks such transparency. Intermediaries bridge the divide between issuers and ultimate investors by delivering post-settlement services in respect of a variety of corporate actions, including in situations where the legal entitlements on the issuer's record and the beneficial entitlements of investors are at variance.[127] Donald and Miraz submit that technology and policy choices of the past, plus the indirect holding

---

[122] The DLT voting system would, however, have to build in some solution for cases of an incorrect voting outcome (eg because securities are transferred by mistake) that must be corrected; see Panisi, Buckley, and Arner, 'Blockchain and Public Companies', VI.B and CSD Working Group on DLT, *Proxy Voting on Distributed Ledger*, 2.4.8, 3.1, 3.2.

[123] CSD Working Group on DLT, *Proxy Voting on Distributed Ledger*, 2.3.3 (Requirement No.120).

[124] See eg CSD Working Group on DLT, *Proxy Voting on Distributed Ledger*, especially at 2.3 and 3.1–2.

[125] ISSA, *Global Principles*, pp 8–9 (Principles 11–13); Shareholder Voting Working Group, *Shareholding Proxy Voting*, 6–7. Cf Art 3c(2) SRD.

[126] ECB Advisory Group, *Potential Use Cases for Innovative Technologies*, ss 3–5; World Economic Forum, *The Future of Financial Infrastructure*, 106–9.

[127] Keijser and Mooney, 'Intermediated Securities Holding System Revisited', 314–5, point to recent European efforts (notably the recast Shareholder Rights Directive and initiatives in the context of T2S) to improve seamless

system, have trapped the post-settlement environment and that it is now up to DLT to provide transparency. This could include the restoration of transparent ownership through direct holding with the issuer.[128] Panisi, Buckley, and Arner take the view that by providing a transparent environment with a clear definition of share ownership, DLT can streamline the entire architecture of tracking share ownership through the complete settlement cycle to enhance shareholder democracy and benefit corporate governance.[129] Keijser and Mooney point out that the application of transparent new technologies, such as DLT, might inspire disintermediation itself, or the abandoning of legal constructs based on tiers of intermediation.[130] Nougayrède highlights that greater transparency, specifically for reasons of corporate governance, is in the public interest.[131] Geis concludes that the impact of traceable securities as enabled by DLT will be profound, as it will alter the allocation of voting rights. He states that a 'well-functioning system of corporate voting is critical to any healthy governance regime'.[132] Mooney calls for a careful analysis of risks, costs, and benefits associated with intermediation and transparency matters, and proposes a new infrastructure model featuring a level of disintermediation based on DLT/fintech.[133]

6.58 Furthermore, any discussion on enhancing transparency by way of new technologies should take into account privacy and confidentiality requirements in connection with information sharing, also in relation to investor identification and corporate actions.[134]

(7) Other factors

6.59 Many concepts, principles, or broader legal issues will require clarification as new technologies develop. The summaries below illustrate just a few of the many other factors that may influence or challenge a decision to use DLT and smart contracts for corporate actions.

6.60 The law and regulatory status of crypto assets (or tokens) is still evolving.[135] The compatibility of the existing legal and regulatory framework of traditional securities with

---

cooperation in the intermediated chain, which should not be confused with the aim of enhancing the transparency of the chain.

[128] Donald and Miraz, 'Multilateral Transparency for Securities Markets through DLT', paras 1, 4.1, 4.3.
[129] Panisi, Buckley, and Arner, 'Blockchain and Public Companies', IV-V.
[130] Keijser and Mooney, 'Intermediated Securities Holding System Revisited', 310–11; see ibid at 15.III.A and IV.A.i on corporate actions as one of several instances of current non-transparency.
[131] Nougayrède, 'Towards a Global Financial Register?', V.2, 4–5, VI, VII.
[132] Geis, *Traceable Shares and Corporate Law*, 276, see also 267–73.
[133] In 'Beyond Intermediation', 419–26, Mooney discusses recent academic articles on the deficiencies of current (indirect) holding systems, inter alia in the area of corporate actions processing, and possible ways for DLT to offer solace. Mooney, at 424–6, criticizes the lack of examination of post-settlement intermediary risk and costs, and points to the fact that no mention is made in these articles of how the investor's rights vis-à-vis an issuer would be exercised without the involvement of an intermediary.
[134] See, eg, CSD Working Group on DLT, *Proxy Voting on Distributed Ledger*, 3.3 and 4.2; Keijser and Mooney, 'Intermediated Securities Holding System Revisited', 334. Cf Art 3a(4)-(6) SRD and recital (12) and Art 10 of Commission Implementing Regulation (EU) 2018/1212.
[135] ISSA, *Crypto Assets*, s 6. On the terms 'crypto asset' and 'token', see Blemus and Guégan, 'ICOs, Tokenization and Corporate Governance', 196–8; CSD Working Group on DLT, *Proxy Voting on Distributed Ledger*, 4.1; ISSA, *Crypto Assets*, 1.2 and Appendix 1.

168   CORPORATE ACTIONS PROCESSING

new crypto assets, representing the rights of crypto-asset holders (or token holders), may pose novel challenges.[136] The legal nature of crypto assets may differ, for example depending on whether the asset is a digital 'native' security token issued directly onto (and existing only on) a DLT platform, or a 'non-native' or 'asset-backed' security token on the DLT that represents underlying securities existing outside the distributed ledger.[137] In the case of 'native' securities tokens, corporate actions will occur at the level of the token only, whereas corporate actions regarding asset-backed securities tokens could arise either because a corporate action is announced by the issuer of the underlying security or because an independent corporate action is initiated by the issuer of the token.[138] It may not be possible to apply standard corporate actions processes for traditional securities one-on-one to tokens. The risks to investors should be considered and addressed.

6.61 Smart contracts are based on elements such as automated execution, the use of immutable, algorithmic code, and 'oracles' to fetch data from the external world. Such 'contracts' should reflect legally binding contractual arrangements and there may be instances when human intervention is necessary.[139] The representation of legal terms in more formal logic presents challenges where some terms are ultimately subjective in nature or where all the different permutations cannot be anticipated.[140] A flexible solution where some parts of the smart contract are expressed in natural language might be advantageous.[141] Suspending automatic performance, but not the contract between parties, could be useful where errors have been identified that need to be corrected or where technical difficulties or hacking has occurred.

6.62 The new division of tasks relating to the use of DLT and smart contracts needs to be clear; for instance, there should be no doubt as to who would be responsible towards investors – the DLT operator, service providers that perform functions under an outsourcing contract, or other actors?[142]

6.63 Present market practices could be impacted. If both the issuer and the investor are on the DLT, they could communicate directly regarding voting rights, income payments, and information;[143] the use of omnibus accounts and intermediation could drop or change;[144] new roles may open up to market players, also in the corporate actions

---

[136] Blemus and Guégan, 'ICOs, Tokenization and Corporate Governance' 204–10.
[137] ISSA, *Distributed Ledger Technology: Principles*, Appendix 1, 3.6; OECD, *Tokenisation of Assets*, 11–15.
[138] ISSA, *Crypto Assets*, s 4.2 and Table 4.
[139] See Clack and McGonagle, *Smart Derivatives Contracts*, s 5.2; ISDA and Linklaters, *Whitepaper*, 17–18. The use of 'soft forks' as open-source code modifications could enable rectification where necessary without creating a new DLT, as the use of 'hard forks' would have done; see Blemus and Guégan, 'ICOs, Tokenization and Corporate Governance', 220–1.
[140] ISDA and Linklaters, *Whitepaper*, 12.
[141] See ISDA and King & Wood Mallesons, *Smart Derivatives Contracts: From Concept to Construction*, 16–18.
[142] Blemus and Guégan, 'ICOs, Tokenization and Corporate Governance', 219–20. The introduction of new actors with new roles (such as a platform operator) changes the analysis of who has what substantive legal rights and obligations and demands a careful analysis of the law that governs them; see ISDA et al, *Private International Law Aspects of Smart Derivatives Contracts Utilizing DLT*, 3; Mooney, 'Beyond Intermediation', 429.
[143] ISSA, *Distributed Ledger Technology: Principles*, Appendix 1, 3.4.
[144] ISSA, *Distributed Ledger Technology: Principles*, Appendix 1, 2.1.

arena;[145] new tax rules may be required;[146] and timelines of corporate actions, inter alia in connection with changes to settlement cycles, may change.[147]

F. Conclusion: Current Status and the Way Forward

In an intermediated setting, the processing of corporate actions regarding voting rights, income, and information may be complex, inefficient, time-consuming, and costly. The position of investors in intermediated securities deserves special attention in light of the possible disconnect between issuers and ultimate investors in intermediated systems, the possible discrepancy between legal and economic interest in intermediated securities, the many details that need to be transmitted to a wide range of participants through long holding chains, and the disenfranchisement of investors that might result.   6.64

Different pathways to address bottlenecks within the current, intermediated market infrastructure include the promulgation of laws and regulations by the State and/or self-regulation. Examples of legislation addressing the issue are Articles 9 and 10 of the GSC and Articles 3a-c of the EU's recast Shareholder Rights Directive. Both initiatives stress the role of intermediaries in facilitating the exercise of rights by investors, but, as such, do not fundamentally address the problems and inefficiencies inherent in tiered, intermediated models. T2S is an example of an initiative that has spurred effective self-regulation among market participants. Whereas legislation and regulation may involve high adaptation costs, a common criticism of self-regulation refers to the substantial influence of the market industry and its vested interests, which do not necessarily favour optimization. When balancing the pros and cons of different approaches, the public interest of the seamless processing of corporate actions within and across borders should be taken into account.[148]   6.65

Ways to improve corporate actions processing within an intermediated setting include enhancing investor identification and 'know your customer' standards; increasing transparency throughout the intermediated chain, while balancing such transparency with privacy concerns; enabling direct links between issuers and investors; improving the technological infrastructure to ensure automated communications throughout the intermediated chain; disclosure of public information on the websites of both issuers and intermediated chain participants; ensuring that information transmitted to and from investors is as concise, complete, and uniform as possible; the adoption by issuers, intermediaries, and other asset services providers of proper internal controls and policies towards optimal corporate actions processing; a default obligation on intermediaries to render certain asset services, such as the execution of instructions by   6.66

---

[145] ISSA, *Distributed Ledger Technology: Principles*, 3.3.5.
[146] ECB Advisory Group, *Potential Impact of DLTs*, pp 84, 114–5; ISSA, *Crypto Assets*, 4.3.
[147] ECB Advisory Group, *Potential Impact of DLTs*, 114; ISSA, *Distributed Ledger Technology: Principles*, Appendix 1, 3.3.
[148] Mooney and Kanda, 'Core Issues', 87–91; Donald, 'Heart of Darkness', 73.

investors and proxy voting; and ensuring minimum compatibility arrangements in a cross-border setting.

6.67 Corporate actions processing may also be improved by the effective use of technology, including new technologies such as DLT and smart contracts. The least disruptive approach would be to optimize the use of technology within existing market infrastructures, combined with proper regulation. Another, and possibly better, approach could be to make use of new technologies to redesign current market infrastructures, and their legal and regulatory underpinnings, in a more thorough fashion with a view to facilitating, *inter alia*, optimum corporate actions processing. DLT and smart contracts, combined with properly implemented governance, have a promising potential to improve corporate actions processing as part of an innovative financial system and industry.

6.68 Some of the possible solutions to the issues set out in this chapter may not be easy to achieve or may be costly for specific role players, but this aspect must be weighed against the overall and long-term benefits for the markets. Specific objectives should be met, such as the flawless exercise of rights, which may benefit from investor identification and improved transparency throughout the holding chain or in a distributed ledger. Ideally, any solution should be compatible across borders: a cross-border investor should be able to exercise rights in the same way as a domestic investor can.[149] Whatever the chosen course for improvements, the interests of investors are a core component, as voting and income rights and rights to proper information are crucial to these parties.

---

[149] Legal Certainty Group, *Second Advice*, 12.3.

7

SUFFICIENT SECURITIES, SEGREGATION, AND LOSS SHARING

A.	Introduction and Terminology	7.01	(3) Reversal of erroneous book entries	7.63
	(1) Introduction	7.01	(4) Use of an intermediary's own securities	7.65
	(2) Terminology	7.02	(5) Buy-in of securities	7.67
B.	Causes of Imbalances	7.07	(6) Shorter settlement cycles	7.69
C.	Requirement of Sufficient Securities	7.13	(7) Regulatory tools	7.70
D.	Segregation of Securities	7.19	F. Loss Sharing in Insolvency	7.71
	(1) Different types of segregation	7.19	(1) Loss-sharing methods: mutualization or individualization?	7.74
	(2) Allocation and segregation under the Geneva Securities Convention	7.26	(2) Loss sharing under the Geneva Securities Convention	7.79
	(3) International regulatory approach	7.33	(3) Four key policy questions in relation to loss sharing	7.82
	(4) Regional approach in the European Union	7.40	(4) Some further issues	7.91
E.	Correction Methods	7.54	G. Outlook: New Technologies	7.94
	(1) Matching of credits and debits	7.55	H. Conclusion	7.108
	(2) Reconciliation	7.61		

A. Introduction and Terminology

(1) Introduction

When more securities are credited to the securities accounts of the account holder than its intermediary actually holds, an imbalance has occurred. As discussed in section B, such an imbalance can occur for different reasons. For example, it may be due to an administrative error or even fraud. Such imbalances can have a disruptive effect on the intermediated holding system. Different solutions are available depending on different factors such as the relevant legal system and the technical infrastructure, including that provided by the securities settlement system (SSS). Section C discusses the requirement that intermediaries should hold sufficient securities to cover the claims of their account holders. Section D examines the allocation of securities to account holders, notably by way of segregation. Such allocation determines 'what belongs to whom' and thus has an impact on which mechanism is appropriate to correct imbalances (section E). Allocation is also a crucial factor when determining how shortfalls should be distributed in insolvency, if such shortfalls nonetheless occur (section F). Section G considers the possible impact of new technology such as distributed ledger technology (DLT).

7.01

(2) Terminology

7.02 An imbalance in the form of a shortfall exists when more securities are credited to the securities accounts of the relevant account holder than its intermediary holds for that account holder.[1] When fewer securities are credited to the accounts of account holders than the intermediary holds for them, there is also an imbalance, but not a shortfall.

7.03 Inflation of securities is closely related to imbalances in the form of a shortfall, as in both cases there is a discrepancy between different tiers of the holding chain. Nonetheless, they are different phenomena. The expression 'inflation of securities' is used to describe the situation where more securities are registered on the accounts of account holders than on the *issuer's register*. Where the number of securities credited to account holders' accounts exceeds the number of securities issued by the issuer, inflation has occurred.[2] As mentioned above, a shortfall refers to the situation where more securities are credited to the securities accounts of the account holders than their *intermediary* holds.

7.04 For the issuer, it is important that the number of investors that can claim rights against it (for example, voting and income rights) be no greater than the number of securities originally issued. In order to maintain the integrity of the issue, mechanisms need to be in place to ensure that no discrepancies occur between the number of securities registered with intermediaries and the total number of issued securities.[3]

7.05 In many instances, imbalances in the form of a shortfall and inflation go hand in hand. The causes of such situations and the mechanisms to correct them are often the same. Therefore, in this chapter, these situations are generally treated together. For ease of reference, the term 'imbalance' is used to describe both situations unless indicated otherwise.

7.06 The occurrence of imbalances is also closely connected to the allocation of losses in the insolvency of the intermediary. If the intermediary enters into an insolvency proceeding and does not hold sufficient securities corresponding to the number of securities registered on its account holders' accounts, someone will have to bear a loss. 'Loss sharing' refers to the situation where the relevant account holders share an irreparable shortfall of securities in the insolvency proceeding of their intermediary.

B. Causes of Imbalances

7.07 Imbalances can have different causes. Without providing an exhaustive list, imbalances may be caused by timing differences, technical or human administrative errors, or even

---

[1] Article 24 GSC uses the terminology 'hold or have available'. As in Kanda et al, *Official Commentary* (see notably paras 24-10 and 24-14), we primarily use the 'hold' terminology in this chapter.
[2] The reverse situation in which *fewer* securities are registered on the accounts of account holders than on the issuer's register can be called 'deflation'.
[3] Legal Certainty Group, *Second Advice*, Recommendation 9. On the difference between integrity of an issue of securities and integrity of the intermediated holding system, see De Vauplane and Yon, 'Integrity', 8.2.

fraud. Innocent acquisitions or rehypothecation may also lead to an imbalance. These different causes of imbalances are discussed in further detail below.[4]

Imbalances may occur as a result of timing differences, for example, where a mismatch occurs between the time when the intermediary receives the securities and the time when the transfer is booked to the securities account of the receiving account holder. The transfer of the securities may be booked to the securities account prior to the actual receipt of the securities. In other words, an irrevocable credit may be made to the account holder's account before the actual settlement takes place. This means that the recipient account holder can dispose of the securities as soon as they have been credited to its securities account irrespective of whether the securities have actually been received.[5] If no securities can be credited to the account due to a default, the question arises how a resulting imbalance should be rectified. Another example relates to the processing of dematerialization or rematerialization orders, where certificates and intermediated securities relating to the same issue may accidentally exist at the same time. 7.08

Imbalances can also be caused by manual or technical errors leading to incorrect book entries in the intermediary's records. Imbalances may, for example, occur in the context of the rounding-off of fractions of securities by the SSS and/or intermediaries. Fractions of securities may be due to account holders in light of a corporate event, for example, where the issuer's bylaws stipulate that an account holder is entitled to one additional share for each three shares it holds. Where fractional interests are not permitted, these must be rounded off upwards or downwards, which may lead to imbalances. Generally, such 'technical' imbalances, even if they involve considerable amounts, can be easily corrected and the records quickly reconciled without any losses or damage to the account holders (with the exception of complications, notably in insolvency).[6] 7.09

The application of a rule protecting innocent acquirers can lead to imbalances when the person that is supposed to bear the loss of the securities cannot be identified.[7] 7.10

Another instance in which an imbalance may occur is where securities are used by the intermediary for its own purposes while they are registered as the property of the account holder on the account holder's securities account. The account holder (as the collateral provider) and the intermediary (as the collateral taker) can agree on such 'rehypothecation' or 'use' of financial collateral in their security agreement.[8] If the intermediary's use of the securities is not properly recorded by registering the securities on a separate account, or by taking other operational measures, the result may be multiple credit entries of the same underlying securities.[9] 7.11

---

[4] See also Yates and Montagu, *Global Custody*, 3.52–4.
[5] Witmer, 'Art. 11 FISA', 242.10 et seq; Yates and Montagu, *Global Custody*, 3.54.
[6] On 'technical causes', see Witmer, 'Art. 11 FISA', 247.36–8.
[7] Kanda et al, *Official Commentary*, 18–1; Legal Certainty Group, *Second Advice*, Example 18.
[8] Article 34 GSC. See also Ch 2, s B(2).
[9] Such multiple credit entries are accepted practice in the US. See Mooney, 'Shortfall', 172–4. See also Johansson, *Investment Securities*, 187; and, critically, EC, *10th Discussion Paper*, esp ss 74–85.

7.12 As a general matter, it should be noted that some imbalances may require an analysis of the intermediary's duty of care. For example, can an account holder hold its intermediary responsible for a shortfall caused by an upper-tier intermediary? Diverging views are held on the relevance of an intermediary's duty of care in such circumstances.[10]

C. Requirement of Sufficient Securities

7.13 One way to prevent imbalances occurring would be to require the intermediary to hold sufficient securities corresponding to the number of securities credited to the account holders' accounts. Many jurisdictions have a regulatory or legal requirement compelling the intermediary to have enough securities on its books to cover the credits it has made to the securities accounts for its account holders.[11]

7.14 This approach, which protects account holders, is reflected in Article 24 GSC.[12] Article 24(1) GSC requires the intermediary to 'hold or have available securities and intermediated securities of an aggregate number or amount equal to the aggregate number or amount of securities of that description' credited to securities accounts that it maintains for its account holders and for itself.[13]

7.15 There are several ways for an intermediary to comply with such a duty. Article 24(2) GSC illustrates this further and provides that an intermediary may:

(a) procure that securities are held on the register of the issuer in the name, or for the account, of [the intermediary's] account holders;
(b) hold securities as the registered holder on the register of the issuer;
(c) possess certificates or other documents of title;
(d) hold intermediated securities with another intermediary; or
(e) apply any other appropriate method.[14]

7.16 The most common method is probably that an intermediary holds intermediated securities with another, upper-tier intermediary.[15] The intermediary may have holdings of the same intermediated securities with several upper-tier intermediaries. Together, such holdings would make up the aggregate number of securities.[16]

---

[10] See Gullifer, 'Ownership of Securities', 1.V.B; Kuhn, 'Art. 19 FISA', 320.9–321.12, 321.14, 324.23; Law Commission, *Second Seminar*, 1.145, 1.164, 1.174–5, 1.261–80; Legal Certainty Group, *Second Advice*, 9.3.2–3; McFarlane and Stevens, 'Interests in Securities', 2.II.C.i; Witmer, 'Art. 11 FISA', 245.23.

[11] On the trustee's duty 'to account' under UK law, see Gullifer, 'Ownership of Securities', 1.V.B; Law Commission, *Second Seminar*, 1.263–70; McFarlane and Stevens, 'Interests in Securities', 2.II.C.i. On the requirements imposed under the US Uniform Commercial Code (UCC) and on registered broker-dealers, see Combs, 'U.C.C. Versus UNIDROIT', 407–8; Law Commission, *Second Seminar*, 1.271–3; Mooney and Kanda, 'Core Issues', 4.III.E (91–3); Mooney, 'Shortfall'.

[12] Kanda et al, *Official Commentary*, Article 24.

[13] On the compatibility of this requirement with US law, see Mooney, 'Shortfall', 7.3.2, 7.3.3.2.

[14] Kanda et al, *Official Commentary*, 24-16 to 24-19; Witmer, 'Art. 11 FISA', 248.40–250.49.

[15] Article 24(2)(d) GSC.

[16] Witmer, 'Art. 11 FISA', 248.41.

A crucial issue is the determination of the timeframe within which to take action to remove any imbalance.[17] Article 24(3) GSC refers this issue to non-Convention law, which may, for example, require 'immediate' or 'prompt' action by the intermediary.[18] From a practical point of view, the timing depends on specific circumstances, such as settlement cycles and the type of securities.[19] **7.17**

Another important issue is the allocation of the cost of ensuring compliance with the requirement of holding sufficient securities. Again, Article 24(4) GSC refers this issue to non-Convention law, the uniform rules of the SSS, or the account agreement.[20] Therefore, where an intermediary or an SSS applies one of the correction mechanisms set out in section E (for example, reversal of erroneous book entries, buy-in, or use of the intermediary's own securities), this does not necessarily settle the question of who ultimately has to bear the cost. The intermediary may be liable to compensate account holders for any loss arising from the failure to comply with the requirement of holding sufficient securities. An alternative approach, notably where the intermediary is not responsible for the deficit (for example, because of an event beyond its control), is to provide that the costs are borne in some other fashion (for example, through allocation to the account holders or an insurance scheme).[21] **7.18**

D. Segregation of Securities

(1) Different types of segregation

When an imbalance occurs, it is important to be able to determine which account holder has what securities. This may be achieved if an intermediary properly allocates securities to account holders, in particular by way of segregation. This enables the correction of imbalances (section E) and the protection of account holders, notably from claims from their intermediary's general creditors in the intermediary's insolvency proceeding (section F).[22] **7.19**

The level of protection for account holders depends on the type of segregation that is available, and is also determined by considerations of cost and bargaining power.[23] Generally, there are two ways in which an intermediary can segregate account holder securities from securities it holds for itself: (i) it can pool account holders' interests in **7.20**

---

[17] UNIDROIT 2010–S78B/CEM/1/Doc 3, 129; UNIDROIT 2011–S78B/CEM/2/Doc 2, 45.
[18] In Switzerland, art 11(2) FISA uses 'without delay'; in the UK, CASS rule 6.5.10 requires correction 'promptly'.
[19] Witmer, 'Art. 11 FISA', 246.30–247.35.
[20] UNIDROIT 2010–S78B/CEM/1/Doc 3, 129; UNIDROIT 2011–S78B/CEM/2/Doc 2, 45.
[21] See Legal Certainty Group, *Second Advice*, 9.3.2–3; Law Commission, *Second Seminar*, 1.277. See also para 7.12.
[22] Article 25 GSC; Kanda et al, *Official Commentary*, commentary on Art 25; ECB and CESR, *Standards for Securities Clearing and Settlement*, Standard 12 (58–61); Law Commission, *Second Seminar*, 1.2–4, 1.31–89; Paech, 'The UNIDROIT Project', 1142; Rogers, 'Policy Perspectives', 1450.
[23] On several instances of an imbalance of bargaining power between investors and intermediaries, see Micheler, 'Perspective of Investors'.

securities of the same type in so-called omnibus accounts (either for all account holders or for groups of them); or (ii) it can hold account holder securities in individually segregated accounts where each account holder's securities of the same type are registered separately from those of other account holders. If the intermediary holds intermediated securities in a securities account with another, upper-tier intermediary, either form of segregation is generally achieved through identification at the upper level.[24] Some jurisdictions distinguish between operational and legal segregation. 'Legal segregation' describes the situation where securities of an account holder are held on a segregated account that is protected by insolvency laws. 'Operational segregation' denotes the situation where securities are held on a segregated account that is reflected on the records or books of the intermediary without necessarily benefiting from the corresponding legal protection.

7.21 In case of segregation of securities on *omnibus accounts*, the intermediary holds its account holders' securities in fungible pools. Often, the intermediary holds its account holders' intermediated securities of the same type in a pooled client account with an upper-tier intermediary. In the upper-tier intermediary's records, the lower-tier intermediary appears to be the holder of the total number of client securities without any attribution of specific securities to identified account holders.[25] Account holders hold securities on a fungible and commingled basis for reasons of cost reduction, simplified administration, and efficiency in the context of portfolio financing and bulk settlements.[26]

7.22 This common practice of commingling in fungible pools raises the question of how the rights of individual account holders should be characterized and treated. Legislation and legal principles have developed in an ad hoc fashion over time to protect account holders' rights in an omnibus account. Solutions include the applicability of trust principles to the pooled assets with protection for account holders as beneficiaries, proprietary co-ownership interests for account holders, and the development of the *sui generis* entitlement notion of Article 8 of the US UCC.[27]

7.23 The problems associated with omnibus accounts are solved differently in so-called transparent systems, which typically envisage 'full' segregation on an individual basis, with separate securities accounts in the name of each individual investor.[28] Individual

---

[24] Article 24(2)(d) GSC; Kanda et al, *Official Commentary*, 25–16; UNIDROIT 2007–Study LXXVIII–Doc 89, s 1.
[25] Benjamin, 'Interests in Securities', 2.73 et seq; Gullifer, 'Ownership of Securities', 1.III; Law Commission, *Second Seminar*, 1.39; Paech, 'The UNIDROIT Project', 2.2.2.
[26] Benjamin, *Interests in Securities*, 2.74; Benjamin, Morton, and Raffan, *The Future of Securities Financing*; Johansson, *Investment Securities*, 3.2.4.
[27] Combs, 'U.C.C. Versus UNIDROIT', III; Einsele, 'Book-entry', I(b); Garrido, 'Loss-sharing', II; Gullifer, 'Ownership of Securities', 1.V.A; Johansson, *Investment Securities*, 3.2.4; Law Commission, *Second Seminar*, 1.37 et seq; Turing, *Clearing and Settlement*, 10.5.
[28] Also referred to as 'direct holding', 'direct ownership', 'securities ownership' models, which exist in various forms in Brazil, China, Colombia, the Czech Republic, Denmark, Finland, Greece, Sweden, etc. See Kanda et al, *Official Commentary*, Int–28 to Int–30, 1–43, commentary on Art 7, 22–19.

segregation also occurs in non-transparent systems where segregated securities accounts are offered to account holders on an optional basis.[29]

7.24 Arguments put forward in favour of individual segregation include enhanced investor identification and protection, reduced misappropriation and insolvency risk, individual allocation of risk in the context of loss sharing, and a more efficient exercise of voting rights and other corporate actions.

7.25 Segregation is dealt with in the private law-oriented Geneva Securities Convention (section D(2)), in international policy guidance issued in the wake of the global financial crisis (section D(3)), and in a range of new directives and regulations adopted in the European Union (section D(4)).

(2) Allocation and segregation under the Geneva Securities Convention

7.26 Article 25 of the GSC, which deals with allocation of securities to different account holders, accommodates different segregation models. The provision illustrates the importance of segregation in the context of insolvency.

7.27 The purpose of Article 25(1) GSC is to protect account holders by ensuring that enough securities and intermediated securities of each description, held by an intermediary under any of the methods listed in Article 24(2) GSC (see paragraph 7.15), are allocated so as to cover the rights of its account holders, other than itself, to the extent necessary to ensure compliance with Article 24(1)(a) GSC.[30] Under this main rule, any securities held pursuant to Article 24(2) are preserved for the benefit of the intermediary's account holders to the extent necessary to ensure that its obligations under Article 24(1)(a) are met. In other words, securities or intermediated securities held by the intermediary must first be allocated to its account holders.[31]

7.28 Article 25(2) GSC establishes the consequences of the allocation rule: securities and intermediated securities allocated under Article 25(1) do not form part of the intermediary's property and are therefore not available to its creditors. This applies notwithstanding the commencement or continuation of an insolvency proceeding in relation to the intermediary (Article 25(6)).

7.29 Article 25(3) allows different methods of allocation, including allocation by way of segregation.[32] Article 25(4) GSC distinguishes between segregation for the benefit of all

---

[29] See, eg, Chilean Security Markets Authority, Circular 1962 (19 January 2010); South Africa's CSD rules on 'segregated depository accounts', especially 5.1.4–8, available at <https://www.strate.co.za/wp-content/uploads/2020/05/lg_strate_pty_ltd_rules_-_october_2018_0.pdf> (accessed 7 July 2021).
[30] Kanda et al, *Official Commentary*, 25–1, 25–12; Kuhn, 'Art 10 FISA', 222.3–223.11.
[31] Kanda et al, *Official Commentary*, 25–12.
[32] Kanda et al, *Official Commentary*, 25–15 to 25–18.

account holders of the intermediary generally, for particular account holders, or for groups of account holders.

7.30 Under Article 25(5) GSC, a Contracting State may declare that, if all securities and intermediated securities held by an intermediary for its account holders, other than itself, are in segregated form, under its non-Convention law the allocation required by Article 25(1) applies only to those securities and intermediated securities and does not apply to securities and intermediated securities held by an intermediary for its own account.

7.31 Such a non-mandatory 'opt-out' declaration[33] does not discharge a State from its obligation to allocate securities to the rights of account holders under Article 25(1) GSC. Nonetheless, the effects of allocation are different where a declaration has been made. While the default rule under Article 25(1) provides that any securities held by the intermediary, whether for itself or for account holders, will be allocated to account holders, Article 25(5) implies that, where the intermediary has segregated securities for its own account and the relevant State has made a declaration, those segregated securities are not available to the intermediary's account holders. The declaration is therefore relevant for jurisdictions that wish to give 'proprietary effect' (legal segregation) to segregation of an intermediary's own securities.[34]

7.32 The main rule of an intermediary's securities being available to account holders applies irrespective of whether the intermediary was responsible for the shortfall in its account holder's account. Since the cause of an imbalance is irrelevant under the GSC, it does not matter whether the imbalance was caused by the relevant intermediary or by an upper-tier intermediary.[35]

(3) International regulatory approach

7.33 The global financial crisis has heightened the awareness of risks associated with various segregation models. The financial crisis resulted in a wide-ranging debate between international and European regulators, the industry, and account holders on the policy choices underlying segregation, also in relation to securities held through a chain of intermediaries. This debate has led to the publication of (joint) guidelines and reports by international standard-setting bodies such as the Basel Committee on Banking Supervision (BCBS),[36] the Committee on Payments and Market Infrastructures (CPMI),[37] the

---

[33] See UNIDROIT 2010–S78B/CEM/1/Doc 3, 66; UNIDROIT 2012–DC11/DEP/Doc 1 rev, 62–5 and Form No 7.
[34] See UNIDROIT 2006–Study LXXVIII–Doc 43, 185; Kanda et al, *Official Commentary*, 25–19, 25–20.
[35] Some, however, take the view that it is difficult to justify an intermediary that made no error having to use its own securities to make up for the imbalance. See Law Commission, *Second Seminar*, 1.145, 1.174–5. See also para 7.12.
[36] BCBS, *Cross-border Bank Resolution* (2010), Recommendation 8, 106, 114; BCBS, *Resolution: Progress So Far* (2011), paras 126–9; BCBS and IOSCO, *Margin Requirements* (2020), 4, 19–21 ('Element 5').
[37] CPMI and IOSCO, *Principles for FMIs*, 3.1.5, 3.11.6, 3.14.1–17, 3.16.2.

Financial Stability Board (FSB),[38] and the International Organization of Securities Commissions (IOSCO);[39] reports, opinions, and level three guidance such as questions and answers by the European Securities and Markets Authority (ESMA);[40] and recommendations by international and European organizations representing various stakeholders in the financial markets, such as the International Securities Services Association (ISSA),[41] the Association for Financial Markets in Europe (AFME),[42] and the European Central Securities Depositories Association (ECSDA).[43]

Different dynamics and policy considerations drive the restructuring and realignment of financial market rules regarding segregation. Views as to whether enhanced segregation at every level of the holding chain enhances asset safety, investor protection, and stability in the financial markets differ. The outcome of the assessment of the pros and cons of segregation varies depending on the specific perspective adopted or the market structure involved. **7.34**

For example, both the BCBS's and FSB's recommendations draw attention to segregation as a mechanism that contributes to investor protection and mitigation of systemic risk.[44] Organizations such as AFME, IOSCO, and ESMA consider segregation as a feature or policy objective of investor protection in the absence of harmonized insolvency laws.[45] A related perspective is the (systemic) impact of different segregation models in connection with individual or mutualized loss sharing. The 2012 CPMI-IOSCO principles for financial market infrastructures (FMIs) impose more onerous requirements on CCPs in terms of segregation.[46] These principles aim at ensuring that FMIs provide sufficient protection to their participants and to the latter's clients, including by way of segregation, so that assets and positions can be identified and, if necessary, ported to **7.35**

---

[38] FSB, *Key Attributes* (2011), ss 3.2(xii), 4, 11.6(v) and Annex I, 7.2(iv); its successor, FSB, *Key Attributes* (2014), with the same provisions in ss 3.2(xii), 4, 11.6(v) and Appendix I-Annex 2, 7.2(iv), and additional guidance especially regarding client asset protection in Appendix II-Annex 3, introduction and ss 2.1(i), 5, 9.1(iii), 10.1(v); FSB, *Re-hypothecation and Collateral Re-use*, 3.1, 4.2.3, 5.2, Annex I(viii).

[39] IOSCO, *Thematic Review of the Adoption of the Principles Regarding the Protection of Client Assets*, 4.2.1; IOSCO, *Standards for the Custody of Collective Investment Schemes' Assets*, paras 17, 29–30, 47–51.

[40] Eg, ESMA, *Consultation Paper: Asset Segregation under the AIFMD* (2014); ESMA, *Opinion: Asset Segregation* (2017).

[41] ISSA, *Financial Crime Compliance Principles*, 3.4.2–4; ISSA, *Financial Crime Compliance Principles: Background*, 2.3, 3.1–3; ISSA, *Transparency*.

[42] AFME, *AFME Principles*.

[43] ECSDA, *Account Segregation Practices*; ECSDA, *CSDs, Asset Segregation, and Custody Services*.

[44] See BCBS, *Cross-border Bank Resolution* (2010), Recommendation 8, 106, 114; BCBS, *Resolution: Progress So Far* (2011), paras 126–9. The FSB's *Key Attributes* (n 38) consider segregation as a means for resolution authorities quickly to identify which assets are client assets. FSB, *Re-hypothecation and Collateral Re-use*, 3.1, 4.2.3, 5.2, Annex I(viii), acknowledges the value of segregation in the context of re-hypothecation of client securities. See also Singh and Aitken, *Deleveraging after Lehman*, IV; Singh and Aitken, *Shadow Banking*, VI; Singh, *Collateral Reuse and Balance Sheet Space*, 25–6.

[45] On segregation of client assets, see AFME, *AFME Principles*, especially ss 4–5; on segregation in intermediary records, see IOSCO, *Thematic Review of the Adoption of the Principles Regarding the Protection of Client Assets*, 4.2.1; on segregation of collective investment schemes' assets, see 'standard 2' in IOSCO, *Custody of Collective Investment Schemes' Assets*, paras 17, 29–30, 47–51; on asset protection under both AIFM and UCITS Directives, see ESMA, *Opinion: Asset Segregation* (2017), paras 11–12, 60–1.

[46] See CPMI and IOSCO, *Principles for FMIs*, 3.1.5, 3.11.6, 3.14.1–17, 3.16.2. Some of the principles refer to CCPs specifically but could apply to FMIs more generally.

other non-defaulting entities in the event of a recovery or resolution proceeding. Yet other organizations, such as ISSA, focus on segregation as a tool to achieve identification and transparency in the context of financial crime.[47] From an issuer's or regulator's perspective, segregation indeed promotes identification of the investor and its claim on securities, while the resulting transparency prevents unauthorized use and enhances compliance with legal and fiscal rules.[48]

7.36 The BCBS and IOSCO have developed segregation requirements specifically for the situation where initial margin is provided under non-centrally cleared OTC derivatives. Rehypothecation of such initial margin by the collecting party is permitted under strict conditions, including additional segregation.[49] In the EU, the BCBS's and IOSCO's margin requirements for non-centrally cleared OTC derivatives have been implemented through EMIR and the Margin RTS[50] (as amended).[51]

7.37 Many intermediaries, CSDs, collateral managers, and trade associations oppose a mandatory segregation model and dispel the notion that segregated accounts are necessary to achieve client asset protection (combined with the facilitation of the prompt return of securities in case of losses), since omnibus accounts also achieve a level of client asset protection. Both ECSDA and AFME argue that the rights of investors are more dependent on the national legal and regulatory framework than additional account segregation practices or other technical record-keeping mechanisms.[52] The industry standard of segregating an intermediary's own securities from client securities at all levels through the intermediary chain is common commercial practice. Intermediaries and other actors in the industry argue that where the account holder requests enhanced levels of account segregation, this should be a matter of commercial negotiation between the parties and not a standard investor protection policy objective. AFME argues that it is critical that the intermediary retain flexibility to utilize the model that is most prudent and practical for a given market, after undertaking regulatory, insolvency, legal, and market analysis.[53] For the industry, there are costs and operational efficiency implications that must be considered when segregation is assessed.[54]

---

[47] ISSA, *Financial Crime Compliance Principles*, 3.4.2–4; ISSA, *Financial Crime Compliance Principles: Background*, 2.3, 3.1–3.
[48] ECSDA, *Account Segregation Practices*, 3.1–3; ISSA, *Transparency*.
[49] BCBS and IOSCO, *Margin Requirements* (2020), 19–21 (Element 5), especially paras 5(iv), 5(v). For a view on initial margin segregation criteria for clients, see ISDA, GFMA, and IIF, *Leverage Ratio Treatment*, 10–11, 26–7. On the related issue of collateral management, see AFME, *AFME Principles*, s 6.
[50] Commission Delegated Regulation (EU) 2016/2251.
[51] See also Ch 2, para 2.45.
[52] For surveys performed by various trade associations, see eg ECSDA, *Account Segregation Practices*, 3.1; AFME, *AFME Principles*. See also ESMA, *Consultation Paper: Asset Segregation* (2014); for the responses to the consultation paper, see <https://www.esma.europa.eu/press-news/consultations/consultation-guidelines-asset-segregation-under-aifmd> (accessed 7 July 2021). ESMA deviated from its original suggestion in 2014 to mandate individual segregation as a general requirement to recommending minimum segregation requirements in 2017; see ESMA, *Opinion: Asset Segregation* (2017), paras 13, 46, 59.
[53] AFME, *AFME Principles*, ss 2, 2.1.
[54] ECSDA, *Account Segregation Practices*, 3.4; ESMA, *Opinion: Asset Segregation* (2017), Annex 1, paras 108–10. EPTF, *Report*, 46–51 (barrier 4) describes the inconsistent application (and the related costs and risks) of asset segregation rules across EU Member States and between different EU regulations.

7.38 ECSDA points out that certain stringent requirements for segregation may have major implications for the regulated environment, for example in cross-border settlement, CSD links, collateral management, and securities lending and borrowing services.[55] A core concern is the removal of liquidity and connected funding from the market if the account structure does not allow for pooling of collateral in omnibus accounts. Such accounts provide a liquid basket from which substitution and realignment of securities portfolios can be performed. Segregation requirements may imply that collateral transactions need to be reflected in the books of all relevant parties through the intermediated chain with more cost, complexities, and delays. Individual segregation then becomes an impediment for the use of triparty agents with a potential knock-on impact on market liquidity and settlement efficiency. Industry stakeholders have therefore warned against imposing unnecessary 'one-size-fits-all' segregation requirements throughout the custody chain.[56]

7.39 Some stakeholders take the view that segregation is not an 'end in itself' and that the regulatory focus should be on the underlying aim of asset segregation, namely investor protection, which may also be achieved by way of proper bookkeeping and reconciliation practices and insolvency protection. Moreover, investors need to be informed about the risks and costs associated with different segregation options so as to be able to make informed decisions.

(4) Regional approach in the European Union

7.40 The afore-mentioned policy considerations are reflected in various EU directives and regulations adopted so as to reduce financial market risk and enhance investor protection. Below is a brief overview of the relevant EU directives and regulations that set out segregation requirements of securities in securities accounts.

7.41 MiFID II permits general omnibus client accounts, provided that the books and records of the investment firm identify the client for whom it is holding the relevant assets and that the sub-custodian account in which clients' assets are held are segregated from the assets of the investment firm.[57] Under Art 16(8) of MiFID II, an investment firm should make adequate arrangements when holding financial instruments belonging to clients to safeguard the ownership rights of its clients, especially in the event of the investment firm's insolvency, and prevent the use of a client's financial instruments for its own account except with the client's express consent.

---

[55] ECSDA, *Account Segregation Practices*, 3.4, specifically the reference at p 26 to the impact of non-harmonised CSD account segregation rules on cross-border T2S settlement; same point made by respondents to ESMA's consultation paper in ESMA, *Opinion: Asset Segregation* (2017), para 49.
[56] AFME, *AFME Principles*, s 6 at p 16; ESMA, *Opinion: Asset Segregation* (2017), paras 62–3.
[57] ESMA, *Opinion: Asset Segregation* (2017), p 55.

7.42 The requirements to safeguard financial instruments of clients are further detailed under Arts 2–3 and 5–8 of the Commission Delegated Directive 2017/593 (MiFID II RTS). Member States shall, for instance, require that investment firms keep records and accounts enabling them at any time and without delay to distinguish assets held for one client from the assets held for any other client and from their own assets. Investment firms must also maintain clients' records and accounts so as to ensure their accuracy, and in particular whether they correspond to the financial instruments held for clients.

7.43 Another requirement is that investment firms must conduct reconciliations between their internal accounts and records and those of any third parties by whom those assets are held on a regular basis. As mentioned above, investment firms must also take the necessary steps to ensure that any client financial instruments deposited with a third party are identifiable separately from the financial instruments belonging to the investment firm and the third party, by means of differently titled accounts on the books of the third party or other equivalent measures that achieve the same level of protection.[58]

7.44 The 2011 Alternative Investment Fund Managers Directive (AIFMD) further illustrates the trend towards segregated accounts.[59] At the level of the depositary, the assets need to be kept safe within segregated accounts on an AIF-by-AIF basis. Third-party custodians may hold multiple AIFs assets in omnibus accounts which need to be segregated from the custodian's, the depositary's, and other clients' assets.

7.45 Article 89 of the AIFMD RTS[60] sets out the safekeeping duties for assets held in custody. A depositary should, for example, ensure that (i) the financial instruments are properly registered, (ii) records and segregated accounts are maintained so as to ensure their accuracy, (iii) reconciliations are conducted on a regular basis between the depositary's internal accounts and records and those of any third party to whom custody functions are delegated, and that (iv) due care is exercised in relation to the financial instruments held in custody in order to ensure a high standard of investor protection.

7.46 On 30 October 2018, the EU Commission's Delegated Regulation (EU) 2018/1618 amending the AIFMD RTS as regards safe-keeping duties of depositaries was published. The amendments follow the publication of ESMA's opinion on asset segregation and depositary delegation in July 2017.[61] Where safekeeping functions have been delegated wholly or partly to a third party (custodian), the depositary must ensure that the third party acts in accordance with the segregation obligations laid down in Art 21(11)(d)(iii) of AIFMD. The depository must ensure that the third party segregates the assets of the depositary's clients from its own assets and from the assets of the depositary

---

[58] See Art 2(1)(a)–(d) of MiFID II RTS.
[59] See recitals (32), (40), and Art 21(8)(a)(ii) and (11)(d)(iii) AIFMD. Similar provisions can be found in Art 22 UCITS V Directive (EU/2014/91).
[60] Commission Delegated Regulation (EU) No 231/2013 of 19 December 2012 supplementing Directive 2011/61/EU of the European Parliament and of the Council with regard to exemptions, general operating conditions, depositaries, leverage, transparency, and supervision (AIFMD RTS).
[61] ESMA, *Opinion: Asset Segregation* (2017).

so that they can be clearly identified at any time as belonging to clients of a particular depositary. It is enough for the third party to commingle the assets of an AIF's clients in the same omnibus account provided its own assets, the assets of the depositary, and assets belonging to other clients of the third party are held in segregated accounts. A similar, delegated regulation has been published which amends the corresponding provisions under the UCITS Directive.[62]

The 2012 European Market Infrastructure Regulation (EMIR) distinguishes between omnibus and individually segregated accounts.[63] Article 39 of EMIR provides that a CCP must enable the segregation of assets and positions held for different clearing members and for itself and, in addition, that it should offer at least two types of segregation of client assets and positions to clearing members: (i) 'omnibus client segregation', enabling each clearing member to distinguish, in accounts with the CCP, the assets and positions of that clearing member from those held for its clients, or (ii) 'individual client segregation', enabling each clearing member to distinguish, in accounts with the CCP, the assets and positions held for one client from those held for other clients.[64] Under Article 39(7) of EMIR, CCPs and clearing members must publicly disclose the levels of protection and the costs associated with the different levels of segregation that they provide and offer those services on reasonable commercial terms. Details of the different levels of segregation must include a description of the main legal implications of the level of segregation that is offered, including information on the insolvency law that applies in the relevant jurisdiction. 7.47

European CCPs typically offer two different types of omnibus account, with different levels of mutualization of risk: (i) net omnibus segregated account (NOSA) and (ii) gross omnibus segregated account (GOSA). In case of a NOSA, clients' margin requirements are calculated and recorded on a net basis, while the corresponding collateral is commingled on the same account. In case of a GOSA, clients' margin requirements are calculated on a gross basis and the corresponding collateral is commingled on the GOSA. 7.48

Individual segregation applies to assets and positions held at the CCP level and does not have to be reflected at the level of the security settlement system, central bank or alternative highly secured arrangements with authorized financial institutions. However, assets belonging to the CCP should be distinguished from assets belonging to clearing members when deposited with a third party.[65] When a client opts for individual segregation, any excess margin should be posted to the CCP.[66] 7.49

---

[62] Commission Delegated Regulation (EU) 2018/1619 of 12 July 2018 amending Delegated Regulation (EU) 2016/438 as regards safe-keeping duties of depositaries.
[63] The EMIR contains, inter alia, rules that provide for mandatory clearing of standardized OTC derivatives transactions through CCPs, reporting of derivatives transactions to trade repositories, as well as authorization, registration, and supervision of CCPs and trade repositories.
[64] For further details, see recital (64) and Art 39 EMIR; Rasheed and Zebregs, 'Segregation in Derivatives Clearing'.
[65] ESMA, *EMIR Q&A*, CCP Question 8.
[66] Article 39(6) EMIR.

7.50 Similarly, the CSD Regulation (CSDR) 'requires CSDs to segregate the accounts of each participant from those of other participants and to enable participants to segregate the accounts of each of the participants' clients', that is, to enable individual client segregation. CSDs can, however, offer different types of individually segregated securities account such as securities accounts with, and securities accounts without, identification of the participant's client at the CSD level.[67]

7.51 Article 38 of CSDR requires participants to offer their clients a choice between omnibus client segregation and individual client segregation and inform them of the costs and risks associated with each option. CSDs and their participants are required to publicly disclose the levels of protection and the costs associated with the different levels of segregation that they provide and must offer those services on reasonable commercial terms. Comparable to EMIR (see paragraph 7.47), the main legal implications of the respective levels of segregation offered should be described, including information on the insolvency law applicable in the relevant jurisdictions.

7.52 The current European segregation rules evidence an inconsistent approach in terms of the requirements regarding account segregation under MiFID II, AIFMD, the UCITS Directive, EMIR, and CSDR, also in relation to the degree of protection at the various levels in the chain of intermediaries.[68] Although segregation does not ensure full protection of investors in all circumstances, given in particular the diverse securities and insolvency laws in different jurisdictions and the lack of harmonization in this area, ECSDA suggests that investors have a level of protection in many instances.[69] It would nonetheless be helpful if the treatment of segregation arrangements were to be further harmonized. From an investor protection perspective, other requirements such as reconciliations and recordkeeping have become increasingly important.

7.53 In a report submitted in 2017, EPTF flagged the urgency of agreeing on a more coherent framework in the EU and called for a segregation model consistent with the principles that (i) investors should have the right to choose between omnibus client segregation and individual client segregation, and (ii) the intermediary's proprietary securities should be segregated from its clients' securities in an insolvency-proof manner. This model would accommodate different business needs and regulatory and legal requirements, while providing a certain degree of flexibility.[70]

---

[67] ESMA, *CSDR Q&A*, CSD Question 5.
[68] AFME, *AFME Principles*, s 4.5; EPTF, *Report*, 46–7, 49; ESMA, *Opinion: Asset Segregation* (2017), paras 94–5. On the differences in segregation requirements for standard links and indirect links with third country CSDs, see ESMA, *CSDR Q&A*, 17.
[69] ECSDA, *Account Segregation Practices*, 3.1 at p 21; ECSDA, *CSDs, Asset Segregation, and Custody Services*, 3–5.
[70] EPTF, *Report*, 46–51. See also AFME, *AFME Principles*, s 5; ESMA, *Opinion: Asset Segregation* (2017), Annex 1, para 8.

E. Correction Methods

Imbalances arising from non-observance of the rule that sufficient securities should be available or for other reasons may place the stability of financial markets at risk. Many practices and legal rules have developed in different jurisdictions over time to rectify such imbalances. The following sections highlight some of those alternatives. **7.54**

(1) Matching of credits and debits

Generally, a distinction can be made between matching and non-matching systems. Matching is the requirement that every credit to a securities account must have a corresponding debit on another account. In matching systems, if a credit cannot be matched with a debit, the credit will be reversed or invalidated.[71] This is also referred to as the 'no-credit-without-debit rule'.[72] **7.55**

The 'no-credit-without-debit rule' is a method that addresses imbalances and safeguards the issue.[73] If an imbalance has occurred and an intermediary has registered too many securities to the accounts of account holders, someone will have to bear a loss. The process of matching generally facilitates the identification of who should bear that loss. **7.56**

There is no international or EU rule with respect to matching of credits and debits. The GSC does not explicitly address the issue, but the Official Commentary makes it clear that Contracting States are permitted to retain the practice of matching as a requirement under non-Convention law.[74] **7.57**

A Consultation Document issued by the European Commission in relation to the proposed Securities Law Legislation (a project that has, unfortunately, not crystallized) suggests that, since crediting and debiting determine the actual number of securities in the holding chain, these methods must be used consistently and in such way as to ensure that the number of securities maintained by the intermediary for the accounts of account holders always corresponds to the number of securities held by the intermediary. Principle 4.1(2) of the Consultation Document puts forward that national law should provide that an intermediary may credit the accounts of its account holders only if it holds a corresponding number of securities. However, the Consultation Document dismisses the introduction of a 'no-debit-without-credit rule'. Rather, if an intermediary **7.58**

---

[71] If the transferee qualifies as an innocent acquirer, the credit and the debit will stand.
[72] Law Commission, *The UNIDROIT Convention: Updated Advice*, 2.33, 2.46–8, 4.51–3; Law Commission, *Second Seminar*, 1.98–100; Legal Certainty Group, *Second Advice*, 9.2.2; Gómez-Sancha, 'Indirect Holdings', 39–40. On the requirements under German law of a corresponding debit and credit and of a transfer from a certain transferor to a certain transferee (without creating securities anew), see Mülbert, 'Depotrecht', I, III.3.5.3; Kronke, 'Das Genfer UNIDROIT-Übereinkommen', V.2; Eichholz, 'Das Genfer Wertpapierübereinkommen', B.II.
[73] EC, *Responses to Second Consultation*, 15.
[74] Kanda et al, *Official Commentary*, 11-4, 15–21, 18–1; Law Commission, *The UNIDROIT Convention: Updated Advice*, 4.51–3.

does not observe Principle 4.1(2), it should 'reverse erroneous credits' (see section E.3) and/or 'provide additional securities of the relevant description' (see sections E.4 and 5) to address the issue.[75]

7.59 The 'no-credit-without-debit rule' is problematic in high-volume international securities markets, where market participants are anonymous and for the most part act through brokers and other intermediaries. It can be extremely difficult for an intermediary to verify corresponding debits and credits through the chain of intermediaries or to establish the party on the 'other side' of a transaction, in which case it may be impossible to apply identification rules such as tracing. Multilateral netting and central counterparty clearing exacerbate the difficulty of matching the credit of a securities account with the debit of another account.[76]

7.60 The principle that an intermediary may not credit the accounts of its account holders unless it continuously holds a corresponding number of securities has also been criticized as overly rigid and imposing costs that are ultimately borne by all the participants in intermediated holding systems. Mooney argues that the absence of flexibility 'would stifle any future efforts to develop creative and innovative approaches that could provide needed flexibility for market participants, while nonetheless providing adequate protection for account holders'.[77]

(2) Reconciliation

7.61 The occurrence of imbalances can be reduced through regular reconciliation of securities holdings between the issuer, the central securities depository (CSD) and each intermediary in the holding chain.[78] Reconciliation is the method used to compare different sets of records and to detect any mismatching figures so as to ensure that the figures are correct. Proper and regular reconciliations can establish whether an imbalance has occurred so that corrective action can be taken. Automated tools may be used to identify and correct imbalances. The internal correction process itself should be compatible with the rules of sound accounting practice.[79]

---

[75] EC, *Second Consultation: Legislation on Securities*, ss 4–5. In the context of innocent acquisitions, the Consultation Document, s 5, states that the question of the creation of 'legally effective excess securities' must be addressed but may be left to the applicable national law. See also De Vauplane and Yon, 'Integrity', 8.2.5, 8.3.1.3, 8.3.2.3.

[76] Kuhn, 'Art. 19 FISA', 321.13–323.20; Law Commission, *Second Seminar*, 1.93; Law Commission, *The UNIDROIT Convention: Updated Advice*, 2.46; Rogers, 'Negotiability, Property and Identity', 491–501. On the tracing aspect, cf Goode et al, *Explanatory Report*, Int–38 to Int–40; Ooi, *Conflict of Laws*, 6.30, 7.47.

[77] Mooney, 'Shortfall', 7.3.4.

[78] See CSDR, recital (2) and Art 37; for level 2 implementation of the operational requirements see Arts 25, 59–65, Commission Delegated Regulation (EU) 2017/392 of 11 November 2016 supplementing Regulation (EU) No 909/2014 of the European Parliament and of the Council with regard to Regulatory Technical Standards on Authorisation, Supervisory and Operational Requirements, OJ L 65.

[79] Kuhn, 'Prel. Cmts Arts. 27–8 FISA', 407.6–7.

Regular reconciliations of securities accounts, not only between each single custodian **7.62**
with its immediate sub-custodian but at all levels throughout the intermediated chain,
and between the securities accounts and the register administered by or for the issuer
are very important.[80]

(3) Reversal of erroneous book entries

'Reversals' are a way of correcting imbalances.[81] In the event of a reversal, the need **7.63**
to correct book entries in certain cases of error must, however, be balanced with the
core principle of absolute irreversibility and finality of book entries.[82] Reversals should,
therefore, only be applied in restricted circumstances. It should be noted that a reversal
may not be possible if the acquirer no longer holds the relevant securities or if the securities involved have been transferred to an innocent acquirer.[83] Where a reversal is
impossible, a claim for damages may ensue.[84]

The GSC does not harmonize the technical and practical reversal rules commonly **7.64**
found in the uniform rules of SSSs or in account agreements. There are currently no
international guidelines that set out requirements for reversals, circumstances where a
reversal is impossible, and the consequences thereof.[85]

(4) Use of an intermediary's own securities

Another way for an intermediary to rectify an imbalance is to credit securities of the re- **7.65**
quired type that it holds for its own account to its account holders' accounts.[86]

However, it is not necessarily a good idea to require intermediaries to hold specific se- **7.66**
curities as a buffer corresponding to each type of security to which its account holders
are entitled. Whereas creating a general financial surplus through some general form
of insurance (see paragraph 7.93) has clear benefits, obliging the intermediary to create
such asset-specific buffers may lead to excessive costs.[87]

---

[80] See Micheler, 'Perspective of Investors', VIII.E. See also Ch 6, paras 6.19 and 6.54.
[81] Article 16 GSC; Legal Certainty Group, *Second Advice*, 9.3.1.
[82] On reversals generally, see Kanda et al, *Official Commentary*, 16–16 to 16–21; Kuhn, 'Prel. Cmts Arts. 27–28'; Kuhn, 'Art. 28 FISA'; Legal Certainty Group, *Second Advice*, 6.4–5; Witmer, 'Art. 11 FISA', 246.28–9. On settlement finality, see Art 27 GSC and the EU Settlement Finality Directive.
[83] Article 18 GSC; Kanda et al, *Official Commentary*, 16–17; Legal Certainty Group, *Second Advice*, Recommendation 7.
[84] See, eg, art 29(1)–(2) of the Federal Intermediated Securities Act (Switzerland) (FISA).
[85] Cf Thévenoz, 'Who Holds?', III.3.
[86] Article 25 GSC; Legal Certainty Group, *Second Advice*, 9.3.3; Witmer, 'Art. 11 FISA', 245.25–27.
[87] See the collated responses to the question regarding the maintenance of own assets in a client account as a 'buffer', in IOSCO, *Consultation Client Assets*, Appendixes A and B; see also Witmer, 'Art. 11 FISA', 245.27.

(5) Buy-in of securities

7.67 'Buy-in of missing securities' is another effective method of addressing an imbalance.[88] In this case, the intermediary acquires additional securities, often in response to regulation, until its total holdings match the aggregate holdings of its account holders. Some flexibility as to timing for buy-in may be required.[89] Where the market is illiquid or the issuer is insolvent, the intermediary will, as a rule, be prevented from using this method and will have to fall back on one of the other methods listed.[90]

7.68 The relevant law may also provide that the intermediary should pay an equivalent sum of money for the missing securities if it cannot find replacement securities.

(6) Shorter settlement cycles

7.69 The standard in many financial markets for settlement cycles varies across countries and in respect of different financial instruments. For instance, in Europe, it typically ranges from T + 0 ('same day settlement', ie, settlement occurs on the same day as the trade date) to T + 2 (settlement occurs two days after the trade date).[91] The setting of the duration of settlement cycles may be influenced by factors such as different back-office processes, market practices, legal requirements, time-zones, liquidity management implications, and technology (on the potential of DLT to speed up settlement, see paragraph 7.104). Shorter settlement cycles of transactions such as T + 1 or even T + 0 can be of assistance in identifying imbalances early on and so in limiting their impact. In addition, a shorter settlement cycle may reduce settlement risk, including counterparty and replacement risk, which exists between the trade and settlement dates. A shorter settlement cycle can also limit the number of outstanding transactions and reduce the aggregate market exposure.[92]

(7) Regulatory tools

7.70 The relevant regulator of the CSD, SSS, or other intermediaries may be empowered to regulate and supervise imbalances. For example, the regulator may prescribe 'matching' of credits and debits, daily reconciliation, reversals, buy-in, or other corrective steps, as well as segregation, restrictions on the use of clients' securities, an appropriate technological infrastructure, daily reporting, audit reports, monetary fines, and other disciplinary measures.

---

[88] Buy-in of securities/financial instruments may also be required in cases that do not solve an imbalance, but rather address settlement failures. See, eg, Article 7 CSDR.
[89] Witmer, 'Art. 11 FISA', 245.21–4 and 246.30–247.35.
[90] Witmer, 'Art. 11 FISA', 245.23, states that the intermediary will in that case not be liable to its account holders. Likewise, Legal Certainty Group, *Second Advice*, 9.3.2, states that liability should be limited, particularly where the event is beyond the intermediary's control. See also para 7.12.
[91] See, eg, Art 5 CSDR; EPTF, *Report*, 133–5.
[92] Yates and Montagu, Global Custody, 8.39–40. See also Ch 9, s D(3)(a).

F. Loss Sharing in Insolvency

Intermediated securities, whether segregated individually or in a pool, are generally subject to custody risk.[93] Custody risk involves the possible 'loss of securities held in custody occasioned by the insolvency, negligence or fraudulent action of the custodian or of a sub-custodian'.[94] If the intermediary has not complied with the requirements regarding the holding of sufficient securities (section C) and proper allocation (section D), the number of securities credited to account holders may in fact exceed the number of securities the intermediary holds for them. Should the intermediary enter into an insolvency proceeding, any shortfall would materialize if there were no further possibilities to correct it (section E). In this case, one or more account holders would have to take a loss.[95]

7.71

The allocation of a shortfall to one or more account holders is a remedy of last resort.[96] The loss-sharing rule should only apply if the intermediary has exhausted all other methods of correcting an imbalance yet it persists. The commencement of an insolvency proceeding usually determines the point in time beyond which it may no longer be possible to remedy the shortfall.[97]

7.72

As a remedy of last resort, the loss-sharing rule should apply in the event of insolvency, but only after the opening of a liquidation procedure, not in the event of a reorganization procedure.[98] The application of the loss-sharing rule where the intermediary is subject to a reorganization procedure may prematurely displace damage from the intermediary to the account holders, despite the intermediary's general duty to cover the imbalance.[99] The intermediary may still be able to correct the imbalance, and in that case there is no reason to transfer the loss to the account holders.[100]

7.73

(1) Loss-sharing methods: mutualization or individualization?

Each State has its own rules on how shortfalls should be distributed in the insolvency proceeding of an intermediary. Three main approaches can be distinguished: (i)

7.74

---

[93] Garrido, 'Loss-sharing', 785; Law Commission, *Second Seminar*, 1.90–1.
[94] CPSS, *Cross-border Securities Settlements*, Annex 1, 38.
[95] Einsele, 'Book-entry', II(c); Garrido, 'Loss-sharing', V; Gullifer, 'Ownership of Securities', 1.V.B; Kuhn, 'Art. 19'; Law Commission, *Second Seminar*, 1.5–10, 1.90–175; McFarlane and Stevens, 'Interests in Securities', 2.II.C; Moss, 'Insolvency', 3.V; Yates and Montagu, *Global Custody*, 3.55.
[96] Garrido, 'Loss-sharing', 787; Kuhn, 'Art. 19 FISA', 324.21; Legal Certainty Group, *Second Advice*, 9.3.4.
[97] Eg, the regime of Art 26 GSC does not relate to non-insolvency situations. See Kanda et al, *Official Commentary*, 26–9.
[98] Kuhn, 'Art. 19 FISA', 324.21.
[99] Legal Certainty Group, *Second Advice*, 9.3.4.
[100] In the GSC, the definition of 'insolvency proceeding' has a broad meaning and includes any 'collective judicial or administrative proceeding, including an interim proceeding, in which the assets and affairs of the debtor are subject to control or supervision by a court or other competent authority for the purpose of reorganization or liquidation' (Article 1(h) GSC; see Kanda et al, *Official Commentary*, 1–46). For the reasons given in the main text and in accordance with the GSC's general principle of account holder protection, the interpretation of the defined term 'insolvency proceeding' should therefore be limited, for the purpose of Article 26 GSC (loss sharing) to liquidation procedures (Article 4 GSC; Kanda et al, *Official Commentary*, 4–8).

mutualization of losses among all account holders holding the same type of security (pro rata loss sharing per issue); (ii) mutualization among all account holders of an intermediary (pro rata loss sharing generally); and (iii) individual allocation of loss per account holder.[101]

7.75 Mutualization of losses can thus be applied to account holders of the same type of security or to all an intermediary's account holders generally, in both cases in proportion to the size of their holdings (without taking into consideration circumstances such as the cause of the loss or the timing of the credit of securities to the securities account).[102] The idea of mutualization is built on the assumption that account holders undertake the common insolvency risk of the relevant intermediary.[103] Mutualization of losses is linked to the account holder's decision to hold certain intermediated securities with a particular intermediary. This is not an arbitrary criterion but has its basis in the account holder's choice.

7.76 However, mutualization of losses may have adverse effects. The application of the sharing rule means that the securities held by the insolvent intermediary and each account holder's position must be determined. As a number of account holders discovered in the Lehman Brothers administration, this may result in the freezing of securities accounts and lead to lengthy and extensive litigation.[104]

7.77 Another method of dealing with shortfalls is to link them to individually segregated client accounts (legal segregation).[105] In this case, the account holder must bear the whole loss related to its account, even if the shortfall was caused entirely by the intermediary's action or omission. Some argue that this may lead to arbitrary allocation of the risk to a specific account holder.[106] This may be true, but an account holder which has rejected the mutualization of risk by opting for individual segregation should not be able to rely on this argument.

7.78 Whereas commingling of securities in omnibus accounts (see paragraphs 7.21–2) generally implies some form of mutualization of loss, losses can be either mutualized or allocated on an individual basis in the case of individually segregated accounts (see paragraphs 7.23–4).

---

[101] The opposed approaches of mutualization and individualization are also apparent in other contexts. For example, the no-credit-without-debit rule and reversals operate on the level of individual transactions (see ss E(1) and (3)), whereas the solution of insurance mutualizes risk (see para 7.93). Other methods of mutualizing losses are included in the EU CCP Recovery and Resolution Regulation and the Bank Recovery and Resolution Directive (BRRD). For CCPs, these measures include the reduction in value of the collateral provided daily to the CCP (so-called variation margin gains haircutting), cash calls to non-defaulting clearing members, and (partial) termination of the CCP's contracts. For credit institutions and investment firms, losses are mutualized through the bail-in mechanism.
[102] Kuhn, 'Art. 19 FISA', 318.1; Law Commission, *Second Seminar*, 1.122–133, 1.161; Legal Certainty Group, *Second Advice*, 9.3.4; Micheler, *Property in Securities*, 203.
[103] Garrido, 'Loss-sharing', 787; Law Commission, *Second Seminar*, 1.132.
[104] See EC, *10th Discussion Paper*, 23–7. See also the account of the Lehman insolvencies in the first edition of this book, Ch 8, s C(3).
[105] See Kuhn, 'Art. 19 FISA', 324.22.
[106] Law Commission, *Second Seminar*, 1.118, 1.123; Rogers, 'Negotiability, Property and Identity', 484–501.

(2) Loss sharing under the Geneva Securities Convention

Article 26 GSC addresses the question of loss sharing in an intermediary's insolvency proceeding. The following brief discussion of this provision illustrates the different mutualization and individualization models mentioned in section F(1).[107] Article 26(2) provides as a main rule: **7.79**

> If the aggregate number or amount of securities and intermediated securities of any description allocated under Article 25(1) GSC to an account holder, a group of account holders or the intermediary's account holders generally (as the case may be) is less than the aggregate number or amount of securities of that description credited to the securities accounts of that account holder, that group of account holders or the intermediary's account holders generally, the shortfall shall be borne:
> (a) if securities and intermediated securities have been allocated to a single account holder, by that account holder; and
> (b) in any other case, by the account holders to whom the relevant securities have been allocated, in proportion to the respective number or amount of securities of that description credited to their securities accounts.

Accordingly, the main rule under Article 26 GSC is mutualization of losses in the intermediary's insolvency, as a remedy of last resort, if the intermediary does not have enough securities to satisfy its account holders' claims.[108] There is an exception to this rule: if securities have been allocated to a single account holder, any shortfall must be borne by that account holder alone. In all other cases, any shortfall must be borne on a pro rata basis in relation to the number or amount of securities of a certain description that have been credited to the account holders' securities accounts. Mutualization under the GSC thus applies on an issue-by-issue basis. **7.80**

However, such mutualization applies in an insolvency proceeding in relation to an intermediary 'unless otherwise provided by any conflicting rule applicable in that proceeding' (Article 26(1) GSC).[109] This wording prioritizes a distributional rule that is conceptually different from the default approach of pro rata mutualization per issue. The non-Convention law could, for example, envisage the individual allocation of losses to account holders that have opted for individual segregation or mutualization of losses among all the intermediary's account holders.[110] **7.81**

---

[107] Extensive information on Art 26 GSC may be found in Kanda et al, *Official Commentary*, Article 26.
[108] Garrido, 'Loss-sharing', 786; Kuhn, 'Art. 19 FISA', 324.21; Legal Certainty Group, *Second Advice*, 9.3.4.
[109] This provision was inserted to reflect the fact that the conflicting distributional rule need not itself be part of the insolvency law. Kanda et al, *Official Commentary*, 26–11; Mooney, *Law and Systems*, 55; Mooney and Kanda, 'Core Issues', 124.
[110] Article 26(3) GSC allows for yet another way of loss sharing, ie, in accordance with uniform rules of a securities settlement system.

(3) Four key policy questions in relation to loss sharing

7.82 From a theoretical standpoint, the application of a loss-sharing rule raises at least four questions. The *first question* is whether the shortfall should be mutualized solely among the account holders of the securities of the same description or whether they should be extended to all the relevant intermediary's account holders.[111] On the one hand, if the sharing rule is based on the assumption that account holders jointly assume the insolvency risk of the intermediary, the type of security that account holders hold with the intermediary is arguably irrelevant.[112] On the other hand, since the account holder decides which type of security to invest in, its exposure should perhaps be limited to the subgroup of account holders that runs the custody risk in respect of the type of securities concerned.[113]

7.83 Regarding the first question, a common approach (with the notable exception of the US)[114] is to share losses among the holders of a specific kind of securities.[115] The (alpha) numeric codes reflected in the International Securities Identification Number (ISIN) and the Committee on Uniform Securities Identification Procedures (CUSIP) accommodate identification of securities of the same type.[116]

7.84 The *second question* is whether pro rata distribution should include the securities booked to a segregated account in the name of the relevant intermediary. While the first question addresses a conflict between account holders, the second question involves the account holders and the creditors of the relevant intermediary. There are arguments both to include and to exclude the intermediary's segregated securities in the pro rata distribution. On the one hand, if segregation is intended as a rule with 'proprietary' effect (legal segregation), the intermediary's segregated securities are part of that intermediary's estate available to its creditors. In addition, some argue that it is unclear why the intermediary and its creditors should be affected if the shortfall arises through an event beyond the intermediary's control.[117] On the other hand, since the intermediary controls the credits in all securities accounts, whether they are made in its own name or in the name of other account holders, it is arbitrary to isolate the intermediary's segregated securities from the shared custody risk. In particular, if a

---

[111] Different answers to this question may even be envisaged within a given jurisdiction. For example, US law envisages the distribution of a shortfall among all the customers of a *broker-dealer intermediary*, whereas losses are shared rateably per issue among account holders of a *bank intermediary*. See Mooney, *Law and Systems*, 16, 83; Mooney, 'Shortfall', 7.3.3.1, 7.3.3.3.

[112] Haentjens, *Harmonisation of Securities Law*, 272; Law Commission, *Second Seminar*, 1.167; Legal Certainty Group, *Second Advice*, 9.3.4; Mooney, *Law and Systems*, 16.

[113] Kuhn, 'Art. 19 FISA', 325.26; Legal Certainty Group, *Second Advice*, 9.3.4.

[114] Mooney, 'Shortfall', 180.

[115] Article 26(2)(b) GSC; Article 19 FISA (Switzerland); Article 154 Texto refundido de la Ley del Mercado de Valores (Spain); L211-10 Code monétaire et financier (France); Article 57.3-bis Testo Unico della Finanza (Italy). Dixon, Legal Nature, 81, considers the mutualization of the shortfall among the account holders of securities of the same description as a feature of co-ownership regimes for intermediated securities.

[116] See Kuhn, 'Art. 19 FISA', 325.27.

[117] See Law Commission, *Second Seminar*, 1.145. Kuhn, 'Art. 19 FISA', 321.12, points out that the FISA does not take this argument into account. See also para 7.12.

shortfall arises as a consequence of a breach of the intermediary's duty for which the intermediary is responsible, the intermediary's securities should arguably be available to cover the shortfall.[118]

Some legal instruments expressly establish that securities booked in a segregated account in the name of the relevant intermediary should be used to cover a shortfall of account holders (Article 25 GSC,[119] 19(1) FISA, and UK CASS 6.6.54[120]). 7.85

The *third question* is whether the distribution should include the securities booked to a segregated account in the name of an individual account holder. By holding their securities in such segregated accounts, account holders seek to limit the risks involved in intermediated securities, particularly in the wake of the financial crisis. Usually, the account holder would pay more for holding its securities in a segregated account as opposed to an omnibus account. Despite strong arguments in its favour, the pro rata loss-sharing rule may produce unsatisfactory results in practice. Account holders subject to an insolvency proceeding have no certainty as to their legal position and cannot dispose of intermediated securities while that position is being determined. 7.86

One possible approach is to give legal effect to such arrangements and to allow the enforceability of individual segregation in insolvency (legal segregation).[121] In line with this approach, the intermediated securities credited to the segregated account should be excluded from the pro rata sharing rule and made available to the relevant account holder by the insolvency administrator.[122] 7.87

However, allowing this approach reduces the advantages for account holders that have opted for mutualization. Individual segregation does not necessarily avoid, but rather shifts, the custody risk. In a 'mixed' scenario of individually segregated and omnibus accounts, those with individually segregated accounts still face custody risk, while those with interests in omnibus accounts must carry the additional losses that would otherwise have been shared with the investors that opted for individual segregation. In a scenario where *all* client assets are segregated on an individual basis, pro rata loss sharing appears to be the only possible solution to cope with losses that cannot be associated with individual accounts. 7.88

---

[118] See Kuhn, 'Art. 19 FISA', 321.12. See also para 7.12.
[119] Under the GSC, segregation of securities that an intermediary holds for itself is intended, as a general principle, neither to have proprietary effect nor to interfere with the intermediary's duty to hold sufficient securities under Article 24. However, Article 25(5) GSC allows segregation with 'proprietary' effect in relation to securities that an intermediary holds for its own account (legal segregation). The securities booked to a segregated account in the name of the relevant intermediary are thus available for distribution among the account holders on an issue-by-issue basis, except in the case where the Contracting State has made a declaration under Article 25(5).
[120] See <https://www.handbook.fca.org.uk/handbook/CASS/6/6.pdf> (accessed 7 July 2021); FCA, Review of the Client Assets Regime for Investment Business (June 2014; Policy Statement, PS14/09), <https://www.fca.org.uk/publication/policy/ps14-09.pdf> (accessed 7 July 2021), 5.83.
[121] Law Commission, *Second Seminar*, 1.108, 1.113; Law Commission, *The UNIDROIT Convention: Updated Advice*, 4.169–70.
[122] Another solution is the enactment of more stringent record-keeping and reporting requirements to facilitate the transfer of client assets in the event of an intermediary's insolvency.

7.89 Moreover, possible systemic implications should be taken into account. This is no straightforward matter. Individual segregation may lead to enormous losses for one single account holder (with possible systemic consequences), whereas the mutualization of losses generally implies smaller losses to be carried by a number of account holders (thus mitigating systemic impact). However, mutualization of losses can play a role in the context of systemic risk, as it may be unclear to market participants where losses will fall (and how extensive they will be). See also Chapter 8, section B(2)(d).

7.90 The *fourth question* is whether the loss-sharing rule only takes into consideration securities credited to a securities account by way of book entry, or whether it also applies to securities for which a credit book entry should have been or is in the process of being made. In some systems, the legal position of the account holders does not depend exclusively on the book entry. For example, if an intermediary receives and accepts financial assets from a client for credit to a securities account and fails to make the credit, the intermediary's negligence or fraud should not preclude the client from benefiting from the protection afforded to an account holder. Although not all legal systems expressly address this issue, in some cases there is support for recognizing the rights of an account holder without a credit having been made.[123]

(4) Some further issues

7.91 The following issues deserve further attention: (i) the application of pro rata loss sharing outside insolvency; and (ii) the role of insurance and comparable schemes.

7.92 While the pro rata rule fits well in an insolvency scenario, there may be cases outside insolvency where its application may also be advantageous. For example, there may be systems in which losses are passed on to account holders if the losses were caused by factors beyond the control of the relevant intermediary. In this situation, a pro rata loss-sharing rule can be applied in order to distribute the losses.[124] While, as a matter of principle, the pro rata rule is one of 'last resort', its application outside insolvency is conceivable.[125]

7.93 An account holder may suffer damages because of the application of a loss-sharing rule. In most cases, the account holder may only have a claim for damages which ranks *pari passu* with the relevant intermediary's unsecured creditors. In some States, this situation is

---

[123] American Law Institute, *UCC Official Text and Comments*, § 8–501 UCC, Comment 2; Mooney, 'Shortfall', 170–1; Mooney and Kanda, 'Core Issues', 124–5 (n 278). For the Hague Securities Convention, see Goode et al, *Explanatory Report*, 1–8. Whether a credit can exist without a book entry under the GSC is not, however, entirely clear. See Kanda et al, *Official Commentary*, 1–22, 11–9, 11–10, 17–7, 18–10. On 'decoupling' an account holder's right to share in its intermediary's insolvency proceeding from the question whether it has a proprietary interest under non-insolvency law, see Ch 8, para 8.22.

[124] See Kuhn, 'Art. 19 FISA', 324.23; Legal Certainty Group, *Second Advice*, Example 34. The GSC takes as a starting point that the cause of imbalances is irrelevant; an intermediary should first use its own securities to remedy any imbalance. See also para 7.12.

[125] Cf Kuhn, 'Art. 19 FISA', 324.23.

mitigated, especially in the case of small investors, by conferring additional protection on account holders.[126] One method to ensure investor protection in the intermediary's insolvency that should be mentioned is an insurance-like mechanism (for example, a private or governmental investor fund, capital reserve, or compensation scheme, based on mandatory or voluntary contributions).[127]

G. Outlook: New Technologies

7.94 The emergence of Bitcoin in 2009 and its explosive growth after 2015 has caught the eye of the financial industry and regulators. Bitcoin uses new technology named 'blockchain': a peer-to-peer network, without central authorities, that 'timestamps transactions by hashing them into an ongoing chain of hash-based proof-of-work, forming a record that cannot be changed without redoing the proof-of-work'.[128] However, blockchain is only one type of distributed ledger technology (DLT), which is an innovation able to establish a new paradigm for the financial markets.[129] DLT has been described as 'the processes and related technologies that enable nodes in a network (or arrangement) to securely propose, validate and record state changes (or updates) to a synchronized ledger that is distributed across the network's nodes'.[130] Core characteristics of DLT are the existence of a decentralized validation system (operating through nodes) and the use of cryptography.[131]

7.95 Originally, it was envisaged that a potential key benefit of applying DLT in a securities market setting would be disintermediation. The direct connection between the issuer and the end-investor, on the one hand, and the direct connection between transacting parties, on the other hand, has the potential of eliminating or reducing the role of third parties providing clearing, settlement, and holding services.[132] However, the technology has given rise to new services offered by intermediaries, such as the custody of private and public keys in omnibus or segregated accounts.[133] The purpose of this section is to describe the potential impact of DLT on the holding of sufficient (crypto) securities (paragraphs 7.96–8), segregation (paragraphs 7.99–101), various correction methods (paragraphs 102–4), and loss sharing (paragraph 7.105). Some attention will

---

[126] For example, in Japan and Spain. See Caballero, *La adquisición a non domino*, 217–23; Mooney and Kanda, 'Core Issues', 125, fns 279–80.
[127] Law Commission, *Second Seminar*, 1.104. In the EU, see the Deposit Guarantee Scheme Directive (recast) and the Investor Compensation Scheme Directive. For insurance-like schemes under US, Canadian, and UK law, see Ch 8, s B(2)(c).
[128] Nakamoto, *Bitcoin*, 1.
[129] ECB Advisory Group, *Potential Impact of DLTs*, 1.
[130] CPMI, *Distributed Ledger Technology*, 2.
[131] ESMA, *Report*, 1.
[132] In the words of Nakamoto: 'What is needed is an electronic payment system based on cryptographic proof instead of trust, allowing any two willing parties to transact directly with each other without the need for a trusted third party' (Bitcoin, 1). See also ESMA, *Report*, 9; Pinna and Ruttenberg, *DLT: Revolution or Evolution?*, 4.1.2; Green and Snagg, *Intermediated Securities and DLT*, 343.
[133] See Mooney, 'Beyond Intermediation', 392, 445 (pointing out that DLT does not eliminate intermediation because investors prefer, for practical reasons, to hold digital assets through custodians. However, DLT could be useful to implement a New Platform System to achieve disintermediation); idem, 'An Essay on Pluralism, 9;

be given to (proposed) legislation on the matter both in the EU and Switzerland (paragraphs 106–7).

7.96 Any analysis of the requirement of sufficient securities and the risk of an imbalance in a DLT environment should distinguish between digital assets originated on the ledger (native assets) and those that represent 'non-crypto', 'real-world' assets electronically on the ledger (non-native assets).[134] In the latter case, the correspondence between the underlying real-world assets and the crypto-assets should be controlled in order to prevent an imbalance. This is not the case for native assets held directly by an end-investor *without a custodian*. As Levin has pointed out: 'Transactions are constructed using previous transactions as inputs to fund transaction outputs. Each output can be thought of as a pipe with some capacity of bitcoin. Each transaction is a fitting, connecting one or more of the existing pipes. The pipe or pipes that are the result of a fitting can at most carry the same capacity of the sum of the pipes that led into the transaction'.[135] However, as explained in paragraph 7.102, if the investor holds the native assets through a custodian, the risk of an imbalance arises and the requirement of sufficient (crypto)securities should be applied.

7.97 In a DLT environment (absent any central entity), each investor can hold and trade its crypto-assets without the participation of an intermediary. This is possible due to the use of cryptography, where each investor is assigned a set of two keys, one public and one private.[136] If an investor owns a crypto-asset and wishes to transfer it, the investor should send a message concerning the transaction containing its public key and the public key of the recipient, and sign the transaction using its private key (without disclosing it). After validation, the transaction is recorded in a new block on the public ledger and the crypto-asset has been (irrevocably) transferred to the recipient.[137]

7.98 The private key is a secret code that facilitates the disposal of crypto-assets and proves the authorization of the transaction by the investor. While the private key gives exclusive control over the crypto-assets (sole owner), the theft or loss of the private key is a major risk. Investors may not wish to take this risk and assign the custody of their crypto-assets to a 'custodial wallet' storing public and private keys.[138]

7.99 Crypto-asset wallets have become an industry that offers a wide range of services. Without claiming to be exhaustive, following are some common examples. A 'software wallet' is an application installed on a computer or mobile phone, while a 'hardware

---

Gullifer, Chong, and Liu, *Client-intermediary Relations in the Crypto-asset World*, 1 ('the vast majority of crypto-assets are kept by intermediaries').

[134] CPMI, *Distributed Ledger Technology*, 2.2.1; UNIDROIT 2021–Study LXXXII–W.G. 3–Doc 2 (rev 1), 85–96.
[135] Levin, *Bitcoin*.
[136] Brito and Castillo, 'Bitcoin', 4; ECB Advisory Group, *Potential Impact of DLTs*, Glossary, 130–1.
[137] ESMA, *Advice*, 23.
[138] ESMA, *Advice*, 25; Hinkes, 'Throw away the Key, or the Key Holder?', 231. Another reason to entrust crypto-assets to a wallet provider is that a private key may be ill-suited where not one, but several persons need to have the control of crypto-assets (ESMA, *Advice*, 58). In this case, a multiple signature wallet may be useful (Hinkes, 'Throw away the Key, or the Key Holder?', 232).

wallet' is a physical device. 'Hot wallets' are connected to the Internet, unlike 'cold wallets'. Hot wallets are considered riskier because of their exposure to cyberattacks. While the precise legal effects of the use of crypto-asset wallets depend on the contract and national law, the investor usually loses partial or full control of the private key.[139] One example is the use of the 'omnibus model'. As Bhutoria explains, a custodian may use a protocol to generate key pairs (public and private) under a tree-like structure (master key, child keys, and grandchild keys), that are maintained by the custodian in its name. Unlike a segregated model, the custodian controls the number of key pairs it manages and defines the percentage of hot and cold storage. The main reason for using this model is liquidity: the custodian may minimize hot wallet storage (and its associated risk) while maintaining enough liquidity to comply promptly with investor instructions without resorting to the cold wallet, and then rebalance the whole custody portfolio to comply with the defined percentage of hot and cold storage.[140]

7.100 The use of segregated and omnibus custody of public and private keys evidences a common practice across the securities industry regardless of the kind of asset or technology used (path dependence).[141] It therefore comes as no surprise that control of the private keys has been considered by ESMA as a safekeeping service.[142] Likewise, an ECB Advisory Group has pointed out that it is technically feasible for a CSD to operate a DLT network that, in line with regulatory requirements, offers both omnibus and individual client segregation.[143]

7.101 As in the case of intermediated securities, the use of segregated and omnibus custody in a DLT environment may give rise to imbalances (cf section B). A requirement of sufficient crypto-assets may help to forestall such imbalances (cf section C), while they may be solved using a variety of corrective methods (cf section E), among which reconciliations, reversals, and settlement cycles in a DLT setting.

7.102 DLT may substitute or improve the reconciliation process. Whereas reconciliation of native assets without a custodian would be superfluous thanks to the 'cryptographic guarantee' of synchronization across the network's nodes (ie, 'no security can be added to or subtracted from the system'),[144] the existence of custodians re-creates the need for reconciliation in order to reduce the risk of imbalance. Moreover, in the case of non-native assets, reconciliation is needed to ensure correspondence between the underlying real-world assets and the crypto-assets.[145]

---

[139] ESMA, *Advice*, 27; SEC-FINRA, *Joint Staff Statement*; GDF, *Crypto Asset Safekeeping*, 2–3.
[140] Bhutoria, *The Omnibus Model for Custody*. The omnibus model casts doubt on the statement of Green and Snagg that 'each crypto-security remains unique and identifiable' ('Intermediated Securities and DLT', 343).
[141] Baty, *Digital Custody*; Werner, *What is Custody of Digital Assets?*.
[142] ESMA, *Advice*, 164. See also SEC-FINRA, *Joint Staff Statement*.
[143] ECB Advisory Group, *Potential Impact of DLTs*, 2.2.3, 15.1. On segregation and pooling of digital assets, see also UNIDROIT 2021–Study LXXXII–W.G. 3–Doc 2 (rev 1), 25–6 (preliminary draft principle C.5(d), Explanation, and Open question#4).
[144] ECB Advisory Group, *Potential Impact of DLTs*, 3.3.2.
[145] ESMA, *Report*, ss 9 and 41; CPMI, *Distributed Ledger Technology*, 3.2.3; ECB Advisory Group, *Potential Impact of DLTs*, 9.2.1. 'Smart contracts' (executable algorithms coded in the ledger) could also reduce or substitute the reconciliation process (ECB Advisory Group, *Potential Impact of DLTs*, 9.2.3).

7.103 As a starting point DLT, after validation, creates irreversible records, at least as designed for Bitcoin. However, the reversibility of the record may be a useful tool to correct erroneous records or unlawful transactions.[146] A restricted (or permissioned) DLT system, with only authorized participants—the model currently prevalent in the financial industry—simplifies the reversal of an erroneous ledger update, where appropriate.[147]

7.104 DLT has the potential of providing instantaneous settlement (T+0). While a shorter settlement cycle is one way of limiting the impact of imbalances, instantaneous settlement (if feasible) may also create liquidity constraints.[148] As part of increased efficiency in post-trade operations in a DLT setting with the appropriate design, a shorter settlement cycle, tailored to suit market needs, could be envisaged.[149]

7.105 In conformity with the possible existence of imbalances, a loss-sharing rule is needed in a DLT environment as a remedy of last resort.[150] The rule raises the same policy issues as those arising in the intermediated securities system.

7.106 In 2020, the EU Commission published a proposal for a Regulation on Markets in Crypto-assets (MiCA).[151] Article 63 of this proposal regards asset safekeeping and determines that 'crypto-asset service providers that hold crypto-assets belonging to clients or the means of access to such crypto-assets shall make adequate arrangements to safeguard the ownership rights of clients, especially in the event of the crypto-asset service provider's insolvency, and to prevent the use of a client's crypto-assets on own account except with the client's express consent'.[152] Article 33 of the proposal also contains fairly detailed rules for custody in the context of 'asset-referenced tokens', a specific type of crypto-asset that purports to maintain a stable value by referring to the value of a 'basket' of underlying reserve assets.[153] To prevent the risk of loss of such asset-referenced tokens and to preserve their value, issuers of asset-referenced tokens should, *inter alia*, ensure that the reserve assets are segregated from the issuer's own assets at all times, that these assets are not encumbered or pledged as collateral, that these assets are held under appropriate custody arrangements, and that the issuer of asset-referenced tokens has prompt access to these reserve assets.

7.107 Also in 2020, the Federal Assembly of the Swiss Confederation adopted the Federal Act on the Adaptation of Federal Law to Developments in Distributed Ledger Technology (Swiss

---

[146] ESMA, *Report*, s 26; CPMI, *Distributed Ledger Technology*, 3.3.5; Clifford Chance and EBRD, *Smart Contracts*, 2.3.6–2.4.1; Gullifer and Hay, *How Final is Final?*, 8. The DAO case has shown the usefulness of reversibility to correct unlawful records in an unrestricted platform (Ethereum).

[147] Pinna and Ruttenberg, *DLT: Revolution or Evolution?*, 2.2.

[148] Ibid, 4.1.3; ECB Advisory Group, *Potential Impact of DLTs*, 6.2.2. and 15.1 at 114.

[149] CPMI, *Distributed Ledger Technology*, 3.3.2; ESMA, *Report*, Appendix, 1–2; FINRA, 'Report on Distributed Ledger Technology, 5–6.

[150] Regarding segregation of crypto-assets in insolvency proceedings, see Zellweger-Gutknecht and Bacharach, 'Segregation of Cryptoassets', 2.2, 3.2, 4.2, and 5.2; Haentjens, de Graaf, and Kokorin, 'Failed Hopes of Disintermediation', 3, 6.4.

[151] Proposal for a Regulation of the European Parliament and of the Council on Markets in Crypto-assets, (Brussels, 24.9.2020; COM(2020) 593 final, 2020/0265 (COD)).

[152] For further guidelines on segregation, see also Article 67(7) MiCA.

[153] See also recital (38) and the definitions of 'asset-referenced token' and 'reserve assets' in Art 3(1)(3) and (21) MiCA.

DLT Law).[154] To protect investors from a custodian's insolvency (custody risk), the Swiss DLT Law enables clients to separate crypto-assets (and data) from the custodian's estate if, *inter alia*, the client crypto-assets are segregated either in omnibus or individual accounts. In case of shortfall, the custodian's crypto-assets of the same kind should cover the deficit. If, after this allocation, the shortfall remains, a pro rata loss-sharing rule applies.[155]

H. Conclusion

Imbalances may occur for a variety of reasons, ranging from technical errors to fraud. One way to prevent them is to impose a duty on the intermediary to hold sufficient securities. When an imbalance occurs, it is important to be able to determine to whom securities have been allocated, including by way of segregation. There are different segregation models, ranging from pooling account holder securities in omnibus accounts to individual segregation of such securities in separate accounts.   **7.108**

A range of mechanisms can be brought into play to correct imbalances as promptly as possible, including matching of credits and debits, reconciliation, reversal of erroneous book entries, use of the intermediary's own securities, buy-in of securities, shorter settlement cycles, and various other regulatory tools.   **7.109**

In insolvency, different approaches are available in relation to losses. These may be shared pro rata among all account holders, pro rata among account holders per issue, or allocated to individual shareholders where these have opted for individual segregation and where such a choice is recognized in insolvency (legal segregation). In addition, insurance or comparable schemes may provide solace. The mutualization of risk, which is inherent in pro rata sharing (and which is the default approach of the GSC), contrasts with a tendency towards segregation per account holder and individualization of risk in the wake of the global financial crisis.   **7.110**

Despite the potential of DLT to contribute to the disintermediation of the securities market, the current trend in the realm of crypto-assets is that investors use the services of third-party custodians. Such custodians typically offer either individual or omnibus account to their clients (in light of path dependence). Therefore, there is still a need for rules to prevent and correct imbalances and to protect investors in case of a shortfall.   **7.111**

The development of a clear set of standardized guidelines on methods of addressing imbalances, segregation, and loss sharing would be helpful for individual States. Consistent application of such guidelines would also lend integrity to and enhance the cross-border compatibility of post-trade processing, and should ensure that account and crypto-asset holders are sufficiently protected while at the same time maintaining flexibility.   **7.112**

---

[154] Federal Assembly, 25 September 2020, available in French, German, and Italian; for the French version, see <https://www.fedlex.admin.ch/eli/fga/2020/2007/fr> (accessed 7 July 2021).
[155] Swiss DLT Law I.2 (amending Arts 242a and 242b Federal Act of 11 April 1889 on Debt Enforcement and Bankruptcy) and I.6 (amending Art 16 n° 1bis and 37d Banking Act of 8 November 1934).

8
PRINCIPLES OF INSOLVENCY LAW FOR INTERMEDIATED SECURITIES

A. Introduction	8.01	(3) Insolvency representative access to information, records, information technology systems, and assets (including securities clearing and settlement systems)	8.67
B. Scope and Objectives of an Effective Insolvency Law Regime for Intermediated Securities	8.17		
(1) Effectiveness of interests in intermediated securities in insolvency proceeding	8.18	(4) Insolvency of operator or participant of securities clearing or settlement system	8.70
(2) Account holder claims in relevant securities intermediary's insolvency proceeding	8.21	C. Related Regimes: Special Resolution of Systemically Important Financial Institutions	8.71
(a) Account holder priority: general	8.21	D. Selected Additional Issues	8.88
(b) *Ex ante* avoidance of losses	8.23	(1) Nature of a securities intermediary's insolvency proceeding: liquidation, reorganization, and other alternatives	8.88
(c) Account holder protection fund or insurance	8.29		
(d) Loss sharing and distributional rules	8.31	(2) Safe harbour protections: automatic stay, avoidance powers, set-off, and close-out netting	8.89
(e) Proof of claims, bar dates, and return of account holder assets and funds	8.50	(3) Set-off: issuer's insolvency proceedings	8.95
(f) Administrative costs	8.55	(4) Choice-of-laws rules	8.100
(g) Transfer of account holder securities accounts to solvent intermediary	8.59	(5) Intermediated holding of digital securities (cryptosecurities)	8.103
(h) Priority of interests granted by intermediary	8.62	(6) Infrastructure modifications: enhanced transparency, disintermediation (direct holding), and priority claims in lieu of property rights	8.116
(i) Limitations on ranking categories of claims and avoidance powers	8.64	(a) Enhanced transparency	8.117
(j) Stay of enforcement and close-out netting	8.65	(b) Post-settlement disintermediation	8.120
(k) Insolvency choice-of-law rules	8.66	(c) Priority in lieu of property rights	8.126
		E. Conclusion	8.132

A. Introduction

8.01 The Introduction to this chapter in the first edition of this book acknowledged the uncertainty as to the future success of the Geneva Securities Convention (GSC or 'Convention'), observing that '[s]uccess may be achieved through States' widespread adoption of the text or by significant influence on reforms of domestic law, including European law, or both.' Widespread adoption of the text clearly has not occurred—the GSC has not yet entered into force.[1] But hope remains that the GSC may provide a significant impact on future law reforms and development dealing with intermediated securities.[2] In this respect the UNIDROIT Legislative Guide on Intermediated Securities, published in 2017, offers additional guidance and support for the future development of the law.[3] The Legislative Guide is especially welcome inasmuch as the GSC does not address comprehensively the law affecting intermediated securities and the corresponding intermediated holding systems.[4] This chapter emphasizes less than its predecessor the specifics of the GSC's provisions and focuses instead on the principles relating to insolvency law and intermediated securities, including those reflected by the GSC and the Legislative Guide. We consider various examples of the treatment of issues under current laws that provide useful illustrations and guidance. We draw primarily in this respect from UK (and English) law and US law (and sometimes law applicable in Canada) because these are the systems that we know best.

The principal goals of this chapter are threefold. First, it will identify the most significant issues involving intermediated securities in the context of insolvency. These issues arise not only in actual insolvency proceedings but also in the contemplation of potential future proceedings. Second, it will provide analysis and offer suggestions for how States might address these issues in their domestic laws, thereby offering a roadmap for the improvement of the relevant legal regimes. The discussion of these issues and the legal treatment benefits greatly from examples drawn from the GSC and the Legislative Guide. Third, it will offer some perspectives on how ongoing and future developments in technology in relation to the financial markets—fintech—may affect the holding of securities in the future. For example, it considers some issues related to the intermediated holding of digital assets such as cryptosecurities. It also addresses how technology-inspired modifications in the financial infrastructure may impact intermediated holding systems and, consequently, the future characteristics and roles of insolvency law. In that context it considers some suggestions that have been raised for more fundamental changes in the securities holding infrastructures. Notwithstanding these developments, this chapter proceeds on the assumption that intermediated holding of securities through intermediaries, such as stockbrokers and banks, will continue to be a significant feature of financial markets throughout the world for holding publicly traded securities.

8.02

---

[1] The GSC has been signed by only one State, Bangladesh, and no State has ratified it. UNIDROIT, GSC, Status, <https://www.unidroit.org/status> (accessed 7 July 2021).

[2] Additional guidance is provided by the GSC's Official Commentary. Kanda et al, *Official Commentary*.

[3] UNIDROIT Legislative Guide on Intermediated Securities (UNIDROIT, 2017) ('Legislative Guide'), <https://www.unidroit.org/instruments/capital-markets/legislative-guide> (accessed 7 July 2021).

[4] The GSC does not deal with all of the relevant private, commercial law, as many matters were left to the non-Convention law or other sources of law outside the GSC, either explicitly or implicitly. This reflects the general view that there were several important matters of private law on which reaching a consensus would be impossible. The Convention leaves those matters to the non-Convention law. See, eg, Art 9(3) GSC (non-Convention law determines limits on rights of an account holder that holds a security interest or limited interest); Art 13 GSC (Convention does not preclude additional methods of acquiring, disposing, or creating interests in intermediated securities under non-Convention law); Art 15(1)(c) GSC (intermediary may debit securities account or remove a designating entry if authorized by non-Convention law). The Legislative Guide contains a detailed list of references in the GSC to the 'non-Convention law', to the 'applicable law', and to rules relating to 'insolvency proceedings'. Legislative Guide, Annex 1 (non-Convention law), Annex 2 (applicable law), Annex 3 (insolvency proceeding). The Legislative Guide addresses many of the matters that the GSC does not cover.

8.03 Market participants utilize such intermediaries (sometimes referred to as 'custodians') for a variety of good reasons.[5] Holding through an intermediated securities holding system exposes an account holder[6] to intermediary risks. The primary intermediary risks are that the intermediary may fail and have insufficient securities to make the account holder whole or that the account holder may suffer a substantial delay in recovering securities in the intermediary's insolvency proceeding.[7] One of the functions of a well-ordered system of financial law is to ensure that account holders' securities are protected in the event of the insolvency of their intermediary. It is an essential function of an insolvency regime to ensure that whatever rights account holders have under the applicable law at the onset of insolvency are essentially preserved in the insolvency proceeding. If before commencement of the insolvency proceeding, however, such rights have already been lost or compromised, it is not necessarily the function of insolvency law to repair the damage.

8.04 Intermediary risk in insolvency could in principle be substantially reduced, if not eliminated, by a change to a direct holding structure under which the names of ultimate investors would appear as holders of record on the books of issuers. Encouraged by the possibility that actual and prospective advances in technology may make this practicable, an increasing number of commentators have in recent years advocated the benefits of disintermediation. We consider this possibility further in section D(6)(b), where we also offer some suggestions regarding the basis on which the merits of any major modification of securities holding infrastructure should be assessed.

8.05 For the present, intermediary risk remains a reality. Even in the absence of insolvency, the practicalities of holding and dealing with a large, varied, and constantly changing collection of account holder securities in numerous countries have led to the evolution of multi-tiered holding structures. As described at more length elsewhere in this book,[8] such structures, for reasons of efficiency and convenience (both practical and legal), typically involve pooling of account holder securities, with securities held in fungible bulk in omnibus accounts with custodians or sub-custodians and individual account holder entitlements being recorded in accounts maintained by the account holder's relevant intermediary.

---

[5] Mooney and Kanda, 'Core Issues', 72–3 (explaining that such intermediation 'is necessary for investors to buy and sell in organised markets').

[6] In this chapter we generally adopt the terminology used in the GSC. See Art 1(a) (defining 'securities'), 1(b) (defining 'intermediated securities'), 1(c) (defining 'securities account'), 1(d) (defining 'intermediary'), 1(e) (defining 'account holder'). However, when discussing US law we usually employ terminology based on definitions in the Securities Investor Protection Act of 1970 (SIPA), as amended, 15 USC §§ 78aaa et seq, such as 'customer' and 'customer property'. Similarly, when discussing English law, we use terminology based on definitions in the Financial Services and Markets Act 2000 and rules of the regulatory authorities under that Act (formerly the Financial Services Authority and, since April 2013, the Financial Conduct Authority and the Prudential Regulation Authority), such as 'client', 'client assets', and 'client money'.

[7] Although some account holders may be protected by compensation schemes under the laws of the relevant States, those protections in general are limited as to the amount and types of claims that are covered. These schemes are discussed below in s B(2)(c).

[8] See para 8.24 and Ch 7, paras 7.20–2.

Even where account holder securities are kept wholly distinct from the intermediary's own property and the intermediary's records and accounts are correct and up to date, the intermediated system substantially increases the role of the insolvency representative when the relevant intermediary becomes subject to an insolvency proceeding. For example, securities held by the relevant intermediary with other intermediaries may be held in the names of nominees controlled by the relevant intermediary, and the insolvency representative's cooperation generally will be necessary for the recovery of account holder securities (for example, by their transfer to a new intermediary chosen by the insolvency representative). Likewise, the records of individual account holder entitlements are held in computerized systems and maintained by persons under the control of the insolvency representative. The insolvency representative's role therefore must go well beyond the theoretical limited role of assisting in the transfer or return of identified account holder securities and funds.[9]

8.06

Even, therefore, in a perfect world where protections of account holder securities are in place and are operated without any delays or errors, a properly functioning system of insolvency law will, in its application to an investment intermediary, have to include a range of additional powers and functions of the insolvency representative. Moreover, experience has shown all too frequently that the world is usually *not* perfect in the circumstances of impending or actual insolvency: account holder securities may not be segregated in sufficient quantity, records may not be clear, accurate and up to date, and many other factors may jeopardize the complete protection, and still more the ready availability, of account holder securities and other client assets. The practical reality is therefore that an insolvency representative tasked with conducting the insolvency of an investment firm with a substantial portfolio of account holder securities usually has to marshal and distribute two separate, though connected, pools of assets: the 'proprietary' estate which is the core focus of the traditional insolvency administration, and the account holder (or 'client') estate of assets held by the failed institution as intermediary. Historically it has often been the case under English law that, precisely because the client estate does not form part of the insolvency administration proper, insolvency representatives have had to carry out this second function without the benefit of a clear framework of rules and powers comparable to that developed over centuries to facilitate their principal function. Too often they have had instead to rely, if necessary with the aid of the courts, on principles and remedies derived from the general law which are much less well-adapted to the task, with results which have been criticized as laborious, expensive, uncertain and, on occasion, arbitrary.

8.07

---

[9] Many difficulties also persist concerning account holder funds, or cash, held by its intermediary. As to account holder funds held by a non-bank securities intermediary, the principle of segregation of account holder funds from 'house' funds continues to apply, but the enormous volume of payments typically handled by such a firm, between itself and other firms on its own behalf and for its account holders, and between clients and itself, may make the maintenance of 'real time' segregated accounts impracticable. In such cases a regime of overnight segregation may apply and this, even if perfectly administered, may entail some commingling of account holder and 'house' funds intra-day, and sometimes overnight.

8.08 Under the insolvency regime for broker-dealers in the United States, dealing with account holder securities is a central theme of the statutory framework. A properly functioning insolvency regime should set out clearly the rules and principles governing account holder securities, and provide the insolvency representative with the range of tools required to deal with them efficiently, in each case in a way that addresses the legitimate expectations of account holders. In the US, the Securities Investor Protection Act of 1970 (SIPA) sets forth the specifics for the administration of liquidation proceedings for registered broker-dealers, including powers and duties of the trustee, notice requirements to customers, claims filing time limits, allocation of customer property, a definition of 'customer', the right to transfer customer accounts without consent of the customer, and circumstances under which the Securities Investor Protection Corporation (SIPC) shall advance funds to the trustee to pay or satisfy net equity claims.[10]

8.09 In Canada, as provided under the Canadian provincial or territorial securities laws, securities regulators that make up the Canadian Securities Administrators (CSA) issued orders approving the Canadian Investor Protection Fund (CIPF).[11] The CIPF's mandate and responsibilities are established through a Memorandum of Understanding among the CSA members.[12] The CIPF Coverage Policy as of 1 April 2014 sets out who and what is protected[13] and the CIPF website details the mechanics of the claims filing procedures.[14]

8.10 Intermediated holding systems, and in particular systems for clearing and settlement[15] of securities transactions, involve other risks for market participants in addition to the type of intermediary risks just mentioned. For example, principal risk in the settlement of securities transactions is the risk that payment is made and the delivery of the security is not forthcoming, or delivery is made and payment is not forthcoming.[16]

---

[10] See 15 USC ss 78fff and 78fff 1–4; see also ss B(2)(c), (d), (g).
[11] See generally, CIPF, History of CIPF, <https://www.cipf.ca/about-us/history-of-cipf> (accessed 7 July 2021).
[12] See Memorandum of Understanding Regarding the Oversight of the Canadian Investor Protection Fund (CIPF), <https://www.cipf.ca/docs/default-source/default-document-library/revised-new-mou-regarding-oversight-of-cipf-effective-jan-1-2021-eng-and-fr.pdf?sfvrsn=f63d8ed_8> (accessed 7 July 2021).
[13] See <https://www.cipf.ca/Public/CIPFCoverage/CoveragePolicy.aspx> (accessed 7 July 2021).
[14] See <https://www.cipf.ca/Public/CIPFCoverage/CoveragePolicy.aspx> (accessed 7 July 2021).
[15] See Mooney and Kanda, 'Core Issues', 73 (footnote omitted):
A system is necessary to verify between the brokers that the trade was in fact made on the exchange and that they agree on the terms (for example, the particular issue of securities, the price, and number of units); this is the 'clearance' function. Next, on a date subsequent to the trade date (in some markets, even on the trade date), the selling broker must 'deliver' (that is make available) the securities to the buying broker and the buying broker must pay the selling broker; this is the 'settlement' function of a system.
For standard definitions of 'settlement', see, eg, Group of Thirty, *Global Clearing and Settlement*, 13 ('Settlement is the process by which the ownership interest in securities is transferred from one investor to another, generally in exchange for a corresponding transfer of funds.'); CPSS and IOSCO, *Recommendations for SSSs*, 48 (defining '[s]ettlement' as '[t]he completion of a transaction through final transfer of securities and funds between the buyer and the seller'); IFSE, *Best Practices*, 10 ('Settlement refers to delivery of securities to the buyer, payment of price to the seller, and all the processes necessary to position assets to allow this to occur, and to deal with the assets which result from delivery or payment'); CPSS, *DVP*, A2–6 (defining 'settlement' as '[t]he completion of a transaction, wherein the seller transfers securities or financial instruments to the buyer and the buyer transfers money to the seller').
[16] See, eg, IFSE, *Best Practices*, 11; CPSS, *DVP*, 3, 13, A2–2, A2–6. Principal risk may be substantially reduced by multilateral netting of payment and delivery obligations. In some cases, depending on the terms of the trades

INTRODUCTION 205

Moreover, even if a seller of securities does not deliver them because payment is not forthcoming, the absence of the expected funds may expose the seller to liquidity risk.[17] It may be forced to borrow funds or sell assets in order to meet its own payment obligations. When a seller is not paid it is also exposed to replacement cost risk. This is the risk that the market value of the securities involved is less than the contract price.[18] A buyer, similarly, is exposed to replacement cost risk if the market price of the securities that are not delivered to the buyer is higher than the contract price.[19] Moreover, these risks in clearing and settlement systems can lead to systemic risk—the risk that an institution's inability to meet its obligations in timely fashion will result in other institutions being unable to meet their own obligations when due.[20] The insolvency-related risks addressed in the various reports on clearing and settlement generally relate to the insolvency of a system participant, an investor's custodian, or a bank through which payments are transmitted.[21]

These and other risks are addressed best by the promulgation of a clear, certain, and principled legal regime for intermediated securities (including relevant aspects of insolvency law), by appropriate regulation of markets, systems, and market participants, and by the construction and operation of securities clearing systems (SCSs) and securities settlement systems (SSSs) designed to reduce such risks. For example, principal risk is normally addressed by settlement systems that ensure 'delivery versus payment' (DvP), so that delivery will not occur except on receipt of payment and payment will not occur except upon delivery.[22] In the US, The Depository Trust and Clearing Corporation (DTCC) subsidiaries National Securities Clearing Corporation (NSCC) and Fixed Income Clearing Corporation (FICC) provide settlement guarantees for most trades. These services eliminate counterparty risk of non-delivery and non-payment.[23]

8.11

This chapter deals with a particular subset of risk reduction and management—insolvency law as it affects intermediated securities. In the main it is not a project of 'comparative' law. However, along the way we take note of aspects of English and US law, and examples from the provisions of the GSC and the Legislative Guide, to illustrate and

8.12

involved, this may result in a participant in a clearing and settlement system being obligated to make both a payment and a delivery of securities, or being entitled to receive both payment and delivery.

[17] See, eg, IFSE, *Best Practices*, 12; CPSS, *DVP*, 3–4, 13–14, A2–4.
[18] See, eg, IFSE, *Best Practices*, 12; CPSS, *DVP*, 13, A2–6.
[19] See, eg, IFSE, *Best Practices*, 12; CPSS, *DVP*, 13, A2–6. A participant in a system may also face counterparty risks in respect of its customers. For example, a seller of a security through a stockbroker may fail to deliver the security to the stockbroker in a manner that will enable the stockbroker to settle the sale transaction by making a delivery; or a buyer of a security may fail to pay its stockbroker. However, in these situations the risks can be controlled by the stockbroker/participant, which may refuse to execute a trade before delivery or payment.
[20] See, eg, IFSE, *Best Practices*, 12; CPSS, *DVP*, 14, A2–7.
[21] See, eg, CPSS and IOSCO, *Recommendations for SSSs*, 39 (risk of securities system participant default resulting from insolvency), 40 (custody risk from failure or default of intermediary and risk of settlement bank failure); CPSS, *DVP*, 14 (risk of settlement bank failure), 18 (risk of SSS participant default in repayment of credit extended within the system).
[22] See CPSS, *DVP*, 15.
[23] See <https://www.dtcc.com/about/businesses-and-subsidiaries/nscc> (accessed 7 July 2021) and <https://www.dtcc.com/clearing-services/ficc-gov/netting> (accessed 7 July 2021).

critique various aspects of insolvency law. Nor does it focus primarily on 'international' or 'cross-border' aspects of intermediated securities systems and transactions. Instead, it is our goal to describe what we believe the relevant insolvency law should achieve and the preferred means by which it should achieve its goals. We present here a roadmap for the reform and improvement of both substantive and procedural aspects of insolvency law as it may affect intermediated securities systems. In some cases there may be more than one approach that commends itself to us.

8.13 The first edition of our chapter expressed an aspiration to 'the substantial harmonization of the insolvency law relevant to intermediated securities'.[24] This chapter is considerably less sanguine. Moreover, harmonization in the insolvency law context is at best directed to reaching the most appropriate results (ie, the 'functional' approach that guided the development of the GSC), not to the creation of uniform texts such as in model laws and conventions. And short of such harmonized results, harmonization of a taxonomy of issues that insolvency law should treat is a worthwhile and likely more achievable goal. We do not aspire to harmonization for its own sake—ie, to reducing differences among the laws of various States, which is much less important than improving the quality of the relevant insolvency laws, however that might be measured (for example, in terms of efficiency, fairness, and certainty). This reflects a more realistic and 'functional' approach to the subject of insolvency law.

8.14 To be clear, our focus here is on securities intermediaries acting in that capacity, as opposed to all aspects of insolvency proceedings of firms that act as securities intermediaries. For example, a securities intermediary may be a deposit-taking commercial bank, an investment bank that is a broker or dealer, or it may act in all of these capacities. The appropriate characteristics of an insolvency proceeding for such a firm depend on the roles that the firm plays. We address primarily the insolvency aspects of the role that such firms have in common—that of a securities intermediary maintaining securities accounts for its account holders.

8.15 This chapter proceeds as follows. Section B provides an overview of the most important insolvency-related issues and principles of insolvency law for intermediated securities. In particular, section B(2) considers the principal subject of this chapter—the treatment of claims of account holders in the relevant securities intermediary's insolvency proceeding. In our view the single most important function of an insolvency proceeding of an intermediary is to ensure the account holders' ability to recover their assets and funds. By way of example, section B discusses some lessons learned in connection with account holder claims in the English administration of Lehman Brothers International (Europe) and in the US liquidation proceeding of Lehman Brothers Inc, a US broker-dealer. Section C addresses the special insolvency regimes for the resolution of systemically important financial institutions that have emerged following the 2008-2009 financial crisis.

---

[24] See the first edition of this book, Ch 8, para 8.09.

SCOPE AND OBJECTIVES OF AN EFFECTIVE INSOLVENCY LAW REGIME   207

Section D addresses some additional insolvency-related matters affecting intermediated holding systems. Section D(1) discusses the issue of the appropriate nature of an insolvency proceeding in which a securities intermediary is the debtor. For example, should a securities intermediary be eligible for a reorganization, subject only to a liquidation, or eligible for either? Section D(2) considers so-called 'safe harbour' provisions for certain financial contracts that involve exceptions to the automatic stay, avoidance powers (for example, preferences and fraudulent transfers), set-off, and close-out netting following commencement of insolvency proceedings. Section D(3) considers the rights (if any) of account holders holding debt securities to set-off their obligations owed to issuers against issuers' obligations on the debt securities in the setting of an issuer's insolvency proceeding. Section D(4) then considers conflict-of-laws rules and in particular choice-of-law issues that may arise in securities intermediary insolvencies in the cross-border situation. Section D(5) identifies some issues related to custody by intermediaries of cryptosecurities and other digital assets. Section D(6) discusses the potential insolvency-related impact of various modifications of the securities holding infrastructures that have been proposed, including the movement toward increased transparency and direct holding. Finally, section E concludes the chapter. 8.16

B. Scope and Objectives of an Effective Insolvency Law Regime for Intermediated Securities

The development of intermediated securities holding infrastructures and their legal implications have been extensively studied over recent decades. The GSC builds on and reflects a great body of work undertaken by national and international experts to develop a clear legal framework. The management of insolvency risk is an important feature of securities markets and, necessarily, of an adequate legal regime. The negotiations over what became the GSC and later work embodied in the Legislative Guide recognized this insolvency risk and the role of insolvency law from the outset of the project. 8.17

(1) Effectiveness of interests in intermediated securities in insolvency proceedings

The integrity of interests in intermediated securities is at the heart of any legal framework for intermediated securities and the GSC recognizes this central feature.[25] Articles 14 and 21 GSC, which provide for the effectiveness of interests in intermediated securities in insolvency proceedings,[26] are the GSC's core insolvency-related provisions. 8.18

---

[25] Articles 11, 12 GSC (acquisition of interests in intermediated securities so as to be effective against third parties).
[26] Note that 'insolvency proceeding' is given a broad meaning in Art 1(h) GSC: 'a collective judicial or administrative proceeding, including an interim proceeding, in which the assets and affairs of the debtor are subject to control or supervision by a court or other competent authority for the purpose of reorganisation or liquidation'.

8.19 We focus initially on Article 21 GSC because a provision similar to that article was included in every draft convention text prepared and circulated during the process leading to the final version of the GSC. Article 21(1) provides that interests in intermediated securities that have become effective against third parties 'are effective against the insolvency administrator and creditors in any insolvency proceeding in relation to the relevant intermediary'.[27] This sensible and intuitive rule reflects the general understanding that the role of an intermediary is functionally analogous to that of a common law bailee of property—the intermediated securities held for the intermediary's account holders belong to the account holders, not the intermediary, and generally should not be available for distributions to, or subject to claims of, the intermediary's creditors. The effectiveness provided by Article 21(1) is not absolute, however. It is subject to avoidance rules for preferences and fraudulent transfers and to procedural rules relating to enforcement of rights to property controlled by the intermediary's insolvency administrator.[28]

8.20 Article 14 has a broader scope than Article 21 GSC. Article 14 provides that interests in intermediated securities that are effective against third parties 'are effective against the insolvency administrator and creditors in *any* insolvency proceeding'.[29] Consider, for example, an account holder-debtor that grants a security interest to a collateral taker to secure a loan. If the collateral taker, debtor, and the relevant intermediary enter into an appropriate control agreement,[30] the collateral taker's interest becomes effective against third parties under Article 12 GSC.[31] Consequently, the collateral taker's security interest would be effective in the account holder's subsequent insolvency proceeding pursuant to Article 14. As is the case under Article 21, Article 14 provides that an interest is subject to avoidance powers for preferences and fraudulent transfers and enforcement is subject to rules as to property controlled by the insolvency administrator.[32] In addition, under Article 14 an interest is subject to rules on 'ranking of categories of claims' that apply in insolvency proceedings.[33]

(2) Account holder claims in relevant securities intermediary's insolvency proceeding

(a) Account holder priority: general

8.21 It is fundamental that in an intermediated holding system the rights of an insolvent intermediary's account holders should be paramount and prevail over the interests of

---

[27] Article 21(1) also provides that such interests are effective 'in relation to any other person responsible for the performance of a function of the relevant intermediary under Article 7'. Under Art 7, '[a] Contracting State may declare that under its non-Convention law a person other than the relevant intermediary is responsible for the performance of a function or functions (but not all functions) of the relevant intermediary under this Convention'.
[28] Article 21(2) GSC. In addition, Art 21(3) GSC does not impair the effectiveness of interests acquired under the non-Convention law.
[29] Article 14(1) GSC (emphasis added). However, Art 14(1) 'does not apply to the rights and interests to which Article 21 applies', ie, in the relevant intermediary's insolvency proceeding: Art 14(3) GSC.
[30] See Art 1(k) GSC (defining 'control agreement').
[31] Article 12(1), (3) GSC.
[32] Article 14(2)(b)–(c) GSC.
[33] Article 14(2)(a) GSC.

the intermediary's general creditors and insolvency administrator,[34] albeit generally subject to avoidance powers and certain procedural rules.[35] The current absence of harmonization arises not so much from disagreement with this principle but from disharmony as to the circumstances that give rise to account holder status and the treatment of account holder claims in the relevant intermediary's insolvency proceeding. In most cases, however, it is an account holder's proprietary interest in underlying securities controlled by its intermediary that invokes the priority in the intermediary's insolvency proceeding.[36] But the absence of a proprietary interest may disqualify an account holder from the priority. For example, Haentjens explained that under Netherlands law an account holder whose intermediary was not a participant of the central securities depository (CSD) formerly obtained only a contractual claim and no proprietary interest.[37] However, Netherlands law was subsequently changed, effective on 1 January 2011, so as to expand proprietary treatment to account holders of all intermediaries lawfully operating in the Netherlands.[38]

In an intermediated holding system, timing and tracing issues may render an account holder's proprietary interest invalid, questionable, or difficult to prove. While in our view a coherent intermediated regime should confer a proprietary interest on account holders, there is also something to be said for decoupling an account holder's right to share in its intermediary's insolvency proceeding from the question whether it has a proprietary interest under non-insolvency law.[39] For example, under US law on broker-dealer insolvencies,[40] an account holder's priority is not dependent on the account holder having a proprietary interest.[41] For example, if the relevant securities are missing because of the intermediary's wrongful conduct or if the account holder provided cash but the intermediary did not acquire the securities, the account holder nonetheless may have 'customer' status in the broker-dealer's insolvency proceeding.[42]

8.22

---

[34] Haentjens, *Harmonisation*, 268; Art 21(1) GSC.
[35] See, eg, Art 21(2) GSC.
[36] A related issue is whether, in case of a shortfall of securities of a particular issue allocated to account holders, the account holders will be afforded a priority right in securities of the same issue held by the intermediary for its own account to the extent necessary to cover the shortfall. This issue is addressed below in s B(2)(d).
[37] Haentjens, *Harmonisation*, 268–9.
[38] NautaDutilh, *Amendment Dutch Book-entry Act*.
[39] See s D(6)(c) for a discussion of more radical suggestions of moving away completely from property concepts as the basis of account holder protection.
[40] Broker-dealer insolvencies in the US are governed by SIPA.
[41] See 15 USC § 78*lll*(2), defining 'customer': (A) In general The term 'customer' of a debtor means any person (including any person with whom the debtor deals as principal or agent) who has a claim on account of securities received, acquired, or held by the debtor in the ordinary course of its business as a broker or dealer from or for the securities accounts of such person for safekeeping, with a view to sale, to cover consummated sales, pursuant to purchases, as collateral, security, or for purposes of effecting transfer. (B) Included Persons The term 'customer' includes—(i) any person who has deposited cash with the debtor for the purpose of purchasing securities; (ii) any person who has a claim against the debtor for cash, securities, futures contracts, or options on futures contracts received, acquired, or held in a portfolio margining account carried as a securities account pursuant to a portfolio margining program approved by the Commission; and (iii) any person who has a claim against the debtor arising out of sales or conversions of such securities.
[42] 15 USC § 78*lll*(2)(B)(i), (iii). In certain circumstances 'customers' are not eligible for SIPC advances (eg if the customer was a broker acting on its own behalf). See 15 USC § 78fff-3(a)(5).

(b) Ex ante avoidance of losses

8.23 As is observed in Chapter 7, the most important risk arising from the intermediated holding of securities is custody risk.[43] Viewed more broadly, custody risk is one of the risks arising from an investor's decision to delegate to a third party authority to carry out one of more of the functions of holding, managing, administering, and dealing with the investor's financial assets. Investors make this decision very frequently because they consider it to be in their interest to procure some or all of a range of services provided by investment professionals. This decision, while entirely reasonable, gives rise to a range of inherent risks, which would classically be analysed as falling partly within the category of agency risk (the risk that the agent, manager, or custodian may deliberately act in a manner that damages the interest of the principal or wrongfully prefer its own interest to that of the principal, for example through fraud or breach of fiduciary duty), and partly within that of operational risk (the risk that the principal's property may be lost or put at risk through inefficiency, error, or some other failure on the part of the agent, manager, or custodian). We return to this broader overview of risk in section D(6), which considers possible structural changes and future developments, because it affects the extent to which structural changes such as a wider use of individual segregation or a return to a system of direct holding may avoid or reduce the risks that must be addressed under the currently prevailing holding patterns.

8.24 As has already been noted, the circumstances which may cause custody risk to crystallize in an insolvency proceeding of an intermediary originate in actions and events that take place earlier. Accordingly, *ex ante* avoidance of loss should be the primary policy objective.[44] The steps that may achieve it are mostly the subject of other chapters,[45] which describe the safeguards that are generally adopted to minimize the custody risks that arise from intermediated holding, and the regimes of regulation, supervision, and oversight that seek to ensure that such safeguards are rigorously applied. As is referred to in more detail in those chapters, the most important such safeguard is the use by each intermediary of separately designated customer securities accounts with a higher-tier intermediary or a central securities depository (or in some cases in the register of the issuer itself). Such accounts may either be 'omnibus' accounts in which securities of a number of underlying investors (but not securities owned by the intermediary itself) are pooled, or individual client securities accounts traceable to particular underlying investors.[46] In either case, authority to operate the securities accounts will rest with the intermediary and not with the customer or customers on whose behalf the

---

[43] Ch 7, para 7.71, which rightly points out that the risk arises whether the basis of segregation of customer securities is pooled or by individual customer.

[44] Although *ex ante* avoidance of loss is the primary objective, policymakers need to recognize that there can be no guarantee of its being wholly achieved in practice and a suitably tailored insolvency regime is therefore essential as a back-up.

[45] See in particular Chs 7 and 9.

[46] See Ch 7, paras 7.19 et seq. The possible benefits of using individual customer securities accounts (referred to as 'full' segregation) are described in para 7.24. Individual segregation is sometimes referred to in terms which imply that it is inherently preferable to the use of omnibus customer securities accounts, but, as discussed in paras

intermediary holds the accounts, and the higher-tier intermediaries with whom the accounts are held will not recognize those customers as having any standing to give instructions (and indeed will generally not be aware of their identity).

In the US, the principal *ex ante* protections for customers of broker-dealers are included in a set of Securities and Exchange Commission (SEC) rules generally known as the 'customer protection rule'.[47] In general, the customer protection rule has three principal components. The first is a requirement that the broker dealer maintain physical possession or control of certain customer securities.[48] Second, in addition to the possession or control requirement, there is a roughly analogous requirement for customer cash balances. A broker-dealer must maintain with a bank or banks a 'Special Reserve Bank Account for the Exclusive Benefit of Customers' ('Reserve Bank Account').[49] A broker-dealer must deposit cash or securities issued by or guaranteed by the US government in amounts calculated from time to time in accordance with a reserve formula.[50] Third, there are restrictions on the aggregate amount of indebtedness that the broker-dealer may secure with customer securities.[51]

8.25

In the UK, the arrangements for *ex ante* protection of client property take the form of arrangements, involving segregation and based on property rights and traditional trust law,[52] which investment firms are required to put in place under the 'Client Assets' (CASS) part of the rules of the Financial Conduct Authority.[53] The current text was put

8.26

7.74–8, the reality is more nuanced. A shortfall of securities underlying an omnibus customer securities account is borne pro rata by all the customers concerned, and a customer whose securities are credited to an individual segregated account will not share in the loss if the records show that the deficiency does not affect the corresponding separate account with the higher-tier intermediary or CSD. But if the records show that the missing securities are, or include, those that should have been credited to that corresponding separate account, the entire loss will fall on the 'fully segregated' customer unless it is possible to correct the position or an overriding rule imposing mutualization of loss applies. The effect of full segregation may therefore be to convert a risk of a shared loss into a smaller risk of a total loss. It seems doubtful whether a fully informed investor would prefer this. One issue with using individual customer accounts is the possibility that the intermediary would favour one or more customers to the disadvantage of the others when a shortfall arises. In the Hanover Sterling insolvency, Hanover attempted to favour certain clients by selling out securities positions that were impacted by the insolvency and placing the positions in accounts of non-favoured customers thus shifting losses among customers. This scheme was recognized and unwound and this permitted a more equitable loss sharing among all customers.

[47] For an overview of the US customer protection rules, see Mooney, 'Shortfall', 166–75. For an in-depth treatment, see Jamroz, 'Customer Protection'. For analysis of US federal and state law relating to the rights of account holders of intermediaries that are banks, as opposed to broker-dealers, see Klees, 'Custodial Bank Insolvency'.
[48] 17 CFR § 240.15c3-3 (fully paid securities and excess margin securities); see Mooney, 'Shortfall', 166–71.
[49] 17 CFR § 240.15c3-3(e)(1). A broker-dealer must maintain its Reserve Bank Account 'separate from any other bank account' of the broker-dealer. In addition, a broker-dealer must obtain from each Reserve Bank Account bank a written notification from the bank stating that the bank was informed that all cash or securities are held in the account for the exclusive benefit of customers of the broker-dealer in accordance with SEC regulations: 17 CFR § 240.15c3-3(f).
[50] 17 CFR § 240.15c3-3(f). The formula is set out at 17 CFR § 240.15c3-3a.
[51] 17 CFR § 240.8c-1(a)(3); 17 CFR § 240.15c2-1(a)(3).
[52] In the case of client cash, the trust is a statutory trust the terms of which are set out in CASS under powers conferred by s 137B of the Financial Services and Markets Act 2000. Uncertainty about the effect of the detailed client money provisions in force at the time of the LBIE insolvency resulted in protracted and complex litigation in the UK courts, ending in a decision of the UK Supreme Court [2012] UKSC 6. This resulted in significant changes to the rules—see FCA Consultation Paper 13/5 and Policy Statement 14/9.
[53] <www.handbook.fca.org.uk> (accessed 7 July 2021).

in place before the UK's departure from the EU, and gave effect to the relevant EU legislation, in particular Article 16(8) of 'MiFID II':[54]

> (8) An investment firm shall, when holding financial instruments belonging to clients, make adequate arrangements to safeguard the ownership rights of clients, especially in the event of the investment firm's insolvency, and to prevent use of a client's financial instruments on own account except with the client's express consent.[55]

8.27 In relation to financial instruments deposited with or held by a third-party custodian, these requirements are supplemented by more detailed provisions in a separate directive,[56] which require separate identification of customer securities, impose duties of care in the selection of the custodian, and in normal cases require the use of a custodian that is locally regulated and supervised.

8.28 The MiFID II requirements are couched in general terms, reflecting the need for detailed implementation under the different legal systems of the Member States. As already noted, protection in the UK is based on trust law, which provides a long-established and sophisticated system governing the holding of property (including intangible property and fungible property held on an unallocated basis)[57] by one person for the benefit of another. It is common for custody agreements to include express language creating the trust and setting out its terms, but even where this is not the case, a trust will readily be inferred.[58]

(c) Account holder protection fund or insurance

8.29 Related to or as a part of an insolvency regime for securities intermediaries, many States have insurance-like schemes to protect account holders against losses from the failure of financial firms. In the US, under SIPA, SIPC provides protection against losses up to USD 500,000 for customer securities and up to USD 250,000 for cash claims.[59] In Canada, pursuant to the CIPF Coverage Policy, individuals holding an

---

[54] Directive of the European Parliament of the Council of 15 May 2014 on markets in financial instruments. For an analysis of the interrelation of regulatory law with private law in various EU jurisdictions in the context of Art 16 of MiFID II, see Haentjens, 'Dispossession and Segregation in Regulatory and Private Law'.

[55] Reproduced, with immaterial changes of defined terms, in CASS 5.2.1.

[56] Commission Delegated Directive (EU) 2017/593 of 7 April 2016 supplementing MiFID II, Arts 2(1)(d) and 3.

[57] Earlier questions about whether fungible custody satisfied the requirement of certainty of subject matter may be regarded as settled following the decision in *Hunter v Moss* [1993] 1 WLR 934 and later cases in which that decision has been followed. For a full discussion see Yates and Montagu, *Global Custody*, 3.37 et seq.

[58] For example, in *In re Lehman Brothers International (Europe) (in Administration)* [2009] EWHC 2545 (Ch), the relevant agreement did not include express trust language, but the existence of a trust was readily inferred from the wording of the agreement, in particular the use of the words 'custody' and 'custodian' and references to securities held in custody 'belong[ing] . . . to the Counterparty and not belong[ing] to the Custodian'. The Bloxham Final Review (para 3.3) commented that 'Custody Assets must be segregated and, although there is no express trust over them [this may be a reference to *statutory* trust, since, as noted above, many modern custody agreements do include express trust language], it is generally considered that the investment firm has no beneficial interest in them'. For a more recent case in which a trust analysis of intermediated holding was affirmed in the face of contrary technical arguments, see *SL Claimants v Tesco plc* [2019] EWHC 2858 (Ch).

[59] 15 USC § 78fff-3(a)(1) (customer securities), (d) (cash). In the US, broker-dealers have several options for managing customers' cash balances in securities accounts. Under a bank sweep arrangement, a customer may elect to have cash at the end of the day automatically swept into one or more interest bearing accounts held at a participating bank. Customer deposits held in a bank sweep program are insured by the Federal Deposit Insurance Corporation (and not covered by SIPC protection), in general up to the limit of USD 250,000 per account as prescribed by FDIC regulations (and to the extent the broker complies with the applicable record keeping requirements). See *Investor Bulletin: Bank Sweep Programs* (5 June 2014), <https://www.sec.gov/oiea/investor-ale

SCOPE AND OBJECTIVES OF AN EFFECTIVE INSOLVENCY LAW REGIME

account or accounts with a member firm, are protected up to CAD 1 million for all general accounts combined (such as cash accounts, margin accounts, and tax free savings accounts), plus CAD 1 million for all registered retirement accounts combined, plus CAD 1 million for all registered education savings plans combined.[60]

There is an analogous system in the UK under the Financial Services Compensation Scheme (FSCS), which is the UK's statutory fund of last resort for customers of financial services firms. The FSCS pays compensation to consumers if a financial services firm is unable, or likely to be unable, to satisfy claims against it.[61] The compensation limit for investments and for deposits is GBP 85,000.[62] The FSCS protects individuals and small firms.[63]   **8.30**

(d) Loss sharing and distributional rules

One of the fundamental issues for an insolvency regime governing a securities intermediary estate is the content of a rule governing the apportionment among account holders of losses arising from any shortfall in the securities held in respect of their account balances. The treatment of this loss allocation issue under the GSC provides a useful point of departure for this discussion. The general, non-insolvency law of a State may address this loss allocation question or it may be addressed in a State's relevant insolvency law itself. This is what Article 26(1) GSC principally has in mind in stating that 'This Article applies in any insolvency proceeding in relation to any intermediary unless otherwise provided in any conflicting rule applicable in that proceeding.' Article 26 GSC addresses loss sharing among account holders when there is a shortfall in the 'aggregate number or amount of securities and intermediated securities of any description allocated under Article 25(1).'[64] An intermediary's failure to maintain sufficient securities as required by Article 24(1) GSC would result in such a shortfall.[65]   **8.31**

If such a shortfall exists the account holders would share pro rata on an issue-by-issue basis. Consider a simple example.   **8.32**

---

rts-bulletins/ib_banksweep.html> (accessed 7 July 2021). Customers that are brokers, dealers, or banks are not eligible for SIPC protection except to the extent that they are claiming on behalf of their own customers (that are not brokers, dealers, or banks), which are treated as separate customers: 15 USC § 78fff-3(a)(5).

[60] See CIPF, Coverage Policy, <https://www.cipf.ca/cipf-coverage/coverage-policy> (accessed 7 July 2021).
[61] The FSCS is an independent body, set up under Pt XV (ss 212–24A) of the Financial Services and Markets Act 2000 (FSMA).
[62] This applies from 1 April 2019; previously claims in respect of securities were subject to a lower limit of GBP 50,000. Many commentators continue to criticize the GBP 85,000 limit as inadequate. For a helpful recent discussion, see the Law Commission's Scoping Paper *Who Owns Your Shares?*, 6.99–105.
[63] FCA and PRA Handbooks of Rules and Guidance, COMP 4.2.
[64] Article 26(2) GSC. Article 25(1) requires an intermediary to allocate securities and intermediated securities to its account holders 'to the extent necessary to ensure compliance with Article 24(1)(a)'. Loss sharing in this setting is also addressed in Ch 7.
[65] Article 24(1) GSC provides:

> An intermediary must, for each description of securities, hold or have available securities and intermediated securities of an aggregate number or amount equal to the aggregate number or amount of securities of that description credited to:
>
> (a) securities accounts that it maintains for its account holders other than itself; and
>
> (b) if applicable, securities accounts that it maintains for itself.

214   PRINCIPLES OF INSOLVENCY LAW

> Calculation of account holder claims in
> intermediary insolvency proceeding under
> Article 26(2) GSC issue-by-issue pro rata loss sharing
>
> ABC Co. AHs = 200 shares × 10 (value) = 2,000
> Actual ABC shares = 150 × 10 (value) = 1,500
> Shortfall = 50 shares, 500 value
>
> XYZ Co. AHs = 100 shares × 10 (value) = 1,000
> Actual ABC shares = 100 x 10 (value) = 1,000
> No shortfall
>
> $$\text{ABC Co. AHs} = \frac{1,500}{2,000} = 75\% = 1,500$$
>
> $$\text{XYZ Co. AHs} = \frac{1,000}{1,000} = 100\% = 1,000$$

Figure 1 Issue-by-issue pro rata loss sharing.

In Figure 1 there is a shortfall in the ABC securities that the insolvent intermediary has allocated to its account holders. Accordingly, the ABC account holders share under Article 26 pro rata according to 'number or amount' of securities and recover 75 per cent of the value or number of shares claimed.[66] The XYZ account holders suffered no shortfall and their claims would be satisfied in full.

8.33   While pro rata, issue-by-issue loss sharing is intuitive and relatively straightforward, it is not the only plausible system and does not necessarily reflect the best policies. The Article 26(1) GSC deference to 'any conflicting rule applicable' in an intermediary's insolvency proceeding recognizes this and the approach taken by US insolvency law, discussed next, provides an example of what this deference contemplates.

8.34   Under SIPA, with the exception of 'customer name securities', which are returned by the trustee to the relevant account holders,[67] all securities the debtor held for its account holders become the fund of 'customer property' (FOCP) and are valued as of the filing date of the petition.[68] The value of all securities of types claimed by the debtor's customers are pooled for the benefit of all customers based on the aggregate value of all such securities; each of the debtor's account holders will share pro rata in the FOCP

---

[66] Claims may be based on, eg, either number of shares or value of shares to which they were entitled, depending on the rule applicable in insolvency proceedings. How these claims would be satisfied, such as by delivery of securities or cash distributions based on securities valuations, is a matter that the GSC leaves to the applicable insolvency law. See s B(2)(e). Uniform Commercial Code (UCC) Art 8 also provides for issue-by-issue sharing. UCC § 8–503(b).
[67] 15 USC § 78*lll*(2) (defining 'customer'), (3) (defining 'customer name securities' to include those held for a customer and 'registered in the name of the customer, or [those]…in the process of being so registered'; however, customer name securities do not include securities which are in negotiable form, such as those that have been endorsed by the customer); 15 USC § 78fff-2(c)(2) (delivery of customer name securities).
[68] 15 USC § 78*lll*(4) (defining 'customer property').

based on its respective 'net equity'.[69] A customer's net equity is the value of the securities and cash credited to its securities account (whether or not the securities are on hand) less the amount of debt, if any, owed to the broker-dealer.[70] From an historical perspective, consider the following regarding the impact of allocation of assets to a shortfall under SIPA:

> Of the approximately 770,400 claims satisfied in completed or substantially completed cases as of December 31, 2020, a total of 355 were for cash and securities whose value was greater than the limits of protection afforded by SIPA. The 355 claims represent less than one percent of all claims satisfied. The unsatisfied portion of claims, $49.7 million, represents less than one percent of the total value of securities and cash distributed for accounts of customers in the 329 completed or substantially completed cases.[71]

This very small number of totally unsatisfied customers reflects the abilities of SIPC trustees to use assets for the greatest benefit of all customers and not only those who purchased any specific asset.

8.35 We would be remiss if we failed to mention at this point the unique circumstances of the liquidation of the Bernard L. Madoff Investment Securities LLC (BLMIS) matter with respect to the calculation of net equity. In that case the SIPA trustee determined a customer's net equity would be based on the real assets that the customers actually deposited with BLMIS less any amounts withdrawn. Adversely affected customers argued instead that the net equity should be based on the amounts shown on the final customer statements issued by BLMIS in November 2008. Other claimants and the SIPA trustee disagreed with the latter basis of calculation and litigation ensued. The SIPA trustee's position was that the statements were fiction. The US Court of Appeals for the Second Circuit affirmed the decision of US Bankruptcy Court for the Southern District of New York that the methodology favoured by the trustee was legally sound, noting that if the shares/amount reflected on the last statement were used then the 'Use of the Last Statement Method' would have the 'absurd effect of treating fictitious and arbitrarily assigned paper profits as real and would give legal effect to Madoff's machinations'.[72] Petitions were filed with the Supreme Court of the US and in 2012 the Supreme Court refused to grant the petitions thus allowing the lower court decision on the net equity methodology calculation to stand.[73]

8.36 Under SIPA, the value of each customer's claim is equal to the value of the securities that are *or should be* credited to its account, and the aggregate value of the securities

---

[69] 15 USC § 78fff-2(c)(1) (allocation of customer property).
[70] 15 USC § 78lll(11) (defining 'net equity'); 15 USC § 78fff-2(b) (payments to customers based on 'net equity'). Each customer's 'net equity' claim must be calculated by taking into account indebtedness of the customer to the debtor on margin loans: 15 USC § 78lll(11)(B) (claims based on 'net equity'). Moreover, within a time set by the trustee, a customer is entitled to repay indebtedness owed to the debtor, thereby increasing its net equity claim: 15 USC § 78lll(11)(C)(1).
[71] SIPC Annual Report 2020, p 9, <https://www.sipc.org/news-and-media/annual-reports> (accessed 7 July 2021).
[72] See *In re Bernard L Madoff Inv Securities LLC*, 654 F 3d 229, 235 (2d Cir 2011).
[73] Sterling Equities Associates v. Picard, certiorari dismissed, 566 US 1032 (4 June 2012); *Ryan v Picard*, 567 US 934 (25 June 2012); *Velvel v Picard*, 567 US 934 (25 June 2012).

is allocated proportionately among the customers.[74] Under this formulation, the fortuity that there may be a shortfall in X securities but not in Y securities does not result in a windfall for Y securities customers and the X securities customers do not bear the entire burden of the shortfall. Similarly, the risk that a firm improperly (and probably fortuitously) failed to acquire securities for, or credit securities to, any particular entitlement holder's account is not borne by that account holder alone. Under this formulation for distribution and eligibility for participation as a customer, each customer holder has a higher likelihood of a lower potential loss.[75]

Figure 2 illustrates the application of the SIPA distributional rule:[76]

Calculation of account holder claims in intermediary insolvency proceeding under the SIPA loss sharing formulation

ABC Co. AHs = 200 shares × 10 (value) = 2,000
Actual ABC shares = 150 × 10 (value) = 1,500
Shortfall = 50 shares, 500 value

XYZ Co. AHs = 100 shares × 10 (value) = 1,000
Actual ABC shares = 100 × 10 (value) = 1,000
No shortfall

ABC Co. AHs + XYZ Co AHs = 2,000 + 1,000 = 3,000
Actual asset values = 1,500 + 1,000 = 2,500

$\dfrac{2{,}500}{3{,}000}$ = 83.33% = ABC Co. AHs = 1,666 value

XYZ Co. AHs = 833 value

Figure 2 The SIPA loss sharing formulation.

8.37 The SIPA distributional scheme may be contrasted with the UK framework, which is based on traditional property law and trust concepts. Because client assets are not property of the insolvent intermediary, they are not available for realization for the benefit of its creditors and are therefore automatically protected. However, the co-operation of the insolvency representative is in practice essential for the efficient marshalling and

---

[74] 15 USC § 78fff-2(c)(1) (allocation of customer property).
[75] Haentjens, *Harmonisation*, 272, states: 'Mooney has convincingly argued, however, that a deficit in a certain type of securities should not only be shared amongst the accountholders entitled to that type of securities, but should be distributed pro rata amongst all the accountholders of the insolvent intermediary, regardless of the type of security in which the deficit occurs. It must be agreed that accountholders are not in a position to assess the likelihood of a deficit in one or another pool of securities held, which will be arbitrary in most situations. The allocation model which Mooney proposes, on the other hand, treats all accountholders equally, and prioritises them over the intermediary's general creditors. In addition, his model *results in a lower risk of large losses and a higher risk of small losses and is therefore also economically more justifiable.*' (emphasis added; footnotes omitted; citing: ISSA, *Recommendations 2000*, 20; Mooney, 'Beyond Negotiability', 305, fn 191; Mooney, 'Practising Safer Lex', 91–3). Haentjens generously but mistakenly refers to '[t]he allocation model which Mooney proposes', but Mooney only advocated for the policy underlying the existing SIPA distributional scheme.
[76] This formulation can be contrasted with the issue-by-issue pro rata loss sharing formulation applicable under the UCC and the GSC, as illustrated by Figure 1. See n 66.

return of client assets, and for dealing with any shortfalls and the resolution of any competing claims. Experience gained in the global financial crisis, in particular in the insolvency of Lehman Brothers International (Europe) (LBIE), revealed some serious gaps in UK insolvency procedures. Resolving the problems that arose entailed substantial delay and expense and gave rise to some complex litigation.

UK policymakers quickly recognized that legislative change was needed, and the 2009 Banking Act, in addition to introducing a special resolution regime[77] and restructuring the UK financial services regulatory system, also empowered the Treasury to make regulations introducing a new form of insolvency proceedings in respect of 'investment banks'.[78] The Treasury was required to have regard to the desirability of the following objectives: **8.38**

(i) identifying, protecting, and facilitating the return of, client assets;[79]
(ii) protecting creditors' rights;
(iii) ensuring certainty for investment banks, creditors, clients, liquidators, and administrators;
(iv) minimizing the disruption of business and markets; and
(v) maximizing the efficiency and effectiveness of the financial services industry in the UK.

In exercise of these powers, the Treasury in February 2011 made the Investment Bank Special Administration Regulations,[80] introducing a new form of insolvency proceeding called the Special Administration Regime (SAR). **8.39**

In view of the short timeframe for the introduction of the new regime and the absence of detailed parliamentary scrutiny, the enabling provisions included a requirement for the Treasury to commission a report from an independent expert, with a brief to consider how far the regime was achieving the objectives referred to above, and whether it should be continued. The review was required to be completed within two years of the new regime's coming into force. **8.40**

To fulfil this requirement, the Treasury instructed Peter Bloxham, an experienced insolvency lawyer and former partner in the international law firm Freshfields Bruckhaus Deringer, to conduct the review. Mr Bloxham's remit was in the event considerably **8.41**

---

[77] See s C.
[78] Part 7 of the Banking Act 2009, ss 232–6. The term 'investment bank' is a little misleading here, since the definition in s 232 is considerably wider than the ordinary use of the term and is in practice likely to include nearly all investment firms which hold client assets.
[79] 'Assets' for this purpose include both client securities and client money. The protection of client money in the UK is separate from that of client securities, being founded on a statutory trust under s 137B of the Financial Services and Markets Act 2000, the detailed terms of which are set out in the CASS section of the FCA's Handbook. Client money falls outside the scope of this chapter, but it may be noted that, as in the case of client securities, the experience of the global financial crisis, in particular the LBIE administration, resulted in substantial changes—see generally the Bloxham Review and FCA Consultation Paper 13/5 (July 2013), Policy Statement 14/9 (June 2014), Discussion Paper 16/2 (March 2016) and Policy Statement 17/18 (July 2017), the last two of which related to the Bloxham Review.
[80] SI 2011/239.

wider than that laid down by the statute. It included a request to take a broader look at whether more could be done, not only in legislation but also in regulation and market practice, to speed up the return of client assets. In recognition that this wider remit, and the additional consultation that it would entail, would require extra time, Bloxham was asked to split his review into two parts: an interim report, to be completed within the two-year deadline and dealing with the points required by the statute, and a final report covering the whole. This two-part structure is now of only historical importance, and references to the Bloxham Final Review in this chapter are to the final report,[81] which was issued in January 2014 and recapitulated the recommendations of the interim report. It also included a number of recommended changes to the regulations, nearly all of which were implemented in 2017.[82]

8.42 A full description of the SAR and the Bloxham Review is beyond the scope of this chapter, but the following points are particularly worth noting:

(i) The administrator is given three 'special administration objectives': to ensure the return of client assets as soon as reasonably practicable;[83] to ensure timely engagement with market infrastructure bodies and the regulatory authorities; and either to rescue the bank as a going concern, or to wind it up in the best interests of the creditors. There is no order of precedence among the three objectives, and the administrator is given a wide discretion on how best to pursue them.[84]

(ii) The administrator is given powers to transfer client assets to a solvent institution free from restrictions and requirements for consent that would normally apply, subject to specified safeguards, in particular where the assets transferred do not comprise the whole of the property, rights and liabilities of the insolvent institution.[85]

(iii) In order to expedite the return of client assets, the administrator is given power to set a binding 'bar date' for the submission of claims of ownership or entitlement to a security interest or other interest in the client assets.[86]

(iv) The regulations provide specifically for any shortfall in the assets available in a client omnibus account to be borne *pro rata* by the clients concerned. This provision operates by reference to 'securities of a particular description'—in other

---

[81] Final Review of the Investment Bank Special Administration Regulations 2011, January 2014 (Bloxham Final Review). The interim report, entitled Review of the Investment Bank Special Administration Regulations 2011, was issued on 7 February 2013 and published in April 2013.

[82] Investment Bank (Amendment of Definition) and Special Administration (Amendment) Regulations 2017, SI 2017/443 (IBSARs). References in this chapter are to the regulations as amended (where applicable) unless otherwise stated.

[83] The administrator is required to work with the Financial Services Compensation Scheme in pursuing this objective—IBSARs, regulation 10A.

[84] IBSARs, regulation 10.

[85] IBSARs, regulations 10B-G.

[86] IBSARs, regulations 11 and 12B to 12F. The absence of such a power in the context of the LBIE administration had posed substantial problems for the LBIE administrators. Having tried without success to use a scheme of arrangement, they were obliged to fall back on a contractual Claims Settlement Agreement.

words, on a security by security basis rather than in respect of the client estate as a whole, as under the US SIPA regime.[87]

(v) Suppliers of IT and data services are not permitted to terminate supply arrangements except where charges remain outstanding and unpaid for at least 28 days, unless the administrator consents of the court's permission is obtained.[88]

8.43 Beyond loss sharing among account holders in case of shortfalls, a potentially more difficult and controversial question is whether the insolvency regime for securities intermediaries should include a general 'account holder preference'[89] rule requiring that any shortfall in the client estate be made good out of the firm estate in priority to the claim of general creditors. This question is closely linked with that of the means by which account holder securities are protected under the general law (ie before any insolvency proceedings). The GSC again provides useful background. The default Convention rule, Article 25(1), provides that securities 'shall be allocated to the rights of . . . account holders' to the extent necessary to ensure compliance with the 'sufficient securities' requirement of Article 24. This allocation is described in the Legislative Guide (paragraph 215) as arising *'ex Conventione'*—in other words it takes effect by operation of law and has the effect of a general client preference. However, Article 25(5) enables a Contracting State, by declaration, to provide that the allocation under Article 25(1) applies only to securities that have been segregated for the benefit of account holders. As the Legislative Guide (paragraph 215) puts it, in terms which, while not inaccurate, are perhaps slightly tendentious: 'However, a State may decide to protect the intermediary's other creditors instead of the intermediary's account holders by giving 'proprietary effect' to the segregation by an intermediary of securities that it holds for its own account.' This is the approach followed in the UK: the duty to return client assets under the SAR is drafted by reference to the relevant clients' beneficial entitlement to assets held on trust.[90] The regulations provide[91] that any shortfall is to be borne by the relevant clients pro rata and ranks as an *unsecured* claim, for which they must prove against the firm's proprietary assets in competition with the general unsecured creditors. If the UK were to ratify the GSC, therefore, it would need to make a declaration under Article 25(5).

8.44 SIPA takes quite a different approach under US law. First, the definition of customer property to be included in the FOCP is broad. For example, if the debtor fails to comply with the customer protection rules so as to have available sufficient securities to meet its obligations for customers' net equity claims based on securities of a particular issue,

---

[87] IBSARs, regulation 12. This provision sidesteps questions that otherwise might continue to be raised about whether *pro rata* loss sharing is always the correct approach under the general rules of common law and equity—as to which see the discussion in the first edition of this book, Ch 8, para 8.57, and paras 6.91–8 of the Law Commission's Scoping Paper *Who Owns Your Shares?*. On the SIPA shortfall regime, see s B(2)(d). On the comparison between the SIPA regime and issue-by-issue pro rata loss sharing, see Figures 1 and 2.
[88] IBSARs, regulation 14.
[89] This useful label is borrowed, slightly modified, from the Bloxham Final Review, 5.14.
[90] IBSARs, regulation 10(5) (definition of 'return of client assets'); see para 8.42.
[91] IBSARs, regulation 12; see n 87.

then the debtor's securities of that type are included in the FOCP to the extent necessary to make up for that shortfall.[92] Moreover, to the extent that the debtor was not in compliance with the customer protection rules, 'any other property of the debtor' will be included in the FOCP to the extent necessary to satisfy the net equity claims.[93] The upshot of this is that to the extent the debtor has free, unencumbered assets sufficient to top off any shortfalls, the customer claims will be satisfied in full.[94]

8.45 There are obvious, and strong, policy arguments in favour of account holder preference and the SIPA formulation. For example, a contrary approach would permit the intermediary to unilaterally allocate securities to itself—and its unsecured creditors. Such a rule could encourage the unscrupulous intermediary (or the normally honest one that seeks to cover its trading losses) to play fast and loose with customer securities.[95] It also would impose stress on account holder protection schemes as a means to make assets available to unsecured general creditors.

8.46 Policies favouring account holder priority, on the other hand, should not preclude consideration of arguments to the contrary, which should be heard for a balanced perspective. The classical contrary argument, based on 'moral hazard', is that it is dangerous to confer too complete a protection against risk, because this encourages irresponsible decisions—in this case, presumably, by encouraging investors to choose custodians without any assessment of their soundness and competence. It is difficult, in our view, to give too much weight to this argument in the current context, because it is unrealistic to expect the majority of investors to make such an assessment, given the disparities of knowledge and expertise involved. Nevertheless, considerations of moral hazard cannot be entirely discounted.

8.47 Two other arguments may carry greater weight. First, the question should be assessed against evidence of relative harm, rather than *a priori*. Second, caution is required because the policy decision entails balancing the conflicting interests of two groups who are, *ex hypothesi*, both innocent sufferers. Both considerations have recently been discussed in important UK papers. The first consideration dissuaded Peter Bloxham from making a recommendation on client preference: 'I do not have any evidence as to the likely differential outcomes for clients (and non-clients) in SAR cases to date of applying a client preference principle and as such cannot find any basis to make a recommendation for client preference'.[96]

---

[92] 15 USC § 78*lll*(4)(A). The UCC provides a similar rule, which would apply when SIPA is not applicable (such as in a bank insolvency). UCC 8–503(b).
[93] 15 USC § 78*lll*(4)(E).
[94] This assumes, of course, that the assets are available to the debtor and not, for example, being blocked by a foreign custodian.
[95] See the case of MF Global where segregated commodity customer funds were used for liquidity purposes: Report of the Trustee's Investigation and Recommendations, In re MF Global Inc., No. 11–2790 (Bankr. S.D.N.Y. June 4, 2012), ECF No. 1865 p. 96.
[96] Bloxham Final Review, 5.16. We interpret Bloxham's careful phrasing here to mean that he did not have before him evidence that would support a recommendation for client preference, not that he considered that there was no possible basis for such a recommendation.

SCOPE AND OBJECTIVES OF AN EFFECTIVE INSOLVENCY LAW REGIME 221

A longer and more substantive discussion in a recent paper from the UK Law Commission[97] is worth quoting at length: **8.48**

> This protection [*ie, that of the segregated pool of client assets*] could be extended so that there would be a larger pool of assets from which to make up the shortfall. For example, intermediated securities owned by the insolvent intermediary and held in its own account, rather than on trust for third parties, could be included in the pool.[98] Alternatively, the ranking of creditors could be changed, so that ultimate investors rank ahead of general creditors. The disadvantage of either of these approaches is that they would reduce the assets available to creditors of the insolvent intermediary. It would be an unusual step to prioritise a particular type of unsecured creditor, and the justification may not be as strong as where preferential status exists elsewhere[99], particularly given the protection afforded by [the UK Financial Services Compensation Scheme].

As this discussion illustrates, this is a complex question involving a number of potentially conflicting policy objectives. For example, while there is general support for protection funds and other schemes for the protection of account holders of insolvent intermediaries, one might seriously question whether they should be relied on to benefit unsecured creditors, albeit indirectly. In sum, different States may rank different considerations in different orders of importance. All will have to be assessed in the light of the overall legal and insolvency systems, and accumulated policy choices, of the State concerned. The US and UK experiences indicate that market participants and insolvency regimes will adjust to either approach. This suggests that it may not be possible to demonstrate that any one particular choice is inherently superior to others. **8.49**

(e) Proof of claims, bar dates, and return of account holder assets and funds

In order to facilitate the efficient and prompt distribution of assets, the insolvency law regime for the firm estate will typically include provision for proof of debts and distributions to creditors, under which creditors whose claims are not proved, or otherwise recognized, by a particular 'bar date' will not be entitled to share in the related distribution (and will deprived of any return at all if their claims are not proved by the final bar date). States should consider whether special provision is needed to ensure that similar procedures can be followed in relation to account holder claims to securities and funds. **8.50**

As already noted, under the SAR in the UK, the administrator is given power to set such a bar date for the submission of claims to beneficial ownership of (or of a security interest asserted over, or other entitlement to) client assets. The effect of this is that the administrator is entitled to distribute client assets by reference to the claims received **8.51**

---

[97] Law Commission, *Who Owns Your Shares?*, 6.76.
[98] A footnote here refers to 'the position in Luxembourg, where, if there is a shortfall in securities held for investors, securities owned by the depository are included in the pooled assets: Loi du 1er août 2001 concernant la circulation de titres et d'autres instruments fongibles, art 7'.
[99] A footnote gives as an example the preferential creditor status of employees under UK general insolvency law.

by the bar date, and such a distribution is not disturbed by any later claims received.[100] The regulations include detailed provisions about the procedure to setting bar dates[101] and the consequences of setting a 'hard' bar date.[102] The administrator is given discretion as to the precise timing, but must allow 'a reasonable time after notice of the special administration has been published . . . for persons to be able to calculate and submit their claims'.[103] Detailed procedural requirements in delegated rules[104] impose further requirements, and in particular include safeguards designed to minimize the risk that client entitlements may be barred unfairly or inadvertently. These include (i) a requirement for the administrator to give notice of an intention to set a bar date to all clients of whose claim to client assets the administrator is aware (this will include clients who are shown in the records of the firm, and should therefore include all or the majority of claimants except in cases where the records of the firm are in serious disorder); (ii) after the bar date has passed, a requirement to give a further notice to any client who has not submitted a claim but is believed, on the basis of the firm's records or other available information, to be eligible to do so; and (iii) a requirement for the administrator to prepare a 'distribution plan' which must be approved by the creditors' committee and the court, and must allow an interval of at least three months from the bar date before distribution of assets (an interval which facilitates late claims).

8.52 Under the UK SAR, client assets are treated as returned where 'the investment bank relinquishes full control over the assets for the benefit of the client to the extent of the client's beneficial entitlement to those assets'.[105] This is wide enough to cover transfer to another intermediary to hold for the client under the power described in paragraph 8.42 or transfer directly to the client. In the latter case, the means of transfer are likely to be set out in the administrator's distribution plan, referred to in paragraph 8.51.

8.53 Under SIPA in the US, the court sets a bar date for customer net equity claims not later than six months after the trustee's publication of a notice of the commencement of the proceeding.[106] The bar date for other creditor claims (including customer cash claims) is six months after publication of the notice.[107] In Canada, the bar date for customers submitting claims under CIPF coverage and supporting documentation is 180 days after commencement of insolvency proceedings.[108]

8.54 In a SIPA proceeding, once a customer claim is filed, the trustee will research and analyse the claim and then mail to the claimant a written determination either allowing or

---

[100] This was one of the more important changes introduced by the SAR, reflecting difficulties encountered in this area in the LBIE administration.
[101] These include a requirement for prior court approval for the setting of a 'hard' bar date—IBSARs, regulation 12B(3).
[102] IBSARs, regulations 11 and 12B.
[103] IBSARS, regulation 11(3).
[104] Investment Bank Special Administration (England & Wales) Rules 2011, Part 5 (rules 139 and following).
[105] IBSARs, regulation 10(5).
[106] 15 USC s 78fff-2(a)(3).
[107] 15 USC s 78fff-2(a)(3).
[108] CIPF, What Happens if a CIPF Member Firm is Insolvent?, <https://www.cipf.ca/Public/CIPFCoverage/WhatHappensifaCIPFMemberFirmisInsolvent.aspx> (accessed 7 July 2021).

disallowing the claim.[109] If the claim is allowed, the trustee will satisfy the claim through the distribution to the claimant of 'customer property' or advances from SIPC, or some combination of the two. How quickly claims are satisfied depends on the complexity of the liquidation and the condition of the failed brokerage firm's records. Delays of several months can arise when the firms' records are not accurate or incomplete. It also is not uncommon for delays to take place when the brokerage firm or its principals were involved in misconduct. When the records of the brokerage firm are accurate, and no misconduct occurred, deliveries of some securities and cash to customers may begin shortly after the trustee receives completed claim forms from customers. Generally, in these cases, customers may receive at least some of their property one to three months after filing a completed claim form.[110] If a customer claim is denied by the trustee, the claimant will be able to seek bankruptcy court review of the trustee's determination.

(f) Administrative costs

8.55 In the insolvency proceeding of a securities intermediary, as in any insolvency proceeding, there should be a clear rule determining how the insolvency representative's costs and other costs of administration are to be borne. In particular, a question arises as to whether the costs of administration should be allocated and borne separately as among the assets held for the account holders and the assets of the intermediary. The Legislative Guide does not take a position on any such allocation, arguably supporting an implication that the better view is that assets of the insolvent intermediary should bear the costs of administration as in the case of insolvency proceedings generally.[111]

8.56 In the US, under the Bankruptcy Code[112] and SIPA, the costs of administration enjoy a priority over the general creditors but the FOCP (customer assets) generally do not bear the burden of these costs. SIPA provides that if necessary SIPC shall advance to the trustee funds necessary to pay all costs and expenses of the administration of the estate of the debtor.[113] In this connection SIPC has some flexibility. For example, in the Madoff case a decision was made that all administrative costs would be borne by SIPC in an effort to ensure that all recovered assets were used to satisfy customer claims.

8.57 In the UK, by contrast, the position until recently was that client assets were treated as a separate 'estate' to bear the costs of administering those assets and that the intermediary's assets would bear the other administrative costs.[114] The

---

[109] See SIPC, 'Investor FAQs, Questions About Liquidations', <https://www.sipc.org/for-investors/investor-faqs> (accessed 7 July 2021).

[110] As to cash claims under bank cash sweep programs in the US, customers should monitor the cash balances. See n 59 (discussing bank cash sweep programs). In the event of a broker-dealer liquidation, a customer will need to deal with the trustee in order to access funds because the bank sweep accounts are held in the name of the broker-dealer and not the customer.

[111] For what it may be worth, the recollection of one of us (Mooney) who was one of the contributing authors of the Legislative Guide, is that no contrary position was advocated or discussed.

[112] 11 USC §§ 101 et seq.

[113] 15 USC § 78fff-3(b).

[114] Investment Bank Special Administration (England and Wales) Rules 2011, rules 134(1)(a) (firm estate), 135(1) (client estate).

Bloxham Final Review explained this, and discussed the possibility of change, as follows:[115]

> The rationale, in insolvency, for costs of dealing with Client Assets to be borne by the fund of which they are part is that this is a fund which is separate from, and does not belong to, the failed firm. It is therefore not fair to the firm's general creditors for the costs to be borne by the general estate.

Bloxham went on to consider the arguments for change as follows:[116]

> Since a preference for costs is built into the current CASS regime[117] and is reflective of the general legal position, I have not found a sufficiently strong reason to justify a general recommendation that the SAR should provide that the Administrator's costs of dealing with Client Assets should be met out of the Firm Estate, when this would create a discrepancy between the SAR and the (current) Client Money Rules. (Clearly, if costs were borne out of the general estate, as occurs in the US, this would favour clients, but I cannot find an objective reason why they should be.)
>
> On the other hand, some at least of the Client Asset costs in any particular case may be directly attributable to failures by the firm (either in terms of non-segregation or of record keeping). I therefore recommend that the Courts be given power, through the SAR, to direct that some Client Asset related costs in the administration can be paid out of the Firm Estate, if the firm's conduct prior to failure has exacerbated the problems associated with the Administrator's dealing with the Client Assets. In making this recommendation, I am anxious that it does not provide scope for further litigation in SAR cases. For this reason, I recommend that guidelines be drawn up by the Insolvency Service in conjunction with the FCA and practitioners as to the factors which would justify the exercise by the Court of any such discretion.

This recommendation was accepted by the UK government and is now incorporated in the regulations.[118] The current, more nuanced, UK position is therefore that costs which are attributable to default by the insolvent intermediary[119] may be payable out of the firm estate.

8.58 Although Bloxham could not to find a reason for the intermediary's assets to bear the burden of administering client assets, others have not been so disabled. Before the intermediary's insolvency proceeding the general creditors presumably enjoyed relationships with the firm and were happy to be paid from income derived from the

---

[115] Para 5.27.
[116] Paras 5.28–9.
[117] Ie, the part of the Financial Conduct Authority rulebook which imposes segregation requirements in respect of client securities and cash and, through the Client Money Rules which form part of CASS, creates a statutory trust over client cash. It seems clear from the context that by 'preference for costs' Bloxham here means the CASS rule that the administrator's costs attributable to the client money pool are payable out of that pool in priority to the claims of clients.
[118] HM Treasury, *Reforms to the investment bank spe0cial administration regime*, March 2016, 4.19–23; IBSARs, regulation 19A.
[119] Not all shortfalls will be attributable to default on the part of the intermediary–for example, shortfalls that arise from insolvency or default on the part of a higher tier intermediary will generally not be.

SCOPE AND OBJECTIVES OF AN EFFECTIVE INSOLVENCY LAW REGIME   225

intermediary's business of maintaining securities accounts. Whether or not the intermediary was in breach of its obligations to account holders before the insolvency proceeding, both account holders and general creditors alike have suffered from a common misfortune, although the bases of their claims as creditors differ in kind. In sum, States ought to consider this allocation question carefully.

(g) Transfer of account holder securities accounts to solvent intermediary

8.59 Account holders' interests will often be better served by transferring their positions to another, solvent, intermediary than by returning them to the account holder directly.[120] This preserves the benefits for the sake of which they employed the failed intermediary in the first place and is likely to be considerably more cost-effective. As paragraph 269 of the Legislative Guide puts it:

> An important technique for the protection of account holders in the insolvency proceeding of an intermediary is the transfer of securities accounts (and the underlying securities) to a solvent intermediary that assumes the insolvent intermediary's duties and obligations to the account holders. An account holder protection fund or insurance typically would provide assurances against loss to the transferee intermediary. A Contracting State should ensure that the relevant insolvency law facilitates this approach.[121]

8.60 In the US, the SIPA trustee is empowered to transfer customer accounts to another broker-dealer and to indemnify the transferee broker-dealer against cash and securities shortfalls.[122] This does not necessarily mean that the customers on the transferred accounts will recover a higher percentage on their net equity claims than the customers that may be left behind. We understand that these bulk transfers are usually made with a 'haircut', to the end that only a certain percentage of the assets in customer accounts are bulk transferred.[123] This structure allows the trustee to transfer substantial portions of a debtor's customer accounts while providing for pro rata customer distributions across all customer accounts. However, the ability to transfer positions promptly

---

[120] As will be apparent, this closely resembles the procedure commonly followed under special resolution regimes. See s C.

[121] Legislative Guide, para 269.

[122] 15 USC § 78fff-2(f) provides:

> In order to facilitate the prompt satisfaction of customer claims and the orderly liquidation of the debtor, the trustee may, pursuant to terms satisfactory to him and subject to the prior approval of SIPC, sell or otherwise transfer to another member of SIPC, without consent of any customer, all or any part of the account of a customer of the debtor. In connection with any such sale or transfer to another member of SIPC and subject to the prior approval of SIPC, the trustee may— (1) waive or modify the need to file a written statement of claim pursuant to subsection (a)(2) of this section; and (2) enter into such agreements as the trustee considers appropriate under the circumstances to indemnify any such member of SIPC against shortages of cash or securities in the customer accounts sold or transferred. The funds of SIPC may be made available to guarantee or secure any indemnification under paragraph (2). The prior approval of SIPC to such indemnification shall be conditioned, among such other standards as SIPC may determine, upon a determination by SIPC that the probable cost of any such indemnification can reasonably be expected not to exceed the cost to SIPC of proceeding under section 78fff-3(a) of this title and section 78fff-3(b) of this title.

[123] Email from Hemant Sharma, Associate General Counsel, SIPC (18 March 2013). However, the bulk transfers of accounts to Barclays in the Lehman Brothers Inc (LBI) SIPA case were made on a 100 per cent basis.

depends on the sanctity and reliability of the books and records of the insolvent. In the LBI matter in the US, for example, there was no issue with the books and records and this permitted an early and significant transfer of positions to another intermediary. Had there been a question about the books and records transfers could not have been accomplished until the records were validated.

8.61 As noted above, in the UK under the SAR the administrator is empowered to transfer client assets to a solvent institution.[124] From the point of view both of clients and of the administrator, this will often be the preferred option.

(h) Priority of interests granted by intermediary

8.62 In a securities intermediary's insolvency proceeding, a shortfall in account holder securities may trigger a priority contest between the affected account holders and creditors to which the intermediary has granted security interests. In a typical transaction, funds borrowed by an intermediary, secured by securities, may be used to fund credit extended by the intermediary to its own account holders (so-called 'margin' loans). Awarding priority to the intermediary's secured creditors in such transactions may benefit account holders of the intermediary by lowering the cost of their borrowings from the intermediary. This priority contest is one best addressed by the private, non-insolvency law. But the actual application of the priority rule is likely to occur primarily in the intermediary's insolvency proceeding.

8.63 Article 20(1) GSC leaves this priority issue to other law except in the case of interests granted by an intermediary and made effective under Article 12—ie, by a control agreement, by a designating entry, or in the case of interests granted to the intermediary's own securities intermediary. Under Article 20(2) GSC such interests have priority over the interests of the intermediary's account holders. A very similar rule applies in the US under UCC 8-511—the transferee's interest has priority over those of entitlement holders if the transferee has control over the relevant security entitlement.[125]

(i) Limitations on ranking categories of claims and avoidance powers

8.64 States should consider whether to make adjustments to otherwise applicable insolvency law rules relating to the ranking of claims and the avoidance of transfers as fraudulent transfers or preferences.[126] For example, protecting payments and transfers made within a securities settlement system may reduce systemic risk in the financial markets.[127]

(j) Stay of enforcement and close-out netting

8.65 In general an automatic or court-ordered stay of enforcement by an insolvent debtor's creditors is an important feature of any insolvency regime. In the context of the

---

[124] See para 8.42(ii); IBSARs, regulations 10B-G.
[125] UCC 8-511(a), (b); 8-106(d) (control of security entitlement).
[126] See Legislative Guide, para 271.
[127] See generally s D(2) (discussing safe harbour protections).

financial markets, however, States also should consider limitations of such stays in connection with financial collateral and, in particular, in connection with the operation of close-out netting procedures.[128] Although controversial, appropriate limitations may enhance market liquidity and offer protections against systemic risk.[129]

(k) Insolvency choice-of-law rules

8.66 Choice-of-law rules need careful consideration in relation to any cross-border insolvency proceeding. We address some of the relevant issues in section D(4).

(3) Insolvency representative access to information, records, information technology systems, and assets (including securities clearing and settlement systems)

8.67 It is essential that an insolvency representative of a securities intermediary have access to all of the information and records available to the intermediary before commencement of an insolvency proceeding.[130] It also requires access to its assets. This access is necessary in order to ensure appropriate protection and treatment of the claims of account holders and other creditors alike. As pointed out in the Legislative Guide: 'A lack of access [to information and records] could be especially problematic in the case of a multinational corporate group in which an affiliate other than the intermediary manages information centrally and may be subject to a separate insolvency proceeding.'[131]

8.68 The Lehman insolvency illustrates the problem. A lack of access to information was particularly problematic in the early stages of the SIPA case of Lehman Brothers Inc (LBI), Lehman's principal US broker-dealer.[132] LBI's operations were substantially disrupted by major clearing organizations and its data screens were frozen by its principal clearing bank, depriving the trustee for LBI of crucial information for several weeks. The trustee learned later that the bank had liquidated collateral that LBI had segregated for the benefit of customers. The trustee also was deprived of access to assets held with other Lehman affiliates. Moreover, after the early sale of LBI's investment business and transfers of customer accounts, the trustee lost access to information technology systems that had been transferred in connection with that sale.

8.69 Once LBI became subject to the SIPA liquidation proceeding it ceased to function as active participant in the various clearing and settlement processes. Under the applicable rules of clearing organizations the trustee had no access to control over LBI's assets

---

[128] See Legislative Guide, para 272; UNIDROIT Principles on the Operation of Close-Out Netting Provisions, <https://www.unidroit.org/instruments/capital-markets/netting> (accessed 7 July 2021); see generally s D(2).
[129] See s D(2) (discussing safe harbour protections).
[130] See generally Legislative Guide, paras 275–6.
[131] Legislative Guide, para 276.
[132] The following summary is based on the discussion of LBI in the first edition of this book, Ch 8, paras 8.72–83. Similar problems were encountered in connection with the administration of LBIE. See the first edition, Ch 8, para 8.92.

and funds held with those organizations. It is appropriate of course that clearing organizations must limit further exposure to an insolvent former participant, protect the interests of other participants and their customers, and take steps to avoid any broader systemic risks. Moreover, the LBI trustee's problems were exacerbated by the sudden nature of the Lehman insolvency and the lack of adequate advance planning. But the lesson is clear that both ex ante provisions and insolvency regimes should address issues of access to information and assets.

(4) Insolvency of operator or participant of securities clearing or settlement system

8.70 An insolvency proceeding of the operator of or participant in a securities clearing systems or securities settlement system presents particular problems. The treatment in the GSC is instructive. Article 27 GSC addresses the finality of transactions under uniform rules of a securities clearing system or a securities settlement system.[133] Article 27(a) GSC applies to system rules that preclude revocation of, and treat as irrevocable, instructions for the disposition of intermediated securities or for making a payment in connection with the acquisition or disposition of intermediated securities. Article 27(b) GSC applies to system rules that preclude invalidation or reversal of entries (debits, credits, designating entries, or removals of designating entries) to securities accounts that are a part of the system. The rules described in Article 27(a) and (b) are effective notwithstanding the insolvency of the operator of a system or the insolvency of a participant in the system and notwithstanding any contrary rule applicable in an insolvency proceeding.[134] Revocation of instructions as a result of an insolvency could be enormously disruptive and require the unwinding of many separate transactions, which implicates systemic risk; Article 27 is intended to ameliorate such risk.[135] Reflecting this policy rationale, many jurisdictions give finality and/or default rules of clearing and settlement systems overriding protection against conflicting rules of insolvency law.[136]

C. Related Regimes: Special Resolution of Systemically Important Financial Institutions

8.71 Perhaps the most important legal innovation resulting from the global financial crisis was the widespread introduction of regimes for the resolution, by means other than

---

[133] See also Art 1(n) GSC (defining 'securities settlement system') and (o) (defining 'securities clearing system').
[134] Article 27 GSC. This effectiveness, however, applies only '[t]o the extent permitted by the law governing a system'.
[135] Kanda et al, *Official Commentary*, 27–5.
[136] See, eg, in the EU, Settlement Finality Directive (98/26/EC), Arts 3 to 5; in the UK, Companies Act 1989, Part VII; in the US, see, eg, DTC Disclosure Framework; NSCC Disclosure Framework, <https://www.dtcc.com/legal/policy-and-compliance> (accessed 7 July 2021).

RESOLUTION OF SYSTEMICALLY IMPORTANT FINANCIAL INSTITUTIONS   229

traditional insolvency proceedings, of the affairs of systemically important financial institutions (SIFIs) in the event of insolvency or threatened insolvency. Such regimes fall outside the scope of this chapter, but a brief explanation of their nature and purpose, and in particular of their approach to the protection of account holder assets, is useful to place them in context. The following discussion addresses examples of relevant reforms in the US, UK, and Europe.

The financial crisis had shown that too many institutions were in practice 'too big to fail': the probable consequences of their failure for the financial system and for society generally were so severe that governments had no alternative but to use public money to support them, thereby bailing out, sometimes at huge cost to the taxpayer, creditors and shareholders who would otherwise have borne the loss. The experience gained from the insolvency of the one large institution that was allowed to fail, Lehman Brothers, reinforced the impression that the systemic risks of allowing normal insolvency proceedings to take their course were too great.   8.72

Statutory resolution regimes were accordingly introduced rapidly in a number of jurisdictions[137], and the concept was approved at global level by the adoption of Key Attributes of Effective Resolution Regimes for Financial Institutions (Key Attributes) by the Financial Stability Board in October 2011[138] and the subsequent endorsement of the Key Attributes at the Cannes Summit meeting of G-20 leaders in November 2011.[139]   8.73

The current (15 October 2014) version of the Key Attributes explains the purpose of resolution regimes as being 'to make feasible the resolution of financial institutions without severe systemic disruption and without exposing taxpayers to loss, while protecting vital economic functions through mechanisms which make it possible for shareholders and unsecured creditors to absorb losses in a manner that respects the hierarchy of claims in liquidation.'[140] The Key Attributes go on to amplify the objectives and to set out in detail the mechanisms by which they are to be achieved. These include appointing new management, transferring assets and liabilities, and writing down ('bailing in') equity and other instruments of ownership and unsecured creditor claims to the extent required to absorb losses. These powers are to be exercised by or under the authority of a public 'resolution authority' rather than an insolvency representative.   8.74

As noted above, resolution regimes are designed to operate wholly or mainly outside traditional insolvency proceedings. This is because the systemic damage against which they are designed to guard is seen as an unavoidable consequence of the delay and complexity inherent in normal insolvency proceedings. Resolution regimes do, however, defer to insolvency proceedings in one key respect: the 'no creditor worse off' principle   8.75

---

[137] See for example Dodd-Frank Wall Street Reform and Consumer Protection Act of 2010, Pub Law No 111–203, 124 Stat 1376 (2010), Title II, codified at 12 USC §§ 5381–5394; UK Banking Act 2009; EU Bank Recovery and Resolution Directive (2014/59/EU).
[138] FSB, *Key Attributes* (November 2011, revised November 2014).
[139] G20 Research Group, *Cannes Summit Final Declaration*, para 28.
[140] FSB, *Key Attributes* (2014), Preamble.

that 'resolution powers should be exercised in a way that respects the hierarchy of claims',[141] subject to some flexibility to depart from the principle of *pari passu* treatment of creditors of the same class. In all cases:

> Creditors should have a right to compensation where they do not receive at a minimum what they would have received in a liquidation of the firm under the applicable insolvency regime ('no creditor worse off than in liquidation' safeguard).[142]

Some of the powers that we have suggested should be conferred by an insolvency regime, such as the power to effect transfers of business to a solvent institution, with protection from obstacles that might ordinarily apply such as a power of termination or a requirement for consent, are also typically among those available in resolution.[143]

8.76 The objectives set out in the preamble to the Key Attributes include 'ensur[ing] the rapid return of segregated client assets'.[144] The detailed treatment of client assets is addressed in Annex 3, entitled 'Client Asset Protection in Resolution', which recommends that:

> The legal framework should include clear and transparent rules on how:
>
> (i) client assets are defined, including the classification of securities held for or on behalf of a client and (where applicable) client money; and
> (ii) client assets are treated in the event of failure of the firm that holds the client assets either directly or indirectly (through one or more intermediaries or custodians).[145]

8.77 The Annex refers to further guidance issued by IOSCO and comments that:

> Given the significant variations in national regimes for client asset protection, the draft guidance is intended to specify outcomes rather than prescribe methods or mandatory rules by which those outcomes should be achieved. Whatever national arrangements apply, client assets should be shielded—in a manner appropriate to those arrangements—from the failure of the firm and, to the extent possible, of any third party custodian. The legal status of client assets and the clients' entitlement to them should not be affected by entry into resolution of the firm.[146]

The Key Attributes are, therefore, consistent with the principles of the GSC, explained above, on the treatment of client assets in insolvency.

8.78 Title II (Title II) of the Dodd-Frank Wall Street Reform and Consumer Protection Act ('Dodd-Frank'),[147] generally implements these Key Attributes. It creates an alternative regime—known as the 'orderly liquidation authority' (OLA)—for the resolution

---

[141] Ibid, 5.1.
[142] Ibid, 5.2.
[143] See s B(2)(g) and FSB, *Key Attributes* (2014), 3.3 (transfer of assets and liabilities).
[144] FSB, *Key Attributes* (2014), Preamble, sub-paragraph (ii) of the second paragraph.
[145] Annex 3, 3.3.
[146] Annex 3, final paragraph of preamble.
[147] Dodd-Frank Wall Street Reform and Consumer Protection Act of 2010, Pub. Law No 111–203, 124 Stat 1376 (2010), codified at 12 USC §§ 5301 et seq. Title II is codified at 12 USC §§ 5381–5394.

RESOLUTION OF SYSTEMICALLY IMPORTANT FINANCIAL INSTITUTIONS   231

of failed financial companies that pose a significant risk to the financial stability of the United States and satisfy other criteria specified in the statute (ie, SIFIs).[148] Under Dodd-Frank, the Federal Deposit Insurance Corporation (FDIC) serves as receiver for any institution placed in a Title II proceeding.[149]

The FDIC and other regulators have expressed a strong preference for the use of Title II at the holding-company level—the 'Single Point of Entry' strategy—in order to minimize the conflicts and complications that inevitably would arise from the resolution in separate proceedings of the numerous operating subsidiaries of any systemically-important financial institution.[150] However, Title II does extend the OLA to 'covered brokers or dealers', defined as those securities broker-dealers that are registered as such with the Securities and Exchange Commission (SEC) and are members of SIPC.[151] Accordingly, it is at least possible that a large, SIPC-member broker-dealer could be resolved through the OLA, rather than SIPA.   8.79

Under Dodd-Frank, a covered broker-dealer may be placed in an OLA proceeding only upon the written recommendation of the SEC and the Board of Governors of the Federal Reserve System, supported by a vote of no less than two-thirds of the members of each institution, and upon the written determination of the Secretary of the Treasury (Secretary) that the firm in question satisfies specified statutory criteria.[152] The statute provides a limited opportunity for the subject firm to seek judicial review of the Secretary's determination.[153]   8.80

If the firm does not challenge the Secretary's determination, or is unsuccessful in doing so, then the Secretary formally commences an OLA proceeding by appointing the FDIC as receiver for the covered broker-dealer.[154] The FDIC then appoints (without court approval) SIPC as trustee for the covered broker-dealer.[155] This differs from the normal practice under SIPA for SIPC to appoint an individual trustee for the liquidation (except in smaller cases where SIPC is the trustee). One would expect that SIPC likely would retain an expert in SIPA bankruptcy proceedings to manage the liquidation and that the manager would no doubt find it essential to retain a large staff of professionals and others. In order to give notice to interested parties that an OLA proceeding has been commenced, SIPC would file in the United States District Court for the district in which the subject firm had its principal place of business a notice and application for a protective decree, which the court must enter.[156]   8.81

---

[148] See 12 USC § 5384.
[149] See 12 USC § 5384(b).
[150] U.S. Department of the Treasury, Orderly Liquidation Authority and Bankruptcy Reform 1, 10–13 (21 February 2018); Resolution of Systemically Important Financial Institutions: The Single Point of Entry Strategy, 78 Fed Reg 76614 (18 December 2013).
[151] See 12 USC §§ 5381(a)(7), 5385.
[152] See 12 USC §§ 5383(a)(1)(B) and (2), 5383(c).
[153] See 12 USC § 5382(a).
[154] See 12 USC § 5382(a)(1)(v).
[155] See 12 USC § 5385(a)(1); 12 CFR § 380.61; 17 CFR § 302.101.
[156] See 12 USC § 5385(a)(2)(A); 12 CFR § 380.62; 17 CFR § 302.102.

8.82 As applied to covered broker-dealers, the OLA procedures essentially amount to an engraftment of the customer protection provisions in SIPA onto the bridge-bank resolution procedures commonly used by the FDIC in large bank resolutions.[157] In accordance with the bridge-bank model, at the inception of an OLA proceeding with respect to a covered broker-dealer, the FDIC forms a bridge broker-dealer, to which the FDIC, in consultation with SIPC, then transfers all or most of the assets of the covered broker-dealer, including the customer accounts and associated property held by the covered broker-dealer.[158] The FDIC then operates the bridge broker-dealer as a full-service broker-dealer, thereby providing customers with rapid access to all or most of their account assets.[159]

8.83 Title II provides expressly that the customers of a covered broker-dealer must receive as much in an OLA proceeding as they would have received had the firm been liquidated under SIPA, and assigns to the FDIC responsibility for covering any shortfall.[160] The transfer of customer accounts and assets to the bridge broker-dealer serves as the primary and immediate source of customer recovery in an OLA proceeding, and performs the same function as the transfer in a liquidation under SIPA of customer accounts and assets to a solvent, third-party broker-dealer.[161]

8.84 Beyond the transfer process, Title II provides customers with the opportunity to recover through a claims process administered by SIPC and the FDIC in the estate of the covered broker-dealer. As a general matter, SIPC is responsible for making all substantive determinations regarding claimant eligibility for 'customer' protection, and must do so in accordance with SIPA.[162] In consultation with SIPC, the FDIC is responsible for the procedural aspects of claims processing and resolution.[163] Customers in an OLA proceeding are eligible for SIPC advances at the same levels, under the same conditions, and subject to the same limits, as under SIPA.[164]

8.85 The UK's legislative response to the global financial crisis included the early introduction of a bank special resolution regime in the Banking Act 2009, enacted on 12 February 2009. This regime, which originally applied only to banks, was extended to investment firms in 2012 and has subsequently been expanded and updated in response to the development of the FSB Key Attributes and other international measures. The most important such measure from a UK perspective is the EU Bank Recovery and Resolution Directive (BRRD),[165] which came into force prior to the UK's departure

---

[157] See FDIC Resolutions Handbook 1, 18 (revised 15 January 2019), <https://www.fdic.gov/bank/historical/reshandbook/> (accessed 7 July 2021).
[158] See 12 USC §§ 5390(a)(1)(O), 5390(h)(2)(H); 12 CFR § 380.63; 17 CFR § 302.103.
[159] See 12 USC § 5390(h)(2)(H)(iv); 12 CFR § 380.63; 17 CFR 302.103.
[160] See 12 USC § 5385(f)(1) and (2).
[161] See 15 USC § 78fff-2(f) (discussed below in B(4)(g)).
[162] See 12 USC §§ 5385(b)(1), 5385(f)(1) and (2); 12 CFR § 380.64(a); 17 CFR § 302.104(a).
[163] See 12 CFR §§ 380.64(b)-(d); 17 CFR 302.104(b)-(d).
[164] See 12 USC § 5385(f)(2); 12 CFR § 380.64(a)(2); 17 CFR § 302.104(a)(2); see s B(2)(c), (e).
[165] 2014/59/EU.

from the EU. As a result, the UK special resolution regime closely parallels that in place in the EU (the core features of which are described below) as regards substantive powers and provisions, subject to detailed and institutional changes to adapt it to the new situation.

The BRRD set up an EU-wide regime modelled on the FSB Key Attributes. By the time it completed its legislative progress (on 15 May 2014), the EU had also nearly completed steps for the creation of a Single Resolution Mechanism as part of the EU's Banking Union. The Banking Union was created by a regulation (the Single Resolution Mechanism Regulation (SRMR))[166] and a separate Intergovernmental Agreement. These provide for the creation of a single mutualized Single Resolution Fund and for a new Single Resolution Board, rather than resolution authorities in individual Member States, to exercise resolution powers. The result is a composite regime creating a resolution system and powers which are administered by different resolution authorities depending on whether the institution's home Member State participates in the Banking Union.[167] At the time of writing (April 2021) all Member States except Sweden, Denmark, and Poland are participants. **8.86**

The EU regimes apply both to credit institutions and to investment firms, and therefore cover all EU institutions which act as intermediaries and have operations of systemic importance. The principal elements are: **8.87**

(i) *Recovery planning*: institutions are required to prepare recovery plans, at both individual institution and group level, providing for measures to be taken by the institution or group to restore its financial position following a significant deterioration.

(ii) *Resolution planning*: resolution authorities are required to draw up for each institution a resolution plan providing for the actions which the authority may take in the event of the institution's meeting the conditions for resolution. In the case of groups, the plan is to be drawn up on a group basis and must provide for resolution of the EU group, either at the level of the parent or through break-up and resolution of subsidiaries.

(iii) *Assessment of resolvability*: resolution authorities are required to assess whether institutions are capable of being resolved without extraordinary public financial support or emergency central bank assistance, and are given powers to require institutions to remove impediments to resolvability. Again, this system operates both at individual entity and group level.

---

[166] 806/2014/EU.
[167] See in particular Art 5 of the SRMR, which provides that, where the Single Resolution Board performs tasks or exercises powers which under the BRRD are to be exercised by the national resolution authority, it is considered to be the national resolution authority for the application of both instruments.

(iv) *Early intervention measures:* the authorities are given a range of powers to require early action to address problems, including powers to remove and replace senior management and appoint a temporary administrator or special manager.

(v) *Resolution tools:* if resolution measures prove to be required, the resolution authority has a range of 'resolution tools', to be used either individually or in any combination. The most important tools are:

- *Sale of business tool:* powers enabling the resolution authority to transfer the shares in the institution, or of all or part of its business or assets, to a private purchaser or purchasers. This power is backed by a range of ancillary powers and safeguards which override legal rules or contractual provisions and suspend the operation of private rights such as rights to enforce security or terminate or close out derivative or securities finance contracts (even rights which normally benefit from 'safe harbours' as mentioned in section D(2)), to the extent required to enable the sale to proceed.
- *Bridge institution tool:* powers enabling the resolution authority to make a corresponding transfer or transfers, backed by a similar range of ancillary powers, to a publicly owned 'bridge institution', generally in order to preserve the business as a going concern with a view to a later sale or sales.
- *Asset separation tool:* power to transfer assets of the institution into the management of a publicly owned asset management institution with a view to maximizing their value through eventual sale or orderly wind-down— broadly speaking, therefore, power to create a 'good bank/bad bank' split and manage or realize both parts with less damage than would be likely to result from conventional insolvency proceedings.
- *Bail-in tool:* power to write off, or write down, shares or other instruments of ownership, and debt securities and ordinary unsecured debts, to the extent required to restore the financial position of the institution. This is the most complicated of the tools, and the provisions relating to it include detailed requirements for the maintenance, prior to resolution, of 'minimum own funds and eligible liabilities' in order to ensure that institutions will have liabilities capable of being bailed in of an amount, priority level, and type sufficient to enable the bail-in tool to be used effectively.

(vi) The exercise of these powers is subject to the overriding 'no creditor worse off' principle. In particular, a valuation must be made, as soon as possible after the exercise of the tools, by an independent person with instructions to compare the treatment that shareholders and creditors would have received under conventional insolvency proceedings with the treatment they have actually received under resolution. If the valuation shows that they would have been better off under ordinary insolvency proceedings, shareholders and creditors have a right to compensation.

D. Selected Additional Issues

(1) Nature of a securities intermediary's insolvency proceeding: liquidation, reorganization, and other alternatives

An insolvency proceeding under SIPA, such as the LBI case, is a liquidation proceeding operating largely under the US Bankruptcy Code. The LBIE proceeding, by contrast, was an administration proceeding under UK law. The difficulties identified in the LBIE administration were an important factor in the decision of the UK authorities to introduce the Special Administration Regime described in section B(2)(d), paragraph 8.37 et seq. More recent UK insolvency proceedings in relation to significant securities intermediaries have taken the form of special administration,[168] and this is likely to be the normal future form of UK insolvency proceedings for any securities intermediary[169]. More generally, the particular form of an insolvency proceeding with respect to a securities intermediary is likely to vary according to a range of factors, including the nature and scope of its overall business (for example whether it is also a deposit-taker), its particular circumstances (for example whether recovery appears a realistic possibility), and the overall legal and insolvency regime of the jurisdiction concerned. Although international harmonization or at least convergence is in principle a desirable objective, it is not a necessity for the purposes of this chapter: rather the key point is that, whatever the form of proceeding adopted, it should provide a framework of rules, procedures, and powers under which account holders' interests are protected, their securities can be returned or transferred to another intermediary quickly and easily, and any issues that arise from shortfalls or disputes can be dealt with clearly, fairly, and expeditiously. We discuss in section B(2) the most important features which we consider that a regime should include in order to achieve this objective.

8.88

(2) Safe harbour protections: automatic stay, avoidance powers, set-off, and close-out netting

Many States have special insolvency law rules for financial contracts such as securities contracts, commodity contracts, forward contracts, repurchase agreements ('repos'), swaps and other derivatives, and master netting agreements.[170] The rights of a party to one of these contracts when its counterparty enters an insolvency proceeding is an important consideration for regulators of markets and for regulators and supervisors of market participants. In the US, the Bankruptcy Code provides special treatment—safe harbours—for these contracts (collectively, 'financial contracts'). This special treatment is considerably more favourable for non-debtor parties to financial contracts than the

8.89

---

[168] The largest of the firms concerned was MF Global UK Limited. For details of this and other special administration proceedings, see the Bloxham Final Review, chapter 2.
[169] As described in s C, the insolvency or threatened insolvency of an institution with a business important enough to be of systemic significance may be addressed in the first instance by the use of special resolution powers.
[170] See also Chs 2 and 3.

rules applicable to non-debtor parties to other contracts with the debtor. The stated motivation for enacting and periodically strengthening the safe harbours in the Bankruptcy Code has been to avoid systemic risk arising from the failure of a financial firm.[171] Other support for these provisions is based on the beneficial enhancement of liquidity.[172]

8.90 Under the Bankruptcy Code a debtor's counterparty may terminate a financial contract and offset and net out the parties' obligations (including enforcement against collateral) under one financial contract or multiple financial contracts free of the restraints of the automatic stay.[173] Moreover, it may terminate the transaction based on the debtor's bankruptcy petition, insolvency, or financial condition under an *ipso facto* clause.[174] The safe harbours also include broad protection from avoidance (for example, as a preference or a constructive fraudulent transfer) for pre-bankruptcy transfers made in connection with financial contracts. The exercise of rights to terminate financial contracts is also protected from avoidance.[175] Finally, certain settlement payments and margin payments are protected from avoidance.[176]

8.91 Likewise in the EU and the UK, close-out netting and collateral arrangements enjoy a substantial degree of protection against avoidance or stay arising from the commencement of insolvency proceedings, principally under special provisions in the 1998 Settlement Finality Directive and the 2002 Financial Collateral Directive and the UK legislation implementing those Directives, which remains in force following the UK's departure from the EU. The relevant provisions are described in more detail in Chapter 2, in particular paragraphs 2.08 to 2.10 and 2.67 to 2.70, and in Chapter 3. In the EU, the policy rationale underlying these protections was reiterated in a recital to the June 2019 'Restructuring and Second Chance' Directive, which provides for the introduction of a new restructuring regime for distressed, but viable, businesses broadly corresponding to the Chapter 11 regime in the US Bankruptcy Code, as follows:

> The stability of financial markets relies heavily on financial collateral arrangements, in particular, when security collateral is provided in connection with participation in designated systems or in central bank operations and when margins are provided to central counterparties (CCPs). As the value of financial instruments given as security may be very volatile, it is crucial to realize their value quickly before it goes down. Therefore, this Directive should be without prejudice to Directive 98/26/EC of the European Parliament and of the Council of 19 May 1998, Directive 2002/47/EC of the European Parliament and of the Council and Regulation (EU) No 648/2012.[177]

---

[171] See Mooney, 'Too Safe', 247–52 (summarizing legislative history and rationale for safe harbours).
[172] See Paech, 'Value'.
[173] 11 USC §§ 362(b)(6) (commodity contract, forward contract, or securities contract); (7) (repo); (17) (swap agreement); (27) (master netting agreement); 555 (securities contract); 556 (commodity contract or forward contract); 559 (repo); 560 (swap agreement); 561 (master netting agreement).
[174] 11 USC §§ 555, 556, 559–61.
[175] 11 USC §§ 555–6, 559–61.
[176] 11 USC § 546(e).
[177] Recital 43 of Directive 2019/1023 of the European Parliament and of the Council of 20 June 2019 on preventive restructuring frameworks, on discharge of debt and disqualifications, and on measures to increase the

8.92 Several scholars have criticized these safe harbours in recent years. During and since the financial crisis in 2008, these critiques have increased in number and sharpness.[178] Contrary to the premise that the safe harbours serve to *reduce* systemic risk, some have argued persuasively that they actually may *increase* systemic risk.[179] Support for the safe harbours based on their facilitation of necessary liquidity in the financial markets also has met with opposition.[180] Yet even some strong critics of the safe harbours concede that *some* special treatment may be warranted, even while maintaining that the package of benefits provided by current US law is excessively protective.[181] We generally agree with this assessment. While some special treatment is appropriate, the experience of the global financial crisis, in particular of the potentially pro-cyclical effect of very broad safe harbour protection, gives grounds to argue that the current safe harbour provisions in Europe and the US are too broad and extend beyond what would be necessary to provide appropriate safeguards against systemic risk. We would therefore support suggestions of a policy review to consider whether the current provisions should be recast and, if so, what more restricted level and scope of safe harbour protection is appropriate.

8.93 The protection of pre-insolvency settlement payments from avoidance in insolvency proceedings generally has been immune from the criticism of the safe harbours. In particular, protection of payments between securities clearing and settlement systems and their participants provide essential finality in the settlement process and further the goal of reducing systemic risk. Risks of such settlement payments being unwound would be significant and costly.[182]

8.94 An analysis of insolvency proceeding safe harbours for financial contracts is beyond the scope of this chapter. Even if, on balance, such favourable treatment provides substantial benefits for the financial markets, the beneficiary firms would not be limited to securities intermediaries. However, intermediated securities are the subject of many financial contracts and are the collateral involved in many others. It follows that any reform of insolvency laws relating to intermediated securities should take account of and address the safe harbours and their benefits and burdens. Likewise, reforms of the safe harbours should consider the impact on the intermediated securities holding systems, including systems for clearing and settlement.

---

efficiency of procedures concerning restructuring, insolvency and discharge of debt, and amending Directive (EU) 2017/1132.

[178] See, eg, Lubben, 'Repeal the Safe Harbors'; Lubben, 'The Bankruptcy Code without Safe Harbors'; Roe, 'Financial Crisis Accelerator'; see also Chs 2 and 3.
[179] See, eg, Mokal, 'Systemic Risk'.
[180] Compare Mokal, 'Systemic Risk' (arguing that safe harbours diminish liquidity and promote overvaluation of assets) with Paech, 'Value' (arguing that safe harbours provide necessary and beneficial liquidity to financial markets).
[181] See, eg, Duffie and Skeel, 'Dialogue on Automatic Stays'; Mooney, '*Too Safe*'.
[182] Unfortunately, case law in the US has extended the protection of settlement payments to transfers far removed for the needs of finality in the settlement process and the protection from systemic risk. See Mooney, '*Too Safe*', 260–5.

(3) Set-off: issuer's insolvency proceedings

8.95 Does an account holder have a right of set-off against the issuer of debt securities (bonds) in the issuer's insolvency proceeding? This question posits that the issuer is indebted (at least indirectly) to the account holder under the bonds and the account holder is indebted to the issuer on a transaction unrelated to the bonds (such as repayment of a loan or an account payable). Under both the non-insolvency law and insolvency law of many jurisdictions a bondholder holding directly on the issuer's books could set-off the bondholder's claim against the issuer on the bonds against the bondholder's obligation to the issuer, thereby reducing (or eliminating) the bondholder's obligation. To the extent of the amount of the set-off, then, the bondholder would recover 100 per cent of its claim against the issuer. Where an account holder's interest in the bonds is held indirectly in a securities account, however, its right to set-off its claim against the issuer's obligation may be questionable or nonexistent. It follows that when set-off is unavailable to an account holder the account holder's rights in that respect clearly are inferior to those of a direct holder of bonds.

8.96 Article 30 of the GSC could change that result. Under Article 30 the fact that the account holder holds in the intermediated system 'shall not of itself... preclude the existence or prevent the exercise of any right of set-off' that the account holder would have had or could have exercised if the account holder had held other than through an intermediary. The Convention, consequently, opts for neutrality and against discrimination based on the manner of holding.[183]

8.97 A creditor's right of set-off is recognized under the US Bankruptcy Code —but only if it exists under non-bankruptcy law (usually the law of a state).[184] Under state law a right of set-off typically requires that the obligations be mutual—ie, between the same parties acting in the same capacity—and that both obligations arise either before or after commencement of the bankruptcy case. Although the relevant case law is not well developed, an account holder in the US wishing to set-off its claim under a bond against a debtor-issuer's claim against the account holder would confront serious obstacles. The account holder normally would not be in a position to assert directly its claim under the bond against the issuer, thereby destroying mutuality. The bonds would be held in an omnibus account by the account holder's relevant intermediary (either with DTC or with another intermediary) and there would be no privity between the account holder and the issuer. Moreover, the structure and terms of the bonds would likely restrict the rights of the account holder in a way that would prevent mutuality. For example, the bonds might contractually prohibit set-off by a bondholder. Most bonds in the US also would be evidenced by a 'global' note registered in the name of DTC's nominee and the

---

[183] Kanda et al, *Official Commentary*, 30–1, 30–7.
[184] 11 USC § 553 (Bankruptcy law 'does not affect any right of a creditor to offset a mutual debt owing by such creditor to the debtor that arose before the commencement of the case ... against a claim of such creditor against the debtor that arose before the commencement of the case.'). To the extent of the amount of a creditor's right of set-off the creditor's claim is treated as a secured claim. 11 USC § 506(a)(1).

obligation of the issuer would run only to the registered holder of that note. Finally, a discrepancy between the amount of bonds credited to an account holder's account and the amount held (directly or indirectly) at DTC might inhibit the ability of the account holder to demonstrate the exact amount of its beneficial holdings. There are workarounds that sometimes permit account holders to enforce bonds directly against issuers, such as consents and assignments by DTC's nominee and the issuance of a certificated bond. But when an issuer files for bankruptcy those steps typically would not have been taken.

Uncertainty also exists under English law as to whether an account holder is entitled to a right of set-off in an issuer's insolvency proceeding.[185] Unlike under US law, set-off in insolvency proceedings (either a liquidation (winding up) or administration) is not dependent on a right under non-insolvency law. Moreover, the rules applicable to insolvency set-off are actually more favourable to a creditor than those applicable under non-insolvency law. For example, the insolvency set-off rights cannot be excluded by the terms of debt securities, apply even if the mutual debts are not due and payable, and operate automatically. However, it is not clear whether insolvency set-off would be applicable to an account holder in the issuer's insolvency proceeding. Although there are 'reasonably strong arguments' that it would be available,[186] it is uncertain whether the requisite mutuality exists between an account holder and the issuer and whether an account holder is a qualifying creditor 'proving or claiming to prove for a debt in the liquidation'.[187] 8.98

A statutory provision along the lines of GSC Article 30 could add useful certainty to the question of account holder set-off rights in an issuer's insolvency proceeding. However, Article 30 addresses only those impediments to set-off arising out of intermediated holding and would not reach other obstructions, such as those arising under the terms of the relevant debt instrument. 8.99

(4) Choice-of-laws rules

A cross-border insolvency proceeding—for example, a proceeding in one jurisdiction that covers account holder assets held by the insolvent intermediary in another jurisdiction—is capable of giving rise to complicated conflict-of-laws issues. In such a proceeding the *ex ante* account holder protection regime in the other jurisdiction may include a loss sharing rule which differs in detail from that applicable in the main insolvency proceeding. The obvious solution is for the law of the main insolvency proceeding to follow Article 26 GSC by recognizing the law of the other jurisdiction to the 8.100

---

[185] The following discussion of set-off under English law draws on Gullifer, 'Debt and Set-off'.
[186] Gullifer, 'Debt and Set-off', 173.
[187] Ibid, 170–3; Rule 14.25 of the Insolvency Rules 2016. Rule 14.24 provides a similar rule applicable in administration.

extent required. However, this may require a change in the choice-of-law rules of the insolvency forum State.[188]

8.101 Several factors complicate the choice-of-laws issues and their resolution. First, insolvency laws differ among States. The discussion in section B of the differing approaches taken in the UK and the US as to loss sharing and allocation among account holders provides an apt example.[189] Second, as among insolvency laws, some insolvency laws dictate the relevant rules and others apply the relevant private-law proprietary rules in insolvency proceedings. For example, loss allocation among account holders is governed by insolvency law both under the UK SAR and under SIPA in the US.[190] On the other hand, in the US, insolvency law for a commercial bank acting as a securities intermediary applies the relevant noninsolvency law private-law rules.[191] Third, the substantive private law relating to proprietary rights in intermediated securities is not harmonized. That the GSC is as yet not in force after more than a decade suggests that harmonisation is unlikely any time soon. Fourth, choice-of-law rules in general, and those relating to intermediated securities in particular, are not harmonized among States—either as to the private law affecting proprietary rights[192] or as to the applicable insolvency law.[193] As to the choice-of-law rules for private law relating to intermediated securities, the meagre acceptance to date of the HSC offers ample grounds for pessimism.[194] There may be more reason for optimism as to harmonising choice-of-law rules for insolvency proceedings, at least in the longer term.[195]

8.102 Consider a securities intermediary that maintains securities accounts in multiple jurisdictions and that is subject to insolvency proceedings in more than one jurisdiction. Each insolvency forum would be obliged to determine, under its rules of private international law, which State's *insolvency* law applies to the relevant securities accounts and, to the extent relevant, which State's *private law* applies to the rights of account holders. Consider as well a securities intermediary subject to a single insolvency proceeding that maintains securities accounts governed by the private law of multiple jurisdictions. Given the lack of harmonisation of private law, insolvency law, and the relevant choice-of-law rules, the *ex ante* uncertainty and the potential for conflicting results and the application of differing rules to different account holders is obvious. Although a detailed discussion of these issues is beyond the scope of this chapter, we note that as a practical matter the potential problems arising out of the absence of harmonisation in

---

[188] Of course, such an optimal approach may never be achieved on the ground.
[189] See s B(2)(d).
[190] See s B(2)(d).
[191] See s B(2)(d).
[192] See generally HSC; Goode et al, *Explanatory Report*.
[193] See, eg, Mooney, 'Harmonizing'.
[194] The HSC entered into force on 1 April 2017 but has been adopted only by Mauritius, Switzerland, and the US. Hague Conference on Private International Law, Status Table, <https://www.hcch.net/en/instruments/conventions/status-table/?cid=72> (accessed 7 July 2021).
[195] See UNCITRAL, Virtual Colloquium On Applicable Law in Insolvency Proceedings (11 December 2020), <https://uncitral.un.org/en/applicablelawcolloquium> (accessed 7 July 2021). Note as well that the EU Insolvency Regulation addresses choice of law in insolvency proceedings, Regulation (EU) 2015/848 of the European Parliament and of the Council of 20 May 2015 on insolvency proceedings, Art 7 (Applicable Law).

these spheres may be substantially ameliorated by the prevailing business models of securities intermediaries. This appears to be so because it is typical is for a securities intermediary to operate in only one jurisdiction. This may result at least in part because multinational investment banks in general maintain securities accounts for account holders through a separate subsidiary in each jurisdiction in which they operate.[196]

(5) Intermediated holding of digital securities (cryptosecurities)

In Chapter 10 Hans Kuhn and Klaus Löber provide an overview and analysis of substantive (private) law and regulatory developments relating to digital assets and, in particular, digital securities (also known as cryptosecurities).[197] In general the digital securities that they address reside in systems based on distributed ledger (including blockchain) technology (DLT) and public key cryptography. Digital securities are relevant to this chapter's focus on insolvency law related to intermediated securities because digital securities often are held through intermediaries—intermediated digital securities. We expect digital securities will continue to be so held for the foreseeable future.[198] Although issues relating to both direct and custodial holding of digital securities (and other digital assets) in general are beyond the scope of this chapter, we consider here the intersections and gaps between the intermediated holding of digital securities and relevant insolvency laws.

8.103

DLT has been widely touted (hyped, perhaps) as a mechanism for disintermediated holding of assets without the involvement of a trusted intermediary.[199] The potential of these technologies underlies some of the proposals and aspirations for disintermediated, direct securities holding infrastructures considered next in section D(6). However, some digital securities are or potentially will be significant investments credited to securities accounts maintained by traditional securities intermediaries (regulated as such). Others, however, may be held through intermediaries subject to no regulation, regulation other than as securities intermediaries, or new specialized regulatory regimes. Indeed, several cryptoasset intermediaries have already been the subject of insolvency proceedings that exposed their customers to losses.[200] Experience with the insolvency regimes for intermediated securities may offer insights and lessons for developing laws and regulations relating to digital assets more generally.

8.104

---

[196] Note, however, that this generally is not the case for the major bank global custodians.
[197] See Ch 10, para 10.14 ('We will be using the term *digital securities* to designate instruments which are issued and transferred on a DLT or comparable technology-based protocol or application, and which are functionally equivalent to physical securities . . .'.)
[198] See Ch 10, para 10.19.
[199] See, eg, Reiff, 'Blockchain Won't Cut Out Intermediaries' (explaining that claims that blockchain technology will eliminate intermediaries are exaggerated and inaccurate).
[200] An early and significant case arose in the Mt. Gox insolvency in Japan, which held that investors in Bitcoin were unable to recover Bitcoin from the insolvent estate of the custodian. For a summary, see Gullifer, Hara, and Mooney, 'English Translation of the Mt Gox Judgment'.

8.105 If digital securities are held through traditional securities intermediaries and subject to legacy regulatory and insolvency regimes for intermediated securities, then existing legal frameworks might be adequate with few adjustments. But in some (perhaps many, or even most) cases the existing securities holding infrastructures may be inadequate or inapplicable from the perspectives of the relevant private-law and regulatory frameworks. For example, digital securities that are securities for some purposes of securities regulation in the US nonetheless are not securities covered by SIPA's customer protection regime for broker-dealer insolvency proceedings.[201] Moreover, the US Securities and Exchange Commission (SEC) has issued a position statement, effective for five years, that would allow a registered broker-dealer to custody 'digital asset securities' only if the broker-dealer's business is restricted to dealing with such assets.[202] Risks associated with access and control of digital securities might impose significant problems in the context of an intermediary insolvency.[203] For example, loss of a private key could call into question the legitimacy of an intermediary's records of a client's position when the position cannot be verified or accessed.

8.106 The development and future impact of crypto-assets is receiving close attention from policymakers in the EU and the UK. The EU approach is set out in two documents published by the European Commission on 24 September 2020: a Communication on a Digital Finance Strategy for the EU, and a Proposal for a Regulation on Markets in Crypto-assets ('MiCA'). The Communication is a wide-ranging document which sets out objectives for future work. In the context of this chapter, two of those objectives are especially worthy of note:

(i) 'By 2024, the EU should put in place a comprehensive framework enabling the uptake of distributed ledger technology and crypto-assets in the financial sector. It should also address the risks associated with these technologies.'[204]

(ii) 'The Commission will, where necessary, adapt the existing conduct and prudential EU legal frameworks so as to continue safeguarding financial stability

---

[201] See 15 USC § 78lll(14) (SIPA definition of 'security').
[202] Securities and Exchange Commission (United States), Release No. 34–90788; File No. S7-25-20, 'Custody of Digital Asset Securities by Special Purpose Broker-Dealers, 86 Federal Register 11627 (26 February 2021). The SEC's goal in so limiting the business of special purpose broker-dealers is to insulate traditional securities customers, broker-dealer counterparties, and other market participants from the perceived risks associated with custody of digital asset securities. 86 Federal Register 11629. Examples of risks noted by the SEC include the possibility of fraud or theft of digital asset securities, loss of a private key, transfer of digital asset securities to an unintended address without the possibility of reversal, and the possibility of malicious activity that would take advantage of the vulnerabilities of DLT. 86 Federal Register 11629. In a similar vein, in 2019 the SEC issued a no-action letter permitting Paxos Trust Company LLC to operate, on a limited, feasibility study basis for a 24-month period, a DLT-based permissioned clearing and settlement system for selected US equity securities. Securities and Exchange Commission (United States), No-action letter re: Clearing Agency Registration Under Section 17A(b)(1) of the Securities Exchange Act of 1934, <https://www.sec.gov/divisions/marketreg/mr-noaction/2019/paxos-trust-company-102819-17a.pdf> (accessed 7 July 2021). Paxos currently plans to apply to become a fully licensed clearing agency. See NASDAQ, 'Paxos Plans to File for a Clearing Firm License' (23 February 2021), <https://www.nasdaq.com/articles/paxos-plans-to-file-for-a-clearing-firm-license-2021-02-23> (accessed 7 July 2021).
[203] In this connection, the FDIC recently issued a request for information concerning 'insured depository institutions' current and potential digital asset activities'. FDIC, Press Release (17 May 2021), <https://www.fdic.gov/news/press-releases/2021/pr21046.html> (accessed 7 July 2021).
[204] Communication, 4.2, first bullet point.

and protecting consumers in line with the 'same activity, same risk, same rules' principle.'[205]

The draft MiCA Regulation includes some strong indications of what the latter point may entail in relation to intermediation, or services corresponding to intermediation, in respect of crypto-assets.[206] Title V, headed 'Authorization and operating conditions for Crypto-Asset Service providers', establishes a regime for the authorization and regulation of firms providing services with respect to crypto-assets. This is modelled on that applicable to conventional investments under MiFID II. It repeats the MiFID II requirement that 'crypto-asset services providers that hold crypto-assets belonging to clients or the means of access to such crypto-assets shall make adequate arrangements to safeguard the ownership rights of clients, especially in the event of the crypto-asset service provider's insolvency',[207] and sets out a list of obligations imposed on firms authorized to provide custody and administration of crypto-assets for clients, including obligations to facilitate the exercise of rights.[208] This seems to imply the view that custody of crypto-assets fits, or can be fitted, within the general legal and conceptual framework governing conventional investment assets.

An important difference between MiCA and the MiFID II regime relates to third country firms. The MiFID II regime includes provision for branches of non-EU firms to be authorized in Member States,[209] and for firms established in third countries whose regulatory system is recognized as 'equivalent' to provide services to non-retail clients on the basis of their home country authorization.[210] There is no equivalent in MiCA: firms providing crypto-asset services must be incorporated and authorized in an EU Member State,[211] the only exception being for cross-border services that are provided 'at the own initiative' of the client—an exception which is likely to be narrowly interpreted where any form of marketing is present.[212] Moreover, EU firms which are already authorized as credit institutions or investment firms will not normally require a new authorization to provide crypto-asset services.[213] It seems likely that these features will impose significant barriers to entry and give a substantial head start to incumbent firms. **8.107**

The UK approach is more cautious. The most recent and, for this purpose, relevant document (a January 2021 H M Treasury consultation document and call for evidence entitled 'UK regulatory approach to cryptoassets and stablecoins') explains that: **8.108**

---

[205] Communication, 4.4 on p 15.
[206] Article 3(2) of the draft Regulation broadly defines 'crypto-asset' as 'a digital representation of value or rights which may be transferred and stored electronically, using distributed ledger technology or similar technology.'
[207] MiCA, Art 63(1); see para 8.26 for the corresponding MiFID II requirement.
[208] MiCA, Art 67.
[209] MiFID II, Art 39.
[210] MiFIR, Arts 46–7.
[211] MiCA, Art 53(1).
[212] MiCA, recital 51.
[213] MiCA, Art 2(5)–(6).

In line with the government's aim to ensure [that] the approach to regulating cryptoassets is proportionate, and to focus on where risks and opportunities are most acute, the government has considered how best to sequence any changes.[214]

Citing consumer research which suggests that consumers' awareness of the risks associated with the purchase of speculative cryptoassets is relatively high, the document proposes that such assets will remain outside the regulatory perimeter for the time being, with the possibility of introducing an authorization regime later, but that stablecoins ('stable tokens used as a means of payment') 'will become subject to minimum requirements and protections as part of a UK authorization regime'.[215] This will include a requirement for firms providing specified services, including 'providing custody and administration of a stable token for a third party', to be authorized,[216] thereby becoming subject to a range of requirements which will include 'Orderly failure and insolvency requirements: requirements to ensure issuers and service providers are prepared for modified resolution or administration, or insolvency'.[217]

8.109 The document is notably more cautious than MiCA in relation to any location requirement, stating that 'Due to the digital, decentralized and cross-border nature of stable tokens, the government and UK authorities are considering whether firms actively marketing to UK consumers should be required to have a UK establishment and be authorized in the UK', and listing a range of possible options.[218]

8.110 The January 2021 document also includes a section seeking views on a range of issues relating to the use of distributed ledger technology generally. This includes seeking views on the advantages and drawbacks of DLT in financial markets and on regulatory and legal barriers to the adoption of DLT, including 'feedback regarding how DLT will interact with existing rules around transfer of title, settlement finality, financial collateral, shareholder rights and corporate actions, and whether there is a need to optimize legislation across these areas . . . '.[219]

8.111 The following discussion identifies several issues that bear on the treatment in insolvency proceedings of digital securities held through intermediaries and that warrant attention from lawmakers, regulators, lawyers, and insolvency professionals. Much of insolvency law and practice deals with assets, claims, and conduct governed by principles of non-insolvency law. Digital securities present significant *sui generis* considerations in this respect. As explained in Chapter 10, work is ongoing in both private-law and regulatory spheres to address digital securities and other digital assets.[220] As also noted in Chapter 10, UNIDROIT is currently developing principles of private law for

---

[214] January 2021 document, 3.1.
[215] January 2021 document, 3.16.
[216] January 2021 document, 3.21.
[217] January 2021 document, 3.23.
[218] January 2021 document, 3.38.
[219] January 2021 document, 4.12.
[220] See Ch 10, ss C, E.

digital assets[221] and a project in the US is currently underway to develop a new article of the Uniform Commercial Code that would address private-law aspects of certain digital assets.[222] In addition to these private-law projects, we would encourage and applaud as well efforts on the international plane to coordinate regulatory initiatives relating to digital securities (and digital assets more generally).

8.112 One set of issues arises out of the vagaries of how digital securities may be held and dealt with directly through public key cryptography, as opposed to holding through a securities intermediary that maintains securities accounts. The cumbersome and risky aspects of these direct holding arrangements in large part account for the need and preference of many investors to hold through an intermediary,[223] But intermediated holding only kicks the can down the road—an intermediary must itself grapple with how to hold digital securities directly on behalf of its account holders.[224]

8.113 In addition to grappling with other aspects of holding digital securities directly, an intermediary must confront the additional and inherent security risks of digital securities arising out of their residence on the internet.[225] The aggregate package of perceived operational and security risks that accompany digital securities underlies the resistance of the SEC in the US to the authorization of traditional broker-dealers to custody and deal with digital securities.[226] Regulators face stiff challenges in determining the duties and standards that securities intermediaries must observe with respect to the custody of digital securities. But those standards should fall considerably short of strict liability. For example, the risk of loss by a 'hacking' attack on an intermediary is a risk that is inherent in digital securities inasmuch as these assets reside and are accessible only via the internet. Assuming an intermediary meets an appropriate standard of care, the residual risk should fall on the investors.

8.114 Even if traditional securities intermediaries are authorized to custody digital securities, the relevant specialized insolvency laws applicable to securities intermediary insolvencies may not apply.[227] And even if parts of such insolvency laws were applicable, as already noted, a State's customer protection scheme might not protect account holders claiming digital securities.[228] Moreover, a State's generally applicable

---

[221] See Ch 10, para 10.04.
[222] See Ch 10, paras 10.45–53.
[223] That said, intermediated holding appears to be antithetical to the normative underpinnings sometimes attributed to DLT as means of eliminating trusted intermediation. See Ch 10, para 10.19. It is interesting that this situation has not motivated innovation that would offer more user-friendly means of direct holding of cryptosecurities. However, lawmakers, regulators, and market participants alike appear for now to accept the cumbersome attributes of these assets which are poorly designed for widespread direct holding in active financial markets.
[224] The same could be said of holding through something like a CSD that would in turn be required to assume the burdens of directly holding the cryptosecurities for its participants who would be acting as intermediaries for investors.
[225] These risks may be reduced but not eliminated when cryptosecurities are held in permissioned systems as opposed to, for example, a permissionless public blockchain platform.
[226] See n 202.
[227] See generally s B(2)(c)–(d).
[228] See generally s B(2)(c).

insolvency laws may or may not provide appropriate protection for account holders. That situation may result, at least in part, because a State's private-law treatment of digital securities may be unclear or ill-suited for the recognition and protection of account holders.

8.115 What amounts to 'custody' of digital securities—ie, intermediated holding as opposed to an investor holding directly? In our view custody risk would exist whenever the insolvency proceedings of a person having power over digital securities would impair an investor's direct, unfettered access to and control over (including the power to dispose of) the digital securities.[229] For example, in a so-called multi-sig arrangement,[230] the participation of one or more persons holding private keys other than a beneficial owner may be required in order to exercise control over digital securities. Such circumstances warrant the attention of lawmakers and regulators for the protection of investors. That is not to say that every multi-sig arrangement gives rise to an intermediated holding arrangement warranting regulation as the intermediated holding of securities. But adjustments in private law and insolvency law should ensure that the rights of beneficial owners are adequately protected in all cases.

(6) Infrastructure modifications: enhanced transparency, disintermediation (direct holding), and priority claims in lieu of property rights

8.116 The discussion that follows briefly considers three approaches (which have become more prominent in recent years) for possible changes to the current intermediated holding systems.

(a) Enhanced transparency

8.117 The first edition of this chapter raised two questions related to the intermediated holding infrastructure:

> First, is today's technology and state of knowledge of and experience with securities holding systems such that, for a reasonable cost, a virtually foolproof, errorless system could be created that would essentially eliminate intermediary risk for account holders? Second, if so, would such an overhaul of any given system be politically or economically feasible?[231]

---

[229] Even if it is clear that intermediated cryptosecurities are not property of the insolvent estate of an intermediary or otherwise subject to claims of an intermediary's creditors, an investor nonetheless might be required to seek permission from an insolvency tribunal or an insolvency representative in order to exercise control over the cryptosecurities.
[230] See, eg, Harper, 'Multisignature Wallets'.
[231] See the first edition of this book, Ch 8, para 8.46.

By way of example, we noted there that affirmative answers to these questions might be given in Brazil,[232] although we offered no definitive answers more generally.[233] We suspect there may be even more support for such infrastructure modifications today, inspired in large part by the perceived potential of distributed ledger (including blockchain) technology (DLT).[234]

8.118 A transparent intermediated holding system may serve to reduce the principal intermediary risks—that if an intermediary fails it would have insufficient securities to make its account holders whole (a shortfall) or that the account holders may suffer a substantial delay in recovering securities in the intermediary's insolvency proceeding. By 'transparent' system we mean one in which the beneficial owner is definitively identified at the CSD level of the intermediated system.[235] In some transparent systems the beneficial owner also has the power to give instructions to the CSD with respect to transfers and withdrawals of assets. Because a transparent system eliminates the 'information gap' between the books of the CSD and those of lower-tier intermediaries in the holding chain, it would ensure (or at least make it more likely) that account holder claims and the securities available to the relevant intermediaries are matched, thereby reducing the likelihood of a shortfall in the event of a relevant intermediary insolvency proceeding.[236] A transparent system also could contribute to evidentiary certainty of account holder claims in the insolvency proceeding of a relevant intermediary.[237]

8.119 Notwithstanding the potential benefits, a transparent intermediated holding system would not insulate account holders from all intermediary risk resulting from a relevant intermediary's insolvency proceeding. This is so in particular because a transparent system would not necessarily entitle account holders to exercise rights directly against the issuers of securities. Even in the absence of shortfalls or any dispute or uncertainty as to account holder claims, account holders would be exposed to the risks of potential delay and expense in dealing with the relevant intermediary's insolvency proceeding.[238]

---

[232] See the first edition of this book, Ch 8, para 8.47 (discussing Brazil's 'final beneficiary model' for identification of beneficial owners at the CSD level).
[233] See the first edition of this book, Ch 8, para 8.49 ('We do not hazard a guess as to whether systems such as the final beneficiary model will eventually become the norm.').
[234] See s D(5) and Ch 10.
[235] Even in a transparent system the information as to beneficial owners would be available only to persons with legal entitlements to access that information.
[236] See Keijser and Mooney, 319. As Keijser and Mooney observe, even in a non-transparent holding system the implementation of a transparent information technology system could eliminate the information gap and thereby address problems of reconciliation among the records of intermediaries and those of a CSD and could identify shortfalls that would impose remedial actions. Keijser and Mooney, 321.
[237] Of course, the books of the relevant intermediary may not be definitive and binding as to account holder claims in the insolvency proceeding. On the other hand, to the extent that the relevant intermediary's records are accurate and undisputed and consistent with those of the CSD, the same results ultimately would obtain even under a non-transparent system.
[238] For example, a form of structural 'transparency' is in place in the US for broker-dealer programs for sweeping customer cash balances into FDIC-insured bank accounts. See s B(2)(c). However, in the absence of any case law, the treatment of such accounts in a broker-dealer insolvency proceeding may not be definitive. A trustee or creditors (or a creditors' committee) might argue that the accounts are assets of the insolvent estate and not those of the customers. Indeed, even if the rights of the customers were upheld, there would nevertheless be substantial delays in the recovery of those assets by the customers. The bank accounts would be in the name of the broker-dealer and only its estate could claim against the bank (or the FDIC) and control distribution of the cash.

These risks were epitomized, for example, by the experiences of many account holders in the LBIE administration proceedings.[239]

(b) Post-settlement disintermediation

8.120 Encouraged by the potential advances in technology, several scholars have advocated the benefits of the disintermediation of the securities holding infrastructures through direct holding systems.[240] As direct holders of securities on the books of issuers, investors would avoid the risks of a relevant intermediary insolvency.[241] Consideration of the merits and drawbacks of such infrastructure modifications is beyond the scope of this chapter. Moreover, we are not of like minds as to various aspects of proposals for infrastructure modifications.[242] That said, given the potential for reductions of intermediary risk, a few comments are in order as to some fundamental points.

8.121 An assessment of the merits of any major modification of the securities holding infrastructure in a given financial market should be based on a rigorous cost-benefit analysis (CBA). The CBA necessarily would involve a comparison of the costs and benefits of generally maintaining the current infrastructures with those of other plausible models involving various approaches to transparency and disintermediation. We note the prevailing view that intermediary risk generally has been managed and dealt with well, with few losses resulting from the failure of securities intermediaries.[243] Even so, a CBA must take account of the costs of such successes in risk reduction under current infrastructures when compared to the costs of similar (or enhanced) risk reduction under various approaches to a modified infrastructure. For example, in the past few years the International Organization of Securities Commissions (IOSCO) has issued two major reports on the protection of client assets.[244] These reports reflect both the reality and the significance of intermediary risk. It is a reasonable assumption that the costs of maintaining the apparatus of client asset protection mechanisms for intermediated holding systems are significant. Perhaps even more significant are the costs imposed by negative externalities resulting from the intermediated holding systems. For example, these might include costs related to shareholder voting, enforcement of bondholder rights, communications between issuers and account holders, and compliance with

---

[239] See the first edition of this book, Ch 8, paras 8.68–70.
[240] Eg Donald and Miraz, 'Multilateral Transparency for Securities Markets through DLT'; Mooney, 'Beyond Intermediation'; Mooney, 'Pluralism'.
[241] We note that provisions exist for a direct registration option within the CSD frameworks in both the US and the UK. See Mooney, 'Beyond Intermediation', 448–9 (discussing The Depository Trust Company's Direct Registration System); *Euroclear UK and Ireland, Personal Membership* (2018), <www.euroclear.com/dam/Brochures/Personal-membership-EUI.pdf> or <https://perma.cc/PP5Z-3ESD> (both accessed 7 July 2021) (discussing CREST personal memberships). However, these options are not practical, cost effective, or convenient for most investors.
[242] We offer these comments in general without assuming any particular attributes of a disintermediated holding infrastructure. For example, it could be implemented through special entries on the books of a CSD that would operate as the records of the relevant issuers.
[243] See para 8.34.
[244] IOSCO, *Recommendations Regarding the Protection of Client Assets*; IOSCO, *Adoption of the Recommendations Regarding the Protection of Client Assets*.

regulations concerning anti-money laundering, terrorist financing and sanctions.[245] On the other hand, current systems generally have served their intended purposes very well. For example, they have provided in particular significant convenience, flexibility and liquidity to intermediaries and account holders alike, including by facilitating the use of account holder securities by intermediaries.

8.122 Many investors employ or rely on professionals to manage the tasks such as recordkeeping, voting, communications, preparation of statements and accounts, and acting on instructions for the acquisition and disposition of investments. In addition, some investors also utilise professionals for investment advice and some delegate authority and discretion for the selection and acquisition of investments.[246] These professional management and administrative services represent significant benefits for investors and offer both convenience and efficiency. Many investors prefer not to be bothered with these tasks or lack the time, skills, and resources to deal with such matters.[247] These services are particularly important in the context of cross-border holdings. Finally, many investors benefit from current intermediated holding systems that facilitate credit extensions to account holders by intermediaries (margin lending) and from securities lending and borrowing. No doubt these services and benefits would continue to be demanded by investors, and provided by professionals and intermediaries, in an environment of increased direct holding.

8.123 Although such arrangements with professionals may impose agency costs and risks of fraud and error, a direct holding environment would be attractive to these investors, and would be politically feasible, *only* if such costs and risks would not be increased. Moreover, a direct holding system would appeal to a broad range of investors, only if it would preserve (or enhance) the existing flexibility, liquidity, and administrative convenience for investors. Indeed, existing direct registration options, such as those offered within the CREST system in the UK and the DTC system in the US, provide a natural experiment that proves this point.[248] Those systems have been designed with attributes that do not offer the benefits currently provided through intermediated holding and, consequently, they are not attractive to most investors.[249]

---

[245] See Mooney, 'Beyond Intermediation', 404–19; see also Davies, 'Investment Claims'; Micheler, 'Intermediated Securities from the Perspective of Investors'.
[246] Of course, providers of these services do not need to be acting as securities intermediaries. The investment advisory industry in the US is enormous and in many cases the advisors are not acting as securities intermediaries for their clients.
[247] Perceptions based on anecdotal communications with customers of firms subjected to SIPA proceedings and whose assets were missing or misused suggests that some customers did not examine their account statements in timely fashion.
[248] See n 236.
[249] We are not aware of empirical studies of account holder attitudes toward these direct holding options, although that data would be welcome indeed. However, we have observed that advocates for the current intermediated holding structures emphatically point to account holder preferences for the convenience of intermediated holding to explain the relatively meagre use of these options for direct holding. Although these advocates may view this explanation as supportive of the status quo, it may actually indicate that the options have not been structured with account holder convenience (and popularity) in mind.

8.124 We hold somewhat differing intuitions and judgments on the feasibility and practicality of technological modifications of the holding infrastructures that would substantially eliminate intermediary risk through direct registration, that would not substantially increase operational or agency risks, and that would preserve currently prevailing benefits. However, we recognize that neither *a priori* reasoning nor empirical evidence of which we are aware[250] would demonstrate one way or the other that these dual goals could or could not be achieved as a practical matter.[251] For this reason we would support subjecting concrete alternatives for improving the holding infrastructure to rigorous cost-benefit analysis and regulatory scrutiny.[252] In this context we emphasize that any successful disintermediated holding infrastructure could not operate without the involvement of intermediaries, which are vital players in the financial markets and which provide significant services and benefits as discussed above. For example, a successful direct holding system might contemplate direct holding only during the post-settlement period (however short or long) before an investor's disposition of a financial asset.[253] Moreover, we see no reason why investors who so choose should not be allowed the option of holding through an intermediary.[254]

8.125 In the absence of regulatory mandates or prodding, the principal impediments to any such reforms are likely to be substantial opposition of interested market participants—primarily securities intermediaries, including CSDs—who benefit from the status quo of deeply intermediated omnibus account-based holding systems. The goal of any reforms would be to preserve (or enhance) the efficiencies and benefits of the current infrastructure in reducing risks (and, perhaps, lowering costs). Properly conceived, a disintermediated post-settlement holding infrastructure would modify but not materially diminish the significant roles of intermediaries, including in the processes of trading and settlement and the provision of other services. While these may be worthwhile goals, whether in a given financial market implementing a direct holding infrastructure would be politically and practically feasible and cost-effective remains to be

---

[250] We are not aware of any studies that would suggest that these goals could not be met.

[251] See Mooney, 'Beyond Intermediation', 436–42 (discussing feasibility of this approach). For a discussion of overcoming complications in connection with debt securities, which in many markets are evidenced by global certificates and issued and held with the involvement of CSDs, see Mooney, 'Beyond Intermediation', 449–50 (discussing feasibility of converting existing debt securities to a direct holding environment); see also Salter, 'Debt Securities'.

[252] Note that in a post-settlement direct registration regime investors would nonetheless be exposed to settlement risks until such time as a direct registration were achieved. For example, the risks of fails to deliver securities on a settlement date would need to be allocated among the investors entitled to receive securities on that date. Accordingly, it also would be important to ensure that investor protection schemes continue to adequately protect against those risks in the case of an intermediary insolvency.

[253] This contemplates that an investor holding directly would put securities back into the intermediated system (ie, under the control of an intermediary) for purposes of disposition and settlement. Such post-settlement holding could involve only the issuer and investor intermediated by the technology that connects them and provides for conventional acquisitions and dispositions with the involvement of intermediaries such as brokers and dealers. This might be contrasted with existing intermediated systems in which the 'same' security is held by multiple intermediaries in tiered holding structures and through redundant record keeping.

[254] We are sceptical that a case could be made that mandating direct holding would be essential for appropriate investor protection.

seen, but we are quite sure that improvements in the infrastructure of *any* variety will not come to pass if they are not seriously considered.

(c) Priority in lieu of property rights

8.126 Another suggestion, more radical than a direct holding infrastructure, is to move away from the property concepts on which the protection of account holder securities is based under the GSC and in most, if not all, States at present. This suggestion is typically prompted by concerns that new types of assets and evolving patterns of holding, particularly in relation to cryptosecurities, are already straining existing concepts, and that this is likely to continue. The Bloxham Final Review referred to this in the following terms:

> 3.15 During the course of my discussions with interested parties, a number of different experts, notably from within the legal profession, forcefully made the point that a fundamental problem with the UK Client Asset Protection Regime is its reliance on general English property and trust law concepts, which are increasingly difficult to apply in the fast moving and intangible rights typically the subject of modern and sophisticated investment markets. The most commonly cited example is the doctrine of tracing, but others (such as the varieties of set-off) exist.
>
> 3.16 One of the objectives of the SAR in the Act is to maximize the efficiency and effectiveness of financial services in the United Kingdom. I consider that in view of this clear and understandable policy objective, it makes sense to listen to those who take the view that a more radical view should be undertaken of the legal basis under which client entitlements can arise and in particular whether trust and property law concepts are still well enough adapted to interests in products in the financial markets. This should be done on the basis of a very specific call for evidence...

8.127 Suggestions of this kind are not entirely new. For example, the rewriting of Article 8 of the UCC in the US in 1994 was based on rather similar concerns. It involved a significant conceptual realignment of holding securities through an intermediary, though it did not completely abandon the use of property concepts. More recent experience and continuing market and technical developments have given such proposals greater prominence in the last few years.[255]

8.128 A wider review of the kind recommended by the Bloxham Final Review would certainly be welcome, though Bloxham's reference to 'a very specific call for evidence' seems to us to be wise, and we do not find it surprising that the UK Government declined to take up the invitation.[256] In this chapter, we confine ourselves to the following general comments.

---

[255] See, eg, Green and Snagg, *DLT*.
[256] HM Treasury, Reforms to the Investment Bank Special Administration Regime (March 2016), 5.22: '... the review recommended that the government consider the merits of a standalone mechanism for determining client asset entitlements. The government does not propose to introduce such a mechanism, as the benefits of overhauling the law in this manner are not proportionate to the disruption and uncertainty it would cause.' Because there is no indication that the Treasury had available evidence which was not known to Bloxham, we take this to be an intuitive assessment.

8.129 First, while the idea of conceptual simplification is undoubtedly attractive in principle, caution is needed on the extent to which the attraction would survive an attempt to formulate a new test in detail. Logically, protection through a simplified structure would involve a more developed, comprehensive, and detailed regime of client preference. The difficulty of articulating the governing principles and then converting them into detailed rules could be considerable, and we think it possible that the final answer to the question 'which client claims should be given priority' might prove to be 'those that would have been classed as proprietary under the old system'.

8.130 Secondly, property law concepts have in the past proved capable of being adapted and developed in the light of changing facts and needs, and any such wider review will need to consider the relative merits (including ones of cost and convenience) of continuing incremental adaptation against those of a more wholesale redesign. The numerous examples of adaptation though legislation include, to name but two, the 1994 reform of the US Uniform Commercial Code, already referred to, and the sweeping statutory reform of Swiss law on intermediated holding in 2008.[257] The framework of trust and equity law in common law jurisdictions has also displayed flexibility and the capacity for its principles to be expanded (and in practice extended, though this tends to be diplomatically left in the shadows) to cover new facts. The various decisions on the Lehman insolvency, and the more recent decisions of the New Zealand courts in relation to the Cryptopia insolvency,[258] are examples of this. The process may give pain to purists, but while it remains effective in practice there is a good deal to be said for letting it continue.

8.131 A further consideration, and in our view not the least important, is that of public perception. Investors' belief that they own securities forms an important underpinning of public confidence in the financial system, both domestically and across borders. Many of the concerns discussed in this book stem from a recognition that under the developed intermediated holding system there a discrepancy between the public perception and the detailed legal reality. But while under the present system there is indeed a considerable difference between what most investors think that they own and what they actually own as a legal matter, this is a difference of degree and detail rather than a difference in kind. It seems to us that there is at least some risk that investor confidence could be undermined by a change of the kind proposed, however carefully it was designed and explained.

E. Conclusion

8.132 This chapter, like its predecessor, has provided an overview of the matters that law—including insolvency law per se—should address in connection with intermediated

---

[257] Bundesgesetz vom 3. Oktober 2008 über Bucheffectken (Buckeffectengesetz, BEG)/Loi Fédérale du 3 octobre 2008 sur les titres intermédiés (LTI)/Legge federale del 3 ottobre sui titoli contabili (Legge sui titole contabili, LTCo) AS 2009, 3577. For a discussion, see Hans Kuhn in Conac, Segna, and Thévenoz, *Intermediated Securities*, Ch 13.

[258] *Ruscoe v Cryptopia Ltd (in Liquidation)* [2020] NZHC 728.

securities in the context of an insolvency proceeding. The focus has remained on the insolvency of securities intermediaries. Indeed, the prospect of securities intermediary insolvencies pervades this volume. For example, in addition to the treatment in this chapter, it figures prominently in Chapters 2 (financial collateral), 3 (close-out netting), 7 (sufficient securities, segregation, and loss sharing), and 9 (regulation, supervision, and oversight). These chapters bear witness to the phenomenon that the role of insolvency law is not limited to the impact on the small percentage of securities intermediaries (and their creditors and account holders) that are the subject of actual insolvency proceedings. Another crucial dimension of insolvency law reflects its instrumental effects on the behaviour of market participants outside of and unrelated to any actual insolvency proceedings. These effects involve contexts such as the availability and cost of credit, investment behaviour and attitudes, the need for and shape of regulation, the content of private-law rules, and in general the level of confidence in the financial markets.

The principal goals of this chapter were summarized in paragraph 8.02; we trust that they have been achieved. The chapter has identified and discussed the most important insolvency law-related issues. It features an expanded section B(2) on the treatment of account holder claims, which lies at the heart of the chapter. It also provides an expanded scope of section D, including treatment of set-off in an insolvency proceeding of an issuer of debt securities and conflict of laws in the cross-border setting. Along the way the chapter offers guidance on how States might best address these issues. Significantly, section D also considers the future impact of technological advances on the securities markets and the implications for the role of insolvency law. Specifically, it considers cryptosecurities and the potential for major modifications of the intermediated securities holding infrastructure. While we make no firm predictions for the future, we note that the evolution of intermediated securities systems has featured continual gains in efficiency and increased attention to the reduction of risks and the protection of account holder rights. We are hopeful that future technology-influenced developments will proceed with an appreciation for the need to preserve the benefits achieved to date. 8.133

9

REGULATION, SUPERVISION, AND OVERSIGHT

A. Introduction		9.01	D. Market-wide Recommendations and Requirements for Intermediaries	9.94
B. Function and Scope of Regulation, Supervision, and Oversight		9.04	(1) Geneva Securities Convention	9.96
(1) Regulated activities		9.04	(2) Client asset protection	9.98
(2) Regulatory policy objectives		9.07	(a) IOSCO high-level principles	9.100
(a) Investor protection		9.08	(b) IOSCO *Recommendations Regarding the Protection of Client Assets*	9.102
(b) Safety and efficiency		9.09		
(c) Financial stability		9.12	(c) FSB guidance on client assets protection in resolution	9.107
(3) The role of international standards		9.14		
(4) Supervision and oversight of central securities depositories and securities settlement systems		9.19	(3) Market-wide recommendations for securities settlement	9.113
			(a) Trade confirmations and settlement cycles	9.115
(5) Supervision of intermediaries		9.25		
(6) Recovery and resolution regimes		9.31	(b) Book-entry securities and protection of customers' securities	9.118
(7) Co-operation and coordination of authorities		9.32	(c) Further recommendations	9.120
C. Requirements for Central Securities Depositories and Securities Settlement Systems		9.37	(4) Requirements for repos and securities lending	9.123
			(a) Enhanced transparency	9.126
(1) CPMI-IOSCO principles for financial market infrastructures		9.38	(b) Regulatory minimum standards for securities lending, re-use, and rehypothecation	9.128
(a) Scope		9.48		
(b) Governance and access		9.51	(c) Collateral management services	9.135
(c) Risk management		9.58	(d) Structural aspects	9.137
(2) Disclosure framework		9.80	(5) Cross-border recognition of resolution actions	9.141
(3) FMI recovery and resolution		9.83		
(a) FMI resolution		9.84	E. Concluding Remarks	9.146
(b) FMI recovery		9.90		

A. Introduction

9.01 Over the past decades, securities trading and settlement volumes have soared, as securities markets have become an increasingly important channel for intermediating flows of funds between borrowers and lenders and as investors have managed their securities portfolios more actively, in part because of declining transaction costs. Volumes of cross-border trades and settlements have grown especially rapidly, reflecting the increasing integration of global markets. Central securities depositories (CSDs), securities settlement systems (SSSs), custodians, and intermediaries constitute the backbone

FUNCTION AND SCOPE OF REGULATION, SUPERVISION, AND OVERSIGHT

of the post-trade securities infrastructure. The smooth and seamless provision of their services contributes to safeguarding the safety and efficiency of financial markets and helps to give market participants confidence that securities transactions are executed properly and in a timely manner, including during periods of extreme stress.[1]

However, weaknesses in the underlying infrastructure for the holding and settlement of securities can be a source of systemic disturbances to securities markets as well as other parts of the financial system. A financial or operational problem at an entity that performs critical functions in the settlement process or at a major user of a settlement infrastructure could result in significant liquidity pressures or credit losses for other market participants. In the securities markets, market liquidity depends critically on confidence in the safety and reliability of the settlement arrangements; traders will be reluctant to trade if they have significant doubts as to whether or when the trade will settle. A particular feature of the settlement infrastructure is its interdependency with other financial market infrastructures (FMIs), such as payments or clearing systems. As an example, a disruption of securities settlement has the potential to spill over to payment systems that settle the corresponding cash leg of transactions as well as any parts of the infrastructure (such as central counterparties) that use the settlement infrastructure to transfer collateral.

9.02

During the global financial crisis of 2007 and also subsequently (for example, in the direct aftermath of the start of the Covid-19 crisis in March 2020), the settlement infrastructure, in particular CSDs and SSSs, generally proved to be highly resilient. Abnormally high settlement volumes could be managed during phases of very high volatility, and FMIs were able to cope even with the default of a large counterparty. There was no visible materialization of systemic risk in FMIs that could have led to spreading disruptions further.[2] To some degree, this was the result of global regulatory efforts over the past 20 years to introduce certain risk mitigants, such as intra-day finality or delivery versus payment structures. However, the global financial crisis also highlighted certain shortcomings, for example in default and liquidity risk management, a severe lack of transparency in some parts of the financial markets such as the repo markets, and inadequate (cross-border) information flows, that have led to continuous efforts to enhance further the resilience of the financial infrastructure.

9.03

B. Function and Scope of Regulation, Supervision, and Oversight

(1) Regulated activities

The securities markets are a core part of the global financial system. A key element of modern economies is that actors no longer necessarily interact directly with each

9.04

---

[1] Padoa Schioppa, Foreword to CPSS, *Central Bank Oversight*.
[2] ECB, *Lessons Learned from the Financial Crisis*, 4.

other, but rely instead on intermediaries. In the securities markets, whether national or international, efficient intermediation fosters an effective and productive allocation of assets. However, intermediation necessarily poses risks, for example, with respect to safeguarding and administering the property of third parties. The intermediation process, to be effective, depends on mutual trust, ie, trust based on confidence in the integrity of institutions and the continuity of markets. That confidence, often taken for granted in well-functioning financial systems, was partially lost in the global financial crisis, in substantial part due to the complexity and opacity of certain market segments. In reaction, there were multiple calls to strengthen regulatory policies and standards, with particular emphasis on standards for governance, risk management, capital, and liquidity, not just for banks, but also for other financial institutions and infrastructures.[3]

9.05 A primary aim of financial regulation is to maintain the stability of the financial system and contain systemic risk. This is usually being achieved by a number of complementary activities,[4] for example subjecting entities that are determined to be systemically important to the highest standards of regulation and ongoing supervision, assuring that critical elements of the infrastructure supporting the financial system, including clearing and settlement systems, and related legal frameworks, are sufficiently robust, and avoiding regulatory or other practices that may have pro-cyclical effects or be detrimental to the maintenance of prudent business practices.

9.06 In its practical application, financial market regulation adopts a variety of structural approaches. There may be institutional approaches, where an entity's legal status (for example, a bank or insurance company) determines which regulatory regime applies and which regulator is tasked with overseeing its activity, in terms of both safety and soundness, and the conduct of business. Alternatively, there may be functional approaches, wherein the type of prudential oversight is determined by the business that is being transacted by the entity, without regard to its legal status. Depending on the jurisdiction, the regulatory authorities can be set up in: a sectoral approach, where separate authorities regulate banking, securities markets, or insurance activities; an integrated approach, in which a single, universal regulator conducts both safety and soundness oversight and conduct-of-business regulation for all the sectors of financial services business; or a 'twin-peaks' approach, in which regulatory functions are separated between one regulator that performs the safety and soundness supervision function and another that focuses on conduct-of-business regulation. Irrespective of the approach taken, it is of paramount importance that the regulatory regime is risk sensitive in a way that all risks emanating from the conduct of financial market activities are adequately addressed.

---

[3] See the Washington declaration of the G20 of 15 November 2008, available at <http://www.g20.utoronto.ca/2008/2008declaration1115.html> (accessed 7 July 2021); see also Tucker, *Building Resilient Financial Systems*.
[4] Group of Thirty, *Financial Reform*, 17 et seq.

(2) Regulatory policy objectives

In the area of intermediated securities, key regulatory policy objectives are (i) to protect investors, (ii) to enhance safety and efficiency of holding and settlement arrangements, and, more broadly, (iii) to limit systemic risk and foster financial stability. 9.07

(a) Investor protection

Regulatory and supervisory frameworks usually emphasize the protection of investors, a major objective of regulatory bodies. However, in response to the increasing intermediation and complexity in financial services, additional dedicated and proportionate policy action to enhance financial consumer protection is also considered necessary to address recent and more structural developments, which have already been implemented in several jurisdictions.[5] Such action includes primarily enhanced safeguards such as customer information requirements or enhanced control and protection mechanisms to safeguard, with a high degree of certainty, investors' proprietary rights in securities and other financial assets, including protection against fraud, misappropriation, or other misuses. New measures also extend to enhanced protection mechanisms for financial and personal information. 9.08

(b) Safety and efficiency

Many regulatory authorities are concerned about the safety as well as the efficiency of the financial markets or entities for which they are responsible. Safety and efficiency, for example in the chain of securities holdings, are not conflicting objectives; rather, they complement each other. While the safety objective is concerned to mitigate risks, efficiency also contributes to well-functioning financial markets. A lack of interconnectivity between services providers, fragmentation of markets, as well as too high a concentration of activities among a small number of players, can result in inefficiencies and higher costs, especially for cross-border transactions.[6] 9.09

To ensure safety, intermediaries (including FMIs for that purpose) should manage their risks robustly. They should identify and understand the types of risks that arise in their services, and determine the sources of those risks. Relevant risks include (but are not limited to) legal, credit, liquidity, general business, custody, investment, and operational risks. Once these risks are properly assessed, appropriate and effective mechanisms should be developed to monitor and manage them. 9.10

An intermediary should not only be safe, but also efficient. Efficiency refers generally to the optimum use of resources by intermediaries and their participants in performing their functions. An intermediary that operates inefficiently may distort financial activity and the market structure, affecting not only its participants but also its participants' customers. These distortions may lead to lower aggregate levels of efficiency and 9.11

---

[5] See OECD, *G20 High-level Principles*; see also IOSCO, *Client Assets Survey*.
[6] ECB, *Eurosystem Oversight Policy Framework*, 2.

safety, as well as increased risks within the broader financial system. In making choices about design and operation, however, intermediaries ultimately should not let other considerations take precedence over the establishment of prudent risk-management practices.

(c) Financial stability

9.12 Financial stability plays a crucial role in the financial system and the wider economy, as the global financial crisis has shown. The crisis revealed that the financial and economic community, in both the private and the public sector, had neglected the system-wide perspective of financial stability, relying instead on the perceived self-correcting mechanisms of the market. With an increasing number of financial institutions active in two or more countries or continents, a global perspective on financial stability has become ever more important.

9.13 Traditional supervision has a micro-prudential focus, in that it looks at the soundness and resilience of an individual institution rather than wider financial market implications. To complement this narrow focus, increased attention has been given to macro-prudential oversight of the financial system in order to contribute to the prevention or mitigation of systemic risks to financial stability that could arise from developments within the financial system, taking account of macro-economic developments, to avoid periods of widespread financial distress. This has led in particular to the establishment of dedicated financial stability authorities on a national (eg, the Financial Stability Oversight Council in the US)[7], regional (eg, the European Systemic Risk Board)[8], and global (the Financial Stability Board (FSB))[9] level.

(3) The role of international standards

9.14 A key challenge in the regulatory process is to ensure global consistency. Financial markets and many large financial entities are global, but financial regulation remains ultimately national or regional. To the extent that national rules differ, they may create overlapping and sometimes conflicting requirements on entities that operate in more than one jurisdiction. These problems are particularly significant for globally active financial institutions.

9.15 To prevent regulatory arbitrage, regulation needs to comprehensively cover global financial markets and entities, while avoiding conflicts, inconsistencies, and unnecessary duplication between national regimes. This does not necessarily mean that

---

[7] See <http://www.treasury.gov/initiatives/fsoc/Pages/home.aspx> (accessed 7 July 2021).
[8] See <http://www.esrb.europa.eu/about/orga/html/index.en.html> (accessed 7 July 2021).
[9] The FSB's role is to identify vulnerabilities in the international financial system, submit proposals on the elimination of such vulnerabilities, monitor the proposals' implementation, coordinate regulatory and prudential policies in financial sector issues at the international level, and intensify cooperation and the exchange of information among the relevant institutions in these fields. See <http://www.financialstabilityboard.org> (accessed 7 July 2021).

FUNCTION AND SCOPE OF REGULATION, SUPERVISION, AND OVERSIGHT 259

different jurisdictions need to have identical regulations, as long as they have similar outcomes. The recent progress in regulatory cross-border cooperation on OTC derivatives provides an example of the type of approach needed. In July 2013, the G20 Finance Ministers and Governors agreed that jurisdictions and regulators should be able to defer to each other's regulatory actions when it is justified by the quality of their respective regulations and enforcement regimes. This is subject to the regimes having essentially identical outcomes, being applied without discrimination, and paying due respect to home country regulations. More widely, across the full spectrum of the financial reform agenda, the FSB promotes outcomes-based approaches to assessing the consistency of implementation of agreed reforms, enabling jurisdictions to defer to each other's rules where they deliver similar outcomes, thus avoiding 'one-size-fits-all' solutions.[10]

In reaction to this, there is the increasingly widespread development of global regulatory standards in the financial domain,[11] which are or are becoming the foundation of national or regional oversight, supervision, and regulatory activities. Such standards are developed by so-called global standard-setters, ie, international bodies that elaborate a set of recommendations or guidance to serve as best practice for the formulation of regulatory policies at a national or regional level. One such widely known set of standards covers the capital adequacy requirements for banks developed by the Basel Committee for Banking Supervision[12] (BCBS) at the Bank for International Settlements[13] (BIS). In the area of intermediated securities, the recognized standard-setting bodies are the International Organization of Securities Commissions[14] (IOSCO) and the Committee on Payments and Market Infrastructures[15] (CPMI) at the BIS. 9.16

International standards and expectations developed by these standard-setters do not have direct legal force. Rather, they are developed and issued by the agreement of their members, in the expectation that individual national and regional authorities will implement them. However, they are broadly accepted as representing minimum 9.17

---

[10] FSB, *Report on Financial Reforms*.
[11] In this context, the term 'standards' is used as a generic term to cover all normative statements such as standards, principles, recommendations, or guidance.
[12] The Basel Committee is the primary global standard-setter for the prudential regulation of banks and provides a forum for co-operation on banking supervisory matters. The Committee formulates supervisory standards and guidelines to promote global financial stability. See <http://www.bis.org/bcbs/> (accessed 7 July 2021).
[13] The BIS is the world's oldest international financial institution, established under a Hague Convention of 1930. The BIS pursues its mission by promoting discussion and facilitating collaboration among central banks and with other authorities responsible for promoting financial stability, conducting research on policy issues confronting central banks and financial supervisory authorities, and providing statistics, hosting committees and secretariats of regulatory bodies, and acting as 'bank for central banks'. See <http://www.bis.org> (accessed 7 July 2021).
[14] IOSCO is recognized as the global standard-setter for the securities sector representing securities regulators. IOSCO develops, implements, and promotes adherence to internationally recognized standards for securities regulation. See <http://www.iosco.org> (accessed 7 July 2021).
[15] The CPMI is a standard-setting body for payment, clearing, and securities settlement infrastructures. It also serves as a forum for central banks to monitor and analyse developments in domestic payment, clearing, and settlement systems as well as in cross-border and multicurrency settlement schemes. Until 1 September 2014, the CPMI was known as Committee on Payment and Settlement Systems (CPSS). See <http://www.bis.org/cpmi/about/overview.htm> (accessed 7 July 2021).

requirements for good practice, which countries are encouraged to meet or exceed. The FSB has identified what it considers to be the key standards for sound financial systems[16] on the basis of the criteria of being (i) relevant and critical for a stable, robust, and well-functioning financial system; (ii) universal in their applicability, by covering areas that are important in nearly all jurisdictions; (iii) flexible in implementation, by being general enough to take account of different national circumstances; (iv) broadly endorsed, namely that such standards should have been issued by an internationally recognized body in the relevant area in extensive consultation with relevant stakeholders;[17] and assessable by competent authorities or by third parties such as IFIs.

9.18 The members of the FSB have committed themselves to the implementation of the global standards (as have the members of the CPMI and IOSCO for their standards). But even beyond the constituencies of these groups, domestic regulation is increasingly based on these standards (which are sometimes also the basis of legislation by way of incorporation) because of the power of the arguments they contain and their recognition as international best practice. Furthermore, in the area of financial markets, the International Monetary Fund (IMF) and the World Bank have adopted these standards as the benchmark for assessments of jurisdictions in the context of their Financial Sector Assessment Programs.[18]

(4) Supervision and oversight of central securities depositories and securities settlement systems

9.19 Due to their position at the end of the settlement process, CSDs and SSSs operated by CSDs are of systemic relevance to the functioning of securities markets. They also serve as an essential tool to control the integrity of an issue, hindering undue creation or reduction of issued securities, and thereby playing an important role in maintaining investor confidence. Moreover, SSSs are often part of the collateralization processes of monetary policy operations as well as between market participants and are, therefore, important actors in the collateral markets. Given this central, systemic role, CSDs and SSSs should be subject to adequate regulation, supervision, and oversight, in

---

[16] See <https://www.fsb.org/work-of-the-fsb/about-the-compendium-of-standards/key_standards/> (accessed 7 July 2021).

[17] To satisfy the latter criterion, the standard should preferably undergo a public consultation process. This criterion would also be satisfied when the standard-setting body has wide representation, or when the standard has been endorsed by International Financial Institutions (IFIs), such as the International Monetary Fund and the World Bank.

[18] The Financial Sector Assessment Program (FSAP) is a joint programme of the IMF and the World Bank. Launched in 1999 in the wake of the Asian financial crisis, the programme brings together World Bank and IMF expertise to help countries reduce the likelihood and severity of financial sector crises. The FSAP provides a comprehensive framework through which assessors and authorities in participating countries can identify financial system vulnerabilities and develop appropriate policy responses. See <http://www.imf.org/external/NP/fsap/fsap.aspx>; <https://www.worldbank.org/en/programs/financial-sector-assessment-program> (both accessed 7 July 2021).

accordance with international best practice. In view of their crucial role, different regulatory authorities have or may have a statutory interest in these FMIs.

9.20 A competent authority in charge of authorizing and supervising CSDs and SSSs operated by CSDs is usually generally empowered to examine how the FMIs operate on a daily basis, to carry out regular reviews, and to take appropriate action when necessary. Depending on the jurisdiction, the role of the authority may be allocated to the central bank, the securities regulator, or, if the FMI is operating under a banking licence (because the function of holding assets on behalf of customers is considered a banking service subject to banking regulation),[19] it may be performed by the banking supervisor.

9.21 In addition to supervisory authorities, central banks are generally also involved with settlement systems if they are not already the regulatory authority in charge in their jurisdiction. Often, central banks operate settlement systems,[20] or provide central bank money as a safe settlement asset for such systems. In addition, central banks are frequently users of settlement systems to implement their monetary policy operations and provide banking services to their own customers. As a consequence, in pursuit of their public policy objectives with respect to monetary and financial stability, central banks have sought to influence the design and function of such systems. The performance of this sort of function towards FMIs is called 'oversight'.

9.22 More specifically, oversight is a 'central bank function whereby the objectives of safety and efficiency are promoted by monitoring existing and planned FMIs, assessing them against these objectives and, where necessary, inducing change'.[21] The concept of central bank oversight of FMIs has become more distinct and formal in recent years as part of a growing public policy concern with financial stability in general. Oversight has developed in part in response to an expansion of the private sector's role in providing payment and settlement systems. Where there has been a risk that the private sector would take insufficient account of negative externalities that could cause systemic risk, central banks have sought to pursue public policy safety and efficiency objectives by guiding and influencing system operators. The increasing attention to oversight also reflects the great increase in the values of transfers cleared and settled, the increasing centralization of activity around a small number of key systems, the increasing technological complexity of many systems, and the consequent concern that systemic risk could increase if the design of key systems did not adequately address various payment and settlement risks.

9.23 The supervision and oversight functions are distinct from each other, but they are conducted in parallel. As noted by the CPSS-IOSCO *Recommendations for Securities Settlement Systems*, '[t]he division of responsibilities for regulation and oversight of securities settlement systems among public authorities varies from country to country

---

[19] This is the case for CSDs operating in, for example, Germany, Austria, Luxembourg, and Belgium.
[20] See Fedwire Securities Service in the United States, NBB SSS in Belgium, etc.
[21] See CPMI, *Central Bank Oversight*, 1.

depending on the legal and institutional framework', so that '[s]ecurities regulators, central banks and, in some cases, banking supervisors will need to work together to determine the appropriate scope of application of the recommendations and to develop an action plan for implementation'.[22]

9.24 There is some degree of overlap in that both the competent supervisory and oversight authorities perform similar tasks, for example: regular reviews to ensure that settlement systems comply at all times with prudential and other rules; collection of necessary data by appropriate means, such as reporting mechanisms or direct access by regulators; review of the arrangements, strategies, processes, and mechanisms implemented by an FMI; organization of on-site inspections, verification, and investigations; early identification of excessive risks through examination, with appropriate testing to assess their resilience in extreme but plausible market conditions, and back testing to assess the reliability of the methodology adopted; ensuring coordination and channelling information flows in emergency situations; and inducing appropriate changes in the organization and governance of an FMI.[23] As a consequence, to avoid overlap, duplications, or conflicting requirements on the supervised and overseen entities, there is a need for relevant competent authorities to consult and cooperate with each other and other relevant authorities (see section B(7)).

(5) Supervision of intermediaries

9.25 Beyond the central role of CSDs and SSSs, a sound prudential and conduct-of-business framework for the holding and transfer of securities relies on strong supervisory regimes for intermediaries, in particular custodian banks.

9.26 Global or local custodians that hold securities for customers, including banks, and which provide related services are key components of the securities holding and settlement infrastructure. Payment and settlement flows may be concentrated in a few large institutions, giving rise to possible (credit and liquidity) concentration and operational risks.

9.27 The issue of such large custodians (sometimes called 'quasi-systems') and the related risks has been analysed in a number of international reports.[24] There is no universally accepted definition of a quasi-system, but the CPSS report on central bank money suggests the following as far as payments are concerned (a parallel definition could apply for securities):

---

[22] CPSS and IOSCO, *Recommendations for SSSs*, 3.84 and 1.10.
[23] However, other public policy objectives (such as data protection, consumer protection, and the fight against money laundering and financing terrorism) are frequently allocated to other authorities having an explicit mandate for such objectives.
[24] See, respectively, Group of Ten, *Financial Sector Consolidation*; CPSS, *Central Bank Money in Payment Systems*.

FUNCTION AND SCOPE OF REGULATION, SUPERVISION, AND OVERSIGHT   263

A commercial institution responsible for clearing and settling payments on behalf of customers which represent, by value, a substantial percentage of payments in a particular currency, a significant proportion of which are internalised by being settled across the books of the institution rather than through an organised payment system.

Such institutions may have certain features of systemically important systems and, in particular, may raise similar risk issues. The values and volumes can, in some cases, be extremely large. There may therefore be a case for treating some aspects of the operations of quasi-systems in a way comparable to CSDs or SSSs.[25] This issue is still under consideration by central banks and other regulators.[26] However, large custodians are usually commercial banks that are subject to banking supervision. In such a situation, the bank supervisors must ensure that risks arising from such activities are properly recognized and controlled.

Beyond the role of large custodians, there is an increasing trend to subject other intermediary activities in respect of holding or transferring securities on behalf of third parties to regulation and, in particular, authorization requirements.[27] In an environment in which securities are held and settled through intermediaries, the protection of the rights of account holders as well as the ability to ensure the continuity of the relationship between the issuer and the investors depend heavily on the careful and diligent exercise of a number of duties by the intermediary.   9.28

Intermediaries play a key role by maintaining accounts on behalf of customers and are a natural part of any acquisition or disposition of securities held in book-entry form. Furthermore, their assistance is vital for the performance of the rights and obligations that exist mutually between an issuer and its investors in any holding structure other than for securities that are directly and exclusively registered with the issuer, and bearer securities where the certificate actually remains in the hands of the investor or in separate safe custody with another person. Against this background an intermediary should act honestly, fairly, and professionally in the best interests of the account holders, and take reasonable steps to ensure continuity and regularity in the performance of its obligations.[28] This entails, for example, the application of sound administrative and accounting procedures, internal control mechanisms, and effective control and safeguard arrangements for information processing systems. The intermediary should implement procedures and arrangements that provide for the prompt, fair, and expeditious   9.29

---

[25] CPSS and IOSCO, *Recommendations for SSSs*, 19.
[26] Group of Ten, *Financial Sector Consolidation*, 9, notes that 'central banks and bank supervisors should carefully monitor the impact of consolidation on the payment and settlement business, and should define safety standards where appropriate. In particular, central banks, in conjunction with bank supervisors, may need to consider various approaches, possibly including standards, that could be used to limit potential liquidity, credit and operational risks stemming from concentrated payment flows through a few very large players participating in payment systems'.
[27] See, eg, EC, *Second Consultation: Legislation on Securities*, Principle 21; see also Art 6(1) and Annex I, s B(1) of Directive 2014/65/EU on markets in financial instruments (recast) (MiFID II), according to which the provision of safekeeping and administration services in respect of financial instruments are considered as ancillary services, thus requiring a licence.
[28] See, eg, Arts 16 and 24(1) MiFID II and Art 5 MiFID Implementing Directive.

execution of the orders of the account holders. To foster such conduct, supervisory authorities should be equipped with sufficient powers to act, and should be able to rely on deterrent sanctioning regimes to be used against any unlawful conduct.

9.30 Arguments in favour of regulating such activities are driven by considerations of investor protection, in this case protection of account holders. It is generally accepted that in the event of the insolvency of the intermediary, its client (the account holder) needs effective protection against the loss of its holdings. From an insolvency point of view there are questions of extending insolvency privileges beyond the narrow scope of regulated financial entities. In practice, however, problems may arise in relation to the delimitation of activities that would fall under such a regulatory regime and those that would not, particularly if the concepts of account provision and securities account were defined in open terms.[29]

(6) Recovery and resolution regimes

9.31 In addition to the established frameworks for supervision and oversight discussed in sections B(4) and (5), there is one comparatively more recent development leading to further requirements to be imposed on intermediaries and CSDs or SSSs. These are requirements stemming from recovery and resolution planning. As a key lesson drawn from the global financial crisis, it was felt necessary to establish a regime that would allow a failing institution to recover, or, failing this, to be wound down in an orderly manner, where default could otherwise lead to systemic effects in the financial markets. Thus, as stipulated by the FSB in its *Key Attributes of Effective Resolution Regimes for Financial Institutions* of October 2011 (which were further completed in 2014), any financial institution that could be systemically significant or critical if it fails should be subject to a resolution regime in accordance with these Key Attributes. In this respect, CSDs and SSSs are deemed to be systemically relevant by default.[30] The classification of systemically relevant institutions entails *inter alia* that such an entity must have in place a recovery and resolution plan including, where relevant, a group resolution plan, containing all elements set out in Appendix I-Annex 4 to the Key Attributes,[31] and that it be subject to regular resolvability assessments.[32] While recovery planning may be incorporated to some degree in the ongoing oversight and supervision by competent supervisory or oversight authorities, resolution planning and assessment entails the involvement of a new category of authorities—dedicated resolution authorities.[33]

---

[29] See Legal Certainty Group, *Second Advice*.
[30] See CPSS and IOSCO, *Principles for FMIs*.
[31] Key Attribute 11.
[32] Key Attribute 10.
[33] On resolution planning, see also Ch 8.

(7) Co-operation and coordination of authorities

The number of authorities involved in the regulation, supervision, oversight, and resolution of intermediaries and infrastructures may cause practical issues. The competences and powers of the authorities need to be clearly defined. To avoid the parallel, repeated application of requirements, or even conflicting rules imposed on supervised and overseen entities, it is essential for relevant competent authorities to share information, consult closely, and co-operate with each other, and, where necessary, to co-ordinate their intended actions to avoid undue burdens being imposed on the entities concerned. There is a particular need for *ex ante* clarification of responsibilities and procedures for cooperation among authorities during crisis situations. **9.32**

While this is true at a national level, it is even more relevant in the case of globally active institutions or infrastructures. In the case of very large or complex, globally active groups, authorities with a statutory interest in the soundness of the regulated entity may not only include the direct domestic supervisors, overseers, and resolution authorities, but also, for example, domestic or foreign authorities responsible for the supervision of major participants. In the case of globally active infrastructures, in addition to the supervisors of major domestic or foreign participants, the supervisors and overseers of linked or interconnected FMIs, or the central banks issuing relevant settlement currencies, could claim a legitimate interest to be associated with any supervision and oversight activities, given the potential systemic impact on the participating or linked institutions or infrastructures, or even their domestic financial markets in general. **9.33**

In such an environment there is an even greater need to align conflicting objectives of authorities and to promote consistency of regulatory requirements and approaches. The cross-border implications increase the need for access to comprehensive and timely information about factors that may impact the safety and resilience of infrastructures, institutions, or markets. There is no global institutionalized framework for cooperation in this field. Given that such a framework would need some enforcement authority, binding disputes settlement, and sanctioning possibilities, it would have to be established by international treaty (comparable, for example, to the World Trade Organization (WTO)). In the absence of such a global construct, co-operation will have to continue to rely on bilateral or multilateral arrangements. **9.34**

Co-operation arrangements can take many forms, depending on the type of entity concerned and the number of authorities involved. They can be based on bilateral or multilateral treaties or memoranda of understanding and follow different approaches, such as home/host supervision structures[34] or primary responsibility overseer models.[35] Various forms of colleges of authorities, which can be based on single institution or group college models and have a national, regional,[36] or global composition, are **9.35**

---

[34] See BCBS, *Home-Host Supervisory Cooperation*, 2 et seq.
[35] See CPSS, *Central Bank Oversight*, 30 et seq.
[36] See Art 18 European Market Infrastructure Regulation (EMIR).

becoming increasingly widespread. Colleges can be formed between supervisors or overseers, or a combination of both.[37] The more complex or layered these cooperation structures are, the greater the need for a clear delimitation of the respective roles and responsibilities of all authorities involved.

9.36 Uncertainties about the treatment of activities (whether of market participants or of infrastructures) under various jurisdictions' regimes continue to be a pressing concern for market participants as regulatory requirements take effect. Where there are conflicts, inconsistencies, and gaps in the regulation of (cross-border) activities, this may create a need for, or otherwise incentivize, market participants or infrastructure providers to reorganize their activity along jurisdictional lines. In such a context, the existence of a globally consistent regulatory regime is also of the utmost relevance. Mutual adoption and recognition of the same internationally recognized standards plays an important role in reducing the risk of inconsistent or conflicting application of national policies and for supporting the resilience of the global financial system.

C. Requirements for Central Securities Depositories and Securities Settlement Systems

9.37 As noted in section B(4), CSDs and SSSs play a critical role in the financial system and the broader economy. These infrastructures facilitate the clearing, settlement, and recording of securities transactions. While safe and efficient FMIs contribute to the maintenance and promotion of financial stability and economic growth, they also concentrate risk. If not properly managed, FMIs can be sources of financial shocks, such as liquidity dislocations and credit losses, or a major channel through which these shocks are transmitted across domestic and international financial markets.

(1) CPMI-IOSCO principles for financial market infrastructures

9.38 In the area of FMIs, the CPMI and IOSCO are the relevant international standard setting bodies as recognized by the FSB.[38] To address the above-mentioned risks, the CPMI (until 2014 as CPSS) and IOSCO have, over the past 25 years, jointly established a series of international risk-management standards.

9.39 In November 2001, the CPSS and IOSCO jointly published the *Recommendations for Securities Settlement Systems* (RSSS). This report proposed 19 recommendations for promoting the safety and efficiency of SSSs.[39] The accompanying assessment

---

[37] They may even involve resolution authorities and ministries of finance in the case of crisis management or resolution groups.
[38] See the FSB's *Key Standards for Sound Financial Systems*, available at <https://www.fsb.org/work-of-the-fsb/about-the-compendium-of-standards/> (accessed 7 July 2021).
[39] The definition of the term 'securities settlement system' in the RSSS is the full set of institutional arrangements for confirmation, clearance, and settlement of securities trades and safekeeping of securities. This definition

methodology for the RSSS was subsequently published in November 2002. The RSSS followed the *Core Principles for Systemically Important Payment Systems* (CPSIPS), published by the CPSS in January 2001, which provided 10 principles for the safe and efficient design and operation of systemically important payment systems, as well as the *Report of the Committee on Interbank Netting Schemes of the Central Banks of the Group of Ten Countries* (also known as the *Lamfalussy Report*),[40] which was published in November 1990. In November 2004, building on the recommendations established in the RSSS, the CPSS and IOSCO published the *Recommendations for Central Counterparties* (RCCP), which provided 15 recommendations addressing the major types of risks faced by central counterparties (CCPs). A methodology for assessing a CCP's observance of each recommendation was included in the report.

In February 2010, the CPSS and IOSCO launched a comprehensive review of the existing sets of standards for FMIs, including the CPSIPS, RSSS, and RCCP, in support of the broader efforts of the G20 and the FSB to strengthen core financial infrastructures and markets by ensuring that gaps in existing international standards are identified and addressed. In March 2011, the CPSS and IOSCO issued a consultative draft and conducted extensive market consultation. The final document was published in April 2012 and incorporated the results of the market consultation as well as lessons learnt from the global financial crisis, the experience of using the existing international standards, and recent policy and analytical work by the CPMI/CPSS, IOSCO, BCBS, and others.

9.40

The new set of standards, the *Principles for Financial Market Infrastructures* (PFMI),[41] are now among the key standards for sound financial systems and are increasingly becoming the foundation of FMI-related regulation, supervision, and oversight activities. The PFMI incorporate the lessons drawn from global crisis experiences, setting more demanding requirements in many areas, and establishing new principles that were not or not fully addressed by previous standards.

9.41

The PFMI aim to offer consistency among requirements for different types of FMIs while reflecting the specific role of certain types of infrastructure (amongst which CSDs/SSSs). They contain 24 principles to be applied by FMIs on an ongoing basis in the operation of their business, including when reviewing their own performance, assessing or proposing new services, or proposing changes to risk controls. In addition, the PFMI contain five responsibilities for central banks, market regulators, and other relevant authorities for FMIs, and provide guidance for consistent and effective regulation, supervision, and oversight of FMIs. Authorities for FMIs should accept and be guided by the responsibilities in this report, consistent with relevant national law. While each individual FMI is responsible for observing these principles, effective

9.42

---

differs from the definition of SSS in the new *Principles for Financial Market Infrastructures* (PFMI), which is more narrowly defined (see s C(1)(a)).

[40] BIS, *Lamfalussy Report*.
[41] CPMI and IOSCO, *Principles for FMIs*.

regulation, supervision, and oversight are necessary to ensure observance and induce change.

9.43 FSB, CPMI, and IOSCO members have undertaken to adopt the principles in the PFMI and put them into effect. Moreover, the PFMI form the basis of assessments by the IMF and the World Bank for Financial Sector Assessment Programs (FSAPs).

9.44 The PFMI differ from previous standards by providing one single set of standards for payment, clearing, settlement, and recording systems. However, they recognize that FMIs differ significantly in terms of their organization, function, and design, and that FMIs can achieve a particular result in different ways. They adopt a functional approach to the applicability of the principles in the PFMI to different types of FMIs. At the same time, they adopt a holistic approach to the principles by having them build on and complement each other.

9.45 As a general theme, the PFMI introduce more demanding requirements and provide greater guidance as compared to previous standards. A number of important issues are addressed across several principles (for example, financial resources, recovery, fair and open access, tiered participation, and interdependencies).

9.46 The CPMI and IOSCO have complemented the PFMI with a number of complementary sets of expectations and guidance. Thus, a disclosure framework and an assessment methodology were published as *Principles for Financial Market Infrastructures: Disclosure Framework and Assessment Methodology* in December 2012.[42]

9.47 To foster completeness and consistency of the implementation process, since April 2013,[43] the CPMI and IOSCO are monitoring jurisdictions' progress towards adopting the legislation and other policies to implement the PFMI, including assessing the consistency of implementation measures in each jurisdiction with the PFMI and consistency of outcomes across jurisdictions.[44] The findings of this monitoring exercise, which revealed some instances of inconsistent implementation or differences of interpretation, in addition to considerations regarding the provision of expanded guidance on some key policy areas, have led to a number of supplementary documents by CPMI and IOSCO, most notably in the areas of FMI cyber resilience and FMI recovery (see sections C(1)(c)(vi) and C(3)(b)). These do not create additional standards for FMIs but provide guidance on how FMIs can observe the existing requirements laid down in the PFMI.

---

[42] CPSS and IOSCO, *FMIs: Disclosure Framework and Assessment Methodology*.
[43] BIS press release of 17 April 2013, available at <http://www.bis.org/press/p130417.htm> (accessed 7 July 2021).
[44] See the overview of activities by CPMI and IOSCO conducted so far under <https://www.bis.org/cpmi/info_mios.htm> (accessed 7 July 2021).

(a) Scope

The PFMI define an FMI as a multilateral system among participating institutions, including the operator of the system, used for the purposes of clearing, settling, or recording payments, securities, derivatives, or other financial transactions. FMIs typically establish a set of common rules and procedures for all participants, a technical infrastructure, and a specialized risk-management framework appropriate to the risks they incur. This definition includes both CSDs and SSSs, irrespective of whether they are publicly[45] or privately owned or operate under a particular form of banking or non-banking licence or authorization.

9.48

(i) Central securities depositories

More specifically, a CSD within the meaning of the PFMI is understood to provide securities accounts, central safekeeping services,[46] and asset services, which may include the administration of corporate actions and redemptions, and plays an important role in helping to ensure the integrity of securities issues. The precise activities of a CSD may, however, vary according to jurisdiction and market practices. For example, the activities of a CSD may depend on whether it operates in a jurisdiction with a direct or indirect holding arrangement, or a combination of both. A CSD may maintain the definitive record of legal ownership for a security; in some cases, however, a separate securities registrar will serve this notary function.[47] A CSD may hold securities either in physical form (but immobilized) or in dematerialized form. In many countries, a CSD also operates a securities settlement system, but, unless otherwise specified, the PFMI adopt a narrower definition of CSD that does not include securities settlement functions.[48]

9.49

---

[45] In exceptional cases the principles are applied differently to FMIs operated by central banks due to requirements in relevant law, regulation, or policy. For example, central banks may have separate public policy objectives and responsibilities for monetary and liquidity policies that take precedence. Such exceptional cases are referenced in (i) Principle 2 on governance, (ii) Principle 4 on credit risk, (iii) Principle 5 on collateral, (iv) Principle 15 on general business risk, and (v) Principle 18 on access and participation requirements. In some cases, FMIs operated by central banks may be required by the relevant legislative framework or by a central bank's public policy objectives to exceed the requirements of one or more principles: see PFMI 1.23, p 13.

[46] This function is characterized by being the central account provider for the entire market of the relevant financial instrument. A CSD enables market participants to deposit their securities by providing securities accounts on which transfers resulting from transactions are recorded. Linked to this function is the central administration of securities, for example, the processing of 'corporate actions' such as interest or dividend distribution, voting, splitting of shares, or tax services. Whether the role of CSDs in formatting corporate actions should be recognized within this central safekeeping function ('central administration'), or whether it should be attributed to the settlement function, is a matter that is open to discussion in many jurisdictions. On corporate actions, see also Ch 6.

[47] From a functional perspective, the notary function is characterized by maintaining the 'central' register for a particular issue to enable the settlement of the corresponding securities. The market refers to this central register for information on settled transactions. This function is present in all securities markets that have established a CSD. Importantly, the notary function should be distinguished from the function of keeping the central register for the issuer, which usually provides information on beneficial owners and/or end-investors, also referred to as the 'shareholders' or 'bondholders'. The latter function is not present in all securities markets (for example, bearer shares or debt instruments). Where it does exist, it can be performed by other entities that are not CSDs, eg, registrars.

[48] Compare this, for example, with the definition of CSD in Art 2(1)(1) of the EU CSD Regulation (CSDR), which defines a CSD by reference to certain core services, which consist of settlement, implying the operation of SSS, notary, and central securities accounts maintenance services. Furthermore, the CSDR contains certain limitation as to what kinds of additional services a CSD may offer; see Arts 2(1)(1) and 52 CSDR.

(ii) Securities settlement systems

9.50 For the purposes of the PFMI, an SSS enables securities to be transferred and settled by book entry according to a set of predetermined multilateral rules.[49] Such systems allow transfers of securities either free of payment or against payment. When a transfer is against payment, many systems provide delivery versus payment (DvP), where delivery of the security occurs if and only if payment occurs. An SSS may be organized to provide additional securities clearing and settlement functions, such as the confirmation of trade and settlement instructions.

(b) Governance and access

9.51 The PFMI emphasize[50] the need for adequate and transparent rules for governance and access in light of the complexity as well as the systemic nature of CSDs and SSSs and in view of the services they provide. The objectives of an FMI should place a high priority on the safety and efficiency of the FMI and explicitly support financial stability and other relevant public interest considerations.

(i) Governance

9.52 A CSD or SSS should have documented governance arrangements that provide clear and direct lines of responsibility and accountability. These arrangements should be disclosed to owners, relevant authorities, participants, and, at a more general level, the public.

9.53 The PFMI contain a number of expectations regarding governance arrangements, such as the clear roles and responsibilities of a board of directors (or equivalent), and documented procedures for its functioning, including procedures to identify, address, and manage members' conflicts of interest. A board should contain suitable members with the appropriate skills and incentives to fulfil its multiple roles. Further, the roles and responsibilities of management should be clearly specified. Management should possess the appropriate experience, a mix of skills, and the integrity necessary to discharge their responsibilities for operation and risk management.

9.54 The PFMI emphasize that the board should establish a clear, documented, risk-management framework that includes the FMI's risk-tolerance policy, assigns responsibilities and accountability for risk decisions, and addresses decision-making in crises and emergencies. Governance arrangements should ensure that the risk management and internal control functions have sufficient authority, independence, resources, and access to the board. Finally, there is an emphasis on transparency to ensure that the legitimate interests of direct and indirect participants and other relevant stakeholders are

---

[49] The definition of an SSS in the PFMI is narrower than that used in the old RSSS, which defined an SSS broadly to include the full set of institutional arrangements for confirmation, clearance, and settlement of securities trades and safekeeping of securities.

[50] Principles 2, 18, 19, and 20.

adequately taken into account, and that major decisions are clearly disclosed to stakeholders and, where there is a broad market impact, the public.[51]

(ii) Access and participation

Access to a CSD or SSS is important because of the critical role such FMIs play in the markets they serve. Access refers to the ability to use the services of a CSD or SSS and includes the direct use of the services by participants, including by other market infrastructures and, where relevant, service providers. To permit fair and open access, CSDs and SSSs should have publicly disclosed, transparent, objective, and non-discriminatory criteria for participation, which allow restricting access to the participants only on the basis of the risks involved.[52] The PFMI also expect the CSD or SSS to monitor compliance with its participation requirements on an ongoing basis and to have clearly defined and publicly disclosed procedures for facilitating the suspension and orderly exit of a participant that breaches, or no longer meets, the participation requirements.

9.55

Unlike previous international standards in this field, the PFMI establish explicit expectations regarding risks resulting from tiered participation. Tiered participation arrangements occur when market participants rely on the services provided by other market participants (that are direct participants) to access the services of a CSD or SSS. Operational dependencies between direct participants and their clients could affect the smooth functioning of the FMI, as in the case of an FMI with a few direct participants and many indirectly connected market participants, or a large client operating through a small direct participant. The failure or default of such a client may affect the credit and liquidity needs of the direct participant, or create uncertainty about whether a client's transactions have been settled or will be settled and whether settled transactions can be unwound. In response, Principle 19 provides guidance on how an FMI should address risks to itself arising from tiered participation arrangements.[53] To the extent that it is expected that an FMI should identify material dependencies between direct participants and their clients that might affect the FMI, this is placing considerable responsibility on a CSD and SSS to identify and, where necessary, mitigate risks, for example, resulting from the concentration of values or volumes with certain indirectly connected clients.

9.56

Moreover, the PFMI address risks resulting from interdependencies, including interoperability between FMIs. Thus, Principle 20 explicitly addresses links (such as links between two CSDs) and their risk management.[54] Linked CSDs should identify, monitor,

9.57

---

[51] See PFMI, pp 26 et seq.

[52] The participation requirements should be tailored to and be commensurate with the FMI's specific risks, and be publicly disclosed. Subject to maintaining acceptable risk control standards, an FMI should endeavour to set requirements that have the least-restrictive impact on access that circumstances permit: see PFMI, Key expectation 2 to Principle 18.

[53] Additional issues relating to indirect participants are addressed in (i) Principle 1 on legal basis, (ii) Principle 2 on governance, (iii) Principle 3 on the framework for the comprehensive management of risks, (iv) Principle 13 on participant-default rules and procedures, (v) Principle 14 on segregation and portability, (vi) Principle 18 on access and participation requirements, and (vii) Principle 23 on disclosure of rules, key procedures, and market data.

[54] In addition, interdependencies are covered in (i) Principle 2 on governance, which states that FMIs should consider the interests of the broader markets, (ii) Principle 3 on the framework for the comprehensive management of risks, which states that FMIs should consider the relevant risks that they incur from and pose to other

and manage the credit and liquidity risks arising from the linked entity. In addition, any credit extensions between CSDs should be covered fully by high-quality collateral and be subject to limits.[55] Further, some practices are seen to merit particularly rigorous attention and controls. In particular, provisional transfers of securities between linked CSDs should be prohibited or, at a minimum, the re-transfer of provisionally transferred securities should be prohibited prior to the transfer becoming final. Further elements considered include robust reconciliation procedures needed to ensure accurate records and the management of risks associated with the use of an intermediary to access another CSD.

(c) Risk management

9.58 Particular attention is paid by the PFMI to the management of risks by FMIs. A sound risk-management framework should identify the range of risks that an FMI faces and should appropriately address these risks. The types of risk to be covered are comprehensive and include legal, credit, liquidity, settlement, general business, operational, custody and investment, and reputational risks. The management of cyber risks as well as risks resulting from the reliance on third-party providers have also become increasingly important. Potential sources of risks can be, for example, direct participants or their customers, other FMIs, or liquidity or service providers. The PFMI consider that there is a need for a holistic risk management view, with the components to address these risks consisting *inter alia* of the FMI design, its policies and procedures, information and control systems, as well as recovery and resolution plans. Some selected aspects of the PFMI's expectations for risk management are presented below.

(i) Legal risk

9.59 A robust legal basis for an FMI's activities in all relevant jurisdictions is critical to an FMI's overall soundness. If the legal basis for an FMI's activities and operations is inadequate, uncertain, or opaque, then the FMI, its participants, and their customers may face unintended, uncertain, or unmanageable credit or liquidity risks, which may also create or amplify systemic risks. Thus, according to the PFMI, an FMI should have a well-founded, clear, transparent, and enforceable legal basis for each material aspect of its activities in all relevant jurisdictions. For a risk management to be effective, the

---

entities, (iii) Principle 17 on operational risk, which states that an FMI should identify, monitor, and manage the risks that other FMIs pose to its operations and the risks its operations pose to other FMIs, (iv) Principle 18 on access and participation requirements, which states that FMIs should provide fair and open access, including to other FMIs, (v) Principle 21 on efficiency and effectiveness, which states that FMIs should be designed to meet the needs of their participants, and (vi) Principle 22 on communication procedures and standards, which states that FMIs should use, or at a minimum accommodate, relevant internationally accepted communication procedures and standards. The combination of these principles is aimed at achieving a strong and balanced approach to interoperability.

[55] In exceptional cases, other adequate collateral may be used to secure credit extensions between CSDs subject to the review and assessment by the relevant authorities. See also Principle 4 on credit risk, Principle 5 on collateral, and Principle 7 on liquidity risk.

enforceability of rights and obligations relating to an FMI and its risk management have to be established with a high degree of certainty.

For a CSD or SSS, the rights and interests of the FMI itself, its participants, and, where relevant, its participants' customers should be clearly articulated and the legal basis should fully protect both a participant's assets held in custody by the CSD or SSS and, where appropriate, a participant customer's assets held by or through the system from the insolvency of relevant parties and other relevant risks. It should also protect these assets when they are held with a custodian or linked FMI. Collateral arrangements may involve either a pledge or a title transfer, including transfer of full ownership, provided there is certainty about their validity and enforceability,[56] including in cases of insolvency.[57]   **9.60**

Particular attention is paid to settlement finality[58] and netting[59] as important building blocks of risk-management systems. The laws of the relevant jurisdictions should support the provisions of the FMI's legal agreements with its participants and settlement banks relating to finality and netting arrangements.[60]   **9.61**

Further, the rules, procedures, and contracts related to an FMI's operation should be enforceable in all relevant jurisdictions[61] and the FMI should identify and analyse potential conflict-of-laws issues and develop rules and procedures to mitigate this risk.[62]   **9.62**

(ii) Credit and liquidity risk

An SSS or its participants may face credit and liquidity risks arising from the system's processes. Credit risk is the risk that a counterparty will be unable fully to meet its financial obligations when due or at any time in the future. Liquidity risk is the risk that a counterparty will have insufficient funds to meet its financial obligations when due, but   **9.63**

---

[56] In case of a pledge, there should be a high degree of certainty that the pledge has been validly created in the relevant jurisdiction and validly perfected, if necessary. If an FMI relies on a title transfer, including transfer of full ownership, it should have a high degree of certainty that the transfer is validly created in the relevant jurisdiction and will be enforced as agreed and not recharacterized, for example, as an invalid or unperfected pledge or some other unintended category of transaction. An FMI should also have a high degree of certainty that the transfer itself is not voidable as an unlawful preference under insolvency law. See also Principle 5 on collateral, Principle 6 on margin, and Principle 13 on participant-default rules and procedures.

[57] For example, the EU Settlement Finality Directive provided for the insulation of a securities settlement system against the disruption caused by insolvency proceedings against a participant in that system.

[58] See also Principle 8.

[59] In the case of CSDs and SSSs, netting arrangements may include close-out netting arrangements with participants, but also, to the extent that a system relies, for example, on net settlement, multilateral netting arrangements on an end-of-day or continuous basis.

[60] See the UNIDROIT Principles on the Enforceability of Close-Out Netting Provisions; and see Ch 3.

[61] The PFMI note that in general there is no substitute for a sound legal basis and full legal certainty. In some practical situations, however, full legal certainty may not be achievable. In this case, the authorities may need to take steps to address the legal framework. Pending this action, an FMI should investigate steps to mitigate its legal risk through the selective use of alternative risk-management tools that do not suffer from the legal uncertainty identified.

[62] These could include, in appropriate circumstances and if legally enforceable, participant requirements, exposure limits, collateral requirements, and prefunded default arrangements. The use of such tools may limit an FMI's exposure if its activities are found to be unsupported by relevant laws and regulations. If such controls are insufficient or infeasible, an FMI could apply activity limits and, in extreme circumstances, restrict access or not perform the problematic activity until the legal situation is addressed: see PFMI, Principle 1.

may be able to do so at some time in the future. Although credit and liquidity risks are distinct concepts, there is often significant interaction between them.

9.64 The PFMI state that an FMI should establish a robust framework to manage its credit exposures to its participants and the credit risks arising from its payment, clearing, and settlement processes. Credit exposure may arise from current exposures (ie, the loss an FMI would face immediately if a participant were to default), potential future exposures (ie, an estimate of credit exposure an FMI could face at a future point in time), or both.[63] In the case of an SSS, a current exposure may result from the extension of intra-day credit by the system to its participants. Further, an SSS faces potential future exposures if the value of collateral securing an extension of intra-day credit could fall below the amount of credit extended, leaving a residual exposure. The PFMI expect an SSS to fully cover exposures to each participant with a high degree of confidence. This means that an SSS must strive to collect collateral or maintain other resources with value equal to or greater than the current and potential future exposures to each participant and should apply 'haircuts' to that collateral to mitigate potential future exposure. For deferred net settlement systems[64] where there is no settlement guarantee (provided either by the SSS itself or by the participants), but where participants face credit exposures arising from the SSS's processes, the SSS should maintain resources to cover the exposures of the two participants and their affiliates that would create the largest aggregate credit exposure in the system.

9.65 Requirements with respect to liquidity risk are similar to those for credit risk, with a few key differences. An SSS, including one employing a deferred net settlement mechanism, is required to maintain sufficient liquid resources in all relevant currencies to effect same-day settlement of payment obligations, and, where appropriate, intra-day or multi-day settlement. The resources should withstand at least the default of the participant and its affiliates that would generate the largest aggregate payment obligation in extreme but plausible market conditions. SSSs are required to perform stress testing of their liquid resources.

(iii) Custody risk and segregation

9.66 The PFMI devote particular attention to the specific and unique risks that could arise in a CSD with regard to the protection of securities and ensuring the integrity of securities issues. Preserving the rights of issuers and holders of securities lies at the heart of the orderly functioning of a securities market. As a general principle, a CSD should have appropriate rules and procedures to help ensure the integrity of securities issues and minimize and manage the risks associated with the safekeeping and transfer of securities.[65]

---

[63] See PFMI, Principle 4.
[64] See PFMI, Principle 4, 3.4.9.
[65] See PFMI, Principle 11. On custody risk and segregation, see also Ch 7.

Specifically, a CSD should employ appropriate procedures and controls to safeguard the rights of securities issuers and holders, prevent the unauthorized creation or deletion of securities, and conduct periodic (at least daily) reconciliation of the securities issues it maintains. This includes in particular the application of robust accounting practices and end-to-end auditing to verify that its records are accurate and provide a complete accounting of its securities issues. **9.67**

Further, to safeguard the integrity of the securities issues, a CSD should conduct periodic (at least daily) reconciliation of the totals of securities issues in the CSD for each issuer (or its issuing agent), and ensure that the total number of securities recorded in the CSD for a particular issue is equal to the amount of securities of that issue held on the CSD's books.[66] It should protect assets against custody risk, including the risk of loss due to the CSD's negligence, misuse of assets, fraud, poor administration, inadequate recordkeeping, or failure to protect a participant's interests in securities, or because of the CSD's insolvency or claims by the CSD's creditors. **9.68**

A CSD should prohibit overdrafts and debit balances in securities accounts to avoid credit risk and to reduce the potential for the creation of securities. This is because if a CSD were to allow overdrafts or a debit balance in a participant's securities account in order to credit another participant's securities account, it would effectively be creating securities and would affect the integrity of the securities issue. **9.69**

A CSD should maintain securities in an immobilized or dematerialized form for their transfer by book entry to the extent possible under applicable law in order to improve efficiency through increased automation and to reduce the risk of errors and delays in processing. **9.70**

As regards segregation requirements, the PFMI expect a CSD to employ a robust system that ensures the segregation of assets belonging to the CSD from securities belonging to its participants. It also stipulates that the CSD should segregate participants' securities from those of other participants by the provision of separate accounts. Where supported by the legal framework, a CSD should also operationally support the segregation of securities belonging to a participant's customers on the participant's books and facilitate the transfer of customer holdings to another participant. **9.71**

(iv) Collateral and money settlement
To the extent that an SSS is using collateral, the PFMI expect it to be subject to the same principles that apply to other types of FMIs. An FMI should routinely only accept assets as collateral that have low credit, liquidity, and market risks.[67] It should establish prudent valuation practices to gain adequate assurance of its collateral's value in the event **9.72**

---

[66] Reconciliation may require coordination with other entities if the CSD does not (or does not exclusively) record the issuance of the security or is not the official registrar of the security. If the CSD is not the official securities registrar for the securities issuer, reconciliation with the official securities registrar should be required.
[67] See PFMI, Principle 5.

of its liquidation. The relevant FMI rules and processes should include daily marking-to-market of collateral, and ensure that haircuts reflect the potential decline in values and liquidity over the interval between their last revaluation and the time when an FMI can reasonably assume that the assets can be liquidated. The FMI should regularly test its valuation practices and incorporate assumptions into stress test scenarios about collateral value during stressed market conditions (including extreme price moves and changes in market liquidity). In order to reduce the need for pro-cyclical adjustments, an FMI should establish stable, conservative haircuts that are calibrated to include periods of stressed market conditions, to the extent that this is practicable and prudent. An FMI should avoid concentrated holdings of certain assets and ensure that the collateral can be used in a timely manner. Further, an FMI should disclose its policies on the re-use of collateral (ie, the use of collateral that has been provided by participants in the normal course of business).[68]

9.73 As regards its money settlements, an SSS should use central bank money, where practical and available, to avoid credit and liquidity risks.[69] The use of central bank money, however, may not always be practical or available.[70] If an SSS instead uses a commercial bank for its money settlements, it should monitor, manage, and limit its credit and liquidity risks arising from the commercial settlement bank.[71] Further, if money settlement does not occur in central bank money and the SSS conducts money settlements on its own books, it should minimize and strictly control its credit and liquidity risks. In such an arrangement, an FMI offers cash accounts to its participants, and a payment or settlement obligation is discharged by providing an FMI's participant with a direct claim on the FMI itself. The credit and liquidity risks associated with a claim on an FMI are therefore directly related to the FMI's overall credit and liquidity risks.[72]

---

[68] The PFMI do not prohibit re-use outright, but an FMI should not rely on the re-use of collateral to increase or maintain profitability. On financial collateral, see also Ch 2.

[69] Central banks have the lowest credit risk and are the source of liquidity in their currency of issue. Indeed, one of the fundamental purposes of central banks is to provide a safe and liquid settlement asset: see PFMI, Principle 9.

[70] For example, an FMI or its participants may not have direct access to all relevant central bank accounts and payment services. A multi-currency FMI that has access to all relevant central bank accounts and payment services may find that some central bank payment services do not operate, or provide finality, at such times as it needs to make money settlements.

[71] For example, an FMI should limit both the probability of being exposed to a commercial settlement bank's failure and the potential losses and liquidity pressures to which it would be exposed in the event of such a failure. An FMI should establish and monitor adherence to strict criteria for its commercial settlement banks that take into account, among other things, their regulation and supervision, creditworthiness, capitalization, access to liquidity, and operational reliability. A commercial settlement bank should be subject to effective banking regulation and supervision. It should also be creditworthy, well capitalized, and have ample liquidity from the marketplace or the central bank of issue.

[72] One way an FMI could minimize these risks is to limit its activities and operations to clearing and settlement and closely related processes. Further, to settle payment obligations, the FMI could be established as a supervised, special-purpose financial institution and limit the provision of cash accounts to participants only. In some cases, an FMI can further mitigate risk by having participants fund and defund their cash accounts at the FMI using central bank money. In such an arrangement, an FMI is able to back the settlements conducted on its own books with balances that it holds in its account at the central bank: see PFMI, Principle 9.

(v) General business and operational risk

As regards the general business risk,[73] the PFMI expect that an FMI should maintain liquid net assets funded by equity equal to at least six months of current operating expenses. The actual amount held (which should be regularly reviewed) should be determined by the FMI's general risk profile and the length of time required to achieve a recovery or orderly wind-down of its critical operations and services (as projected in its recovery or orderly wind-down plan). The actual amount held should be reviewed periodically using a variety of scenarios and the calculation of operating expenses for these purposes may exclude depreciation and amortization expenses. Liquid net assets held for these purposes cannot be used for any other purpose. However, equity held under international risk-based capital standards should be included where relevant and appropriate to avoid duplicate capital requirements. Further, an FMI's capital plan should specify how it would raise new capital if its equity capital were to fall close to or below the amount needed.

9.74

In respect of operational risk, the PFMI[74] expect CSDs and SSSs to take a holistic approach when establishing their operational risk-management framework. Here, operational risk is the risk that deficiencies in information systems, internal processes, and personnel, or disruptions from external events will result in the reduction, deterioration, or breakdown of services provided by an FMI. Operational failures may damage an FMI's reputation, lead to legal consequences, result in financial losses, and may even cause systemic risk.

9.75

In consequence, particular emphasis is given to an FMI's operational risk-management framework, which should be reviewed, audited, and tested periodically as well as after significant changes. Specific requirements are set as to the scalable capacity of an FMI adequately to handle increasing stress volumes and to achieve its service-level objectives. Of growing practical relevance are the comprehensive physical and information security policies that address all potential vulnerabilities and threats, including cyber attacks (see paragraphs 9.77–9). In order to avoid potentially systemic disruptions, an FMI should have a business continuity plan that addresses events posing a significant risk of disrupting operations. This plan should entail a number of key elements, including the use of a secondary site. It should be designed to ensure that critical IT systems can resume operations within two hours following disruptive events and enable the FMI to complete settlement by the end of the day of the disruption, even in extreme circumstances.

9.76

(vi) Cyber resilience of FMIs

Cyber security has become a topic of critical importance for FMIs and the broader financial sector. Disruptions in one FMI may spread to a multitude of other connected entities. Furthermore, cyber threats tend to be cross-jurisdictional in nature, posing

9.77

---

[73] See PFMI, Principle 3.
[74] See PFMI, Principle 17.

challenges for risk mitigation efforts conducted solely at national or single-institution level. Given the critical role of FMIs, in 2014, the CPMI analysed the relevance of cyber security issues for FMIs and their overseers within the context of the PFMI.[75] The CPMI noted that while cyber resilience has increasingly become a top priority within FMIs, there are differences as to the form and maturity of FMIs' approaches to cyber resilience. Approaches frequently attempt to combine different factors, such as people, technology, processes, and communication. Furthermore, a variety of preventive, detective, and recovery measures may be deployed to cope with different forms of threats, ranging from threats to confidentiality and availability of services to integrity of data.

9.78 In June 2016, CPMI and IOSCO released a guidance on cyber resilience for FMIs.[76] The guidance aims to contribute to the ongoing efforts of industry and authorities to enhance the FMIs' ability to pre-empt cyber attacks, to respond rapidly and effectively to them, and achieve faster and safer target recovery objectives if they succeed. In doing so, the guidance sets out the kind of measures that FMIs should undertake to enhance their cyber resilience capabilities in order to limit the risks that cyber threats pose to FMIs and thereby to financial stability. It also provides authorities with a set of internationally agreed guidelines to support consistent and effective oversight and supervision of FMIs in the area of cyber risk. The guidance builds on and is supplemental to the PFMI, primarily in the context of governance (Principle 2), the framework for the comprehensive management of risks (Principle 3), settlement finality (Principle 8), operational risk (Principle 17), and FMI links (Principle 20).

9.79 The guidance highlights a number of key considerations that are deemed central to an efficient cyber resilience framework. As for any type of operational risk, the ability of an FMI to resume operations quickly and safely after a successful cyber attack is paramount. This entails rigorous planning and pre-established processes. FMIs should make use of good-quality threat intelligence and rigorous testing and have an established process of continuous improvements. CPMI and IOSCO consider that board and senior management attention is critical to a successful cyber resilience strategy. A further key element of the guidance is the emphasis on cooperation and information sharing, as cyber resilience is not achievable by an FMI in isolation; rather it is a market-wide collective endeavour. The cyber guidance complements, but does not establish additional standards for FMIs beyond those already set out in the PFMI.

(2) Disclosure framework

9.80 Public dissemination of rules, key procedures, and market data promotes the understanding of an FMI by all stakeholders, underpins investor protection, and facilitates the exercise of market discipline. This is reflected in the PFMI, which in Principle 23

---

[75] CPMI, *Cyber Resilience*.
[76] CPMI and IOSCO, *Guidance on Cyber Resilience*.

inter alia require FMIs to provide sufficient information to enable participants to have an accurate understanding of the risks, fees, and other material costs they incur by participating in the FMI. Further, all relevant rules and key procedures should be publicly disclosed.

To complement Principle 23, the CPSS and IOSCO provided further guidance to FMIs regarding the expected disclosure framework, prescribing the form and content of the disclosures expected of FMIs. This guidance was published together with an assessment methodology for the PFMI in December 2012 and titled *Principles for Financial Market Infrastructures: Disclosure Framework and Assessment Methodology*. The disclosure framework outlines the basic information that an FMI should disclose to increase transparency of its governance, risk management, and operations. Disclosure should aim at providing participants, authorities, and the public with a comprehensive understanding of the FMI with a view to facilitate comparisons across FMIs, including the FMI's organization, markets served, key metrics, recent changes to the FMI's design and services, and, more generally, the FMI's approach to observing each of the applicable principles in the PFMI. 9.81

Principle 23 of the PFMI expects FMIs to complete the disclosure framework on a regular basis and to disclose answers publicly. A template sets out the elements the FMI should provide: an executive summary of the key points for disclosure; a summary of major changes since the last update; a description of the FMI's function and the markets it serves; basic data and performance statistics on its services and operations; a description of the FMI's general organization, legal and regulatory framework, and system design and operations; a comprehensive narrative disclosure for each applicable principle with sufficient detail and context to enable a reader to understand the FMI's approach to observing the principle; and a list of publicly available resources, including those referenced in the disclosure, which may help a reader understand the FMI and its approach to observing each applicable principle. 9.82

(3) FMI recovery and resolution

Another, complementary work stream relates to the provision of further guidance on the protection against disorderly failures of FMIs, including CSDs and SSSs. Recovery and resolution of FMIs are closely interrelated, with the set of tools and resources that are available strongly overlapping or even being identical. Thus, CPMI and IOSCO as the relevant bodies for regulatory standards on FMI recovery and the FSB being responsible for global guidance on resolution of FMIs coordinated their approaches in this regard. 9.83

(a) FMI resolution
The global work in the domain of resolution is being led by the FSB, which has been working on principles for the resolution of systemically important financial institutions, 9.84

leading to the publication of the *Key Attributes of Effective Resolution Regimes for Financial Institutions* of November 2011, with further work being undertaken on a related Assessment Methodology.[77] The Key Attributes are an 'umbrella' standard for resolution regimes for all types of financial institutions that are potentially systemically significant or critical in failure.[78]

9.85 When the FSB adopted the Key Attributes in 2011, it was agreed to develop further guidance on their implementation, taking into account in particular sector-specific considerations, such as for insurers or FMIs, to promote effective and consistent implementation across jurisdictions. Towards this end, a CPSS-IOSCO consultative report of July 2012[79] looked at recovery and resolution tools and further issues to be taken into account for different types of FMIs, including CSDs and SSSs, when putting in place effective recovery and resolution regimes for FMIs. Consequently, in October 2014, the FSB published a revision of the Key Attributes[80] including sector-specific guidance that sets out how the Key Attributes should be applied in the context of insurers, FMIs, and the protection of client assets in resolution. The FMI Annex to the Key Attributes[81] is complemented with FMI-related specifications in the updated Assessment Methodology to the Key Attributes.

9.86 The FMI annex to the Key Attributes contains guidance elements for the resolution of FMIs and is complemented by an additional section on the resolution of FMI participants.[82] While the key objective for FMIs remains to ensure continuity of critical FMI functions without exposing taxpayers to loss from solvency support,[83] there may be instances where restoring the ability of the FMI to perform those functions as a going concern is not possible and instead it is necessary to ensure the performance of those functions by another entity or arrangement coupled with the orderly wind-down of the FMI in resolution.[84] This requires FMIs to be subject to resolution regimes that apply the objectives and provisions of the Key Attributes in a manner as appropriate to FMIs and their critical role in financial markets.

9.87 Accordingly, such resolution regimes should empower the resolution authority to enable the timely completion of payment, clearing and settlement functions by an FMI throughout the period that it is in resolution, including the day it enters into resolution. The regime should also enable authorities to preserve critical functions by restructuring and restoring the FMI's ability to provide those services as a going concern, arranging

---

[77] FSB, *Consultative Document: Key Attributes Assessment Methodology*.
[78] On insolvency regimes in the US and the UK following the insolvency of Lehman Brothers, see Ch 8.
[79] CPSS and IOSCO, *Recovery and Resolution of FMIs: Consultative Report* (2012).
[80] FSB, *Key Attributes* (2014).
[81] FSB, *Key Attributes* (2014), Appendix II-Annex 1, 57 et seq.
[82] FSB, *Key Attributes* (2014), Appendix II-Annex 1, 71–4.
[83] This key objective is also expressed in FSB, *Key Attributes Assessment Methodology*, 16.
[84] FSB, *Key Attributes* (2014), Appendix II-Annex 1, 58, s 1.1. Thus, entry into resolution should be possible, subject to determination by the relevant authorities, if the recovery plan and loss allocation procedures have failed to return the FMI to viability or have not been implemented in a timely manner, or if, even though the recovery plan may not yet have been fully implemented, recovery measures are not reasonably likely to return the FMI to viability or would otherwise be likely to compromise financial stability.

their orderly transfer to another FMI or bridge institution, or provide participants sufficient time to establish and move to an alternative arrangement.

Key issues in the FMI annex include the continuity of the process for settlement and application of the relevant finality rules; tools for the application of margin haircuts and contract tear-ups, the continuity and timely completion of critical payment, clearing, and settlement functions, and the settlement of obligations due to participants and to any linked FMI and the non-application of moratoria in that respect; and the temporary stay on early termination rights. The FMI annex further addresses the issue of the powers of resolution authorities, appropriate resolution strategies and plans, as well as guidance on access to information and information sharing. 9.88

Particular attention has been paid to the exercise of early termination rights (such as under close-out netting arrangements) by FMI participants. In accordance with Key Attribute 4,[85] early termination rights should not be exercisable by any participant in an FMI or other counterparties under a financial contract solely by virtue of the entry into resolution of, or the exercise of any resolution power in relation to, an FMI. However, such rights should remain exercisable where the FMI (or the authority, administrator, receiver, or other person exercising control over the FMI in resolution) fails to meet payment or delivery obligations, including collateral transfers, when due in accordance with its rules, but subject to any application of loss allocation to margin or collateral under the rules of the FMI or through the exercise of statutory loss allocation powers. Further, in accordance with Key Attribute 4, the resolution authority should have the power temporarily to stay any early termination rights exercisable by FMI participants and other relevant counterparties, and, where appropriate, regarding the objectives of the resolution procedure, by the FMI itself. When considering whether to impose a temporary stay on the exercise by FMI participants and other relevant counterparties of early termination rights and set-off rights triggered by entry into resolution of the FMI, the resolution authority should take into account the impact on the financial markets and on the safe and orderly operations of the FMI and any linked FMI.[86] 9.89

(b) FMI recovery
CPMI and IOSCO have been looking at the appropriate framework for FMI recovery and the requirements for recovery planning by FMIs. Following the consultative report on recovery and resolution of July 2012[87] (see paragraph 9.85), a draft report on FMI recovery planning issued for consultation in August 2013,[88] and taking into account 9.90

---

[85] Key Attribute 4.2 proposes that the 'entry into resolution and the exercise of any resolution powers should not trigger statutory or contractual set-off rights' or constitute an event enabling 'any counterparty to exercise contractual acceleration or early termination rights provided the substantive obligations under the contract continue to be performed'. Key Attribute 4.3 further provides that in the event that such rights are nonetheless exercisable, the resolution authority shall be entitled to temporarily stay such rights 'where they arise by reason only of entry into resolution or in connection with the exercise of any resolution powers'.
[86] Principle 8 of the 2013 UNIDROIT Principles on the Operation of Close-Out Netting Provisions recognizes these regulatory developments. See also Ch 2, s C and Ch 3, s D(6).
[87] CPSS and IOSCO, *Recovery and Resolution of FMIs: Consultative Report* (2012).
[88] CPSS and IOSCO, *Recovery of FMIs: Consultative Report* (2013).

comments received,[89] this resulted in the final report by CPMI and IOSCO on FMI recovery of October 2014.[90] This report supplements the PFMIs by providing guidance on how FMIs can observe the requirements laid down in Principle 3 of the PFMIs to have effective recovery plans. The CPMI-IOSCO report on FMI recovery was published simultaneously with the FMI annex on resolution (see paragraph 9.85 et seq) to provide a comprehensive set of guidance on recovery and resolution for systemically important FMIs.

9.91 The aim of the CPMI-IOSCO FMI recovery report is to provide additional guidance to FMIs on the development of comprehensive plans to enable them to recover from threats to their viability and financial strength which may prevent them from continuing to provide critical services, such as clearing and settlement, to their participants and the markets they serve. The report also aims to provide guidance to relevant authorities in carrying out their responsibilities associated with the development and implementation of recovery plans and tools. Given the criticality of the functions performed by FMIs, particular emphasis is given to maintaining or restoring the viability of a FMI as opposed to its winding-down.

9.92 The report further provides guidance on the recovery planning process and the content of recovery plans. It provides an overview of tools that an FMI may include in its recovery plan,[91] including a discussion of scenarios that may trigger the use of recovery tools and characteristics of appropriate recovery tools in the context of such scenarios (including tools to allocate uncovered losses caused by participant default; tools to address uncovered liquidity shortfalls; tools to replenish financial resources; or tools to allocate losses not related to participant default). Some or all of these tools may be used, also taking into account regulatory guidance in that respect, in different combinations or sequences by different FMIs and under different scenarios.

9.93 The basic principle is that an FMI should have a set of recovery tools that is comprehensive and effective in allowing the FMI, where relevant, to allocate any uncovered losses and cover any liquidity shortfalls. The set of tools should include plausible means of addressing unbalanced positions and replenishing financial resources, including the FMI's own capital, in order to continue to provide critical services. Each tool should be effective in the sense of being timely, reliable, and having a strong legal basis. The tools should be transparent and designed to allow those who would bear losses and liquidity shortfalls to measure, manage, and control their potential exposure. They should create appropriate incentives for the FMI's owners, participants, and other relevant stakeholders to control the amount of risk that they bring to or incur in the system, monitor the FMI's risk-taking and risk-management activities, and assist in the FMI's default management process. Finally, the tools should also be designed to minimize

---

[89] <http://www.bis.org/publ/cpss109/comments.htm> (accessed 7 July 2021).
[90] CPMI and IOSCO, *Recovery of FMIs: Final Report* (2014).
[91] CPMI and IOSCO, *Recovery of FMIs: Final Report* (2014), 12 et seq.

D. Market-wide Recommendations and Requirements for Intermediaries

Regulatory obligations imposed on intermediaries and market participants more widely are an essential corollary of, and are interrelated with, any regulatory regime applicable to CSDs and SSSs. Only to the extent that there are consistent and appropriate regulatory rules covering the full chain of securities holding or transfer will there be some assurance that the rights of holders of intermediated securities are adequately safeguarded.

9.94

However, compared to the comprehensive and detailed set of international principles for CSDs and SSSs (see section C), the global regulatory regime for the conduct of activities of securities intermediaries appears to be still more high-level and focused on specific aspects rather than on a holistic perspective.

9.95

(1) Geneva Securities Convention

In this respect, it is recalled that the GSC contains an enumeration of key obligations towards account holders with which an intermediary should comply. While Article 10(1) GSC contains a general duty of the intermediary to 'take appropriate measures to enable its account holders to receive and exercise the rights specified in Article 9(1)', Article 10(2) contains a non-exhaustive list of six core obligations that are deemed to be relevant for the protection and exercise of the rights of account holders.[92]

9.96

---

[92] Article 10 GSC, on 'Measures to enable the exercise of rights', states:
  2. An intermediary must, at least:
  (a) protect securities credited to a securities account, as provided in Article 24;
  (b) allocate securities or intermediated securities to the rights of its account holders so as to be unavailable to its creditors, as provided in Article 25;
  (c) give effect to any instructions given by the account holder or other authorised person, as provided by the non-Convention law, the account agreement or the uniform rules of a securities settlement system;
  (d) not dispose of securities credited to a securities account without authorisation, as provided in Article 15;
  (e) regularly pass on to account holders information relating to intermediated securities, including information necessary for account holders to exercise rights, if provided by the non-Convention law, the account agreement or the uniform rules of a securities settlement system; and
  (f) regularly pass on to account holders dividends and other distributions received in relation to intermediated securities, if provided by the non-Convention law, the account agreement or the uniform rules of a securities settlement system.

9.97 It should be noted that the wording of Article 10 GSC deviates somewhat from the approach taken in the remainder of the Convention, in that it specifies obligations in a way that could not be directly implemented.[93] Instead, Article 10 has to be read in conjunction with Article 28 GSC, which stipulates that the obligations of an intermediary under the Convention, including the manner in which it has to comply, may be specified in non-Convention law and, if permitted, by contractual agreements. Typically, such obligations are specified in regulatory regimes set by competent supervisory authorities in charge of supervising the conduct of business of intermediaries.

(2) Client asset protection

9.98 Some of the aspects enumerated in the GSC are being addressed by global regulatory standards, in particular as regards client asset protection. The main international standard-setting body in this sphere is IOSCO.[94]

9.99 Client assets are held by different types of entities in the course of different financial activities and services, including safeguarding, administration and custody, and collateral taking in connection with other financial transactions. National regimes for client asset protection vary significantly in the methods by which client assets are protected because such protection depends on the particularities of the laws defining property rights and resolution and insolvency regimes in each jurisdiction. IOSCO[95] classifies client asset protection regimes in three broad categories, 'custodial regimes', 'trust regimes', and 'agency regimes', based on the legal nature of the relationship between the firm and its clients with respect to client assets. Moreover, the definition of a 'client asset' that is subject to a particular form of protection and rights varies across jurisdictions.

(a) IOSCO high-level principles

9.100 As early as 1996, IOSCO issued a report on high-level principles for client asset protection[96] in recognition of its importance to investor protection and to confidence in markets in which customers know that their assets will be protected so far as practicable from the risk of loss at the level of an intermediary. The report outlines the techniques that can be used to protect clients' assets in the event of the insolvency of an authorized firm and analyses three types of techniques, which seek to ensure that client assets are treated in a more favourable way than the other obligations of a firm in the event of insolvency, which aim to compensate clients of insolvent firms, and which customers themselves can use to minimize their exposure to authorized firms. The report recognizes the importance of appropriate information in relation to customers, internal controls, and supervision of intermediaries, but leaves the mechanisms of ensuring

---

[93] See Kanda et al, *Official Commentary*, 10–9.
[94] See <http://www.iosco.org> (accessed 7 July 2021).
[95] IOSCO, *Client Assets Survey*, Introduction.
[96] IOSCO, *Client Asset Protection*.

protection entirely to national law and regulation. In 2004, IOSCO established further specifications in *Principles on Client Identification and Beneficial Ownership for the Securities Industry*, which detail beneficial owner identification and omnibus account requirements for certain intermediaries.

In June 2010, IOSCO issued *Objectives and Principles of Securities Regulation*. This document sets out 38 principles of securities regulation, based on three objectives: protecting investors (understood as including customers or other consumers of financial services); ensuring that markets are fair, efficient, and transparent; and reducing systemic risk. The principles are divided into nine categories, of which one category, (H), specifically addresses principles for market intermediaries. These principles establish minimum entry standards for intermediaries and initial and ongoing capital and other prudential requirements that are commensurate with the risks undertaken by intermediaries. Further, the document states that intermediaries should be required to establish an internal compliance system with the aim of protecting the interests of clients and their assets and ensuring proper management of risk. In addition, procedures should be established to minimize damage and loss to investors caused by an intermediary and to contain systemic risk. However, these principles remain high-level and no details are provided regarding their national implementation. 9.101

(b) IOSCO Recommendations Regarding the Protection of Client Assets
Following the IOSCO 2010 document, and taking into account lessons learned from the insolvencies of Lehman Brothers and MF Global, the regulatory community has considered how it might enhance the supervision of intermediaries holding client assets by clarifying the respective roles of the intermediary and the regulator in protecting client assets. In January 2014, IOSCO published a set of *Recommendations Regarding the Protection of Client Assets*.[97] 9.102

Particular emphasis is given to proper customer records and information. An intermediary is expected to establish systems and controls for maintaining accurate and up-to-date records of client asset holdings, including information specifying the amount, location, and ownership status of client assets. The intermediary's systems and controls should provide, on a regular basis, for reconciliations between internal accounts and records in relation to the client assets and those of any third party with which such assets are held. In the context of reconciliations between an intermediary and a central securities depository, such reconciliations should take place daily. The records and accounts should enable an intermediary, at any time and without delay, to specify each client's rights and the intermediary's obligations to each client with respect to client assets. The records should also be maintained in such a way that they may be used as an 9.103

---

[97] IOSCO, *Recommendations Regarding the Protection of Client Assets* (January 2014), <https://www.iosco.org/news/pdf/IOSCONEWS318.pdf> (accessed 7 July 2021).

audit trail.[98] Further, an intermediary should provide a regular statement to each client, as well as on request, detailing the client assets held for or on behalf of such client.[99]

9.104 As regards the mechanisms for safeguarding client assets, an intermediary is under the obligation to identify and understand risks resulting from any available options for holding client assets, and take into account the levels of client asset protection (both pre- and post-default) through in-house analysis as well as through external advice, with the ultimate aim of minimizing the risk of loss and misuse.[100] To the extent that third parties are involved, this includes the exercise of due skill, care, and diligence in selection and appointment (where applicable), and periodic review of any third party and of the arrangements for safeguarding client assets. Further, an intermediary should be aware of the effect of liens and other encumbrances on client assets and consider the best interest of the clients to the extent that it has a choice in agreeing to liens or encumbrances. Overall, an intermediary should ensure clarity and transparency in the disclosure of the relevant client asset protection regime(s) and arrangements, and the consequent risks involved.[101]

9.105 Two scenarios are seen to pose regulatory challenges: where a client has knowingly or unknowingly waived or modified the degree of protection applicable to client assets or otherwise opted out of the application of the client asset protection regime (where permitted by law); and where an intermediary has placed or deposited assets in a foreign jurisdiction.[102] To address the former issue, and to provide greater clarity regarding the status of client assets, documentary requirements should apply. The intermediary should be required to obtain the client's explicit, written consent to any waiver of, modification to, or opting-out of the client asset protection regime. Where such a waiver, modification, or opt-out is permitted by law, any client consent should be set out in a separate document that addresses only the provision of consent. The consent should be affirmative and explicit and should not be 'deemed' or 'implied'. It is important that clients are aware of the possible effects of a waiver or modification of the degree of protection applicable to client assets or opt-out of the application of the client asset protection regime, especially in the context of a default, resolution, or insolvency. In addition, the documentation could help clarify the status of client assets at a particular point in time and, if necessary, facilitate return of any client assets in a default, resolution, or insolvency. Further, where an intermediary has placed or deposited assets in a foreign jurisdiction, the regulator should, to the extent necessary to perform its supervisory responsibilities, consider information sources that may be available to it, including information provided by the intermediaries it regulates and/or assistance from local regulators in the foreign jurisdiction.

---

[98] IOSCO, *Recommendations Regarding the Protection of Client Assets*, Principle 1.
[99] IOSCO, *Recommendations Regarding the Protection of Client Assets*, Principle 2.
[100] IOSCO, *Recommendations Regarding the Protection of Client Assets*, Principle 3.
[101] IOSCO, *Recommendations Regarding the Protection of Client Assets*, Principle 5.
[102] IOSCO, *Recommendations Regarding the Protection of Client Assets*, p 1.

9.106 The recommendations emphasize that it is first and foremost the intermediary's responsibility to ensure compliance with these rules, including through the development of internal systems and controls to monitor compliance. Where the intermediary places client assets with third parties, it should reconcile its accounts and records with those of the third party. While the intermediary must comply with the client asset protection regimes, the regulator has a role in supervising the intermediary's compliance with the applicable domestic rules and maintaining a regime that promotes effective safeguarding of client assets.

(c) FSB guidance on client assets protection in resolution

9.107 As part of the global attempts to establish a framework for the recovery and resolution of systemically relevant financial institutions led by the FSB and CPMI-IOSCO (see section C(3)), particular attention has been given to holdings of client assets in the context of resolution regimes. The FSB Key Attributes of November 2011[103] stated that the legal framework governing the segregation of client assets should be clear, transparent, and enforceable during a crisis or resolution and should not hamper the effective implementation of resolution measures. Effective resolution regimes should allow for the rapid return of segregated client assets or the transfer of the client asset holdings to a third party or bridge institution.

9.108 In February 2013, the FSB proposed further guidance on client asset protection in resolution,[104] building on IOSCO's *Recommendations Regarding the Protection of Client Assets*. This resulted in an annex on client asset protection in resolution as part of the 2014 revision of the FSB Key Attributes.[105] This annex is meant to provide guidance on the interpretation and implementation of the FSB Key Attributes relating to elements in resolution regimes that are necessary to resolve a financial firm that directly or indirectly holds client assets. Given the variations in national regimes, the annex specifies outcomes[106] rather than prescribing methods or mandatory rules by which those outcomes should be achieved.

9.109 The annex contains a number of recommendations and principles regarding standards of client asset protection, including those relating to safeguarding, administration, management, and the deposit of client assets in a foreign jurisdiction, waivers of client asset protection, rights of use, and disclosure to clients. Whatever national arrangements apply, client assets should be shielded, in a manner appropriate to those arrangements, from the failure of the firm and, to the extent possible, of any third-party custodian. The legal status of client assets and the clients' entitlement to them should

---

[103] FSB, *Key Attributes*, Key Attribute 4.1.
[104] FSB, *Consultative Document: Application of the Key Attributes*.
[105] FSB, *Key Attributes* (2014), Appendix II-Annex 3, 85 et seq.
[106] FSB, *Key Attributes* (2014), Appendix II-Annex 3, 86: 'Whatever national arrangements apply, client assets should be shielded–in a manner appropriate to those arrangements–from the failure of the firm and, to the extent possible, of any third party custodian. The legal status of client assets and the clients' entitlement to them should not be affected by entry into resolution of the firm.' [footnotes omitted].

not be affected by the firm's resolution.[107] To achieve the objectives of ensuring clients' prompt access to their assets, the rapid return to the client of identifiable and segregated client assets, or the transfer of the client asset holdings of a firm in resolution to a performing third party or bridge institution, institutions should be required to maintain adequate arrangements for the identification and safeguarding of client assets.

9.110 The new annex further stipulates that there should be effective arrangements such as segregation mechanisms,[108] information systems, and controls,[109] to identify quickly which assets are client assets and to ascertain the nature of claims and entitlements of individual clients to those assets, including with respect to client assets held in a holding chain. The clients should be informed on these arrangements and their consequences. Moreover, the transfer powers under the Key Attributes 3.2 (vi) and (vii) and 3.3 No. 4 should extend to the transfer of client assets.[110]

9.111 The annex contains considerations on rehypothecation and re-use of client assets. Where a firm lends client securities as agent, it should keep adequate records of outstanding transactions, including counterparties, contract terms, legal documentation, collateral details, and location of collateral.[111] Further, to the extent that rehypothecation and re-use of client securities by the firm or third parties acting as principal is permitted by a jurisdiction, such techniques should be governed by clear frameworks, and transactions should be adequately recorded.[112] In any case, there should be adequate disclosure to clients of the effects of such transactions on the protection of their assets and the nature of their legal claims in resolution.[113]

9.112 Finally, the new annex reiterates that jurisdictions should have clear rules in place on how losses are shared between clients in the event of shortfalls in a pool of client assets, and that there should be clarity as regards the role of investor protection schemes and other guarantee schemes or funds supporting the transfer of client assets and addressing shortfalls. To support the effective exercise of transfer powers, resolution authorities should have the power to require changes to a firm's business practices, information management systems, and contractual arrangements relating to the holding and protection of client assets.[114]

---

[107] FSB, *Key Attributes* (2014), Appendix II-Annex 3, p 86.
[108] FSB, *Key Attributes* (2014), Appendix II-Annex 3, 89, s 5. The annex does not take a position on the form such segregation should take (eg client omnibus accounts or individual client accounts). On these forms of segregation and their impact in the event of loss sharing in insolvency, see Ch 7, ss D and F.
[109] FSB, *Key Attributes* (2014), Appendix II-Annex 3, 92–3, s 10.
[110] FSB, *Key Attributes* (2014), Appendix II-Annex 3, 88–9, s 4.
[111] FSB, *Key Attributes* (2014), Appendix II-Annex 3, 90, s 6. 'Those records should be sufficient to enable clients to unwind outstanding transactions to which they are principal or, in the event of resolution, to enable outstanding transactions to be transferred to a qualified transferee. Particular consideration should be given to ensuring that the firm holds adequate records of collateral allocation where securities collateral is held for multiple clients on a pooled basis and where cash collateral is reinvested on a pooled basis.'
[112] FSB, *Key Attributes* (2014), Appendix II-Annex 3, 90, s 6. 'In particular, in order to facilitate resolution, it should be clear how the exercise of the right of use is recorded and what quantity of assets can be re-hypothecated or used.' [footnote omitted].
[113] On repos and securities lending, see also s D(4).
[114] FSB, *Key Attributes* (2014), Appendix II-Annex 3, 91–2, s 9.

(3) Market-wide recommendations for securities settlement

When assessing risks related to securities settlement in the early 2000s, the CPSS and IOSCO looked at the full set of institutional arrangements for confirmation, clearance, and settlement of securities trades, and the safekeeping of securities. This was to take account of the fact that beyond SSSs and CSDs, a number of institutions perform functions that are critical to the settlement of securities trades. The confirmation of trade details is often performed by a stock exchange or trade association, or by counterparties bilaterally, rather than by a CSD. In some markets, a central counterparty (CCP) interposes itself between buyers and sellers, becoming, in effect, the buyer to every seller and the seller to every buyer. Although funds may be transferred through internal accounts at the CSD, in many cases accounts at the central bank or at one or more private commercial banks are used. Finally, not all buyers and sellers of securities hold accounts at the CSD; instead, they may hold their securities and settle their trades through a custodian, and the custodian may, in turn, hold its customers' securities through a sub-custodian. In some markets in which intermediaries and investors hold their securities through a very small number of custodians, those custodians may settle transactions between clients through book-entry transfers on their own books rather than on the books of the CSD.

9.113

Thus, when setting up the *Recommendations for Securities Settlement Systems* (RSSS) in 2001, the CPSS and IOSCO took a broader perspective, establishing a number of so-called market-wide recommendations, the scope of which went beyond CSDs and SSSs. These recommendations address trade confirmations, settlement cycles, central counterparties, securities lending, immobilization and dematerialization of securities, and protection of customers' securities. Since the new CPMI-IOSCO *Principles for Financial Market Infrastructures* (see section C(1)) focus more narrowly on CSDs and SSSs, the wider recommendations in the RSSS have not been superseded by the PFMI and remain in effect. However, given that the financial markets have developed significantly over the last decade, the CPSS and IOSCO have indicated that they may conduct a full review of the market-wide standards in the future.[115] Such update has not yet taken place.

9.114

(a) Trade confirmations and settlement cycles

The RSSS (in recommendation 2) recommend that confirmation of trades between direct market participants should occur as soon as possible after trade execution, but no later than trade date (T + 0). Confirmation of trades by indirect market participants (such as institutional investors) should occur as soon as possible after trade execution, preferably on T + 0, but no later than T + 1. This recommendation ensures that any errors and discrepancies can be discovered early in the settlement process. Early detection should help to avoid errors in recording trades, which could result in inaccurate

9.115

---

[115] PFMI, p 6.

books and records, increased market and credit risk, and increased costs. Rapid, accurate verification of trades and matching settlement instructions is an essential precondition for avoiding settlement failures, especially when the settlement cycle is relatively short. Over time, trade confirmation systems have become increasingly automated. In many cases, manual intervention was eliminated from post-trade processing altogether through the implementation of straight through processing (STP). As a result, immediate confirmation of trades has become the norm in many parts of the securities markets.

9.116 Particular attention is given by the RSSS to the issue of settlement cycles (recommendation 3). In order to ensure the safety of settlement, market participants buying or selling financial instruments should settle their obligation on the intended settlement date. Longer periods cause uncertainty and increased risk for the counterparties to such trades, as one of the parties may become insolvent or default on the trade. The larger the number of unsettled trades, the greater the opportunity for the prices of the securities to move away from the contract prices, thereby increasing the risk that non-defaulting parties will incur a loss when replacing the unsettled contracts. Furthermore, to the extent that the length of settlement periods remains non-harmonized across jurisdictions, this may hamper reconciliation and be a source of error for issuers, investors, and intermediaries. Consequently, the RSSS recommend that 'final settlement should occur no later than T+3' (ie, trade date plus three days). This is understood as a minimum standard, and markets that have not yet achieved a T + 3 settlement cycle should identify impediments to achieving T + 3 and actively pursue the removal of those impediments.[116] Many markets are already settling at a shorter interval than T + 3 or are considering a move in that direction.[117] This standard is likely to be adapted in a revision.[118]

9.117 Irrespective of the applied settlement cycle, the RSSS suggest close monitoring of the frequency and duration of settlement failures. The benefits achieved in terms of risk reduction by harmonizing and shortening settlement cycles may be jeopardized by a lack of settlement discipline in a market. Risk implications of high failure rates should be analysed in such circumstances. The RSSS do not prescribe concrete measures but identify a range of tools to be considered, such as financial penalties for failing to settle that could be imposed contractually or by competent authorities; alternatively, failed trades could be marked to market and, if not resolved within a specified timeframe,

---

[116] At the time the RSSS were being finalized, a number of markets still operated with settlement at the end of an 'account period'.

[117] For example, in the EU, Art 5 CSDR mandates the harmonization of settlement cycles in Europe at T + 2, although shorter settlement periods are allowed. In a number of jurisdictions, government securities even settle on T + 1 or T + 0.

[118] Although it is noted that reducing the cycle is neither costless nor without certain risks. This is especially true for markets with significant cross-border activity because differences in time zones and national holidays, and the frequent involvement of multiple intermediaries, make timely trade confirmation and settlement more difficult. In most markets, a move to T + 1 (perhaps even to T + 2) would require a substantial reconfiguration of the trade settlement process and an upgrade of existing systems.

closed out at market prices. This list of possible options is not meant to be exhaustive, and there are further tools that could be considered, such as subjecting market participants that fail to deliver securities on the intended settlement date to a mandatory 'buy-in' procedure, which may be executed by a CCP in the case of a cleared transaction, or otherwise included in trading venues' own rules.[119]

(b) Book-entry securities and protection of customers' securities

9.118 The RSSS contain a general recommendation for securities to be immobilized or dematerialized and transferred by book entry in CSDs to the greatest extent possible.[120] The immobilization or dematerialization of securities and their transfer by book entry are viewed by the CPSS and IOSCO as significantly improving the speed and efficiency of settlement, supporting the repo and securities lending markets, and reducing the total costs associated with securities settlements and custody. Thus, it is understood as a contribution to enhancing market efficiency.[121] It is also considered to improve safety by reducing or eliminating certain risks, for example, destruction or theft of certificates, and by facilitating DvP through book entries.

9.119 There is a further recommendation laying out key elements regarding the protection of customers' securities,[122] in particular by requiring that entities holding securities in custody should employ accounting practices and safekeeping procedures and that customers' securities should be protected against the claims of a custodian's creditors. There should be adequate protection against all forms of custody risk,[123] including segregation of customer securities on the books of the custodian (and of all sub-custodians, and, ultimately, the CSD).[124] Further, the RSSS consider that even when customer securities are segregated from a custodian's own securities, customers may still be at risk of loss if the custodian does not hold sufficient securities to satisfy all customer claims or if an individual customer's securities cannot be readily identified.[125] Thus, entities that hold securities in custody (or maintain records of balances of securities) should reconcile their records regularly to keep them current and accurate. Other ways to safeguard or protect customers against misappropriation and theft include internal controls and insurance or other compensation schemes. Furthermore, it is noted that, ideally, a customer's securities should be immune from claims made by third-party creditors of the custodian. This requires a supportive applicable legal framework that prioritizes a customer's rights in case of a custodian's insolvency.

---

[119] See Art 7 CSDR.
[120] Recommendation 6.
[121] Recognizing, however, that effective governance is necessary to ensure that these benefits are not lost as a result of monopolistic behaviour by a CSD.
[122] Recommendation 12.
[123] Ie, the risk of a loss on securities held in custody occasioned by a custodian's (or sub-custodian's) insolvency, negligence, misuse of assets, fraud, poor administration, inadequate record keeping, or failure to protect a customer's interests in securities (including voting rights and entitlements).
[124] The RSSS consider identification on the books of the custodian as a potential alternative, if the legal protection were comparable.
[125] See Arts 24 and 25 GSC, discussed in Ch 7, ss C–D.

Finally, particular expectations are placed on global custodians in selecting and overseeing foreign sub-custodians.[126]

(c) Further recommendations

9.120 The RSSS contain two further, more general recommendations regarding (i) the promotion of repurchase and securities lending arrangements and (ii) the use of central counterparties in a market.

9.121 As regards repurchase and securities lending arrangements, the CPSS and IOSCO consider that, given the perceived advantages of such arrangements (allowing sellers ready access to securities needed to settle transactions, offering an efficient means of financing securities portfolios, and supporting participants' trading strategies), barriers[127] that inhibit these practices should be removed. When conducting repos or securities lending, counterparties should employ appropriate risk management policies, including conducting credit evaluations, collateralizing exposures, marking-to-market daily exposures and collateral, and employing master agreements. See further section D(4).

9.122 Finally, the RSSS contain a somewhat ambivalent recommendation on the use of central counterparties, stating that '[t]he benefits and costs of a CCP should be evaluated. Where such a mechanism is introduced, the CCP should rigorously control the risks it assumes'.[128] The RSSS in 2001 thus took a comparatively cautious approach to the introduction of CCPs in securities markets compared to the call for the establishment of mandatory central clearing of certain types of OTC derivatives transactions by the G20 in 2009.[129]

(4) Requirements for repos and securities lending

9.123 Another crucial area relating to intermediated securities that has been the subject of regulatory attention by international standard setting bodies are the securities lending and repo markets. They play crucial roles in supporting secondary market liquidity for a variety of securities issued by both public and private agents. These markets also facilitate the implementation of various risk management and collateral management strategies. However, in the aftermath of the global financial crisis, concerns have been raised that securities lending and the repo market may be conducive to financial stability risks, in particular when securities lending and repos are being used in 'bank-like'

---

[126] For example, by ascertaining that local sub-custodians protect customer securities adequately and employ appropriate accounting, safekeeping, and segregation procedures for customer securities.
[127] Barriers were seen to include unsupportive tax or accounting policies, inadequate legal underpinnings, and ambiguities about the treatment of such transactions in insolvency.
[128] Recommendation 4.
[129] See Leaders' statement at the Pittsburgh G20 summit, September 2009, 9: 'All standardized OTC derivative contracts should be traded on exchanges or electronic trading platforms, where appropriate, and cleared through central counterparties by end-2012 at the latest. OTC derivative contracts should be reported to trade repositories.'

RECOMMENDATIONS AND REQUIREMENTS FOR INTERMEDIARIES   293

activities, such as creating 'money-like' liabilities, carrying out maturity or liquidity transformation, and obtaining leverage, including short-term financing of longer-term assets, some of which may run the risk of becoming illiquid or losing value. These perceived risks fall within what is generally described as the 'shadow banking system'.[130]

The main global regulatory activity regarding shadow banking is performed by the FSB. The objective of the FSB's work in this regard is to ensure that shadow banking is subject to appropriate oversight and regulation in order to address bank-like risks to financial stability emerging outside the regular banking system, while not inhibiting sustainable non-bank financing models that do not pose such risks. It also provides a process for monitoring the shadow banking system so that any rapid growth in new activities that pose bank-like risks can be identified early and, where needed, the risks addressed. **9.124**

Based on initial recommendations set out in its report of October 2011 to the G20,[131] the FSB assessed financial stability risks and developed draft policy recommendations to strengthen the regulation of securities lending and repos. Following a public consultation, in August 2013 the FSB published a policy framework for addressing shadow banking risks in securities lending and repos.[132] This document sets out 11 recommendations for addressing financial stability risks in this area, including enhanced transparency, regulation of securities financing, and improvements to market structure. It also includes consultative proposals on minimum standards for methodologies to calculate haircuts on non-centrally cleared securities financing transactions and a framework of numerical haircut floors. Subsequently, the FSB has specified some of the recommendations in its 2013 policy framework, which is reflected in further regulatory guidance in the area of enhanced transparency and collateral valuation. The FSB monitors the implementation of the recommendations and their consistency across jurisdictions. **9.125**

(a) Enhanced transparency

The first set of policy recommendations in the 2013 policy framework[133] addresses improvements in transparency. This is a response to a perceived opacity in these market segments, where, comparable to what was being done in the area of OTC derivatives, authorities should obtain sufficient information and data to be able to identify and mitigate risks to financial stability, for example arising from excessive leverage and maturity transformation. The FSB recommends authorities to collect more granular data on securities lending and repo exposures among large international financial institutions. **9.126**

---

[130] The FSB defines the shadow banking system in its report, *Shadow Banking: Strengthening Oversight and Regulation*, 1, as 'credit intermediation involving entities and activities [fully or partially] outside the regular banking system' or 'non-bank credit intermediation'. Such intermediation, appropriately conducted, provides a valuable alternative to bank funding and supports real economic activity. Experience from the crisis, however, demonstrates the capacity of some non-bank entities and transactions to operate on a large scale in ways that create bank-like risks to financial stability (longer-term credit extension based on short-term funding and leverage).
[131] FSB, *Shadow Banking: Strengthening Oversight and Regulation*, 22–4.
[132] FSB, *Shadow Banking: Securities Lending and Repos*.
[133] FSB, *Shadow Banking: Securities Lending and Repos*, Recommendations 1–5; see also Annex I, p 20.

294   REGULATION, SUPERVISION, AND OVERSIGHT

This includes trade-level (flow) data and regular snapshots of outstanding balances (position/stock data) for repo and securities lending markets. To achieve this, it is suggested that authorities leverage the existing data collection infrastructure, for example regarding clearing agents, central securities depositories, and/or central counterparties. However, in view of the experience gained in the field of OTC derivatives, national or regional authorities may also rely on trade repositories to collect comprehensive repo and securities lending market data. Regulatory reporting was subsequently developed as a viable alternative approach.

9.127   Following a public consultation,[134] in November 2015 the FSB issued final standards and processes defining the data elements for repos, securities lending, and margin lending that authorities will be asked to report as aggregates to the FSB for financial stability purposes.[135] These standards and processes describe data architecture issues related to the data collection and transmission from the reporting entity to the national/regional authority and then from the national/regional to the global level. To ensure consistency and to derive meaningful global aggregates, six recommendations to national/regional authorities are set out.[136] Despite having announced to complement these standards with detailed operational arrangements in order to initiate the official global data collection and aggregation at the end of 2018, no further related guidance has yet been released by the FSB.

(b) Regulatory minimum standards for securities lending, re-use, and rehypothecation

9.128   A second set of recommendations in the 2013 policy framework[137] deals with the regulation of securities financing. Regulatory authorities for non-bank entities that engage in securities lending should implement regulatory minimum standards for cash collateral reinvestment in their jurisdictions to limit liquidity risks arising from such activities. The minimum standards include high level principles; considerations addressing liquidity risk, maturity transformation, concentration, and credit risks; implementation guidelines (including recommended metrics for supervisory reporting and monitoring); stress testing; and disclosure requirements. Further, safeguard requirements are specified for rehypothecation,[138] whereby financial intermediaries should provide sufficient disclosure to clients in relation to rehypothecation of assets so that clients can understand their exposures in the event of a failure of the intermediary. In jurisdictions where client assets may be rehypothecated (for example, for the purpose of financing clients' long positions and covering short positions), they should not be

---

[134] FSB, *Consultative Document: Standards and Processes for Global Securities Financing Data Collection and Aggregation* (2014).
[135] FSB, *Standards and Processes for Global Securities Financing Data Collection and Aggregation* (2015).
[136] FSB, *Standards and Processes for Global Securities Financing Data Collection and Aggregation* (2015), 32–3.
[137] FSB, *Shadow Banking: Securities Lending and Repos*, Recommendations 6–9.
[138] 'Rehypothecation' and 're-use' of securities are terms that are often used interchangeably. The FSB defines 're-use' as any use of securities delivered in one transaction in order to collateralize another transaction, and 'rehypothecation' more narrowly as re-use of client assets. On this terminology, see also Ch 2, para 2.27.

rehypothecated for the purpose of financing the intermediary's own-account activities; and only entities subject to adequate regulation of liquidity risk should be allowed to engage in the rehypothecation of client assets.[139] Finally, authorities should adopt minimum regulatory standards[140] for collateral valuation and management for all securities lending and repo market participants.

9.129 Following up on its initial recommendations, in January 2017, the FSB published a report[141] describing potential financial stability issues associated with, and explains the evolution of market practices and current regulatory approaches relating to, rehypothecation of client assets and collateral re-use. The report looks at the different regulatory approaches to rehypothecation in use in various jurisdictions, noting that the approaches differ reflecting their roots in national/regional securities laws and other legal regimes that vary across jurisdictions, but that nevertheless all such regulatory approaches are designed to protect rehypothecated client assets within their jurisdictions. The report also highlights improvements in risk management practices associated with rehypothecation by market participants such as prime brokers and their clients, as well as that regulators have also strengthened the relevant client asset protection regimes. Based on these observations, the FSB concluded that there is no immediate case for harmonizing regulatory approaches to rehypothecation.

9.130 With respect to collateral re-use, the FSB considers that appropriately monitoring collateral re-use at the global level will be an important step towards obtaining a clearer understanding of global collateral re-use activities in the securities financing markets. It reaffirms the importance of implementing its *Standards and Processes for Global Securities Financing Data Collection and Aggregation* of November 2015, which now include data elements related to a non-cash collateral re-use measure and to some associated indicators (ie metrics). These non-cash collateral re-use measure and metrics are defined in a further report of January 2017.[142] The FSB furthermore encourages authorities to consider monitoring collateral re-use activities beyond securities financing transactions as appropriate. Since market practices evolve, the FSB highlights the need to review the scope, measure and metrics of collateral re-use.

9.131 With regard to collateral valuation, in November 2015, the FSB released a document on *Transforming Shadow Banking into Resilient Market-based Finance: Regulatory Framework for Haircuts on Non-centrally Cleared Securities Financing Transactions*,[143]

---

[139] See the discussion in Ch 2.
[140] These standards entail the following: (i) Securities lending and repo market participants (and, where applicable, their agents) should only take collateral types that, following a counterparty failure, they are able to: hold for a period without breaching laws or regulations; value; and risk manage appropriately. (ii) Securities lending and repo market participants (and, where applicable, their agents) should have contingency plans for the failure of their largest market counterparties, including in times of market stress. These plans should include how they would manage the collateral following default and the capabilities to liquidate it in an orderly way. (iii) Collateral and lent securities should be marked to market at least daily and variation margins collected at least daily where amounts exceed a minimum acceptable threshold.
[141] FSB, *Re-hypothecation and Collateral Re-use*.
[142] FSB, *Non-cash Collateral Re-use: Measure and Metrics*.
[143] The 2015 framework was updated in July and November 2019 and in September 2020.

which contains the finalized framework for applying numerical haircuts on certain non-centrally cleared securities financing transactions. The final framework builds on a consultative FSB document of October 2014,[144] taking also into account the responses received during the consultation period.[145]

9.132 Consistent with the 2014 consultative report, the final framework includes recommendations on (i) qualitative standards for methodologies used by market participants that provide securities financing to calculate haircuts on the collateral received; and (ii) a framework of numerical haircut floors for non-centrally cleared securities financing transactions. The numerical haircut floors set upper limits on the amount that non-banks can borrow against different categories of collateral other than government securities. The framework also includes an implementation approach for applying the numerical haircut floors to non-bank-to-non-bank transactions; details of an enhanced monitoring of implementation of the framework through the FSB; and technical guidance on the implementation of the framework.

9.133 Compared to the 2014 consultative report and based on the assessment of consultative responses received, the FSB extended the scope of the numerical haircut floors to non-bank-to-non-bank transactions to limit regulatory arbitrage and prevent the build-up of excessive leverage and liquidity mismatch in the non-bank financial system.

9.134 Finally, as part of this framework, the FSB recommended that the Basel Committee on Banking Supervision (BCBS) incorporates the haircut floors into the capital requirements for non-centrally cleared SFTs by setting significantly higher capital requirements for transactions with haircuts traded below the haircut floors. Taking up this recommendation, in November 2015, the BCBS issued a consultative document on haircut floors for non-centrally cleared SFTs,[146] followed by final guidelines issued in December 2019.[147]

(c) Collateral management services

9.135 The movement of securities and the settlement of transactions for collateral management purposes rely on existing clearing and settlement infrastructure. Motivated by expected increases in demand for collateral stemming from regulatory changes and a greater preference for secured transactions, collateral management service providers have been adapting their services with the aim to enhance efficiency and enable market participants to meet collateral demands with existing and available securities. In a report published in September 2014,[148] the CPMI analysed the existing range of collateral

---

[144] FSB, *Regulatory Framework for Haircuts on Non-centrally Cleared Securities Financing Transactions* (October 2014).
[145] <http://www.financialstabilityboard.org/2014/12/public-responses-to-the-consultative-proposal-included-in-the-october-2014-document-regulatory-framework-for-haircuts-on-non-centrally-cleared-securities-financing-transactions/> (accessed 7 July 2021).
[146] BCBS, *Consultative Document: Haircut Floors*.
[147] BCBS, *CRE56*, as updated.
[148] CPMI, *Developments in Collateral Management Services*.

management services as well as what innovation is under way to respond to the higher demands for collateral.

The report identifies a number of benefits resulting from the innovations, furnishing customers with better tools to monitor their securities holdings and increase efficiencies in the deployment of those securities. At the same time, it highlights that proposed services may lead to increased complexity and potential settlement-related risks by creating extensive networks of interconnections among financial market infrastructures and custodian banks active in providing collateral management services. The CPMI notes that both the public and the private sector need to understand, monitor, and appropriately manage the associated risks, as innovations in collateral management services are introduced and as partnerships and operational connections are established, implemented, and used. **9.136**

(d) Structural aspects

The last two recommendations in the 2013 FSB policy framework[149] concern structural aspects of the securities financing markets, namely the possible introduction of central clearing requirements or changes to the insolvency and resolution treatment of repos. In these areas, the FSB takes a more restrained view. **9.137**

As regards central clearing and the introduction of repo CCPs, the FSB has been looking into experiences with existing securities and derivatives markets that are served by a CCP. Benefits are seen to include greater transparency, multilateral netting of exposures of CCP participants, and more robust collateral and default management processes. The FSB considers that some repo market segments, such as the inter-dealer market, may profit more from the benefits than other areas, such as the dealer-to-customer repo markets or the markets for less-liquid securities. Consequently, the FSB urges authorities, with a view to mitigating systemic risks, to evaluate the costs and benefits of proposals to introduce CCPs in their inter-dealer repo markets where CCPs do not exist. Where CCPs exist, authorities should consider the pros and cons of broadening participation, in particular of important funding providers in the repo market. However, existing incentives to use CCPs in these markets are seen to be sufficiently strong (for example, balance sheet netting) and no further regulatory or other action appears necessary to the FSB at this stage. **9.138**

Finally, the FSB has been looking into whether changes may be warranted to the insolvency (or resolution) treatment of repos in some jurisdictions. Under the insolvency laws in a number of jurisdictions, repos are either fully exempt from the 'automatic stay' or are exempt subject to limited qualifications.[150] This means that in case of a financial institution's insolvency, its repo counterparties are allowed to exercise contractual **9.139**

---

[149] FSB, *Shadow Banking: Securities Lending and Repos*, Recommendations 10 and 11.
[150] Since 1985, repos have been exempt from the 'automatic stay' provisions of the US Bankruptcy Code. In the EU, Art 77 of the Bank Recovery and Resolution Directive provides for an exemption of collateral protected under the Financial Collateral Directive, with some limited qualifications.

rights to terminate the contract immediately, set off remaining mutual debts and claims, and liquidate any collateral held. This special treatment was introduced to reduce the contagion risk in the repo market. However, since the global financial crisis, a number of academics[151] have argued that the 'safe harbour' status of repos may in fact increase systemic risk, because, in their view, it may: (i) increase the 'money-likeness' of repos and result in a rapid growth in cheap and potentially unstable short-term funding; (ii) facilitate the fire sales of collateral upon default; and (iii) reduce creditors' incentives to monitor the credit quality of repo counterparties.[152]

9.140 The FSB considers that the proposals made by these academics,[153] while theoretically viable in addressing some financial stability issues, can involve substantial practical difficulties, particularly the need for fundamental changes in insolvency laws, and therefore should not be prioritized for further work at this stage due to significant difficulties in implementation.

(5) Cross-border recognition of resolution actions

9.141 Cross-border recognition of resolution actions in relevant foreign jurisdictions is critical for an orderly and successful resolution process. This holds true in particular for certain resolution tools, namely temporary restrictions or stays on early termination and cross-default rights in financial contracts; and the 'bail-in' of debt instruments that are governed by the laws of a jurisdiction other than that of the issuing entity. In the absence of global harmonization of the relevant laws, for example through an international instrument such as a model law or a convention, alternative measures have to be pursued to enhance the degree of certainty for the cross-border effectiveness of these resolution tools.

9.142 In order to enhance the cross-border recognition of resolution actions and remove impediments to cross-border resolution, the FSB decided to develop alternative policy proposals on how legal certainty in cross-border resolution can be further enhanced, focusing on contractual recognition clauses in financial contracts. Following a public consultation in September 2014[154] on a set of policy measures and guidance consisting of elements that jurisdictions should consider including in their statutory cross-border recognition frameworks to facilitate effective cross-border resolution and on contractual approaches to cross-border recognition, in November 2015, the FSB released its final *Principles for Cross-border Effectiveness of Resolution Actions*.

---

[151] For details, see, eg, Acharya and Öncü, 'Resolution of Systemically Important Assets and Liabilities'; Duffie and Skeel, 'Dialogue on Automatic Stays'; Perotti, *Systemic Liquidity Risk*.
[152] See also the discussion in Ch 3.
[153] The proposals include, for example, that repos backed by risky or illiquid collateral should either not be exempt from automatic stay or should be so exempt but subject to a tax, which could be varied as a macro-prudential tool; or, that in the event of default, lenders of such repos should be able to sell collateral only to a 'repo resolution authority' (RRA) at market prices minus pre-defined haircuts specified by asset class by the RRA. The RRA would then seek to liquidate the collateral in an orderly manner.
[154] FSB, *Cross-border Recognition of Resolution Action: Consultative Document*.

9.143 These Principles set out statutory and contractual mechanisms that jurisdictions should consider including in their legal frameworks to give cross-border effect to resolution actions in accordance with the FSB *Key Attributes*. While emphasizing the importance of implementing comprehensive statutory frameworks, these Principles are aimed to support contractual approaches to cross-border recognition, which the FSB considers critical pending the adoption of such statutory frameworks and which may also complement such regimes once they are in place. The guidance focuses on the resolution of banks, however, many of the legal issues and principles may be relevant to other types of financial institutions as well as to financial market infrastructures.

9.144 Whilst the Principles stress that jurisdictions should consider the development of statutory frameworks and legal processes that would enable to give prompt effect to foreign resolution actions,[155] following the principle of equal treatment of creditors, they also recommend authorities to require, or provide incentives for, firms to adopt, where appropriate, contractual approaches to fill the gap until statutory approaches have been fully implemented and to complement such approaches by reinforcing the legal certainty and predictability of cross-border recognition under statutory frameworks that are in place.[156]

9.145 The FSB conducted its activities on the principles in close interaction with the industry, which worked in parallel to establish contractual solutions to enforcing stays in resolution. Examples for such contractual clauses are the 2015 ISDA Universal Resolution Stay Protocol[157] or the 2016 LMA bail-in clauses, as updated.[158] Generally, adherence to these contractual provisions is voluntary and they are only binding between the parties that have adhered or agreed to them. However, relevant industry associations are strongly encouraging and some authorities even require the use of such contractual provisions in financial transactions.

E. Concluding Remarks

9.146 The post-trade infrastructure supporting the intermediated holding and transfer of securities, consisting of CSDs, SSSs, custodians, and intermediaries, is a pivotal element of modern financial markets. Its safe and efficient functioning is indispensable to

---

[155] Including eg the conditions for recognition, enforcement, or support actions; the grounds for refusal of such actions, which should be limited; and the process for taking such actions.

[156] FSB, *Principles for Cross-border Effectiveness of Resolution Actions*, 13 et seq. In line with the Principles, 'contractual cross-border recognition of temporary stays on early termination rights should be framed as a contractual agreement by the parties to a financial contract to be bound by temporary stays on early termination that are imposed under the resolution regime applicable to the counterparty, subject to safeguards that are consistent with the Key Attributes'. Further, '[c]apital or debt instruments that are governed by the laws of a jurisdiction other than that of the issuing entity should include legally enforceable provisions recognising a write-down, cancellation or conversion of debt instruments in resolution ('bail-in') by the relevant resolution authority if the entity enters resolution.'

[157] See Ch 3, para 3.68.

[158] <https://www.lma.eu.com/documents-guidelines/documents/category/bailin-clause#> (accessed 7 July 2021).

safeguard the stability of financial markets and to maintain market participants' confidence about the way they own and dispose of securities.

9.147 One of the lessons learned from the global financial crisis is that systemically relevant segments of the financial markets require enhanced regulatory attention. Reliance on self—or light-touch regulation has not always proven to yield entirely satisfactory results. To raise the bar when it comes to providing a regulatory regime for risk management of critical market participants has been at the heart of regulatory reform across the globe, as emphasized not the least by the G20 heads of State, finance ministers, and central banks, as well as the FSB.

9.148 Given the increasingly cross-border nature of the securities markets, solutions can no longer function by looking at domestic environments in isolation. Infrastructures and intermediaries are becoming global in outreach, while serving markets, issuers, and investors in a wide number of jurisdictions. This calls for globally consistent approaches to resolution, supported by effective and efficient mechanisms for competent authorities to cooperate, exchange relevant information, and coordinate actions where relevant.

9.149 In this respect, the efforts by the relevant international standard-setting bodies in this field, namely the CPMI and IOSCO over the past 20 years, as well as the coordinating initiatives by the FSB following the emergence of the global financial crisis, are instrumental to foster a globally consistent, holistic regulatory framework to protect investors, to enhance safety and efficiency of holding and settlement arrangements, and more broadly, to limit systemic risk and foster financial stability.

10

CRYPTO SECURITIES AND OTHER DIGITAL ASSETS: ASPECTS OF SUBSTANTIVE AND REGULATORY LAW

A. Introduction	10.01
B. Definitions and Key Concepts	10.06
(1) Blockchain and DLT	10.06
(2) Smart contracts	10.09
(3) Tokens	10.10
(4) Digital securities, crypto securities, intermediated securities	10.14
C. Legislative Developments in Selected Jurisdictions	10.20
(1) Overview	10.20
(2) France	10.21
(3) Luxembourg	10.27
(4) Liechtenstein	10.32
(5) Switzerland	10.38
(6) United States of America	10.45
(7) Germany	10.54
D. Core Elements of a Legal Framework for Digital Securities	10.68
(1) Overview	10.68
(2) Requirements for the securities registry	10.69
(a) Overview	10.69
(b) Manipulation resistance	10.72
(c) Publicity	10.75
(d) Data integrity and business continuity	10.78
(e) Technological neutrality	10.80
(3) Creation of digital securities	10.82
(4) Transfer of digital securities	10.85
(5) Good-faith acquisition of digital securities	10.90
(6) Security interests in digital securities	10.93
(7) Conflict of laws regarding digital securities	10.95
E. Regulation of Crypto Securities	10.103
(1) Introduction	10.103
(2) Function and scope of regulation	10.106
(a) Regulatory policy objectives	10.108
(b) Function of regulation	10.111
(3) Regulatory classification	10.120
(a) Absence of common terminology and categorization	10.120
(b) Emergence of a basic taxonomy	10.122
(4) Application of securities regulation to digital securities	10.127
(a) Regulatory considerations on issuance and registration	10.128
(b) Regulatory considerations on trading of digital securities	10.132
(c) Regulatory considerations applicable to digital securities intermediaries (custodians, wallet providers)	10.135
(d) Regulatory considerations applicable to digital securities clearing and settlement infrastructures	10.142
(e) Regulatory considerations applicable to digital securities service providers	10.149
(5) Regulatory approaches to digital securities in selected jurisdictions	10.150
(a) Prohibitive approaches	10.156
(b) Application of existing regulation	10.159
(c) Focus on anti-money laundering	10.163
(d) Technology specific regulation (DLT)	10.165
(e) Regulatory attempts to provide a comprehensive framework for digital assets and services	10.174
(6) The role of global standard-setters and global regulatory initiatives	10.182
(a) Financial Stability Board (FSB)	10.185
(b) Financial Action Task Force (FATF)	10.188
(c) Basel Committee on Banking Supervision (BCBS)	10.192
(d) International Organization of Securities Commissions (IOSCO)	10.195
(e) Committee on Payments and Market Infrastructures (CPMI)	10.199
(f) Organisation for Economic Co-operation and Development (OECD)	10.203
F. Conclusions	10.204

A. Introduction

10.01 The dematerialization of securities has been the dominant topic in securities law and regulation since the paper crunch[1] in the late 1960s. The driving force behind this process is and was the digitization of value chains, where the existence of a physical information carrier (ie a physical certificate in a case of certificated securities) is a disruptive and costly factor, preventing to realize the full benefits of digitization. From a conceptual point, the dematerialization of securities is not very fastidious and consists, at its core, in the mere substitution of the certificate by an electronic database or registry. However, unlike physical goods, digital information can be replicated and distributed at marginal cost of almost zero. Exclusivity and rivalry—fundamental prerequisites for the creation of private goods—are not satisfied under these conditions.[2] Dematerialization of securities therefore required the intervention of trustworthy intermediaries or government agencies up to now.[3]

10.02 The blockchain or distributed ledger technology (DLT) now permits to overcome these limitations. The essential innovation of DLT is that it can make digital goods scarce and exclusive by means of its technical design.[4] Due to these properties, DLT systems are ideally suited to documenting, securing, and transferring digital goods as well as ownership rights in such goods. Many therefore see the issuance, custody, administration, and transfer of securities and other financial instruments as one of the most promising use cases for DLT-based systems.[5] There is also a consensus emerging that these applications will fundamentally change the trading and post-trading infrastructure of capital markets,[6] much like the internet has radically changed the distribution of books and other media content, travel, shoes and clothing, and many other goods and services. The driving force behind the adoption of DLT-based systems as a technical infrastructure for securities markets and services is the expectation of significant efficiency gains resulting from the consolidation of previously separated

---

[1] Ledrut and Upper, 'Changing Post-trading Arrangements', p 88 ('The US paper crunch').

[2] See Wildmann, *Einführung*, 58 et seq; Hens and Pamini, *Grundzüge*, 231 et seq ('Öffentliche Güter'). A good is rivalrous if the consumption/use of the good or service by one person reduces the availability of the good or service to another person. It is exclusive (or excludable) if a person can be prevented from accessing or using it if that person does not pay for it.

[3] See Hopf, Loebbecke, and Avital, *Blockchain Technology*.

[4] Meisser, Meisser, and Kogens, 'Bitcoins im Konkurs', para 15; Miscione, 'Blockchain-Hype'.

[5] See OECD, *Tokenisation*; ECB Advisory Group, *Potential Use Cases*; OECD, *Initial Coin Offerings*; CPMI, *Distributed Ledger Technology in Payment, Clearing and Settlement*; Swift, *Blockchain*; Pinna and Ruttenberg, *Distributed Ledger Technologies in Securities Post-trading*.

[6] OECD, *Tokenisation*, 3: 'Distributed ledger technologies (DLTs) are poised to become a transformative feature of financial markets, both in financial products and in the underlying market infrastructure itself. The tokenisation of assets, involving the digital representation of real assets on distributed ledgers or the issuance of traditional asset classes in tokenised form, is a core part of this technology's revolutionary potential. Though the technology and practice of tokenisation are nascent, its theoretical benefits include: efficiency gains driven by automation and disintermediation; transparency; improved liquidity potential and tradability of assets with near-absent liquidity; and faster and potentially more efficient clearing and settlement. It suggests a reconsideration of core financial market activities, from trading, pricing and liquidity of securities, to processes such as clearing and settlement, and activities such as repo and securities lending'.

infrastructures for the issuance, the custody, the trading, and the clearing and settlement of securities transactions on one single platform.[7] This evolution might also permit faster and cheaper corporate actions and possibly a direct interaction between issuer and investor.[8]

One necessary, but not sufficient, condition for the widespread adoption of DLT-based securities is a clear and transparent legal framework. This is particularly true for jurisdictions like Germany, Switzerland, or Austria where a physical certificate is still a key component of the concept of securities. Perhaps surprisingly, this is equally true for jurisdictions like France or the Nordic States, where securities have been dematerialized at an early stage, but which had to rely on trusted third parties in order to guarantee exclusivity and rivalry.

10.03

Several jurisdictions have recently enacted legislations to facilitate or enable the application of DLT for the issuance and transfer of digital securities, including, in approximate chronological order, France (see section C(2)), Luxembourg (section C(3)), Liechtenstein (section C(4)) and Switzerland (section C(5)), some US states (section C(6)), and Germany (section C(7)). While the legislative actions taken by these jurisdictions are differing widely in terms of format and scope, they clearly converge with respect to the concepts underpinning the codification of securities issued on the basis of a DLT system (hereinafter referred to as digital or crypto securities). In particular, most reform acts are relying heavily on notions and concepts of traditional securities law. On the international level, UNIDROIT, in cooperation with UNCITRAL, is developing a set of principles that address private-law aspects of digital assets (in particular, proprietary interests).[9]

10.04

The remainder of this chapter is organized as follows: a first part provides some important key concepts and definitions (section B) followed by an overview of development in selected jurisdictions (section C). The first main part will then discuss common issues in the substantive legal framework for digital securities (section D). The second main part provides an overview over the regulation of digital securities (section E). This chapter is limited to a high-level overview, since developments in this field are too diverse and quick to be fully captured. A few conclusions in section F will complete the chapter.

10.05

---

[7] OECD, Tokenisation, 32: 'If tokenisation of assets were to take off, a potential disruption in the market structure could involve the replacement of CSDs by the distributed ledger as a decentralised version of such depositories. Similarly, central clearing houses could, in theory, ultimately be made redundant by the use of the blockchain platform itself as the clearing entity, acting as the common counterparty for the completion of trades. Trades will effectively be settled through the validation of transactions by participants of the network'. See also Chiu and Koeppl, Blockchain-*based Settlement for Asset Trading*: '... estimates based on the market for US corporate debt show that gains from moving to faster and more flexible settlement are in the range of 1 to 4 basis points relative to existing legacy settlement systems.'

[8] On corporate actions processing, see Ch 6.

[9] UNIDROIT, Study LXXXII–Digital Assets and Private Law Project, <https://www.unidroit.org/work-in-progress/digital-assets-and-private-law> (accessed 21 July 2021).

B. Definitions and Key Concepts

(1) Blockchain and DLT

10.06 Although blockchain or distributed ledger technology (DLT) is on everyone's lips, a correct and concise definition is anything but trivial. This is due to the fact that there is not one single, but many types of blockchains and that its technical development is still at an early stage. Some experts therefore question whether it makes sense at all to refer to it as a uniform technology.[10]

10.07 DLT refers to a group of technologies which have in common that a database is shared across a network of multiple sites, with all participants within a network having their own identical copy of the ledger.[11] Any changes to the ledger are validated by participants in accordance with an agreed-upon validation mechanism and are reflected in all copies of the ledger. The security and accuracy of the assets stored in the ledger are maintained by using crypto technologies, in particular keys and signatures to control changes to the state of the ledger. The blockchain is one of several possible data structures in a DLT system, characterized by the fact that its entries are combined (linked) in blocks.[12]

10.08 It is neither possible nor useful to comprehensively discuss technical aspects of DLT in the present context. What is relevant is that this technology offers the possibility of digitally mapping information in such a way that, under certain conditions, it can neither be copied nor manipulated and can be securely transmitted between people. In doing so, it solves a central problem that previously prevented the digitization of property rights. Unlike physical goods, digital goods can be replicated and distributed at marginal costs close to zero. This means that basic prerequisites for the creation of private goods (excludability and rivalry) are not met. Therefore, up to now, trustworthy intermediaries or government agencies had to be called in to create, transfer and store private digital goods. The essential innovation of DLT is that it can make digital goods scarce and exclusive by means of technical precautions.[13] Due to these properties, DLT systems are ideally suited for documenting, securing, and transferring ownership rights in digital goods.

(2) Smart contracts

10.09 Some blockchains are supporting smart contracts, computer programs, or a transaction protocol which can automatically execute, control, or document legally relevant events

---

[10] See Kaminska, I and Walker, M, Written evidence, Submission to the House of Commons Treasury Committee–Digital Currencies Inquiry (12 April 2018), <http://data.parliament.uk/writtenevidence/committeeevidence.svc/evidencedocument/treasury-committee/digital-currencies/written/82032.html> (accessed 21 July 2021).
[11] For a comprehensive discussion, see Schär and Berentsen, *Bitcoin, Blockchain, and Cryptoassets*.
[12] See ISSA, *Distributed Ledger Technology: Principles*; World Bank, *DLT and Blockchain*.
[13] Brekke and Fischer, 'Digital Scarcity'.

and actions.[14] For example, if the transfer of a digital security is contingent on the approval by the issuer, the token digitally representing the security can be programmed in such a way that a transfer is effective only once the approval has been given. To execute automatically, smart contracts need to be able to interface with external data sources, usually referred to as an 'oracle'. According to a popular saying, smart contracts are neither contracts nor particularly smart.[15] Moreover, not all clauses of an agreement are susceptible to automation and self-execution. Even where a clause might technically be capable of being automated, it might not always be desirable to automate it.[16] Also the possibility to formally represent an agreement in a non-ambiguous way is clearly limited, reducing the scope in which smart contract might be usefully applied even further.[17] Despite these limitations smart contracts are an important element to realize efficiency gains in securities transactions. This is particularly true for transactions where payments and deliveries are heavily dependent on conditional logic, including securities and derivatives transactions.[18]

(3) Tokens

A key concept in the context of DLT-based digital goods are so-called 'tokens'. In computer science, a token describes an object (software or hardware) that contains the right or instructions to carry out a certain operation (for example, to access tokens). In connection with DLT applications, tokens are smart contacts used to process transactions, for example by defining the rules according to which assets assigned to a public key can be transferred. In legal terminology, the term token is understood more narrowly, namely as a 'digital representation of an intrinsic or market-related value'.[19] The concept of tokens was also developed as part of the Ethereum blockchain, where widely-used standards such as the ERC-20[20] for fungible and the ERC-721[21] for non-fungible tokens have emerged. Standardization allows tokens to be created quickly and cheaply.

10.10

In supervisory practice a distinction has emerged between payment, investment, and utility tokens. This 'holy trinity' was first formulated in guidelines of Switzerland's Financial Market Supervisory Authority (FINMA) on Initial Coin Offerings.[22] It is now

10.11

---

[14] Fries and Paal, *Smart Contracts*; Savelyev, *Contract Law 2.0*; Schär and Hübner, 'Blockchain und Smart Contracts'; Clack, Bakshi, and Braine, *Smart Contract Templates*.
[15] ISDA and Linklaters, *Whitepaper*, 5.
[16] Ibid, 10.
[17] ISDA and Linklaters, *Whitepaper*, 12.
[18] Ibid, 19 et seq.
[19] Fußwinkel and Kreiterling, 'Blockchain-Technologie', 54; see also Kaulart and Matzke, 'Die Tokenisierung des Rechts'; Koch, 'Tokenisierung'; Veil, 'Token-Emissionen', 348 et seq. See also Art 2(c) Liechtenstein Blockchain Act (TVTG).
[20] See Vogelsteller and Buterin, *ERC-20*.
[21] Entriken et al, *ERC-721*.
[22] See Eidgenössische Finanzmarktaufsicht (FINMA), *Aufsichtsmitteilung 04/2017: Aufsichtsrechtliche Behandlung von Initial Coin Offerings* (29 September 2017); Eidgenössische Finanzmarktaufsicht (FINMA), *Wegleitung für Unterstellungsanfragen betreffend Initial Coin Offerings (ICOs)* (16 February 2018).

largely established internationally.[23] Broadly speaking, the token categories can be defined as follows:

> (i) Payment tokens are intended to be used as a means of payment, ie serve as a medium of exchange, store of value, and/or unit of account. They usually have no intrinsic value. In AML regulations, the payment token corresponds to the term 'virtual currency' or 'crypto currency'.[24] The most prominent example of a crypto currency is Bitcoin, the first major application of a blockchain and in terms of market capitalization still by far the most important crypto asset.
> (ii) Investment tokens (or asset tokens, securities tokens) are representing monetary or non-monetary claims or rights against an issuer and/or membership or corporate rights under company laws, or derivatives of any of such rights. Investment tokens can be a digital representation of financial assets like a bond, a share, or a derivative financial instrument. Investment tokens can also represent rights or interests in non-financial assets like real estate, diamonds, or fine art.
> (iii) Utility tokens are providing access to a digital service and can only be used in the issuer's network to purchase goods or services.

10.12 The classification of tokens as payment, investment, or utility tokens may be useful as a first approximation for determining the regulatory framework applicable to the issuance, public offering, or trading of tokens. Investment tokens may be classified as securities for regulatory purposes, whereas payment tokens are usually subject to the regulation of payment services providers and/or anti-money laundering laws. However, the trifurcation of payment, securities, and utility tokens is not suitable for a reliable assessment of the regulatory legal framework applicable to tokens or other DLT-based assets. Only the relevant supervisory categories can provide a reliable point of reference for a regulatory assessment of a given token. Furthermore, many tokens have properties of one and the other class (so-called 'hybrid tokens'). In particular, the demarcation between payment and investment tokens is entirely blurred since, on the one hand, hardly any of the numerous crypto currencies effectively fulfils any of the functions of money, and on the other hand, many buyers of payment tokens are motivated by speculative expectations.[25]

10.13 Even more dubious is the term stablecoin. Stablecoins are, broadly speaking, crypto currencies which are somehow backed by, or linked to, an underlying reference asset (like an

---

[23] See EBA, *Report on Crypto-assets*, 7; ESMA, *Advice on Initial Coin Offerings and Crypto-assets*, para 19; ABA, *Digital and Digitized Assets*, 27 et seq; Blandin et al, *Global Cryptoasset Regulatory Landscape Study*, 121 et seq. See also Global Digital Finance, *Taxonomy*, 6.

[24] See Eidgenössische Finanzmarktaufsicht (FINMA), *Wegleitung für Unterstellungsanfragen betreffend Initial Coin Offerings (ICOs)* (16 February 2018), 3; see also the definition of 'virtual currency' in Art 3(18) Directive 2018/843 (5th AML Directive): '"virtual currencies" means a digital representation of value that is not issued or guaranteed by a central bank or a public authority, is not necessarily attached to a legally established currency and does not possess a legal status of currency or money, but is accepted by natural or legal persons as a means of exchange and which can be transferred, stored and traded electronically.'

[25] See Kuhn, 'Taxonomie', para 7 et seq.

official currency or precious metals) in order to limit the volatility against official currencies which is typical for crypto currencies.[26] A broad variety of stabilization mechanisms is being used, ranging from an immediate backing with full convertibility through numerous more or less intermediate backings with restricted convertibility to stablecoins where stabilization is achieved (or not achieved) with trading or hedging strategies.[27] In view of this very wide spectrum, the term stablecoin is void of any tangible common characteristics and should therefore, at least in a legal context, best be avoided.

(4) Digital securities, crypto securities, intermediated securities

Assets or securities issued on the basis of a DLT system are sometimes referred to as digital or crypto assets or securities (as in the title of this chapter). We will be using the term *digital securities* to designate instruments which are issued and transferred on a DLT or comparable technology-based protocol or application, and which are functionally equivalent to physical securities (which will be referred to as *certificated* securities). We fully recognize that the term as such is not very concise since virtually all relevant forms of financial assets have been in existence in only digital or electronic form for decades. However unprecise, the term digital asset or digital securities is more and more used with this meaning. The term *crypto securities* emphasizes the widespread use of crypto technology in DLT systems and is employed synonymously to digital securities.

10.14

Digital securities are controlled through a private key infrastructure. The holder of the private key, and only the holder,[28] has the power to change the status of the distributed database, ie to effect a transaction. The holder of the private key has therefore a power similar to dominion, control, or possession in relation to a movable, physical asset.[29] The holder of the private key has also the power to directly transfer such control to another person (peer-to-peer).[30]

10.15

Digital or crypto securities must be distinguished from dematerialized securities in the broader sense, usually referred to as *uncertificated* (or *electronic* or *register*) securities.

10.16

---

[26] See Moin, Gün Sirer, and Sekniqi, *Classification Framework*; see also Bullmann, Klemm, and Pinna, *Are Stablecoins the Solution?*.
[27] Moin, Gün Sirer, and Sekniqi, *Classification Framework*.
[28] A private key can be controlled by one or several persons, requiring two or more signatures for authorizing a transaction ('multisig infrastructure').
[29] This is clearly recognized by the Liechtenstein Blockchain Act which in Art 5(1) makes a distinction between control of tokens ('*Verfügungsgewalt*') and ownership ('*Verfügungsberechtigung*'). A person having control is supposed to have ownership (Art 5(2) TVTG). The concept of control or possession in relation to digital securities is also acknowledged by the Swiss DLT Act, although less clear than in the Liechtenstein Act; see Art 973d(1) CO (Switzerland).
[30] See, eg, Art 967(1) CO (Switzerland) (providing that the transfer of ownership in certificated securities, or the perfection of a pledge or another limited right in rem, requires in any case the transfer of possession of the certificate). A peer-to-peer transfer is not possible in a legal system with mandatory dematerialization such as, eg, under French law.

Like digital securities, uncertificated securities have no physical representation, but unlike digital securities the ledger or registry can be based on any kind of technology (for example, an excel sheet maintained by the issuer or a centralized database). If they are not issued on a DLT protocol, they will usually not have the properties distinctive for digital securities (see paragraphs 10.68 et seq).

10.17 Digital or crypto securities must also be distinguished from *intermediated* securities, even though intermediated securities also exist in electronic or digital form only. Intermediated securities are—very much simplified—credits to securities accounts maintained by a securities intermediary (a custodian, a bank, a securities firm, a central securities depository or CSD), representing securities, or rights in securities, that the securities intermediary is holding for the account holder (the 'investor').[31] The name derives from the fact that intermediaries are interposed between the issuer and the investor, and that the investor can transfer securities or assert rights in relation so such securities only through its own securities intermediary.

10.18 The legal frameworks for digital and intermediated securities are dealing with different legal relationships at different levels. Intermediated securities are representing legal positions resulting from the custody of (physical or dematerialized) securities by securities intermediaries. The law of digital securities, on the other hand, is tackling the completely different issue of how the person controlling an entry in a distributed database is identified by the issuer as the legitimate creditor, how payment to such person discharges the issuer, and how the position of such person is transferred to another person. Digital securities are therefore performing exactly the same functions as certificated securities.[32]

10.19 A clear conceptual distinction between intermediated and digital securities is all the more important as it is absolutely conceivable that digital securities are held with securities intermediaries, thus serving as an underlying for the creation of intermediated securities. While this seems to be outlandish at first sight, it is highly relevant in practice because institutional investors in particular are still wary of holding relevant assets in self-custody, and holding digital securities with custodians makes it easier to use existing infrastructure. Many other investors also resort to intermediated holding because the infrastructure for holding digital securities directly still is not very user friendly and also comes with certain risks. An explicit interface between digital and intermediated securities therefore is a key requirement for a well-defined legal infrastructure for digital securities.

---

[31] See Art 9(1) Geneva Securities Convention ('Intermediated securities'); see also Law Commission (UK), *Who Owns Your Shares?*, 1.14 et seq.

[32] See Kuhn, 'Registerwertrechte', para 24 et seq.

C. Legislative Developments in Selected Jurisdictions

(1) Overview

The following chapter is providing a high-level overview of legislative developments in selected jurisdictions relevant for the emergence of a legal framework for digital securities. The jurisdictions are presented in chronological order.

10.20

(2) France

France was one of the first jurisdictions to introduce a mandatory dematerialization of securities in the 1980s.[33] Since then, securities have been issued exclusively in the form of book-entry securities and transferred by way of an entry into a securities account maintained by the central securities depository or a financial intermediary.[34] The securities account could also be maintained by the issuer, especially for non-listed securities.[35] Dematerialization is mandatory under French law; it is not possible to hold securities other than through financial intermediaries or the issuer.[36]

10.21

It goes without saying that such a closed and centralized system is difficult to reconcile with the decentralized approach of the blockchain. The French government therefore started earlier than others to make the legal framework for the issue and custody of securities compatible with decentralized ledgers. A first step was taken with Ordinance n° 2016-520 of 28 April 2016[37] ('Minibons Ordinance'), which created the possibility of issuing so-called minibons on the basis of DLT systems.[38] Minibons are fungible borrower's notes that are issued by small and medium-sized companies through crowdfunding platforms (Article L.223-6 et seq CMF). Regulation n° 2017-1674 of 8 December 2017[39] ('DLT Regulation') then extended the possibility to issue and transfer securities on the basis of a DLT system to all unlisted securities. The DLT Regulation is supplemented by a decree n° 2018-1226 of 24 December 2018,[40] which specifies technical requirements for DLT systems.

10.22

---

[33] See Art 94-II Loi de finance n° 81-1160 of 30 December 1981, now codified as Art L.211-4 Code monétaire et financier (CMF) and Art L.229-1 Code de commerce.
[34] See Art L.211-3(1) CMF.
[35] Ibid.
[36] For a comprehensive review of dematerialization in France, see Vauplane, *20 ans de dématérialisation*; see also Foyer, 'Dématérialisation', 21 et seq.
[37] Ordonnance n° 2016-520 du 28 avril 2016 relative aux bons de caisse, JORF n° 0101 du 29 avril 2016, texte n° 16.
[38] The legislation uses the technologically neutral term 'dispositif d'enregistrement électronique partagé' or 'DEEP'; see Art 120 Loi Sapin II. The legislative materials make it clear that this includes DLT systems and blockchains.
[39] Ordonnance n° 2017-1674 du 8 décembre 2017 relative à l'utilisation d'un dispositif d'enregistrement électronique partagé pour la représentation et la transmission de titres financiers, JORF n° 0287 du 9 décembre 2017.
[40] Décret n° 2018-1226 du 24 décembre 2018 relatif à l'utilisation d'un dispositif d'enregistrement électronique partagé pour la représentation et la transmission de titres financiers et pour l'émission et la cession de minibons, JORF n° 0298 du 26 décembre 2018.

10.23 From a legislative point of view, these amendments were made by modifying the relevant provisions of the Code monétaire et financier (CMF) on the management of securities accounts (Article L.211-3 et seq CMF) and the pledging of securities accounts (Article L.211-20 et seq CMF). The issuance and transfer of securities on the basis of DLT systems is therefore now legally equivalent to the crediting of securities in securities accounts maintained by intermediaries or the issuer. The scope of the DLT regulation therefore corresponds to the scope of the regulations on securities held by intermediaries (Article L.211-3 et seq CMF).

10.24 The substantive scope of the DLT Regulation is limited to non-listed securities (Article L.211-1 CMF). The use of DLT system is therefore currently permitted for the following classes of securities:

(i) Debt securities, namely bonds, commercial paper and the French Billets de Trésorerie and Certificats de Dépôt;
(ii) Units or shares in undertakings for collective investment (UCITS) and alternative investment funds (AIF);
(iii) Securities issued by special purpose vehicles and companies in accordance with Ordinance n° 2017-1432 of 4 October 2017;
(iv) Shares of joint-stock companies (Société Anonyme, SA).

10.25 The decision to issue securities on the basis of a DLT registry is taken by the issuer (Article L.211-7 CMF). A legal basis in the articles of association is required in the case of shares, and a corresponding clause in the terms and conditions for debt securities. The issuer can then enter the financial instruments in a DLT registry in the name of the holder (Article L.211-4 CMF).

10.26 French law regulates in some detail the technical and functional requirements a DLT system must meet in order to be used for the issuance of securities. Minimum requirements must be met in particular with regard to authentication, which correspond to those of a securities account (Article L.211-3 CMF). These conditions are further specified by a decree of the State Council of 24 December 2018.[41] The decree names a total of four requirements that a DLT system must meet: integrity; identification of the owner and the type and number of financial instruments it owns; a business continuity plan; and ensuring access to transaction data. The types of DLT systems that can be used for the issuance and transfer of financial instruments are not specified in the decree itself, but the result of these requirements most likely is the exclusion of public blockchains.

---

[41] Décret n° 2018-1226 du 24 décembre 2018 relatif à l'utilisation d'un dispositif d'enregistrement électronique partagé pour la représentation et la transmission de titres financiers et pour l'émission et la cession de minibons. See also Rapport au Président de la République relatif à l'ordonnance n° 2017-1674 du 8 décembre 2017 relative à l'utilisation d'un dispositif d'enregistrement électronique partagé pour la représentation et la transmission de titres financiers, JORF n° 0287 du 9 décembre 2017. The Décret has been codified in Arts R.211-1-5, R.211-9-4, and R.211-9-7 CMF.

(3) Luxembourg

Luxembourg is home to an international central securities depository and a central hub for the European securities and fund business. It created a modern legal framework for intermediated securities in 2001.[42] This act was amended in 2019 to create a legal basis for the use of secure electronic registry systems ('*dispositifs d'enregistrement électroniques sécurisés*') for the custody and transfer of securities.[43] In 2020, the government submitted a further amendment that allows issuer accounts to be managed on a DLT basis and allows credit institutions and investment firms from the EEA to do so.[44]

10.27

The 2001 Securities Act applies to securities that are credited to a securities account and can be transferred by way of debits and credits to securities accounts (Article 1(1)-(2) L.1.8.2001). Only banks, investment firms, and other financial intermediaries are permitted to act as account operator ('*teneur de comptes*') and to maintain securities accounts (Article 3(7) L.1.8.2001).[45]

10.28

Article 18bis L.1.8.2001, introduced in 2019, equates booking and transfer processes in DLT systems with credits to conventional securities accounts and transfers in securities clearing and settlement systems. According to the explanations on the draft law, DLT systems are understood as a new way of managing securities accounts and as an alternative to established forms of dematerialization.[46]

10.29

Only fungible securities can be held in securities accounts under the 2001 Securities Act (Article 1(3) L.1.8.2001).[47] Article 18bis L.1.8.2001 explicitly states that this requirement also applies to securities held on the basis of a DLT system. By way of explanation the legislative materials state that tokens are by definition fungible, a statement which is incorrect in this generality.

10.30

The Luxembourg regime is a good example for a legislative approach which tries to integrate DLT into the organization and operational framework of the existing securities industry. Securities accounts maintained by financial intermediaries are the bedrock of a manner of industrial organization, which has emerged over the last decades, and which is essentially based on centralized IT systems and communication networks. The big promise of DLT in the securities industry is an alternative, decentralized industrial organization. The horse is therefore behind the cart when DLT is squeezed into centralized structures. It is moreover questionable from a legal perspective whether it is

10.31

---

[42] Loi du 1 août 2001 concernant la circulation de titres et d'autres instruments fongibles. The securities act was amended in 2013 in order to comply with the requirements of the Geneva Securities Convention. See Loi du 6 avril 2013 relative aux titres dématérialisés.

[43] See Mémoire au Projet de Loi n° 7363 v. 6.11.2018, 2. This term, which can best be translated as 'secure electronic register system', as evidenced by the explanations of draft law n° 7363, also means DLT systems and, in particular, blockchain applications.

[44] Projet de loi n° 7637 portant modification (i) de la loi modifiée du 5 avril 1993 relative au secteur financier; (ii) de la loi du 6 avril 2013 relative aux titres dématérialisés.

[45] Prüm, 'Dématerialisation', 273.

[46] See Mémoire au Projet de Loi n° 7363 v. 6.11.2018, at 2.

[47] Prüm, 'Dématerialisation', 276. See also Prussen, 'Le régime des titres et instruments fongibles'.

appropriate to regulate tokens in an intermediated securities act. Intermediated securities laws address issues and risks that arise from the fact that the direct relationship between the (end)investor and the issuer has been dissolved beyond recognition through the interposition of intermediaries.

(4) Liechtenstein

10.32 Liechtenstein was one of the first States to enact a comprehensive legislative framework dealing with the DLT-based token economy. The parliament of the small principality edged between Switzerland and Austria adopted the act with the rather cumbersome name 'Token and Trustworthy Technology Service Provider Act' (TVTG) on 3 October 2019; it has entered into force on 1 January 2020.[48] The TVTG includes a legal framework for the issuance and transfer of tokens (Articles 3–10 TVTG) on the one hand, and a part dealing with the regulation and supervision of service providers in a token economy (TT service provider; Articles 11–29 TVTG) on the other hand. The law also stipulates transparency regulations for tokens similar to prospectus regulations for transferable securities (Articles 30 et seq TVTG). The scope of the TVTG is limited in so far as it does not deal with any issues covered by financial market regulations. Since Liechtenstein is an EEA Member State, it is bound by the EEA financial market acquis.

10.33 According to Article 1, the TVTG defines 'the legal framework for transaction systems based on trustworthy technologies'. The term 'trustworthy technologies' is defined as technologies that guarantee the integrity of tokens, their allocation, and secure exchange (Article 2(a) TVTG). The law does not elaborate on these requirements. However, the legislative materials indicate that they mean technologies which 'guarantee the uniqueness and manipulation security of the tokens . . . It must not be possible for tokens to be copied or changed without authorization; in particular, the TT System must ensure the integrity of the tokens. The term "integrity" comes from computer science and is usually used for the correctness and integrity of data. Systems that do not guarantee this uniqueness and security against manipulation by unauthorized persons are not trustworthy. ...'[49] It is therefore clear that currently only DLT systems can meet the Act's requirements for trustworthy technologies.

10.34 The private law part comprises Articles 3–10 TVTG. The innovative core of this part is the recognition of tokens as an asset in relation to which legal subjects can have ownership rights, and which can be disposed of. A token is defined as information on a

---

[48] See Gesetz vom 3. Oktober 2019 über Token und VT-Dienstleister (Token- und VT-Dienstleister-Gesetz; TVTG), LGBl. 2019 Nr 301, <https://www.gesetze.li/konso/2019301000> (accessed 21 July 2021). For the legislative history, see Bericht und Antrag der Regierung an den Landtag des Fürstentums Liechtenstein betreffend die Schaffung eines Gesetzes über Token und VT-Dienstleister (Token- und VT-Dienstleister-Gesetz; TVTG), BuA 54/2019; and Vernehmlassungsbericht der Regierung betreffend die Schaffung eines Gesetzes über auf vertrauenswürdigen Technologien (VT) beruhende Transaktionssysteme (Blockchain-Gesetz; VT-Gesetz; VTG) (28 August 2018).
[49] Bericht und Antrag, BuA 54/2019, 130 et seq.

TT system that can represent fungible claims or membership rights vis-à-vis a person, rights to property, or other absolute or relative rights and that is allocated to one or more TT identifiers—meaning the public key[50] (Article 2(1)(c) TVTG). The holder of the TT key (private key)[51] has power of disposal over the token (Article 5(1) TVTG); and the person who has power of disposal is presumed to be the person entitled to be the owner of the token (Article 5(2) TVTG). Article 3(3) TVTG makes it clear that Articles 4–6 and 9 also apply *mutatis mutandis* to tokens that do not represent any rights against a third party (native tokens). In this context, the legislative materials are using the image of a container, which can also be empty.[52] The law, including the civil law part, therefore clearly also applies to crypto currencies such as Bitcoin.[53]

10.35 The disposition of tokens requires first the completion of the technical transfer process in accordance with the rules of the relevant DLT system (Article 6(2)(a–c) TVTG). The transfer must be based on an agreement between the transferor and the transferee that ownership be transferred (Article 6(2)(a–c) TVTG; *dingliche Einigung*). Only dispositions of an authorized person effect the transfer of ownership; if the transferor does not have the required authority, the transferee can acquire ownership by virtue of good faith (Articles 6(1)(c) and 9 TVTG).

10.36 Article 7 TVTG defines the effects of a disposition of the token with regard to the right represented in such token. Article 7(1) TVTG specifies in a programmatic way that the 'transfer of the token shall effect the transfer of the right represented by the token'. However, this is only true if the law governing the represented right follows suit. If this is not the case, Article 7(2) TVTG obliges the issuer to ensure that the transfer of a token directly or indirectly results in the transfer of the represented right; and that conflicting dispositions of represented rights are prevented. Article 8 TVTG provides that the issuer shall acknowledge the holder of a token as evidenced by the system as the legitimate creditor, and that payment to that holder shall discharge him. Finally, Article 10 TVTG provides for a judicial process to invalidate tokens if a private key is lost, or if the token becomes inoperable for other reasons.

10.37 The TVTG also codified the concept of dematerialized securities by amending the Final Clauses of the Persons and Company Act (see § 81a SchlA PGR), creating the possibility to issue bearer or order securities in fully dematerialized form, called register securities ('*Wertrechte*'). Register securities are issued by way of an entry in a book maintained by the issuer, where the number and the nominal value of the securities as well as the creditors are registered (§ 81a(1) SchlA PGR). The book may or may not be maintained on the basis of a DLT system; if not, it must in any case be organized in such a manner that unauthorized interventions by the issuer are being prevented. Register securities are transferred by way of an entry into the securities book (§ 81a(4) SchlA

---

[50] Ibid, 20.
[51] Ibid, 20.
[52] Ibid, 141.
[53] Ibid, 140.

PGR). Register securities can also be acquired by virtue of good faith from the person registered in the book (§ 81a(5) SchlA PGR). Finally, the issuer is only obliged to pay to the creditor entered in the book and is discharged by making payments to that creditor (§ 81a(3) SchlA PGR).

(5) Switzerland

10.38 Switzerland is home to one of the largest blockchain clusters and was one of the epicentres of the Initial Coin Offering (ICO) hype in 2017/18. The Swiss Financial Market Supervisory Authority (FINMA) therefore had to position itself earlier than other regulators and was one of the first authorities to issue clear regulatory guidance for the treatment of ICOs and tokens.[54] The Swiss Federal government has taken a pronounced positive stance in relation to DLT early on. In 2018 it started a comprehensive review of the federal law in order to identify and remove entry barriers and obstacles for the use of DLT systems.[55] A preliminary draft for a Federal Act on Adapting Federal Law to Developments in Distributed Ledger Technology (DLT Act) was submitted to public consultation in spring 2019.[56] A revised version was sent to Parliament in December 2019[57] and was adopted unanimously by both chambers in September 2019.[58] Both the speed of the legislative process–lightning speed for Switzerland—as well as the overwhelming support by the parliament for the DLT Act are clear evidence for a very positive political environment for DLT in Switzerland.

10.39 The DLT Act is not aimed at creating a bespoke legal framework for DLT applications but is rather an umbrella act with the purpose of removing obstacles for DLT applications. It is amending a total of ten existing Federal acts, with a focus on the Code of Obligations (CO) where DLT-based register securities are codified as a new form to issue securities, on insolvency law where the segregation of crypto assets in the insolvency of a custodian is clarified, and on financial market regulations where a license for a DLT trading system is introduced.

10.40 Swiss securities law is in principle still relying on physical (certificated) securities. Uncertificated securities (*Wertrechte*; *droits-valeurs*) have been used since the 1980s

---

[54] See para 10.10.
[55] See Bundesrat, Rechtliche Grundlagen für Distributed Ledger-Technologie und Blockchain in der Schweiz: Eine Auslegeordnung mit Fokus auf dem Finanzsektor, 14 December 2018 (Federal Council report on legal foundations of DLT and blockchain in Switzerland;'DLT-Report').
[56] See Eidgenössisches Finanzdepartement, Bundesgesetz zur Anpassung des Bundesrechts an Entwicklungen der Technik verteilter elektronischer Register, Erläuternder Bericht zur Vernehmlassungsvorlage, 22. März 2019 (Federal Department of Finance, Explanatory Report on preliminary draft of DLT Act).
[57] See Botschaft vom 27. November 2019 zum Bundesgesetz zur Anpassung des Bundesrechts an Entwicklungen der Technik verteilter elektronischer Register, BBl 2020, 233–328 (Federal Council bill on the DLT Act submitted to the parliament).
[58] Bundesgesetz zur Anpassung des Bundesrechts an Entwicklungen der Technik verteilter elektronischer Register [Federal Act on the Adaptation of Federal Law to Developments in the Technology of Distributed Electronic Registers], 25 September 2020, AS 33 (2021) (the 'DLT Act'), amending Obligationenrecht ('Code of Obligations', 'CO'), Art 973d et seq.

LEGISLATIVE DEVELOPMENTS IN SELECTED JURISDICTIONS 315

as a substitute for physical registered shares of listed companies (*Namenaktien mit aufgeschobenem oder aufgehobenem Titeldruck*). The concept has been codified in 2010 by the Federal Intermediated Securities Act (FISA), as an underlying component for the creation of intermediated securities.[59] However, the concept of uncertificated securities was never fully developed, and was therefore not suitable for capital market instruments. Uncertificated securities are created by way of an entry into an uncertificated securities book, which may be maintained in physical or electronic form (for example as an excel sheet) and is not public. They are transferred by way, and with the effects, of an assignment,[60] and are pledged in accordance with provisions governing the pledge of claims.[61] Both the assignment of and the pledge of uncertificated securities require the execution of the assignment and the pledge, respectively, in writing.[62]

In 2010, the Federal Intermediated Securities Act codified and modernized the legal framework for intermediated securities, mostly in line with the Geneva Securities Convention. The concept of intermediated securities (*Bucheffekten, titres intermédiés*) was introduced as a new form of property to reflect the rights resulting from a credit of securities to a securities account.[63] According to Article 3(1) FISA, intermediated securities are (i) personal or corporate rights of a fungible nature against an issuer; (ii) credited to a securities account; (iii) that may be disposed of by the account holder in accordance with the provisions of the FISA (ie, by way of credit to a securities account[64] or by way of a control agreement[65]). According to Article 6(1) FISA, intermediated securities are created by (i) the deposit of certificated securities (which may be a global certificate) into collective custody with a custodian or by registering uncertificated securities in the main registry of a single custodian and (ii) the credit of such securities to one or several securities accounts. The main registry, which is different from the uncertificated securities book, is maintained by a custodian (normally by the central securities depository) and is public.[66]

10.41

The DLT Act completed the dematerialization of securities law and introduced the concept of register, or ledger-based, securities as a new form of truly digital securities fulfilling all functions of certificated bearer or order securities.[67] Register securities are issued on the basis of a securities registry which must meet certain minimum requirements set forth in Article 973d(2) CO. These requirements include (i) control by the creditor, but not the debtor; (ii) protection of the integrity of the registry by appropriate technical or organizational measures; (iii) availability of information regarding

10.42

---

[59] Art 973c(1) CO.
[60] Art 973c(4) CO.
[61] Art 899 et seq Schweizerisches Zivilgesetzbuch ('Swiss Civil Code', 'CC').
[62] Art 165(1) CO; Art 900(1) CC.
[63] See Bundesgesetz über Bucheffekten ('Federal Intermediated Securities Act', 'FISA'), 3 October 2008, AS 2009, 3577.
[64] Art 24 FISA.
[65] Arts 25–6 FISA.
[66] Art 6(2) FISA.
[67] Art 973d et seq CO.

the registered right and the operation of the registry; and (iv) the creditor's right to read relevant information and verify relevant content. It is generally agreed that these requirements, under the current state of technology, can be met only by DLT-based systems. The securities registry can be either a public blockchain (like the Bitcoin or the Ethereum blockchain) or a permissioned blockchain (like Corda or Hyperledger Fabric). The registration is based on an agreement (called a registration agreement) which includes the consent of the parties to issue securities in the form of register securities and information about the securities registry.[68]

10.43 Register securities (unlike simple uncertificated securities, see paragraph 10.16) are functionally fully equivalent to certificated bearer or order securities. They are transferred by way of an entry in the securities registry in accordance with the registration agreement.[69] The obligor of register securities is obliged to pay, and is discharged only by paying, the creditor registered in the securities registry.[70] A purchaser in good faith from the person registered in the securities registry is protected even if the seller had no power to dispose of the register securities.[71] The obligor of register securities may raise against the claim of the person registered in the securities registry only defenses (i) that relate to the validity of the registration or that are derived from the securities registry; (ii) that the obligor is personally entitled to raise against the registered creditor; or (iii) that are based on the direct relations between the obligor and a former creditor, if the current registered creditor intentionally acted to the detriment of the obligor when acquiring the register securities.[72]

10.44 The DLT Act expressly acknowledges that register securities can be used as collateral similar to certificated securities.[73] A security interest in register securities can either be a possessory or a non-possessory security interest. In each case, the security interest can be a full-title security interest or a pledge. A possessory security interest is created by way of transferring control over the register securities to the secured party, based on a security agreement. The perfection requirements are the same as for certificated securities.[74] Non-possessory security interests are perfected by flagging the security interest in the securities registry and providing that the secured party can assume control over the register securities in case of a default by the debtor.[75]

(6) United States of America

10.45 Most issues in connection with the private law framework for securities fall within the legislative competence of US states. The relevant legal provisions are largely

---

[68] Art 973d(1) CO.
[69] Art 973f(1) CO.
[70] Art 973e(1)-(2) CO.
[71] Art 973e(3) CO.
[72] Art 973e(4) CO.
[73] Art 973g CO.
[74] Art 973g(2) CO (referring to Arts 899 et seq CO).
[75] Art 973g(1) CO.

harmonized by the Uniform Commercial Code (UCC). The UCC is a uniform law developed by the Uniform Law Commission (ULC) in collaboration with the American Law Institute (ALI). It only becomes legally binding by virtue of being adopted by the individual states, which are free to make more or less extensive modifications. Article 8 UCC has been adopted in all states, the District of Columbia, and Puerto Rico with a few non-uniform variations.[76]

Private law for securities is codified in Article 8 UCC, which covers both physical securities (certificated securities, § 8-102(4) UCC) as well as uncertificated securities (§ 8-102(18) UCC) and securities held with intermediaries (Part 5: § 8-501 et seq UCC). While uncertificated securities (similar to certificated securities) are based on the idea of a direct legal relationship between investor and the issuer, Part 5 (added in 1994) codified the concept of securities held with an intermediary as a separate type of property interest, called 'security entitlement'. A security entitlement comes into existence when financial assets are credited to a securities account (§ 8-501 UCC) managed by a securities intermediary. The securities entitlement can be understood as a bundle of rights that can only be asserted in relation to the account-holding securities intermediary, but not in relation to the issuer or other intermediaries.

10.46

The UCC has so far not been amended to take into account securities issued on the basis of DLT systems (although that work is underway, as described below). However, the ULC adopted a uniform law regulating crypto service providers in 2017, the Uniform Regulation of Virtual-Currency Businesses Act, or URVCBA.[77] The URVCBA applies to the trading, transfer, and custody of virtual currencies (§ 102(25) URVCBA) and essentially deals with supervisory issues. An exception can be found in § 502 URVCBA, which tries to clarify the legal relationship under property law when a crypto service provider has virtual currencies under its control. According to the official commentary on § 502 URVCBA, the provision is based on § 8-503 and 8-504 UCC, ie on the provisions on security entitlements.[78] § 502 URVCBA stipulates that virtual currencies that a crypto service provider holds or transfers for its customers are the property of the customers and not of the service provider, and that accordingly creditors of the service provider cannot access these assets. However, the customer has no direct ownership right to the virtual currencies held for him, but only a right that corresponds to the securities entitlement within the meaning of § 8-501 UCC. Accordingly, the URVCBA also reproduces the tiered safekeeping relationships of securities and obliges the crypto service provider to cover customer stocks with corresponding credits with other service providers (§ 502(a) URVCBA). If the crypto service provider does not comply with this obligation, the customers acquire proportional claims to the service provider's portfolio (§ 502(b) URVCBA).

10.47

---

[76] See website of the Uniform Law Commission: <https://www.uniformlaws.org/committees/community-home?CommunityKey=f93a92b2-020f-4bfa-880b-5f80d24d018d> (accessed 21 July 2021).
[77] Uniform Regulation of Virtual-Currency Businesses Act; Annual Conference Meeting in its One-Hundred-And-Twenty-Sixth Year (San Diego, California: 14–20 July 2017).
[78] See Official Comment 1 to Section 502 URVCBA.

10.48 § 502 URVCBA was replaced in 2018 by another uniform law entitled Supplemental Commercial Law for the Uniform Regulation of Virtual-Currency Businesses Act (SCL-URVCBA).[79] The purpose of this supplement was to make the provisions of Part 5 of Article 8 UCC directly applicable, so that the rights of customers of crypto service providers correspond in every respect to a security entitlement.[80]

10.49 The URVCBA and the 2018 SCL-URVCBA have been enacted by only one US state, Rhode Island. At least one state (Wyoming) made a deliberate decision against adopting these uniform laws based on the reasoning that the legal framework for securities held with intermediaries is not suitable in the DLT context.[81] Wyoming is one of the most active states in its attempts to create a favourable legal and regulatory framework for crypto businesses. The state has passed and amended no fewer than 13 laws to date to create a legal framework that aims to enable and facilitate digital assets and related business models.

10.50 Of particular relevance in the present context are provisions of Wyoming law that endeavour to fit digital assets into the taxonomy and structure of Articles 8 and 9 of the Wyoming Uniform Commercial Code (UCC-Wyoming).[82] Digital assets are defined as 'a representation of economic, proprietary or access rights that is stored in a computer readable format' (WS 34–29–101(a)(i)). In addition to virtual currencies, this definition also includes digital securities and usage tokens (digital consumer assets, WS 34–29–101(a)(i)-(ii)).

10.51 Under UCC-Wyoming, digital securities are considered securities within the meaning of § 8-102(a)(15) UCC; ie they are treated by analogy to physical securities or dematerialized securities (WS 34-29-102(a)(ii)). The law allows the parties to treat digital securities as subject to security entitlements within the meaning of Part 5 of Article 8 UCC. However, the Wyoming legislature's reluctance to accept this regime and its preference for direct custody is reflected in the duty imposed on securities service providers to inform investors about the risks of indirect custody (WS 34-29-104(g)). UCC-Wyoming also clarifies that security interests in digital assets may be subject to control. Control is synonymous with possession, so that a security interest may be perfected by control (WS 34–29–103(e)(i), (f)).

10.52 The different approaches taken by Wyoming and the law harmonization organizations illustrate nicely the fundamental differences between a legal framework for securities held with an intermediary and the framework for directly held digital securities.

---

[79] Uniform Supplemental Commercial Law for the Uniform Regulation of Virtual-Currency Businesses Act, Adopted at the Annual Conference Meeting in its One-Hundred-And-Twenty-Seventh Year (Louisville, Kentucky: 20–26 July 2018).

[80] Official Comment 1 to Section 502 of the URVCBA.

[81] See letter of Wyoming Blockchain Task Force to Uniform Law Commission, 27 February 2019 (on file with the authors): 'The inherent nature of digital assets largely obviates the need for intermediaries. The Model Acts also have left a gaping hole in this space by neglecting to address the direct ownership and peer-to-peer nature of digital assets.'

[82] SF0125–Digital assets-existing law.

Whereas multi-tiered custody chains arise in the first case, the holder of digital securities can control them directly and immediately.

10.53 The ULC and ALI currently are preparing revisions to the UCC that would add a new Article 12 dealing with certain digital assets, defined as 'controllable electronic records' (CERs), including conforming amendments to UCC Articles 8 and 9.[83] The draft provisions include a definition of 'control' of CERs that is functionally the rough equivalent of 'possession' of tangible movables. Control also would be a method of third-party effectiveness (perfection) of security interests in CERs and a necessary element for qualifying for protection as an innocent acquirer of CERs (a 'qualified purchaser').

(7) Germany

10.54 Germany has recognized the concept of dematerialized securities already since the late nineteenth century,[84] but only in relation to Government debt securities.[85] For securities issued by private entities German law has staunchly maintained the requirement of a physical certificate.[86] This is even true for securities held with an intermediary, for which a global certificate must be deposited with the central securities depository Clearstream Banking.[87] A first step to permit the dematerialization of privately issued securities has been taken by the Bundestag on 6 May 2021 with the adoption of the Act on Electronic Securities (eWpG).[88]

10.55 The law consists of two parts which must clearly be distinguished. First, it creates a legal basis for the complete dematerialization of securities held with an intermediary through the introduction of so-called central register securities (§ 4(2) eWpG). The registry for central register securities can only be maintained by central securities depositories or financial institutions admitted to the custody business in Germany (§ 12(2) eWpG). The practical significance of this part is limited since it permits only to waive the need to deposit a global certificate with Clearstream Banking. A second, possibly much more relevant part provides for the introduction of decentralized electronic securities (so-called crypto securities). A crypto security is an electronic security that is entered in a crypto security registry (§ 4(3), § 16 eWpG). This part creates a legal basis for the tokenization of securities.

10.56 The material scope of the eWpG is initially limited to bearer bonds (§ 1 eWpG), fund units (§ 95 Capital Investment Code), and covered bonds (*Pfandbriefe*; § 4(5), § 8(3)

---

[83] Memorandum from Steven Harris to the Committee on the Uniform Commercial Code and Emerging Technologies regarding Controllable Electronic Records, 22 January 2021 (on file with the authors).
[84] See Gesetz betreffend das Reichsschuldbuch vom 31.5.1891, RGBl 1891, 321.
[85] Cf Bundesschuldenwesengesetz vom 12. Juli 2006, BGBl I 1466.
[86] For securities under transport law (consignment notes, waybills, warehouse receipts, and bills of lading), there may already be a separate electronic form under commercial law (§§ 443(3), 475c(4), and 516(2)–(3) HGB).
[87] Entwurf eines Gesetzes zur Einführung von elektronischen Wertpapieren, Drucksache 19/26925.
[88] Gesetz über elektronische Wertpapiere vom 3. Juni 2021, BGBl I S 1423.

320 CRYPTO SECURITIES AND OTHER DIGITAL ASSETS

Covered Bond Act). The dematerialization of shares was considered too complex to be codified at this stage, due to interfaces with company law, where problems were identified primarily in connection with the incorporation of the company, the issuance and transfer of shares, the general meeting of shareholders, corporate actions, and the dissemination of information from the company to the shareholder. For checks and bills of exchange, the Federal Government is of the opinion that an electronic form cannot be considered from the outset due to international agreements.

10.57 § 2 eWpG regulates the basic properties of electronic securities. § 2(2) eWpG first clarifies that 'an electronic security [deploys] the same legal effect as a security that has been issued by means of a certificate'. This sentence makes it clear that electronic securities are not a new type of security, just a new form to issue debt or any other right. While the eWpG does not explicitly state the effects, the approach is the same as the one taken in Liechtenstein (section C(4)) and Switzerland (section C(5)).

10.58 § 2(3) eWpG then succinctly states that 'an electronic security ... is an asset within the meaning of § 90 of the German Civil Code'. Electronic securities are therefore considered to be a corporeal movable (*bewegliche Sache*) for property law purposes. This fiction is highly remarkable from a dogmatic point of view since German (as well as Swiss, Austrian, and Liechtenstein) property law has been firmly constricted to corporeal movables, but not to choses in action or other non-physical assets.[89] The Liechtenstein and Swiss legislators have shied away from breaking with this dogma, leaving issues about the legal nature of digital securities unresolved. Under German law, it is now clear that ownership interests can be created in electronic securities (see also § 27 eWpG: presumption of ownership). Electronic securities can also be segregated in the insolvency of a custodian based on general insolvency law principles (§ 47 InsO), without the need for further adjustments of insolvency laws.

10.59 Electronic securities are issued when the issuer makes an entry in an electronic securities registry (§ 2(1) eWpG), which is called the crypto securities registry in the case of crypto securities (§ 4(1)-(2) eWpG). The Act establishes only very general requirements for the crypto securities registry and places the burden for compliance squarely on the issuer. According to § 16 eWpG, the registry must be kept on a manipulation-proof recording system on which the data are logged in chronological order and secured against unauthorized deletion and subsequent changes. Further requirements will be set forth in an ordinance the Ministries of Justice and Finance will issue (§ 23 eWpG).

10.60 A key feature of the Electronic Securities Act is that it places responsibility for compliance with these requirements with the body maintaining the registry (*Registerführer*; registrar). According to § 16(2) eWpG, this is the body that the issuer designates as such; if there is no designation, the issuer is deemed to be the registrar. According to § 7 eWpG the registrar must maintain the crypto securities registry in such a way that the

---

[89] Regierungsentwurf eWpG, 43. In the opinion of the Federal Government, this fiction is necessary because only a new form of issuance will be introduced and the legal nature of the security will not be changed.

confidentiality, integrity, and authenticity of the data are guaranteed (§ 7(1) eWpG). It is also responsible for any damage caused by an incorrect management of the registry (§ 7(2)-(3) eWpG). The registrar has also the duty to provide an extract from the registry in text form to the holder of a crypto security if this is necessary to exercise its rights (§ 19(1) eWpG).

The issuer must publish the entry of crypto securities in a crypto securities registry in the Federal Gazette—the official publication organ of the Federal Republic of Germany (§ 20(1) eWpG). The issuer must furthermore notify the German Federal Financial Supervisory Authority (BaFin) of any publication; BaFin maintains a public list of published entries (§ 20(2)-(3) eWpG). Similar publication requirements do not apply to the issuance of physical securities. **10.61**

The Act and the legislative materials do not clarify the critical issue of what the legal consequences are if a system used for the issuance of crypto securities is found not to meet the very general standards set forth in the eWpG. One obvious conclusion would be to conclude that a right registered in a system which does not meet the minimum requirements set forth in the act are not crypto securities at all. However, such an approach would be clearly against the best interests of investors who might be left with nothing but a liability claim against the issuer. What seems clear, however, is that any issue not published in the Federal Gazette and notified to BaFin does not qualify as an issue of crypto securities. This leaves BaFin in the uncomfortable situation of having to review such notification and intervene in cases where it concludes that the basic requirements of § 16 eWpG have not been met. **10.62**

The Electronic Securities Act also makes the commercial management of crypto securities registries for third parties a regulated activity subject to the supervision of BaFin. Entities maintaining crypto securities registries are deemed to be a financial services institution within the meaning of § 1(1a) KWG and are therefore subject to the supervision of BaFin. § 2(7b) KWG provides for exceptions, but the regulatory burden is still considerable. In addition, the registries are subject to anti-money laundering requirements and must comply with regulations on internal controls (§ 25h KWG) as well as increased due diligence (§ 25k KWG). **10.63**

The federal government justifies this supervision 'on grounds of investor protection, market integrity, transaction security and the functionality of the markets'.[90] However, it fails to recognize that DLT systems can guarantee integrity and transaction security due to their architecture and their properties without the need for trustworthy third parties. The draft for an EU Regulation on Markets in Crypto-assets (MiCA) therefore does not include the maintenance of a crypto registries in the list of crypto services subject to licensing requirements and supervision. It remains to be seen whether the authorization requirement under the eWpG will therefore prevail over future EU law. **10.64**

---

[90] Regierungsentwurf eWpG, 86.

10.65 Overall, the regulatory burden for the registration of crypto securities and the keeping of the registry is very high. Whereas German law does not regulate self-issuance in the context of physical securities, the registrar of crypto securities is subject to numerous duties and responsibilities under the eWpG, which are accentuated by strict civil liability. The obligation to publish a registration in the Federal Gazette also seems anachronistic. It is therefore more than doubtful whether this approach is technologically neutral.

10.66 The Electronic Securities Act regulates the disposition of electronic securities (including crypto securities) in §§ 24 et seq. A disposition (including the perfection of a pledge or another limited right and the disposition of rights arising from electronic securities) first requires an entry in the crypto securities registries. The entry must be made on the basis of a person having the power to issue such an instruction, and both the transferor and the transferee must agree that ownership shall be transferred or a limited right be perfected (*dingliche Einigung*). Until the transfer to the transferee has been completed, the transferor does not loose its ownership (§ 25 eWpG).

10.67 § 26 eWpG makes it clear that ownership of electronic securities can be acquired based on the good faith of the transferee. For this purpose, the content of the electronic securities registry is deemed complete and correct, and the owner is deemed to be the authorized person. § 27 codifies the presumption of ownership in favour of the holder of an electronic security. According to § 28 eWpG, the holder of an electronic security is entitled to be recognized as the legitimate creditor by the debtor, and the debtor is discharged by paying this person.

D. Core Elements of a Legal Framework for Digital Securities

(1) Overview

10.68 The following sections will discuss in more detail core elements of a legislative framework for digital securities. A first issue virtually all jurisdictions are struggling with are the requirements the technical infrastructure underpinning digital securities has to meet. This is a multi-dimensional discussion at the cross-roads of technical, legal, and regulatory considerations (section D(2)). Section D(3) discusses the creation of digital securities. The transfer thereof, including the acquisition of digital securities based on the good faith of the acquirer, and the creation of security interests in digital securities, is another core element (sections D(4)–(6)). Thorny conflict-of-laws issues that arise in the context of digital securities are discussed in section D(7).

(2) Requirements for the securities registry

(a) Overview

10.69 Probably the greatest challenge in designing a legal framework for digital securities is to define the requirements an electronic registry needs to satisfy in order to ensure full functional equivalence with certificated securities. As explained in paragraph 10.08, the registry must be designed in a manner that it ensures exclusivity and rivalry as fundamental prerequisites for the creation of private goods. A centralized digital database run by the issuer will hardly meet these conditions, even if fully secured, encrypted, and audited, if the issuer maintains the power to unilaterally change entries in the registry or tamper with the transaction history or if the holder of a security depends on the issuer for transferring it to a transferee. This is the reason why electronic securities registries so far had to be operated by trusted third parties, ie a governmental organization or a financial intermediary. It is the most important feature of DLT that it enables the design of registries which are tamper-proof and permit direct control and verification by the holders of securities without involvement of a trusted third party.

All reform bills taken into consideration in this chapter are trying to define these requirements in a more or less extensive manner. The Liechtenstein Blockchain Act applies only to 'Trustworthy Technologies' ('*vertrauenswürdige Technologien*'), which are defined as technologies 'ensuring the integrity of tokens, the unequivocal allocation of tokens to public keys, and the disposition of tokens' (Article 2(a) TVTG). In its bill to the Liechtenstein parliament, the government emphasized that this definition refers to technologies which are trustworthy based on their design, without the need for a central operator.[91] However, the Liechtenstein Blockchain Act did not try to define more precisely the features of 'Trustworthy Technologies'. As explained in the government bill, the codification of specific features would quickly result in interpretation issues and legal uncertainty.[92] The French State Council Decree of 24 December 2018 (codified in Articles R.211-1-5, R.211-9-4, and R.211-9-7 CMF) names a total of four requirements a DLT system must meet: (i) integrity; (ii) identification of the owner and the type and number of financial instruments; (iii) a business continuity plan; and (iv) ensuring access to transaction data. The Swiss DLT Act also requires that a database meets at least four conditions in order to qualify as a digital securities registry: (i) the creditors, but not the debtor, have control over the digital securities; (ii) the integrity of the securities registry is protected; (iii) the securities registry provides publicity in relation to the securities and the operation of the registry; and (iv) creditors have inspection rights in order to verify the integrity of the registry (see Article 973d(2) CO). The preliminary draft of the DLT Act had included even more constitutive requirements, including that the operational capacity and integrity be ensured in accordance with the latest state of technology. This overbroad approach was fiercely criticized in the consultation process,[93] and in the bill submitted to parliament the government made a clear distinction between the four constitutive requirements referred to in Article 973d(2) CO, which are also defining the scope of application of the securities law provision of the DLT Act, and other, non-constitutive requirements, which may result in the issuer's liability if not met (Article 973d(3) CO). The German Electronic Securities Act requires that a

10.70

---

[91] Bericht und Antrag, BuA 2019/54, 130.
[92] Ibid, 130.
[93] Kuhn et al, 'Wertrechte als Rechtsrahmen', 8 et seq, 15 et seq.

crypto securities registry must be kept on a tamper-proof recording system in which data are logged in time sequence and are protected against unauthorized deletion and subsequent changes (§ 16 eWpG). The crypto securities registry must provide detailed information about the crypto securities registered, including third-party rights (§ 17 eWpG), and about any change in ownership (§ 18 eWpG). Liability for damages caused by insufficient or malfunctioning securities registries are also dealt with by different reform bills (see Article 973d(3) CO, § 7 eWpG).

10.71 In view of the early stage and the quick evolution of distributed ledger technology, legislators should avoid the temptation to design a perfect registry and limit statutory requirements to what is indispensable in order to ensure full functional equivalence of digital with certificated securities. It is also crucial to clearly distinguish requirements determining the application of the statutory framework for digital securities and requirements which are a statutory or contractual obligation of the issuer and which may trigger the issuer's liability if not complied with. Requirements which must be met in order to make the statutory framework applicable must be defined as clearly and as narrowly as possible since investors will normally be left worse off if an instrument does not qualify as a digital security. It must also be possible to determine compliance with these criteria in advance and without the cooperation of the issuer or another third party. In our view, only two criteria are truly indispensable functional requirements for an electronic securities registry: manipulation resistance and publicity.

(b) Manipulation resistance

10.72 The first and most important functional requirement for a digital securities registry is that it protects against manipulation by the issuer or the administrator of the system. Physical securities are per se protected against tampering because they are under the control of the creditor (or a custodian acting for the creditor) after issuance. In order to be functionally equivalent, the digital securities registry must be designed in a manner that any unauthorized changes in the transaction history or the reallocation of control rights not provided for in the functional description are prevented.

10.73 Manipulation resistance goes beyond integrity in the technical sense, which generally refers to the accuracy and completeness of data.[94] Manipulation resistance also requires protection against changes to registry entries not authorized by the holder of the securities, or a person authorized by the holder. The parties must also be able to verify the integrity of a registry entry without the involvement of the issuer.

10.74 In DLT systems, manipulation resistance is achieved by way of decentralization.[95] In a distributed ledger, no single entity in the network can amend past data entries in the ledger, and no single entity can approve new additions to the ledger. Instead, a predefined, decentralized consensus mechanism is used to validate new data entries that are added to the blockchain and thus form new entries in the ledger. However,

[94] Ghallab, Saif, and Mohsen, 'Data Integrity and Security'.
[95] Bericht und Antrag, BuA 2019/54, 130.

CORE ELEMENTS OF A LEGAL FRAMEWORK FOR DIGITAL SECURITIES   325

centralization or decentralization is problematic as a qualification criterion for a securities registry because decentralization of a DLT system is not a simple binary property.[96] The degree of decentralization depends, among other things, on the number and type of validators (nodes) and any dependencies between them. It can also be shown that if a ledger is required to deal with the failure of a single participant, it must consist of at least three participants.[97] Closed networks (permissioned blockchains) are potentially more susceptible to manipulation than open ones (unpermissioned blockchains), but these shortcomings may be balanced out by appropriate governance structures. The number and distribution of validators can also change over time. Any attempt of a legislator to substantiate the criterion of manipulation resistance through technical specifications will therefore result in unintended consequences or will become quickly obsolete.

(c) Publicity

A second set of requirements securities registries should meet results from the fact that they are designed to reflect property rights in a legally conclusive manner. A property right (a right *in rem*) is, by definition, a right effective against third parties (*erga omnes*), including secured and unsecured creditors of, and acquirers from, the holder of a security. Third parties must be capable, in principle, to recognize existing rights. Publicity of existing rights which shall have priority against competing rights is therefore another key condition a digital securities registry must meet in order to provide full equivalence with certificated securities. Just like the possession of a certificated security reflects the holder's ownership, the holder of a digital security must be able to prove its legal position independently and without the involvement of the issuer to any third party. DLT-based securities registries are uniquely well suited to provide publicity in relation to existing property rights, at least if a public blockchain is being used. This is less clear in the case of private or permissioned blockchains, since the access to such systems is controlled by a gate-keeper and thus limited. However, read-only functions may be granted to persons who have no writing or administration rights.   10.75

From a securities law perspective, the information to be provided by the securities registry in order to satisfy the publicity requirement is limited. What is required, from a functional perspective, is first that the object of a transfer can clearly and univocally be identified and, secondly, that a transferor could identify any right or encumbrance which would have priority over the right he acquires.   10.76

---

[96] Rauchs et al, *Distributed Ledger Technology Systems*, 44.
[97] See Swiss Blockchain Federation, *Circular 2021/01: Register Securities*, 6: 'Although such requirements are met by a typical Blockchain, they can conceivably be satisfied by other systems, too. For example, the Paxos algorithm is often used in IT systems with strict system availability and integrity requirements. In general, it can be proven that a system that is supposed to be robust when f equal-ranking participants are compromised must consist of at least 2*f + 1 participants. If a ledger is required to deal successfully with the failure of a single participant, it must consist of at least three participants. Exceptionally, decentralization is assured if there are only two equal-ranking participants, providing that there is a mechanism of resolving a contradiction between the two participants with the involvement of a third party.' (footnote omitted).

10.77 Publicity, as it is understood here, must clearly be distinguished from other transparency requirements relating to the rights represented by the security. Specifics about the right represented is provided by terms of issue, offering memoranda or prospectuses, or (in the case of equity instruments) from company registries, but not the securities registry (even though the registry may include a hyperlink to such documents). Nor can transparency obligations regarding the architecture and functionality of the registry be justified by the publicity requirement, as it is understood here. While it is wholly sensible to impose transparency obligations upon the issuer in this respect, they should by no means be codified as systemic, application-defining requirements.

(d) Data integrity and business continuity

10.78 Whether rights represented in digital securities can effectively be controlled and transferred depends entirely on the possibility to access the system on a continuous basis. Most reform acts therefore impose certain duties and obligations upon the issuer or the system operator to ensure data integrity and business continuity. The Swiss DLT Act therefore places the obligation upon the issuer 'that the securities ledger is organized in accordance with its intended purpose' and that in particular 'it must be ensured that the ledger operates in accordance with the registration agreement at all times' (Article 973d(2) CO). The German Electronic Securities Act requires the issuer to 'take the necessary technical and organizational measures to ensure the integrity and authenticity of the crypto securities' (§21(1) WpG). If the issuer fails to comply with this duty, BaFin may request it to transfer the crypto securities to another (centralized) securities registry (§21(2) eWpG).

10.79 While the emphasis on data integrity and business continuity is fully justified in relation to DLT-based securities registry (as is true for any kind of electronic database), it is important not to define such requirements as a condition for the application of a legal framework. If data integrity, business continuity, or other technical requirements are part of the legal definition of a securities registry, a DLT system does not qualify as a securities registry if the requirements are not met. This, however, would be against the best interest of investors, since they would be left in limbo, without the protection of a well-defined legal framework. Moreover, technology and risks are evolving so quickly that a set-up meeting best-practice standards at the time of issue may be considered to be outdated shortly thereafter.

(e) Technological neutrality

10.80 Legislators have mostly tried to draft the minimum requirements for securities registries in a technologically neutral manner, rightly trying to avoid relying on technologies which may be outdated in short order. However, at the current stage of technological development it appears that only DLT can fully meet all of the constitutive requirements for a securities registry. According to the current state of the art, it can therefore be assumed that the systemic, application-determining requirements of the law can only be satisfied if the securities registry is based on some form of a DLT protocol.

The Swiss Federal Council's bill to the parliament includes a detailed discussion of **10.81**
blockchain or DLT protocols, which are basically suitable for meeting the requirements
of Article 973d(2) CO. Accordingly, both the Bitcoin and the Ethereum blockchain are
suitable for guaranteeing the integrity of the data it contains. The prerequisite, however,
is that the relevant protocol 'actually provides a minimum level of decentralization and
thus resilience at all times'.[98] For this, the system must have several participants who, in
turn, actually participate in the consensus mechanism used and who are independent
of one another. In addition, the bill also mentions proof-of-stake mechanisms that can
meet the requirements of a value rights registry, namely the Cardano blockchain or
Algorand.[99] Finally, the bill makes it clear that DLT systems with a limited group of participants (so-called permissioned blockchains) can in principle meet the requirements
of a value rights registry. Two protocols, namely Corda and Hyperledger Fabric, are
expressly mentioned in this context, which protocols delegate the decision to resolve
conflicts to special participants who ensure that only one of the set of conflicting transactions is considered binding.[100]

(3) Creation of digital securities

Creating a digital security means that a right (a claim, a corporate right etc.) is entered **10.82**
into a registry meeting the statutory minimum requirements for securities registries.
The registration has the legal effect that the right is subject to specific rules for the
transfer and assertion of the right, as defined by the underlying system.

The technical modalities for the registration depend on the DLT protocol and appli- **10.83**
cation layers being used. If the securities registry is based on the Ethereum protocol,
the registration is effected by way of publishing a token smart contract which incorporates the key terms of the relevant instrument (type of instrument, number of securities issued, nominal amount). A token contract is a special kind of smart contract
that defines a token and keeps track of its balance across user accounts. Ethereum has
two main technical standards for the implementation of tokens, known as the ERC20
standard for fungible tokens and the ERC721 standard for non-fungible tokens. The
standardization allows contracts to operate on different tokens seamlessly, while also
fostering interoperability between contracts. Since the information which can reasonably be stored on a blockchain is limited, additional documentation like a whitepaper, a
private placement memorandum, or even a prospectus are linked to the smart contract
(usually by way of a hash link).

The publication of the smart contract is a unilateral act performed by, or on behalf of, **10.84**
the issuer. In itself, it does not create a digital security. What is required in addition is

---

[98] Botschaft, BBl 2020, 281.
[99] Ibid, 281.
[100] Ibid, 282.

the consent of the first acquirer (who may be the issuer) to have the relevant right represented in a digital security and therefore subject it to the rules for the transfer and assertion of such right as defined by the underlying system. The Swiss DLT Act emphasizes this consent requirement by introducing the concept of a 'registration agreement' as a necessary condition for the creation of digital securities (Article 973d(1) CO). The registration agreement covers the agreement of the parties that the right be registered in a securities registry, and can be transferred and asserted only by way of an entry into such registry.[101]

(4) Transfer of digital securities

10.85   The registration of a right in a securities registry has the legal effect that the right is transferred by way of an entry in the securities registry. The technical modalities for the transfer depend on the DLT protocol being used and can vary considerably. In the case of an ERC-20 token, one of the most common standards for fungible tokens, a token is transferred by the holder sending the token to the transferee's public address. The transaction is authorized by the transferor signing it with its private key. The signature is an expression of the transferor's will to transfer the token to the transferee.

10.86   Only the person holding the private key for the tokens can initiate a transfer. The holder of the private key may or may not be the legal owner of digital securities. What is therefore transferred from a legal and conceptual perspective is the right to control entries in the securities registry, similar to the possession of certificated securities.

10.87   Since it is possible to transfer a physical copy of the private key, it is also possible that a transfer takes place outside the DLT system (off chain).[102] This is, for example, the case when the transferee receives a physical copy of the private key from the transferor. The assumption that every transfer of tokens is directly reflected in the registry is therefore not correct. However, unless and until the transferee updates the registry by using the private key, the transferor keeps the power to transfer the token a second time to a second transferee (who will then prevail over the first transferee). Moreover, as long as the registry is not updated, the original transferor qualifies as the legitimate owner of the token. Payment to the registered owner discharges the issuer, and a purchaser in good faith from that person acquires full title.

10.88   The rules of a DLT protocol can also make the completion of the transfer dependent on further requirements, such as its approval by the issuer or certain authorities. Such conditions and requirements can be easily integrated into the token smart contract, with the effect that a transfer is technically not possible unless the condition has been met.

---

[101] See Art 973e(1) CO; Kuhn, 'Registerwertrechte', para 102.
[102] Kuhn, 'Registerwertrechte', para 119.

CORE ELEMENTS OF A LEGAL FRAMEWORK FOR DIGITAL SECURITIES   329

The transfer of digital securities is completed once the transaction has been validated by the number of participants (nodes) required by the rules of the underlying protocol. Depending on the degree of decentralization and other properties, the validation can take a certain amount of time (block time). Block time is a measure of the time it takes to produce a new block, or data file, in a blockchain network. Each protocol has its own defined block time. For instance, the Bitcoin network's block time is around 10 minutes[103] while the Ethereum network's block time is about 13 seconds.[104] The actual time necessary for the validation of a transaction may also depend on the traffic on a particular DLT system and other factors like transaction pricing.[105] A legislative framework must take such factors into account when providing for the finality of transactions.   10.89

(5) Good-faith acquisition of digital securities

Dispositions of digital securities are only effective if made by, or on behalf of, the owner. In other word, the 'nemo dat' or 'nemo plus' rule also applies to transfers of digital securities. Securities laws have always provided strong protections to good faith purchasers in order to shield commercial transactions.[106] The legislation on digital securities also protects a purchaser who acquires digital securities from a transferor who is registered in the securities registry.[107]   10.90

The protection of the good faith purchaser of physical securities is based on the transferor's possession of the instrument. In the case of digital securities, it is founded on the entry of the transferor in the securities registry. As a result, a transferee who acquires from the person registered in the securities registry acquires good and valid title even if the registered holder had no power to dispose of the securities. In accordance with general securities law principles this is true even if the securities have been stolen by the person registered as the holder.[108]   10.91

In line with general commercial principals, a transferee is protected only if it acted in good faith in relation to the transferor's ownership. The legislation on digital securities tends to follow the relatively general test developed for order securities where good faith is denied only if the transferee knew of ought to have known that the transferor lacked the required power to dispose of the securities.[109]   10.92

---

[103] Bitcoin, 'Vocabulary: Block', <https://bitcoin.org/en/vocabulary#block> (accessed 21 July 2021).
[104] Etherscan, 'Ethereum Average Block Time Chart', <https://etherscan.io/chart/blocktime> (accessed 21 July 2021).
[105] For a theoretical framework see Chiu and Koeppl, 'Blockchain-based Settlement for Asset Trading', 20 et seq.
[106] See Gilmore, 'Good Faith Purchase'; Art 18 Geneva Securities Convention (Acquisition by an innocent person).
[107] See Art 973e(3) CO (Switzerland); Art 9 TVTG (Liechtenstein); § 26 eWpG (Germany).
[108] This seems to be true at least for Swiss law where the 'good faith purchaser' provision in the DLT Act has been modelled after Art 935 CO (providing that cash and bearer securities cannot be reclaimed even if taken against the holder's will). See Kuhn, 'Registerwertrechte', para 124.
[109] See Art 973e(3) CO (Switzerland); Art 9 TVTG (Liechtenstein); § 26 eWpG (Germany).

(6) Security interests in digital securities

10.93 Digital securities can also be subject to security interests in accordance with general principles of secured transaction laws. Since digital securities are regulated in analogy to certificated securities for purposes of transferring ownership, it is also possible to create and perfect a security interest in digital securities by transferring control to the secured party. It is, in other words, possible to create possessory security interests in digital securities.

10.94 Since ownership of digital securities is reflected in a public registry, it is moreover possible to create non-possessory security interests. This is expressly recognized by both the Swiss and the Liechtenstein Acts, although under slightly different conditions.[110] Both acts require that the security interest is made public by way of an entry in the securities registry, ie can be recognized when searching the registry. The time when the security interest is perfected must also be clearly recognizable.[111] Since a timestamp is part of the basic equipment of any blockchain, this requirement is easy to comply with. The Swiss Act finally requires that in case of a default the secured party has the exclusive right to dispose of the securities. In order to enforce a non-possessory security interest in case of default, the security arrangement must provide for a procedure or a process for removing control from the debtor. Since digital securities can be programmed, the underlying smart contract can automatically transfer control to the secured party if an oracle determines that the debtor is in default.

(7) Conflict of laws regarding digital securities

10.95 The use of DLT systems also raises major challenges for determining the law applicable to the transfer of digital securities.[112] The main reason is that the decentralization of many blockchains make it difficult or impracticable to determine a jurisdiction with which the system, or a transaction made on this system, has a relevant or close relationship. Traditional connecting factors relying on an objective 'closest relationship'-test are therefore difficult to apply to DLT-based digital securities. However, these challenges are not new. They have in particular also arisen in relation to intermediated securities where the determination of the applicable law is still a largely unresolved issue in cross-border situations, at least for the jurisdictions which have not yet ratified the Hague Securities Convention.

---

[110] See Art 973g(1) CO (Switzerland) (providing that a security interest in register securities can also be perfected without transferring the register securities if the security interest is made public in the securities registry and if only the secured party can dispose of the register securities in the event of default); see also Art 6(2)(a) TVTG (Liechtenstein) (providing that a pledge of a token can also be perfected without transfer provided it can be recognized by a third party and the time of perfection can be clearly determined).
[111] See Art 6(2)(a) TVTG.
[112] On this topic, see also Ch 11, s K.

10.96 In a context where no clear relationship to a specific jurisdiction can be established based on an objective connecting factor, party autonomy[113] is a tried and tested means for ensuring legal certainty.[114] It is globally recognized that granting the parties the freedom to choose the applicable law is—in principle—an efficient approach solution for determining the applicable law.[115] Assuming equal negotiation powers and the absence of information asymmetries, the parties are best suited to make a rational choice of the law governing a contractual relationship.[116]

10.97 Party autonomy is much more limited in international property law for a variety of reasons,[117] including the protection of persons not privy to a transaction and public policy interests like the publicity of rights in rem.[118] Party autonomy has in particular been acknowledged by the Hague Securities Convention as the primary connecting factor, even if the laws which may be chosen by the parties are limited (Article 4 Hague Securities Convention).

10.98 In the case of DLT-based securities, the issue of the protection of third parties does not arise in the same way as in the case of movable objects or physical securities, because third parties can only participate in transactions if they have directly or indirectly become system participants. This requires them to have agreed to the terms and conditions for participants, which may include a choice of law. The interests of the creditors, supervisory authorities, or the public are adequately safeguarded by the reservations of the *lex fori concursus* or supervisory regulations (which usually qualify as *loi d'application immédiate*) and *ordre public*.

10.99 The Swiss DLT Act includes an amendment to the Private International Law Act (PILA) which recognizes party autonomy in relation to rights represented by a (physical or electronic) title (see Article 145a PILA). The provision is drafted in a rather cumbersome manner, but according to the legislative materials its clear purpose is to acknowledge the parties' right to freely choose the law applicable to the transfer of digital securities, at least if the security represents a contractual right. Party autonomy in international property law has long been recognized in Swiss conflict of laws (see Articles 105, 106 PILA), but the choice of law was not effective against third parties.

10.100 The Liechtenstein DLT Act does not provide a universal conflict-of-laws provision, but rather a unilateral provision regulating the territorial scope of the TVTG's private law provisions. According to Article 3(2) TVTG, the private law provisions are applicable

---

[113] The reference to party autonomy here is to the freedom of the parties to choose the law applicable to their relationship (conflict-of-laws party autonomy), which needs to be distinguished from the party autonomy granted under a specific legal system (internal party autonomy). Conflict-of-laws party autonomy displaces also mandatory provisions under different laws, unless those are applicable as international mandatory provisions.
[114] See Mills, *Party Autonomy*; Ruhl, *Party Autonomy*.
[115] See, eg, Garcimartín, 'Regulatory Competition', 251; Guzman, 'Choice of Law: New Foundations', 913–15; Muir Watt, 'Choice of Law', 386–7; O'Hara and Ribstein, 'From Politics to Efficiency in Choice of Law', 1151; O'Hara and Ribstein, 'Conflict of Laws and Choice of Law', 631.
[116] Ruhl, *Party Autonomy*, 32–3.
[117] See Westrik and Weide, *Party Autonomy*. D'Avout, *Solutions*; reviewed by Stoll, *RabelsZ*, 73 (2009), 383–95.
[118] Flessner, 'Choice of Law in International Property Law', 26.

to tokens generated or issued by a service provider or an issuer in Liechtenstein (letter a) or if the parties to a transaction in relation to tokens have expressly agreed to its application (letter b). Article 4 TVTG provides moreover that a token qualifies as an asset located in Liechtenstein if it is governed by Liechtenstein law in accordance with Article 3. This fiction permits to establish the jurisdiction of the Liechtenstein courts, which have jurisdiction in relation to assets located in Liechtenstein. Article 3(2)(b) TVTG permits parties to a transaction in relation to tokens (whether or not issued by an issuer in Liechtenstein) to freely choose Liechtenstein law to govern their transaction and thus to establish the jurisdiction of the Liechtenstein courts.

10.101 The German eWpG also includes a conflict-of-laws rule and provides in § 32 that rights to an electronic security and disposal of an electronic security are subject to the law of the State which supervises the electronic securities registry. The Federal Government explains correctly that the connection to the location (lex cartae sitae, Chapter IV margin no. 201 et seq) is ruled out in the case of electronic securities and that the securities registry is difficult to locate in the case of electronic registry management. So far, however, no State has declared the maintenance of DLT registries to be an activity requiring a license; MiCA does not count this activity as crypto services either. In addition, DLT systems are precisely characterized by the fact that a single, central point cannot be determined. § 32 eWpG will therefore not lead to clear results in many, if not most, cases. It would make more sense to make dispositions of electronic securities subject to the law of the State under which the relevant registry is organized.

10.102 The discussion about conflict-of-law issues in connection with the blockchain and in particular the determination of the best connecting factor is only at the beginning. A quick consensus is not expected, so that there will be considerable uncertainty in this regard for the time being. In this respect, digital securities do not differ from intermediated securities, where the determination of the law applicable to cross-border securities transactions is still causing considerable problems, at least in States that have not ratified the Hague Securities Convention.

E. Regulation of Crypto Securities

(1) Introduction

10.103 As financial technology evolves and the trend towards digitization, including tokenization of assets and the use of platforms based on distributed ledger technology, accelerates, the regulation of financial services has to adapt as well.

10.104 Existing securities regulation predates the advent of new technologies and services leveraging such technology. Concepts that are traditionally applied in the regulation of securities and related activities often presuppose certain functions and services to be provided in specific ways (such as centralized governance, specific form requirements, intermediation) and usually rely on identifiable responsible actors to be the focal point of regulatory requirements.

Given that digital assets may entail a high degree of decentralization, an absence of intermediaries, or a blurring of traditionally segregated functions such as trading, clearing, and settlement, as a result, many jurisdictions have encountered challenges when addressing regulatory issues resulting from digital assets such as crypto securities.[119]

10.105

(2) Function and scope of regulation

There are some fundamental issues that arise when trying to apply traditional concepts and classifications to digital assets and related activities. A general benchmark on whether and how to apply regulatory requirements is the principle that if a particular asset, activity, or service is economically equivalent to an already regulated one and entails the same types and degrees or risk, then the same regulatory standards should apply.[120]

10.106

However, this necessitates that regulatory authorities have a comprehensive understanding of the structure, complexity, and intricacies of digital assets and the underlying technology used, such as DLT. This in turn requires regulators to follow closely the quickly emerging field of technical innovation in the financial sphere and acquire a thorough knowledge of technical features of digital assets and services that are being developed.

10.107

(a) Regulatory policy objectives
The primary aim of financial regulation is to maintain the stability of the financial system and contain risks. As noted in Chapter 9, paragraph 9.07, as concerns securities, key regulatory policy objectives are (i) investor protection, (ii) enhanced safety and efficiency of holding and settlement arrangements, and, more broadly, (iii) limiting systemic risk. Whilst not necessarily creating new types of risks, the use of new technologies might create new sources or emanations of risks that are not yet included in the scope of existing regulatory frameworks. In the area of securities, an enhanced reliance on digitization, distribution, and cryptography may raise issues as regards various types of risks. For instance, as regards operational risk, there may be issues of cyber resilience (reliability of cryptography) and maturity of technology (role of nodes in a DLT arrangement), operational capacity, and scalability. There may be issues of data integrity, privacy and confidentiality, or concerning the immutability of

10.108

---

[119] For further discussion, see UNSGSA FinTech Working Group and CCAF, *Early Lessons on Regulatory Innovations to Enable Inclusive FinTech*.
[120] See FSB, *Regulation, Supervision and Oversight of 'Global Stablecoin' Arrangements*, p 31; and also Expert Group on Regulatory Obstacles to Financial Innovation, *Thirty Recommendations on Regulation, Innovation and Finance: Final Report to the European Commission*, p 13.

data (error handling). There may be new aspects not known to the traditional securities infrastructure, such as modes of settlement relying on consensus or proof-of-work as well as probabilistic finality that are not yet addressed in existing regulatory requirements. Distributed record keeping or transaction processing may blur regulatory and legal responsibilities that were traditionally based on bilateral principal-agent relationships.

10.109 This poses challenges to regulatory authorities trying to cover, address, and mitigate these risks in an appropriate manner. Apart from a radical approach of banning digital assets outright, there are three basic approaches to regulation and authorization of digital assets and services surrounding them: A regulatory authority may try to apply existing regulation such as regulation surrounding the issuance, trading, holding, and settlement of securities to digital assets that are considered to be financial instruments. Alternatively, a regulator may try to adjust existing regulatory frameworks to provide adjustments for specific activities based on new technology. Lastly, a regulator may decide to create a bespoke new regime specific to digital securities (for example, for DLT based exchanges or depositories or for custodial wallet service providers).

10.110 All of these approaches may come with their own challenges, even if the aim of all is to provide certainty on the applicable rules and mitigate risks related to the performance of activities surrounding digital securities. On the one hand, the application of existing regulation may lead to problems of interpretation and application to the extent that new technology may entail features not falling clearly within known regulatory definitions. On the other hand, an adapted or tailor-made regime may give rise to a non-level playing field between incumbents and new market entrants, either by providing a more lenient or a more stringent regime for services based on new technology.

(b) Function of regulation

10.111 Looking at the application of securities regulation to digital securities and services based on new technology, beyond the basic concepts of 'same business, same risk, same regulation' and ensuring a level playing field, the regulatory discourse centres around a number of central considerations, in particular technological neutrality, proportionality, and regulatory perimeter.

10.112 (i) Technological neutrality The principle of technology neutrality is meant to describe the principle that regulation should 'neither impose[s] nor discriminate[s] in favour of the use of a particular type of technology',[121] ie rules should not require or assume a particular technology and should not hinder the use or development of technologies in the future. This principle enjoys wide acceptance in principle but its practical application is not always straightforward. Whilst direct requirements of the use of a certain technology exist to a certain extent (such as the usage of specific message formats in the

---

[121] Recital 18 of Directive 2002/21/EC on a common regulatory framework for electronic communications networks and services.

transmission of transaction data),[122] in many instances the exclusion of certain technologies may be less evident.

One such example is the underlying regulatory assumption in the field of securities issuance and settlement that certain activities such as the maintenance of issuance registries or settlement systems are a given, implying centralized operations under the governance of a responsible legal entity (the operator).[123] A platform or network arrangements relying on fully decentralized DLT set-ups without any identifiable entity responsible for the governance, access rules, or risk management is likely to run afoul of requirements concerning such a centralized set-up when trying to provide registration or settlement of digital securities. Another example is the question whether a digital security issued in tokenized form would qualify as traditional security in the meaning of traditional securities law and regulation in a specific jurisdiction. A change in the form of an asset does not necessarily change its economic substance, but may result in a different legal and regulatory classification (should a digital bond be treated similarly to a bond written on paper? Should a digital asset in tokenized form be considered as property and transferred as such or not?). To resolve such issues, recourse may be needed to interpretation of rules, entailing legal uncertainties in the absence of legal clarification or regulatory guidance. **10.113**

(ii) **Proportionality** A further regulatory consideration when it comes to the application of requirements to new products and new service providers is the principle of proportionality. In regulation, a proportionate approach means tailoring regulatory requirements to a financial institution's size, systemic importance, complexity, and risk profile. The aim is to avoid an excessive regulatory burden for smaller and non-complex financial institutions that could unduly hamper their competitive positions without a clear prudential justification.[124] **10.114**

Indeed, the costs of regulatory compliance can be prohibitive for a small start-up. To the extent that the scope and size of activities of a particular entity entails less risk than for instance a globally active complex financial institution, it could be envisaged to apply a lighter targeted regulatory regime commensurate to the particular risk profile. This is being done for instance in EU payments regulation, where depending on the concrete activities, lighter specific authorization regimes apply for e-money institutions or payment institutions.[125] However, the application of such proportional regimes requires specific attention, as for instance in the field of digital finance, the financial situation and risk profile of a small fintech start-up may be very different to the one of a global technology firm entering the financial services domain by leveraging on their massive internet platforms. **10.115**

---

[122] See for instance the use of ISO 20022 standards in Regulation (EU) 260/2012 establishing technical and business requirements for credit transfers and direct debits in euro.
[123] See for instance the definition of 'financial market infrastructure' in CPSS and IOSCO, *Principles for Financial Market Infrastructure* (2012), p 176.
[124] Lautenschläger, *Is Small Beautiful?*.
[125] For more details, see <https://ec.europa.eu/info/business-economy-euro/banking-and-finance/consumer-finance-and-payments_en> (accessed 21 July 2021).

10.116 A specific consideration to address the specificities of new market entrants is around the creation of so-called regulatory sandboxes. Regulatory sandboxes enable a direct testing environment for innovative products, services, or business models pursuant to a specific testing plan, which usually includes some degree of regulatory lenience combined with certain safeguards.[126] Regulatory sandboxes (which should be distinguished from so-called innovation hubs primarily aimed to promote a particular financial market as a centre for financial innovation) bring along potential benefits and risks. For regulators, sandboxes allow enhancing understanding of new or changed risks brought by new technology which can facilitate an adequate policy response. For innovators, they can reduce regulatory uncertainties and help lower the high barriers to entry in the sector. However, among the main possible risks, some are specific to innovation facilitators and regulatory sandboxes such as level playing field concerns, whereas another risk relates to regulatory arbitrage to the extent that strategies applied by jurisdictions to raise their attractiveness as a fintech hub may lead to a race to the bottom when it comes to appropriate risk management.

10.117 **(iii) Regulatory perimeter** Traditionally, regulatory approaches in the financial domain are entity based, ie the application of a particular regulatory regime is linked to the authorization or license for a specific entity to provide a defined set of financial services. Depending on the business model, an entity can be subject to regulatory requirements in relation to the carrying out of regulated financial services; for other activities that are not regulated financial services, the entity may or may not be subject to regulatory requirements.[127]

10.118 Questions may arise if a particular activity does not squarely fall within the remit of a defined regulated financial service, for instance, for activities relating to digital assets (such as issuance and trading of digital securities), because of such activity failing to qualify for a constitutive element (for example a particular form requirement) of the regulatory framework in question despite being equal in terms of economic purpose and effect. In such situation, a determination needs to be made whether such activity is permissible without authorization and application of regulatory rules because it is falling outside the regulatory remit or whether regulatory responses are needed. In the latter case, some jurisdictions have considered bans whereas others have been looking at adjusting the regulatory perimeter by extending the need for a regulatory license or authorization explicitly to new types of digital financial assets or services.

10.119 One particularly interesting response that is increasingly discussed by competent authorities is a shift from traditional entity-focused regulation to a more functional approach, whereby a defined service or activity is subject to specific requirements irrespective of the regulatory status of the entity or entities performing the activity or

---

[126] European Parliament, *Regulatory Sandboxes and Innovation Hubs for FinTech*, p 19.
[127] EBA, *Report on Regulatory Perimeter, Regulatory Status and Authorisation Approaches in Relation to FinTech Activities*.

service. An example for this approach is the proposed new Eurosystem oversight framework for electronic payment instruments, schemes, and arrangements.[128] The Eurosystem follows a functional and holistic approach to oversight, which covers all types of payment instruments resulting in a transfer of value (whether credit transfers, card payment, e-money transfers, or tokenized payments) and includes the governance function and the functionalities of a payment arrangement, as well as all the functions of a payment scheme. The approach covers both licensed and non-licensed governance bodies. For cases in which a governance body is responsible for the functioning of several payment schemes or arrangements, the overseer may assess these jointly.

(3) Regulatory classification

(a) Absence of common terminology and categorization

10.120 A major impediment to the analysis and the formulation of clear policies for the emerging digital asset industry is the lack of clear and common terminology. As of today, there are no commonly accepted definitions, or a generally agreed classification of digital assets. Terms used differ considerably depending on the background and often the motivations of the user, whether it is crypto asset, virtual asset, crypto security, digital token, or other variants. The absence of consensus over terminology is a key obstacle to certainty over legal characterization and in turn the regulatory treatment, which frequently, but not necessarily follows a legal qualification. Regulators therefore face the challenge to identify the terminology most suitable for their regulatory objectives and to develop suitable and robust definitions and classifications. This is usually done by gathering empirical evidence and engaging key stakeholders, followed by engagement among competent authorities and regulators.

10.121 However, even if a particular jurisdiction were to develop a consistent and comprehensive approach to the legal and regulatory categorization, given the inherent cross-border nature of digital assets and services transactions, diverging terms and concepts among regulatory bodies may facilitate regulatory arbitrage. The lack of harmonized and coordinated regulatory responses allows actors in the digital assets space to exploit regulatory loopholes and circumvent stringent regulations. Thus, there is a need for global co-ordination aligning domestic approaches.

(b) Emergence of a basic taxonomy

10.122 Taxonomy is the science of classification by identifying different entities or objects, establishing criteria for classifying them into distinct categories and sub-categories, and naming them.[129] This practice introduces common definitions, terminologies, and

---

[128] Draft for public consultation (October 2020), <https://www.ecb.europa.eu/paym/intro/cons/pdf/pisa/ecb.PISApublicconsultation20201027_2.en.pdf> (accessed 21 July 2021).
[129] <https://www.macmillandictionary.com/dictionary/british/taxonomy> (accessed 21 July 2021).

semantics which can be used across multiple systems. A common system of categorization allows to provide a harmonized view and facilitates the handling of new and evolving additions as they appear. The existence of a taxonomy for digital securities, in particular in a DLT environment is pivotal to understanding the landscape of digital assets. However, the categorization of assets available on distributed ledgers still poses significant challenges for market regulators.

10.123 Some basic questions are relevant to support the development of a conceptual framework. First the extent to which digital assets are similar in nature to traditional assets such as securities needs to be assessed. If so, a determination has to be made whether the existing regulatory framework can be applied directly or whether adaptations are required due to specific technical features such as the use of open and permissionless distributed ledgers. Further, should a differentiation be made between digital assets that are a tokenized representation of traditional assets and those that constitute new assets by themselves? What will happen if a digital asset entails hybrid features such as being usable both as a security or as a means of payment? Should sectoral regulation be applied cumulatively, or only the stricter requirements, or would a new set of requirements be appropriate?

10.124 At this juncture, a common system of categorization for digital assets is still emerging. A number of regulators have issued classification frameworks for digital assets, which have been generally inspired by the particularities of open and permissionless networks and the usage of tokens, and which typically consist of three broad types categorized by the primary use cases/functions: payment/exchange tokens (a means of value exchange), utility tokens (granting access to a digital platform or service), and security tokens (an investment instrument).[130]

10.125 This three-category classification has been useful as a first guidance for regulatory responses to digital assets. However, there remain considerable practical difficulties with this basic framework to capture the complexities of a quickly evolving innovation landscape. First, this classification may not cover all digital assets (see paragraphs 10.117-9 on the regulatory perimeter). Securities tokens failing to meet one of the constitutive elements of a traditional financial instrument may remain outside the regulators' scope. Second, some tokens could fall under more than one of these categories. For such so-called hybrid tokens, it may be unclear whether the legal and regulatory requirements associated with each category should be applied cumulative or hierarchical.

10.126 For example, for a security token that is also a payment token, regulators could adopt different positions. They could apply a cumulative approach, whereby the hybrid token has to comply with both securities and payment regulation (which may be difficult to do as some requirements may be conflicting). Alternatively, they may take a hierarchical

---

[130] For instance in Switzerland, see *FINMA Guidelines for enquiries regarding the regulatory framework for initial coin offerings (ICOs)* (February 2018), <https://www.finma.ch/en/news/2018/02/20180216-mm-ico-wegleitung/> (accessed 21 July 2021), p 3. See also para 10.11.

approach whereby hybrid tokens have to comply with either securities or payment regulation. In the latter case, the regulator may be either looking at the predominant feature (is the token mainly a payment or an investment instrument?) or apply the more stringent regime (which in most jurisdictions would be securities regulation). A further element of differentiation applied by regulatory authorities may be whether a digital security in the form of a securities token is native to a distributed ledger (ie it is only constituted by the token on the ledger itself) or whether it is a reference to a security which has been issued and recorded in a traditional manner. A few regulators have specified their approach in this regard (see section E(5), paragraphs 10.150 et seq), however, in many jurisdictions there is still no clarification or guidance available.

(4) Application of securities regulation to digital securities

10.127 The application of existing regulation pertaining to securities issuance, trading, and settlement to assets in the digital space comes with a number of challenges as highlighted in the previous sections. Most activities related to digital securities resemble closely existing traditional activities found in securities markets, such as exchange and trading platforms, custodians or service providers. However, the use of new technologies entails a number of novel elements such as decentralization, the use of cryptographic keys, mining activities, etc., that do not fit always seamlessly into existing regulatory regimes. Even where regulation is to a large extent formulated in a manner that is technology agnostic, the particular characteristics of given designs of digital assets and the underlying technologies used can give rise to uncertainties on the application of specific regulatory requirements.

(a) Regulatory considerations on issuance and registration
10.128 When it comes to the application of issuance requirements, traditional regulation is looking at a responsible entity, a legal or natural person, to be identified as the legal issuer of a security. Such identified issuer is the obligor of rights arising from the security, whether it is a debt or a participation right. Such assignation of an issuer role is also the precondition for the application of a number of subsequent responsibilities such as distribution limitations or anti-money laundering obligations. Digital assets, however, may be created not only by any individual or entity that has been granted access to the data layer[131] (for example, where an application is run on a DLT), by corporations, public-sector institutions, and enterprise consortia among others, but also by informal groups (for example, an open source community of developers) or associations without legal personality. This may raise challenges for regulators, such as identifying who can be held liable for a breach of securities regulation such as limitations on investor types. Regulation may need to be adapted to clarify whether such forms of issuance are

---

[131] See Rauchs et al, *Distributed Ledger Technology Systems*, p 33 et seq.

permissible or not and whether stricter requirements may apply to certain variants of digital issuance.

10.129 Once digital securities have been created, there are various means for distributing these to potential holders, such as initial offerings, mining, air drops, or forks.[132] Depending on the technical environment used, the access to such methods may be limited. This may give rise to regulatory compliance questions such as whether the issuer has to issue a prospectus or what additional documentation[133] is needed for the distribution of digital assets (such as underwriting/purchase agreements, limitations on classes of investors). This in turn raises issues as to whether there should be stricter requirements for the distribution of digital securities and how these requirements are checked, and if necessary, enforced.

10.130 When it comes to registration requirements, in traditional ledger, registry, or account-based systems, the entry of information into an official information repository plays a constitutive role in the creation of a financial asset,[134] and provides the top-tier level based on which subsequent secondary market operations with digital assets can be carried out. In such traditional models, specific entities, often centralized for a specific market, are authorized to maintain the relevant registry(/ies) which record securities issuances. The operator of such register has the legal duty to ensure that the registry is accurate (ie reflects the legal position at the relevant time) and that all changes to the registry are made in accordance with the law.

10.131 In a digitized environment, for instance where tokens representing securities are created on a distributed ledger, the question arises whether there is an identifiable entity that can be attributed with the requirements of an operator of a securities registry. Given that the performance of such operator function usually requires some form of authorization by a competent authority, there may be uncertainties whether for example a distributed ledger is subject to such authorization requirement and whether a responsible operator could (or should) be identified. On a more technical level, existing regulation may need to be reviewed in view of the need for specific requirements regarding digital registries such as operational or cyber resilience.

(b) Regulatory considerations on trading of digital securities

10.132 Once created and distributed, digital securities can be traded, exchanged, and transferred in multiple ways on secondary market. The trading of digital securities, in particular if done over-the-counter, raises first and foremost questions on the substantive law regime for holding and transferring digital securities.

---

[132] See Blandin et al, *Global Cryptoasset Regulatory Landscape Study*, p 24.
[133] On specific issues that may arise if the documentation is embedded in so-called 'smart contracts', see ECB Advisory Groups, *Use of DLT in Post-trade Processes*, p 8.
[134] Allen et al, *Legal and Regulatory Considerations for Digital Assets*, p 31.

10.133 However, increasingly digital securities are traded through exchange platforms, ie digital marketplaces that provide transfer and exchange services, with or without requiring corresponding on-chain transfers. Whether such a marketplace qualifies as a traditional stock exchange, with the consequence of triggering licensing or authorization requirements for operators of such exchanges, may depend on the specific features of the exchange platform, such as whether it entails price discovery elements or bid and sell matching, but also on the legal qualification of the digital assets traded on such exchange. Given the differences in approach to the legal qualification of digital assets, regulatory authorities across jurisdictions have developed a wide variety of regulatory response to regulate trading activities. For instance, regulators may regulate entities differently depending on whether they are offering exchange services against digital asset and/or against a fiat currency.[135]

10.134 The regulatory qualification of the exchange service in turn may lead to the application of other requirements such as investor protection rules (fraud prevention), monitoring and reporting of transactions, or price transparency rules.

(c) Regulatory considerations applicable to digital securities intermediaries (custodians, wallet providers)

10.135 Traditional financial market structures involve intermediaries holding financial assets in custody on behalf of clients. This is particularly prevalent in the domain of securities. The complexities of intermediated holdings of securities, both domestically and in particular cross-border, are well known. These entail property law issues, often compounded by the dematerialization of financial assets. In intermediated holding structures, there is often a split of possession/control and ownership, or, in some legal systems, between 'legal' and 'beneficial' title. Sometimes, property rights in a financial asset are functionally replaced by obligational rights against an intermediary in complex, layered structures.

10.136 Whilst dematerialization also is an obvious inherent feature of digital securities, the additional element of decentralization (and the implied discarding of traditional forms of trusted intermediaries) originally dominated the digital securities space such as securities tokens based on DLT technology. However, mirroring earlier developments in the traditional securities markets, the crypto ecosystem has seen a rapid emergence of a variety of intermediaries. These often operate without being authorized by regulators; in many cases because there was, at least initially, no legal requirement for them to do so.[136]

10.137 Some variants, in particular in the context of what is generally labelled as the provision of 'digital wallets',[137] do pose particular issues in this regard as they enable new types

---

[135] For further details, see Blandin et al, *Global Cryptoasset Regulatory Landscape Study*, p 45 et seq.
[136] Nevertheless, existing regulation has sometimes been directly applied to actors that perform tasks similar to traditional intermediaries, see s E(2), paras 10.106 et seq.
[137] Software that stores private keys used to initiate transactions and provides additional customizable services, eg, an overview of asset balance and transaction history; cf ECB Advisory Groups, *Use of DLT in Post-trade Processes*, Glossary, p 31.

of custody, such as wallet services where the provider technically cannot move funds without user action[138] or services such as decentralized exchanges that do not entail a central operator and thus do not offer a regulatory anchor point for the application of regulatory requirements such as client asset protection rules.

10.138 From a risk perspective, the holding of any financial asset entails an element of risk, and the storage of digital securities is no exception. With the emergence of digital securities, existing tools for custody are replaced by new technical solutions to address the risk of misappropriation of those digital assets, with a different risk profile compared to traditional securities. A widespread technique in digital securities holdings is the use of cryptographic encryption consisting of private and public keys. Such keys can be stolen by attackers, or hacked from wallets or exchanges, if not properly secured. Similarly, keys can be lost, which prevents holders (or their legal successors) from accessing their assets permanently.

10.139 As the secure key storage and management is a cumbersome and complex task which requires a high level of technical proficiency, it is often outsourced to third-party custodial service/wallet providers.[139] This re-introduces a layer of intermediation to the way that digital assets are being held, which necessitates adequate regulatory rules to ensure client asset protection, handling of positions, and accurate records for instance in the event of disruptions, cyberattacks, or insolvency of the service provider.

10.140 Furthermore, given that the providers of wallet services or digital securities custody frequently also conduct transactions in own positions, the distinction between self-custody and third-party custody may become blurred. This warrants the application of regimes for the avoidance of conflicts of interests and client asset protection.

10.141 Finally, and more generally, the potentially highly tiered or opaque holding patterns that may result from the interposition of various players performing diverse functions in intermediating digital securities supports the application of stringent transparency requirements for involved entities outlining the risk profiles and the rights and obligations of holders of intermediated digital securities.

(d) Regulatory considerations applicable to digital securities clearing and settlement infrastructures

10.142 The ecosystem for digital assets in many instances relies on specific technical platforms such as distributed ledger arrangements for the storage of the assets. If such arrangement serves also as a facilitator for the transfer of digital securities between entities that are directly or indirectly connected to such platform, this 'transfer function' closely

---

[138] It is commonly assumed that having control over private keys in a public-private key cryptographic system can be described as 'custody', but, given the impossibility of traditional possession of intangible objects, important questions arise in the context of relationships described as 'custodial'. From a legal perspective, other concepts, such as 'control', could provide an alternative to possession (eg involving storage of private keys).
[139] Rauchs et al, *Distributed Ledger Technology Systems*, p 52.

resembles from an operational and regulatory perspective a traditional securities settlement system (SSS). This holds particularly true if the arrangement entails a set of rules for the transfer of digital assets among participants, and a mechanism for validating transactions. This gives rise to the question to which extent such transfer arrangements should be subject to licensing or authorization requirements applicable to SSSs and if so, how such arrangement would have to comply with applicable regulation and relevant international standards for financial market infrastructures (FMIs).[140] Triggered by the advent of potentially systemically relevant stablecoin arrangements, the global standard-setting community has been reflecting on the applicability of existing global standards for financial services to novel arrangements leveraging innovative technology and whether additional guidance may be necessary to foster compliance with relevant regulatory expectations (see section E(6), paragraphs 10.182 et seq).

10.143 The application of existing requirements for FMIs may not be straightforward due to specific novel features compared with existing FMIs, such as the degree of decentralization of operations and/or governance, and the potentially large-scale deployment of emerging technologies such as distributed ledger technology (DLT) or automated process protocols ('smart contracts'). Other such features are the potential use of settlement assets that are neither central bank money nor commercial bank money and that carry additional financial risk, or the interdependencies between multiple functions performed by the arrangement. The applications of FMI rules may also be contingent on the legal qualification of the digital assets, ie whether in a particular jurisdiction, a securities token or a digital representation of a security that exists external to a digital platform would be qualified as a security in the meaning of FMI regulation.

10.144 In order to comply with regulatory expectations for governance,[141] a systemically important[142] arrangement for the transfer and settlement of digital securities would need to have a governance structure allowing for clear and direct lines of responsibility and accountability, which may entail the identification of responsible legal or natural persons. These entities would be responsible for the management and mitigation of all types of risks (whether legal, operational, financial, or others) related to the transfer function.[143] This also entails responsibility for defining and policing access rules as well as a potential liability for fraud, cyber attacks, erroneous transfers, or weaknesses of smart contract protocols or the underlying technology.

---

[140] In this instance, CPSS and IOSCO, *Principles for Financial Market Infrastructures* (PFMI). The PFMI define an FMI as 'a multilateral system among participating institutions, including the operator of the system, used for the purposes of clearing, settling, or recording payments, securities, derivatives, or other financial transactions. FMIs typically establish a set of common rules and procedures for all participants, a technical infrastructure, and a specialized risk-management framework appropriate to the risks they incur. FMIs provide participants with centralized clearing, settlement, and recording of financial transactions among themselves or between each of them and a central party to allow for greater efficiency and reduced costs and risks.'
[141] Cf Principle 2, key considerations 2, 6, and 7 of the PFMI.
[142] As evidenced eg by the number of users, volume and value of transactions, nature and risk profile, interconnectedness, business, structural, and operational complexity, as well as substitutability.
[143] Cf Principle 3, key consideration 3 of the PFMI.

10.145 A particular challenge with complex arrangements based on for example DLT is that—beyond the transfer function—the arrangement may also integrate other functions such as an issuance and registration function, an end-user interface function, or a stability mechanism (such as an underlying pool of assets) which may trigger the application of specific other sets of regulation such as investor protection rules, anti-money laundering regimes, prospectus requirements, etc. This entails an additional challenge for the responsible entities to consider the material risks that the transfer function bears from and poses to other functions and the entities (such as other FMIs, settlement banks, liquidity providers, or service providers) which perform other functions or on which the arrangement relies for its transfer function. At the same time, regulators should consider whether additional guidance may be warranted to avoid overlaps or duplications of potentially relevant regulation.

10.146 Similar issues arise in case of interdependencies with other infrastructure functions such as payments. To the extent that the payment function is integrated in the same technical platform as the securities settlement to support delivery-versus-payment (DvP), questions arise as to whether the platform will have to comply with payment system rules or security settlement system regulation or both regimes at the same time. Furthermore, as with traditional systems, there may be links between a digital securities settlement arrangement and other post-trade infrastructures (for payment, clearing, or settlement, traditional or innovative) to enable DvP or delivery-versus-delivery. This necessitates an appropriate framework for the management of risks posed by or to external infrastructures and the alignment of rules for settlement processes and cross-system finality.

10.147 In all instances, particular attention should be paid to the assets used for money settlement purposes. In accordance with the PFMI, settlement assets should have little or no credit or liquidity risk,[144] such as claims on a central bank (central bank money) or credit institution (commercial bank money). In particular to the extent that the money settlement asset constitutes a new form of representing monetary value (such as a cash/payment token), such usage would not be ruled out per se by the PFMI, but the risk presented by the money settlement asset would need to be carefully assessed. This includes an analysis of whether the money settlement asset provides its holders with a direct legal claim on the issuer and/or claim on, title to, or interest in underlying assets for timely convertibility into other liquid assets such as central bank or commercial bank money, as well as clear and robust processes for fulfilling a holder's claim in both normal and stressed times.

10.148 Finally, it would have to be determined whether the specific architecture of an arrangement such as DLT-based platforms using consensus mechanisms may only provide

---

[144] PFMI Principle 9, key considerations 2, 4, and 5.

probabilistic finality (where there is always a possibility of transaction reversal due to the nature of the consensus model) may be compatible with the expectation to clearly define the point at which a transfer on the ledger becomes irrevocable and technical settlement happens. It should be transparent whether and to what extent there could be a misalignment between technical settlement and legal finality.

(e) Regulatory considerations applicable to digital securities service providers

A last set of considerations that may be relevant in the context of regulation of digital securities is the role that third-party service providers may play in providing ancillary services to the issuers, intermediaries, infrastructures, or holders of digital securities. For instance, such role may be performed by the developers of DLT platforms or the providers of non-custodial wallet services. These activities may raise questions as to whether they require some form of license, for instance if the services were to be considered critical for a settlement infrastructure and subsequent supervision or oversight. This may be driven by risk concerns comparable to traditional outsourcing of risk, with a focus on the ability of the user of such services to understand and control risks stemming from the service. To the extent that DLT platforms are developed by anonymous groups of programmers, additional governance issues may occur such as questions of liability for cyber-attacks or weaknesses of the underlying technology. Specific attention needs to be paid to digital operational resilience, the availability of fall-back solutions, and financial stability considerations (single point of failure).[145]

10.149

(5) Regulatory approaches to digital securities in selected jurisdictions

As noted in section E(3), paragraphs 10.120 et seq, regulatory approaches towards digital securities vary across jurisdictions. This holds true for the regulation of the issuance process, for trading and settlement platforms, or custody and secondary trading.

10.150

The approaches taken are reflections of various factors, including national market developments or underlying legal and regulatory frameworks as well as policy objectives and wider economic considerations. Attitudes as to whether preference is given to the mitigation of risks or to fostering financial innovation or supporting financial inclusion play a role as much as the societal consensus on the role of the private sector versus the public offering of certain functions as a public good.

10.151

Thus, on the one side of the spectrum, one can see outright bans on certain transactions or at least prohibitions for certain actors to engage in such activities, on the other end one can see permissive behaviour of regulators or cautious exploration through forbearance to active encouragement through the creation of regulatory sandboxes for

10.152

---

[145] Cf the EU digital services package, especially the proposed Directive on digital operational resilience; see para 10.181.

new types of actors or services. In between, one can observe attempts to either adjust existing regulation for specific activities or extension of the scope of existing regulation to services leveraging new technologies or business models.

10.153 In the securities field, the regulatory treatment is very closely dependent on questions of legal qualification of certain assets as securities or derivatives and, in particular when it comes to applying existing securities regulation (such as market transparency, prospectus requirements, custody or segregation rules) and enforcement mechanisms. This impacts the determination of whether no new regulation may be needed or whether digital securities and services surrounding them may call for bespoke regulation. The latter may also be determined by fundamental positions on whether financial services should seek to conform with existing regulation (even if services have been designed to function outside established regulatory frameworks) or whether regulation should follow financial developments.

10.154 Overall, those jurisdictions which were primarily concerned about risks were the quickest to act, for instance by clarifying the application of AML rules or by issuing prohibitions. Otherwise, many jurisdictions applied some 'quick fixes' to specific areas by clarifying the applicable regulatory regime for certain activities, with only a small number of jurisdictions starting to try to take a more comprehensive view at the digital asset ecosystem and its integration into the wider financial market regulatory framework.

10.155 The below references to actions taken by specific countries and their relevant regulators is meant only to illustrate some prominent cases for different approaches and is by no means meant to be exhaustive.

(a) Prohibitive approaches

10.156 A number of regulatory authorities have banned specific activities related to digital assets, albeit with different scope, sometimes focusing on prohibiting only specific entities to engage in certain activities and sometimes banning certain activities altogether.

(i) India

10.157 In 2018, the Reserve Bank of India (RBI) prohibited any dealings in crypto assets by regulated financial entities, including banks, non-bank financial companies, or payment system providers. However crypto asset trading through other channels is still permitted.[146]

(ii) China

10.158 In the same vein, a 2017 joint statement[147] by the People's Bank of China (PBC) and other government ministries, building on an earlier notice directed at virtual

---

[146] Reserve Bank of India, *Prohibition on Dealing in Virtual Currencies* (April 2018), <https://www.rbi.org.in/scripts/FS_Notification.aspx?Id=11243&fn=2&Mode=0> (accessed 21 July 2021).
[147] Announcement of the Banking Regulatory Commission, the Securities Regulatory Commission and the Insurance Regulatory Commission of the General Administration of Industry and Commerce, the Ministry of Industry and Information Technology, the Central Network of the People's Bank of China on preventing the risk of issuing and financing tokens (2017).

currencies,[148] banned trading platforms from offering crypto assets to fiat currency exchanges and reiterated that Initial Coin Offerings (ICOs) are considered unauthorized public financing. However, trading platforms could still offer crypto-asset-to-crypto-asset exchange activities. In a 2018 notice,[149] the PBC reiterated China's cautionary stance on crypto assets and ICOs as illegal financing.

(b) Application of existing regulation

10.159 Other jurisdictions have, at least for the time being, refrained from amending their regulatory requirements or introducing new rules, focusing instead in some instances on providing some degree of guidance on the applicability of existing securities regulation.

(iii) Australia

10.160 In 2017, the Australian Securities and Investments Commission (ASIC) released an information sheet, subsequently updated in May 2019,[150] providing guidance on the regulation of ICOs and crypto assets. The information sheet clarified that crypto assets qualifying as financial products under the Corporations Act will attract relevant regulatory obligations. ASIC stated its primary aim[151] is to ensure that products are not misleading or deceptive.

(iv) United States of America

10.161 The US regulatory landscape entails both the federal level and the state level. In the area of securities regulation, at the federal level, the primary regulator is the Securities and Exchange Commission (SEC). So far, the SEC has not yet issued any regulation specific to digital securities. So the question whether existing securities regulation would apply to certain types of digital assets, their custody and trading, depends on whether a particular digital asset would qualify as a security in the meaning of the Securities Act of 1933.[152] In making that determination, the SEC applies the 'Howey test' as established by the US Supreme Court.[153] The Howey test defines securities as investment contracts that involve investment of money or property, in a common enterprise, with profits coming from the sole efforts of people other than the investor. Depending on the

---

[148] Notice of the China Securities Regulatory Commission of the China Banking Regulatory Commission of the Ministry of Industry and Information Technology of the People's Bank of China on Preventing Bitcoin Risk (2013).

[149] People's Bank of China, *Continued Prevention of the Risks in ICO and Virtual Currency Trading* (2018).

[150] Australian Securities and Investments Commission, *Initial Coin Offerings and Crypto-assets* (2019), <https://asic.gov.au/regulatory-resources/digital-transformation/initial-coin-offerings-and-crypto-currency/> (accessed 21 July 2021).

[151] Australian Securities and Investments Commission, *ASIC Acts Against Misleading Initial Coin Offerings and Crypto-asset Funds Targeted at Retail Investors* (September 2018), <https://asic.gov.au/about-asic/news-centre/find-a-media-release/2018-releases/18-274mr-asic-acts-against-misleading-initial-coin-offerings-and-crypto-asset-funds-targeted-at-retail-investors/> (accessed 21 July 2021).

[152] An act to provide full and fair disclosure of the character of securities sold in interstate and foreign commerce and through the mails, and to prevent frauds in the sale thereof, and for other purposes (27 May 1933), 74, <https://govtrackus.s3.amazonaws.com/legislink/pdf/stat/48/STATUTE-48-Pg74.pdf> (accessed 21 July 2021).

[153] *SEC v Howey Co*, 328 US 293 (1946), <https://supreme.justia.com/cases/federal/us/328/293/> (accessed 21 July 2021).

determination of digital assets as securities, issuers, custodians, and other relevant parties will have to comply with the relevant securities regulation. In 2020, the SEC issued a statement describing certain conditions under which a broker-dealer could comply with relevant requirements the Securities Exchange Act with respect to digital asset securities.[154]

(v) Canada

10.162 Key guidance issued by the Canadian Securities Administrators (CSA) in 2018[155] outlines how Canadian securities laws and 'substance over form' tests may apply to ICOs and crypto asset investment funds and exchanges. The staff notice noted that many purported 'utility' tokens were not eligible to be exempt from securities laws, therefore requiring both a prospectus and the registration of the securities issuer. Under the 'Pacific Coin Test', based on the US 'Howey Test', a crypto asset is a security if it involves an 'investment of money in a common enterprise with the expectation of profit that is to come significantly from the efforts of others'.

(c) Focus on anti-money laundering

10.163 In a few instances, the focus of supervisory authorities was limited so far on clarifications concerning the applicability of AML and terrorist financing requirements.

(vi) Hong Kong

10.164 Following the introduction of a virtual asset (VA) exchanges regulatory regime by the Hong Kong Securities and Futures Commission (SFC) in 2019,[156] the SFC issued a proposal outlining a new regulatory framework that would bring operators of VA exchanges within the formal regulatory perimeter of the SFC, and aims to enhance anti-money laundering and counter-terrorist financing (AML/CTF) regulations in Hong Kong.[157]

(d) Technology specific regulation (DLT)

10.165 Having in mind the desire to enhance regulatory certainty and promoting the attractiveness of their financial centres for fintech companies and start-ups in the field of digital financial services, other jurisdictions have taken efforts to provide specific

---

[154] SEC statement describing certain conditions under which a broker-dealer could comply with the requirements of Rule 15c3-3 under the Securities Exchange Act of 1934 (hereinafter the 'Customer Protection Rule' or 'Rule 15c3-3') with respect to digital asset securities, <https://www.sec.gov/rules/policy/2020/34-90788.pdf> (accessed 21 July 2021).

[155] CSA Staff Notice 46-308: Securities Law Implications for Offerings of Tokens (June 2018), <https://www.osc.gov.on.ca/documents/en/Securities-Category4/csa_20180611_46-308_implications-for-offerings-of-tokens.pdf> (accessed 21 July 2021).

[156] SFC Position Paper: Regulation of Virtual Asset Trading Platforms (November 2019), <https://www.sfc.hk/-/media/EN/files/ER/PDF/20191106-Position-Paper-and-Appendix-1-to-Position-Paper-Eng.pdf> (accessed 21 July 2021).

[157] FSTB Public Consultation on Legislative Proposals to Enhance Anti-money Laundering and Counter-terrorist Financing Regulation in Hong Kong (2020).

tailor-made regulation focusing on supporting and regulating the use of specific innovative technologies and technology supported financial services, primarily the use of distributed ledger technology and tokenization.

(vii) Liechtenstein
As part of a comprehensive legislative project to support a DLT-based token economy (Law on Tokens and Trustworthy Technology Service Providers),[158] in 2019, Liechtenstein addressed the regulation and supervision of technology service providers supporting a token ecosystem by providing specific transparency requirements for tokens similar to prospectus regulations for transferable securities[159] and by setting expectations for 'trustworthy technologies', namely DLT technology, as regards the integrity of tokens, their allocation, and exchange.[160] The scope of the TVTG does not deal with any issues covered by other existing financial market regulations.

10.166

(viii) Luxembourg
Luxembourg took a rather specific approach to adapting its legal and regulatory framework to digital securities based on novel technologies such as DLT. It is reviewing its existing legal framework for intermediated securities through amendments to create a legal basis for the use of secured distributed registries, electronic ledgers and databases for the issuance, registration, and circulation of digital securities[161] as well as allowing issuer accounts to be managed by EEA credit institutions and investment firms on a DLT basis without altering the regulatory framework and requirements for the security itself.

10.167

(ix) Gibraltar
Gibraltar developed a bespoke regulatory framework regime for providers of DLT technology, which took effect in 2018.[162] It applies to firms conducting activities that use DLT for the transmission or storage of value belonging to others and that are not subject to any other regulatory framework. Types of activities that require a DLT license include operating a crypto exchange, custodian service providers and asset storage service providers, crypto wallet providers, and operating DLT-based marketplaces that facilitate the buying and selling of goods and services. Firms carrying out such DLT activities need to be authorized and licensed as DLT Providers by Gibraltar's Financial Services Commission (GFSC).

10.168

---

[158] Gesetz über Token und VT-Dienstleister (Token- und VT-Dienstleister-Gesetz; TVTG), LGBl 2019 Nr 301.
[159] Articles 30 et seq TVTG.
[160] Article 2(a) TVTG.
[161] Projet de loi n° 7637 portant modification (i) de la loi modifiée du 5 avril 1993 relative au secteur financier; (ii) de la loi du 6 avril 2013 relative aux titres dématérialisés, <https://legilux.public.lu/eli/etat/projet/pl/20170306> (accessed 21 July 2021).
[162] Gibraltar Financial Services Commission, Financial Services (Distributed Ledger Technology Providers) Regulations 2017.

(x) Malta

10.169 Malta in 2018 issued specific regulation, the Virtual Financial Assets Act,[163] concerning specific classes of DLT based assets, namely: (i) virtual tokens;[164] (ii) virtual financial assets;[165] (iii) electronic money; or (iv) financial instruments, that are intrinsically dependent on or utilize DLT. Where a DLT based asset is classified under the VFAA as a financial instrument or as e-money, then relevant EU legislation, namely the Prospectus Directive, MiFID II, and the E-money Directive applies. Otherwise, issuers are required to establish a legal entity in Malta, properly register a whitepaper, and comply with governance, security, and ongoing disclosure requirements. VFA Service Providers (which includes VFA exchanges) require a license from the Malta Financial Services Authority (MFSA), with licencing requirements including competency, capital, prudential, governance, risk management, conduct of business, and reporting requirements.

10.170 Furthermore, the Innovative Technology Arrangements and Services Act (ITASA)[166] regulates innovative technology arrangements (ITAs), such as DLT software and architecture or smart contracts, and designated innovative technology services providers (ITSPs), requiring recognition by the Malta Digital Innovation Authority (MDIA), whose role is to function as a regulator.

(xi) France

10.171 Following-up on the legal recognition of DLT-based so-called minibonds ('minibons') under the French Commercial Code and the French Monetary and Financial Code by Ordinance n° 2016-520,[167] in 2017 a specific DLT regulation (regulation n° 2017-1674,[168] the 'DLT Regulation') extended the possibility to issue and transfer securities on the basis of a DLT system to all unlisted securities. The DLT Regulation was supplemented by dedicated regulation (decree n° 2018-1226)[169] which specifies further requirements for DLT systems, such as integrity, identification of the owner and the type and number of financial instruments it owns, a business continuity plan, and ensuring access to transaction data.

---

[163] Government of Malta, Virtual Financial Assets Act (VFAA) (November 2018), <https://legislation.mt/eli/cap/590/eng/pdf> (accessed 21 July 2021).

[164] Defined as a form of digital medium recordation whose utility, value, or application is restricted solely to the acquisition of goods or services, either solely within the DLT platform on or in relation to which it was issued or within a limited network of DLT platforms.

[165] Defined as any form of digital medium recordation that is used as a digital medium of exchange, unit of account, or store of value and that is not: (i) electronic money; (ii) a financial instrument; or (iii) a virtual token.

[166] Government of Malta, Innovative Technology Arrangements and Services Act (ITASA) (November 2018), <https://legislation.mt/eli/cap/592/eng/pdf> (accessed 21 July 2021).

[167] Ordonnance n° 2016-520 relative aux bons de caisse, JORF n° 0101 du 29 avril 2016, texte n° 16, <https://www.legifrance.gouv.fr/loda/id/JORFTEXT000032465520/> (accessed 21 July 2021).

[168] Ordonnance n° 2017-1674 relative à l'utilisation d'un dispositif d'enregistrement électronique partagé pour la représentation et la transmission de titres financiers, JORF n° 0287 du 9 décembre 2017, <https://www.legifrance.gouv.fr/loda/id/JORFTEXT000036171908/> (accessed 21 July 2021).

[169] Décret n° 2018-1226 relatif à l'utilisation d'un dispositif d'enregistrement électronique partagé pour la représentation et la transmission de titres financiers et pour l'émission et la cession de minibons, JORF n° 0298 du 26 décembre 2018, <https://www.legifrance.gouv.fr/loda/id/LEGIARTI000037904725> (accessed 21 July 2021).

10.172 Furthermore, in 2019, France regulated the issuance of digital assets not classified as financial instruments (such as Initial Coin Offerings) and intermediaries providing crypto asset services through legislation for markets in digital assets (the 'PACTE law').[170] Issuers have the ability, but not the obligation to apply for a 'visa' from the French Financial Markets Regulator (AMF) in return for filing an information document and by complying with anti-money laundering (AML) duties. Likewise, intermediaries such as custodian wallet providers and crypto/fiat exchange service providers are subject to a mandatory AML registration, while all intermediaries including platforms and investment advisers may apply for an optional license.

(xii) Germany

10.173 In 2021, Germany adopted a law on digital securities and the custody of such digital securities.[171] This legislation aims to provide a framework for issuing securities without issuing a certificate, including through the use of DLT or blockchain technologies, whilst submitting these securities are subject to the same legal requirements as certificated securities. It includes requirements relating to entry into specific digital securities registries. The respective digital registries may be operated by licensed central securities depositories (*Wertpapiersammelbanken*) or a new type of digital registrar, which will be subject to licensing, specific requirements for the administration and safeguarding of digital securities, as well as supervision by the German supervisory authority (BaFin).[172] This new regime is meant to apply to any custody service providers operating in Germany, regardless of whether they are physically established in the country.

(e) Regulatory attempts to provide a comprehensive framework for digital assets and services

10.174 Finally, a group of jurisdictions has been trying to review and overhaul their regulatory frameworks to provide a comprehensive set of requirements for digital assets and digital asset services, including digital securities, digital payments, hybrid instruments, and related activities.

(xiii) Singapore

10.175 The Monetary Authority of Singapore (MAS) in 2017 issued comprehensive guidance on the application of relevant laws and regulation administered by MAS in relation to offerings or issuance of digital assets in Singapore (A Guide to Digital Token Offerings).[173] Whilst the guidance is 'not exhaustive, has no legal effect and does not

---

[170] Loi n° 2019-486 du 22 mai 2019 relative à la croissance et la transformation des entreprises, <https://www.legifrance.gouv.fr/jorf/id/JORFTEXT000038496102/> (accessed 21 July 2021).

[171] Bundesministerium der Justiz, Gesetz zur Einführung von elektronischen Wertpapieren (eWpG) vom 3. Juni 2021, BGBl. I p 1423, <https://www.bmjv.de/SharedDocs/Gesetzgebungsverfahren/Dokumente/Bgbl_elektronische_Wertpapiere.pdf;jsessionid=AAA2FFD0E42B80898C14BA712F97B8C2.1_cid289?__blob=publicationFile&v=2> (accessed 21 July 2021).

[172] See Art 6 eWpG.

[173] MAS, Guide to Digital Token Offerings (the MAS Guide) (2017), <https://www.mas.gov.sg/regulation/explainers/a-guide-to-digital-token-offerings> (accessed 21 July 2021).

modify or supersede any applicable laws, regulations or requirements', it clarifies in a detailed manner that digital assets and related services that qualify as capital markets products must comply with the Securities and Futures Act (SFA).[174] MAS is focussing on the concept of token,[175] considering that a token is a capital markets product under the SFA if it resembles either an ownership interest in a corporation or a product, debt, or a share in an investment scheme. Correspondingly, digital payment token services (account issuance, domestic money transfer, cross-border money transfer, merchant acquisition, e-money issuance, digital payment token, and money-changing services) are subject to payments oversight requirements issued by MAS.

10.176 If a digital token is deemed to be a capital market product, the offer or issue of such digital security will be treated by MAS identically to any other capital market product under the SFA, which includes the requirement that the offer be accompanied by a properly prepared prospectus registered with MAS, subject to certain exemptions.[176] MAS stressed that exemptions are subject to certain conditions, which includes advertising restrictions, authorization, and recognition requirements (when an offer is made in relation to units of a collective investment scheme).

10.177 The Guide further specified that certain intermediaries might be required to hold certain licenses or seek approval from MAS, unless otherwise exempt.[177] Any intermediary which facilitates primary offers or issues of digital securities tokens must hold a Capital Markets Services License for that regulated activity under the SFA. Further, any intermediary that establishes or operates a trading platform in Singapore in relation to digital securities tokens must be approved by MAS as an approved exchange or recognized by MAS as a recognized market operator under the SFA. SFA requirements apply to a person that operates a primary platform, or trading platform, partly in or partly outside of Singapore, or outside of Singapore.

(xiv) European Union

10.178 The European Commission in 2020 adopted a 'Digital Finance Package',[178] which includes inter alia legislative proposals on crypto assets and digital operational resilience. The aim is to make Europe's financial services more digital-friendly and to stimulate responsible innovation and competition among financial service providers in the EU.

10.179 The proposed legislation on crypto assets (defined as a digital representation of values or rights that can be stored and traded electronically) consists of a draft Regulation on Markets in Crypto-assets (MiCA).[179] It aims to provide legal clarity and certainty for

---

[174] Securities and Futures Act (Chapter 289), revised edition 2006, <https://sso.agc.gov.sg/Act/SFA2001> (accessed 21 July 2021).
[175] Defined as 'a cryptographically-secured representation of a token-holder's rights to receive a benefit or to perform specified functions in several of its statements'.
[176] Sections 2.5 et seq MAS Guide.
[177] Sections 2.8 et seq MAS Guide.
[178] <https://ec.europa.eu/info/sites/info/files/business_economy_euro/banking_and_finance/documents/2019-financial-services-digital-resilience-consultation-document_en.pdf> (accessed 21 July 2021).
[179] <https://eur-lex.europa.eu/legal-content/EN/TXT/?uri=CELEX:52020PC0593> (accessed 21 July 2021).

crypto asset issuers and providers and allow operators authorized in one Member State to provide their services across the EU ('passporting'). It foresees specific safeguards including capital requirements, rules for the custody of assets, a mandatory complaint procedure available to investors, and rights of the investor against the issuer.

The package also contains a 'DLT pilot regime'[180] for market infrastructures that wish to try to trade and settle transactions in financial instruments in crypto asset form. The pilot regime foresees a so-called 'sandbox' approach that allows temporary derogations from existing rules applicable to exchanges and SSSs so that regulators can gain experience with the use of distributed ledger technology in market infrastructures, while ensuring that they can deal with risks to investor protection, market integrity, and financial stability. The intention is to allow companies to test and learn more about how existing rules fare in practice.

10.180

Another element of relevance is a legislative proposal on digital operational resilience, called 'Digital Operational Resilience Act' (DORA).[181] The proposed legislation will require all firms to ensure that they can withstand all information and communication technology (ICT) related disruptions and threats and introduces an oversight framework for ICT providers, such as cloud computing service providers.

10.181

(6) The role of global standard-setters and global regulatory initiatives

As outlined above, approaches taken by regulatory authorities in response to the advent of digital financial innovations can differ considerably. Fintech firms, in particular those which are highly agile and mobile, may converge towards jurisdictions with regulatory frameworks that are perceived to be comparably light-touch and accommodating. At the same time, in particular with the entry of major global players into the digital financial service markets, there may be an emergence of innovative arrangements leveraging digital technology and global customer bases to offer services in multiple jurisdictions. The results may lead to regulatory arbitrage and asymmetries which could be significant across jurisdictions if national regulatory responses continue to differ substantively and gaps, overlaps, and conflicts occur. Ultimately, there could be global policy inconsistencies if economically equivalent assets are treated differently for regulatory purposes.

10.182

International regulatory collaboration and co-operation can mitigate potential harms of regulatory arbitrage by creating a more consistent, harmonized, and co-ordinated regulatory framework, in addition to enforcement measures across jurisdictions. These have been the key objectives of global standard-setting bodies in the financial

10.183

---

[180] <https://eur-lex.europa.eu/legal-content/EN/TXT/?uri=CELEX:52020PC0594> (accessed 21 July 2021).
[181] <https://eur-lex.europa.eu/legal-content/EN/TXT/?uri=CELEX:52020PC0595> (accessed 21 July 2021).

regulatory sphere, such as the Financial Stability Board, the Financial Action Task Force, the Basel Committee on Banking Supervision, the Committee on Payments and Market Infrastructures, the International Organization of Securities Commissions, or the Organisation for Economic Co-operation and Development. Digital asset related policy making and regulations at the domestic level can be shaped by global standards and best practices issued by these bodies, leading to regulatory convergence which, in turn, may facilitate international regulatory cooperation.

10.184 Global standard-setting bodies are working actively on a variety of issues relating to digital assets, with a particular focus on investor and consumer protection, market integrity, risk management, financial stability monitoring, and AML/CFT.

(a) Financial Stability Board (FSB)

10.185 The FSB mandate is to promote international financial stability; it does so by co-ordinating national financial authorities and international standard-setting bodies as they work toward developing strong regulatory, supervisory, and other financial sector policies. It fosters a level playing field by encouraging coherent implementation of these policies across sectors and jurisdictions.[182]

10.186 Starting in 2018, the FSB undertook work to consider risks to financial stability from crypto assets. Its work concluded that based on the available information, crypto assets do not pose a material risk to global financial stability at this time. However, vigilant monitoring is seen necessary in light of the speed of market developments. Should the use of crypto assets continue to evolve, it could have implications for financial stability in the future. Such implications may include: confidence effects and reputational risks to financial institutions and their regulators; risks arising from direct or indirect exposures of financial institutions; risks arising if crypto assets became widely used in payments and settlement; and risks from market capitalization and wealth effects.[183] The FSB is constantly monitoring the regulatory work undertaken by regulators,[184] however, since 2020 with a primary focus on global stablecoin arrangements, issuing 10 high-level recommendations concerning the regulation of such arrangements.[185]

10.187 The FSB also prepared a directory of relevant regulators and other authorities in FSB jurisdictions and international bodies who are dealing with crypto asset issues, and the aspects covered by them.[186]

(b) Financial Action Task Force (FATF)

10.188 The FATF is the inter-governmental body setting the international standards for anti-money laundering and countering terrorist financing (AML/CFT), the FATF

---

[182] Cf FSB Mandate: <https://www.fsb.org/about/> (accessed 21 July 2021).
[183] FSB, *Crypto-assets: Report to the G20*.
[184] FSB, *Crypto-assets: Work Underway*.
[185] FSB, *Regulation, Supervision and Oversight of 'Global Stablecoin' Arrangements*.
[186] FSB, *Crypto-assets Regulators Directory*.

REGULATION OF CRYPTO SECURITIES   355

Recommendations,[187] working to generate the necessary political will to bring about national legislative and regulatory reforms in these areas.

10.189 In 2018, the FATF adopted changes to its Recommendations to explicitly clarify that they apply to financial activities involving virtual assets, and also added two new definitions in the Glossary, 'virtual asset' (VA) and 'virtual asset service provider' (VASP). The amended FATF Recommendation 15[188] requires that VASPs be regulated for anti-money laundering and combating the financing of terrorism (AML/CFT) purposes, licenced or registered, and subject to effective systems for monitoring or supervision. In June 2019, the FATF adopted an Interpretive Note to Recommendation 15 to further clarify how the FATF requirements should apply in relation to VAs and VASPs,[189] in particular with regard to the application of the risk-based approach (RBA) to VA activities or operations and VASPs; supervision or monitoring of VASPs for AML/CFT purposes; licensing or registration; preventive measures, such as customer due diligence, recordkeeping, and suspicious transaction reporting, among others; sanctions and other enforcement measures; and international co-operation. The FATF also clarified the application of requirements on accurate originator information and required beneficiary information on virtual asset transfers, the so-called 'travel rule' to VASPs.

10.190 Whilst primarily covering digital representation of value that can be digitally traded, transferred, or used for payment, the Recommendations may also apply to securities service providers as well as virtual assets considered as securities in a particular jurisdiction.[190]

10.191 The FATF is also actively looking into the opportunities that new technology can offer to improve AML/CFT efforts. In this regard, the FATF is focussing on innovative skills, methods, and processes that are used to achieve goals relating to the effective implementation of AML/CFT requirements by the private sector and innovative ways to use established technology-based processes to comply with AML/CFT obligations.[191]

(c) Basel Committee on Banking Supervision (BCBS)

10.192 The Basel Committee on Banking Supervision (BCBS) is the primary global standard setter for the prudential regulation of banks. Consequently, its primary interest in digital assets is to consider the risk implications for banks engaging in activities related to such assets.

10.193 In 2019, the BCBS published a number of high-level supervisory expectations for banks engaging in crypto assets,[192] relating in particular to due diligence analysing the risks

---

[187] FATF, *Recommendations*.
[188] FATF, *Recommendations*, Recommendation 15.
[189] FATF, *Virtual Assets and Virtual Asset Service Providers*.
[190] FATF, *Securities Sector*.
[191] For more details, see <https://www.fatf-gafi.org/publications/digitaltransformation/digital-transformation.html?hf=10&b=0&s=desc(fatf_releasedate)> (accessed 21 July 2021).
[192] BCBS, *Statement on Crypto-assets*.

to crypto assets, governance and risk management, disclosure of material crypto asset exposures or related services, and a supervisory dialogue.

10.194 Furthermore, in 2021 the BCBS released a consultative document on the prudential treatment of crypto asset exposures,[193] which suggests to classify crypto asset exposures in two categories. Group 1 are assets which fulfil a set of classification conditions and as such are eligible for treatment under the existing Basel Framework (with some modifications and additional guidance), including certain tokenized traditional assets and stablecoins. Group 2 are crypto assets such as bitcoin that do not fulfil the classification conditions. Since these are seen to pose additional and higher risks, they should be subject to a new conservative prudential treatment.

(d) International Organization of Securities Commissions (IOSCO)

10.195 IOSCO is the international body for securities regulators and is recognized as the global standard setter for the securities sector. IOSCO develops, implements, and promotes adherence to internationally recognized standards for securities regulation. In line with its mandate, IOSCO has been focusing so far mainly on investor protection issues related to offerings of digital assets and trading platforms that facilitate the secondary trading of crypto assets.

10.196 Building on earlier research work on financial technologies,[194] in particular DLT, IOSCO considered crypto assets as a type of private asset that depends primarily on cryptography and DLT or similar technology as part of its perceived or inherent value, and can represent an asset such as a currency, commodity, or security, or be a derivative of a commodity or security. Where a regulatory authority has determined that a crypto asset or an activity involving a crypto asset falls within its regulatory remit, the IOSCO's Objectives and Principles of Securities Regulation (the IOSCO Principles)[195] should apply in principle.

10.197 In a report of 2020,[196] IOSCO provided more detailed guidance on issues and risks associated with the trading of crypto assets on crypto asset trading platforms (CTPs). The report provides key considerations and toolkits that are intended to assist regulatory authorities who may be evaluating CTPs within the context of their regulatory frameworks, in particular as regards access to CTPs, safeguarding participant assets, conflicts of interest, operations of CTPs, market integrity, price discovery, and technology.

10.198 IOSCO has also been focusing on investor protection, providing an overview of securities regulators' statements on the risks of initial coin offerings.[197] Moreover, in 2020, IOSCO published a report on education of retail investors regarding risks of crypto

---

[193] BCBS, *Prudential Treatment of Cryptoasset Exposures*.
[194] IOSCO, *Financial Technologies (Fintech)*.
[195] IOSCO, *Objectives and Principles of Securities Regulation*.
[196] IOSCO, *Issues, Risks and Regulatory Considerations Relating to Crypto-asset Trading Platforms*.
[197] IOSCO, <https://www.iosco.org/publications/?subsection=ico-statements> (accessed 21 July 2021).

assets,[198] outlining types of crypto assets and the main risks associated with these instruments and offering guidance on education and information of the public.

(e) Committee on Payments and Market Infrastructures (CPMI)

10.199 The CPMI is the international standard-setter in the area of payment, clearing, settlement and related arrangements. In line with its mandate, the main focus of the CPMI on matters related to digital assets has been in the areas of payments and financial market infrastructures (FMIs).

10.200 When it comes to digital assets, one key focal area is on payments-related emanations such as central bank digital currencies,[199] but also on the risks and implications of other form of digital means of payment such as crypto currencies or stablecoins.[200] However, there is also the wider area of FMIs, which include security settlement systems and central securities depositories. Here, the work of the CPMI focussed in particular on the implications of new technologies such as DLT for FMIs.

10.201 In this respect, the CPMI has prepared an analytical framework[201] for central banks and other authorities to review and analyse the use of this technology for payment, clearing, and settlement. The main aim of the framework is to help understand the uses of DLT and, in doing so, identify both the opportunities and challenges associated with this technology in a critical part of the financial system. Whilst this is helpful in itself and also is a contribution to the dialogue on how industry can use innovation to support robust, efficient, and safe payment, clearing, and settlement systems, the primary purpose of this framework is that it can serve as a blueprint for central banks and other relevant authorities to structure regulatory requirements for the use of DLT technology. The framework looks at the safety and efficiency of FMIs as well as wider financial markets implications. Safety considerations include operational and security risk, settlement issues, legal risk, governance, data management and protection, while efficiency considerations encompass speed of settlement, costs of processing, reconciliation, credit and liquidity management, as well as automated contract tools.

10.202 Additionally, through a joint working group with IOSCO, the CPMI monitors innovations in clearing and settlement and their impact on the current standards for financial market infrastructures (the PFMIs),[202] with a view on potential guidance on the application of the PFMIs to transfer arrangements involving digital assets. Key issues of attention here are governance and risk management, the regulatory perimeter, settlement assets, finality, participation and access.

---

[198] IOSCO, *Investor Education on Crypto-assets*.
[199] See for instance CPMI, *Central Bank Digital Currencies*.
[200] G7, IMF, CPMI, *Investigating the Impact of Global Stablecoins*.
[201] CPMI, *Distributed Ledger Technology in Payment, Clearing and Settlement*.
[202] Cf FSB, *Crypto-assets: Work Underway*.

(f) Organisation for Economic Co-operation and Development (OECD)

10.203 The OECD and its Committee on Financial Markets worked on crypto assets and applications of DLT in the financial markets. The Committee examined ICOs as one of the most prominent applications of DLT for financing, leading to the publication of a report in 2019[203] looking at the potential benefits from the use of regulated ICOs for small business capital formation, issuing and trading of tokens, limitations in the structuring of ICOs, as well as risks to which investors subscribing to ICO offerings and small and medium-sized enterprises issuing tokens are exposed to. The report examined policy implications of such activity related to regulation and supervision of token issuances on a national and cross-border basis, financial consumer protection, and financial education, and called for clarity and proportionality in the regulatory and supervisory framework applied to ICOs.

F. Conclusions

10.204 DLT is a young, still developing technology that has only started to find broad, commercially significant application in commercial practice. It is therefore notable that legislators in several jurisdictions have been trying to create favourable framework conditions for this technology. The breadth and depth of this reform movement is extraordinary and possibly without parallel in the history of technical innovations. The backdrop of these developments is a widely shared understanding that DLT has the potential to fundamentally change the way securities are issued, held in custody, traded, and managed, as well as an emerging consensus that these applications will fundamentally change the trading and post-trading infrastructure of capital markets.

10.205 An appropriate private law framework for DLT-based securities is a necessary, but not sufficient condition for realizing the full potential of this new technology. While the scope and the technical approach of the reforms undertaken so far differs considerably, they are mostly based on concepts and notions of traditional securities law. Like certificated securities, digital securities are conceptualized as digital representations of a claim, a right, or another financial or non-financial asset. Like certificated securities, digital securities can be controlled by the holder of the private key in a manner which is fully equivalent to the direct possession of physical securities. The person reflected in the distributed ledger as the holder is considered to be the legitimate creditor, and the transfer of the digital security in accordance with the rules of the underlying DLT protocol transfers the right represented to the transferee. Digital securities therefore assume all relevant functions certificated securities have assumed so far.

10.206 Compared to the process for the codification and regulation of intermediated securities the legal framework for digital securities is much more straightforward. The complexity

---

[203] OECD, *Initial Coin Offerings (ICOs) for SME Financing*.

resulting from multi-tiered holding systems, which are typical for intermediated securities and which are greatly exacerbated in cross-border situations, is mostly absent in the holding structure of digital securities. The private-public-key infrastructure which is a core component of any blockchain or DLT system permits to distinguish factual control and legal ownership, again very similar to certificated securities. At the same time, the registration of the holder of digital securities in a public blockchain provides effective publicity, unlike the securities account to which intermediated securities are credited and which are accessible only to the securities intermediary maintaining the account and the account holder (if at all).

10.207 From a legal and operational perspective it seems highly likely that future generations of the infrastructure for the issuance, custody, trading, and the clearing and settlement of securities transactions will be built on the basis of DLT systems. They promise to be more efficient and much more interoperable than current systems and will therefore gradually replace the existing intermediated infrastructure in due course. This will put pressure on other jurisdictions to make their securities law fit for the future.

10.208 From a regulatory perspective, the emergence of digital securities is raising some fundamental questions on the scope and function of regulation as well as on the perimeter of existing regulatory requirements in view of novel arrangements or services crossing sectoral boundaries.

10.209 Key challenges triggered by technological innovation leveraging digitization, cryptography, tokenization, and decentralization in the field of financial markets and securities regulation encompass the determination of the regulatory addressee and the avoidance of gaps, overlaps, and duplication of requirements, in particular if new services or activities cross the boundaries of traditional regulatory categories.

10.210 Regulatory frameworks need to be constantly reviewed to ensure their continued effective functioning in a rapidly evolving market environment. This, in turn, requires legislators, regulators, and supervisors to acquire and keep up-to-date the relevant knowledge to comprehensively understand technology, underlying protocols/codes, and to adequately assess their functioning. The work of global standard-setters is instrumental here to identify international best practice and to provide harmonized regulatory standards to avoid regulatory fragmentation and arbitrage.

10.211 Furthermore, the intrinsic borderless nature of service offerings using the digital space raises questions as to the regulatory perimeter. The cross-sectoral and cross-jurisdictional dimension puts a particular emphasis on the need for authorities to closely co-operate and co-ordinate their respective regulatory and supervisory authorities. This holds true for the co-operation across different types of authorities within a given jurisdiction that have a legitimate interest in digital assets and related arrangements and services, such as securities market regulators, central bank overseers, bank supervisors, AML authorities, consumer protection authorities, data protection authorities, and competition authorities. But it also holds true for the need of those authorities from relevant jurisdictions having an interest in an arrangement or service with cross-border relevance, which may entail the creation of tailor-made co-operative arrangements ranging from bilateral co-operation to global colleges for global systemic digital securities arrangements.[204] As the FSB notes: 'Authorities should cooperate and coordinate with each other, both domestically and internationally, to foster efficient and effective communication and consultation in order to support each other in fulfilling their respective mandates and to ensure comprehensive regulation, supervision, and oversight . . . '.[205]

---

[204] See Responsibility E of the PFMI; and for more details CPMI and IOSCO Board, *Responsibility E: A Compilation of Authorities' Experience*.
[205] FSB, *Regulation, Supervision and Oversight of 'Global Stablecoin' Arrangements*, High-level Recommendation no 3, p 4.

11

CONFLICT-OF-LAWS RULES

A. Introduction	11.01	G. Factors to be Disregarded When Determining the Applicable Law	11.41
B. Internationality of a Situation Involving Intermediated Securities	11.02	H. Third-party Rights	11.43
		(1) Change of the applicable law	11.44
C. History of the Hague Securities Convention	11.06	(2) Opening insolvency proceedings	11.48
(1) Object of the Hague Securities Convention	11.06	I. Relationship between the Hague Securities Convention and the UNIDROIT Instruments for Intermediated Securities	11.51
(2) Status of the Hague Securities Convention	11.09	(1) Sphere of application of the Geneva Securities Convention	11.52
D. Scope of the Hague Securities Convention	11.11	(2) Interaction between the Hague Securities Convention and the Geneva Securities Convention	11.56
(1) Definition of 'securities held with an intermediary'	11.12	(3) Consistency of the international instruments: the 'tier-by-tier approach' as the building block	11.62
(2) Issues falling within the scope of the Hague Securities Convention	11.14	J. Problems of the Hague Securities Convention: the European Debate	11.65
(3) Issues excluded from the scope of the Hague Securities Convention	11.18	(1) Status quaestionis	11.66
E. Choice of Law as the Primary Rule	11.22	(2) Substantive debate	11.78
(1) Law designated by the parties to an account agreement	11.24	(a) Protection of third-party rights	11.79
(2) Requirement of qualifying office	11.29	(b) Interaction with substantive law	11.86
F. Fall-back Rules	11.36	(c) Interaction with public law	11.94
(1) Law of the place of the relevant intermediary's office	11.38	(d) Diversity of laws in securities settlement systems	11.96
(2) Law under which the relevant intermediary is incorporated or otherwise organized	11.39	(3) The way forward for intermediated securities	11.98
(3) Law of the relevant intermediary's principal place of business	11.40	K. Outlook: New Technologies	11.103

A. Introduction

The vast majority of transactions in securities held with an intermediary take place in an international context. The notion of internationality is therefore defined in section B. The Hague Convention of 5 July 2006 on the Law Applicable to Certain Rights in Respect of Securities Held with an Intermediary ('the Hague Securities Convention' or HSC) has been drafted to clarify the law applicable to a situation involving intermediated securities. After a brief résumé of the history of the HSC in section C, section D defines the scope of the Convention's application. Section E examines the choice-of-law rule set out in the HSC, while section F deals with the other rules that may be taken

11.01

into consideration in order to find the applicable law. Section G discusses the factors that are not relevant to determining the applicable law. Section H deals with the protection of third-party rights under the HSC, which may be compromised in case of a change of law or the opening of insolvency proceedings. Section I examines the relationships between the HSC and the UNIDROIT instruments for intermediated securities, notably the UNIDROIT Convention of 9 October 2009 on Substantive Rules for Intermediated Securities ('the Geneva Securities Convention' or GSC) and the 2017 UNIDROIT Legislative Guide on Intermediated Securities. Section J analyses the main problems raised by the HSC from a European perspective, and possible ways forward. Finally, section K examines the challenges posed by new technologies, such as distributed ledger technology (DLT), from a conflict-of-laws perspective.

B. Internationality of a Situation Involving Intermediated Securities

11.02 The HSC applies when a situation involving intermediated securities is international. The Convention refers to an autonomous notion of internationality by stating that there is an international situation in all cases that involve 'a choice between the laws of different States' (Article 3 HSC).

11.03 In other words, the applicable law is a debatable issue arising from the presence of one or several foreign elements. The situation is international, for example, if: an intermediary has its registered office or domicile in another State; the securities account is maintained in another State; the issuing company has its registered office in another State or is subject to foreign law; the register of account holders is kept in another State; or the securities are held with a central depository located in another State. The decisive factor in determining whether a situation is 'international' is whether the foreign element creates some doubt as to which law should apply to a right in intermediated securities.

11.04 In practice, nearly all situations involving intermediated securities have a sufficient foreign element causing them to fall within the scope of the HSC. It seldom occurs that intermediated securities issued by a company with a registered office in State A, held with a central depository in State A, are the subject of a transaction between two persons both domiciled in State A, both of whose intermediaries are also located in State A and hold the securities account in State A. However, any situation other than this is 'international'. Furthermore, the mere designation of a foreign legal regime by the parties to an account agreement is sufficient to make the situation 'international'.

11.05 A situation involving intermediated securities may be domestic to begin with but become international when a certain event occurs. For example, granting a security interest in intermediated securities in favour of a person domiciled abroad introduces a sufficiently foreign element to make the entire situation international. Any person participating in a transaction involving intermediated securities must therefore expect the HSC to apply at some time, by virtue of the appearance of a foreign element.

C. History of the Hague Securities Convention

(1) Object of the Hague Securities Convention

The classic rules of private international law refer to the law of the place where the security is located ('*lex rei sitae*' or '*lex chartae sitae*'). While this connecting factor is suited to a direct holding system based on the physical transfer of securities, it is inappropriate to an indirect holding system based on the immobilization and dematerialization of securities. Any attempt to apply this factor to such a system is likely to produce unexpected or even unmanageable results in practice. For example, in the context of a transaction involving a portfolio of securities located in different States, the idea of referring each security to the law of the place where it is located has the unfortunate effect of multiplying the applicable laws. If this factor is applied to the granting of a security interest in a securities account, it is in practice impossible for the beneficiary to fulfil the perfection requirements of all the laws applicable to all the securities. The development of an intermediated system for holding securities has therefore given rise to significant legal uncertainty in private international law. **11.06**

It is in this context that an international review was launched early in 2000 under the aegis of the Hague Conference on Private International Law. It followed a joint proposal by Australia, the UK, and the US to set up an international convention with a view to establishing modern conflict rules reflecting the fact that securities are now held, transferred, and pledged indirectly. Harmonizing the rules of private international law seemed to be the best way of guaranteeing legal certainty. **11.07**

The work of the Hague Conference was based on two guiding principles: on the one hand, the need to modernize the traditional conflict-of-laws rules that exist in most States, and, on the other, to set up a system of connecting factors that would guarantee legal predictability and thus provide legal certainty. Given the urgent needs of practitioners, the States rapidly reached an agreement, and the text of a new Hague Convention was adopted in December 2002.[1] **11.08**

(2) Status of the Hague Securities Convention

The HSC was signed jointly by Switzerland and the US on 5 July 2006. Switzerland was the first State to ratify the HSC, on 14 September 2009.[2] It was followed by the Republic **11.09**

---

[1] Goode et al, *Explanatory Report*, Int-1 to Int-15.
[2] The HSC was incorporated into the Swiss Private International Law Act (article 108c), which entered into force on 1 January 2010. See Guillaume, 'Preliminary Remarks', 6.9–7.11.

of Mauritius on 15 October 2009 and by the United States of America on 15 December 2016. Although no other State has signed or ratified the Convention as yet, this was sufficient for the HSC to enter into force as of 1 April 2017.[3]

11.10 Within the European Union, ratification of the HSC has been postponed because the system of connecting factors relating to rights in securities held with an intermediary adopted in European law is different from the system finally adopted in the HSC. Whereas the Convention refers to the law designated by the parties to an account agreement, the European legislator chose to subject the rights in securities held with an intermediary to the law of the place where the securities account is located.[4] This connecting factor is based on the 'place of the relevant intermediary approach' (PRIMA) conflict rule, which was used as the basis for initial discussion during the process of drafting the HSC. It refers to the place where the account holder's direct intermediary—described as the 'relevant intermediary'—maintains the former's securities account. In the course of negotiations at the Hague, the PRIMA conflict rule was long retained as the principal connecting factor to be used for the purposes of the HSC. The formulation of this connecting factor gave rise to numerous problems, however, arising from the practical difficulty of identifying the location of the relevant intermediary or of the securities account it maintains for the account holder. It is not unusual for the various activities involved in maintaining a securities account to be dispersed among offices located in a number of different States, or distributed among a number of sub-contractors located in different States. Moreover, the location of a securities account may easily be changed. The PRIMA conflict rule was not adopted ultimately because the negotiators considered that it was too difficult—or even impossible—to determine, in practice, the place where a securities account is located.[5] The subjective, rather than the objective, approach has therefore been preferred in the HSC. See further section J.

D. Scope of the Hague Securities Convention

11.11 The HSC applies to 'securities held with an intermediary'. The Convention is the first international legal text to define this term (section D(1)). The HSC determines the law applicable to issues falling within its scope of application (section D(2)). Since the scope of the HSC is limited to determining the applicable law, it does not apply to questions relating to the competence of judicial authorities, nor to the recognition and enforcement of foreign decisions. These matters must be dealt with according to the private international law rules of each State. Furthermore, some issues have been explicitly excluded in order to precisely circumscribe the scope of the HSC (section D(3)).[6]

---

[3] See <https://www.hcch.net/en/instruments/conventions/status-table/?cid=72> (accessed 7 July 2021).
[4] See s J(1).
[5] Goode et al, *Explanatory Report*, Int–41 to Int–46. See also paras 11.70–2.
[6] Sections D–H are inspired by Guillaume, 'Convention', 29–81 (Arts 1–11 HSC).

(1) Definition of 'securities held with an intermediary'

The HSC applies only to securities held with an intermediary. In order for a security to be an 'intermediated security', it must be entered into an indirect holding system by being credited to a securities account held with an intermediary. The account holder may be an investor or another financial intermediary, or the intermediary itself. The Convention is not applicable as long as a security is held directly; nor does it apply to cash.

11.12

According to Article 1(1)(f) HSC, 'securities held with an intermediary means the rights of an account holder resulting from a credit of securities to a securities account'. This definition gains in substance when read in the context of the other definitions in Article 1. Securities held with an intermediary are thus securities, that is, 'any shares, bonds or other financial instruments or assets (other than cash), or any right to such securities' (Article 1(1)(a)), held with an intermediary, that is, 'a person that in the course of a business or other regular activity maintains securities accounts for others or both for others and for its own account and is acting in that capacity' (Article 1(1)(c)). Central securities depositories are intermediaries (Article 1(4)), as are banks, securities dealers, and other financial intermediaries that maintain securities accounts in the course of their business activity. By contrast, persons who act as registrars or transfer agents for an issuer of securities, as well as those who act purely as managers or administrators of securities accounts, are not intermediaries within the meaning of the HSC (Article 1(3)).

11.13

(2) Issues falling within the scope of the Hague Securities Convention

Article 2(1) HSC provides an exhaustive list of issues that fall within the scope of the HSC. This list is meant to include all issues in respect of rights in intermediated securities that are of practical importance, irrespective of the way these issues are treated in the private international law rules of the States concerned. Often, the same matter falls under two different letters of the list in Article 2(1). It is not necessary to determine precisely which letter governs any particular matter. If it falls within at least one of the topics listed, then the HSC applies.[7]

11.14

The law designated by the HSC applies to the following issues:

11.15

(i) the legal nature and effects against the intermediary and third parties of the rights resulting from a credit of securities to a securities account (Article 2(1)(a));
(ii) the legal nature and effects against the intermediary and third parties of a disposition of intermediated securities (Article 2(1)(b));

---

[7] Goode et al, *Explanatory Report*, 2–9.

(iii) the requirements for perfection of a disposition of intermediated securities (Article 2(1)(c));
(iv) the priority among competing rights (Article 2(1)(d));
(v) the obligations of an intermediary in cases where a competing right is invoked (Article 2(1)(e));
(vi) the requirements for the realization of an interest in an intermediated security (Article 2(1)(f)); and
(vii) whether the disposition of an intermediated security extends to entitlement to dividends and other proceeds of that security (Article 2(1)(g)).

11.16 The rights specified in Article 2(1) relate either to the intermediated security itself, or to its disposition. Within the context of the HSC, the disposition of a security held with an intermediary refers to (i) any transfer of title, whether outright or by way of security, and (ii) any grant of a security interest, whether possessory or non-possessory (Article 1(1)(h)). Its scope therefore includes sales and purchases of securities, repurchase agreements, sell/buy-back transfers, stock loans, and security interests. Non-possessory security interests that fall within the scope of the HSC are those that can be granted without crediting the securities to the collateral taker's securities account, simply by means of an agreement between the account holder and an intermediary that grants control over the securities to the collateral taker. A disposition of securities may refer either to the transfer of all or some of the securities in a securities account, or to the transfer of the securities account itself (Article 1(2)(a)). This may be done in favour of either the account holder or its intermediary (Article 1(2)(b)). A lien by operation of law in favour of an intermediary, such as a right of retention, is also considered a disposition within the meaning of the HSC (Article 1(2)(c)).

11.17 The HSC applies whether or not the designated law is that of a contracting State (Article 9). The law designated by the HSC may be refused only if the effects of its application would be manifestly contrary to the public policy of the forum (Article 11(1)). Bearing in mind the adverb 'manifestly', the public policy exception can only be invoked, with reserve, in situations where the application of a foreign substantive law rule would be diametrically opposed to the essential principles of the legal system of the forum. This limitation of the scope of public policy is intended to reinforce legal certainty.[8]

(3) Issues excluded from the scope of the Hague Securities Convention

11.18 Anything not included in the list of Article 2(1) HSC is not governed by the law designated by the HSC.

11.19 In particular, the HSC does not apply to purely contractual or personal rights (Article 2(3)(a) and (b)). These rights derive from the legal contractual status and are governed

---

[8] Goode et al, *Explanatory Report*, 11–6.

by the contract rules of the private international law of each State. All rights arising exclusively from the contractual relationship between an account holder and its intermediary (or between two intermediaries) fall outside the scope of the HSC. These include, for example, matters relating to the degree of diligence expected of the intermediary in maintaining securities accounts; the content and frequency of account statements; risk of loss; securities prices; the date on which securities must be transferred against payment; and the consequences of a violation by one of the parties in the course of a disposition of securities or in payment for securities at maturity. Contractual rights between parties to a disposition of intermediated securities likewise do not fall within the scope of the HSC.

11.20 The HSC does not apply to the rights and obligations of an issuer of securities, whether in relation to the holder of the securities or to any other person (Article 2(3)(c)). These rights depend on the legal status of the issuing company and are governed by the law applicable to the latter in accordance with the private international law rules of each State. The law applicable to the issuing company determines, for example, entitlement to income payments (for example, dividends or interest); the type of voting right attaching to securities; and the requirements with regard to granting free shares.

11.21 The regulation of financial markets does not fall within the scope of the HSC.[9] The regulatory provisions relating to the issue or trading of securities as well as those relating to supervision of financial markets contained in the law of the forum are thus applicable regardless of the law designated by the HSC. Such mandatory provisions of the forum, whose application is required regardless of the law designated by the HSC (in other words, 'internationally mandatory rules' or 'lois d'application immédiate'), are expressly reserved at Article 11(2). Among the forum laws that could apply on grounds of public policy are also its regulations on the prevention of financial crime and money laundering, including the degree of diligence required of financial intermediaries; tax rules; and rules intended to safeguard banking secrecy.

E. Choice of Law as the Primary Rule

11.22 The HSC refers primarily to the choice of applicable law by the parties to an account agreement (section E(1)). This subjective connecting factor has the great advantage of avoiding the need to localize a securities account held with an intermediary in order to determine the law applicable to the rights arising from a credit to the account. However, the parties to an account agreement have only limited freedom to choose the law applicable to issues falling within the scope of the HSC. Such a choice is valid only if the intermediary has a qualifying office in the State whose law has been designated by the parties (section E(2)).

---

[9] Sigman and Bernasconi, 'Myths', esp. 31–2.

11.23 When a transaction in intermediated securities involves a chain of intermediaries, the applicable law is not determined globally for the entire chain. It is designated separately for each securities account. The HSC does not permit the designation of a single law to govern all matters falling within its scope in respect of all the securities accounts maintained by the intermediaries located between the investor and the issuing company. A single transaction (for example, the acquisition of securities) may thus be governed by different laws at each level in the chain of intermediaries.[10] Even if a single intermediary performs the transaction by debiting and crediting two or more securities accounts that it maintains for different investors, it is still possible—if only in theory—for a different law to apply to each securities account.

(1) Law designated by the parties to an account agreement

11.24 The law applicable to rights in intermediated securities is the law designated by the account holder and its direct intermediary by means of an express *electio juris* in the account agreement between them (Article 4(1) first sentence HSC).

11.25 The account holder's direct intermediary, which maintains its securities account, is deemed to be the 'relevant intermediary' (Article 1(1)(g)). The word 'relevant' highlights the fact that this intermediary is decisive in defining the connecting factor. The intermediary that maintains a securities account is always the relevant intermediary in respect of that account. This is true even if a disposition of securities is made in its favour (Article 4(3)).

11.26 To be valid pursuant to the HSC, the choice of law must be explicit. It cannot derive implicitly from the provisions of the account agreement or from external circumstances. It may be contained in the account agreement in the broader sense: it may appear in an annex, such as terms and conditions.[11] Although Article 4(1) does not require the choice of law to be made in writing, it is difficult to imagine a situation in which it could validly be made orally.

11.27 The choice of law may be either (i) general, in which case it applies to all legal relationships between the parties, including issues falling within the scope of the HSC, or (ii) specific, applying only to issues falling within the scope of the HSC. The law applicable to issues falling within the scope of the HSC is therefore not necessarily the same as that governing other aspects of the legal relationship between the parties to the account agreement. The parties can choose the law of State A for their contractual relationships and the law of State B for issues specified in Article 2(1). The choice of law governing the parties' contractual relationships must comply with the private international law rules of the forum if it is to be valid. If the parties have chosen a single applicable law

---

[10] Goode et al, *Explanatory Report*, 4–43 to 4–51.
[11] Goode et al, *Explanatory Report*, 4–18.

without specifying a different law to govern issues falling within the scope of the HSC, then that law also applies automatically to these issues. In that case, the choice of law must, if it is to be valid, comply not only with the HSC requirements but also with those of the private international law rules of the forum.

A single law governs all legal issues specified in Article 2(1) relating to intermediated securities that are credited to a particular securities account. The applicable law cannot be fragmented by stipulating that a different law shall apply to some of the issues specified in Article 2(1).[12] **11.28**

(2) Requirement of qualifying office

The parties to an account agreement cannot choose just any law. The choice of law is valid only if the intermediary has a qualifying office in the State whose law has been designated by the parties (Article 4(1) second sentence HSC). **11.29**

An intermediary is deemed to have an 'office' at any place of business in which any of its activities are carried on (Article 1(1)(j)). Therefore, it has an office at any place in which it has a registered office, branch, or agency. A place of business which is intended to be merely temporary or a place of business of any person other than the intermediary is not an office within the meaning of the HSC (Article 1(1)(j) *in fine*). The place of business of a subsidiary or another company belonging to the intermediary's group is thus not an 'office' as defined in the HSC.[13] **11.30**

An intermediary has a 'qualifying office' if it has an office in the State whose law has been designated in the account agreement and this office is either (i) engaged in a business or other regular activity relating to the maintenance of securities accounts (Article 4(1)(a)), or (ii) identified as holding securities accounts in that State by an account number, bank code, or other specific means of identification (Article 4(1)(b)). In any event, an office will not be deemed to be a qualifying office if it engages only in limited activities related to the maintenance of securities accounts (for example, processing electronic data or operating a call centre) in the State whose law has been chosen in the account agreement (Article 4(2)(a)–(c)). Moreover, an office that engages solely in representational or administrative functions and does not have authority to enter into an account agreement cannot be deemed a qualifying office (Article 4(2)(d)). **11.31**

An intermediary's qualifying office need not necessarily maintain the securities account in respect of which a question arises. The choice of law is valid as long as the intermediary has an office that engages in an activity relating to the maintenance of securities accounts in the State whose law has been chosen.[14] The securities account **11.32**

---

[12] Goode et al, *Explanatory Report*, 4–10.
[13] Goode et al, *Explanatory Report*, 1–25.
[14] Goode et al, *Explanatory Report*, 4–23.

in respect of which a question is raised may therefore be held by any other office of the intermediary or even by one or more sub-contractors, regardless of their locations. For example, if the parties to an account agreement have chosen the law of State B for issues within the scope of the HSC, this choice is valid if the intermediary has an office in State B, even if the securities account in question is held partly in State C by another office of the intermediary and partly in State D by one of its sub-contractors.

11.33 The qualifying office requirement must be fulfilled at the time the choice of law is agreed (Article 4(1) second sentence). This is generally at the same time as the account agreement is entered into. If the intermediary has no qualifying office in the State whose law has been chosen by the parties at that time, the choice of law is not valid. In such a case, the law applicable to rights in intermediated securities credited to the account in question must be determined pursuant to Article 5.[15] If the intermediary later sets up a qualifying office in the State whose law is designated in the account agreement, this does not remedy the initial defect. In such a case, the choice of law must be made afresh in the account agreement, or at least the existing choice-of-law clause must be expressly confirmed if the choice of law is thenceforth to be valid.[16] Conversely, if at the time the choice of law was agreed the intermediary had a qualifying office in the State whose law was chosen, but this office later ceases to be a qualifying one, the choice of law remains valid.

11.34 The qualifying office requirement is intended to prevent parties from choosing a law solely for the advantages it offers them. It must be acknowledged, however, that this requirement can very easily be fulfilled by the intermediary, the more so because it is not necessary for the securities account to be held by the qualifying office. Since it is unlikely that any private investor will be in a position to oppose a choice of law proposed by its direct intermediary, the latter has a degree of freedom to choose the law that best serves its interests in its relationships with investors. However, the power relationship may be reversed in the case of institutional investors. Such investors are in a better position to impose the law of their choice on their intermediary, for example, in order to subject all their transactions to the same law. Likewise, in the context of relationships between two financial intermediaries, the intermediary that holds the securities account on behalf of the other intermediary is not necessarily the one that is in a position to impose the applicable law.

11.35 The qualifying office requirement is the only limitation to the freedom of the parties to an account agreement to choose the applicable law to issues falling within the scope of the HSC. To a certain extent the qualifying office requirement addresses the risk of fraud. Therefore, it should not be possible to invoke fraud as grounds for invalidating the choice of law made by the parties to an account agreement.[17] However, the

---

[15] See s F.
[16] Goode et al, *Explanatory Report*, 4–27.
[17] Goode et al, *Explanatory Report*, 3–10 and 11–5.

intermediary may be forced to choose a specific law by regulatory provisions;[18] it may even be a precondition to participation in a system. Such regulatory provisions would apply on grounds of public policy (Article 11(2)).

F. Fall-back Rules

11.36 The choice-of-law rule is supplemented by a cascade of fall-back rules that apply in the event that (i) the parties have not designated the applicable law in their account agreement, or (ii) the choice of law is not valid (Article 5 HSC). The fall-back rules provided in Article 5 are objective rules based on the PRIMA connecting factor, which refers to the place where the account holder's direct intermediary—described as the 'relevant intermediary'—maintains the former's securities account.[19] More precisely, it refers to the law of the place where the intermediary has an office (section F(1)), the law under which it is incorporated or otherwise organized (section F(2)), or the law of the place where it has its principal place of business (section F(3)). The decisive moment is the time the account agreement was entered into, or the time the securities account was opened if there is no account agreement.

11.37 The fall-back rules are of only marginal importance, since cases where there has been no choice of law or no valid choice of law are rare in practice. The main case where a choice of law is not valid is where the direct intermediary did not have an office in the State whose law was chosen by the parties at the time the choice of law was made (ie, it did not comply with the qualifying office requirement).[20]

(1) Law of the place of the relevant intermediary's office

11.38 The first fall-back rule designates the law in force in the State where the office of the relevant intermediary, which has unambiguously entered into a written account agreement, is located (Article 5(1) HSC). In order for this fall-back rule to apply, the account agreement must expressly state that it has been entered into through a particular office. Moreover, this office must be a qualifying office within the meaning of Article 4 HSC.

(2) Law under which the relevant intermediary is incorporated or otherwise organized

11.39 The second fall-back rule designates the law in force in the State under whose law the relevant intermediary is incorporated or otherwise organized (Article 5(2) HSC). This rule is

---

[18] Sigman and Bernasconi, 'Myths', 32.
[19] See para 11.10.
[20] See s E(2).

subsidiary to the preceding one, meaning that it can only be invoked if the office through which the account agreement was entered into cannot be determined with certainty, or if there was no qualifying office within the meaning of Article 4 HSC. It applies, of course, only to intermediaries that are companies.

(3) Law of the relevant intermediary's principal place of business

11.40 The third fall-back rule designates the law of the State in which the relevant intermediary has its principal place of business (Article 5(3) HSC). This rule is subsidiary to the two preceding ones. Thus, it can only be invoked if the relevant intermediary has not been validly incorporated or otherwise organized. In fact, however, it is difficult to imagine that a company might be considered an intermediary without being validly incorporated or organized in accordance with the law of a given State. Arguably, even though this last fall-back rule was clearly drawn up for companies, it should only be applied to intermediaries that are individuals. In practice, therefore, the rule should not often apply.

G. Factors to be Disregarded When Determining the Applicable Law

11.41 Article 6 HSC supplements Articles 4 and 5 by drawing up a negative list of connecting factors that are to be disregarded when determining the law applicable to rights in intermediated securities. This provision is intended unambiguously to exclude all connecting factors traditionally applied to determining the law applicable to securities held within a direct holding system.[21] The irrelevance of these criteria is already apparent from an *a contrario* interpretation of Articles 4 and 5.

11.42 The law applicable to the matters specified in Article 2(1) cannot be determined with regard (i) to the place where the issuing company is incorporated, otherwise organized, or has its statutory seat, registered office, or principal place of business, or (ii) to the place where the securities are located, or (iii) to the place where a register of holders of securities maintained by or on behalf of the issuing company is located (Article 6(a)–(c)). Furthermore, only the account holder's direct intermediary is decisive in determining the applicable law (Article 6(d)). It is not possible to take account of another intermediary in the chain. In particular, the applicable law cannot be found by treating the direct intermediary as transparent and referring to another higher-level intermediary, or by referring directly to the issuing company. The so-called 'look-through approach' is not applicable.[22]

---

[21] Goode et al, *Explanatory Report*, 6–1.
[22] Goode et al, *Explanatory Report*, 6–2 and Int–37 to Int–40.

H. Third-party Rights

The system of connecting factors enshrined in the HSC centres on the specific relationship between an account holder and the direct intermediary that maintains its securities account. These two persons may choose which law shall apply to their rights in the intermediated securities credited to the account (Article 4 HSC). This choice of law will nevertheless affect the rights of third parties. The chosen law will apply to the rights of any other person (for example, a creditor) in the same intermediated securities (Article 2(1)). For example, the requirements for perfection of a disposition of intermediated securities, as well as priority among competing rights, are governed by the law designated by the HSC. It should be added that requirements arising from a law other than that determined under the HSC cannot be imposed over and above that law on grounds of public policy (Article 11(3)). For example, a procedure for registering securities in a special register stipulated by a law other than that designated by the HSC cannot be imposed on grounds of public policy. The HSC provides special rules to protect third-party rights in two situations where they are particularly vulnerable. The first situation occurs when the parties to an account agreement agree to change the applicable law (section H(1)). The second comes into play when insolvency proceedings have been opened against one of the participants in the indirect holding system (section H(2)).

11.43

(1) Change of the applicable law

The issue of third-party rights upon a change of applicable law arises if the parties to the account agreement decide to change the law applicable to interests in intermediated securities by making a choice of law. They may, for example, insert a choice-of-law clause into an account agreement that did not previously include one. They may also insert into an account agreement that already contains a general choice-of-law clause, a special clause designating the law applicable to the issues specified in Article 2(1) HSC. They may also change the law designated in a pre-existing clause.

11.44

If the conditions for choosing a law as specified in Article 4 HSC are satisfied,[23] the new law designated by the parties to the account agreement will apply retroactively, replacing *ab initio* the law that was previously applicable (Article 7(3)). The new law will thus govern all interests in the intermediated securities that were credited to the securities account both before and after the change of the applicable law. Therefore, the rights of third parties may be endangered if they are not informed of the change of law agreed upon by the parties to an account agreement.[24]

11.45

The risk of harm to third parties' rights in such situations is reduced by Article 7(4), which provides that interests acquired by third parties prior to the change of law are

11.46

---

[23] See s E.
[24] Guillaume, '*Electio juris*', esp 75–6; Sigman and Bernasconi, 'Myths', 34.

neither restricted nor set aside if the parties to an account agreement agree to change the applicable law. The old law remains applicable in principle to third parties for all issues in respect of (i) the existence of an interest in intermediated securities arising before the change of law, (ii) interests arising from a disposition of securities that were perfected before the change of law, and (iii) priority as between parties whose interests arose before the change of law (Article 7(4)(a)–(c)). However, if an interest in an intermediated security that arose before the change of law was not perfected under the old applicable law but was subsequently perfected under the new applicable law, then the latter applies to issues of priority (Article 7(5)).

11.47 Article 7(4) applies only to third parties that have not been informed of the change of applicable law agreed upon by the parties to an account agreement. The new applicable law is thus applicable to third parties that were informed of and consented to the change of law made by the parties to the account agreement (Article 7(4) *cum* Article 7(3)). It is not necessary to protect the rights of an informed third party, inasmuch as the latter itself has the means to protect them. For example, if the collateral taker was informed of and consented to the change of law made by the parties to the account agreement, the newly chosen law applies to the collateral taker's rights in the pledged securities. This new law applies in respect of the collateral taker, and does so retroactively, as soon as it has given its consent. This means that it must make its security interest effective in accordance with the requirements of the new law designated by the parties to the account agreement.

(2) Opening insolvency proceedings

11.48 The issue of third-party rights where insolvency proceedings are opened against one of the participants in the indirect holding system (for example, an investor, an intermediary, a depository, or an issuing company) is a sensitive one. The opening of insolvency proceedings makes it necessary to determine whether and to what extent the rights a creditor has acquired in intermediated securities before the proceedings commenced are maintained and may be enforced after they have opened.[25]

11.49 The HSC provides that all rights acquired pursuant to the law that it designates must be recognized in the context of subsequent insolvency proceedings (Article 8(1)). For example, if an intermediated security was credited to a securities account before the opening of bankruptcy proceedings against the intermediary maintaining the securities account, the rights of the account holder continue to be governed by the law designated by the HSC. Therefore, the place where the insolvency proceedings have been opened does not affect the law applicable to the perfection of rights in the intermediated securities.

---

[25] For a detailed analysis of the consequences of the opening of insolvency proceedings in respect of the rights of third parties, see Guillaume, '*Electio juris*', 77–82.

However, the HSC has no effect on 'the application of any substantive or procedural **11.50**
insolvency rules, including any rules relating to a) the ranking of categories of claim or
the avoidance of a disposition as a preference or a transfer in fraud of creditors; or b)
the enforcement of rights after the opening of an insolvency proceeding' (Article 8(2)).
Only the insolvency law (ie, in principle, the law of the place where the bankruptcy proceedings have been opened) can determine the effects of rights in intermediated securities in the context of such proceedings. In the above example, it is the insolvency law
that determines, among other things, whether or not the rights of the account holder in
the securities credited to its account have priority over the rights of other creditors of
the bankrupt intermediary.

I. Relationship between the Hague Securities Convention and the UNIDROIT Instruments for Intermediated Securities

This section analyses the relationship between the HSC and the UNIDROIT instruments **11.51**
on intermediated securities, primarily the Geneva Securities Convention.[26] Although
the GSC has not (yet) entered into force, its approach is reflected in the guidelines for
legislators set out in the UNIDROIT Legislative Guide on Intermediated Securities.[27]
Moreover, the examination of the interaction between the HSC and the GSC brings to
light a number of general issues concerning the interoperability of conflict of laws and
substantive law regimes for intermediated securities. First, we describe the key idea—
the fact that the sphere of application of the GSC is not determined by itself but by the
conflict-of-laws rules applicable in each State (the conflict-of-law rules of the forum)
(section I(1)). Secondly, we point out that the manner in which the scope of conflict-of-laws rules relates to the scope of substantive law rules for intermediated securities
merits consideration (section I(2)). Finally, we explain the consistency of the tier-by-tier approaches adopted by the HSC and the UNIDROIT substantive law instruments
(section I(3)).

(1) Sphere of application of the Geneva Securities Convention

The GSC deals with substantive law, not with private international law. However, even if **11.52**
this Convention were to be adopted by all States, including by way of implementation of
the UNIDROIT Legislative Guide on Intermediated Securities, the conflict-of-laws rules
would continue to play a very important role since many aspects are still left to the
'non-Convention law'.

---

[26] See Bernasconi and Keijser, 'The Hague and Geneva Securities Conventions'.
[27] The text of this chapter, then numbered 10, s I in the first edition of this book inspired Chapter VIII of the Legislative Guide.

11.53 The GSC does not lay down any connecting factor that triggers its application, which is determined instead by the conflict-of-laws rules of the forum. This idea is stated in Article 2(a) GSC. The Convention applies whenever the applicable conflict-of-laws rules designate the law in force in a Contracting State as the applicable law. The reason for this approach is clear. Once the GSC has been ratified by a State, it becomes part of the substantive national law of that State. Therefore, the rules of the GSC will apply insofar as the substantive law of that State is the applicable law under the conflict-of-laws rules of the forum.[28]

11.54 As a consequence, even if the forum is a Contracting State to the GSC, this text does not apply when its conflict-of-laws rules point to the law of a non-Contracting State as the applicable law on an issue. And *vice versa*: even if the forum is a non-Contracting State, the GSC will apply (as part of the *lex causae*) if the conflict-of-laws rules of that State point to the law of a Contracting State as the applicable law.[29]

11.55 Together with Article 2 GSC, Article 3 clarifies the effect of conflict-of-laws rules on declarations. Since the declarations established by the GSC are related to its substantive rules, mainly allowing Contracting States to opt into or out of the uniform rules, the application of such declarations is also determined by the conflict-of-laws rules of the forum.

(2) Interaction between the Hague Securities Convention and the Geneva Securities Convention

11.56 The HSC and the GSC are texts of a different nature. The former is a conflict-of-laws instrument, the latter is a material-law instrument. Application of the GSC is, therefore, determined by the HSC.

11.57 However, the substantive scope of application of the HSC is not exactly the same as the substantive scope of the GSC. Article 2(1)(a)–(g) HSC contains an exhaustive list of all the issues falling within the scope of the HSC, which is narrower than the scope of the GSC.[30] The HSC applies to rights that relate either to the securities themselves and result from a credit of securities to a securities account, or to the disposition of securities held with an intermediary. Although the concept is avoided, the HSC applies mainly to 'proprietary' issues. However, purely contractual or personal rights that arise solely from the contractual relationship between the account holder and its intermediary or the parties to a disposition *inter se* are not included within the scope of the HSC (Article 2(3)(a)).[31]

11.58 Assuming the HSC were in force in a Contracting State, all the issues mentioned in Article 2(1)(a)–(g) would be governed by the applicable law determined under Article

---

[28] Kanda et al, *Official Commentary*, 2–6.
[29] Kanda et al, *Official Commentary*, 2–7 and 2–9.
[30] See paras 11.14–17.
[31] Goode et al, *Explanatory Report*, 2–4. See also para 11.19.

4 or one of the fall-back rules provided in Article 5. Furthermore, it is important to note that the *same law* applies to all Article 2(1) issues. It is not possible, therefore, for some of these issues to be governed by one law while others are governed by a different one.[32]

Conversely, the GSC contains rules of a very different nature. Rules on: (i) the effectiveness against the intermediary and third parties of the account holder's rights over the securities (for example, Articles 9, 11, and 12); (ii) the effectiveness against the insolvency administrator (for example, Articles 14 and 21); (iii) the contractual relationships between the intermediary and its account holder (for example, Article 10); or (iv) even the exercise of certain rights against the issuer (for example, Article 29). There is no single, all-encompassing conflict-of-laws rule applicable to all these issues. From a conflict-of-laws perspective, each of these issues has to be filed in one of the legal categories used by the conflict-of-laws rules of the forum to determine the applicable law and, accordingly, whether the GSC applies.[33] **11.59**

Having said that, the interaction between the HSC and the GSC is easy to understand. Within its substantive scope of application, ie, with regard to Article 2(1) HSC issues,[34] the HSC determines the applicable law. If the law is that of a Contracting State to the GSC, this instrument will govern all substantive issues included within that substantive scope. As an example, let us assume that State A has ratified the HSC and, according to this instrument, State B's law is applicable. All issues included in Article 2(1) HSC are therefore governed by the law of State B. If State B is a party to the GSC, then the GSC will apply to those issues (or, where appropriate, the 'non-Convention law' as defined in Article 1(m) GSC). Note that because the HSC has a universal scope of application (Article 9), the question of whether State B is a party to the HSC is not relevant. **11.60**

The law applicable to other issues that are outside the substantive scope of the HSC but may fall within the scope of the GSC is determined by the corresponding conflict-of-laws rules of the forum. For example, the law applicable to the contractual obligations of the intermediary vis-à-vis its account holder is determined by the conflict of law rules on contractual obligations; in the EU, this is the Rome I Regulation. If the applicable law is that of a Contracting State to the GSC, the GSC's provisions on contractual obligations will apply, for example, Article 10. **11.61**

(3) Consistency of the international instruments: the 'tier-by-tier approach' as the building block

As substantive-law instruments, the GSC and the UNIDROIT Legislative Guide are neutral from a conflict-of-laws perspective. The UNIDROIT instruments do not determine the **11.62**

---

[32] Kanda et al, *Official Commentary*, 4–10. See also para 11.28.
[33] See, with further details, Garcimartín, 'The Geneva Convention'.
[34] See para 11.15.

conflict-of-laws rule that a forum has to adopt nor, for the same reason, do they determine whether or not *renvoi* is acceptable.[35] Nonetheless, the approach adopted by the UNIDROIT instruments fits better with the conflict-of-laws approach of the HSC than with others, and vice versa: the conflict-of-laws approach followed by the HSC fits better with the substantive rules designed by the UNIDROIT instruments.[36]

11.63 The UNIDROIT instruments follow a 'tier-by-tier approach'. They divide the holding chain into tiers and look at each link in that chain: *for each account holder there is one, and only one, relevant intermediary*. The building block of the UNIDROIT instruments is each relationship between an account holder and *its relevant (or immediate) intermediary*. This concept of 'relevant intermediary' refers to the intermediary that keeps a particular securities account for a particular account holder, enabling that intermediary to be distinguished from any other intermediary in the holding chain. This lets the UNIDROIT instruments focus on each tier individually and as independently as possible from what happens in other tiers of the same holding chain.[37]

11.64 This substantive approach works well with a conflict-of-laws approach whereby the applicable law is determined separately for each tier in the chain of intermediaries, as in the HSC.[38] Both the HSC rule and the EU rules determine the applicable law separately for each tier in the holding chain, ie, for each relationship between an account holder and its relevant intermediary.[39] There may only be one applicable law for each tier and, therefore, in a multi-tier structure there may be two or more layers of laws. This perfectly suits a substantive law regime that establishes the rules governing each relationship. As a result, a conflict-of-laws approach based on the relevant intermediary (ie, a 'tier-by-tier approach') rule sits easily with the substantive regime of the UNIDROIT instruments. Conversely, a tier-by-tier approach is more difficult to reconcile with a substantive law regime based on the idea that the ultimate account holder has a direct ownership or co-ownership right over the underlying securities. This is one of the issues discussed more extensively in section J.

J. Problems of the Hague Securities Convention: the European Debate

11.65 The purpose of this section is to analyse the main problems raised by the HSC from a EU perspective. Section J(1) describes the *status quaestionis*, while section J(2) covers

---

[35] Kanda et al, *Official Commentary*, 2–8.
[36] Chun, *Cross-border Transactions*, 422–3; Einsele, 'Das Haager Übereinkommen', 2354; Einsele, 'Modernising', 254–61; Einsele, 'Security Interests', 361–2; Garcimartín, 'The Geneva Convention', 754–5; Rögner, 'Inconsistencies', 104–5; Thévenoz, 'Intermediated Securities', 419–20.
[37] Kanda et al, *Official Commentary*, 1–38, 1–44; UNIDROIT Legislative Guide, 304–6; see also Thévenoz, 'Intermediated Securities', 420.
[38] See para 11.23.
[39] Thévenoz, 'Intermediated Securities', 420: 'While they differ in respect of a subjective, choice-oriented test as opposed to an objective, location-oriented-test, the two rules converge in relying on the account to which the securities are credited and on the relevant intermediary who maintains that account'. See also para 11.71.

the debate on the merits of the HSC solutions. In addition, we examine ways to move forward (section J(3)).

(1) Status quaestionis

Three EU legal acts lay down a rule to determine the law applicable to rights in intermediated securities. These rules on the European *acquis* are worded slightly differently but are based on the same formula: the law is that of the Member State (or in some cases third State) in which the securities account that records the existence of those rights is located (held, maintained, or recorded). The relevant provisions are the following. **11.66**

Article 9(2) of the EU Settlement Finality Directive (SFD): **11.67**

> Where securities including rights in securities are provided as collateral security to participants, system operators or to central banks of the Member States or the European Central Bank as described in paragraph 1, and their right or that of any nominee, agent or third party acting on their behalf with respect to the securities is legally recorded on a register, account or centralised deposit system located in a Member State, the determination of the rights of such entities as holders of collateral security in relation to those securities shall be governed by the law of that Member State.

Article 24 of the Banks Insolvency Directive (BID): **11.68**

> *Lex rei sitae*
>
> The enforcement of proprietary rights in instruments or other rights in such instruments, the existence or transfer of which presupposes their recording in a register, an account or a centralised deposit system held or located in a Member State, shall be governed by the law of the Member State where the register, account, or centralised deposit system in which those rights are recorded is held or located.

Article 9(1) of the Financial Collateral Directive (FCD): **11.69**

> Any question with respect to any of the matters specified in paragraph 2 arising in relation to book entry securities collateral shall be governed by the law of the country in which the relevant account is maintained. The reference to the law of a country is a reference to its domestic law, disregarding any rule under which, in deciding the relevant question, reference should be made to the law of another country.

Both the conflict-of-laws rule adopted by the HSC and the regime that is currently applied in the European Union have a common starting point, but differ in the way in which they formulate the connecting factor. **11.70**

Both may be deemed sub-species of the PRIMA rule, since they are not based on the look-through approach but on the general principle that the immediate intermediary should in some way be the focus of the account holder's rights. As explained above, **11.71** both converge on a 'tier-by-tier approach'.[40] In fact, they are likely to produce identical results in most situations.[41]

11.72 The HSC, however, is based on the law chosen in the account agreement between the account holder and the relevant intermediary, provided the 'qualifying office test' is met.[42] The PRIMA rule is based on an objective connecting factor: the location of the relevant account. The applicable law should be the law of the place where the record of title is maintained and where, therefore, orders in respect of the property can be effectively enforced.[43] *Ceteris paribus*, the main advantage of the HSC rule is that it offers a clear, easily ascertainable solution to those situations where the intermediary has different branches involved in the maintenance of securities accounts; with computer records it is not always clear where a securities account is located.[44] The choice of law eliminates this uncertainty.

11.73 It should also be noted that the scope of application of the HSC and that of the EU rules are very different. The HSC has a much broader scope: it provides a comprehensive treatment of all conflict-of-laws issues in respect of rights in intermediated securities that are of practical importance.[45] Conversely, the EU rules are mainly limited to situations where securities are used as collateral. In addition, the HSC attempts to offer an exhaustive private international law regime for intermediated securities, whereas the EU rules do not.

11.74 In December 2003, the EU Commission proposed that the Community sign the HSC.[46] This proposal sparked a wide-ranging debate about the merits of adopting the HSC. In July 2006, the EU Commission presented a working document on the consequences for the EU of adopting the HSC and explicitly concluded that the 'adoption of the Convention would be in the best interests of the Community'.[47] In this document, the Commission also suggested that the SFD, BID, and FCD would need to be changed and an amendment made to the SFD to ensure that only one law should be expressly chosen by all participants in an EU securities settlement and payment system.

11.75 However, in December 2006 the European Parliament adopted a resolution on the implication of signing the HSC.[48] The Parliament pointed out some of the drawbacks associated with the solutions of the HSC and called for a comprehensive impact study on such drawbacks before it was signed on behalf of the EU. Three years later, in 2009, the Commission withdrew its proposal to sign the HSC.[49]

---

[40] See paras 11.62–4.
[41] Thévenoz, 'Geneva Securities Convention', 11.
[42] See s E.
[43] See EC, Reflection Paper DG MARKT, 2, quoting materials produced early in the negotiation process leading to the HSC.
[44] See para 11.10.
[45] See para 11.15.
[46] EC, *Signing the Hague Convention*.
[47] EC, *Legal Assessment HSC*.
[48] OJ 2006 C317/904 (hereafter, 'European Parliament Resolution').
[49] OJ 2009 C71/17.

11.76 The EU Commission has considered the issue in the context of work on securities law legislation – a project that is now off the table, despite many years of work devoted to it. In this context, the Commission considered the following options: (i) including a conflict-of-laws rule for intermediated securities that would retain the location of the account criterion but clarify its application when multiple branches are concerned ('Where an account provider has branches located in jurisdictions different from the head offices' jurisdiction, the account is maintained by the branch which handles the relationship with the account holder in relation to the securities account, otherwise by the head office');[50] (ii) and/or opting for ratification of the HSC; or (iii) introducing a new approach.[51]

11.77 Most recently, the issue of conflict-of-laws rules for intermediated securities was considered in the context of the EU's flagship project of a Capital Markets Union. This time round, the Commission looked at an even more modest route in the form of a non-legally binding 'communication' with a 'proportionate response' to the difficulties surrounding a coherent EU regime.[52] This approach, however, was broadly criticized as inadequate.[53]

(2) Substantive debate

11.78 The European Parliament Resolution of December 2006 and the Opinion of the European Central Bank of March 2005[54] summarize the main concerns raised by the HSC in Europe. These concerns revolve around four aspects: (a) protection of third-party rights, (b) interaction with substantive laws, (c) interaction with public law, and (d) the diversity of laws within a single securities settlement system (SSS).

(a) Protection of third-party rights
11.79 The HSC determines the impact of the applicable law on third parties' rights.[55] In this regard, it has been argued that the choice of law made by an account holder and its intermediary would disadvantage third parties either because they (i) would not know about it (problem of transparency), or (ii) would find it detrimental to their interests (problem of abuse).

---

[50] EC, *Second Consultation: Legislation on Securities*, Principle 14. The issue was also considered in the context of the drafting of the EU CSD Regulation (CSDR). Article 46 of the 2012 draft CSDR (COM(2012) 73 final) contained detailed conflict-of-laws rules tailored to the context of CSDs. However, this draft provision is not reflected in the final text of the CSDR. Instead, recital 57 CSDR refers the issue to 'future Union legislative acts'.
[51] See paras 11.98–102.
[52] EC, *Communication on the applicable law*.
[53] Letter by ISDA of 22 May 2018 to the European Commission regarding the assignment of claims and transactions in intermediated securities; Keijser, 'Financial Collateral Arrangements' (2017), s 22; Keijser and Mooney, 'Transparency', III.B especially fn 64; Ch 2, n 26.
[54] ECB, 'Opinion'.
[55] See s H.

11.80 **(i) Transparency** It has been said that when the applicable law is chosen within the agreement between an account holder and its intermediary, it is not easy for third parties to discover that law: the account agreement is not a public document. This can be contrasted with the current situation in which the law can often be ascertained from objective facts, ie, the location of the relevant securities account, that do not require further enquiry.[56]

11.81 This argument, however, is not convincing. On the one hand, with regard to third parties seeking to gain an interest in securities by agreement, for example, potential collateral takers, these parties already need to obtain information about the existence of a securities account and its location. Under the HSC, these third parties will also want to know the law chosen by the account holder and the intermediary. As the cooperation of the account holder and its intermediary is always necessary, the need to obtain this additional information will not constitute a significant change.[57] In general, third parties who wish to acquire a proprietary right over the securities will always obtain information about which law governs such securities, whether under the current EU PRIMA rule or the HSC rule.

11.82 Other third parties may have had no prior dealings with the account holder as such, for example, ordinary public or private creditors seeking to attach securities to enforce a debt. In order to attach securities, a creditor, or the competent authority, generally needs to establish the existence of a securities holding and the jurisdiction to which it is subject. Under the current EU PRIMA rule, that creditor needs to know where the securities account of its debtor is located. The HSC will not significantly alter this. The key issue is that establishing the location of a securities account usually requires the cooperation of the account holder and/or the intermediary (or intermediaries). In fact, in order to enforce the attachment, the competent authority will normally approach the intermediary to provide certain information and block the account. Therefore, the need to obtain a single piece of additional information, ie, the law chosen, would not materially compromise an attaching creditor's current position.[58]

11.83 **(ii) Abuse** It has also been alleged that the possibility of choosing the applicable law may be used by intermediaries to select a law more favourable to them than to account holders or by both parties vis-à-vis secured creditors.[59]

---

[56] EC, *Legal Assessment HSC*, 11; ECB, 'Opinion', 15; Ooi, 'Critical Reading', 471; Ooi, 'Intermediated Securities', 226; Rögner, 'Inconsistencies', 104.
[57] EC, *Legal Assessment HSC*, 12; Sigman and Bernasconi, 'Myths', 34.
[58] EC, *Legal Assessment HSC*, 12; Sigman and Bernasconi, 'Myths', 34. There may be cases, nevertheless, where an objective connecting factor, such as a diagnostic number (similar to the International Bank Account Number), may make things easier for third parties in general and for potential attaching creditors and local authorities in particular. Thus, for example, if the jurisdictional rules remain based on the location of the account, under the HSC the number of cases in which the local authorities should have to apply a foreign law may increase *ceteris paribus*: see ECB, 'Opinion', 14. But this is a common scenario in cross-border situations and has to be balanced against the advantage of a global, standardized solution; see EC, *Legal Assessment HSC*, 13.
[59] European Parliament Resolution, 8.

11.84 It is true that the HSC may facilitate 'law shopping strategies': in principle, it would appear to be easier to include a choice of law in the account agreement than to register or maintain the account in a particular place.[60] The situation under the HSC, however, is not very different from the current EU PRIMA rule. Under this rule, nothing prevents a domestic account holder from opening a securities account in a foreign jurisdiction with a local intermediary. There is no prohibition on locating accounts abroad. Parties already have the freedom, at least from a private international law standpoint, to choose where their securities accounts are held or maintained. By the same token, nothing prevents an intermediary from locating its clients' accounts in a particular office.[61]

11.85 Finally, the idea that secured creditors may be disadvantaged by any subsequent changes to the choice of applicable law made without their consent is also unfounded. The pre-acquired rights of secured creditors are preserved by Article 7 HSC, the effect of which is that rights created under the applicable law may not be restricted or swept aside when that law changes by agreement of the parties. Their agreement to change the Convention law may not be imposed on a third party that had acted in reliance on the first account agreement.[62]

(b) Interaction with substantive law

11.86 The HSC is a pure conflict-of-laws Convention and does not affect or give rise to substantive law applicable to intermediated securities.[63] It is neutral on issues such as the nature of an account holder's rights or the requirements for creating or disposing of such rights. Nevertheless, as pointed out above, it has been argued that the solutions of the HSC are more attuned to certain legal systems and, therefore, may *indirectly* affect the substantive law rules. These indirect effects have been considered in two areas: company law and securities law.

11.87 The first issue is whether the Convention would jeopardize existing rules applying to companies. If the law governing corporate actions, such as the exercise of voting rights or payment of income, differs from the law chosen by the account holder and its intermediary, this will cause difficulties. By way of example, it has been suggested that an issuer will be prevented from knowing who the ultimate investor is, or that a situation could arise where, in order to determine who is entitled to exercise the rights arising from securities, an issuer would need to require each claimant to provide proof of entitlement, including the relevant account agreement. This would involve additional complications and expense.[64]

11.88 However, the Convention expressly provides that it does not determine the law applicable to the rights and duties of an issuer of securities, whether in relation to the holder

---

[60] See para 11.34.
[61] Potok, 'Hague Securities Convention', 219; Sigman and Bernasconi, 'Myths', 34.
[62] See para 11.46.
[63] Goode et al, *Explanatory Report*, 2-1.
[64] EC, *Legal Assessment HSC*, 13.

of securities or any other person (Article 2(3)(c) HSC).[65] This exclusion encompasses the duties of the issuer with respect to all corporate actions, including voting rights and income. These matters would continue to be subject to the applicable corporate law, and would not be affected by ratification of the HSC.[66] On the other hand, the difficulties of identifying the person entitled to exercise corporate rights derive from the very nature of intermediated holding systems. The preamble to the EU Shareholders' Rights Directive states: 'Where financial intermediaries are involved, the effectiveness of voting upon instructions relies, to a great extent, on the efficiency of the chain of intermediaries, given that investors are frequently unable to exercise the voting rights attached to their shares without the cooperation of every intermediary in the chain, who may not have an economic stake in the shares'. The complexity is inherent in the chain of intermediaries. The problem, therefore, is basically the same, regardless of whether the applicable law to the intermediated securities follows the HSC rule or the current EU PRIMA rule.

11.89 With regard to securities law, the argument has more weight yet the conclusion is very similar. The HSC fits well with substantive laws based on a *trust* mechanism or on the creation of a new entitlement for each account holder vis-à-vis its intermediary. Conversely, it does not fit as well with substantive laws based on a direct proprietary right of the final investor—either an individual right or a pro rata collective right—over the securities deposited or registered at the issuer central securities depository (CSD). The same, it has been argued, holds with regard to transparent systems, where the names of the ultimate account holders are registered in individual segregated accounts at the level of the issuer CSD, and not at the level of their custodian only.

11.90 The reason can be summarized as follows.[67] The HSC is based on a tier-by-tier approach. The applicable law is determined separately for each tier in accordance with the choice of law made between the corresponding account holder and its intermediary.[68] This law determines the nature and effects of the rights of the account holder against its intermediary and third parties. Naturally, the nature of these rights may be different in each of those tiers. Along the chain of intermediaries, there is no one, single overarching law, just different layers of laws. This fragmentation at the conflict-of-laws level, however, does not fit well with those legal systems which, at the substantive law level, recognize a direct, individual, or collective ownership right of the (ultimate) investors over the original securities. Suppose that the issuer CSD is located in a jurisdiction that recognizes an investor's right to direct pro rata ownership of the securities. However, the investor's securities are held through a custodian in another jurisdiction where the law attributes to the account holder a bundle of rights only against its intermediary that may crystallize in a 'security entitlement' in an insolvency. These two systems are hard

---

[65] See para 11.20.
[66] EC, *Legal Assessment HSC*, 14; Goode et al, *Explanatory Report*, 2–34.
[67] See n 37.
[68] Goode et al, *Explanatory Report*, 2–26; Ooi, 'Intermediated Securities', 237.

to reconcile. At least conceptually, it is difficult to understand how the investor may have a direct ownership right over the securities registered at the issuer CSD and, at the same time, have a 'security entitlement' enforceable only against its intermediary.

To some extent, a similar problem arises in a dynamic situation. The HSC fits well with legal systems where a transfer of intermediated securities implies that the transferor's rights are discharged and the transferee's rights are newly created. Conversely, it does not fit as well with legal systems where rights *in rem* over the securities are directly transferred and, therefore, what is acquired by the transferee derives directly from the transferor. The transferee acquires what the transferor loses, ie, under these substantive law systems, the rights *in rem* acquired by the transferee are the same as those lost by the transferor.[69] However, if each part of the transaction is governed by different laws, as may be the case under the HSC, the acquisition by the transferee can, and should, be analysed independently from the question of whether the transferor has lost its rights. The acquisition side and disposition side of the transaction may be governed by different laws and therefore analysed independently. As in the static example, this may lead to conceptually conflicting results, for example, the so-called 'double interest' situation.[70]

11.91

Nevertheless, this is not a problem arising specifically from the HSC. It is, again, an issue linked to the PRIMA rule.[71] This rule, whether the HSC or the current EU version, creates different layers of laws. If the chain of intermediaries crosses different jurisdictions, different laws will apply, one to each intermediary. This means that problems of cross-border compatibilities may always arise, like those mentioned above. That is why the HSC calls for a Convention on substantive law ensuring the compatibility between the conflict and the material law levels.[72]

11.92

Finally, with regard to *transparent systems*, the solution offered by the HSC seems appropriate. According to Article 1(3)(b) HSC mere account operators are not considered intermediaries. If a financial institution opens a securities account with a third party in the name of the customer, the financial institution itself, even if it keeps a parallel record of the customer's holding, will not be considered an intermediary under the HSC.[73] If the investor has an individually segregated securities account under its name at the level of the issuer CSD, this will be the relevant account from a conflict-of-laws standpoint. This avoids problems of substantive incompatibilities, since the rights of the investor in the securities are governed by one single law, not by different layers of laws. Therefore, if the intention is to give final investors the option to open individually

11.93

---

[69] Einsele, 'Modernising', 255.
[70] EC, *Legal Assessment HSC*, 10; Einsele, 'Modernising', 255; Garcimartín, 'Disposition and Acquisition', 749–50; Rögner, 'Inconsistencies', 104; Ooi, 'Critical Reading', 484–7; Ooi, 'Intermediated Securities', 227. Goode et al, *Explanatory Report*, 4–43 to 4–51 deal with this problem, but only from a conflict-of-laws perspective.
[71] Chun, *Cross-border Transactions*, 416–17; Goode et al, *Explanatory Report*, 4–49; Haentjens, *Harmonisation*, 233, 290; Morton, 'Security Interests', 370–1.
[72] *Inter alia*, Einsele, 'Modernising', 256; Thévenoz, 'Intermediated Securities', 426–30.
[73] Goode et al, *Explanatory Report*, 1–35.

segregated accounts at the issuer CSD level, Article 1(3)(b) HSC may also provide an adequate solution.

(c) Interaction with public law

11.94 It has been argued that the HSC may interfere with the enforcement of public laws. In particular, concern has been voiced as to a possible risk of conflict between the HSC and reporting duties imposed on EU intermediaries in the areas of money laundering and market abuse, and laws preserving the confidentiality of client's affairs arising under a chosen non-EU law, especially when those duties are based on the location of the account.[74] It has also been said that the autonomy of the parties may be used to disempower supervisory authorities. The promotion of party autonomy under the HSC may interfere, directly or indirectly, with the application of public laws based on the location of the account.[75]

11.95 However, the HSC deals only with private law issues (Article 2). Regulatory measures are excluded, and the HSC therefore affects the scope neither of the application of public laws nor of the powers of national authorities.[76] Generally speaking, these laws are based on personal and/or territorial rules, which use objective connecting factors to determine their scope of application, independent of private agreements. The choice of law of a non-EU State will therefore have no impact on the transaction reporting or tax obligations imposed on an intermediary, account holder, or any other person concerned with securities held in the relevant securities account.[77] For the same reason, the HSC has no effect on supervisory authorities' powers: it limits neither the substantive scope nor the geographical reach of the power of a supervisory authority.[78] Furthermore, the exception for mandatory rules of public policy in the HSC makes it clear that transaction reporting obligations and similar public law based obligations would not be affected in any event (Article 11).

(d) Diversity of laws in securities settlement systems

11.96 It has also been argued that the HSC would jeopardize the stability of SSSs. Since the HSC allows the choice of law, an SSS and its members could use a variety of laws. Different laws may be applicable to different participants which do not coincide with the law governing the system, and this could destroy the commonality needed for settlement operations within the system.[79]

11.97 The argument is theoretically correct, but not realistic. The system operator and all participants have a shared interest in a smoothly operating system. This makes it highly

---

[74] EC, *Legal Assessment HSC*, 15; ECB, 'Opinion', 16
[75] ECB, 'Opinion', 16.
[76] See para 11.21.
[77] EC, *Legal Assessment HSC*, 15; Sigman and Bernasconi, 'Myths', 31.
[78] Sigman and Bernasconi, 'Myths', 31.
[79] EC, *Legal Assessment HSC*, 17; European Parliament Resolution, 14; Ooi, 'Critical Reading', 471; Ooi, 'Intermediated Securities', 233.

unlikely that any system operator would agree to different laws among its members.[80] Furthermore, regulatory or supervisory authorities also have the power, if necessary, to compel system operators to ensure that no unacceptable legal or systemic risk can arise from the application of diverse laws. Those authorities may, for example, require that all participants in a national system choose the same law.[81]

(3) The way forward for intermediated securities

It is not easy to predict the future of the law applicable to intermediated securities, but it is possible to describe the different alternatives and to weigh up each of them, taking into account their main advantages and drawbacks.

11.98

The simplest option is that the EU ratifies the HSC, an option initially favoured by the European Commission.[82] It would solve the main difficulties associated with the location of the relevant account when different branches are concerned and, therefore, bring more certainty as to which law applies. If need be, the problem of a diversity of laws in EU securities settlement and payment systems could be resolved by amending the definition of 'system' or by imposing an obligation on all participants to choose the same law. Naturally, this would also call for the amendment of EU directives so as to remove the location of the account formula as a connecting factor. At this stage, however, this option seems remote since there does not appear to be sufficient support for ratification of the HSC, either in the Council or the European Parliament or the ECB.[83]

11.99

The other option is to keep the current EU PRIMA rule, extending it to all uses of securities and refining its application to ensure that it is implemented in the same way in all EU Member States. In addition, other solutions different from the choice of law could be explored to put the location of an account beyond doubt, such as the adoption of securities account codes including a reference to a State.[84] The main problem is that this option would not provide an international solution, so uncertainty as to the applicable law would persist in the case of proprietary issues concerning non-EU States. While EU law may be able to provide certainty as to which law applies when all aspects of a securities transaction are located within the EU, it would still be unclear which law applies in cases involving aspects related to States outside the EU, at least with regard to States that do not apply the location of the account criteria.[85]

11.100

---

[80] EC, *Legal Assessment HSC*, 18; Rank, W., *Assessment: Does the Hague Securities Convention Offer Greater Certainty in International Securities Transactions?* (on file with the authors), 18.
[81] EC, *Legal Assessment HSC*, 18; Sigman and Bernasconi, 'Myths', 32.
[82] EC, *Legal Assessment HSC*, 23.
[83] The situation is the same as reflected in 2007 by EC, Reflection Paper DG MARKT, 4.
[84] See EC, Reflection Paper DG MARKT, 5; Paech, 'Conflict of Laws', II.B.iii.
[85] EC, *Legal Assessment HSC*, 22.

11.101 A third option would be to amend the HSC and partially re-establish the original drafts based on the location of the account as a main connecting factor.[86] This, however, would require the consensus of many States, including the Hague Conference itself. If the rationale for departing from that original approach was difficulties in identifying the location of the relevant account in modern global trading, it is not easy to imagine what new arguments could be brought to bear to rebut that reasoning.

11.102 Finally, if the EU is not willing to change its views, a fourth option would be a 'dual-system approach' worldwide—one based on the location of the account (current EU PRIMA rule with additional clarifications) and another based on the choice of law by the parties (HSC rule). The application of either approach would be determined by each intermediary. If the securities are held with an EU intermediary, the first system applies. If the securities are held with a non-EU intermediary, the second system applies. In fact, this is currently the (de facto) status quo. It is not clear whether the current version of the HSC allows for this option, ie, whether the EU could ratify the HSC but exclude the choice of law for EU intermediaries.[87] If this dual-system approach were acceptable, the ambiguity could be resolved by a minor amendment to the current text of the HSC (or by other mechanisms such as a declaration by the Secretary General of the Hague Conference or a Special Commission). The entry into force of the HSC in 2017 has, however, made this a thornier way forward.

K. Outlook: New Technologies

11.103 New conflict-of-laws questions have arisen in light of the ongoing development of crypto-assets, including crypto-securities. Such assets incorporate new technologies, such as distributed ledger technology (DLT) and smart contracts, which are described in more detail in earlier chapters.[88] The market for crypto-assets is taking shape at a rapid pace and shows a wide variety of different applications of new technologies. The corresponding legal framework, including conflict-of-laws rules for crypto-assets, is still in its infancy. For example, in 2018, the EBRD and Clifford Chance called for 'co-ordinated international efforts' to address the relevant conflict-of-laws issues as a 'longer term ambition'.[89] Early in 2020, a report on the conflict-of-laws intricacies in the context of smart derivatives contracts based on DLT called for 'adapting or developing global legal standards aimed at ensuring the safe, transparent and consistent regulation of DLT-based financial transactions'.[90] Both the Hague Conference and a

---

[86] See para 11.10.
[87] For some authors, the answer is clearly positive. See Sigman and Bernasconi, 'Myths', 31, who argue that the HSC does not prevent Contracting States from prohibiting intermediaries 'from choosing any governing law'. It is, nevertheless, at least doubtful whether such a radical and absolute prohibition would not contravene the *'effet utile'* of the Convention.
[88] See Ch 5, s C; Ch 6, s E; Ch 7, s G; Ch 8, s D(5); Ch 10.
[89] EBRD and Clifford Chance, Legal Framework, 2.5 at p 40.
[90] ISDA et al, *Private International Law Aspects of Smart Derivatives Contracts*, 30.

UNIDROIT Working Group on Digital Assets and Private Law have in the meantime initiated projects concerning different conflict-of-laws questions with regard to crypto-assets (including jurisdiction, applicable law, and recognition and enforcement), but these projects need to mature; no established guidelines are yet available.[91] In light of this 'moving target', we here limit ourselves to a number of general considerations, in line with the UNIDROIT project primarily concerning the applicable law, although the practical need for appropriate rules is growing more pressing by the day.

Initially, the debate on the appropriate conflict-of-laws regime focused on the platform (or network), consisting of connected 'nodes', on which crypto-assets are typically represented and traded. The initial idea was that issuers and investors would be directly connected on such platforms and that a degree of disintermediation might take place. One plausible connecting factor put forward to determine the applicable law in this context is the law of the platform.[92] The conflict-of-laws analysis of the insolvency of a platform operator (if any) or a platform participant also deserves attention.[93]

11.104

However, custodians started fulfilling a role in this context fairly early on.[94] Investors began to look for ways to place their 'private keys' (or other code or information allowing them to trade 'their' crypto-assets) in safe custody with third parties. A market of crypto-custody services thus developed, raising additional conflict-of-laws queries. Apart from queries such as that regarding the forum should the custodian become insolvent,[95] the relevant connecting factor to determine the law applicable to an investor's claims (of a contractual and/or proprietary nature) towards its custodian should be determined. Possible connecting factors, to name but a few, are the place of incorporation or business of the custodian, the place of the physical carrier (the 'private key' as represented on, for example, an online computer or in 'cold', off-line storage), an account number given to the relevant DLT code (possibly with a country identifier), and a choice-of-law agreement between the investor and the custodian. Some of these possible connecting factors may be difficult to ascertain in a virtual context.

11.105

Moreover, it would seem advantageous for the 'conflict-of-laws worlds' of intermediated securities and crypto-securities to be in tune. As phrased by Haentjens, De Graaf, and Kokorin: 'The problem of having to localize the unlocalizable is not new and has been addressed where it regards financial instruments that are credited to accounts. It therefore seems appropriate to investigate the conflict-of-laws rules that have been developed for proprietary claims in financial instruments as inspiration for proprietary claims in crypto-currency.'[96] If one were to apply the analysis relating to intermediated

11.106

---

[91] Hague Conference on Private International Law, Prel Doc No 4 (November 2020) on 'Developments with respect to PIL implications of the digital economy, including DLT'; UNIDROIT 2021–Study LXXXII–W.G. 2–Doc 2 (rev 1) (March 2021; Issues Paper), paras 124–7.
[92] Keijser and Mooney, 'Transparency', II.E; Paech, *Securities, Intermediation and the Blockchain*, IV.D.1; UNIDROIT 2021–Study LXXXII–W.G. 2–Doc 2 (rev 1), p 38 s A.
[93] UNIDROIT 2021–Study LXXXII–W.G. 2–Doc 2 (rev 1), p 38 s B.
[94] See, eg, Art 63 of the proposed MiCA concerning the safekeeping of clients' crypto-assets and related funds.
[95] Haentjens, De Graaf, and Kokorin, *Failed Hopes of Disintermediation*, 5.2.
[96] Ibid, p 26.

securities to crypto-securities involving some form of custody, one might consider an account-based approach (possibly with additional attributes such as a country identifier), as is common in Europe, or a (conditioned) choice-of-law approach along the lines of the HSC.[97] Policy issues similar to those outlined in paragraph 11.102 regarding the 'dual-system approach' for intermediated securities are thus appearing on the horizon.

11.107 An additional complication in the context of crypto-assets is that such assets come in different guises. 'Native' crypto-assets are assets that exist on a DLT platform only. Other crypto-assets (sometimes labelled 'non-native', 'asset-backed', 'tethered', or 'twinned' crypto-assets) represent assets that are outside the DLT platform.[98] Ideally, the underlying 'non-crypto' or 'real-world' assets are congruent with the assets in the crypto domain: the 'real' assets should, for example, not be disposed of if this untethers the crypto-assets. When designing a conflict-of-laws framework, the question should be addressed as to whether the conflict rules for the 'real' assets should correspond with, or may deviate from, those for the crypto-assets.[99]

---

[97] Haentjes, De Graaf, and Kokorin, *Failed Hopes of Disintermediation*, 5.3 especially at 27–8. See also Kalderon, Snagg, and Harrop, 'Distributed Ledgers', 247–8 ('Conflict of laws'); Keijser, 'Financial Collateral Arrangements' (2017), 291.
[98] Crypto-assets that are 'directly' connected with real-world assets should not be confused with digital assets that are 'backed' by a basket of real-world assets to stabilize their value, such as in the case of stablecoins.
[99] UNIDROIT 2021–Study LXXXII–W.G. 2–Doc 2 (rev 1), p 39 s C.

Bibliography

Acharya, V, Adler, B, Richardson, M, and Roubini, N, 'Resolution Authority', in Acharya, V, Cooley, T, Richardson, M, and Walter, I, *Regulating Wall Street: The Dodd-Frank Act and the New Architecture of Global Finance* (Hoboken, New Jersey: Wiley, 2010), 213–40.

Allen, J, Rauchs, M, Blandin, A, Bear, K, *Legal and Regulatory Considerations for Digital Assets* (Cambridge Centre for Alternative Finance, 2020), <https://www.jbs.cam.ac.uk/faculty-research/centres/alternative-finance/publications/legal-and-regulatory-considerations-for-digital-assets/> (accessed 21 July 2021).

Acharya, V and Öncü, S, 'A Proposal for the Resolution of Systemically Important Assets and Liabilities: The Case of the Repo Market', *International Journal of Central Banking*, 9 (2013; Supplement 1), 291–349.

Adams, S, *Derivatives Safe Harbors in Bankruptcy and Dodd-Frank: A Structural Analysis* (2013), <http://dash.harvard.edu/handle/1/10985175> (accessed 21 July 2021).

AFME, Post Trade Division, Client Asset Protection Task Force, *AFME Principles on Asset Segregation, Due Diligence and Collateral Management* (September 2016), <http://www.afme.eu/globalassets/downloads/publications/afme-position-and-proposed-principles-on-asset-segregation-07.09.16.pdf> (accessed 21 July 2021).

American Bar Association (ABA), Derivatives and Futures Law Committee, Innovative Digital Products and Processes Subcommittee & Jurisdiction Working Group, *Digital and Digitized Assets: Federal and State Jurisdictional Issues* (2019).

American Law Institute, *UCC Official Text and Comments* (Thomson Reuters, 2012).

Architzel, P and Walker, P, *CFTC's Rulemaking on the Segregation of Cleared Swaps: Customer Collateral: LSOC and Beyond* (New York City Bar, 3 May 2012).

Austen-Peters, A, *Custody of Investments: Law and Practice* (Oxford: Oxford University Press, 2001).

Avgouleas, E and Kiayias, A, 'The Promise of Blockchain Technology for Global Securities and Derivatives Markets: The New Financial Ecosystem and the "Holy Grail" of Systemic Risk Containment', *European Business Organization Law Review*, 20 (2019), 81–110.

Ayotte, K and Skeel, D, 'Bankruptcy or Bailouts?', *The Journal of Corporation Law*, 35/3 (2010), 469–98.

Bank of England, Prudential Regulation Authority, *Collateral Upgrade Transactions and Asset Encumbrance: Expectations in Relation to Firms' Risk Management Practices* (April 2013; Supervisory Statement LSS2/13).

Bates, S and Gleeson, S, 'Legal Aspects of Bank Bail-ins', *Law and Financial Markets Review*, 5/4 (2011), 264–75.

Baty, J, *Digital Custody: Is Custody of Digital Securities 'Different'?* (January 2020), <https://thefintechtimes.com/digital-custody-is-custody-of-digital-securities-different/> (accessed 21 July 2021).

Bazinas, S, 'The UNCITRAL Legislative Guide on Secured Transactions: Key Objectives and Fundamental Policies', *Uniform Commercial Code Law Journal*, 42/2 (2010), 123–55.

Bazinas, S, 'Towards Global Harmonization of Conflict-of-laws Rules in the Area of Secured Financing: the Conflict-of-laws Recommendations of the UNCITRAL Legislative Guide on Secured Transactions', in The Permanent Bureau of the Hague Conference on Private International Law (ed), *A Commitment to Private International Law: Essays in Honour of Hans van Loon* (Cambridge: Intersentia, 2013), 1–16.

Bazinas, S, 'The Law Applicable to Third-party Effects of Assignments of Claims: the UN Convention and the EU Commission Proposal Compared', *Uniform Law Review*, 24/4 (2019), 609–32.

Bazinas, S, 'Does the World Need Another Uniform Law on Factoring?', in Benicke, C and Huber, S (eds), *National, International und Transnational: Harmonischer Dreiklang im Recht: Festschrift für Herbert Kronke zum 70. Geburtstag* (Giesenking Verlag, 2020), 679–92.

Bazinas, S, Kohn, R, and Del Duca, L, 'Facilitating a Cost-free Path to Economic Recovery: Implementing a Global Uniform Receivables Financing Law', *Uniform Commercial Code Law Journal*, 44/3 (2012), 277–316.

Bazinas, S and Smith, E, 'UNCITRAL Model Law and UCC Article 9 Conflict-of-laws Rules Compared', *Uniform Commercial Code Journal*, 49/3 (2020), 387–428.

BCBS, *Basel I: International Convergence of Capital Measurement and Capital Standards* (July 1988), <http://www.bis.org/publ/bcbs04a.htm> (accessed 21 July 2021).

BCBS, *Basel Capital Accord: The Treatment of the Credit Risk Associated with Certain Off-balance-sheet Items* (July 1994; 1994 Amendment), <http://www.bis.org/publ/bcbs12a.htm> (accessed 21 July 2021).

BCBS, *Basel Capital Accord: Treatment of Potential Exposure for Off-balance-sheet Items* (April 1995; 1995 Amendment), <http://www.bis.org/publ/bcbs18.htm> (accessed 21 July 2021).

BCBS, *Basel II: International Convergence of Capital Measurement and Capital Standards: A Revised Framework: Comprehensive Version* (June 2006), <http://www.bis.org/publ/bcbs128.pdf> (accessed 21 July 2021).

BCBS, *Principles for Home-Host Supervisory Cooperation and Allocation Mechanisms in the Context of Advanced Measurement Approaches (AMA)* (November 2007), <http://www.bis.org/publ/bcbs135.pdf> (accessed 21 July 2021).

BCBS, *Report and Recommendations of the Cross-border Bank Resolution Group* (March 2010), <http://www.bis.org/publ/bcbs169.pdf> (accessed 21 July 2021).

BCBS, *Basel III: A Global Regulatory Framework for More Resilient Banks and Banking Systems* (June 2011; revised version), <http://www.bis.org/publ/bcbs189.htm> (accessed 21 July 2021).

BCBS, *Resolution Policies and Frameworks: Progress So Far* (July 2011), <http://www.bis.org/publ/bcbs200.pdf> (accessed 21 July 2021).

BCBS, *Capital Requirements for Bank Exposures to Central Counterparties* (July 2012), <http://www.bis.org/publ/bcbs227.pdf> (accessed 21 July 2021).

BCBS, *Consultative Document: Haircut Floors for Non-centrally Cleared Securities Financing Transactions* (November 2015), <http://www.bis.org/bcbs/publ/d340.htm> (accessed 21 July 2021).

BCBS, *Statement on Crypto-assets* (March 2019), <https://www.bis.org/publ/bcbs_nl21.htm> (accessed 21 July 2021).

BCBS, *Prudential Treatment of Cryptoasset Exposures: Consultative Document* (June 2021), <https://www.bis.org/bcbs/publ/d519.pdf> (accessed 21 July 2021).

BCBS, *CRE56: Minimum Haircut Floors for Securities Financing Transactions* (July 2021; update of versions of December 2019 and March 2020), <https://www.bis.org/basel_framework/timeline.htm?st=CRE&ch=56> (accessed 21 July 2021).

BCBS and IOSCO Board, *Margin Requirements for Non-centrally Cleared Derivatives* (April 2020; revised version), <https://www.bis.org/bcbs/publ/d499.pdf> (accessed 21 July 2021).

Beale, H, Bridge, M, Gullifer, L, and Lomnicka, E, *The Law of Security and Title-based Financing* (Oxford: Oxford University Press, 2012; 2nd edn).

Benjamin, J, *Interests in Securities* (Oxford: Oxford University Press, 2000).

Benjamin, J, *Financial Law* (Oxford: Oxford University Press, 2007).

Benjamin, J, Morton, G, and Raffan, M, 'The Future of Securities Financing', *Law and Financial Markets Review*, 7/1 (2013), 4–8.

Bergman, W, Bliss, R, Johnson, C, and Kaufman, G, 'Netting, Financial Contracts, and Banks: The Economic Implications', in Kaufman, G (ed), *Market Discipline in Banking: Theory and Evidence* (Amsterdam: Elsevier, 2003), 303–34.

Bernasconi, C and Keijser, T, 'The Hague and Geneva Securities Conventions: A Modern and Global Legal Regime for Intermediated Securities', *Uniform Law Review*, 17/3 (2012), 549–60.

Bertrams, R, 'EU-richtlijn sanering en liquidatie van kredietinstellingen en de Nederlandse uitvoeringswet: Wijzigingen in de Wtk 1992 en Fw', *Tijdschrift voor Insolventierecht*, 11/4 (2005), 112–25.

Bhutoria, R, *The Omnibus Model for Custody* (January 2020), <https://www.fidelitydigitalassets.com/articles/the-omnibus-model-for-custody> (accessed 21 July 2021).

Biggins, J and Scott, C, 'Public-Private Relations in a Transnational Private Regulatory Regime: ISDA, the State and OTC Derivatives Market Reform', *European Business Organization Law Review*, 13 (2012), 309–46.

Birnhak, D, 'Online Shareholder Meetings: Corporate Law Anomalies or the Future of Governance?', *Rutgers Computer and Technology Law Journal*, 29/2 (2003), 423–46.

BIS, *Report on Netting Schemes* (February 1989; *Angell Report*; prepared by the Group of Experts on Payment Systems of the central banks of the Group of Ten countries), <http://www.bis.org/publ/cpss02.pdf> (accessed 21 July 2021).

BIS, *Report of the Committee on Interbank Netting Schemes of the Central Banks of the Group of Ten Countries* (1990; reformatted and repaginated 1999 website version; *Lamfalussy Report*), <http://www.bis.org/publ/cpss04.pdf> (accessed 21 July 2021).

BIS, *Statistical Release: OTC Derivatives at End-December 2019* (May 2020), <https://www.bis.org/publ/otc_hy2005.pdf> (accessed 21 July 2021).

BIS, *Statistical Release: OTC Derivatives at End-December 2020* (May 2021), <https://www.bis.org/publ/otc_hy2105.pdf> (accessed 21 July 2021).

Blandin, A, Cloots, A, Hussain, H, Rauchs, M, Saleuddin, R, Allen, J, Zhang, B, and Cloud, K, *Global Cryptoasset Regulatory Landscape Study* (Cambridge Centre for Alternative Finance, 2019), <https://www.jbs.cam.ac.uk/faculty-research/centres/alternative-finance/publications/cryptoasset-regulation/#.YP6hDY4zY2w> (accessed 21 July 2021).

Blemus, S and Guégan, D, 'Initial Crypto-asset Offerings (ICOs), Tokenization and Corporate Governance', *Capital Markets Law Journal*, 15/2 (2020), 191–223.

Bliss R and Kaufman, G, 'Derivatives and Systemic Risk: Netting, Collateral, and Closeout', *Journal of Financial Stability*, 2 (2006), 55–70.

Block-Lieb, S and Halliday, T, *Global Lawmakers: International Organizations in the Crafting of World Markets* (Cambridge: Cambridge University Press, 2017).

Bloxham, P, *Review of the Investment Bank Special Administration Regulations 2011* (United Kingdom: April 2013).

Böger, O, 'Close-out Netting Provisions in Private International Law and International Insolvency Law (Part I)', *Uniform Law Review*, 18/2 (2013), 232–61.

Böger, O, 'Close-out Netting Provisions in Private International Law and International Insolvency Law (Part II)', *Uniform Law Review*, 18/3–4 (2013), 532–63.

Bolton, P and Oehmke, M, 'Should Derivatives Be Privileged in Bankruptcy?', *Journal of Finance*, 70/6 (2015), 2353–93.

Boros, E, 'Virtual Shareholder Meetings: Who Decides How Companies Make Decisions?', *Melbourne University Law Review*, 28 (2004), 265–89.

Brekke, J and Fischer, A, 'Digital Scarcity', *Internet Policy Review*, 10/2 (2021), <https://doi.org/10.14763/2021.2.1548> (accessed 21 July 2021).

Brink, U, 'New German Legislation Opens Door to Ratification of UNIDROIT Factoring Convention', *Uniform Law Review*, 3/4 (1998), 770–5.

Brito, J and Castillo, A, 'Bitcoin: A Primer for Policymakers', *Policy*, 29/4 (Summer 2013–2014), <https://www.cis.org.au/app/uploads/2015/04/images/stories/policy-magazine/2013-summer/29-4-13-jbrito-acastillo.pdf> (accessed 21 July 2021), 3–12.

Broad Stakeholder Group, *Dismantling Giovannini Barrier 3: The Market Standards for Corporate Actions Processing & General Meetings* (February 2013; 5th Implementation Progress Report), <https://www.ebf.eu/wp-content/uploads/2017/07/000141B-2013-5th-BSG-Implementation-Progress-Report-February-2013.pdf> (accessed 21 July 2021).

Broadridge, *Shareholder Rights Directive II: Lessons Learned, Ongoing Challenges and Planning for the Future* (2021).

Bullmann, D, Klemm, J, and Pinna, A, *In Search for Stability in Crypto-assets: Are Stablecoins the Solution?* (August 2019; ECB Occasional Paper No. 230).

Chan, D, Fontan, F, Rosati, S, and Russo, D, *The Securities Custody Industry* (August 2007; Occasional Paper Series 68), <http://www.ecb.europa.eu/pub/pdf/scpops/ecbocp68.pdf> (accessed 21 July 2021).

Chiu, J and Koeppl, T, *Blockchain-based Settlement for Asset Trading* (Ottawa: Bank of Canada, 2018; Bank of Canada Staff Working Paper 2018-45).

Chun, C, *Cross-border Transactions of Intermediated Securities* (Heidelberg, New York, Dordrecht, London: Springer, 2012).

Clack, C, Bakshi, V, and Braine, L, *Smart Contract Templates: Foundations, Design Landscape and Research Directions* (2016, revised March 2017).

Clack, C and McGonagle, C, *Smart Derivatives Contracts: The ISDA Master Agreement and the Automation of Payments and Deliveries* (2018–19), <https://arxiv.org/pdf/1904.01461.pdf> (accessed 21 July 2021).

Clark, R, 'The Four Stages of Capitalism: Reflections on Investment Management Treatises', *Harvard Law Review*, 94/3 (1981), 561–82.

Clifford Chance and EBRD, *Smart Contracts: Legal Framework and Proposed Guidelines for Lawmakers* (October 2018).

Cohan, W, *House of Cards: How Wall Street's Gamblers Broke Capitalism* (London: Allen Lane, 2009).

Collins, H, 'Flipping Wreck: *Lex Mercatoria* on the Shoals of *Ius Cogens*', in Grundmann, S, Möslein, F, and Riesenhuber, K (eds), *Contract Governance: Dimensions in Law and Interdisciplinary Research* (Oxford: Oxford University Press, 2015), 383–406.

Combs, V, 'The Law of Intermediated Securities: U.C.C. Versus UNIDROIT', *Alabama Law Review*, 58/2 (2006), 399–415.

Conac, P-H, Segna, U, and Thévenoz, L (eds), *Intermediated Securities: The Impact of the Geneva Securities Convention and the Future European Legislation* (Cambridge: Cambridge University Press, 2013).

Constâncio, V, *Introductory Remarks to the ECB Workshop—Repo Market and Securities Lending: Towards an EU Database* (3 December 2012), <http://www.ecb.europa.eu/press/key/date/2012/html/sp121203.en.html#footnote.2> (accessed 21 July 2021).

Corradin, S, Heider, F, and Hoerova, M, *On Collateral: Implications for Financial Stability and Monetary Policy* (2017; ECB Working Paper Series 2107).

CPMI, *Developments in Collateral Management Services* (September 2014), <https://www.bis.org/cpmi/publ/d119.pdf> (accessed 21 July 2021).

CPMI, *Cyber Resilience in Financial Market Infrastructures* (November 2014), <http://www.bis.org/cpmi/publ/d122.pdf> (accessed 21 July 2021).

CPMI, *Distributed Ledger Technology in Payment, Clearing and Settlement: An Analytical Framework* (February 2017), <https://www.bis.org/cpmi/publ/d157.pdf> (accessed 21 July 2021).

CPMI, Markets Committee, *Central Bank Digital Currencies* (March 2018), <https://www.bis.org/cpmi/publ/d174.pdf> (accessed 21 July 2021).

CPMI and IOSCO Board, *Recovery of Financial Market Infrastructures: Final Report* (October 2014), <http://www.bis.org/cpmi/publ/d121.htm> (accessed 21 July 2021).

CPMI and IOSCO Board, *Guidance on Cyber Resilience for Financial Market Infrastructures* (June 2016), <http://www.bis.org/cpmi/publ/d146.pdf> (accessed 21 July 2021).

CPMI and IOSCO Board, *Responsibility E: A Compilation of Authorities' Experience with Cooperation* (December 2019), <https://www.iosco.org/library/pubdocs/pdf/IOSCOPD644.pdf> (accessed 21 July 2021).

CPSS, *Delivery Versus Payment in Securities Settlement Systems* (September 1992), <http://www.bis.org/publ/cpss06.htm> (accessed 21 July 2021).

CPSS, *Cross-border Securities Settlements* (March 1995), <http://www.bis.org/publ/cpss12.pdf> (accessed 21 July 2021).

CPSS, *Core Principles for Systemically Important Payment Systems* (January 2001), <http://www.bis.org/publ/cpss43.htm> (accessed 21 July 2021).

CPSS, *The Role of Central Bank Money in Payment Systems* (August 2003), <http://www.bis.org/publ/cpss55.pdf> (accessed 21 July 2021).

CPSS, *Central Bank Oversight of Payment and Settlement Systems* (May 2005), <http://www.bis.org/publ/cpss68.htm> (accessed 21 July 2021).

CPSS and IOSCO Technical Committee, *Recommendations for Securities Settlement Systems* (November 2001), <http://www.bis.org/publ/cpss46.pdf> (accessed 21 July 2021).

CPSS and IOSCO Technical Committee, *Recommendations for Central Counterparties* (November 2004), <http://www.bis.org/publ/cpss64.pdf> (accessed 21 July 2021).

CPSS and IOSCO Technical Committee, *Principles for Financial Market Infrastructures* (April 2012), <http://www.bis.org/publ/cpss101a.pdf> (accessed 21 July 2021).

CPSS and IOSCO Board, *Recovery and Resolution of Financial Market Infrastructures: Consultative Report* (July 2012), <http://www.bis.org/publ/cpss103.pdf> (accessed 21 July 2021).

CPSS and IOSCO Board, *Principles for Financial Market Infrastructures: Disclosure Framework and Assessment Methodology* (December 2012), <http://www.bis.org/publ/cpss106.pdf> (accessed 21 July 2021).

CPSS and IOSCO Board, *Recovery of Financial Market Infrastructures: Consultative Report* (August 2013), <http://www.bis.org/publ/cpss109.pdf> (accessed 21 July 2021).

CRMPG III, *Containing Systemic Risk: The Road to Reform* (August 2008), <http://www.crmpolicygroup.org/docs/CRMPG-III.pdf> (accessed 21 July 2021).

CSD Working Group on DLT, *General Meeting Proxy Voting on Distributed Ledger* (November 2017; Version 2.1), <https://www.issanet.org/e/pdf/2017-11_General_Meeting_Proxy_Voting_on_Distributed_Ledger_v2-1.pdf> (accessed 21 July 2021).

Crockett, A, 'Discussion of "A Proposal for the Resolution of Systemically Important Assets and Liabilities: The Case of the Repo Market"', *International Journal of Central Banking*, 9 (2013; Supplement 1), 351–7.

Davidoff, S and Zaring, D, 'Regulation by Deal: The Government's Response to the Financial Crisis', *Administrative Law Review*, 61/3 (2009), 463–541.

Davies, P, 'Investment Claims and Corporate Governance', in Gullifer, L and Payne, J (eds), *Intermediation and Beyond* (Oxford: Hart Publishing, 2019), 187–214.

Davis Evans, A, 'A Requiem for the Retail Investor?', *Virginia Law Review*, 95/4 (2009), 1105–29.

D'Avout, L, *Sur les solutions du conflit de lois en droit des biens* (Paris: Economica, 2006).

Deschamps, M, 'The Security Interest Provisions of the UNIDROIT Convention on Intermediated Securities', *Uniform Law Review*, 15/2 (2010), 337–56.

Deschamps, M, 'The Geneva Securities Convention: Selected Issues Left to Law outside the Convention', *Uniform Law Review*, 15/3–4 (2010), 703–12.

Deschamps, M, 'Conflict-of-laws Rules on Assignments of Receivables in the United States and Canada', *Zeitschrift für Finanzmarktrecht*, Heft 5 (2019), nr 101.

Digital Asset, *The Digital Asset Platform: Non-technical White Paper*, (December 2016), <https://hub.digitalasset.com/hubfs/Documents/Digital%20Asset%20Platform%20-%20Non-technical%20White%20Paper.pdf> (accessed 21 July 2021).

Dixon, V, 'The Legal Nature of Intermediated Securities: An Insurmountable Obstacle to Legal Certainty?', in Gullifer, L and Payne, J (eds), *Intermediation and Beyond* (Oxford: Hart Publishing, 2019), 47–84.

Donald, D, *The Rise and Effects of the Indirect Holding System: How Corporate America Ceded Its Shareholders to Intermediaries* (26 September 2007), <http://ssrn.com/abstract=1017206> (accessed 21 July 2021).

Donald, D, 'Heart of Darkness: The Problem at the Core of the US Proxy System and Its Solution', *Virginia Law & Business Review*, 6/1 (2011), 41–100.

Donald D and Miraz, M, 'Multilateral Transparency for Security Markets Through DLT', *Fordham Journal of Corporate & Financial Law* 25 (2019), 97–153, <https://ir.lawnet.fordham.edu/jcfl/vol25/iss1/2/> (accessed 21 July 2021).

Duffie, D and Skeel, D, 'A Dialogue on the Costs and Benefits of Automatic Stays for Derivatives and Repurchase Agreements', in Scott, K and Taylor, J (eds), *Bankruptcy Not Bailout: A Special Chapter 14* (Stanford, California: Hoover Institution Press, 2012), 133–73.

Dupont, P, 'Rights of the Account Holder Relating to Securities Credited to Its Securities Account', in Conac, P-H, Segna, U, and Thévenoz, L (eds), *Intermediated Securities: The Impact of the Geneva Securities Convention and the Future European Legislation* (Cambridge: Cambridge University Press, 2013), 90–104.

EBA, *Report with Advice for the European Commission on Crypto-assets* (January 2019).

396 BIBLIOGRAPHY

EBA, *Report on Regulatory Perimeter, Regulatory Status and Authorisation Approaches in Relation to FinTech Activities* (July 2019), <https://www.eba.europa.eu/sites/default/documents/files/documents/10180/2551996/810d55c1-9866-4422-84ca-d78270b66452/Report%20regulatory%20perimeter%20and%20authorisation%20approaches.pdf> (accessed 21 July 2021).

EBRD and Clifford Chance, *Smart Contracts: Legal Framework and Proposed Guidelines for Lawmakers* (October 2018).

EC, *Communication from the Commission: Implementing the Framework for Financial Markets: Action Plan* (Brussels, 11 May 1999; COM(1999) 232 final).

EC, *Proposal for a Council Decision Concerning the Signing of the Hague Convention on the Law Applicable to Certain Rights in Respect of Securities Held with an Intermediary* (Brussels, 15 December 2003; COM(2003) 783 final).

EC, *Commission Staff Working Document: Legal Assessment of Certain Aspects of the Hague Securities Convention* (Brussels, 3 July 2006; SEC(2006) 910)).

EC, *Conflict of Laws: Modernisation of the PRIMA-rule for Intermediated Securities* (22 June 2007; Reflection Paper DG MARKT).

EC, *An EU Framework for Cross-border Crisis Management in the Banking Sector* (Brussels, 20 October 2009; COM(2009) 561 final).

EC, *An EU Framework for Crisis Management in the Financial Sector* (Brussels, 20 October 2010; COM(2010) 579 final).

EC, *Bank Resolution Funds* (Brussels, 26 May 2010; COM(2010) 254 final).

EC, *Legislation on Legal Certainty of Securities Holding and Dispositions* (Brussels, 2010; DG Markt G2 MET/OT/acg D(2010) 768690; Second Consultation Document of the Services of the Directorate-General Internal Market and Services).

EC, *Legislation on Legal Certainty of Securities Holding and Dispositions: Summary of Responses to the Directorate-General Internal Market and Services' Second Consultation* (2011), <https://ec.europa.eu/finance/consultations/2010/securities/docs/extended_summary_responses_en.pdf> (accessed 21 July 2021).

EC, *Technical Details of a Possible EU Framework for Bank Recovery and Resolution* (2011; DG Internal Market and Services Working Document).

EC, *Discussion Paper on the Debt Write-down Tool: Bail-in* (2012; DG Internal Market and Services Working Document).

EC, *Commission Staff Working Document, Impact Assessment Accompanying the document Proposal for a Directive of the European Parliament and of the Council establishing a framework for the recovery and resolution of credit institutions and investment firms and amending Council Directives 77/91/EEC and 82/891/EC, Directives 2001/24/EC, 2002/47/EC, 2004/25/EC, 2005/56/EC, 2007/36/EC and 2011/35/EC and Regulation (EU) No 1093/2010* (6 June 2012; SWD(2012) 166 final).

EC, *Legislation on Legal Certainty of Securities Holding and Dispositions: 10th Discussion Paper of the Services of the Directorate-General Internal Market and Services* (Brussels, 16 October 2012; 6th meeting of the Member States Working Group).

EC, *Communication from the Commission on the applicable law to the proprietary effects of transactions in securities* (Brussels, 12 March 2018; COM(2018) 89 final).

ECB, *Opinion of the European Central Bank of 17 March 2005 at the request of the Council of the European Union on a proposal for a Council decision concerning the signing of the Hague Convention on the Law applicable to certain rights in respect of securities held with an intermediary* (COM(2003) 783 final; CON/2005/7), OJ 2005 C81/10.

ECB, *Report on the Lessons Learned from the Financial Crisis with Regard to the Functioning of European Financial Market Infrastructures* (April 2010), <http://www.ecb.europa.eu/pub/pdf/other/reportlessonslearnedfinancialcrisis201004en.pdf> (accessed 21 July 2021).

ECB, *Eurosystem Oversight Policy Framework* (July 2011), <http://www.ecb.europa.eu/pub/pdf/other/eurosystemoversightpolicyframework2011en.pdf> (accessed 21 July 2021).

ECB Advisory Group on Market Infrastructures for Securities and Collateral, *The Potential Impact of DLTs on Securities Post-trading Harmonisation and on the Wider EU Financial Market Integration* (September 2017), <https://www.ecb.europa.eu/paym/groups/ami/shared/pdf/201709_dlt_impact_on_harmonisation_and_integration.pdf> (accessed 21 July 2021).

ECB Advisory Group on Market Infrastructures for Securities and Collateral, *Potential Use Cases for Innovative Technologies in Securities Post-trading* (January 2019), <https://www.ecb.europa.eu/paym/intro/publications/pdf/ecb.miptopical190111.en.pdf> (accessed 21 July 2021).

ECB Advisory Groups on Market Infrastructures for Securities and Collateral and for Payments (AmiSeCo/AmiPay), *The Use of DLT in Post-trade Processes* (April 2021), <https://www.ecb.europa.eu/pub/pdf/other/ecb.20210412_useofdltposttradeprocesses~958e3af1c8.en.pdf> (accessed 21 July 2021).

ECB and CESR, *Standards for Securities Clearing and Settlement in the European Union* (September 2004), <http://www.ecb.europa.eu/pub/pdf/other/escb-cesr-standardssecurities2004en.pdf> (accessed 21 July 2021).

ECSDA, *Response to the Giovannini Report: Barrier 3, Corporate Actions* (June 2005).

ECSDA, *Account Segregation Practices at European CSDs* (October 2015), <https://www.ecsda.eu/wp-content/uploads/2015_10_13_ECSDA_Segregation_Report.pdf> (accessed 21 July 2021).

ECSDA, *CSDs, Asset Segregation, and Custody Services under UCITS and AIFMD* (September 2016), <https://ecsda.eu/wp-content/uploads/2016_09_23_ECSDA_ESMA_asset_segregation.pdf> (accessed 21 July 2021).

Edwards, F and Morrison, E, 'Derivatives and the Bankruptcy Code: Why the Special Treatment?', *Yale Journal on Regulation*, 22/1 (2005), 91–122.

Eidenmüller, H, '*Lex Mercatoria*, The ISDA Master Agreement, and *Ius Cogens*: Comment on H. Collins, "Flipping Wreck: *Lex Mercatoria* on the Shoals of *Ius Cogens*"', in Grundmann, S, Möslein, F, and Riesenhuber, K (eds), *Contract Governance: Dimensions in Law and Interdisciplinary Research* (Oxford: Oxford University Press, 2015) 407–13.

Einsele, D, 'Das Haager Übereinkommen über das auf bestimmte Rechte im Zusammenhang mit zwischenverwahrten Wertpapieren anzuwendende Recht', *WM Zeitschrift für Wirtschafts- und Bankrecht*, 57/49 (2003), 2349–56.

Einsele, D, 'The Book-entry in a Securities Account: Linchpin of a Harmonised Legal Framework of Securities Held with an Intermediary', *Uniform Law Review*, 9/1 (2004), 41–50.

Einsele, D, 'Modernising German Law: Can the UNIDROIT Project on Intermediated Securities Provide Guidance?', *Uniform Law Review*, 10/1–2 (2005), 251–61.

Einsele, D, 'Security Interests in Financial Instruments', in Eidenmüller, H and Kieninger, E-M (eds), *The Future of Secured Credit in Europe* (Munich: De Gruyter Recht, 2008), 350–64.

Einsele, D, 'Intermediär-verwahrte Wertpapiere: Rechtsharmonisierung versus Systemneutralität', *Zeitschrift für das gesamte Handelsrecht und Wirtschaftsrecht*, 177/1 (2013), 50–89.

Enriques, L, Gargantini, M, and Novembre, V, 'Mandatory and Contract-based Shareholding Disclosure', *Uniform Law Review*, 15/3–4 (2010), 713–42.

Entriken, W, Shirley, D, Evans, J, and Sachs, N, *EIP-721: ERC-721 Non-fungible Token Standard*, (24 January 2018), <https://eips.ethereum.org/EIPS/eip-721> (accessed 21 July 2021).

ESMA, *Consultation Paper: Guidelines on Asset Segregation under the AIFMD* (December 2014), <https://www.esma.europa.eu/sites/default/files/library/2015/11/2014-1326_cp_-_guidelines_on_aifmd_asset_segregation.pdf> (accessed 21 July 2021).

ESMA, *Opinion: Asset Segregation and Application of Depositary Delegation Rules to CSDs* (July 2017), <https://www.esma.europa.eu/sites/default/files/library/esma34-45-277_opinion_34_on_asset_segregation_and_custody_services.pdf> (accessed 21 July 2021).

ESMA, *Report: The Distributed Ledger Technology Applied to Securities Markets* (February 2017), <https://www.esma.europa.eu/sites/default/files/library/dlt_report_-_esma50-1121423017-285.pdf> (accessed 21 July 2021).

ESMA, *Advice: Initial Coin Offerings and Crypto-assets* (January 2019), <https://www.esma.europa.eu/sites/default/files/library/esma50-157-1391_crypto_advice.pdf> (accessed 21 July 2021).

ESMA, *Questions and Answers: Implementation of the Regulation (EU) No 909/2014 on improving securities settlement in the EU and on central securities depositories* (February 2020).

ESMA, *Questions and Answers: Implementation of the Regulation (EU) No 648/2012 on OTC derivatives, central counterparties and trade repositories (EMIR)* (March 2021).

European Parliament, *Regulatory Sandboxes and Innovation Hubs for FinTech* (2020; study requested by the ECON committee), <https://www.europarl.europa.eu/RegData/etudes/STUD/2020/652752/IPOL_STU(2020)652752_EN.pdf> (accessed 21 July 2021).

European Post Trade Forum (EPTF), *EPTF Report* (May 2017), <https://ec.europa.eu/info/sites/default/files/170515-eptf-report_en.pdf> (accessed 21 July 2021).

Expert Group on Cross-border Voting in Europe, *Final Report* (Wetenschappelijk Onderzoek- en Documentatiecentrum, 2002; WODC Onderzoeksnotities 2002/6).

Expert Group on Regulatory Obstacles to Financial Innovation (ROFIEG), *Thirty Recommendations on Regulation, Innovation and Finance: Final Report to the European Commission* (2019), <https://ec.europa.eu/info/publications/191113-report-expert-group-regulatory-obstacles-financial-innovation_en> (accessed 21 July 2021).

Fairfax, L, 'Virtual Shareholder Meetings Reconsidered', *Seton Hall Law Review*, 40 (2010), 1367–432, <http://ssrn.com/abstract=1787297> (accessed 21 July 2021).

FATF, *Guidance for a Risk-Based Approach: Securities Sector* (October 2018), <http://www.fatf-gafi.org/publications/fatfrecommendations/documents/rba-securities-sector.html> (accessed 21 July 2021).

FATF, *Guidance for a Risk-Based Approach: Virtual Assets and Virtual Asset Service Providers* (June 2019), <https://www.fatf-gafi.org/media/fatf/documents/recommendations/RBA-VA-VASPs.pdf> (accessed 21 July 2021).

FATF, *The FATF Recommendations: International Standards on Combating Money Laundering and the Financing of Terrorism & Proliferation* (last updated 2020), <https://www.fatf-gafi.org/media/fatf/documents/recommendations/pdfs/FATF%20Recommendations%202012.pdf> (accessed 21 July 2021).

Faubus, B, 'Narrowing the Bankruptcy Safe Harbor for Derivatives to Combat Systemic Risk', *Duke Law Journal*, 59/4 (2010), 801–42.

FCA, *Consultation Paper 13/5: Review of the Client Assets Regime for Investment Business* (July 2013).

FCIC, *The Financial Crisis Inquiry Report: Final Report of the National Commission on the Causes of the Financial and Economic Crisis in the United States* (January 2011; Official Government Edition).

FDIC, 'The Orderly Liquidation of Lehman Brothers Holdings Inc. under the Dodd-Frank Act', *FDIC Quarterly*, 5/2 (2011), 31–49.

Ferrarini, G and Saguato, P, 'Reforming Securities and Derivatives Trading in the EU: From EMIR to MIFIR', *Journal of Corporate Law Studies*, 13/2 (2013), 319–59.

Ferrarini, G and Saguato, P, 'Regulating Financial Market Infrastructures', in Moloney, N, Ferran, E, and Payne, J (eds), *The Oxford Handbook of Financial Regulation* (Oxford: Oxford University Press, 2015), 568–95.

FINRA, *Report: Distributed Ledger Technology: Implications of Blockchain for the Securities Industry* (January 2017), <https://www.finra.org/sites/default/files/FINRA_Blockchain_Report.pdf> (accessed 21 July 2021).

Firth, S, *Derivatives: Law and Practice* (London: Sweet & Maxwell, 2008–2013; loose-leaf).

Flessner, A, 'Choice of Law in International Property Law: New Encouragement from Europe', in Westrik, R and Weide, J van der (eds), *Party Autonomy in International Property Law* (Munich: Sellier European Law Publishers, 2011), 11–40.

FMLC, *Issue 3: Property Interests in Investment Securities* (July 2004) <http://fmlc.org/wp-content/uploads/2018/02/Issue-3-Background-paper-on-Article-8-of-the-Uniform-Commercial-Code.pdf> (accessed 21 July 2021).

Foyer, J, 'La dématérialisation des valeurs mobilières en France', in Dutoit, B, Hofstetter, J, and Piotet, P, *Mélanges Guy Flattet* (Lausanne: Payot, 1985), 21 et seq.

Franciosi, L, 'Commercial Reasonableness in Financial Collateral Contracts: a Comparative Overview', *Uniform Law Review*, 17/3 (2012), 483–95.

Fries, M and Paal, B, *Smart Contracts* (Mohr Siebeck, 2019; in German).

FSA, *Consultation Paper 12/22: Client Assets Regime: EMIR, Multiple Pools and the Wider Review* (September 2012).

FSB, *Key Attributes of Effective Resolution Regimes for Financial Institutions* (October 2011), <http://www.financialstabilityboard.org/publications/r_111104cc.pdf> (accessed 21 July 2021).

FSB, *Key Attributes of Effective Resolution Regimes for Financial Institutions* (October 2014; revision of the version of October 2011), <http://www.financialstabilityboard.org/wp-content/uploads/r_141015.pdf> (accessed 21 July 2021).

FSB, *Recovery and Resolution Planning: Making the Key Attributes Requirements Operational: Consultative Document* (November 2012), <https://www.financialstabilityboard.org/publications/r_121102.pdf> (accessed 21 July 2021).

FSB, *Consultative Document: Application of the Key Attributes of Effective Resolution Regimes to Non-bank Financial Institutions* (August 2013), <https://www.fsb.org/wp-content/uploads/r_130812a.pdf> (accessed 21 July 2021).

FSB, *Consultative Document: Assessment Methodology for the Key Attributes of Effective Resolution Regimes for Financial Institutions* (August 2013), <https://www.fsb.org/wp-content/uploads/r_130828.pdf> (accessed 21 July 2021).

FSB, *A Narrative Progress Report on Financial Reforms: Report of the Financial Stability Board to G20 Leaders* (September 2013), <http://www.financialstabilityboard.org/publications/r_130905a.pdf> (accessed 21 July 2021).

FSB, *Shadow Banking: Strengthening Oversight and Regulation* (October 2011), <http://www.financialstabilityboard.org/publications/r_111027a.pdf> (accessed 21 July 2021).

FSB, *Strengthening Oversight and Regulation of Shadow Banking: Policy Framework for Addressing Shadow Banking Risks in Securities Lending and Repos* (August 2013), <http://www.financialstabilityboard.org/publications/r_130829b.pdf> (accessed 21 July 2021).

FSB, *Transforming Shadow Banking into Resilient Market-based Financing: An Overview of Progress and a Roadmap for 2015* (November 2014), <http://www.fsb.org/wp-content/uploads/Progress-Report-on-Transforming-Shadow-Banking-into-Resilient-Market-Based-Financing.pdf> (accessed 21 July 2021).

FSB, *Transforming Shadow Banking into Resilient Market-based Finance: An Overview of Progress* (November 2015), <http://www.fsb.org/wp-content/uploads/shadow_banking_overview_of_progress_2015.pdf> (accessed 21 July 2021).

FSB, *Strengthening Oversight and Regulation of Shadow Banking: Regulatory Framework for Haircuts on Non-centrally Cleared Securities Financing Transactions* (October 2014), <http://www.fsb.org/wp-content/uploads/r_141013a.pdf> (accessed 21 July 2021).

FSB, *Transforming Shadow Banking into Resilient Market-based Finance: Regulatory Framework for Haircuts on Non-centrally Cleared Securities Financing Transactions* (November 2015; updated in July 2019, November 2019, and September 2020), <https://www.fsb.org/wp-content/uploads/P070920-1.pdf> (accessed 21 July 2021).

FSB, *Consultative Document: Standards and Processes for Global Securities Financing Data Collection and Aggregation* (November 2014), <http://www.fsb.org/wp-content/uploads/Global-SFT-Data-Standards-Consultative-Document.pdf> (accessed 21 July 2021).

FSB, *Transforming Shadow Banking into Resilient Market-based Finance: Standards and Processes for Global Securities Financing Data Collection and Aggregation* (November 2015), <http://www.fsb.org/wp-content/uploads/FSB-Standards-for-Global-Securities-Financing-Data-Collection.pdf> (accessed 21 July 2021).

FSB, *Transforming Shadow Banking into Resilient Market-based Finance: Possible Measures of Non-cash Collateral Re-use* (February 2016), <http://www.fsb.org/wp-content/uploads/Report-on-possible-measures-of-non-cash-collateral-reuse.pdf> (accessed 21 July 2021).

FSB, *Transforming Shadow Banking into Resilient Market-based Finance: Non-cash Collateral Re-use: Measure and Metrics* (January 2017), <https://www.fsb.org/2017/01/non-cash-collateral-reuse-measure-and-metrics/> (accessed 21 July 2021).

FSB, *Transforming Shadow Banking into Resilient Market-based Finance: Re-hypothecation and Collateral Re-use: Potential Financial Stability Issues, Market Evolution and Regulatory Approaches* (January 2017), <https://www.fsb.org/wp-content/uploads/Re-hypothecation-and-collateral-re-use.pdf> (accessed 21 July 2021).

FSB, *Cross-border Recognition of Resolution Action: Consultative Document* (September 2014), <http://www.fsb.org/wp-content/uploads/c_140929.pdf> (accessed 21 July 2021).

FSB, *Principles for Cross-border Effectiveness of Resolution Actions* (November 2015), <http://www.fsb.org/wp-content/uploads/Principles-for-Cross-border-Effectiveness-of-Resolution-Actions.pdf> (accessed 21 July 2021).

BIBLIOGRAPHY

FSB, *Principles on Loss-absorbing and Recapitalisation Capacity of G-SIBs in Resolution: Total Loss-absorbing Capacity (TLAC) Term Sheet* (November 2015), <https://www.fsb.org/wp-content/uploads/TLAC-Principles-and-Term-Sheet-for-publication-final.pdf> (accessed 21 July 2021).

FSB, *Crypto-assets: Report to the G20 on the Work of the FSB and Standard-setting Bodies* (July 2018), <https://www.fsb.org/2018/07/crypto-assets-report-to-the-g20-on-the-work-of-the-fsb-and-standard-setting-bodies/> (accessed 21 July 2021).

FSB, *Crypto-assets Regulators Directory* (April 2019), <https://www.fsb.org/2019/04/crypto-assets-regulators-directory/> (accessed 21 July 2021).

FSB, *Crypto-assets: Work Underway, Regulatory Approaches and Potential Gaps* (May 2019), <https://www.fsb.org/2019/05/crypto-assets-work-underway-regulatory-approaches-and-potential-gaps/> (accessed 21 July 2021).

FSB, *Regulation, Supervision and Oversight of 'Global Stablecoin' Arrangements: Final Report and High-level Recommendations* (October 2020), <https://www.fsb.org/2020/10/regulation-supervision-and-oversight-of-global-stablecoin-arrangements/> (accessed 21 July 2021).

Fußwinkel, O and Kreiterling, C, 'Blockchain-Technologie: Gedanken zur Regulierung', *BaFin Perspektiven*, 1 (2018), 48–67.

G7, IMF, CPMI, *Investigating the Impact of Global Stablecoins* (October 2019), <https://www.bis.org/cpmi/publ/d187.pdf> (accessed 21 July 2021).

G20 Research Groups, *Cannes Summit Final Declaration: Building Our Common Future: Renewed Collective Action for the Benefit of All* (4 November 2011), <http://www.g20.utoronto.ca/2011/2011-cannes-declaration-111104-en.html> (accessed 21 July 2021).

Garcimartín, F, 'Regulatory Competition: A Private International Law Approach', *European Journal of Law and Economics*, 8 (1999), 251.

Garcimartín, F, 'Disposition and Acquisition of Intermediated Securities: The Geneva Convention and Traditional Property Law', *Uniform Law Review*, 15/3–4 (2010), 743–50.

Garcimartín, F, 'The Geneva Convention on Intermediated Securities: A Conflict-of-Laws Approach', *Uniform Law Review*, 15/3–4 (2010), 751–77.

Garcimartín, F, 'The Geneva Securities Convention: A Spanish Perspective', in Conac, PH, Segna, U, and Thévenoz, L (eds), *Intermediated Securities: The Impact of the Geneva Securities Convention and the Future European Legislation* (Cambridge: Cambridge University Press, 2013), 269–87.

Garcimartín, F, *Derivatives in Cross-border Insolvency Proceedings* (2016), <https://papers.ssrn.com/sol3/papers.cfm?abstract_id=2731772> (accessed 21 July 2021).

Garrido, J, 'The Loss-sharing Rule in the Insolvency of Financial Intermediaries', *Uniform Law Review*, 15/3–4 (2010), 779–90.

Geis, G, 'Traceable Shares and Corporate Law', *Northwestern University Law Review*, 113/2 (2018), 227–78, <https://scholarlycommons.law.northwestern.edu/cgi/viewcontent.cgi?article=1354&context=nulr> (accessed 21 July 2021).

Ghallab, A, Saif, M, and Mohsen, A, 'Data Integrity and Security in Distributed Cloud Computing: A Review', in Gunjan, V, Zurada, J (eds), *Proceedings of International Conference on Recent Trends in Machine Learning, IoT, Smart Cities and Applications* (Singapore: Springer, 2021; Advances in Intelligent Systems and Computing Volume 1245), <https://doi.org/10.1007/978-981-15-7234-0_73> (accessed 21 July 2021), 767–84.

Giacomet, F, 'Is the Ordinary Treatment of Client Assets in Prime Brokerage Consistent with the Recognition of a Trust upon Insolvency of the Prime Broker?', *Capital Markets Law Journal*, 8/2 (2013), 205–23.

Gilmore, G, 'The Commercial Doctrine of Good Faith Purchase', *Yale Law Journal*, 63/8 (1953-1954), 1057–1122.

Gilson, R and Gordon, J, 'The Agency Costs of Agency Capitalism: Activist Investors and the Revaluation of Governance Rights', *Columbia Law Review*, 113 (2013), 863–927.

Giovannini Group, *Cross-border Clearing and Settlement: Arrangements in the European Union* (Brussels, November 2001), <https://ec.europa.eu/info/publications/giovannini-reports_en> (accessed 21 July 2021).

Giovannini Group, *Second Report on EU Clearing and Settlement Arrangements* (April 2003), <https://ec.europa.eu/info/publications/giovannini-reports_en> (accessed 21 July 2021).

Global Digital Finance (GDF), *GDF Code of Conduct Part VIII(i): Principles for Custody: 'Custodial Wallets'* (without date), <https://www.gdf.io/wp-content/uploads/2020/06/GDF-Code-of-Conduct-Part-IX-Principles-for-Custody-Custodial-Wallets.pdf> (accessed 21 July 2021).
Global Digital Finance, *Taxonomy for Cryptographic Assets* (October 2018).
Gómez-Sancha Trueba, I, 'Indirect Holdings of Securities and Exercise of Shareholder Rights (a Spanish Perspective)', *Capital Markets Law Journal*, 3/1 (2008), 32–57.
Goode, R, Kanda, H, Kreuzer, K, with the assistance of Bernasconi, C, *Hague Securities Convention: Explanatory Report* (The Netherlands: Martinus Nijhoff Publishers, 2005).
Goodhart, C and Avgouleas, E, *A Critical Evaluation of Bail-ins as Bank Recapitalisation Mechanisms* (July 2014; Centre for Economic Policy Research Discussion Paper 10065).
Graziadei, M, 'Financial Collateral Arrangements: Directive 2002/47/EC and the Many Faces of Reasonableness', *Uniform Law Review*, 17/3 (2012), 497–506.
Green, S, 'To Have and to Hold? Conversion and Intangible Property', *Modern Law Review*, 71(1) (2008), 114–31.
Green, S and Snagg, F, 'Intermediated Securities and Distributed Ledger Technology', in Gullifer, L and Payne, J (eds), *Intermediation and Beyond* (Oxford: Hart Publishing, 2019), 337–58.
Group of Ten, *Report on Consolidation in the Financial Sector* (January 2001), <http://www.bis.org/publ/gten05.htm> (accessed 21 July 2021).
Group of Thirty, *Global Clearing and Settlement: A Plan of Action* (2003), <https://group30.org/images/uploads/publications/G30_GlobalClearingSettlement.pdf> (accessed 21 July 2021).
Group of Thirty, *The Structure of Financial Supervision: Approaches and Challenges in a Global Marketplace* (2008), <https://group30.org/images/uploads/publications/G30_StructureFinancialSupervision2008.pdf> (accessed 21 July 2021).
Group of Thirty, *Financial Reform: A Framework for Financial Stability* (2009), <https://group30.org/images/uploads/publications/G30_FinancialReformFrameworkFinStability.pdf> (accessed 21 July 2021).
Grove, R, 'Valuation in the Context of Derivatives Litigation', *Capital Markets Law Journal*, 6/2 (2011), 149–62.
Guillaume, F, *'L'electio juris* comme règle de rattachement des titres intermédiés, ses effets sur les droits des tiers et ses conséquences dans une procédure d'insolvabilité', in Bonomi, A, Cashin Ritaine, E, and Volders, B (eds), *La loi applicable aux titres intermédiés: La Convention de La Haye du 5 juillet 2006: Une opportunité pour la place financière Suisse?* (Schulthess Verlag: Zurich, 2006), 67–83.
Guillaume, F, 'Conflict of Laws: Preliminary Remarks', in Kuhn, H, Graham-Siegenthaler, B, and Thévenoz, L, *The Federal Intermediated Securities Act (FISA) and the Hague Securities Convention (HSC)* (Berne: Stampfli Publishers Ltd, 2010), 1–7.
Guillaume, F, 'Convention on the Law Applicable to Certain Rights in Respect of Securities Held with an Intermediary', in Kuhn, H, Graham-Siegenthaler, B, and Thévenoz, L, *The Federal Intermediated Securities Act (FISA) and the Hague Securities Convention (HSC)* (Berne: Stampfli Publishers Ltd, 2010), 27–111.
Gullifer, L (ed), *Goode on Legal Problems of Credit and Security* (London: Sweet & Maxwell, 2008; 4th edn).
Gullifer, L, 'Ownership of Securities: The Problems Caused by Intermediation', in Gullifer, L and Payne, J (eds), *Intermediated Securities: Legal Problems and Practical Issues* (Oxford: Hart Publishing, 2010), 1–32.
Gullifer, L, 'What Should We Do about Financial Collateral?', *Current Legal Problems*, 65 (2012), 377–410.
Gullifer, L (ed), *Goode on Legal Problems of Credit and Security* (Sweet & Maxwell/Thomson Reuters, 2013; 5th edn).
Gullifer, L, 'Two Consequences of the Intermediated Holding of Debt Securities: Examining Discharge of Debt and Set-off', in Gullifer, L and Payne, J (eds), *Intermediation and Beyond* (Oxford: Hart Publishing, 2019), 155–74.
Gullifer, L, Chong, H, and Liu, H, *Client-intermediary Relations in the Crypto-asset World* (2020; University of Cambridge Faculty of Law Research Paper 18/2021), <https://ssrn.com/abstract=3697946> or <http://dx.doi.org/10.2139/ssrn.3697946> (both accessed 21 July 2021).

Gullifer, L, Hara, M, and Mooney, C, 'English Translation of the Mt Gox Judgment on the Legal Status of Bitcoin prepared by the Digital Assets Project' (6 February 2019), <https://www.law.ox.ac.uk/research-subject-groups/commercial-law-centre/blog/2019/02/english-translation-mt-gox-judgment-legal> (accessed 21 July 2021).

Gullifer, L and Hay, R, 'How Final is Final? Settlement Finality, Blockchains and DLT', *Journal of International Banking and Financial Law*, 35/1 (January 2020), 8–14.

Gullifer, L and Payne, J (eds), *Intermediated Securities: Legal Problems and Practical Issues* (Oxford: Hart Publishing, 2010).

Gullifer, L and Payne, J (eds), *Intermediation and Beyond* (Oxford: Hart Publishing, 2019).

Guttman, E, 'Transfer of Securities: State and Federal Interaction', *Cardozo Law Review*, 12/2 (1990), 437–69.

Guzman, A, 'Choice of Law: New Foundations', *Georgetown Law Journal*, 90 (2002), 883 et seq.

Haentjens, M, *Harmonisation of Securities Law: Custody and Transfer in European Private Law* (Alphen aan den Rijn: Kluwer Law International, 2007).

Haentjens, M, 'European Harmonisation of Intermediated Securities Law: Dispossession and Segregation in Regulatory and Private Law', in Gullifer, L and Payne, J (eds), *Intermediation and Beyond* (Oxford: Hart Publishing, 2019), 259–87.

Haentjens, M (ed), *Financial Collateral: Law and Practice* (Oxford: Oxford University Press, 2020).

Haentjens, M and De Gioia-Carabellese, P, *European Banking and Financial Law* (Oxford: Routledge, 2020; 2nd edn), chapter 13 ('Collateralised finance').

Haentjens, M, De Graaf, T, and Kokorin, I, *The Failed Hopes of Intermediation: Crypto-custodian Insolvency, Legal Risks and How to Avoid Them* (2020; Hazelhoff Research Paper Series 9).

Harper, C, 'Multisignature Wallets Can Keep Your Coins Safer (If You Use Them Right)', (10 November 2020, updated 14 November 2020), <https://www.coindesk.com/what-is-a-multisignature-crypto-wallet> (accessed 21 July 2021).

Harris, D, 'Use of Customer Securities by UK Prime Brokers: The Road Ahead', *Law and Financial Markets Review*, 7/2 (2013), 107–11.

Hens, T and Pamini, P, *Grundzüge der analytischen Mikroökonomie* (Berlin, Heidelberg: Springer, 2008).

Herring, R, 'The Challenge of Resolving Cross-border Financial Institutions', *Yale Journal on Regulation*, 31/3 (2014), 853–81.

Hertig, G, Kraakman R, and Rock, E, 'Issuers and Investor Protection', in Kraakman, R et al (eds), *The Anatomy of Corporate Law: A Comparative and Functional Approach* (Oxford: Oxford University Press, 2009; 2nd edn), 275–302.

High Level Group of Company Law Experts, *Report on a Modern Regulatory Framework for Company Law in Europe* (Brussels: 2002).

Hinkes, A, 'Throw away the Key, or the Key Holder? Coercive Contempt for Lost or Forgotten Cryptocurrency Private Keys, or Obstinate Holders', *Northwestern Journal of Technology and Intellectual Property*, 16/4 (2019), 225–63, <https://scholarlycommons.law.northwestern.edu/njtip/vol16/iss4/1> (accessed 21 July 2021).

HLS Forum on Corporate Governance and Financial Regulation, *Istanbul Stock Exchange Moves First on Mandatory Electronic Voting* (2012), <https://corpgov.law.harvard.edu/2012/11/06/istanbul-stock-exchange-moves-first-on-mandatory-electronic-voting/> (accessed 21 July 2021).

Hoek, M van den, 'Voorkomt Ulpianus de crisis?', in Graaf, F, Maatman, R, and Silverentand, L (eds), *Lustrumbundel 2012 Vereniging voor Effectenrecht: Gedurfde essays over financieel toezichtrecht* (Deventer: Kluwer, 2012; Serie vanwege het Van der Heijden Instituut 113), 413–27.

Hopf, S, Loebbecke, C, and Avital, M, *Blockchain Technology Impacting Property Rights and Transaction Cost Regimes* (New Orleans: 2018; proceedings of the twenty-fourth Americas Conference on Information Systems).

Hull, J, *Options, Futures, and Other Derivatives* (Harlow: Pearson, 2012; 8th edn).

Hull, J, *Risk Management and Financial Institutions* (Hoboken, New Jersey: Wiley, 2018; 5th edn).

Hynes, R and Watt, S, 'Why Banks Are Not Allowed in Bankruptcy', *Washington and Lee Law Review*, 67/3 (2010), 985–1051.

IFSE, *Clearing and Settlement Best Practices* (1996).

Iglesias-Rodríguez, P, 'The Regulation of Cross-border Clearing and Settlement in the European Union from a Legitimacy Perspective', *European Business Organization Law Review*, 13/3 (2012), 441–74.

IOSCO Technical Committee, *Client Asset Protection* (August 1996), <http://www.iosco.org/library/pubdocs/pdf/IOSCOPD57.pdf> (accessed 21 July 2021).

IOSCO, *Principles on Client Identification and Beneficial Ownership for the Securities Industry* (May 2004), <http://www.iosco.org/library/pubdocs/pdf/IOSCOPD167.pdf> (accessed 21 July 2021).

IOSCO, *Objectives and Principles of Securities Regulation* (June 2010), <http://www.iosco.org/library/pubdocs/pdf/IOSCOPD323.pdf> (accessed 21 July 2021).

IOSCO Technical Committee, *Survey of Regimes for the Protection, Distribution and/or Transfer of Client Assets: Final Report* (March 2011; FR05/11).

IOSCO, *Multilateral Memorandum of Understanding Concerning Consultation and Cooperation and the Exchange of Information* (May 2012; revised version), <http://www.iosco.org/library/pubdocs/pdf/IOSCOPD386.pdf> (accessed 21 July 2021).

IOSCO Board, *Recommendations Regarding the Protection of Client Assets: Consultation Report* (February 2013; CR02/13).

IOSCO, *Recommendations Regarding the Protection of Client Assets* (2014).

IOSCO Board, *Standards for the Custody of Collective Investment Schemes' Assets: Final Report* (November 2015; FR25/2015), <https://www.iosco.org/library/pubdocs/pdf/IOSCOPD512.pdf> (accessed 21 July 2021).

IOSCO, *IOSCO Research Report on Financial Technologies (Fintech)* (February 2017), <https://www.iosco.org/library/pubdocs/pdf/IOSCOPD554.pdf> (accessed 21 July 2021).

IOSCO, *Objectives and Principles of Securities Regulation* (May 2017), <https://www.iosco.org/library/pubdocs/pdf/IOSCOPD561.pdf> (accessed 21 July 2021).

IOSCO Board, *Thematic Review of the Adoption of the Principles set forth in IOSCO's Report: Recommendations Regarding the Protection of Client Assets: Final Report* (July 2017; FR16/17), <https://www.iosco.org/library/pubdocs/pdf/IOSCOPD577.pdf> (accessed 21 July 2021).

IOSCO Board, *Issues, Risks and Regulatory Considerations Relating to Crypto-asset Trading Platforms: Final Report* (February 2020; FR02/2020), <https://www.iosco.org/library/pubdocs/pdf/IOSCOPD649.pdf> (accessed 21 July 2021).

IOSCO Board, *Investor Education on Crypto-assets: Final Report* (December 2020; FR12/2020), <https://www.iosco.org/library/pubdocs/pdf/IOSCOPD668.pdf> (accessed 21 July 2021).

ISDA, Collateral Law Reform Group, *Collateral Arrangements in the European Financial Markets: The Need for National Law Reform* (London: 2000).

ISDA, *Memorandum on the Implementation of Netting Legislation: A Guide for Legislators and Other Policy-makers* (2006).

ISDA, *Legal Guidelines for Smart Derivatives Contracts: Collateral* (September 2019), <https://www.isda.org/a/VTkTE/Legal-Guidelines-for-Smart-Derivatives-Contracts-Collateral.pdf> (accessed 21 July 2021).

ISDA, *ISDA Legal Guidelines for Smart Derivatives Contracts: Equity Derivatives* (2020), <https://www.isda.org/a/CLXTE/ISDA-Legal-Guidelines-for-Smart-Derivatives-Contracts-Equities.pdf> (accessed 21 July 2021).

ISDA, *Coronavirus and the SIMM* (April 2020), <https://www.isda.org/2020/04/08/coronavirus-and-the-simm/> (accessed 21 July 2021).

ISDA, *Navigating Initial Margin Documentation: Where Do I Begin* (May 2020), <https://www.isda.org/a/Z47TE/ISDA_Initial-Margin-Documentation-Where_to_Begin_FINAL.pdf> (accessed 21 July 2021).

ISDA, *Whitepaper: Collaboration and Standardization Opportunities in Derivatives and SFT Markets* (October 2020), <https://www.isda.org/a/wVrTE/Collaboration-and-Standardization-in-Derivatives-and-SFT-Markets.pdf> (accessed 21 July 2021).

ISDA, *Netting Legislation: Status* (April 2021), <https://www2.isda.org/functional-areas/legal-and-documentation/opinions/> (accessed 21 July 2021).

ISDA, Clifford Chance, R3, and Singapore Academy of Law, *Private International Law Aspects of Smart Derivatives Contracts Utilizing Distributed Ledger Technology* (January 2020), <https://www.

isda.org/a/4RJTE/Private-International-Law-Aspects-of-Smart-Derivatives-Contracts-uitilizing-DLT.pdf> (accessed 21 July 2021).

ISDA, GFMA, and IIF, *Leverage Ratio Treatment of Client Cleared Derivatives* (January 2019), <https://www.isda.org/a/nDiME/Leverage-ratio-treatment-of-client-cleared-derivatives.pdf> (accessed 21 July 2021).

ISDA and King & Wood Mallesons, *Whitepaper: Smart Derivatives Contracts: From Concept to Construction* (October 2018), <https://www.isda.org/a/cHvEE/Smart-Derivatives-Contracts-From-Concept-to-Construction-Oct-2018.pdf> (accessed 21 July 2021).

ISDA and Linklaters, *Whitepaper: Smart Contracts and Distributed Ledger: A Legal Perspective* (August 2017), <https://www.isda.org/a/6EKDE/smart-contracts-and-distributed-ledger-a-legal-perspective.pdf> (accessed 21 July 2021).

ISDA, MFA, and SIFMA, *Independent Amounts* (March 2010; Release 2.0).

ISSA, *Recommendations 2000* (June 2000).

ISSA, *Global Principles for Corporate Actions and Proxy Voting* (June 2012), <https://www.issanet.org/e/pdf/ISSA_WG_CA-PV_Final_Report_June2012.pdf> (accessed 21 July 2021).

ISSA, *Discussion Paper: Transparency in Securities Transactions and Custody Chains* (April 2014), <issanet.org/e/pdf/2014_ISSA_Discussion_Paper_Transparency_in_Securities_Transaction.pdf> (accessed 21 July 2021).

ISSA, *Distributed Ledger Technology: Principles for Industry-wide Acceptance* (June 2018; Version 1.0 Report), <https://www.issanet.org/e/pdf/2018-06_ISSA_DLT_report_version_1.0.pdf> (accessed 21 July 2021).

ISSA, *Financial Crime Compliance Principles for Securities Custody and Settlement* (May 2019; second revision), <https://www.issanet.org/e/pdf/2019-05-21_ISSA_FCC%20Principles_second_revision.pdf> (accessed 21 July 2021).

ISSA, *Financial Crime Compliance Principles for Securities Custody and Settlement: Background & Overview* (May 2019), <https://www.issanet.org/e/pdf/2019-05-21_ISSA_Background_Overview.pdf> (accessed 21 July 2021).

ISSA, *Crypto Assets: Moving from Theory to Practice* (November 2019), <https://issanet.org/e/pdf/2019-11_ISSA_Report_Crypto-Assets_Moving_from_Theory_to_Practice.pdf> (accessed 21 July 2021).

Jamroz, M, 'The Customer Protection Rule', *Business Lawyer*, 57/3 (2002), 1069–125.

Janssen, L, 'Bail-in from an Insolvency Law Perspective', *Norton Journal of Bankruptcy Law and Practice*, 26/5 (2017), 457–505.

Johansson, E, *Property Rights in Investment Securities and the Doctrine of Specificity* (Berlin, London: Springer, 2009).

Johansson, E, 'Reuse of Financial Collateral Revisited', in Gullifer, L and Payne, J (eds), *Intermediated Securities: Legal Problems and Practical Issues* (Oxford: Hart Publishing, 2010), 151–65.

Johnson, C, 'Derivatives and Rehypothecation Failure: It's 3:00 p.m, Do You Know Where Your Collateral Is?', *Arizona Law Review*, 39 (1997), 949–1001.

Johnson, C, 'Collateral', in Ali, P (ed), *Secured Finance Transactions: Key Assets and Emerging Markets* (London: Globe Law and Business, 2007), 57–68.

Johnson, V, 'International Financial Law: The Case Against Close-out Netting', *Boston University International Law Journal*, 33 (2015), 101–25.

Judge, K, 'Intermediary Influence', *The University of Chicago Law Review*, 82/2 (2015), 573–642.

Kahan, M and Rock, E, 'The Hanging Chads of Corporate Voting', *The Georgetown Law Journal*, 96/4 (2008), 1227–81.

Kalderon, M, Snagg, F, and Harrop, C, 'Distributed Ledgers: A Future in Financial Services?' (2016) 31 *Journal of International Banking Law and Regulation*, 243–8.

Kanda, H, 'Legal Rules on Indirectly Held Investment Securities: The Japanese Situation, Common Problems, and the UNIDROIT Approach', *Uniform Law Review*, 10/1–2 (2005), 271–6.

Kanda, H, 'Case No. 19: Supreme Court 7 December 2010, Case No. 2010 kyo 9, *Media Exchange Case*', in Bälz, M et al, *Business Law in Japan: Cases and Comments* (The Netherlands: Wolters Kluwer, 2012), 199–204.

Kanda, H, Mooney, C, Thévenoz, L, Béraud, S, assisted by Keijser, T, *Official Commentary on the Unidroit Convention on Substantive Rules for Intermediated Securities* (Oxford: Oxford University Press, 2012).

Kaulartz, M and Matzke, R, 'Die Tokenisierung des Rechts', *Neue Juristische Wochenschrift*, 45 (2018), 3278.

Kay, J, *The Kay Review of UK Equity Markets and Long-term Decision Making: Final Report* (July 2012), <https://assets.publishing.service.gov.uk/government/uploads/system/uploads/attachment_data/file/253454/bis-12-917-kay-review-of-equity-markets-final-report.pdf> (accessed 21 July 2021).

Keijser, T, *Financial Collateral Arrangements: The European Collateral Directive Considered from a Property and Insolvency Law Perspective* (Deventer: Kluwer, 2006; Law of Business and Finance 9).

Keijser, T (ed), *Report on a Right of Use for Collateral Takers and Custodians* (Rome: July 2003).

Keijser, T, 'Non-intermediated Securities: A European View on the Draft UNCITRAL Model Law on Secured Transactions', *European Company Law*, 12/1 (2015), 7–12.

Keijser, T, 'Financial Collateral Arrangements in the European Union: Current State and the Way Forward', *Uniform Law Review*, 22/1 (2017), 258–300.

Keijser, T, 'The Potential Impact of Technology on the Enforcement of Security Interests', in Jansen, C, Schuijling, B, and Aronstein, I (eds.), *Onderneming en Digitalisering* (Deventer: Wolters Kluwer, 2019; Serie Onderneming en Recht 116), 189–200.

Keijser, T, Kyrkousi, M, and Bakanos, A, 'Financial Collateral: The Legal Framework of the European Union and Unidroit Compared', *Uniform Law Review*, 19/3 (2014), 429–58.

Keijser, T and Mooney, C, 'Intermediated Securities Holding Systems Revisited: A View Through the Prism of Transparency', in Gullifer, L and Payne, J (eds), *Intermediation and Beyond* (Oxford: Hart Publishing, 2019), 309–35.

Kettering, K, 'Repledge and Pre-default Sale of Securities Collateral under Revised Article 9', *Chicago-Kent Law Review*, 74/3 (1999), 1109–55.

Kettering, K, 'Repledge Deconstructed', *University of Pittsburgh Law Review*, 61/1 (1999), 45–239.

Klees, E, 'How Safe Are Institutional Assets in a Custodial Bank's Insolvency?', *Business Lawyer*, 68/1 (2012), 103–35.

Kobler, G, 'Shareholding Voting over the Internet: A Proposal for Increasing Shareholder Participation in Corporate Governance', *Alabama Law Review*, 49/2 (1998), 673–700.

Koch, P, 'Die "Tokenisierung" von Rechtspositionen als digitale Verbriefung', *Zeitschrift für Bankrecht und Bankwirtschaft*, 6 (2018), 359 et seq.

Kohn, R, 'The Case for Including Directly Held Securities within the Scope of the UNCITRAL Legislative Guide on Secured Transactions', *Uniform Law Review*, 15/2 (2010), 413–18.

Kraakman, R, Arnour, J, Davies, P, Enriques, L, Hansmann, H, Hertig, G, Hopt, K, Kanda, H, and Rock E, *The Anatomy of Corporate Law: A Comparative and Functional Approach* (Oxford: Oxford University Press, 2009; 2nd edn).

Kronke, H, 'Das Genfer Unidroit-Übereinkommen über materiellrechtliche Normen für intermediär-verwahrte Wertpapiere und die Reform des deutschen Depotrechts', *WM Zeitschrift für Wirtschafts- und Bankrecht*, 64/35 (2010), 1625–76.

Kuhn, H, 'Art. 10 FISA', in Kuhn, H, Graham-Siegenthaler, B, and Thévenoz, L, *The Federal Intermediated Securities Act (FISA) and the Hague Securities Convention (HSC)* (Berne: Stampfli Publishers Ltd, 2010), 219–37.

Kuhn, H, 'Art. 19 FISA', in Kuhn, H, Graham-Siegenthaler, B, and Thévenoz, L, *The Federal Intermediated Securities Act (FISA) and the Hague Securities Convention (HSC)* (Berne: Stampfli Publishers Ltd, 2010), 317–26.

Kuhn, H, 'Prel. Cmts Arts. 27–28 FISA', in Kuhn, H, Graham-Siegenthaler, B, and Thévenoz, L, *The Federal Intermediated Securities Act (FISA) and the Hague Securities Convention (HSC)* (Berne: Stampfli Publishers Ltd, 2010), 406–13.

Kuhn, H, 'Art. 28 FISA', in Kuhn, H, Graham-Siegenthaler, B, and Thévenoz, L, *The Federal Intermediated Securities Act (FISA) and the Hague Securities Convention (HSC)* (Berne: Stampfli Publishers Ltd, 2010), 438–47.

Kuhn, H, Graham-Siegenthaler, B, and Thévenoz, L, *The Federal Intermediated Securities Act (FISA) and the Hague Securities Convention (HSC)* (Berne: Stampfli Publishers Ltd, 2010).

Kuhn, H, 'Taxonomie', in Weber, R and Kuhn, H, *Entwicklungen im Schweizer Blockchainrecht* (Basel: Helbing Lichtenhahn, 2021), 35-50.

Kuhn, H, 'Registerwertrechte', in: Weber, R and Kuhn, H, *Entwicklungen im Schweizer Blockchainrecht* (Basel: Helbing Lichtenhahn, 2021), 51-130.

Kuhn, H, Stengel, C, Meisser, L, and Weber, R, 'Wertrechte als Rechtsrahmen für die Token-Wirtschaft', *Jusletter IT* (23 May 2019).

Lamfalussy et al, *Final Report of the Committee of Wise Men on the Regulation of European Securities Markets* (February 2010), <https://www.esma.europa.eu/sites/default/files/library/2015/11/lamfalussy_report.pdf> (accessed 21 July 2021).

Lautenschläger, S, *Is Small Beautiful? Supervision, Regulation and the Size of Banks*, (Washington DC: 2017; speech at an IMF seminar), <https://www.ecb.europa.eu/press/key/date/2017/html/ecb.sp171014.en.html> (accessed 21 July 2021).

Law Commission (UK), *Law Commission Project on Intermediated Investment Securities, First Seminar: Objectives for a Common Legal Framework* (2006).

Law Commission (UK), *Law Commission Project on Intermediated Investment Securities, Second Seminar: Issues Affecting Account Holders and Intermediaries* (2006).

Law Commission (UK), *Law Commission Project on Intermediated Investment Securities, Third Seminar: Issues Affecting Transferees of Intermediated Securities* (2006).

Law Commission (UK), *The UNIDROIT Convention on Substantive Rules regarding Intermediated Securities: Further Updated Advice to HM Treasury* (May 2008).

Law Commission (UK), *Intermediated Securities: Who Owns Your Shares? A Scoping Paper* (November 2020), <https://s3-eu-west-2.amazonaws.com/lawcom-prod-storage-11jsxou24uy7q/uploads/2020/11/Law-Commission-Intermediated-Securities-Scoping-Paper-1.pdf> (accessed 21 July 2021).

Ledrut, E and Upper, C, 'Changing Post-trading Arrangements for OTC Derivatives', *BIS Quarterly Review* (December 2007), 83–95.

Legal Certainty Group, *Second Advice of the Legal Certainty Group: Solutions to Legal Barriers Related to Post-trading within the EU* (August 2008), <https://ec.europa.eu/info/sites/default/files/legal-certainty-group-2nd-advice_en.pdf> (accessed 21 July 2021).

Lehmann, M, 'Résolution et le droit international privé', *Revue de droit bancaire et financier*, 4 (2014), 88–95.

Lehmann, M, 'National Blockchain Laws as a Threat to Capital Markets Integration', *Uniform Law Review*, 26/1 (2021), 148-79.

Levels, A and Capel, J, *Is Collateral Becoming Scarce? Evidence for the Euro Area* (2012; DNB Occasional Studies 10/1).

Levin, J, *Bitcoin: New Plumbing for Financial Services* (updated version of 2 December 2014), <https://www.coindesk.com/bitcoin-new-plumbing-financial-services> (accessed 21 July 2021).

Loizou, S, 'Close-out Netting and an Introduction to the UNIDROIT Principles on Its Enforceability', *Journal of International Banking Law and Regulation*, 27/10 (2012), 429–32.

Lubben, S, 'Derivatives and Bankruptcy: The Flawed Case for Special Treatment', *University of Pennsylvania Journal of Business Law*, 12/1 (2009), 61–78.

Lubben, S, 'Systemic Risk & Chapter 11', *Temple Law Review*, 82/2 (2009), 433–48.

Lubben, S, 'Repeal the Safe Harbors', *American Bankruptcy Institute Law Review*, 18/1 (2010), 319–35.

Lubben, S, 'The Bankruptcy Code without Safe Harbors', *American Bankruptcy Law Journal*, 84/2 (2010), 123–44.

Lubben, S, 'Transaction Simplicity', *Columbia Law Review Sidebar*, 112 (2012), 194–205.

Lucas, R and Stokey, N, *Liquidity Crises: Understanding Sources and Limiting Consequences: A Theoretical Framework* (Federal Reserve Bank of Minneapolis, May 2011; Economic Policy Paper 11–3).

Mangano, R, 'Blockchain Securities, Insolvency Law and the Sandbox Approach', *European Business Organization Law Review*, 19 (2018), 715–35.

Manning, M, Sutton, M, and Zhu, J, 'Distributed Ledger Technology in Securities Clearing and Settlement: Some Issues', *The Finsia Journal of Applied Finance* (2016), 30–6.

Marks, D, 'Regulating Financial Services and Markets in the EU', in Moss, G, Fletcher, I, and Isaacs, S (eds), *The EC Regulation on Insolvency Proceedings: A Commentary and Annotated Guide* (Oxford: Oxford University Press, 2009; 2nd edn), 175–224.

Mayer Brown, *The ISDA Resolution Stay Protocol* (November 2014), <http://www.mayerbrown.com/The-ISDA-Resolution-Stay-Protocol-11-25-2014/> (accessed 21 July 2021).

McDowell, H, 'ASX to Replace Equity Post-trade Systems with Blockchain', *Global Custodian*, (7 December 2017), <https://www.globalcustodian.com/asx-to-replace-equity-post-trade-systems-with-blockchain/> (accessed 21 July 2021).

McFarlane, B and Stevens, R, 'Interests in Securities: Practical Problems and Conceptual Solutions', in Gullifer, L and Payne, J (eds), *Intermediated Securities: Legal Problems and Practical Issues* (Oxford: Hart Publishing, 2010), 33–59.

McKendrick, E (ed), *Goode on Commercial Law* (London: Penguin Books, 2010; 4th edn).

Meisser, C, Meisser, L, and Kogens, R, 'Verfügungsmacht und Verfügungsrecht an Bitcoins im Konkurs', *Jusletter IT* (24 May 2018).

Mengle, D, *The Importance of Close-out Netting* (2010; ISDA Research Notes 1).

Micheler, E, *Doctrinal Path Dependence and Functional Convergence: The Case of Investment Securities* (January 2006), <http://ssrn.com/abstract=880110> (accessed 21 July 2021).

Micheler, E, *Wertpapierrecht zwischen Schuld- und Sachenrecht: Zu einer kapitalmarktrechtlichen Theorie des Wertpapierrechts* (Vienna: Springer Verlag, 2004).

Micheler, E, *Property in Securities: A Comparative Study* (Cambridge: Cambridge University Press, 2007).

Micheler, E, 'The Legal Nature of Securities: Inspirations from Comparative Law', in Gullifer, L and Payne, J (eds), *Intermediated Securities: Legal Problems and Practical Issues* (Oxford: Hart Publishing, 2010), 131–49.

Micheler, E, 'Custody Chains and Asset Values: Why Crypto-securities Are Worth Considering', *Cambridge Law Journal*, 74 (2015), 505–33.

Micheler, E, 'Intermediated Securities from the Perspective of Investors: Problems, Quick Fixes and Long-term Solutions', in Gullifer, L and Payne, J (eds), *Intermediation and Beyond* (Oxford: Hart Publishing, 2019), 237–58.

Mills, A, *Party Autonomy in Private International Law* (Cambridge University Press, 2019).

Miscione, G, 'Der Blockchain-Hype: braucht es "Ockhams Rasiermesser"?', *Inside-IT* (6 February 2019; blog contribution).

Moin, A, Gün Sirer, E, and Sekniqi, K, *A Classification Framework for Stablecoin Designs* (18 September 2019), arXiv:1910.10098v1 [q-fin.GN].

Mokal, R, 'Liquidity, Systemic Risk, and the Bankruptcy Treatment of Financial Contracts', *Brooklyn Journal of Corporate, Financial & Commercial Law*, 10 (2015), 15–96, <https://brooklynworks.brooklaw.edu/bjcfcl/vol10/iss1/2> (accessed 21 July 2021).

Mooney, C, 'Beyond Negotiability: A New Model for Transfer and Pledge of Interests in Securities Controlled by Intermediaries', *Cardozo Law Review*, 12/2 (1990), 305–427.

Mooney, C, 'Practising Safer Lex: The Proper Domain of Property, Secured Transactions and Insolvency Laws in the Regulation of Securities Intermediaries', in Ferrarini, G (ed), *European Securities Markets* (London, The Hague: Kluwer Law International, 1998), 85–94.

Mooney, C, *Law and Systems for Intermediated Securities and the Relationship of Private Property Law to Securities Clearance and Settlement: United States, Japan, and the UNIDROIT Draft Convention* (2008; IMES Discussion Paper 2008-E-7).

Mooney, C, 'The (UNIDROIT) Geneva Securities Convention on Intermediated Securities', *Butterworths Journal of International Banking and Financial Law*, 24/10 (2009), 596–8.

Mooney, C, 'Private Law and the Regulation of Securities Intermediaries: Perspectives under the Geneva Securities Convention and United States Law', *Uniform Law Review*, 15/3-4 (2010), 801–13.

Mooney, C, 'The Truth about Shortfall of Intermediated Securities: Perspectives under the Geneva Securities Convention, United States Law, and the Future EU Legislation', in Conac, P.-H, Segna, U, and Thévenoz, L (eds), *Intermediated Securities: The Impact of the Geneva Securities Convention and the Future European Legislation* (Cambridge: Cambridge University Press, 2013), 160–92.

Mooney, C, 'Harmonizing Choice-of-Law Rules for International Insolvency Cases: Virtual Territoriality, Virtual Universalism, and the Problem of Local Interests', *Brooklyn Journal of Corporate, Financial and Commercial Law*, 9/1 (2014), 120–51, <https://papers.ssrn.com/sol3/papers.cfm?abstract_id=2491070> (accessed 21 July 2021).

Mooney, C, 'The Bankruptcy Code's Safe Harbors for Settlement Payments and Securities Contracts: When Is Safe *Too* Safe?', *Texas International Law Journal*, 49/2 (2014), 243–67.

Mooney, C, 'Beyond Intermediation: A New (Fintech) Model for Securities Holding Infrastructures', *University of Pennsylvania Journal of Business Law*, 22 (2020), 386–456, <https://papers.ssrn.com/sol3/papers.cfm?abstract_id=3444269> (accessed 21 July 2021).

Mooney, C, 'An Essay on Pluralism in Financial Infrastructure Design: The Case of Securities Holding in the United States', in Binder, J-H and Saguato, P (eds), *Financial Market Infrastructure: Law and Regulation* (Oxford: Oxford University Press, forthcoming), <https://papers.ssrn.com/sol3/papers.cfm?abstract_id=3581864> (accessed 21 July 2021).

Mooney, C and Kanda, H, 'Core Issues under the UNIDROIT (Geneva) Convention on Intermediated Securities: Views from the United States and Japan', in Gullifer, L and Payne, J (eds), *Intermediated Securities: Legal Problems and Practical Issues* (Oxford: Hart Publishing, 2010), 69–130.

Moore, M and Petrin, M, *Corporate Governance: Law, Regulation and Theory* (London: Palgrave 2017).

Morrison, E and Riegel, J, 'Financial Contracts and the New Bankruptcy Code: Insulating Markets from Bankrupt Debtors and Bankruptcy Judges', *American Bankruptcy Institute Law Review*, 13 (2010), 641–64.

Morrison, E, Roe, M, and Sontchi, C, 'Rolling Back the Repo Safe Harbors', *The Business Lawyer*, 69/4 (2014), 1015–48.

Morton, G, 'Security Interests in Financial Instruments: Commentary', in Eidenmüller, H and Kieninger, E-M (eds), *The Future of Secured Credit in Europe* (Munich: De Gruyter Recht, 2008), 364–72.

Moss, G, 'Intermediated Securities: Issues Arising from Insolvency', in Gullifer, L and Payne, J (eds), *Intermediated Securities: Legal Problems and Practical Issues* (Oxford: Hart Publishing, 2010), 61–8.

Moss, G, Wessels, B, and Haentjens, M, *EU Banking and Insurance Insolvency* (Oxford: Oxford University Press, 2017).

Muir Watt, H, 'Choice of Law in Integrated and Interconnected Markets: A Matter of Political Economy', *Columbia Journal of European Law*, 9 (2003), 383 et seq.

Mülbert, P, 'Vom Ende allen sachenrechtlichen Denkens im Depotrecht durch UNIDROIT und die EU', *Zeitschrift für Bankrecht und Bankwirtschaft*, 22/6 (2010), 445–58.

Murphy, D, *OTC Derivatives: Bilateral Trading & Central Clearing* (Basingstoke: Palgrave MacMillan, 2012).

Murray, E, 'The ISDA Credit Support Documents', in Tyson-Quah, K (ed), *Cross-border Securities: Repo, Lending and Collateralisation* (London: Sweet & Maxwell, 1997), 197–219.

Murray, E, 'Financial Collateral Arrangements and the Financial Markets', in Dahan, F (ed), *Research Handbook on Secured Financing in Commercial Transactions* (Edward Elgar Publishing, 2015) 286–325.

Murray, E, 'Use of Close Out Netting and Financial Collateral in Relation to Derivatives (Including ISDA Documentation)', in Yeowart G and Parsons, R, *Yeowart and Parsons on the Law of Financial Collateral* (Edward Elgar Publishing, 2016), 434–60.

Muscat, B, *Insolvency Close-out Netting: A Comparative Study of English, French and US Laws in a Global Perspective* (Leiden, 2020; PhD thesis).

Myners, P, *Review of the Impediments to Voting UK Shares: Report by Paul Myners to the Shareholder Voting Working Group* (January 2004).

Myners, P, *Review of the Impediments to Voting UK Shares: Report by Paul Myners to the Shareholder Voting Working Group: An Update on Progress Three Years on* (July 2007).

Nakamoto, S, *Bitcoin: A Peer-to-peer Electronic Cash System* (2008), <https://bitcoin.org/bitcoin.pdf> (accessed 21 July 2021).

Nauta Dutilh, *Amendment to the Dutch Securities Book-entry Administration and Transfer Act* (January 2011; Banking and Finance Update).

Nijenhuis, A, 'Close-out netting en insolventie: Close-out netting bepalingen in swaps en valutatermijncontracten en de rol van de artikelen 38 en 237 Faillissementswet', in Kortmann, S et al (eds), *Onderneming en effecten* (Deventer: Tjeenk Willink, 1998), 601–16.

Nijenhuis, A and Verhagen, H, '"Netting": een beschouwing naar Nederlands recht', *De Naamlooze Vennootschap*, 4 (1994), 96–103.

Nolan, R, 'Indirect Investors: A Greater Say in the Company?', *Journal of Corporate Law Studies*, 3/1 (2003), 73–121.
Nolan, R, 'The Continuing Evolution of Shareholder Governance', *Cambridge Law Journal*, 65/1 (2006), 92–127.
Nougayrède, D, 'Towards a Global Financial Register? The Case for End Investor Transparency in Central Securities Depositaries', *Journal of Financial Regulation*, 4 (2018), 276–313.
OECD, *G20 High-level Principles on Financial Consumer Protection* (October 2011), <http://www.oecd.org/daf/fin/financial-markets/48892010.pdf> (accessed 21 July 2021).
OECD, *Initial Coin Offerings (ICOs) for SME Financing* (January 2019) <https://www.oecd.org/finance/initial-coin-offerings-for-sme-financing.htm> (accessed 21 July 2021).
OECD, *The Tokenisation of Assets and Potential Implications for Financial Markets* (January 2020), <https://www.oecd.org/finance/The-Tokenisation-of-Assets-and-Potential-Implications-for-Financial-Markets.htm> (accessed 21 July 2021).
O'Hara, E and Ribstein, L, 'Conflict of Laws and Choice of Law', in Bouckaert, B and Geest, G de (eds), *Encyclopedia of Law and Economics*, vol 5 (Cheltenham, Northampton: Edward Elgar Publishing, 2000), 631 et seq.
O'Hara, E and Ribstein, L, 'From Politics to Efficiency in Choice of Law', *University of Chicago Law Review*, 67 (2000), 1151 et seq.
Ooi, M, *Shares and Other Securities in the Conflict of Laws* (Oxford: Oxford University Press, 2003).
Ooi, M, 'The Hague Securities Convention: A Critical Reading of the Road Map', *Lloyd's Maritime & Commercial Law Quarterly*, 4 (2005), 467–90.
Ooi, M, 'Intermediated Securities: The Choice of a Choice of Law Rule', in Gullifer, L and Payne, J (eds), *Intermediated Securities: Legal Problems and Practical Issues* (Oxford: Hart Publishing, 2010), 219–44.
Osborn, T, 'Too Much Choice: The Problems with Europe's Plethora of Segregation Models', *Risk Magazine* (May 2013).
Oxera, *Corporate Action Processing: What Are the Risks?* (May 2004; sponsored by The Depository Trust & Clearing Corporation), <https://www.oxera.com/wp-content/uploads/2018/03/Corporate-action-processing-3.pdf> (accessed 21 July 2021).
Paech, P, 'Harmonising Substantive Rules for the Use of Securities Held with Intermediaries as Collateral: The UNIDROIT Project', *Uniform Law Review*, 7/4 (2002), 1140–61.
Paech, P, 'Systemic Risk, Regulatory Powers and Insolvency Law: The Need for an International Instrument on the Private Law Framework for Netting' (Frankfurt: March 2010; Institute for Law and Finance, Working Paper Series 116), <https://www.ilf-frankfurt.de/fileadmin/_migrated/content_uploads/ILF_WP_116.pdf> (accessed 21 July 2021).
Paech, P, 'Enforceability of Close-out Netting: Draft UNIDROIT Principles to Set New International Benchmark', *Butterworths Journal of International Banking and Financial Law*, 28/1 (2013), 13–19.
Paech, P, 'Market Needs as Paradigm: Breaking up the Thinking on EU Securities Law', in Conac, P-H, Segna, U, and Thévenoz, L (eds), *Intermediated Securities: The Impact of the Geneva Securities Convention and the Future European Legislation* (Cambridge: Cambridge University Press, 2013), 22–64.
Paech, P, 'The Value of Financial Market Insolvency Safe Harbours', *Oxford Journal of Legal Studies*, 36/4 (2016), 855–84.
Paech, P, *Securities, Intermediation and the Blockchain: An Inevitable Choice between Liquidity and Legal Certainty?* (June 2016, updated version; LSE Law, Society and Economy Working Paper 20/2015).
Paech, P, 'Securities, Intermediation and the Blockchain: An Inevitable Choice Between Liquidity and Legal Certainty?', *Uniform Law Review*, 21/4 (2016), 612–39.
Paech, P, 'The Governance of Blockchain Financial Networks', *Modern Law Review*, 80 (2017), 1073–110.
Paech, P, 'Conflict of Laws and Relational Rights', in Gullifer, L and Payne, J, *Intermediation and Beyond* (Oxford: Hart Publishing, 2019), 289–307.

Paech, P and Löber, K, 'Interconnecting Law of Securities Holding and Transfer: A Chance for Seamless International Improvements', *Butterworths Journal of International Banking and Financial Law*, 22/1 (2007), 9–15.

Panetta, F and Schnabel, I, *The Provision of Euro Liquidity through the ECB's Swap and Repo Operations* (19 August 2020, ECB blog), <https://www.ecb.europa.eu/press/blog/date/2020/html/ecb.blog200819~0d1d04504a.en.html> (accessed 21 July 2021).

Panisi, F, Buckley, R, and Arner, D, 'Blockchain and Public Companies: A Revolution in Share Ownership Transparency, Proxy Voting and Corporate Governance?', *Stanford Journal of Blockchain Law & Policy 2 (2019), University of Hong Kong Faculty of Law Research Paper 2019/039, UNSW Law Research Paper 19-100*, <https://papers.ssrn.com/sol3/papers.cfm?abstract_id=3389045> (accessed 21 July 2021).

Partnoy, F and Skeel, A, 'The Promise and Perils of Credit Derivatives', *University of Cincinnati Law Review*, 75 (2007), 1019–51.

Payne, J, 'Intermediated Securities and the Right to Vote in the UK', in Gullifer, L and Payne, J (eds), *Intermediated Securities: Legal Problems and Practical Issues* (Oxford: Hart Publishing, 2010), 187–218.

Perdana, A et al, 'Distributed Ledger Technology: Its Evolutionary Path and the Road Ahead', *Information & Management*, 58 (2021), 103316 (pre-print).

Perotti, E, *Systemic Liquidity Risk and Bankruptcy Exceptions* (2010; Centre for Economic Policy Research, Policy Insight No 52).

Pinna, A and Ruttenberg, W, *Distributed Ledger Technologies in Securities Post-trading: Revolution or Evolution?* (April 2016; ECB Occasional Paper Series 172), <https://www.ecb.europa.eu/pub/pdf/scpops/ecbop172.en.pdf> (accessed 21 July 2021).

Pirrong, C, *A Bill of Goods: CCPs and Systemic Risk* (without year), <https://capital-markets.law.columbia.edu/sites/default/files/content/docs/Pirrong_Paper.pdf> (accessed 21 July 2021).

Potok, R (ed), *Cross Border Collateral: Legal Risk and the Conflict of Laws* (London: Butterworths, 2002).

Potok, R, 'The Hague Securities Convention: Closer and Closer to a Reality', *Journal of Banking and Finance Law and Practice*, 15 (2004), 204–20.

Priem, R, 'Distributed Ledger Technology for Securities Clearing and Settlement: Benefits, Risks and Regulatory Implications', *Financial Innovation*, 6/11 (2020), 1–25.

Provost, C and Kenard, M, 'The World Bank Is Supposed to Help the Poor: So Why Is It Bankrolling Oligarchs? The Bank's Private Investment Arm Is Increasingly Chasing Profits at the Expense of Its Anti-poverty Mission' (2016), <https://www.motherjones.com/politics/2016/03/world-bank-ifc-fund-luxury-hotels/> (accessed 21 July 2021).

Prüm, A, 'La dématerialisation des titres fongibles en droit luxembourgois', in: Vauplane, H. de, *20 ans de dématérérialisation des titres en France* (Paris: 2005), 271–87.

Prussen, Y, 'Le régime des titres et instruments fongibles', in Association Luxembourgeoise des Juristes de Droit Bancaire (ed), *Droit bancaire et financier au Luxembourg: recueil de doctrine* (Brussels: Larcier, 2004), 1287–318.

Rachman, N, 'Securities Trading Meets Corporate Law: What are "Securities" and Who Holds Them?: Trends and Patterns in Brazilian Law', *Uniform Law Review*, 15/3-4 (2010), 833–44.

Rasheed, T and Zebregs, B, 'Can a House Divided Between Itself Stand?: Segregation in Derivatives Clearing', *Butterworths Journal of International Banking and Financial Law*, 27/5 (2012), 293–300.

Rauchs, M, Glidden, A, Gordon, B, Pieters, G, Recanatini, M, Rostand, F, Vagneur, K, and Zhang, B, *Distributed Ledger Technology Systems: A Conceptual Framework* (Cambridge Centre for Alternative Finance, August 2018), <https://ssrn.com/abstract=3230013> or <http://dx.doi.org/10.2139/ssrn.3230013> (both accessed 21 July 2021).

Rauchs, M, Blandin, A, Bear, K, and McKeon, S, *2nd Global Enterprise Blockchain Benchmarking Study* (Cambridge Centre for Alternative Finance, 2019), <https://papers.ssrn.com/sol3/papers.cfm?abstract_id=3461765> (accessed 21 July 2021).

Reiff, N, 'Blockchain Won't Cut Out Intermediaries After All', *Investopedia* (16 December 2020), <https://www.investopedia.com/tech/blockchain-wont-cut-out-intermediaries-after-all/> (accessed 21 July 2021).

Ringe, W-G and Ruof, C, *The DLT Pilot Regime: An EU Sandbox, at Last!* (19 November 2020), <https://www.law.ox.ac.uk/business-law-blog/blog/2020/11/dlt-pilot-regime-eu-sandbox-last> (accessed 21 July 2021).

Rodríguez de las Heras Ballell, T, 'Digital Technology-based Solutions for Enhanced Effectiveness of Secured Transactions Law: The Road to Perfection?', *Law and Contemporary Problems*, 81 (2018), 21–44.

Roe, M, 'The Derivatives Market's Payment Priorities as Financial Crisis Accelerator', *Stanford Law Review*, 63/3 (2011), 539–90.

Rögner, H, 'Inconsistencies between the Hague Securities Convention and German Law', *Zeitschrift für Bankrecht und Bankwirtschaft*, 2 (2006), 98–106.

Rogers, J, 'Negotiability, Property and Identity', *Cardozo Law Review*, 12 (1990), 471–508.

Rogers, J, 'Policy Perspectives on Revised UCC Article 8', *UCLA Law Review*, 43/5 (1996), 1431–545.

Ruhl, G, *Party Autonomy in the Private International Law of Contracts: Transatlantic Convergence and Economic Efficiency* (Osgoode Hall Law School, 2007; Research Report 4/2007), <http://digitalcommons.osgoode.yorku.ca/clpe/227> (accessed 21 July 2021).

Salter, R, 'Enforcing Debt Securities', in Gullifer, L and Payne, J (eds), *Intermediation and Beyond* (Oxford: Hart Publishing, 2019), 129–54.

Savelyev, A, *Contract Law 2.0: 'Smart' Contracts as the Beginning of the End of Classic Contract Law* (December 2016), <https://papers.ssrn.com/sol3/papers.cfm?abstract_id=2885241> (accessed 21 July 2021).

Schär, F and Berentsen, A, *Bitcoin, Blockchain, and Cryptoassets* (Cambridge MA, London: 2020).

Schär, F and Hübner, P, 'Blockchain und Smart Contracts im Kontext der Prozessautomatisierung', in Bruhn M and Hadwich, K (eds), *Automatisierung und Personalisierung von Dienstleistungen* (Berlin: 2020), 297–316.

Schelo, S, *Bank Recovery and Resolution* (Kluwer Law International, 2020; 2nd edn).

Schillig, M, 'Bank Resolution Regimes in Europe—Part I: Recovery and Resolution Planning, Early Intervention', *European Business Law Review*, 24/6 (2013), 751–79.

Schillig, M, 'Bank Resolution Regimes in Europe—Part II: Resolution Tools and Powers', *European Business Law Review*, 25/1 (2014), 67–102.

Schuster, E, 'Cloud Crypto Land', *Modern Law Review*, 84/5 (2020), 974-1004.

Schwarcz, S, 'Intermediary Risk in a Global Economy', *Duke Law Journal*, 50/6 (2001), 1541–607.

Schwarcz, S, 'Distorting Legal Principles', *The Journal of Corporation Law*, 35/4 (2010), 697–727.

Schwarcz S and Sharon, O, 'The Bankruptcy-law Safe Harbor for Derivatives: A Path-dependence Analysis', *Washington and Lee Law Review*, 71/3 (2014), 1715–55.

Scott, H, *Interconnectedness and Contagion* (November 2012), <https://www.capmktsreg.org/wp-content/uploads/2014/11/2012.11.20_Interconnectedness_and_Contagion.pdf> (accessed 21 July 2021).

SEC-FINRA, *Joint Staff Statement on Broker-Dealer Custody of Digital Asset Securities* (July 2019), <https://www.sec.gov/news/public-statement/joint-staff-statement-broker-dealer-custody-digital-asset-securities> (accessed 21 July 2021).

Segna, U, 'The Geneva Securities Convention, the Future European Legislation, and Their Impact on German Law', in Conac, P-H, Segna, U, and Thévenoz, L (eds), *Intermediated Securities: The Impact of the Geneva Securities Convention and the Future European Legislation* (Cambridge: Cambridge University Press, 2013), 248–68.

Senior Supervisors Group, *Risk Management Lessons from the Global Banking Crisis of 2008* (October 2009), <http://www.financialstabilityboard.org/publications/r_0910a.pdf> (accessed 21 July 2021).

Shabsigh, G, Khiaonarong, T, and Leinonen, H, *Distributed Ledger Technology Experiments in Payments and Settlements* (International Monetary Fund, June 2020; Fintech Notes Note/20/01).

Shareholder Voting Working Group, *Shareholding Proxy Voting: Discussion Paper on Potential Progress in Transparency* (July 2015), <https://www.investorforum.org.uk/wp-content/uploads/securepdfs/2020/06/SVWG-Shareholder-Proxy-Voting-DP-July-2015.pdf> (accessed 21 July 2021).

Sigman, H and Bernasconi, C, 'Myths about the Hague Convention Debunked', *International Finance Law Review*, 24/11 (2005), 31–5.

Simmons, M and Dalgleish, E, *Corporate Actions: A Guide to Securities Event Management* (Chichester, West Sussex: Wiley, 2006).

Singh, M and Aitken, J, *Deleveraging after Lehman: Evidence from Reduced Rehypothecation* (March 2009; IMF Working Paper WP/09/42).

Singh, M and Aitken, J, *The (Sizable) Role of Rehypothecation in the Shadow Banking System* (July 2010; IMF Working Paper WP/10/172).

Singh, M, *Making OTC Derivatives Safe: A Fresh Look* (March 2011; IMF Working Paper WP/11/66).

Singh, M, *Velocity of Pledged Collateral: Analysis and Implications* (November 2011; IMF Working Paper WP/11/256).

Singh, M, *The (Other) Deleveraging* (July 2012; IMF Working Paper WP/12/179).

Singh, M, *The Changing Collateral Space* (January 2013; IMF Working Paper WP/13/25).

Singh, M, *Collateral and Financial Plumbing* (Risk Books, 2014).

Singh, M, *Collateral Reuse and Balance Sheet Space* (May 2017; IMF Working Paper 17/113).

Skeel, D, 'Bankruptcy Boundary Games', *Brooklyn Journal of Corporate, Financial and Commercial Law*, 4/1 (2009), 1–21.

Skeel, D and Jackson, T, 'Transaction Consistency and the New Finance in Bankruptcy', *Columbia Law Review*, 112 (2012), 152–202.

Smethurst, J and Benjamin, J, 'Restatement of the Law Relating to Client Securities', *Capital Markets Law Journal*, 4/3 (2009), 311–22.

Sołtysiński, S, *Draft Principles and Rules on the Netting of Financial Instruments (Report of the Chairman of the Group)*, UNIDROIT 2012–CD (91) 15, Appendix IV.

Sołtysiński, S, 'The Importance of the Principles of Equality of the EU Member States and Economic Actors in EU Law', *ELTE Law Journal*, 2/1 (2014), 73–97.

Sorkin, A, *Too Big to Fail: Inside the Battle to Save Wall Street* (London: Penguin Books, 2010).

Struycken, T and Schim, B, 'Vermogensscheiding in ondernemingsrechtelijk perspectief: aandelen houden vanachter het girale gordijn', in Rank, W (ed), *Vermogensscheiding in de financiële praktijk* (Amsterdam: NIBE SVV, 2008; Bankjuridische Reeks 56), ch 7.

Summe, K, 'An Examination of Lehman Brothers' Derivatives Portfolio Postbankruptcy: Would Dodd-Frank Have Made a Difference?', in Scott, K and Taylor, J (eds), *Bankruptcy Not Bailout: A Special Chapter 14* (Stanford, California: Hoover Institution Press, 2012), 85–129.

Swift, *Blockchain: Progression in Securities Markets?* (January 2018), <https://www.swift.com/news-events/news/blockchain-progression-securities-markets> (accessed 21 July 2021).

Sykes, J, *Regulatory Reform 10 Years After the Financial Crisis: Systemic Risk Regulation of Non-bank Financial Institutions* (12 April 2018; Congressional Research Service 7–5700/R45162).

The Company Law Review Steering Group, *Modern Company Law for a Competitive Economy: Final Report* (2001).

Thévenoz, L, 'New Legal Concepts Regarding the Holding of Investment Securities for a Civil Law Jurisdiction: The Swiss Draft Act', *Uniform Law Review*, 10/1–2 (2005), 301–37.

Thévenoz, L, 'Intermediated Securities, Legal Risk, and the International Harmonization of Commercial Law', *Stanford Journal of Law, Business & Finance*, 13/2 (2008), 384–452.

Thévenoz, L, 'Who Holds (Intermediated) Securities?: Shareholders, Account Holders, and Nominees', *Uniform Law Review*, 15/3–4 (2010), 845–59.

Thévenoz, L, 'The Geneva Securities Convention: Objectives, History, and Guiding Principles', in Conac, P-H, Segna, U, and Thévenoz, L (eds), *Intermediated Securities: The Impact of the Geneva Securities Convention and the Future European Legislation* (Cambridge: Cambridge University Press, 2013), 3–21.

Thévenoz, L, 'Transfer of Intermediated Securities', in Conac, P-H, Segna, U, and Thévenoz, L (eds), *Intermediated Securities: The Impact of the Geneva Securities Convention and the Future European Legislation* (Cambridge: Cambridge University Press, 2013), 135–59.

Tröger, T, *Too Complex to Work: a Critical Assessment of the Bail-in Tool under the European Bank Recovery and Resolution Regime* (2017; SAFE Working Paper No. 179).

Tröger, T, *Why MREL Won't Help Much* (2017; SAFE Working Paper No. 180).

Tucker, P, *Building Resilient Financial Systems: Macroprudential Regimes and Securities Market Regulation* (2011; speech at the International Council of Securities Associations), <https://www.bis.org/review/r110525a.pdf> (accessed 21 July 2021).

Tuckman, B, *Amending Safe Harbors to Reduce Systemic Risk in OTC Derivatives Markets* (Center for Financial Stability, 2010; CFS Policy Paper), <http://www.centerforfinancialstability.net/research/Safe-Harbor-Systemic-Risk-20100422.pdf> (accessed 21 July 2021).

Turing, D, *Clearing and Settlement in Europe* (West Sussex: Bloomsbury, 2012).

Twemlow, C, 'Why Are Securities Held in Intermediated Form?', in Gullifer, L and Payne, J (eds), *Intermediation and Beyond* (Oxford: Hart Publishing, 2018), 85–107.

UNCITRAL, Hague Conference, and UNIDROIT, *Texts on Security Interests: Comparison and Analysis of Major Features of International Instruments Relating to Secured Transactions* (2012), <https://uncitral.un.org/en/texts/securityinterests/explanatorytexts/UNIDROIT_texts_on_security_interests> (accessed 21 July 2021).

UNSGSA FinTech Working Group and CCAF, *Early Lessons on Regulatory Innovations to Enable Inclusive FinTech: Innovation Offices, Regulatory Sandboxes, and RegTech* (2019), <https://www.jbs.cam.ac.uk/wp-content/uploads/2020/08/2019-early-lessons-regulatory-innovations-enable-inclusive-fintech.pdf> (accessed 21 July 2021).

Van der Elst, C and Lafarre, A, 'Blockchain and Smart Contracting for the Shareholder Community', *European Business Organization Law Review*, 20 (2019), 111–37.

Vauplane, H de (ed), *20 ans de dématérialisation des titres en France* (AEDBF, RB Revue banque, 2005).

Vauplane, H de and Yon, J-P, 'The Concept of Integrity in Securities Holding Systems', in Conac, P-H, Segna, U, and Thévenoz, L (eds), *Intermediated Securities: The Impact of the Geneva Securities Convention and the Future European Legislation* (Cambridge: Cambridge University Press, 2013), 193–213.

Veil, R, 'Token-Emissionen im europäischen Kapitalmarktrecht', *Zeitschrift für das gesamte Handels- und Wirtschaftsrecht*, 183/02-03 (2019), 346-87.

Vogelsteller, F and Buterin, V, *EIP-20: ERC-20 Token Standard* (19 November 2015), <https://eips.ethereum.org/EIPS/eip-20> (accessed 21 July 2021).

Werlen, T and Flanagan, S, 'The 2002 Model Netting Act: A Solution for Insolvency Uncertainty', *Butterworths Journal of International Banking and Financial Law*, 17/4 (2002), 154–64.

Werner, S, *What Is Custody of Digital Assets?* (without date), <https://www.globalcustodian.com/blog/custody-digital-assets/> (accessed 21 July 2021).

Westrik, R and Weide, J van der (eds), *Party Autonomy in International Property Law* (Sellier, 2011).

Wildmann, L, *Einführung in die Volkswirtschaftslehre, Mikroökonomie und Wettbewerbspolitik* (München, Wien: De Gruyter Oldenbourg, 2014).

Witmer, J, 'Art. 11 FISA', in Kuhn, H, Graham-Siegenthaler, B, and Thévenoz, L, *The Federal Intermediated Securities Act (FISA) and the Hague Securities Convention (HSC)* (Berne: Stampfli Publishers Ltd, 2010), 238–50.

Wood, P, *Set-off and Netting, Derivatives, Clearing Systems* (London: Sweet & Maxwell, 2007).

World Bank, *Principles for Effective Insolvency and Creditor/Debtor Regimes* (2016), <https://documents1.worldbank.org/curated/en/518861467086038847/pdf/106399-WP-REVISED-PUBLIC-ICR-Principle-Final-Hyperlinks-revised-Latest.pdf> (accessed 21 July 2021).

World Bank, *Distributed Ledger Technology (DLT) and Blockchain* (2017).

World Economic Forum, *The Future of Financial Infrastructure: An Ambitious Look at How Blockchain Can Reshape Financial Services* (August 2016), <http://www3.weforum.org/docs/WEF_The_future_of_financial_infrastructure.pdf> (accessed 21 July 2021).

Wymeersch, E, Hopt, K, and Ferrarini, G (eds), *Financial Regulation and Supervision: A Post-crisis Analysis* (Oxford: Oxford University Press, 2012).

Yates, M and Montagu, G, *The Law of Global Custody* (West Sussex: Bloomsbury Professional, 2013; 4th edn).

Yeowart, G, Parsons, R, Murray, E, and Patrick, H, *Yeowart and Parsons on the Law of Financial Collateral* (Edward Elgar Publishing, 2016).

Zacaroli, A, 'Taking Security over Intermediated Securities: Chapter V of the UNIDROIT (Geneva) Convention on Intermediated Securities', in Gullifer, L and Payne, J (eds), *Intermediated Securities: Legal Problems and Practical Issues* (Oxford: Hart Publishing, 2010), 167–86.

Zellweger-Gutknecht, C and Bacharach, J, 'Segregation of Cryptoassets in Insolvency Proceedings' (forthcoming; draft kindly provided by the authors).

Zetzsche, D, *Corporate Governance in Cyberspace: A Blueprint for Virtual Shareholder Meetings* (Heinrich-Heine-Universität Düsseldorf, 2005; Center for Business and Corporate Law Research Paper Series 11), <http://ssrn.com/abstract=747347> (accessed 21 July 2021).

Zetzsche, D, 'Shareholder Passivity, Cross-border Voting and the Shareholder Rights Directive', *Journal of Corporate Law Studies*, 8/2 (2008), 289–336.

Index

account holders:
  concept 1.07
  intermediaries' duties towards 1.22, 4.39, 7.12, 9.28–9.30, 9.96–9.97
    client assets protection, *see* client assets protection
    sufficient securities requirement 7.13–7.18, 7.96–7.98, 9.119
  'securities entitlement' of 1.10, 10.46, 11.90
  see also intermediated securities
Acharya, Viral V. 3.49
AFME (Association for Financial Markets in Europe) 7.35, 7.37
allocation of securities, *see* segregation of securities
alternative dispute resolution 4.89–4.101
applicable law, *see* choice of law; conflict-of-laws
arbitrage 3.49, 9.15, 10.121
Arner, Douglas W. 5.16, 6.57
assets, *see* client assets
assignments of securities, *see* transfers of securities
Association for Financial Markets in Europe (AFME) 7.35, 7.37
Australia, crypto securities regulation 10.160
Austria, negotiability of securities in 5.26
avoidance of loss, *ex ante* 7.13-53, 8.23–8.28
  see also correction of imbalances
avoidance rules for preferences and fraudulent transfers 8.19, 8.20, 8.64
  safe harbour protection 8.90–8.93

bail-ins for banks 2.76–2.77, 2.80, 3.77–3.78, 8.87
bail-outs for banks 2.72
Bank Recovery and Resolution Directive:
  on close-out netting 2.83, 2.88, 3.75–3.79
  conflicts-of-laws rules 3.56–3.58, 11.68
  generally 2.71, 2.73, 8.85–8.87
  limitations to termination rights 2.86–2.88
  resolution tools 2.76–2.77, 2.79–2.84, 3.77–3.78, 8.87
bank resolution regimes:
  bail-ins 2.76–2.77, 2.80, 3.77–3.78, 8.87
  contracts modification 2.84
  cross-border recognition of 9.141–9.145
  EU regime, *see* Bank Recovery and Resolution Directive
  and financial collateral transactions 2.74–2.75, 2.77, 2.83–2.84, 2.88, 2.94
  Financial Stability Board recommendations 2.78, 3.48, 3.67–3.68, 3.79
  generally 2.71–2.73, 9.31
  limitations to termination rights 2.85–2.89
  loss-absorbing capacity assurance 2.78–2.81
  no-creditor-worse-off principle 2.74, 2.77, 3.79, 8.75, 8.87
  for systemically important financial institutions 2.72, 2.78, 8.71–8.87
  transfers of assets/liabilities 2.82–2.83
  see also Lehman Brothers insolvency
bankruptcy:
  institutional, *see* insolvency
  transfer of securities on 1.25, 1.40–1.55, 1.63
Bankruptcy Code (US):
  costs of administration 8.56
  creditors' set-off rights 8.97
  safe harbours 2.70, 3.34, 3.46, 3.49, 3.54, 8.89–8.90, 8.92
  see also broker-dealer insolvencies, US regime
banks, *see* bank resolution regimes; central banks; intermediaries
bare security arrangements 2.49, 2.53
Basel Committee on Banking Supervision:
  capital requirements of 3.37–3.38, 9.134
  on close-out netting 3.37, 3.54, 3.65–3.66
  on crypto securities and DLT 10.192–10.194
  generally 9.16–9.17
  on rehypothecation 2.58
  on segregation of securities 7.35, 7.36
  on systemic risk mitigation 2.75, 3.48
bearer securities 1.15, 1.31
Benjamin, Joanna 2.31
Bergman, William J. 3.54
Bernard L. Madoff Investment Securities LLC liquidation 8.35, 8.56
Bhutoria, Ria 7.99
Bitcoin 5.18–5.19, 7.94, 7.103, 10.81, 10.89; *see also* distributed ledger technology (DLT)

416 INDEX

Blemus, Stéphane 6.46
blockchain, *see* distributed ledger technology (DLT)
Bloxham, Peter (and Bloxham Review) 8.41–8.42, 8.47, 8.57–8.58, 8.126
Brexit 5.37
broker-dealer insolvencies, US regime:
  account holders' priority 8.22
  administration of claims and return of assets 8.53–8.54
  bank broker-dealers 2.73, 8.78–8.81
  costs of administration 8.56
  customer protection rule 8.25
  and Lehman Brothers Inc, *see* Lehman Brothers insolvency
  loss sharing 2.35, 8.34–8.36
  summary of 8.08
  transfer of securities to solvent intermediary 8.60
  transparency rules 8.119
  see also Bankruptcy Code (US)
BRRD, *see* Bank Recovery and Resolution Directive
Buckley, Ross P. 5.16, 6.57
buy-in of securities 7.67–7.68

Canada, crypto securities regulation 10.162
Canadian Investor Protection Fund 8.09, 8.29
capital requirements 3.37–3.38, 9.134
CARIT, *see* Receivables Convention (CARIT) (UN)
central banks:
  emergency assistance by 2.20, 2.27, 8.87
  financial regulation by 9.21–9.23, 9.33
  securities settlement systems, central bank money use 9.73
central clearing:
  central counterparties 2.71, 9.39, 9.122, 9.138
  of OTC derivatives 2.20, 2.39, 2.42, 3.55
central securities depositories:
  distributed ledger technology, impact on 5.23, 5.24, 5.32, 7.100
  ECSDA (European Central Securities Depositories Association) 7.33, 7.37, 7.38, 7.52
  generally 6.01, 9.01, 9.49
  in global financial crisis 9.03
  and imbalances 7.61, 7.70, 7.100, 9.66–9.71
  recovery and resolution of 9.31, 9.83–9.93
  regulation of 9.19–9.24, 9.37
    crypto securities infrastructure 10.142–10.148
    FMI Principles, *see* Principles for Financial Market Infrastructures (CPMI-IOSCO)
  and segregation of securities 7.37, 7.50–7.51, 9.71
  transparency of holdings in 8.118, 8.125, 9.54
  see also clearing; settlement
certificated securities:
  bearer securities 1.15, 1.31
  certificate possession requirement 1.21
  concept 1.14
  conflict-of-laws rules 1.98–1.103
  horizontal priority rules 1.60–1.63
  transfers, effectiveness against issuers 1.33
  transfers, effectiveness against third parties (perfection) 1.44, 1.48–1.51, 1.63
China, crypto securities regulation 10.158
choice of law:
  for enforcement of debt securities 4.104
  Hague Securities Convention on 10.97, 11.10, 11.22–11.23
    change of choice, third party rights 11.44–11.47
    conditions 11.24–11.35
  insolvency law for intermediated securities 8.100–8.102, 11.48–11.50
  see also conflict-of-laws
clearing:
  central clearing, *see* central clearing
  CSDs for, *see* central securities depositories
  distributed ledger technology for 5.23, 5.32
  insolvency of system operators or participants 8.70
  risks for market participants 8.10–8.11
  and systemic risk 8.10, 8.64
  see also settlement
client assets:
  digital assets, *see* crypto securities
  in omnibus accounts 7.21–7.23, 7.37, 7.41, 7.48, 7.78
  and prime brokerage agreements 2.05
  protection of, *see* client assets protection
  rehypothecation of, *see* rehypothecation
  return of assets, insolvency context 8.50–8.54
  segregation of, *see* segregation of securities
client assets protection:
  correction of imbalances 7.54–7.70, 7.102–7.104, 7.109
  Financial Stability Board on 9.107–9.112
  investor protection funds or insurance 8.08–8.09, 8.29–8.30
  IOSCO on 8.76–8.77, 8.121, 9.98–9.106
  and loss sharing 7.93, 9.112
  and omnibus accounts 7.37

close-out netting 3.01–3.81
  concept and terminology 2.64–2.65, 3.08–3.09, 3.11, 3.26, 3.64
  and credit risk 3.36–3.38
    market risk interacting with 3.39–3.42
  enforceability, *see* close-out netting: enforceability
  harmonized regimes, *see* close-out netting: harmonized regimes
  restrictions on 8.65
  types, *see* close-out netting: types
close-out netting: enforceability:
  legal obstacles 3.26–3.31, 3.41–3.42
  safe harbours 2.66–2.70, 2.88, 3.34, 3.46, 3.49, 3.54, 8.91
  and single agreement concept 3.32–3.35
  for systemic risk mitigation 3.43–3.52
  UNIDROIT Principles on 3.70–3.74
close-out netting: harmonized regimes:
  BCBS and FSB recommendations 3.37, 3.54, 3.65–3.68, 3.79
  EU law measures 2.10, 2.83, 2.88, 3.06, 3.56–3.61, 3.75–3.79
  generally 3.53–3.55
  Geneva Securities Convention 3.06, 3.59–3.61, 4.44
  ISDA Master Agreements 3.19, 3.25, 3.28, 3.33, 3.78
  ISDA Model Netting Acts 3.04, 3.68
  Legislative Guide on Insolvency Law (UNCITRAL) 3.06, 3.62–3.64
  UNIDROIT Principles, *see* Principles on the Operation of Close-Out Netting Provisions (UNIDROIT)
close-out netting: types:
  common elements 3.10
  selection of type 3.23–3.25
  Type A: 'close-out set-off' 3.11–3.12, 3.64
  Type B: set-off of accelerated and converted obligations 3.13–3.17
  Type C: netting of replacement values 3.18–3.22
collateral, *see* financial collateral
collateral management services 9.135–9.136
Committee on Payments and Market Infrastructures (CPMI, formerly CPSS) 9.16–9.18, 9.149
  CPMI-IOSCO cyber resilience guidance 9.78–9.79
  CPMI-IOSCO FMI Principles, *see* Principles for Financial Market Infrastructures (CPMI-IOSCO)
  CPMI-IOSCO FMI recovery report 9.90–9.93

CPSS-IOSCO Recommendations for Securities Settlement Systems 9.23, 9.39, 9.113–9.122
  on crypto securities and DLT 10.199–10.202
'competing claimant' term 1.17, 1.41
conflict-of-laws rules 11.01–11.107
  choice of law, *see* choice of law
  for crypto securities and DLT 10.95–10.102, 11.103–11.107
  of EU law 3.56–3.58, 11.10, 11.61, 11.64, 11.66–11.73
    HSC from EU perspective, *see* Hague Securities Convention: EU perspective
  on financial collateral arrangements 2.12
  and financial market infrastructures 9.62
  of Geneva Securities Convention 4.06, 11.52–11.55
    Hague Securities Convention, relationship with 11.56–11.64
  of HSC, *see* Hague Securities Convention
  of MLST, *see under* Model Law on Secured Transactions (UNCITRAL)
  on non-intermediated securities 1.96–1.107
  of Receivables Convention (CARIT) 4.30
  renvoi 4.06, 11.62
control agreements 1.53–1.54, 1.66, 1.69–1.72, 1.106, 4.39–4.40, 4.65, 8.20
Convention on the Assignment of Receivables in International Trade, *see* Receivables Convention (CARIT) (UN)
corporate actions processing 6.01–6.68
  distributed ledger technology and smart contracts for 6.45–6.49, 6.67
    benefits and challenges 6.50–6.63
  EU law on 6.08, 6.65, 11.88
  general meetings, participation and voting 6.10–6.23
  Geneva Securities Convention on 6.07, 6.65
  Hague Securities Convention on 11.87–11.88
  income distributions 6.24–6.32
  information provision 6.33–6.44
correction of imbalances 7.54–7.70, 7.102–7.104, 7.109
Covid-19 pandemic 2.25, 6.22, 9.03
CPMI (formerly CPSS), *see* Committee on Payments and Market Infrastructures (CPMI, formerly CPSS)
creditors, *see* judgment creditors
crypto securities 10.01–10.211
  concept and terminology 10.14–10.19, 10.120–10.126
  conflict-of-laws rules 10.95–10.102, 11.103–11.107
  creation of 10.82–10.84, 10.128–10.131

crypto securities (*cont.*)
   cyber security risk 8.113, 10.149
   DLT, *see* distributed ledger technology (DLT)
   good-faith acquisition of 10.90–10.92
   imbalances, correction of 7.102–7.104, 7.111
   initial coin offerings 10.38, 10.158, 10.172, 10.198
   and insolvency, *see* crypto securities and insolvency
   legal frameworks, *see* crypto securities: legal frameworks
   property rights in 10.08, 10.47, 10.58, 10.75
   registries of, *see* crypto securities registries
   regulation of, *see* crypto securities regulation
   security interests in 10.93–10.94
   smart contracts, *see* smart contracts
   sufficient securities requirement 7.96–7.98
   tokens 10.10–10.13, 10.30, 10.85–10.88, 10.125–10.126
   transfers of 10.85–10.89, 10.93–10.94
   'wallets' for 7.98–7.100, 10.137–10.141, 10.149

crypto securities and insolvency:
   loss sharing, DLT for 7.105–7.107
   overview 8.103–8.115
   segregation of securities, DLT for 7.98–7.101

crypto securities: legal frameworks:
   crypto securities registries, requirements for, *see* crypto securities registries
   EU proposed Regulation (MiCA) 7.106, 8.106–8.107, 10.64, 10.101, 10.178–10.181
   French measures 10.21–10.26, 10.70, 10.171–10.172
   generally 4.127, 6.60, 10.03–10.04
   German measures 10.54–10.67, 10.70, 10.78, 10.101, 10.173
   Liechtenstein measures 10.32–10.37, 10.70, 10.94, 10.100, 10.166
   Luxembourg measures 10.27–10.31, 10.167
   Swiss measures, *see* Swiss crypto securities and DLT measures
   UK measures 8.108–8.110
   US measures 10.45–10.53, 10.161
   see also crypto securities regulation

crypto securities registries:
   creation of securities by registration 10.82–10.83
   data integrity and business continuity requirement 10.78–10.79
   general requirements 10.69–10.71
   manipulation resistance requirement 10.72–10.74
   publicity requirement 10.75–10.77, 10.94

   technological neutrality requirement 10.80–10.81

crypto securities regulation 10.103–10.211
   classification issues 10.120–10.126
   conflict-of-laws rules 10.95–10.102, 11.103–11.107
   of financial market infrastructures 10.142–10.148
   of intermediaries and service providers 10.135–10.141, 10.149
   by international standards-setting bodies 10.182–10.184
     Basel Committee on Banking Supervision 10.192–10.194
     Committee on Payments and Market Infrastructures 10.199–10.202
     Financial Action Task Force 10.188–10.191
     Financial Stability Board 10.185–10.187, 10.211
     IOSCO 10.195–10.198
     OECD 10.203
   of issuance and registration 10.128–10.131
   policy objectives 10.108–10.110
   proportionality requirement 10.114–10.116
   scope of 10.117–10.119
   in selected jurisdictions 10.150–10.155
     anti-money laundering focus 10.163–10.164
     comprehensive framework efforts 10.174–10.181
     existing regimes extended 10.159–10.162
     prohibitive approaches 10.156–10.158
     technology specific regulation 10.165–10.173
   technological neutrality requirement 10.112–10.113
   of trading 10.132–10.134
CSDs, *see* central securities depositories
custodians, *see* intermediaries

debt securities:
   conflict-of-laws rules 1.101–1.102, 1.105–1.107
   issuer's insolvency, set-off right 8.95–8.99
defective transfers, third party effectiveness, *see* innocent acquisition of securities
dematerialized securities, *see* intermediated securities; uncertificated securities
Denmark, right of use devices in 2.31
derivatives:
   characteristics 2.07
   close-out netting, *see* close-out netting
   ISDA standard documentation 2.03

INDEX

credit support annexes 2.04, 2.30, 2.43–2.45
OTC derivatives, *see* OTC derivatives
systemic risks 2.18, 3.44
Deschamps, Michel 4.06
digital securities, *see* crypto securities
'directly held securities' term 1.12; *see also* non-intermediated securities
disintermediation 8.04, 8.120–8.125
  DLT for, *see* distributed ledger technology (DLT)
distributed ledger technology (DLT):
  characteristics and applications 7.94–7.95, 8.104, 10.02, 10.06–10.08, 10.69
  conflict-of-laws issues 10.95–10.102, 11.103-107
  for corporate actions processing 6.45–6.49, 6.67
    benefits and challenges 6.50–6.63
  DLT-based securities registries, *see* crypto securities registries
  for imbalances management 7.94–7.107, 7.111
  for intermediated securities management 5.15–5.28
    barriers to adoption 5.29–5.36
  legal frameworks, *see* crypto securities: legal frameworks
  manipulation resistance 10.74
  protocols 10.81, 10.83, 10.85, 10.88–10.89
  regulation of, *see* crypto securities regulation
  smart contracts, *see* smart contracts
  see also crypto securities
dividend distributions 6.24–6.32
DLT, *see* distributed ledger technology (DLT)
Dodd-Frank Act Title II 2.73, 8.78–8.81
Donald, David 5.21, 6.57

ECSDA (European Central Securities Depositories Association) 7.33, 7.37, 7.38, 7.52
Edwards, Franklin R. 3.50
electronic voting 6.22
Elst, Christoph Van der 5.16
enforceability of close-out netting, *see* close-out netting: enforceability
enforcement of security interests under uniform law 4.01–4.132
  Geneva Securities Convention provisions 2.89, 4.44–4.49, 4.111
  Hague Securities Convention provisions 4.50–4.51
  MLST provisions, *see* Model Law on Secured Transactions: enforcement regime

  Receivables Convention (CARIT) provisions 4.108–4.110
  scope and terminology of instruments 4.04–4.31
  comparisons 4.32–4.43
  UNCITRAL Legislative Guide provisions 4.73–4.88
  UNIDROIT project 4.120–4.127, 4.132
England, *see* United Kingdom
enhanced transparency rules:
  proposed 8.117–8.119
  for shadow banking sector 9.126–9.127
ESMA (European Securities and Markets Authority) 7.33, 7.100
EU law:
  bank resolution regime, *see* Bank Recovery and Resolution Directive
  on business restructuring 8.91
  on close-out netting 2.10, 2.83, 2.88, 3.06, 3.56–3.61, 3.75–3.79
  conflict-of-laws rules 3.56–3.58, 11.10, 11.61, 11.64, 11.66–11.73
    HSC from EU perspective, *see* Hague Securities Convention: EU perspective
  on corporate actions processing 6.08, 6.65, 11.88
  on crypto securities and DLT
    Commission Communication on EU Digital Finance Strategy 8.106–8.107
    proposed Regulation (MiCA) 7.106, 8.106–8.107, 10.64, 10.101, 10.178–10.181
  ex ante avoidance of loss rules 8.26–8.28
  on financial collateral transactions 2.08–2.13, 2.30, 2.32, 2.36, 2.67–2.69, 2.88
  on rehypothecation 2.59
  on segregation of securities 7.40–7.53
  on settlement 2.08, 3.57
European Central Securities Depositories Association (ECSDA) 7.33, 7.37, 7.38, 7.52
European Commission Communication on EU Digital Finance Strategy 8.106
European Master Agreement 2.03
European Securities and Markets Authority (ESMA) 7.33, 7.100
Eurosystem 10.119
Evouleas, Emilios 5.16
***ex ante* avoidance of loss** 8.23–8.28
  see also correction of imbalances

Financial Action Task Force 10.188–10.191
financial collateral 2.01–2.95
  collateral management services 9.135–9.136

financial collateral (*cont.*)
  documentation, market standard 2.02–2.03, 2.04
  enforcement in insolvency context 2.63–2.65
    bank resolution, impact of 2.74–2.75, 2.77, 2.83–2.84, 2.88, 2.94
    close-out netting, *see* close-out netting: enforceability
    MLST and UNCITRAL Legislative Guides on 4.71–4.88
  enforcement under uniform law, *see* enforcement of security interests under uniform law
  financial market infrastructures using 9.72
  'haircuts' of 2.37, 2.47, 9.64, 9.72, 9.131–9.134
  legal framework 2.06–2.07
    EU law 2.08–2.13, 2.30, 2.32, 2.36, 2.67–2.69
    Geneva Securities Convention 2.14–2.15, 2.30, 2.32, 4.11
    proposed reforms 2.51–2.56
  MTM (mark-to-market/mark-to-model) exposure 2.37, 2.47, 3.39–3.40
  overcollateralization, *see* overcollateralization
  re-use of 2.17, 9.72, 9.111, 9.130
  regulation
    post-crisis reforms 2.05, 2.16–2.20, 2.57–2.62, 3.55
    right to use devices, US regulation 2.35, 2.57, 2.62
  right of use attached to, *see* right of use devices
  types 2.04–2.05
  undercollateralization 2.26–2.29, 2.41, 2.47, 2.77
  see also derivatives; repurchase (repo) agreements; securities financing transactions; title transfer collateral agreements
financial crisis of 2008-09, *see* global financial crisis
financial market infrastructures, *see* central securities depositories; securities settlement systems
financial regulation 9.01–9.149
  approaches to 9.06, 9.15
  of bank insolvencies, *see* bank resolution regimes
  co-operation by authorities 9.15, 9.32–9.36
  of crypto securities, *see* crypto securities regulation
  of financial collateral
    post-crisis reforms 2.05, 2.16–2.20, 2.57–2.62, 3.55
    right to use devices, US regulation 2.35, 2.57, 2.62
  of financial market infrastructures 9.19–9.24, 9.37
    crypto securities infrastructure 10.142–10.148
    FMI Principles, *see* Principles for Financial Market Infrastructures (CPMI-IOSCO)
    recovery and resolution 9.31, 9.83–9.93
  intermediaries' duties to account holders 1.22, 4.39, 7.12, 9.28–9.30, 9.96–9.97
    client assets protection, *see* client assets protection
    sufficient securities requirement 7.13–7.18, 7.96–7.98, 9.119
  international standards 9.14–9.18, 9.36
  policy objectives 9.08–9.13, 9.30
  regulated activities 9.04–9.05
  regulatory arbitrage 3.49, 9.15, 10.121
  of rehypothecation 2.57–2.62, 9.111, 9.128–9.129
  of settlement 9.113–9.122
  of shadow banking sector, *see* shadow banking sector regulation
Financial Stability Board:
  on bank resolution 2.78, 3.48, 3.67–3.68, 3.79, 8.73–8.77, 9.84
    cross-border recognition principles 9.142–9.145
  on client assets protection 9.107–9.112
  on crypto securities and DLT 10.185–10.187, 10.211
  on financial market infrastructures resolution 9.31, 9.85–9.89
  on key standards 9.17
  outcomes-based regulation promoted by 9.15
  on rehypothecation 2.58, 9.111
  role 9.13, 9.149
  on segregation of securities 7.35, 9.107
  on shadow banking sector, *see* shadow banking sector regulation
financial stability risk, *see* systemic risk
fire sales 3.48, 9.139
France, crypto securities and DLT measures 10.21–10.26, 10.70, 10.171–10.172
FSB, *see* Financial Stability Board

Geis, Georg 5.16, 6.57
general meetings, participation and voting 6.10–6.23
Geneva Securities Convention:
  on bank resolution 2.89

on clearing/settlement system
 transactions 8.70
on close-out netting 3.06, 3.59–3.61, 4.44
concepts and terminology 1.07, 1.11, 1.18,
 4.34–4.39, 4.41
conflict-of-laws rules 4.06, 11.52–11.55
 Hague Securities Convention, relationship
  with 11.56–11.64
on corporate actions processing 6.07, 6.65
on enforcement of security interests 2.89,
 4.44–4.49, 4.111
on financial collateral transactions 2.14–2.15,
 2.30, 2.32, 4.11
generally 1.04, 4.02, 4.05, 4.128, 8.01
on innocent acquisition 1.29, 1.37–1.39, 1.75,
 1.79, 1.91–1.94
insolvency law regime, *see* Geneva Securities
 Convention: insolvency law regime
on intermediaries' duties to account
 holders 9.96–9.97
scope of application 4.06–4.12, 4.32
status 2.15, 8.01, 8.101, 11.51
on sufficient securities
 requirement 7.14–7.18
on transfers of securities 1.26–1.27, 4.10
 effectiveness against third parties
  (perfection) 1.44, 1.52–1.54, 1.75, 1.88
**Geneva Securities Convention: insolvency law
 regime:**
bank resolution 2.89
integrity of interests principle 8.18–8.20
loss sharing rules 7.79–7.81, 8.31
priority rules 1.65, 1.75, 4.09, 4.41,
 8.43, 8.63
segregation of securities 7.26–7.32
set-off rights 8.96, 8.99
Germany:
bank resolution regime 2.73
crypto securities and DLT measures 10.54–
 10.67, 10.70, 10.78, 10.101, 10.173
negotiability of securities in 5.26
right of use devices in 2.31
Gibraltar, crypto securities regulation 10.168
global financial crisis:
financial market infrastructures, performance
 in 9.03
lessons offered by 2.01, 2.22–2.23, 9.12, 9.147
 on bank bail-outs 2.72
 on close-out netting, *see* Principles on
  the Operation of Close-Out Netting
  Provisions (UNIDROIT)
 on overcollateralization, *see*
  overcollateralization
 on segregation of securities 7.33
post-crisis regulatory reforms

on bank resolution, *see* bank resolution
 regimes
on financial collateral 2.05, 2.16–2.20,
 2.57–2.62, 3.55
on shadow banking sector, *see* shadow
 banking sector regulation
**Global Master Repurchase Agreement
 (GMRA)** 2.03, 2.04, 2.65
on close-out netting 3.14, 3.15, 3.16, 3.28
**Global Master Securities Lending Agreement
 (GMSLA)** 2.03, 2.04, 2.65
global regulatory standards 9.14–9.18, 9.36
GMRA, *see* Global Master Repurchase
 Agreement (GMRA)
**GMSLA (Global Master Securities Lending
 Agreement)** 2.03, 2.04, 2.65
good-faith acquisition of securities:
crypto securities 10.90–10.92
intermediated securities 1.29, 1.37–1.39,
 1.75, 1.79, 1.91–1.94, 7.10
Graaf, Tycho de 11.106
gratuitous transfers 1.74–1.83, 1.93–1.95
Green, Sarah 5.24–5.25
Grove, Rick 3.42
GSC, *see* Geneva Securities Convention
Guégan, Dominique 6.46
Gullifer, Louise 2.31, 2.56

Haentjens, Matthias 8.21, 8.36, 11.106
Hague Securities Convention:
adoption of 11.06–11.08
choice of law as primary rule 10.97, 11.10,
 11.22–11.23
 change of choice, third party
  rights 11.44–11.47
 conditions 11.24–11.35
concepts and terminology 1.11, 4.14, 4.34,
 11.12–11.13
on enforcement of security
 interests 4.50–4.51
EU perspective on, *see* Hague Securities
 Convention: EU perspective
fall-back rules 11.36–11.40
generally 1.04, 11.01
Geneva Securities Convention, relationship
 with 11.56–11.64
negative list of connecting
 factors 11.41–11.42
scope of application 4.13–4.14, 4.32, 11.02–
 11.05, 11.11–11.17
 excluded issues 11.18–11.21, 11.95
status 8.101, 11.09–11.10
on third party rights 11.43–11.50,
 11.79–11.85
see also conflict-of-laws rules

422   INDEX

Hague Securities Convention: EU perspective:
 future EU-HSC relationship 11.98–11.102
 public law impact concerns 11.94–11.95
 securities settlement systems impact concerns 11.96–11.97
 status quaestionis 11.10, 11.66–11.77
 substantive law impact concerns 11.86–11.93
 third party rights protection concerns 11.79–11.85
'haircuts' of collateral 2.37, 2.47, 9.64, 9.72, 9.131–9.134
Hoek, Marc van den 2.60
Hong Kong, crypto securities regulation 10.164
horizontal priority rules:
 certificated securities 1.60–1.63
 generally 1.56–1.59, 1.91
 qualifications and exceptions 1.73
  judgment creditor or insolvency administrator 1.78, 1.84–1.89
  transfer not-for-value 1.74–1.83, 1.95
 uncertificated securities 1.64–1.72, 1.76
Howey test 10.161
HSC, *see* Hague Securities Convention
hybrid tokens 10.12, 10.125–10.126

IA (independent amount) collateral 2.37–2.49, 7.36
imbalances 7.01–7.112
 causes 7.07–7.12
 concept and terminology 7.02–7.06
 correction methods 7.54–7.70, 7.102–7.104, 7.109
 and distributed ledger technology 7.94–7.107, 7.111
 and financial market infrastructures 7.09, 7.70, 9.66–9.71
 on insolvency of intermediary
  loss sharing, *see* loss sharing
  segregation of securities, *see* segregation of securities
 sufficient securities requirement 7.13–7.18, 7.96–7.98, 9.119
income distributions to shareholders 6.24–6.32
independent amount (IA) collateral 2.37–2.49, 7.36
India, crypto securities regulation 10.157
indirect holdings, *see* no-look-through principle
inflation of securities 7.03; *see also* imbalances
information provision, corporate 6.33–6.44

initial coin offerings 10.38, 10.158, 10.172, 10.198
initial margin collateral 2.39, 7.36
innocent acquisition of securities:
 crypto securities 10.90–10.92
 intermediated securities 1.29, 1.37–1.39, 1.75, 1.79, 1.91–1.94, 7.10
insolvency:
 financial collateral enforcement 2.63–2.65
  bank resolution, impact of 2.74–2.75, 2.77, 2.83–2.84, 2.88, 2.94
  and close-out netting, *see* close-out netting: enforceability
  MLST and UNCITRAL Legislative Guides on 4.71–4.88
 insolvency proceeding types 3.29, 8.88
 of intermediaries, *see* insolvency law for intermediated securities
 recovery and resolution
  of failing banks, *see* bank resolution regimes
  of financial market infrastructures 9.31, 9.83–9.93
 US law, *see* Bankruptcy Code (US); broker-dealer insolvencies, US regime
insolvency administrators:
 access to information, records, and assets 8.67–8.69
 interests in intermediated securities, effectiveness against 8.18–8.20
 priority disputes with, *see* horizontal priority rules
 transfers, effectiveness against 1.40–1.55, 1.63
 transfers to 1.25
insolvency law for intermediated securities 8.01–8.133
 account holder priority 8.21–8.22, 8.43–8.49
 account holder protection fund or insurance 8.29–8.30
 administration of claims and return of assets 8.50–8.54
 administrator access to information, records, and assets 8.67–8.69
 bank intermediaries, *see* bank resolution regimes
 choice of law rules 8.100–8.102, 11.48–11.50
 clearing/settlement system operators or participants 8.70
 costs of administration 8.55–8.58
 crypto securities, *see* crypto securities and insolvency
 ex ante avoidance of loss rules 8.23–8.28
  correction of imbalances 7.54–7.70, 7.102–7.104, 7.109

INDEX

GSC regime, *see* Geneva Securities
  Convention: insolvency law regime
  harmonization, prospect of 8.13, 8.88, 8.101
  integrity of interests principle 8.18–8.20
  issuers' insolvency, set-off right 8.95–8.99
  loss sharing rules, *see* loss sharing
  potential reforms 8.116
    enhanced transparency 8.117–8.119
    post-settlement
      disintermediation 8.120–8.125
    priority in lieu of property
      rights 8.126–8.131
  priority of interests granted by
    intermediary 8.62–8.63
  restricted acts 8.64–8.65
  safe harbours, *see* safe harbours
  segregation rules, *see* segregation of securities
  transfer of securities to solvent
    intermediary 8.59–8.61
  UK regime, *see* Special Administration
    Regime (UK)
  US regime, *see* broker-dealer insolvencies,
    US regime
interest, distributions to
  shareholders 6.24–6.32
intermediaries:
  corporate actions processing by, *see* corporate
    actions processing
  crypto securities intermediaries 10.135–
    10.141, 10.149
  distributed ledger technology, expected
    opposition to 5.32
  insolvency of, *see* bank resolution regimes;
    insolvency law for intermediated securities
  large custodians (quasi-systems) 9.27
  own security holdings 7.65–7.66
  'qualifying offices' of 11.29–11.35
  regulation of, *see* financial regulation
intermediated securities:
  concepts and terminology 1.07, 1.09–1.11,
    10.17–10.19
  corporate actions processing, *see* corporate
    actions processing
  disintermediation 8.04, 8.120–8.125
    DLT for, *see* distributed ledger
      technology (DLT)
  enforcement of, *see* enforcement of security
    interests under uniform law
  generally 1.01
  imbalances of, *see* imbalances
  innocent acquisition of 1.29, 1.37–1.39, 1.75,
    1.79, 1.91–1.94, 7.10
  insolvency law for, *see* insolvency law for
    intermediated securities

  intermediaries, *see* intermediaries
  legal framework, *see* Geneva Securities
    Convention; Hague Securities Convention
  no-look-through principle, *see* no-look-
    through principle
  priority rules 1.65, 1.75, 1.91
  property model, proposed
    abandonment 8.126–8.131
  property rights in 1.09–1.11, 4.09, 8.19,
    10.41, 10.46
  transfers of 1.16
    effectiveness against third parties
      (perfection) 1.44, 1.52–1.54, 1.75, 1.88
    to solvent intermediaries 8.59–8.61
    validity between parties 1.26–1.27
International Monetary Fund 9.18, 9.43
International Organization of Securities
  Commissions (IOSCO):
  on client assets protection 8.76–8.77, 8.121,
    9.98–9.106
  CPMI-IOSCO cyber resilience
    guidance 9.78–9.79
  CPMI-IOSCO FMI Principles, *see* Principles
    for Financial Market Infrastructures
    (CPMI-IOSCO)
  CPMI-IOSCO FMI recovery
    report 9.90–9.93
  CPSS-IOSCO Recommendations for
    Securities Settlement Systems 9.23, 9.39,
    9.113–9.122
  on crypto securities and DLT 10.195–10.198
  on rehypothecation 2.58
  role 9.16–9.18, 9.149
  on segregation of securities 7.35, 7.36
international regulatory standards 9.14–
  9.18, 9.36
International Swaps and Derivatives
  Association (ISDA):
  Master Agreements 2.03
    on close-out netting 3.19, 3.25, 3.28,
      3.33, 3.78
    credit support annexes 2.04, 2.30,
      2.43–2.45
  Model Netting Acts 3.04, 3.68
  Resolution Stay Protocols 3.68
invalid transfers, third party effectiveness, *see*
  innocent acquisition of securities
investment tokens 10.11–10.12
investor protection funds or insurance 7.93,
  8.08–8.09, 8.29–8.30
IOSCO, *see* International Organization of
  Securities Commissions (IOSCO)
ISDA, *see* International Swaps and Derivatives
  Association (ISDA)

issuers:
    corporate actions processing by, *see* corporate actions processing
    insolvency, set-off right 8.95–8.99
    transfers, effectiveness against 1.30–1.39
Italy, right of use devices in 2.31

Johansson, Erica 2.60
Johnson, Christian A. 2.31
judgment creditors:
    interests in intermediated securities, effectiveness against 8.18–8.21
    priority disputes with, *see* horizontal priority rules
    transfers, effectiveness against 1.40–1.55, 1.63
    transfers to 1.25

Kanda, Hideki 6.10, 8.10
Keijser, Thomas 6.57, 8.118
Kettering, Kenneth C. 2.31
Khaionarong, Tanai 5.32
Kiayias, Aggelos 5.16
Kokorin, Ilya 11.106

Lafarre, Anne 5.16
large custodians 9.27
Legislative Guide on Insolvency Law (UNCITRAL):
    on close-out netting 3.06, 3.62–3.64
    on enforcement of security interests 4.73–4.88
    scope and terminology 4.23–4.25
Legislative Guide on Intermediated Securities (UNIDROIT) 8.01, 8.43, 8.59, 11.51, 11.62–11.63
Legislative Guide on Secured Transactions (UNCITRAL):
    on enforcement of security interests 4.73–4.88
    scope of application 4.21–4.22, 4.32
Lehman Brothers insolvency:
    administrator's access to assets 8.68–8.69
    bail-out efforts 2.72
    effects of 2.19, 2.85
    inferred trust finding 8.28
    mutualization of losses 7.76
    overcollateralization 2.26, 2.33–2.36
Leinonen, Harry 5.32
Levin, Jonathan 7.96
Liechtenstein, crypto securities and DLT measures 10.32–10.37, 10.70, 10.94, 10.100, 10.166
liquidation, *see* insolvency

liquidity:
    and close-out netting 3.47, 3.50
    liquidity risk 2.58, 8.10, 9.57, 9.59, 9.63, 9.65, 9.73, 9.128, 10.147
loss avoidance, *ex ante* 8.23–8.28
    correction of imbalances 7.54–7.70, 7.102–7.104, 7.109
loss sharing:
    client assets protection 7.93, 9.112
    distributed ledger technology for 7.105–7.107
    generally 7.06, 7.71–7.73, 7.110
    Geneva Securities Convention on 7.79–7.81, 8.31
    methods 7.74–7.78, 8.32–8.33
    outside insolvency context 7.92
    policy questions 7.82–7.90
    and segregation of securities 7.77, 7.86–7.89, 8.43
    UK Special Administration Regime 8.37–8.43
    US SIPA scheme 2.35, 8.34–8.36
    see also imbalances; insolvency law for intermediated securities; segregation of securities
Lubben, Stephen J. 3.34, 3.49
Luxembourg, crypto securities and DLT measures 10.27–10.31, 10.167

Madoff liquidation case 8.35, 8.56
Malta, crypto securities regulation 10.168–10.170
mark-to-market/mark-to-model (MTM) exposure 2.37, 2.47, 3.39–3.40
market discipline 3.51, 9.80
market risk 3.39–3.42
Markets in Crypto-Assets Regulation (proposed) (MiCA) 7.106, 8.106–8.107, 10.64, 10.101, 10.178–10.181
Mengle, David 3.55
MiCA (EU Proposal for a Regulation on Markets in Crypto-assets) 7.106, 8.106–8.107, 10.64, 10.101, 10.178–10.181
minimum requirement for own funds and eligible liabilities (MREL) principles 2.79–2.81
Miraz, Mahdi 5.21, 6.57
MLST, *see* Model Law on Secured Transactions (UNCITRAL)
MNAs (Model Netting Acts) (ISDA) 3.04, 3.68
Model Law on Secured Transactions (UNCITRAL):
    concepts and terminology 1.08, 1.14, 1.15, 1.17, 4.15, 4.33, 4.35–4.40, 4.42

conflict-of-laws rules 1.97, 4.06, 4.19, 4.118
   for debt securities 1.101–1.103,
      1.105–1.107
   enforcement, applicable law 4.72,
      4.102–4.107
   on effectiveness against third parties
      (perfection) 1.40, 1.43, 1.49, 1.51, 1.55
   enforcement regime, *see* Model
      Law on Secured Transactions:
      enforcement regime
   generally 1.05, 1.19, 4.129–4.130
   horizontal priority rules 1.61, 1.67,
      1.87, 1.89
   scope of application 4.15–4.20, 4.31,
      4.32, 4.127
Model Law on Secured Transactions:
   enforcement regime:
   and alternative dispute resolution 4.89–4.101
   applicable law 4.72, 4.102–4.107
   generally 4.52–4.70
   in insolvency context 4.71–4.88
   as non-Convention law under GSC 4.08,
      4.16, 4.17, 4.19, 4.47, 4.111–4.119, 4.132
Model Netting Acts (ISDA) 3.04, 3.68
Mooney, Charles W. 5.22, 5.32, 6.57, 8.10,
   8.36, 8.118
Morrison, Edward R. 3.50
mortgages 1.42
**MREL (minimum requirement for own
   funds and eligible liabilities)
   principles** 2.79–2.81
**MTM (mark-to-market/mark-to-model)
   exposure** 2.37, 2.47, 3.39–3.40
mutualization of losses 7.74–7.76, 7.80–7.81,
   7.88–7.89

negotiable instruments law 1.38, 1.45–1.48,
   1.50, 1.92, 1.94, 1.98
nemo dat **rule** 1.42–1.44, 1.82, 10.90
Netherlands:
   account holder priority in 8.21
   bank resolution regime 2.73, 2.88
netting:
   close-out, *see* close-out netting
   by financial market infrastructures 9.61
   netting agreements 3.47, 4.24, 4.29, 4.34
   UNCITRAL recommendations on 4.77
no-credit-without-debit rule 7.55–7.60
no-creditor-worse-off principle 2.74, 2.77,
   3.79, 8.75, 8.87
no-look-through principle 5.01–5.51
   concept and advantages 5.01–5.10
   problem arising 5.11–5.14
   suggested solutions 5.37–5.50

technological alternative, *see* distributed
   ledger technology (DLT)
non-intermediated securities 1.01–1.108
   certificated, *see* certificated securities
   concepts and terminology 1.07–1.19
   conflict-of-laws rules 1.96–1.107
   creation of 1.20–1.22
   enforcement of, *see* enforcement of security
      interests under uniform law
   horizontal priority rules, *see* horizontal
      priority rules
   MLST on, *see* Model Law on Secured
      Transactions (UNCITRAL)
   transfers of 1.16
      effectiveness against issuers 1.30–1.39
      effectiveness against third parties
         (perfection) 1.40–1.55, 1.63, 1.80
      validity between parties 1.23–1.29
   uncertificated, *see* uncertificated securities
   vertical priority rules 1.56, 1.90–1.95
not-for-value transfers 1.74–1.83, 1.93–1.95
Nougayrède, Delphine 5.17, 6.57

**OECD on crypto securities and
   DLT** 10.02, 10.203
omnibus client accounts 7.21–7.23, 7.37, 7.41,
   7.48, 7.78
operational risk 2.49, 8.23, 9.10, 9.26, 9.74–
   9.76, 10.108
**OSLA (Overseas Securities Lender's
   Agreement)** 2.03
OTC derivatives:
   central clearing requirement 2.20, 2.39,
      2.42, 3.55
   close-out netting of, *see* close-out netting
   collateralization of 2.30, 2.37–2.49, 7.36
   cross-border co-operation on 9.15
   systemic risks 2.18, 3.44
outright assignments of receivables 1.43, 1.87,
   1.89, 1.101, 4.18
over-the-counter derivatives, *see* OTC
   derivatives
overcollateralization:
   generally 2.26–2.29
   independent amount (IA)
      collateral 2.37–2.49
   Lehman Brothers case 2.26, 2.33–2.36
   proposed responses 2.50–2.62, 2.93
**Overseas Securities Lender's Agreement
   (OSLA)** 2.03
oversight, *see* financial regulation

Pacific Coin test 10.162
Paech, Philipp 5.18, 5.20

Panisi, Frederico 5.16, 6.57
partial property transfers 2.82, 2.83, 3.76
party autonomy, *see* choice of law
payment tokens 10.11–10.12, 10.126
perfection (effectiveness against third parties):
  intermediated securities 1.44, 1.52–1.54, 1.75, 1.88
  non-intermediated securities 1.40–1.55, 1.63, 1.80
PFMI, *see* Principles for Financial Market Infrastructures (CPMI-IOSCO)
pooled client accounts 7.21–7.23, 7.37, 7.41, 7.48, 7.78
Priem, Randy 5.23
prime brokerage agreements 2.05, 2.30
Principles for Financial Market Infrastructures (CPMI-IOSCO):
  adoption of 9.40–9.47
  on collateral and money settlement 9.72–9.76
  on credit and liquidity risk 9.63–9.65
  on custody risk and segregation 9.66–9.71
  on cyber-security 9.77–9.79
  disclosure framework and assessment methodology 9.46, 9.80–9.82
  'financial market infrastructures' definition 10.142
  on governance and access 9.51–9.57
  on legal risk 9.59–9.62
  on risk management generally 9.56–9.58
  scope 9.48–9.50, 10.202
  on segregation of securities 7.35
  see also central securities depositories; securities settlement systems
Principles on the Operation of Close-Out Netting Provisions (UNIDROIT):
  on 'close-out netting' concept 3.08, 3.11, 3.26
  on enforceability of close-out netting 3.70–3.74
  generally 3.06, 3.69
  and Geneva Securities Convention 2.89
priority/priorities:
  account holder priority 8.21–8.22, 8.43–8.49
  collateral providers, proposals for 2.55
  disputes over 1.17
  Geneva Securities Convention on 1.65, 1.75, 4.09, 4.41, 8.43
  horizontal rules, *see* horizontal priority rules
  interests granted by intermediaries 8.62–8.63
  'priority' definitions 4.41–4.43
  vertical rules 1.56, 1.90–1.95
private international law, *see* conflict-of-laws
property rights in securities:
  crypto securities 10.08, 10.47, 10.58, 10.75
  intermediated securities 1.09–1.11, 4.09, 8.19, 10.41, 10.46
  priority in lieu of (proposal) 8.126–8.131
  transfers of, *see* transfers of securities
proxy voting 6.12–6.15, 6.22, 6.53, 6.54

'qualifying offices' of intermediaries 11.29–11.35
quasi-systems 9.27

re-use of collateral 2.17, 9.72, 9.111, 9.130
  see also rehypothecation, right of use devices
Receivables Convention (CARIT) (UN):
  concepts and terminology 4.28, 4.34, 4.36–4.39, 4.43
  conflict-of-laws rules 4.30
  on enforcement of security interests 4.108–4.110
  scope of application 4.16, 4.17, 4.26–4.31
  status 4.130
receivables, outright assignments of 1.43, 1.87, 1.89, 1.101, 4.18
reconciliation of imbalances 6.54, 7.61–7.62, 7.102
recovery and resolution:
  of failing banks, *see* bank resolution regimes
  of financial market infrastructures 9.31, 9.83–9.93
registries for crypto securities, *see* crypto securities registries
regulation, *see* financial regulation
regulatory arbitrage 3.49, 9.15, 10.121
rehypothecation:
  concept 2.27
  imbalances caused by 7.11
  of initial margin collateral 7.36
  Lehman Brothers case 2.33–2.36
  regulation of 2.57–2.62, 9.111, 9.128–9.129
  see also overcollateralization, re-use of collateral, right of use devices
renvoi 4.06, 11.62
replacement values, close-out netting of 3.18–3.22, 3.23
repurchase (repo) agreements:
  characteristics 2.07
  close-out netting of 3.13–3.17
  CPSS-IOSCO guidance on 9.121
  Global Master Repurchase Agreement (GMRA) 2.03, 2.04, 2.65
    on close-out netting 3.14, 3.15, 3.16, 3.28
  regulation of, *see* shadow banking sector
  safe harbours for 9.139–9.140
  systemic risks 2.19, 3.44, 9.139

see also securities lending agreements, securities financing transactions
resolution and recovery:
of failing banks, *see* bank resolution regimes
of financial market infrastructures 9.31, 9.83–9.93
reversal of book entry errors 7.63–7.64
right of use devices:
concept 2.04, 2.27
credit exposure risk 2.18, 2.48
EU law on 2.10, 2.30, 2.32, 2.36
Geneva Securities Convention on 2.30, 2.32
proposed abolition 2.53–2.54
rehypothecation based on, *see* rehypothecation
title transfer collateral agreements compared 2.30–2.32
US regulation of 2.35, 2.57, 2.62
see also re-use of collateral

safe harbours:
for close-out netting 2.66–2.70, 2.88, 3.34, 3.46, 3.49, 3.54, 8.91
generally 8.94
for repurchase (repo) agreements 9.139–9.140
of UK and EU law 8.91–8.93
of US Bankruptcy Code 2.70, 3.34, 3.46, 3.49, 3.54, 8.89–8.90, 8.92
Schuster, Edmund 5.19–5.20
Secured Transactions Model Law, *see* Model Law on Secured Transactions (UNCITRAL)
'securities entitlement' term 1.10, 10.46, 11.90
securities financing transactions:
agreements for, *see* repurchase (repo) agreements; securities lending agreements
close-out netting of, *see* close-out netting
concept 3.39
'haircuts' of collateral 2.37, 2.47, 9.64, 9.72, 9.131–9.134
risks 2.17–2.19
see also financial collateral
Securities Investor Protection Act regime, *see* broker-dealer insolvencies, US regime
securities lending agreements:
CPSS-IOSCO guidance on 9.121
Global Master Securities Lending Agreement (GMSLA) 2.03, 2.04, 2.65
regulation of 9.123–9.125
see also repurchase (repo) agreements
securities settlement systems:
CPSS-IOSCO Recommendations for 9.23, 9.39, 9.113–9.122

finality of settlements principle 4.77, 7.63, 8.70, 8.93, 9.61
generally 6.26, 8.11, 9.01, 9.50
Geneva Securities Convention on 4.12, 7.18, 7.64
in global financial crisis 9.03
Hague Securities Convention, impact on 11.96–11.97
and imbalances 7.09, 7.70, 9.66–9.71
recovery and resolution of 9.31, 9.83–9.93
regulation of 9.19–9.24, 9.37
crypto securities infrastructure 10.142–10.148
FMI Principles, *see* Principles for Financial Market Infrastructures (CPMI-IOSCO)
see also settlement
'securities' term 1.18
segregation of securities:
by central securities depositories 7.37, 7.50–7.51, 9.71
distributed ledger technology for 7.99–7.101
EU law on 7.40–7.53
Financial Stability Board on 7.35, 9.107
generally 8.24
Geneva Securities Convention on 7.26–7.32
international regulatory approach 7.33–7.39
and loss sharing 7.77, 7.86–7.89, 8.43
types 7.19–7.25
see also imbalances; insolvency law for intermediated securities; loss sharing
set-off:
close-out netting technique of 3.11–3.12, 3.64
and insolvency of issuers 8.95–8.99
UNCITRAL recommendations on 4.77
settlement:
by central banks 9.21
concept 8.10
CSDs for, *see* central securities depositories
distributed ledger technology for 5.21, 5.23, 5.28, 5.32–5.34
EU law on 2.08, 3.57
finality of settlement principle 4.77, 7.63, 8.70, 8.93, 9.61
insolvency of system operators or participants 8.70
regulation of 9.113–9.122
risks for market participants 8.10–8.11
shorter cycles of 7.69
SSSs for, *see* securities settlement systems
and systemic risk 8.10, 8.64
Taurus project (UK) 5.33, 5.36
see also clearing

Shabsigh, Ghiath 5.32
shadow banking sector regulation:
  central clearing
    central counterparties 2.71, 9.39, 9.122, 9.138
    of OTC derivatives 2.20, 2.39, 2.42, 3.55
  of collateral management services 9.135–9.136
  enhanced transparency rules 9.126–9.127
  generally 9.123–9.125
  minimum standards for securities lending, re-use, and rehypothecation 9.128–9.134
  safe harbours for repos 9.139–9.140
  see also OTC derivatives; repurchase (repo) agreements; securities lending agreements
shareholder rights processing, *see* corporate actions processing
shortfalls 7.02–7.03; *see also* imbalances
Singapore, crypto securities regulation 10.175–10.177
SIPA regime, *see* broker-dealer insolvencies, US regime
smart contracts:
  automatic transfers via 10.94
  concept 6.46, 10.09
  for corporate actions processing 6.45–6.49, 6.67
    benefits and challenges 6.50–6.63
  creation of securities with 10.84
  tokens 10.10–10.13, 10.30, 10.85–10.88, 10.125–10.126
  see also crypto securities; distributed ledger technology (DLT)
Snagg, Ferdisha 5.24–5.25
Special Administration Regime (UK):
  administration of claims and return of assets 8.51–8.52
  costs of administration 8.57–8.58
  issuers' insolvency, set-off right 8.98
  loss sharing 8.37–8.43
  transfer of securities to solvent intermediary 8.61
SSSs, *see* securities settlement systems
stablecoins 10.13
sufficient securities requirement 7.13–7.18, 7.96–7.98, 9.119
supervision, *see* financial regulation
Swiss crypto securities and DLT measures:
  conflict-of-laws issues 10.99
  creation of crypto securities and security interests 10.84, 10.94
  crypto securities registries 10.70, 10.78
  DLT protocols 10.81
  overview 10.38–10.44
  segregation of crypto securities 7.107
systemic risk:
  bank insolvencies posing 2.72, 2.75, 9.27
    resolution regimes, *see* bank resolution regimes
  clearing and settlement causing 8.10, 8.64
  and close-out netting 3.43–3.52
  and financial collateral arrangements 2.18–2.19, 3.44
  regulation of, *see* financial regulation
  and safe harbours 3.49, 8.92, 9.139

TARGET2-Securities (T2S) corporate actions standards 6.08, 6.51, 6.65
Taurus project (UK) 5.33, 5.36
third parties:
  Hague Securities Convention on third party rights 11.43–11.50, 11.79–11.85
  innocent acquisition of securities by crypto securities 10.90–10.92
  intermediated securities 1.29, 1.37–1.39, 1.75, 1.79, 1.91–1.94, 7.10
  interests in intermediated securities, effectiveness against 8.18–8.20
  transfers, effectiveness against, *see* perfection (effectiveness against third parties)
  transfers to 1.25
tiered participation arrangements 9.56
title to land 1.42, 1.86
title transfer collateral agreements:
  credit exposure risk 2.18, 2.48
  EU law on 2.10
  generally 2.04
  proposed reforms 2.53
  rehypothecation based on, *see* rehypothecation
  right of use devices compared 2.30–2.32
tokens 10.10–10.13, 10.30, 10.85–10.88, 10.125–10.126
Total Loss-Absorbing Capacity (TLAC) principles 2.78–2.79
transfers of securities:
  concept 1.16
  crypto securities 10.85–10.89, 10.93–10.94
  intermediated securities, *see* intermediated securities, transfers of
  invalid transfers, third party effectiveness, *see* innocent acquisition of securities
  non-intermediated securities, *see* non-intermediated securities, transfers of
  not-for-value 1.74–1.83, 1.93–1.95

outright assignments of receivables 1.43, 1.87, 1.89, 1.101, 4.18
perfection, *see* perfection (effectiveness against third parties)
title transfer collateral agreements, *see* title transfer collateral agreements
and voting rights 6.23
transparency:
of crypto securities holdings 10.75–10.77, 10.94
enhanced rules
proposed 8.117–8.119
for shadow banking sector 9.126–9.127
trustees in bankruptcy, *see* insolvency administrators

UCC, *see* Uniform Commercial Code (United States)
UN Convention on the Assignment of Receivables in International Trade, *see* Receivables Convention (CARIT) (UN)
unauthorized transfers 1.28–1.29, 1.36–1.39
uncertificated securities:
concept 1.15, 10.16
conflict-of-laws rules 1.104–1.107
horizontal priority rules 1.64–1.72, 1.76
transfers, effectiveness against issuers 1.34
transfers, effectiveness against third parties (perfection) 1.52–1.55
UNCITRAL:
Legislative Guides, *see* Legislative Guide on Insolvency Law (UNCITRAL); Legislative Guide on Secured Transactions (UNCITRAL)
MLST, *see* Model Law on Secured Transactions (UNCITRAL)
undercollateralization 2.26–2.29, 2.41, 2.47, 2.77
Unidroit:
on close-out netting, *see* Principles on the Operation of Close-Out Netting Provisions (Unidroit)
enforcement of security interests, forthcoming guidelines 4.120–4.127, 4.132
GSC, *see* Geneva Securities Convention
Legislative Guide on Intermediated Securities 8.01, 8.43, 8.59, 11.51, 11.62–11.63

Uniform Commercial Code (United States):
on crypto service providers 10.47–10.49
generally 1.19, 10.45
horizontal priority rules 1.61, 1.62
on non-intermediated bearer securities 1.15
reforms to 8.127, 8.130, 10.53
on securities 10.46
vertical priority rules 1.94
United Kingdom:
bank resolution regime 2.73, 2.88, 8.85
Brexit 5.37
crypto securities and DLT measures 8.108–8.110
ex ante avoidance of loss rules 8.26
investor protection in 8.30
no-look-through principle, *see* no-look-through principle
right of use devices in 2.31
SAR, *see* Special Administration Regime (UK)
Taurus project 5.33, 5.36
United States:
bank resolution regime 2.73, 8.78–8.81
Bankruptcy Code, *see* Bankruptcy Code (US)
broker-dealer insolvency in, *see* broker-dealer insolvencies, US regime
crypto securities and DLT measures 10.45–10.53, 10.161
investor protection in 8.08, 8.29
right of use devices in 2.31, 2.35, 2.57, 2.62
UCC, *see* Uniform Commercial Code (United States)
unregistered title to land or mortgages 1.42, 1.86
utility tokens 10.11–10.12

valuation:
of closed-out transactions 3.15, 3.20, 3.28, 3.33, 3.41–3.42, 3.61, 3.73–3.74, 3.78
of financial collateral 9.72, 9.128, 9.131
vertical priority rules 1.56, 1.90–1.95
voting rights at general meetings 6.10–6.23

'wallets' for crypto securities 7.98–7.100, 10.137–10.141, 10.149
withholding tax 6.32
World Bank 4.123, 4.126, 9.18, 9.43
Wyoming, crypto securities and DLT measures 10.49–10.52